THE WRITE STUFF
Thinking Through Paragraphs

Marcie Sims

How important is critical thinking to the writing course?

 Critical thinking is the foundation for everything in the writing course.

 Critical thinking should be applied to every writing and reading assignment.

Critical thinking would figure even more prominently in the course if it were easier to implement

The Write Stuff: Thinking Through Paragraphs focuses on teaching students the critical thinking skills they need to interpret and analyze information and express their ideas clearly and logically in writing. Critical thinking provides the theme that integrates the instruction throughout the text.

THE WRITE STUFF
Thinking Through Paragraphs

Marcie Sims

Critical thinking is the foundation for everything in the writing course.

"I appreciate the author's pedagogical approach. Critical thinking is rarely emphasized in developmental texts and her approach is refreshing and exciting."
—**Loraine Anderson,** *Linn-Benton Community College*

- **Part I: Critical Thinking.** The two critical thinking chapters in Part I are the foundation on which *The Write Stuff* is built. Chapter 1 (Critical Thinking in Writing and Reading) defines critical thinking and explains the meaning and function of specific critical thinking terms and tools used throughout the book. Chapter 2 (Critical Thinking and Reading Techniques) equips developing writers with the critical thinking skills they need to interpret and analyze information so they can understand and evaluate textbook and other reading materials.

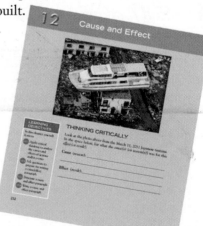

- **Chapter Openers/Thinking Critically questions.** Each chapter opens with an image accompanied by questions or prompts designed to get students thinking critically. This provides students with the opportunity to think about what they already know about the chapter material before they use it and helps them to engage with the chapter content.

THE WRITE STUFF
Thinking Through Paragraphs

Marcie Sims

Critical thinking should be applied to every writing assignment.

"I love that critical thinking is presented as being so important in the learning and writing process and that it is so well presented with adequate exercises, so students will see its importance."

—**Josh M. Beach,** *Central Texas College*

- **Critical Thinking Checklists.** Featured in the writing chapters, these checklists reinforce the critical thinking–writing connection and ensure that students are thinking critically about all the elements of their essays.

- **Applying Critical Thinking boxes.** These boxes either briefly define the critical thinking tools relevant to specific sections of the chapter (and explain how students can apply them) or demonstrate practical applications of the tools. In the writing chapters, students are taught to think critically about writing structures and how to express ideas clearly. In the grammar chapters, students are prompted to think critically about key sentence elements.

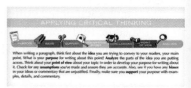

- **Step-by-step writing instruction in the modes.** The writing chapters each contain three major sections ("Preparing to Write . . ."; Structuring . . . "; "Writing . . . ") that isolate the steps in the writing process, getting students to think critically about the importance of each step, and how to put them together in the culminating writing activities.

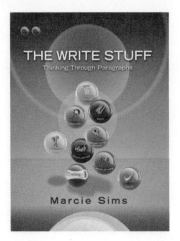

Critical thinking would be even more important if I could easily integrate it into my course.

"I never knew how to use critical thinking skills. This text spells it out perfectly so that even a person who has been out of school for YEARS can understand and grasp the concepts."

—**Patricia Cunningham,** *Student*

Visual cues throughout the text. Critical thinking terms may be unfamiliar to many students and seem abstract and hard to grasp. In order to make the connection between these terms and their application to writing paragraphs that clearly articulate and support ideas and arguments, the author has assembled a "Critical Thinking Toolbox" in which each of the critical thinking terms is linked to a specific tool icon. This provides students with visual cues that identify critical thinking tools they can use whenever they embark on a writing assignment.

Critical Thinking and your course. The 40-page Instructor's Guide written by Elizabeth Barnes (Daytona State College) located in the Instructor's Resource Manual (ISBN: 0132243083) includes help on integrating critical thinking into your classroom through small group work, in-class activities, peer review, portfolios, student seminars, projects, games, and more.

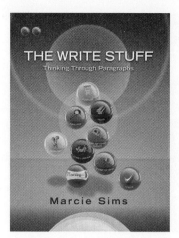

The Write Stuff: Thinking Through Paragraphs Reviewers

The author and Pearson would like to thank the following instructors who have helped craft *The Write Stuff: Thinking Through Paragraphs*. The reviewers below often reviewed multiple stages of the manuscript, helping the author refine and improve upon instructional content for this first edition. We are most grateful for their comments.

Althea Allard
Community College of Rhode Island

Andrew S. Andermatt
Clinton Community College

Lorraine Anderson
Linn-Benton Community College

Joe W. Anguiano
Riverside Community College

Josh M. Beach
Central Texas College

Michael Bodek
Bergen Community College

Crystal W. Brantley
Vance-Granville Community College

Kristin Brunnemer
Pierce College

Patricia Colville
Orange County Community College

Karen L. Feldman
Seminole State College of Florida

Patricia Golder
Victor Valley College

Kathryn Hake
Linn-Benton Community College

Carrie Harrison
Pittsburgh Technical Institute

Mariama S. Hodari
Kennedy-King College

Maria Jackson
Albany Technical College

Stanley W. Johnson
Southside Virginia Community College

Mandy Kallus
Kingwood College

Paulette Longmore
Essex County College

Nicole Lovejoy
Cerritos College

Elizabeth Marsh
Bergen Community College

Jan Modisette
Jacksonville College

Catherine Moran
Bristol County Community College

Debbie Naquin
Northern Virginia Community College

David Nelson
Glendale Community College

Mary Nielsen
Dalton State College

Christie Okocha
Cuyahoga Community College

Karen Petit
Community College of Rhode Island

Anne Marie Prendergast
Bergen Community College

Jessica Rabin
Anne Arundel Community College

Christa Raney
University of North Alabama

Sharon M. Taylor
Western Wyoming Community College

Kathy Tyndall
Wake Technical Community College

Ralph Velazquez
Rio Hondo College

Nikka Harris Vrieze
Rochester Community and Technical College

Jon A. Yasin
Bergen Community College

Gregory Zobel
College of the Redwoods

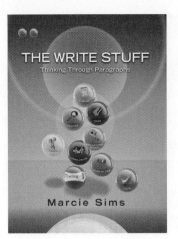

THE WRITE STUFF
Thinking Through Paragraphs

Marcie Sims

Praise for
The Write Stuff: Thinking Through Paragraphs

Throughout the entire three-year writing and development process, reviewers liked what they saw. Below is just a sample of what was said.

"I feel the author has created a detailed, comprehensive, accessible, and valuable teaching tool that successfully incorporates critical and analytical thinking in both reading samples and writing activities."

—Mary Nielsen, *Dalton State College*

"The activities in Chapter 4 regarding marking the parts of a paragraph are effective and helpful for students to think about the construction of an effective paragraph."

—Kathryn Hake, *Linn-Benton Community College*

"With these critical thinking activities, [students] will have adequate practice in responding to all types of questions that really test how they can apply knowledge."

—Paulette Longmore, *Essex County College*

"I think too often in developmental texts the focus becomes solely on the grammar and mechanics of writing, but it doesn't touch upon critical thinking. Students may be able to write a structurally-sound paragraph, but if they cannot think critically about what they read, hear, and see, they will have nothing about which to write."

—Nikka Harris, *Vrieze Rochester Community and Technical College*

"I believe that the author's pedagogical approach to teaching writing is sound. The approach is simple and direct, beginning with basic exposition in paragraph writing and progressing through modes of paragraph writing onto a simple essay, and, in the process, providing practice in the critical thinking skills so necessary for interpretation and analysis in writing."

—Jan Modisette, *Jacksonville College*

THE WRITE STUFF
Thinking Through Paragraphs

Marcie Sims
Green River Community College

PEARSON

Boston   Columbus   Indianapolis   New York   San Francisco   Upper Saddle River
Amsterdam   Cape Town   Dubai   London   Madrid   Milan   Munich   Paris   Montreal   Toronto
Delhi   Mexico City   Sao Paulo   Sydney   Hong Kong   Seoul   Singapore   Taipei   Tokyo

Senior Acquisitions Editor: Matthew Wright
Senior Development Editor: Gillian Cook
Senior Marketing Manager: Kurt Massey
Senior Supplements Editor: Donna Campion
Senior Media Producer: Stefanie Liebman
Project Coordination, Text Design, and
   Electronic Page Makeup: Laserwords Maine
Art Director, Cover: Anne Nieglos

Cover Designer: Ilze Lemesis
Cover Illustration: Slamer/Shutterstock
Photo Researcher: Lily Ferguson
Permissions Researcher: Jennifer Kennett
Procurement Specialist: Mary Ann Gloriande
Printer and Binder: Quad Graphics-Taunton
Cover Printer: Lehigh-Phoenix Color Corporation

Credits and acknowledgments borrowed from other sources and reproduced, with permission, in this textbook appear on page 631.

1 2 3 4 5 6 7 8 9 10—QG-T—14 13 12 11

Student Edition

ISBN-13: 978-0-13-224306-3
ISBN-10: 0-13-224306-7

Annotated Instructor's Edition

ISBN-13: 978-0-13-224307-0
ISBN-10: 0-13-224307-5

www.pearsonhighered.com

Brief Contents

Detailed Contents

PART III   WRITING AND CRITICAL THINKING IN THE MODES 125

To the Instructor

The Write Stuff: Thinking Through Paragraphs is an all-in-one writing text designed for developmental and pre-college-level composition courses. *The Write Stuff* provides all the basic information students need to develop their paragraph and short essay writing skills—including the information and practice they need for doing so using correct grammar and an appropriate style—and to build their ana-  lytical reading skills. Most developmental composition texts do not provide the basic instruction and exercises needed, while at the same time developing more difficult-to-grasp analytical skills: interpretation and analysis. This text does! It not only provides students with the basic tools for writing well-organized and developed paragraphs that are grammatically and mechanically correct, but it also focuses on teaching students the critical thinking skills they need to interpret and analyze information and express their ideas clearly and logically in writing. Critical thinking provides the theme that integrates the instruction throughout the text.

Students in developmental composition courses need detailed instruction on how to write paragraphs and essays; how to spot and correct their spelling, usage, and sentence-level errors; and how to correctly include quotes from other writers. However, students also need instruction on how to interpret what they read, how to go deeper into the topics they've chosen to write about, how to choose the best approach for communicating their ideas to their target audience, and how to pull all of these aspects together into a meaningful purpose for writing. *The Write Stuff* encourages students to engage in an active critical thinking process during all stages of reading and writing and helps them to move beyond defending the obvious in their understanding of others' ideas as well as their own.

CRITICAL THINKING

Critical thinking is defined in Chapter 1, which also includes clear explanations of the meaning and function of specific writing and critical thinking terms and tools that are used in almost every chapter of the book. These terms include *purpose, ideas, support, assumptions and biases, analysis, conclusions,* and *point of view.*

Critical thinking terms may be unfamiliar to many students and seem abstract and hard to grasp at first. In order to make explicit the connection between these terms and their application to writing para-

graphs and essays that clearly articulate and support ideas and arguments, the concept of a **critical thinking toolbox** is used. Each of the terms listed above is linked to a specific tool icon. The idea is to provide students with visual cues that identify critical thinking tools and writing concepts they can use whenever they embark on a writing or reading assignment. For example, *blueprints* are used to represent purpose, and *beams* to represent the main ideas expressed in topic sentences to support a thesis. *Nails* are used to represent the support (examples, details, facts) a writer uses to underpin ideas, while a *camera* represents the importance of looking closely at and analyzing the elements of an argument, a paragraph, or even an individual sentence.

These icons are used consistently throughout the text to make explicit to students the connection between the critical thinking tools and writing concepts they have learned about in Chapter 1 and their application to real-world writing. The icons work not only on a visual identification level, alerting students that a specific tool is being used, but also on a subliminal level, so that students begin to automatically connect the icons with important writing and critical thinking concepts. As they progress through the text, students will become increasingly familiar with these critical thinking concepts and tools and develop confidence in using them in their writing assignments.

CONTENT

The Write Stuff speaks to students who are pre-college-level readers and writers. The user-friendly tips and exercises help students develop the tools they need to succeed in reading and writing, and the critical thinking focus throughout the book helps them move past rote learning and summary into true interpretation and analysis of what they are reading or what they are writing about.

The Write Stuff includes the following features:

- **Critical thinking skills defined and applied** with critical thinking pointers, prompts, and exercises throughout the text
- **Critical reading and analysis techniques** for reading pre-college- and college-level assignments including visual aids
- **Critical thinking boxes** that either briefly define the critical thinking tools and writing concepts relevant to specific sections of the chapter and explain in concrete terms how students can apply them or demonstrate practical applications of the tools and concepts
- **Critical thinking icons** that keep terminology and tools discussed in Chapter 1 fresh in students' minds, integrating them into the ongoing instruction, and showing they have practical use in all aspects of writing
- **Learning Objectives** boxes at the beginning of each chapter that list the major topics to be discussed
- **Learning Objective Review** boxes at the end of each chapter that provide a summary of the major topics in a format that allows students to review and test their recall of what they have learned
- Thorough coverage of the basics for writing paragraphs
- Introductory coverage of the basics for writing essays
- Separate chapters on each of the modes, including argument
- Annotated student paragraphs that provide achievable models for student writers
- Professional paragraphs with writing prompts for analysis
- Two chapters that cover how to paraphrase, summarize, and avoid plagiarism, as well as how to research, evaluate, and cite sources using MLA documentation style
- A chapter of reading selections with critical thinking and writing prompts for skill application

- A section on sentence construction and common sentence construction errors with ample practice exercises
- A handbook that provides information and helpful tips on correct use of grammar, spelling, vocabulary, and style, plus plentiful sentence- and paragraph-length exercises

ORGANIZATION

Part I introduces students to the concept of critical thinking, defines important terms, and outlines critical thinking skills and how they apply to reading and writing.

In **Part II** students are given a review of how to write expository paragraphs. They learn about paragraph structure and how to clarify their purpose for writing, assess their audience, generate ideas, provide details and

support for their paragraph's purpose, and ensure order, unity, and coherence. In Chapter 5, they learn the basic building blocks of essays and how to apply what they have learned to the essay writing process.

In **Part III** students learn about various modes, or paragraph types, including narration, description, process, classification, definition, example/illustration, cause and effect, comparison and contrast, and argument and persuasion. Each chapter contains specific instruction on how to write in a particular mode; critical thinking pointers; an annotated student paragraph that provides a realistic and level-appropriate model; practice activities for specific skills as well as linked activities that walk students through the writing process; a professional example paragraph written in the mode with exercises; and writing assignments.

Chapter 15 provides instruction in how to take short-answer and timed exams.

In **Part IV** students learn how to write from sources including readings and articles as well as how to summarize, paraphrase, and analyze other writers' work. They also learn how to find sources to support their own ideas (research), how to evaluate them, and how to cite them correctly in their own writing (MLA citation format).

Chapter 18 provides students with a wide range of selections to use for practicing their critical reading and writing skills. All of the reading selections are followed by exercises and writing prompts that emphasize critical thinking and encourage deeper understanding and analysis.

Part V provides a review of sentence parts and common sentence construction errors, and contains tips and exercises for avoiding sentence fragments, run-ons, comma splices, and common shift and construction errors.

Part VI, a grammar handbook, covers the following topics and provides a wealth of sentence- and paragraph-level exercises for each:

- Punctuation
- Spelling and mechanics
- Tone, style, diction, and usage
- ESL tips
- Vocabulary tips

Hopefully, you and your students will find that this text provides *the right stuff* to help them successfully dive deeper into their critical thinking abilities and learn how to apply them in every aspect of their writing and reading.

Pearson Writing Resources for Instructors and Students

Book-Specific Ancillary Material

Annotated Instructor's Edition for The Write Stuff: Thinking Through Paragraphs, 1/e

ISBN 0132243075

The Annotated Instructor's Edition for *The Write Stuff: Thinking Through Paragraphs* includes general teaching tips and answers to all exercises in the student edition of the book.

Instructor's Resource Manual for The Write Stuff: Thinking Through Paragraphs, 1/e

ISBN 0132243083

Prepared by Elizabeth Barnes, Daytona State College, the Instructor's Resource Manual offers general teaching tips, guidance on tailoring instruction for English language learners, additional exercises, an Answer Key for all exercises, and a 40-page Instructor's Guide on how to include critical thinking instruction in the developmental writing course.

The Pearson Writing Package

Pearson is pleased to offer a variety of support materials to help make teaching writing easier for teachers and to help students excel in their coursework. Many of our student supplements are available free or at a greatly reduced price when packaged with *The Write Stuff: Thinking Through Paragraphs*. Visit www.pearsonhighereducation.com, contact your local Pearson sales representative, or review a detailed listing of the full supplements package in the *Instructor's Resource Manual* for more information.

MEDIA RESOURCES PEARSON mywritinglab

MyWritingLab: Where better practice makes better writers (www.mywritinglab.com)!
MyWritingLab, a complete online learning program, provides better practice exercises to developing writers.
What makes the practice in MyWritingLab better?

- **Diagnostic Testing:** MyWritingLab's diagnostic test comprehensively assesses students' skills in grammar. Students are given an individualized learning path based on the diagnostic's results, identifying the areas where they most need help.

- **Progressive Learning:** The heart of MyWritingLab is the progressive learning that takes place as students complete the Recall, Apply, and Write exercises within each topic. Students move from literal comprehension (Recall) to critical understanding (Apply) to the ability to demonstrate a skill in their own writing (Write). This progression of critical thinking, not available in any other online resource, enables students to truly master the skills and concepts they need to become successful writers.

- **Online Gradebook:** All student work in MyWritingLab is captured in the Online Gradebook. Students can monitor their own progress through reports explaining their scores on the exercises in the course. Instructors can see which topics their students have mastered and access other detailed reports, such as class summaries, that track the development of their entire class and display useful details on each student's progress.

E-Book

The Write Stuff: Thinking Through Paragraphs e-text is accessed through MyWritingLab. Students now have the e-text at their fingertips while completing the various exercises and activities within MyWritingLab. Students can highlight important material in the e-text and add notes to any section for reflection and/or further study throughout the semester.

ACKNOWLEDGMENTS

I am grateful to all of my students, colleagues, friends, and family who have supported me in the process of writing *The Write Stuff: Thinking Through Paragraphs*.

First, I would like to thank Matthew Wright, senior acquisitions editor, and Gillian Cook, senior development editor, for their support, vision, and encouragement throughout the development of this text. Thanks to Bruce Hobart and the staff at Laserwords for their valuable design and production work; Tom DeMarco, senior marketing manager, for his support and vision; and to all the editorial assistants, design staff, marketing representatives and others at Pearson who made this book possible.

I am grateful to my colleagues at Green River Community College for their support and encouragement as I wrote this text and to fellow teachers throughout the country who helped review chapters and the preliminary and final drafts of the manuscript. I am particularly indebted to the following reviewers for their thoughtful, candid, and insightful comments and suggestions, which have guided me in the development of this book:

Andrew S. Andermatt, Clinton Community College; Lorraine Anderson, Linn-Benton Community College; Joe W. Anguiano, Riverside Community College; Josh M. Beach, University of Texas, San Antonio; Patricia Colville, Orange County Community College; Karen L. Feldman, Seminole State College of Florida; Patricia Golder, Victor Valley College; Kathryn Hake, Linn-Benton Community College; Mariama Jackson, Albany Technical College; Stanley W. Jackson, Southside Virginia Community College; Paulette Longmore, Essex County College; Nicole Lovejoy, Cerritos College; Elizabeth Marsh, Bergen Community College; Jan Modisette, Jacksonville College; Catherine Moran, Bristol County Community College; Christie Okocha, Cuyahoga Community College; Karen Petit, Community College of Rhode Island; Anne Marie Prendergast, Bergen Community College; Jessica Rabin, University of North Alabama; Kathy Tyndall, Wake Technical Community College; Ralph Velazquez, Rio Hondo College; Nikka Harris Vrieze, Rochester Community and Technical College; Gregory Zobel, College of the Redwoods

I am extremely grateful to my students, past and present, who inspired me in the classroom and who inspired me to begin writing textbooks. Thank you also to those students who have given me permission to use their work and to those who provided their feedback on this text and its exercises. *The Write Stuff* would not be if not for you.

A special thanks to the artists and photographers who let me feature their beautiful visuals in this text. I am especially indebted to Tom Shugrue,

Wayne Buck, Fred Huston, Annie Musselman, Zoe Close, Paul Metivier, Hank Galmish, and the other artists featured in the book.

Finally, I want to thank my family for their patience and support as I worked on this text. Special thanks to my sons, Marcus and Thomas. Thanks also to my mother, Delores Sims, and to my brothers and sister and their families: Nick, Charlie, Dolly, Diana, Jerith, Mathew, Krysta, and Ashley Sims. Thanks also to Douglas T. Cole; Sharon Thornton and Fumitaka Matsuoka; Doug and Nancy Cole; Halvor and Ilona Cole; Traci Cole and David and Rachel Haygood; Katharine deBaun; Sandy Johanson; Jaeney Hoene; Jennifer Whetham; Julie Moore; Lori Vail; Amanda Schaefer; Walter Lowe; Joyce Hammer; Jim Wood; Neal Vasishth; Richard, Cara, and Josh Berman; Jeb, Darci, Levi, and Jaspar Wyman; Tom and Hannah Shugrue; and all of my extended family across the country.

Marcie Sims

ABOUT THE AUTHOR

Marcie Sims has been teaching pre-college and college-level composition for 20 years. She is the author of *The Write Stuff: Thinking Through Essays* and *The Write Stuff: Thinking Through Paragraphs* (Pearson). She is a tenured faculty member at Green River Community College in Auburn, Washington. She lives in Seattle, Washington, with her two sons Marcus and Thomas.

Picture by Jennifer Whetham

Preface to the Student

The Write Stuff is designed to provide you with the basic skills you will need for successful college writing, reading, and critical thinking—skills you will continue to use after college, in your career, and beyond. A Critical Thinking Toolbox in Chapter 1 that defines critical thinking icons and writing terms used throughout the text and Applying Critical Thinking boxes in every chapter will help you apply critical thinking skills in your reading and writing. Notes in the margin will also direct you to related information or expanded explanations for specific topics.

As you build your skills in writing and analysis, *The Write Stuff* weaves critical thinking practice throughout the chapters. You will learn about the basic components of critical thinking in Chapter 1. In Chapter 2, you'll learn how to apply critical thinking skills to reading. Then, in the chapters on writing paragraphs and essays, patterns of organization, and writing from sources, as well as in the reading selections themselves, you will find critical thinking questions and writing prompts to hone your analysis skills. Finally, in the handbook section, critical thinking is woven into the instruction on sentence construction and grammar skills and information is provided on vocabulary and style.

The Write Stuff: Thinking Through Paragraphs is a tool, so remember to use it in a way that best serves your purpose. You don't need to read the chapters in order. Read them in the order assigned by your instructor, but don't forget to use the index to look up answers to problems you need help with and to answer questions that arise as you study. The critical writing and reading skills you learn in this book will help you do better in courses you will take throughout your college career (not just in English or writing classes). This all-in-one textbook provides what you'll need to succeed in your college writing and reading tasks and in your professional career.

Marcie Sims

1 Critical Thinking in Writing and Reading

Moieties: Eagle and Raven on Blue Ice   Zoe Close

LEARNING OBJECTIVES

In this chapter, you will learn

 LO1 What critical thinking is and why it is important

LO2 What critical thinking tools you can use to write well

THINKING CRITICALLY

Look at the picture above. Then answer the questions that follow.

1. On first glance, what strikes you in this image? What is your eye drawn to?

   _____

   _____

2. Now take a closer look, paying attention to each detail of the photograph. How do the individual parts of the photo (the glacier, the birds, the sky, the water) come together to make an overall image that blends or contrasts shapes and colors? How can breaking down the parts of an image or a reading help you get a better understanding of the overall message?

   _____

   _____

LO 1   CRITICAL THINKING

Critical thinking is a term you will hear quite a bit in college because it refers to the kind of thinking you'll be asked to do in your courses and later in your career. You'll be happy to know that you are already a critical thinker! You use your critical thinking skills every day. Whenever you make a decision, solve a problem, or prioritize tasks, you are using critical thinking. For instance, when you choose your classes each term, you have to think carefully about your schedule. What classes are open this term? Which classes count toward my degree or certificate goals? How many classes can I take in one term and still be successful? Which classes are most important for me to take first? Engaging in the process of making these decisions, weighing the choices, and prioritizing all involve critical thinking. Even on a day-to-day basis, you engage your critical thinking skills. When you shop for groceries, when you decide which bills you should pay first on a limited budget, when you work out problems and arguments between you and your friends or you and your coworkers, you are being a critical thinker.

This chapter provides you with critical thinking tools and tips designed to help you read and write analytically. (When you analyze, you break down ideas into their basic parts and work out how they relate to each other.) These tools will also aid you in evaluating your reading and writing processes. Critical thinking skills are essential for effective reading and writing. Good thinking and good writing go hand in hand. In fact, the word *critical* comes from the Greek word *kritikos*, meaning "to question or to analyze." Many teachers and experts today emphasize the importance of critical thinking in college courses.

Various experts define critical thinking differently, but **critical thinking** is always a process that involves actively thinking through and evaluating all the steps in your thinking process or the thinking process of others. You must also be aware of any biases or assumptions (see page 15) you have and how they affect your conclusions.

Critical thinking skills are essential for good analytical reading and clear, fair-minded analytical writing. You can use critical thinking skills to understand and evaluate the writings of others and to discover the strengths and weaknesses in their arguments. As you learn and practice these skills, your own thinking and writing will improve. Develop the habit of a step-by-step process of thinking about each part of an argument or idea. Once you get hooked on the power that comes from using your critical thinking skills, you may not be able to stop—you will find yourself using them everywhere: while reading the newspaper, listening to the radio, reading a novel, even watching a movie.

Think of each step in the critical thinking process as a domino in a long line of dominoes set up to fall in a certain pattern and to end in a specific place. Knock over one domino, and it will knock over the next. But if one domino is out of place, it will keep all the others that follow it from falling correctly. In the same way, one error in your reasoning can throw off your whole chain of thinking and interrupt the flow and logic of your ideas. So line up each step in your critical thinking process carefully: Weigh each piece of evidence you provide, your reasons and conclusions, and make sure no point you make is out of line. Otherwise, your chain of thought and evidence will be thrown off and your end result will be derailed. You want your dominoes to fall into place perfectly, one idea sparking the next: a perfect process.

LO 2 CRITICAL THINKING TOOLS

The following critical thinking tools are used throughout this textbook to help you evaluate your thinking, reading, and writing processes; to explore your ideas, arguments, and conclusions; and to analyze the arguments and writing decisions of other writers. The icons (pictures) that accompany these key critical thinking tools alert you to when they are being used in the text and remind you when to use them yourself as you read selections and practice your writing skills.

These critical thinking terms are essential to the critical thinking process, but they are also the tools of argument. *Most college writing contains some level of argument:* You always have a purpose to explain and illustrate for your reader.

Now read the following explanations of each of these terms and the questions related to them that you should ask yourself as you read and write in order to think more critically and analyze more thoroughly.

CRITICAL THINKING TOOLBOX

Icons	Critical Thinking Terms	Definitions	Writing Terms
PURPOSE (Blueprints/plans)	Purpose	What you want to say about your topic: the point(s) you are making. The purpose is the plan or blueprint for what you want to say in your essay.	Thesis statement
IDEAS (Support/beams)	Ideas	The foundation for your argument: Ideas develop your purpose. They form the structure of your overall sentences (beams), develop your thesis (plans), and hold up your conclusion.	Topic sentences
SUPPORT (Nails)	Support	Examples, details, and evidence illustrate the ideas you use to support your purpose. They provide support (nails) for the ideas (beams) that support your purpose.	Major and minor details
ASSUMPTIONS BIASES (Tape measure)	Assumptions and Biases	Assumptions (information you take for granted) and biases (personal beliefs you have about particular topics) need to be carefully measured for accuracy and validity. Always evaluate them when making an argument.	
CONCLUSIONS (Finished house)	Conclusions	The results of your argument or purpose. The result of carefully building your argument (using plans, beams, and nails) is a well-thought-out conclusion (house).	Conclusion
POINT OF VIEW (Camera)	Point of View	How you see the subject you are discussing, your particular view, like looking through a camera lens and seeing a specific version of an image	
ANALYSIS (Magnifying glass)	Analysis	Breaking down an idea and working out the meaning of the individual parts and how they relate to the whole: like looking at something through a magnifying glass to see in detail all the parts it is made up of	

1. **Purpose.** Purpose is your reason for writing a paragraph or essay. It is what you want to explain or prove to your readers. It should be stated in the topic sentence of a paragraph or the thesis sentence in an essay. Everything else you include in a piece of writing should develop that purpose.

    When you read, ask yourself:

    ■ What is the author's purpose for writing?

    ■ What argument(s) is the author putting forth?

    ■ What direct or implied questions is he or she addressing?

    When you write, ask yourself:

    ■ What is my purpose in this writing assignment?

    ■ What is my argument for this topic?

    ■ What conclusion(s) have I reached related to it?

    ■ How will I argue this conclusion or these conclusions?

2. **Ideas and Information.** You develop your purpose using your own ideas, personal knowledge, and information. Later, you develop these ideas using examples, ideas, details, and commentary.

    When you read, ask yourself:

    ■ What ideas does the author include to support his or her purpose?

    ■ What background information does he or she provide?

    When you write, ask yourself:

    ■ What ideas do I want to include to support my purpose?

    ■ What background or personal information can I use to help develop my purpose?

3. **Support.** You need to provide information to support your purpose. You can draw on your personal experiences or those of others, use facts and statistics you have researched, provide examples and specific details, or supply information provided by your instructor to support

your reasoning. Always evaluate the information provided by other writers. Include comments that explain the importance of the examples and details you provide.

When you read, ask yourself:

- What evidence or examples is the author using to support his or her reasoning?
- Are the examples and support believable and clearly explained?
- Do they adequately support the author's purpose?

When you write, ask yourself:

- What evidence or examples can I provide to back up my ideas?
- Are they believable and clearly explained?
- Do they support my purpose?

4. **Assumptions and Biases.** Be sure that the assumptions you or an author make about a topic or idea are not based on misinformation. Check for any biases in your thinking or that of an author. Any mistakes in the ideas that your reasoning is based on can cause problems in your argument. Although assumptions and biases can be well-founded, they must be measured for accuracy and logic.

When you read, ask yourself:

- Is there an error in the idea the author is explaining?
- Does the author include assumptions or biases that are flawed or unfair?

When you write, ask yourself:

- Is there an error in the idea I'm explaining?
- Are the assumptions I make or the biases I brought into thinking about my topic based on false information?

5. **Conclusions and Consequences.** The conclusion is the final point in your argument. Consequences are all the results of the conclusion you've made. For instance, if you argue that the music program should

be cancelled at your school and the money used to add more parking spaces on campus, be sure to address all the possible consequences of your position. The consequences could be a loss in the artistic identity of your school, fewer students who want to focus on music applying to your college, and so on.

When you read, ask yourself:

- What are the author's conclusions in this reading?
- Are the consequences of his or her arguments acceptable?

When you write, ask yourself:

- What are my conclusions in this paper?
- Are the consequences of my ideas acceptable and clearly thought out?

Back to the domino idea again: Think of the concluding argument in your writing not as the last domino falling over in the chain but as one near the end. The consequences of your argument are the last few dominoes that follow that one. They might not be directly stated in your paper: You'll have to imagine those last dominoes falling and what they mean. For instance, will canceling the music program lead to a decrease in enrollment and hurt the overall budget of the school and therefore the quality of the education it provides?

POINT
OF VIEW

6. **Point of View.** Your point of view is your perspective on a topic. Be sure to check the assumptions your point of view is based upon are correct and unbiased.

When you read, ask yourself:

- What point of view does the author have on his or her topic?
- Did he or she consider other points of view that might be relevant?
- Is the point of view one-sided or biased?

When you write, ask yourself:

- What is my point of view on the topic?
- Have I considered other points of view that might be relevant?
- Is my point of view too biased for my intended audience?

7. **Analysis.** Analysis involves breaking down an idea and working out the meaning of its individual parts and how they relate to the whole. It is an in-depth look at every detail of an idea or argument, like using a magnifying glass to examine something up close and carefully.

When you read, ask yourself:

- What is the author saying?
- Does the author develop his or her ideas well using specific ideas, support, and analysis?

When you write, ask yourself:

- What ideas am I developing, and have I broken them down into all their separate parts?
- Do I develop all the ideas well using specific ideas, support, and analysis?

Using these critical thinking tools for reading and writing will help you focus on the basic parts of your written arguments. With practice, these skills will become an automatic and natural part of your reading and writing processes.

CRITICAL THINKING CHECKLIST

Using the critical thinking skills defined in this chapter will help you get into the habit of analyzing and evaluating the ideas and techniques you and other writers use to present arguments. Throughout this book, you will see critical thinking questions based on the concepts covered here. Be sure to use the general Critical Thinking Checklist that follows to evaluate your critical thinking process or the process of another writer.

CRITICAL THINKING CHECKLIST

PURPOSE

1. What is the *purpose* of this piece of writing? Is it clear?

_____

_____

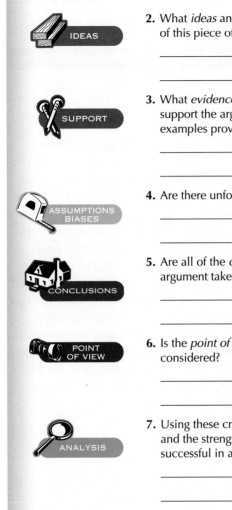

2. What *ideas* and background information are provided to support the purpose of this piece of writing?

_____

_____

3. What *evidence* and *examples* are used to explain and develop the ideas that support the argument made in this piece of writing? Are the evidence and examples provided sufficient?

_____

_____

4. Are there unfounded *assumptions* or unreasonable *biases*?

_____

_____

5. Are all of the *conclusions* and *consequences* of the argument (the results of the argument taken to their furthest extreme) considered?

_____

_____

6. Is the *point of view* clear and consistent, and have other points of view been considered?

_____

_____

7. Using these critical thinking tools, *analyze* the overall structure of this essay and the strength of the author's argument, ideas, and support. Was the author successful in accomplishing the purpose? Why or why not?

_____

_____

CRITICAL THINKING IN ACTION

In order for critical thinking to become second nature, you need to practice using the tools described above in your writing and when you read. Practice these skills on the following reading.

ACTIVITY 1-1   **Using the Critical Thinking Checklist**

Directions: *Review the critical thinking terms, and read the article "Does Johnny Really Need a Cell Phone?" Then, answer the seven questions in the Critical Thinking Checklist after the article.*

READING

Does Johnny Really Need a Cell Phone?

Karen Haywood Queen

For Diane Matheson, the financial breaking point of keeping her teen in technology was the $360 her daughter spent to download music and horoscopes onto her cell phone. For "Ellen," who is too embarrassed to use her real name, it was back-to-back cell phone bills totaling $1,100 for her daughter's text messages and excess minutes.

Back when today's parents struggled to join the "in" crowd, being cool meant wearing the right clothes and sneakers, having a phone in your room and listening to the right music on eight-track or cassette tapes. For this generation of teens and 'tweens, the cost of being cool and connected has soared. Cell phones are the main expense: Teens, 'tweens and younger kids want cell phones to talk to and text their friends. "It's about being cool—having that cell phone so you can whip it out," says Claudine Jalajas, adding there's no way her 10-year-old son is getting a cell phone anytime soon, despite his constant pleas. "When we were kids, we saw adults with cigarettes in their hands, and we thought that made you look cool. Now it's cell phones."

Have phone, will text

At one time, kids without cell phones were on the other side of a digital divide, based on a 2002 study by Context-Based Research Group in Baltimore. "Now, the real dividing line is whether you're texting or not texting," says Robbie Blinkoff, the principal anthropologist and managing director of Context. Parents end up feeling ambushed by high cell phone bills with charges for hundreds of minutes, thousands of texts and other options they didn't even know existed. Keeping up with the Joneses' cool kids has never been so costly. "Apparently, it is very expensive to have access to the Web," Matheson says wryly. "That wasn't explained to me. My daughter downloaded four songs, and those four songs cost me $280. I was really upset. I canceled the service right away."

Unlimited headaches

The next company's plan offered Matheson's teen 200 minutes and unlimited texting for $39.99 a month. But then a bill came for texting a five-digit code to get horoscopes—an additional $80 in charges. "I didn't realize getting a cell phone was going to be so complex," Matheson says. "I didn't realize what was really involved. You'd think the phone companies would tell you these things."

Unfortunately, you have to know to ask about opt-out options. "Ellen" and her husband hit the roof when they got a $500 phone bill for their daughter's excess minutes and texting. "She had sent over 3,000 text messages and spent almost 12 hours on the cell phone," Ellen says. "My husband checked on the next bill, which we hadn't gotten yet, and it was even higher—$600. We told her she was going to have to pay it off." Matheson's and Ellen's girls are paying back their parents by baby-sitting and forking over birthday cash, but their families are footing the bills in the meantime. "Maybe I should take a second job," says a still-steaming Ellen. "Parents are doing ridiculous things to finance the status symbols of their children," says Marybeth Hicks, the author of *Bringing Up Geeks*.

Comparison-shop

Check price plans online before you go phone shopping, says Matheson, who found a better deal on the Internet after signing a contract at a carrier's brick-and-mortar store. Consider different service levels, options and charges for extra minutes and services. For example, Sprint offers a variety of voice, text, Web and other plans, company spokeswoman Emmy Anderson says.

There are two schools of thought on texting. One is that kids are going to send hundreds, even thousands of text messages anyway, so you might as well get unlimited texting. On the other hand, do you really want your child sending that many text messages? "One relative of mine sent 6,000 text messages the first month she had a cell phone," Hicks says. "If you send that many text messages, you're spending way too much time texting."

After you choose a plan, you can also check online to find out what parental control features your carrier has. If your carrier isn't listed, options listed by the other carriers will at least give you topics for conversation. "Carriers are offering tools to help parents encourage responsible cell phone use as well as protect kids from questionable content," says Shannon Nix, a spokeswoman for CTIA—The Wireless Association.

Set expectations, then check up

Phones are all about communication, so discuss your expectations about texting, minutes used, downloads and other issues with your child before handing over a phone. "Talk to the child before getting the phone, about how you expect them to use the features, what you will or won't be allowing," Anderson says. "But sometimes that discussion comes after they get the first bill." Then, check up on your child. "You can dial in and check, log in and check or do it right on the phone itself," Anderson says. "If your child hasn't had a cell phone before, checking on how the phone is used is a very good idea."

Determine an age limit

Set an age or school grade for when your child can get a cell phone. At $20 a month, that's an extra $240 in your savings account every year that you delay. In Hicks' family, each child gets a cell phone the summer before freshman year of high school. "I don't want a cell phone that lands in my wash," she says. "That's where a sixth-grader's cell phone goes." Blinkoff advocates waiting as long as possible. "There's no need for the kids to have the things they have at the ages they have them," he says.

Limit use by paying in advance. "Get a pay-as-you-go phone, not one that is on anybody's family plan," says a wiser Ellen. "Once you run out of those minutes, they're gone. I don't think kids today see things as being 'gone.' They think: 'We can go buy some more. We can get unlimited.' That's sending the wrong message—that everything is free."

Make them pay

Clear up that everything-is-free idea and be frank about costs.

"My kids used to say, 'But the cell phone is free,'" Hicks says. "They were truly surprised that I had to sign a contract and pay every month. We can't put our kids in a bubble and have them not know about the costs of things." Have your child foot the bills for any extras, whether cell phone minutes or games or designer clothes. For some reason, $20 of a child's own money is worth more than $20 out of Mom's or Dad's wallet. "Allowance really does help," Jalajas says. "I'll say, 'That will cost 20 weeks of allowance.' My policy is, I'm your mother, and I will provide you with everything you need—food, clothes, a home. Anything above and beyond that, which includes video games, you'll pay for yourself."

Buy pre-loved items

Jalajas' son, who used to insist on all-new books and games, now realizes he can buy a used computer game for $10 or the same game, new, for $35. The Mathesons also shop for used games for their Nintendo Wii, often trading in old ones for credit. "It's a rarity we'll buy a brand-new game," Diane Matheson says.

A friend in deed

Friends can make a difference in encouraging or curbing materialism. One of Jalajas' son's friends is an only child with a nice bedroom, a cell phone, an iPod, a big-screen TV in the basement and more. "He comes home and says, 'How come I have to share a room with my brother?'" Jalajas says. But a new friend has made Jalajas' son more appreciative of what he has. "He came home and said, 'Do you know he has to share a room with his three sisters?'" she says. "We need more of those friends."

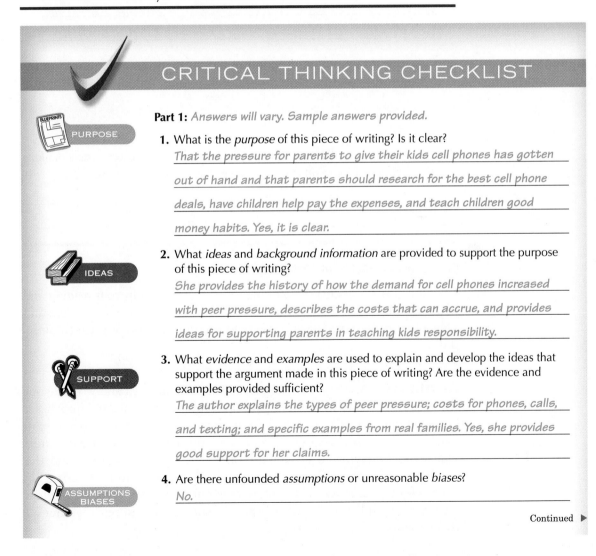

CRITICAL THINKING CHECKLIST

Part 1: *Answers will vary. Sample answers provided.*

PURPOSE

1. What is the *purpose* of this piece of writing? Is it clear?

   That the pressure for parents to give their kids cell phones has gotten

   out of hand and that parents should research for the best cell phone

   deals, have children help pay the expenses, and teach children good

   money habits. Yes, it is clear.

IDEAS

2. What *ideas* and *background information* are provided to support the purpose of this piece of writing?

   She provides the history of how the demand for cell phones increased

   with peer pressure, describes the costs that can accrue, and provides

   ideas for supporting parents in teaching kids responsibility.

SUPPORT

3. What *evidence* and *examples* are used to explain and develop the ideas that support the argument made in this piece of writing? Are the evidence and examples provided sufficient?

   The author explains the types of peer pressure; costs for phones, calls,

   and texting; and specific examples from real families. Yes, she provides

   good support for her claims.

ASSUMPTIONS BIASES

4. Are there unfounded *assumptions* or unreasonable *biases*?

   No.

Continued ▶

5. Are the *conclusions* and *consequences* of the argument (the results of the argument taken to their furthest extreme) considered?

Yes, although she could say parents could say no completely to kids having cell phones.

6. Is the *point of view* clear and consistent, and have other points of view been considered?

Yes, and she also looks at the kids' point of view.

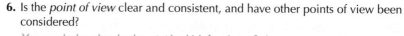

7. Using these critical thinking tools, *analyze* the overall structure of this essay and the strength of the author's argument, ideas, and support. Was the author successful in accomplishing her purpose? Why or why not?

She sets up the problem with details and a background history, and she provides specific examples, and finally, a plan for a solution. She was successful because she provides adequate, logical support for her arguments and purpose.

Part 2: *What effect did knowing that you would have to answer critical thinking questions afterwards have on the way you read the article?* Answers will vary.

_____

_____

Glossary of Critical Thinking Terms

Here is a glossary of critical thinking terms to help you in your reading and writing. Some of these terms have already been covered in the chapter, and some of them are new but will also help you in using your critical thinking skills.

ANALYSIS   Analysis involves breaking down an idea and working out the meaning of the individual parts and how they relate to the whole. For example, if you were asked to analyze a paragraph or a poem, you would go through each line or sentence and figure out what each individual part is saying; then you'd look at the overall meaning and the connections between the parts. Think back to the Thinking Critically opener for this chapter: The picture may not have been completely clear until you carefully analyzed each part of the image and put together all the evidence.

ARGUMENT   In most college writing, you are making an argument(s) and presenting a conclusion about a topic using reasons and evidence to convince your readers of your point. Arguments in writing can be casual and entertaining (such as arguing for the best place in town to go for a first date), or they can be more formal and structured (such as arguing for the need for a new science building on your campus).

ASSUMPTIONS   An assumption is a belief or claim that you take for granted or that society, particular people, or an author you are reading takes for granted without providing or asking for evidence or proof to support the idea. Almost everything you believe and do is based on assumptions; for instance, you assume the sun will rise each morning and set each evening. Some, however, are more individual assumptions that you take for granted but that not everyone would agree with. It is important to learn to separate the assumptions that have a basis in fact from ones that don't. When reading other people's writing, look carefully for the assumptions, the ideas they take for granted, and consider whether these are an undeniable truth.

BIAS   Bias is a particular viewpoint that you or an author has about an idea or a topic. All ideas or opinions reflect a bias. Sometimes you (or an author) are conscious of the biases in your ideas, and sometimes you are not. Having biases is not necessarily a bad thing (it is inevitable), but when one's biases are founded on misinformation or unrealistic assumptions they can get in the way of good critical thinking.

CONCLUSION   A conclusion is the end result of an argument. It is the main point you make in your paper and should be the logical result of the reasons you provide to support your argument. When you read an author's argument, you are looking for their conclusion about the topic they have chosen and how well they have developed it using reasons, examples, and details as support.

EVALUATION   Evaluation is looking at the strength of your reasoning, support, and conclusions (or those of another writer) and how well those ideas are developed and explained. Evaluate the arguments you put forth and how well you supported them with examples, reasons, and details. Also, consider the counterarguments—what people who argue for a different stand might say against your conclusion on the issue—and evaluate how well those arguments are constructed.

IMPLY/IMPLICATION   To imply means to hint that something is so, to say it indirectly. For instance, if your aunt visits you and says, "My, aren't you looking filled out these days!" she may be implying, or hinting, that you need to go on a diet.

INFERENCE   Inference involves tapping into your ability to read between the lines and figure out, or infer, what someone means based on clues in what they say or write. For instance, in the example above, your aunt has implied that you are getting fat, and you, in receiving those clues from her language, have inferred her meaning.

INTERPRETATION   Interpretation involves decoding an idea so you understand its meaning. When you interpret an author's idea, you decode it using your own words. You need to interpret and understand an author's ideas before you can analyze their meanings and evaluate them.

OPINION   Your opinion is what you (or another writer) believe about an idea, question, or topic. Opinion involves thinking about an idea or question and coming to your own conclusions about it. An opinion is based on weighing information and deciding where you stand on a question.

POINT OF VIEW   Point of view in critical thinking refers to the perspective you are coming from in your reasoning and writing (or the perspective of the author you are reading). Be aware of your own point of view and the biases, assumptions, and opinions that make up that point of view, and be prepared to think of potential points of view that differ from yours (or from the views of the author you are reading).

PURPOSE   The term purpose refers to the reason you are writing a paragraph or essay. It is what you (or the author you are reading) have set out to explain or prove to your readers. It is stated in the topic sentence of a paragraph and the thesis sentence of an essay.

SYNTHESIS   Synthesis involves pulling together your ideas, and sometimes the ideas of others, in order to make or support an argument. Often, synthesis involves pulling together ideas from different authors that connect on a particular subject or argument to give a bigger picture.

Critical thinking skills are essential for developing good arguments in paragraphs and essays. You need to engage your critical thinking skills to evaluate the writing of others: classmates, authors you read for class, and sources you consult. As with any new language, the language of critical thinking gets easier with familiarity and practice. Training yourself to use critical thinking skills is challenging, but using these skills will significantly improve your reading and writing abilities and will become a treasured, lifelong habit.

The critical thinking terms and tools discussed in this chapter are used in different places throughout the book (watch for the icons), and you will need to use some or all of them in the writing assignments, reading selection activities, and grammar exercises. Use this chapter when you need a quick reminder of what a term means or how to apply it.

Applying these critical thinking terms and tools as you write helps you better understand and analyze what you read.

ACTIVITY 1-2 Critical Thinking Review and Practice

Directions: *Answer the following questions.* *Answers will vary.*

1. Reread the definition for critical thinking on page 2. Then write a definition of critical thinking using your own words.

   _____

   _____

   _____

   _____

2. List three assumptions you have made during the last three months related to events in your life. Then write a line or two about whether each assumption ended up being valid (true) or invalid (not true or unfounded) and why.

   Assumption 1: _____

   True or unfounded: _____

   _____

   _____

   Assumption 2: _____

   True or unfounded: _____

   _____

   _____

   Assumption 3: _____

   True or unfounded: _____

   _____

   _____

3. Describe your purpose for going to college. What do you hope to accomplish?

   _____

   _____

4. What is your point of view about the cost of attending college?

   _____

   _____

5. List any biases you think you had about college life before coming to college. Were they founded or not?

_____

_____

6. List two benefits you predict you will gain from learning and applying the critical thinking tools and terms explained in this chapter.

1. _____

_____

2. _____

_____

ACTIVITY 1-3   Applying Critical Thinking Terms to a Reading

Directions: *Review the reading from Activity 1-1 on pages 9–13, "Does Johnny Really Need a Cell Phone?", and then answer the questions that follow. Refer back to the glossary of critical thinking terms on pages 14–16 for help with this exercise.*   Answers will vary. Sample answers provided.

1. What **point of view** is this piece of writing told from? How do you know?

   From the point of view of the author who is reporting on what parents go through when their kids get cell phones. I know because the reporter is using third person and giving examples from various families in her report.

2. What **assumptions** does the author make? Give an example and provide evidence to support it.

   She assumes that most parents are overwhelmed by the costs of the new demand for cell phones from their teens. Examples include the bills Diane Matheson and "Ellen" paid for their children's texting, downloading photos and horoscopes, and accessing the Web.

3. What **inferences** are made by the author in this excerpt? Explain.

   She infers that the cell phone craze has placed a burden on parents. The examples show that parents are suffering because of their children's demand for and use of cell phones.

4. What **conclusions** are reached through the details and comments in this excerpt?

She concludes that parents should research for the best cell phone deals,

have children help pay the expenses, and teach children good money habits.

LEARNING OBJECTIVES REVIEW

LO1 What is critical thinking, and why is it important? (See pp. 2–3)	**Critical thinking** is actively thinking through and evaluating all the steps in your thinking process or the thinking process of others. It is essential for good analytical reading and clear, fair-minded analytical writing. You can use critical thinking skills to understand and evaluate the writings of others and to discover the strengths and weaknesses in their arguments. You can also use them to examine your own thinking, your biases and assumptions, and to evaluate the strength and logic of the reasons you provide for an argument.
LO2 What critical thinking terms are included in the Critical Thinking Toolbox, and what do they mean? (See pp. 3–8)	The **critical thinking terms** discussed in this chapter are *purpose* (your reason for writing), *ideas* (the ideas, personal knowledge, and information used to develop your purpose), *support* (facts, statistics, examples, and research used to support your reasoning), *assumptions and biases* (errors in your ideas or those of others that you need to be aware of when reading and writing), *conclusions* (the results of your argument), *point of view* (the way you see an issue), and *analysis* (breaking an idea into its individual parts to see how they relate and contribute to overall meaning).

PEARSON
mywritinglab

For support in meeting this chapter's objectives, log in to www.mywritinglab.com and select **Critical Thinking: Responding to Text and Visuals.**

Critical Thinking
and Reading Techniques

In this chapter, you will learn to

 LO1 Apply critical thinking to reading

LO2 Read actively and interact with the text

LO3 Use six steps for active reading

LO4 Use the T-KED method for marking

  LO5 Annotate your texts

THINKING CRITICALLY

Of course good reading skills and good critical thinking skills go hand-in-hand. Would the image poster on the building above be as effective without the words that go with it? Reading takes focus. Have you ever read an article or chapter of a book, or part of an article or chapter, and then not remembered or absorbed anything that you read? Before you read this chapter, what do you think you can do to increase your retention of information as you read? List some ideas in the lines below.

_____

_____

_____

CRITICAL THINKING AND THE READING PROCESS

The critical thinking tools discussed in Chapter 1 can help you go beyond basic comprehension of what you read. If you get into the habit of asking critical thinking questions as you read a selection, you will be able to understand it better and reach deeper analytical conclusions about its content. Not only will you be able to assess the conclusions and arguments an author is making in a story or essay, but you will also be able to recognize the writing techniques used and the ideas that the author is building his or her arguments and conclusions upon. You can also check to see if there are any flaws in the introduction or in the conclusions an author reaches. Here are some questions to ask as you read that will help you think more critically about an assignment.

APPLYING CRITICAL THINKING

PURPOSE   IDEAS   SUPPORT   ASSUMPTIONS BIASES   CONCLUSIONS   POINT OF VIEW   ANALYSIS

Questions to Ask as You Read

1. What is the author's **purpose** or *goal* in this reading selection? What does he or she set out to explain, argue, or prove?

2. What are the *implied* or *stated* questions the author is answering in this reading selection?

3. What **ideas** and **support** (*evidence, data, experience,* or *facts*) does the author use to explain and illustrate his or her purpose? Is the support adequate? Convincing?

4. Does the author present alternative **points of view** when needed?

5. What **assumptions** does the author make in this reading selection? (**Assumptions** are ideas or reasons the author takes for granted and upon which he or she bases judgments or develops his or her reasoning.) Are the assumptions valid?

6. What are the *implications* or *consequences* of the author's ideas and arguments? What **conclusions** does the author reach?

7. When you break down, or **analyze**, the author's argument is it logical and well-founded?

(LO 2) ACTIVE READING

To be a good reader, you have to take an active role. You have to focus your mind, ask questions, and create an internal conversation in your head between yourself and the words as you read. The difference between *passive* and *active* reading is like the difference between *hearing* and *listening*. You can hear what someone says without listening to the words, and you can read words passively without actively engaging in understanding what they mean. Good listening takes concentration, and so does active reading. Active reading involves communication between you and the text: it's a dialogue, not a monologue.

This chapter explains how to use two active reading systems. They will provide you with the tools you need to create a dialogue with a text, so that you can understand and analyze the meaning of what you read. Many assigned college readings require you to think critically and analyze and break down the ideas, arguments, and techniques of the authors. Try out these active reading techniques to see which one works best for you or combine and customize them into a system of your own. Active reading improves your understanding of content and increases your ability to remember what you have learned. With practice, you will get faster at active reading, analyzing as you read and retaining information more easily.

(LO 3) SIX STEPS FOR ACTIVE READING

Applying the following six steps will turn your reading process into an active dialogue between you and a reading. You will need a notebook to keep as your Reading Log. For each textbook chapter, article, or essay, go through the six steps that follow and record them in your Reading Log. Mark each entry in your log with the date, name of the chapter or article, and page numbers before you begin the six steps. The sample entries from the student log that follow are based on the reading "The Windowsill as a Front Row to Life's Pageant," by Andy Newman and Cassi Feldman (in Chapter 18, p. 394).

Reading Log

Date: 10-10-10

Reading: "The Windowsill as a Front Row to Life's Pageant," by Andy Newman and Cassi Feldman

Step One: Preview the Reading

Previewing what's coming in a chapter or article helps increase your retention as you read—it's like glancing at a whole picture before you study its individual parts.

Preview the entire chapter or article before you begin reading it, and be sure to do the following:

1. **Read the chapter or article title and any subtitles.**
2. **Read the introduction** (or at least the first paragraph of the chapter or article if there is not a formal introduction).
3. **Read the first sentence of each paragraph.** In textbooks this is often the topic sentence and will tell you the main point of the paragraph.
4. **Take note of the format.** Look for text that is in boldface or italic font, underlined, or presented in a bulleted or numbered format. Key words that are defined in the text are often in boldface and authors use italics or underlining to emphasize important information.
5. **Review any graphics.** Look at any photographs, graphs, charts, diagrams or other visual aids, as these are included to provide additional information that supports and illustrates the text.
6. **Read the summary** at the end of the chapter or article (if there is no summary, then read the last paragraph).

Step Two: Think About What You Already Know About the Topic

After you have previewed the reading, ask yourself what you already know about the topic. Chances are you have already heard or read some things about the topic. If you don't know anything about the specific topic itself, what do you know about related topics, subtopics, or ideas within the article? For instance, if you are reading an article about how your community is increasing its recycling efforts, ask yourself, "What do I already know about different types of recycling? What kinds of recycling do I do?" Even a little bit of background information will help you feel more comfortable with a new topic and retain new information better.

Reading Log

Date: 10-10-10

Reading: "The Windowsill as a Front Row to Life's Pageant," by Andy Newman and Cassi Feldman

Prior knowledge/background: I know from the title that this article is probably going to be about viewing life from a window.

Step Three: Create Questions to Begin Your Dialogue with the Text

Creating questions helps keep you active and engaged in your reading as you look for answers. Turn the title and subheadings into questions and look for answers to them as you read. This active process will help you build a more detailed picture of the reading. Then, when you've finished this step, ask yourself the following two questions and write your responses down in your Reading Log. Don't worry that you might get some of the information wrong. When you read through the entire chapter or article (Step Four), you'll be able to adjust your answers; the process helps you understand more as you go.

1. What is the chapter or article about?
2. What major topics or ideas are covered in the chapter or article?

Then, create two more questions *of your own* that come to mind based on your preview of the chapter or article (e.g., What is photosynthesis? or Why do we have the electoral college system?).

Write the two questions you've created in your Reading Log and as you read through the entire piece (Step Four) look for the answers to all four questions, adding to or changing your answers to the first two and recording the answers to the second two.

Reading Log

Date: 10-10-10

Reading: "The Windowsill as a Front Row to Life's Pageant," by Andy Newman and Cassi Feldman

Prior knowledge/background: I know from the title that this article is probably about viewing life from a window.

Questions made from title/subtitles:
1. What do the authors mean by "pageant"?
2. Is this article about one person who looks out of his or her window?
3. Is it a positive or a negative article about looking out windows?
4. Is the article going to focus on people in New York?

Step Four: Read in Blocks

Either read from one subtitle to the next or if there are no subtitles read one to two paragraphs at a time, and then, after each section, complete Step Five.

▶ NOTE   Reading in blocks instead of straight through a chapter without stopping keeps you focused and careful and helps prevent the "I just read the whole chapter and I have no idea what I read" syndrome.

Step Five: Write in Your Reading Log

Write the following in your Reading Log for each block of text you read:

1. **Write a two- to three-sentence summary** of the main ideas from each section or one to two paragraph block(s), as you finish it.
2. **Write the answers** to all of the questions you created in Step Three as you discover them—or amend your questions if you find your questions were off track.
3. **Write down any vocabulary words** from each block that you don't know. If you can't figure out their meanings by the end of the block, then look them up after finishing the block (not understanding a key word or term can sabotage your understanding of that section).

Once you are sure you have understood the section you have read, place a check mark at the end of it and move on to the next one.

Reading Log

Date: 10-10-10

Reading: "The Windowsill as a Front Row to Life's Pageant," by Andy Newman and Cassi Feldman

Prior knowledge/background: I know from the title that this article is probably about viewing life from a window.

Questions made from title/subtitles:

1. What do the authors mean by "pageant"?

   They mean that the windowsill watchers see a parade of life pass by their windows and they are entertained by just watching life go on outside of their windows.

2. Is this article about one person who looks out of his or her window?

   No, this article talks about several people with the habit of windowsill gazing and then provides specific examples for different people.

3. Is it a positive or a negative article about looking out of windows?

   It's positive.

4. Is the article going to focus on people in New York?

   It focused on people in the greater New York City area.

Step Six: Review Summaries and Answer Your Own Questions

This final step tests your comprehension and retention by using your summaries and the questions about the reading you generated in Step Three to see if you have retained the information you read. When you've finished reading the entire article or essay and finished writing your summary statements, answers, and new vocabulary for each section of it, **go back and read (review)** all of the summary statements, answers, observations, and vocabulary words with definitions that you wrote in your Reading Log.

Next, in your Reading Log, **answer all the questions that you generated in Step Three without looking** at the chapter or article or your notes from Step Five. If you can't answer the questions, then review your Step Five notes, and, if necessary, the relevant sections of the piece.

▶ FINAL NOTE   If you follow all these steps, you will have engaged in an active reading process. Also, you will have notes for review to use later for class discussions, tests, or writing assignments. At first, the Six Steps for Active Reading will take longer than passively reading straight through a chapter or article. However, with lots of practice, you will be able to go through these steps quickly, sometimes doing Steps One, Two, and Six completely in your head as you get into the habit of reading as a dialogue. Finally, this process can actu-ally *save you time* by preventing you from having to reread whole chapters or articles because you didn't understand or retain informa-tion the first time through.

Example of the Six Steps in Action

Read through the excerpt below and see how the Six Steps process works for one student.

Reading Log

Step One: I have previewed the entire excerpt and read the title, introduction, first sentence of each paragraph, and the last paragraph.

Step Two: I already know that her book gives advice for how to help someone get started in writing.

READING

Excerpt from *Wild Mind: Living the Writer's Life*

Natalie Goldberg

The rules of writing practice

For fifteen years now, at the beginning of every writing workshop, I have repeated the rules of writing practice. So I will repeat them again here. And I want to say why I repeat them: Because they are the bottom line, the begin-
✓ ning of all writing, the foundation of learning to trust your own mind. . . .

Step Three, Question 1:
What are the rules of writing practice?

1. *Keep your hand moving.* When you sit down to write, whether it's for ten minutes or an hour, once you begin, don't stop. If an atom bomb drops at your feet eight minutes after you have begun and you were going to write
✓ for ten minutes, don't budge. You'll go out writing.

Step Three, Question 2:
Why should I keep my hand moving?

What is the purpose of this? Most of the time when we write, we mix up the editor and the creator. Imagine your writing hand as the creator and your other hand as the editor. Now bring your two hands together and lock your fingers. This is what happens when we write. . . . If you keep your creator hand moving, the editor can't catch up with it and lock it. It gets to write out what it wants. "Keep your hand moving" strengthens the creator and gives little space for the editor to jump in. Keeping your hand moving is the main structure for writing practice.   ✓

Step Three, Question 3:

How can losing control help in writing?

2. *Lose control.* Say what you want to say. Don't worry if it's correct, polite, appropriate. Just let it rip . . . it is remarkable how I can tell students, "Okay, say what you want, go for it," and their writing takes a substantial turn toward authenticity.   ✓

Step Three, Question 4:

Are there some exam-ples of being specific?

3. *Be specific.* Not car, but Cadillac. Not fruit, but apple. Not bird, but wren. . . But don't chastise yourself as you are writing, "I'm an idiot; Natalie said to be specific and like a fool I wrote 'tree.'" Just gently note that you wrote "tree," drop to a deeper level, and next to "tree" write "sycamore." Be gentle with yourself. Don't give room for the hard grip of the editor.

Notes from Reading Log

Step Four: I went through the article and read in blocks and turned most topic sentences into questions.

Step Five, Summary: This section of the reading is explaining some sug-gested rules for writing practice to help keep your writing flowing and keep it authentic.

Answers, Question 1: The three rules from this section are (1) keep your hand moving, (2) lose control, and (3) be specific. **Question 2:** Keeping your hand moving as you write helps the creator in you flow and helps quiet your inner editor. **Question 3:** Losing control helps you write what you really want to say. **Question 4:** Yes, some examples included Cadillac instead of car and wren instead of bird.

Step Six: My answers to my questions were accurate, so I will review them. Vocabulary words: (1) authentic: real, not phony; (2) wren: a small brownish songbird; (3) sycamore: a type of tree, with hand-shaped leaves and round knobby fruit.

ACTIVITY 2-1   Six Steps Practice

Directions: *Apply the Six Steps method to the next section of the chapter that is annotated above. Write your questions in the margin of the reading, place check marks after each section after you have read and understood it, and write the answers to your questions, your summary, and any unfamiliar vocabulary words in your Reading Log or on a separate sheet of paper. Then, explain below* *what effect this process had on the way you read the section and your under-standing of it.* Answers will vary.

Excerpt 2 from *Wild Mind: Living the Writer's Life*

Natalie Goldberg

4. *Don't think.* We usually live in the realm of second or third thoughts, thoughts on thoughts, rather than in the realm of first thoughts, the real way we flash on something. Stay with the first flash. Writing practice will help you contact first thoughts. Just practice and forget everything else. . .

5. *Don't worry about punctuation, spelling, grammar.*

6. *You are free to write the worst junk in America.* You can be more specific, if you like: the worst junk in Santa Fe; New York; Kalamazoo, Michigan; your city block; your pasture; your neighborhood restaurant; your family. Or you can get more cosmic: free to write the worst junk in the universe, galaxy, world, hemisphere, Sahara Desert.

7. *Go for the jugular.* If something scary comes up, go for it. That's where the energy is. Otherwise, you'll spend all your time writing around whatever makes you nervous. It will probably be abstract, bland writing because you're avoiding the truth.

_____

_____

_____

_____

_____

ACTIVITY 2-2   **More Six Steps Practice**

Directions: *Pick an article or essay from the reading section of this textbook or from outside of class, or from a chapter in a textbook from one of your other classes, and apply the Six Steps method. Then, on a separate sheet of paper, explain what effect this process had on the way you read the chapter, article, or essay and your understanding of it.* Answers will vary.

To be a good reader, you also need to know how to annotate (mark, high-light, and make notes) throughout your assigned reading. The T-KED method that follows gives you some codes you can use, in addition to high-lighting and using regular symbols (examples given following the explana-tion of the T-KED method).

LO 4   THE T-KED METHOD FOR MARKING TEXTBOOKS AND ARTICLES

The T-KED method is a system designed to help you mark your text as you read. It works best for nonfiction: articles, textbook chapters, or essays. The process involves marking the **Thesis** ("**T**") or main point of the article or essay, the **Key Ideas** ("**K**") in each body paragraph, the **Examples** ("**E**") that support those Key Ideas, and the **Details** ("**D**") that support those examples. By marking these elements as you read, you will increase your comprehension and your ability to distinguish main ideas and arguments from supporting examples and details.

T = Thesis

The **thesis** is the main idea, argument, or point of the article or essay. It is the purpose statement of the piece. A thesis can be one sentence, or it can be a few sentences depending on the length and complexity of the piece. Usually, the thesis is located in the first or second paragraph of an article or essay, but sometimes it is stated at the end.

Sometimes the thesis is never stated and is only implied. In an **implied thesis**, the author provides many ideas and examples and details about a subject that will lead you to a conclusion about that topic. If you find the thesis is implied instead of directly stated, write out a sentence of your own that explains what the main idea or argument is for the reading after you have read all the information and examples (clues).

▶ TRY THIS   After reading the first two paragraphs of an article or essay, **circle** the one to three sentences that you think state the main argument. **Mark a "T"** in the left margin next to the sentences you have circled as the thesis statement.

▶ NOTE   As you read through the article or essay, you may find you were wrong about the thesis statement and will have to mark the correct one. Or, if it turns out the thesis was implied, you might have to write it in yourself.

K = Key Idea

For each paragraph of the article or essay, **underline** the one- to two-sentence key idea for that paragraph. **Mark a "K"** in the left margin next to each underlined key idea. The **key idea** is the *topic sentence* for the paragraph.

▶ **TIP**   Read the entire paragraph before you underline the key idea. Often the key idea or topic sentence for a paragraph is the first or second sentence of the paragraph, but sometimes it's in the middle or even the end.

E = Examples

In each paragraph, **put an "E"** over each sentence or part of a sentence that provides an **example to support** the key idea or topic sentence of that paragraph.

D = Details

In each paragraph, **put a "D"** over any **detail that supports** an example used to support the paragraph's key idea or topic sentence.

T (again!)

Double-check your "T" (thesis) to make sure it still works as the main idea of the article or essay. If not, circle the real thesis or write in the implied thesis of the article.

▶ **TIP**   Answer this question: What was the essay or article trying to explain, show through implied ideas or conclusions, or prove though evidence provided? The answer to that question is the thesis.

LO 5 ANNOTATE AS YOU READ

Whether or not you choose to use one of the specific active reading systems discussed above when you read, you need to get into the habit of using highlighting or underlining, codes, and other annotating methods.

Both highlighting and underlining are a way to separate the main ideas from the rest of the sentences in a reading. Use highlighting or underlining on the thesis, topic sentences, and major ideas for each section. You can also use a highlighter to mark words you don't know and then fill in their definitions in the margins.

Be sure to use the margins to write notes to yourself throughout the reading. You can use the margin spaces for the following purposes:

- **To write what you already know about the subject** or any insights that you have as you read
- **To number subpoints or examples** given in support of the main idea of a paragraph or reading as a whole

- **To write in definitions of unfamiliar vocabulary** words you've marked
- **To write in questions** you have as you read
- **To make comments about graphics** (photos, charts, diagrams, cartoons, etc.)
- **To make comments when you notice an author's biases or assumptions**
- **To add codes** (see some suggestions below)
- **To note any other reminders to yourself** that will help your understanding as you review later

Codes You Can Use

You can customize your own list of symbols and codes to annotate text as you read. Here are a few commonly used symbols or codes:

?	Use a question mark whenever you don't understand a term or a concept in a particular section. It will remind you later to double-check that part to make sure you understand it.
paternalism	Use boxes around key words—you can write the definitions for them in the margins.
analysis breaking something down into parts	Or, use a circle around key terms and add the definitions in the margins.
1, 2	Use numbers to indicate listed points that are not numbered already, or use numbers to mark the numbers of examples given for each main idea.
☆ * ☺	Use symbols such as stars, asterisks, or smiley faces to indicate important points or sections you particularly enjoyed.

Example of Using T-KED, Highlighting, and Codes as You Read

Note the codes, highlighting, and T-KED notations in yellow and *blue* in the following excerpt from "How to Mark a Book," by Mortimer Adler.

*K   If you're a die-hard anti-book-marker, you may object that the margins, the space between the lines, and the end-papers don't give you room enough. All right. How about using a scratch pad slightly smaller than the page-size of the book—so that the edges of the sheets won't protrude? Make your index, outlines and even your notes on the pad, and then insert these sheets permanently inside the front and back covers of the book.

K   Or, you may say that this business of marking books is going to slow up your reading. It probably will. That's one of the reasons for doing it. Most of us have been taken in by the notion that speed of reading is a measure of our intelligence. There is no such thing as the right speed for intelligent reading. Some things should be read quickly and effortlessly and some
                                                      E
should be read slowly and even laboriously. The sign of intelligence in read-ing is the ability to read different things differently according to their worth.
   E
In the case of good books, the point is not to see how many of them you can get through, but rather how many can get through you—how many you
                   D
can make your own. A few friends are better than a thousand acquain-tances. If this be your aim, as it should be, you will not be impatient if it takes more time and effort to read a great book than it does a newspaper.☺

K   You may have one final objection to marking books. You can't lend them to your friends because nobody else can read them without being
                           E
distracted by your notes. Furthermore, you won't want to lend them
                               D
because a marked copy is kind of an intellectual diary, and lending it is almost like giving your mind away.☺

ACTIVITY 2-3   **T-KED Practice**

Directions: *Pick another chapter from this text, an article from outside of class, or a chapter from a textbook from one of your other classes, and apply the T-KED method. Then, on a separate sheet of paper, explain what effect this process had on the way you read the chapter or article and your understanding of it.* Answers will vary.

USE THE CRITICAL THINKING CHECKLIST

In order to ensure that you are thinking critically as you read, analyzing the writer's arguments and techniques, answer the critical thinking checklist questions below immediately after reading a large section or the whole read-ing if it is not too long.

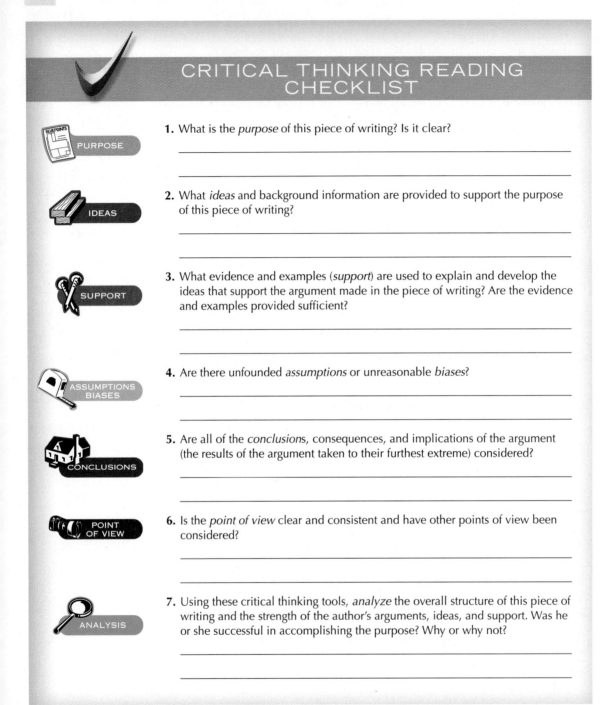

CRITICAL THINKING READING CHECKLIST

PURPOSE

1. What is the *purpose* of this piece of writing? Is it clear?

_____

_____

IDEAS

2. What *ideas* and background information are provided to support the purpose of this piece of writing?

_____

_____

SUPPORT

3. What evidence and examples (*support*) are used to explain and develop the ideas that support the argument made in the piece of writing? Are the evidence and examples provided sufficient?

_____

_____

ASSUMPTIONS BIASES

4. Are there unfounded *assumptions* or unreasonable *biases*?

_____

_____

CONCLUSIONS

5. Are all of the *conclusions*, consequences, and implications of the argument (the results of the argument taken to their furthest extreme) considered?

_____

_____

POINT OF VIEW

6. Is the *point of view* clear and consistent and have other points of view been considered?

_____

_____

ANALYSIS

7. Using these critical thinking tools, *analyze* the overall structure of this piece of writing and the strength of the author's arguments, ideas, and support. Was he or she successful in accomplishing the purpose? Why or why not?

_____

_____

LEARNING OBJECTIVES REVIEW

LO1 Why is it useful to apply critical thinking skills to reading? (See p. 21)	It is **useful to apply critical thinking skills** to reading because it increases your overall understanding of the author's purpose, and you can come to deeper analytical conclusions about the reading, its arguments, and the author's techniques.
LO2 What does it mean to read actively? (See p. 22)	When you **read actively**, you interact with the text by creating a dialogue with it as you read, asking and answering questions about the material, which helps you understand and remember it.
LO3 What are the six steps for active reading? (See pp. 22–29)	The **six steps for active reading** are (1) preview the material; (2) think about what you already know about the topic; (3) create questions from titles and headings; (4) read in blocks; (5) write in your reading log; and (6) review your summaries and answer your questions.
LO4 What is the "T-KED" method for marking and why is it useful? (See pp. 30–31)	The **T-KED method** involves marking key elements in a selection as you read (T = thesis, K = key ideas, E = examples, D = details), which increases your understanding of the content and your ability to identify the thesis and distinguish main ideas from supporting examples and details.
LO5 Why is it important to annotate as you read, and what are some ways you can do so effectively? (See pp. 31–33)	**Annotation** increases your understanding of what you read, helps you identify main ideas and details, note unfamiliar vocabulary, ask questions, and make comments. **Types of annotation** include highlighting, underlining, using codes and symbols, and writing definitions and comments in the margins.

PEARSON
mywritinglab

For support in meeting this chapter's objectives, log in to **www.mywritinglab.com** and select **Critical Thinking: Responding to Text and Visuals.**

3 Paragraphs: Building Blocks and Order, Unity, and Coherence

Cave View   Tom Shugrue

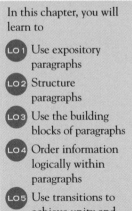

THINKING CRITICALLY

Look at the picture above and then answer the questions that follow.

When you first looked at this photo, did you immediately realize that it was a shot taken looking out from a cave? Could you tell that the dark frame was rock, or were you confused by the dark and light of the photo?

_____

_____

Writing a paragraph involves having a clear purpose; providing support in the form of examples, details, and comments; and arranging the paragraph parts in an effective order so that you can clearly communicate your point to your intended audience.

LO 1 EXPOSITORY PARAGRAPHS

A **paragraph** is a structured unit of writing composed of a topic sentence with a focused purpose and several sentences that provide support to develop that purpose. The Latin term "expository" means "to explain." Therefore, an expository paragraph or essay always has a purpose or message that it tries to *explain*. Paragraphs should always have a point, an analytical idea, or an argument the writer is putting forth to the reader.

The **support** you use can come in the form of personal experience, the experience of others, research, facts, statistics, or quotations from assigned readings. You also need to use your critical thinking skills to evaluate the strength of your argument and how well you have organized your support.

Paragraphs can be stand-alone units of writing or they can be building blocks in an essay. They can be adapted, depending on the purpose of your assignment, your topic, and your audience, the same way essays can. Once you are familiar with paragraph structure, you can focus on your purpose for writing and how to support your main idea.

APPLYING CRITICAL THINKING

BLUEPRINTS						
PURPOSE	IDEAS	SUPPORT	ASSUMPTIONS BIASES	CONCLUSIONS	POINT OF VIEW	ANALYSIS

When writing a paragraph, think first about the **idea** you are trying to convey to your readers, your main point. What is your **purpose** for writing about this point? **Analyze** the parts of the idea you are putting across. Think about your **point of view** about your topic in order to develop your purpose for writing about it. Check for any **assumptions** you've made and ensure they are accurate. Also, see if you have any **biases** in your ideas or commentary that are unjustified. Finally, make sure you **support** your purpose with examples, details, and commentary.

LO 2 PARAGRAPH STRUCTURE

In the classic paragraph form, the topic sentence comes first. The middle section provides examples, details, and analysis of and commentary about the support you provide, and the concluding sentence restates the main point of the paragraph or serves as a transition to the following paragraph.

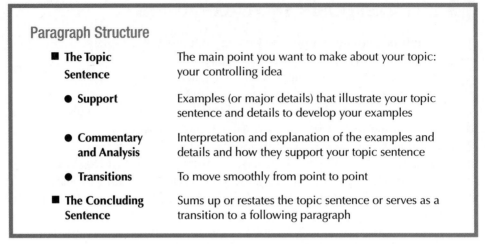

Paragraph Structure

- **The Topic Sentence** — The main point you want to make about your topic: your controlling idea
- **Support** — Examples (or major details) that illustrate your topic sentence and details to develop your examples
- **Commentary and Analysis** — Interpretation and explanation of the examples and details and how they support your topic sentence
- **Transitions** — To move smoothly from point to point
- **The Concluding Sentence** — Sums up or restates the topic sentence or serves as a transition to a following paragraph

In most cases, this pattern will be your best bet when writing one or two paragraphs. It is also the most common pattern for body paragraphs within essays. While it is true that some authors construct paragraphs that place the topic sentence further toward the middle or end of a paragraph, most writers choose to have a clear, strong topic sentence at the beginning of the paragraph, as in the sample below. Note that transitions are highlighted.

Sample Paragraph (annotated)

David Macey

Professor Anderson

English 090

22 October 2010

Topic sentence

College years are a time for students to gain valuable life skills. Although many students focus on the specific information they will learn in college classes, such as how to solve mathematical equations or how to write an essay, they often do not realize that the most valuable skills they learn may have more to do with basic ways of dealing with others, communication, and critical thinking. One of the most

Example 1

important skills students can learn in college is how to work with

others to accomplish a task. For instance, in small group projects stu-

Detail supporting
example 1

dents learn to work out problems together, communicate, negotiate,

and follow through on specific tasks. An example of this would be a

Detail supporting
example 1

project in which a group is assigned a task that involves researching

and presenting a topic. They would have to come up with a specific

plan and divide up the research and presentation tasks. Also, through

Example 2

participation in group assignments, students learn and practice

problem-solving and critical thinking skills as well as how to strategize

and follow through on assigned tasks. For example, in a sociology

Detail supporting
example 2

class, a group of students may be asked to consider the issues related

to handicap access by borrowing a wheelchair, using it to move

around campus, identifying the obstacles they encountered, and com-

ing up with solutions to make access easier. In conclusion, these valu-

Concluding sentence

able life skills are useful not only in college but also in daily life and

will contribute to success in all work situations.

ACTIVITY 3-1   Marking the Basic Parts of a Paragraph

Directions: *To better understand the elements of the basic paragraph form, complete these tasks using the following paragraph.*

1. *Underline the topic sentence and label it TS.*
2. *Write E above sentences that provide examples that support the topic sentence.*
3. *Write D above details used to illustrate and develop examples.*
4. *Underline the concluding sentence and label it CS.*

L'Tanya Johnson

Ms. Wobst

English 090

1 November 2010

<u>Registering for college classes requires thinking ahead and</u>
<u>planning for the long haul.</u> To begin with, it is wise to take all
prerequisite classes as soon as possible. If students wait to take their
prerequisites (the required classes they need to complete before taking harder or more specialized classes), then it may be more difficult
for them to get into those higher level classes later. Also, if students
put off taking prerequisite classes, they take the risk that they will
be unavailable or full when they are ready to take them. Students
should also avoid taking all of their "dessert" classes early on in
their college careers. If they take all of their favorite courses the
first year of college, then they will not have the option to do so later,
when they would benefit from being able to take some classes they
enjoy. Furthermore, students should always have a back-up plan
when they register for classes. They should be prepared for the
chance that the schedule they have created is not possible. For
instance, if they plan to take biology in the fall, but all the sections
are full when they go to register, then they will need to have considered other options. For instance, they could take a different science
course or decide to meet their science requirement during the next
quarter or semester. Finally, students should always check with an
advisor as they plan their initial strategy for registering and continue to do so intermittently as they register for classes in following
years. Advisors help students ensure they have taken all the

necessary courses they need to successfully complete their intended
degrees. In brief, the main idea that students should keep in mind
the first time they register for classes is that they should look at the
big picture and their long-term goals and not just focus on classes
for one quarter or semester.

THE BUILDING BLOCKS OF AN EXPOSITORY PARAGRAPH

LO 3

Here are the essential building blocks that you will find in all expository
paragraphs.

The Topic Sentence

The **topic sentence** is the *controlling idea* of a paragraph. It establishes the
paragraph's **topic** and **purpose**. Like the driver of a car, it controls where the
paragraph is going and how it gets there. An effective, focused topic sentence
should make a clear point or state an opinion about the topic. It is basically
what you want to explain or prove about your topic: the argument you put forth.

Your topic sentence should be more than just a fact or detail; it should
state an idea or *opinion* about your topic, and the goal of your paragraph
should be to convince your readers of the truth or validity of your idea or
opinion by supporting it with examples and details that prove your point.
For example, if you started with the subject of "winter sports" and narrowed
it down to the topic of "snowboarding," you could then come up with an
opinion about snowboarding that would serve as the basis for a topic sentence. For instance, you could say "Snowboarding has replaced skiing as the
favorite snow sport for people my age because it is more exciting and challenging." (See Chapter 4, pages 66–73, for prewriting techniques you can
use to help broaden or narrow your topic sentence.)

Essentially, a topic sentence needs to be broad enough that it can be
developed into a full paragraph about your topic and narrow enough to be
covered well in the scope of one paragraph. A topic sentence is **too broad** if
it is too general to develop and support in one paragraph.

Too broad:	Winter sports are adventurous.
Focused:	Snowboarding is a great workout for the whole body.
Too broad:	The world is a big place with lots to see.
Narrowed:	The San Francisco waterfront features many interesting and exciting attractions.

A topic sentence is **too narrow** if it is just a fact or detail because once you have stated the fact or detail, there is nothing else to say.

Too narrow:	A snowboard is like a surfboard for snow.
Focused:	Snowboards are designed for a maximum workout at a maximum speed.
Too narrow:	You can buy fish and chips at San Francisco's waterfront.
Broadened:	San Francisco's waterfront boasts many great places to get lunch.

Use prewriting techniques such as freewriting or brainstorming to generate some ideas about your topic. Then, come up with a focus and an opinion that need to be developed through examples and details

ACTIVITY 3-2   Creating Good Topic Sentences

Directions: *Mark the following topic sentences as* **TB** *(too broad),* **TN** *(too narrow), or* **TS** *(good topic sentence). If a topic sentence is too broad or too narrow, rewrite it on the line provided so that it makes a specific point you can support in the space of a paragraph.*   Answers will vary. Sample answers provided.

Example

___TB___   Fruit is a delicious category of food.

Revised: *Star fruit is an unusual and tasty fruit that provides surprising health benefits.*

___TB___   **1.** Trees add to our lives.

Trees help the environment in several ways.

___TN___   **2.** One piece of equipment needed for baseball is a glove.

A few basic items are required in order to play baseball.

___TN___   **3.** Hang gliding requires buying or renting a hang glider.

Hang gliding is a fun but pricey hobby.

___TB___   **4.** Football is a popular sport.

Football fans are the most intense fans in American sports.

___TB___   **5.** Cats and dogs are very different.

        Cats and dogs require different care and diets.

___TN___   **6.** Pizza is a food made with cheese and bread.

        Pizza is popular with kids for many reasons.

___TN___   **7.** Taking online classes requires a computer.

        Online classes require certain skills and some basic equipment.

___TB___   **8.** Worms benefit the planet.

        Worms improve soil in several beneficial ways.

___TN___   **9.** Some people are allergic to peanuts.

        There are a few common food allergy culprits.

___TS___   **10.** American teens are struggling with obesity.

Support

When you make a claim or state an opinion in a topic sentence, you need to **support** it—explain and illustrate it using your own knowledge about and personal experience with the subject, examples from other people or writers, and/or facts, statistics, and quotations from other sources. (If you use quotations or statistics, be sure to acknowledge their source.)

Be sure the examples and details you use clearly illustrate or explain your point. If their relevance is not obvious, explain their significance to the reader. You also need to provide **analysis** of the support you provide, breaking down the meaning and significance of the examples and details and explaining how they support your topic sentence:

Topic Sentence → Example → Details → Comments and Analysis

One way to ensure you provide effective support for your topic sentence is to use the Ice Cream Sandwich model described below.

Creating an Analytical Ice Cream Sandwich

An **ice cream sandwich** consists of two chocolate cookies that surround an ice cream filling. Think of the facts, examples, or details you include in your paragraphs and your interpretation and analysis of them as the ice cream filling. You need to surround that filling with two cookies to hold it together. The top cookie is your topic sentence, which sets up the point you want to

Cross Reference

See Chapter 17 for more on using the Analytical Ice Cream Sandwich for framing quotes and facts.

make in the paragraph, and the bottom cookie is your concluding sentence, which frames your examples with interpretation and analysis.

The Analytical Ice Cream Sandwich

Top cookie   Topic sentence (controlling idea of paragraph)

Ice cream filling   Facts, examples, or details that develop the topic sentence and interpretation and analysis of those examples and details (two to four supporting examples with details and analysis per paragraph)

Bottom cookie   Concluding sentence that reiterates the topic sentence

---

Here is an example of the ice cream sandwich using the topic sentence from page 42:

Top cookie   Snowboarding is a great workout for the whole body.

Ice cream filling   To snowboard successfully, you must use your core muscles as well as your leg muscles to keep your balance and make good turns. As you turn and move down the mountain, your quads, abdominal muscles, back muscles, and arm muscles are working hard to keep you balanced.

Bottom cookie   As a result of all of your muscles working together to get you down the mountain with speed and balance, snowboarding provides an excellent whole-body workout.

ACTIVITY 3-3 **Providing Support: Examples, Details, and Comments and Analysis**

Directions: *Provide a specific example to illustrate each of the topic sentences below. Then, provide at least one detail that explains or illustrates the example and one comment analyzing the significance of the example and detail. Answers will vary.*

Example

Topic Sentence: Good time management skills are necessary for college success.

Specific Example: *For instance, keeping a calendar of all scheduled test dates and major assignment due dates helps you to plan your writing and study time.*

Detail(s): *Specifically, you should write down exact dates of quizzes, tests, and major assignments and then schedule study times and mini assignment deadlines before the due dates.*

Comment (analyzing the significance of the example and detail provided to support the topic sentence):

By scheduling the actual dates and pre-assignments beforehand, you can avoid procrastination and do better on assignments and tests.

1. There are a few great things to do in the city/town where I live.

   Specific example: _____

   _____

   Detail(s): _____

   _____

   Comment: _____

   _____

2. Background music in grocery stores creates a certain mood.

   Specific example: _____

   _____

   Detail(s): _____

   _____

Comment: _____

_____

3. Video games have become increasingly popular over the years.

Specific example: _____

_____

Detail(s): _____

_____

Comment: _____

_____

Transitional Words and Phrases

Cross Reference
See pp. 53–57 for more about transitions and a table of the most common transitions.

Transitions are words, phrases, or sometimes even complete sentences that help move the reader smoothly from one example to the next. They provide **coherence**—a logical, organized flow—to a paragraph, and point the reader in the direction you want to take them. Transitions also provide clues for your readers about the way you have organized your examples and content. For instance, if you arranged your examples from least to most important, you might use a transition after your first support statement that says, "Even more important is . . . "

The Concluding Sentence

End your paragraph with a **concluding sentence** that re-emphasizes the focus and *purpose* of the topic sentence. Do not repeat your topic sentence word for word. Also, be careful not to introduce a completely new idea or argument in your concluding sentence that changes the focus of your original topic sentence. Look at the following topic sentences and corresponding concluding sentences from earlier in this chapter. Notice how the concluding sentences restate the original topic sentence without repeating it word for word or introducing a new or contradictory idea.

Topic Sentence: Registering for college classes requires thinking ahead and planning for the long haul.

Concluding Sentence: In brief, the main idea that students should keep in mind the first time they register for classes is that they should look at the big picture and their long-term goals and not just focus on classes for one quarter or semester.

Topic Sentence: College years are a time for students to gain valuable life skills.

Concluding Sentence: In conclusion, these valuable life skills are useful not only in college but also in daily life and will contribute to success in all work situations.

Sometimes, the concluding sentence in a paragraph can serve as a transition to the next paragraph if you are writing several paragraphs or an entire essay.

ACTIVITY 3-4   Creating a Good Concluding Sentence

Directions: *Use the three topic sentences you created support and examples for in Activity 3-3, and create a concluding sentence that connects to the topic sentence and highlights the examples, details, and comments you added and leaves the reader with an ending thought.* Answers will vary.

Example

Topic sentence: Good time management skills are necessary for college success.

Concluding sentence: As you can see, using specific time management skills will help you plan your work and schedule your study time, which will increase your success with assignments and tests.

1. Topic sentence: _____

   _____

   Concluding sentence: _____

   _____

2. Topic sentence: _____

   _____

   Concluding sentence: _____

   _____

3. Topic sentence: _____

   _____

   Concluding sentence: _____

   _____

Model Paragraph

Jessi Blake

Dr. Reeves

English 091

15 March 2010

Topic sentence.

Example 1

Note order of importance used to organize paragraph.

Supporting detail

Supporting detail

Supporting detail

Example 2

Supporting detail

Example 3

Supporting detail

Supporting detail

Example 4

Supporting detail

Supporting detail

Supporting detail

Supporting detail

    Farmer's Markets are the best place to get fresh, high quality, and varied produce. The most important reason for shopping for produce at a farmer's market instead of a regular grocery store is the freshness factor. Because local farmers bring their own fruit and vegetables to the market, the products are fresh; sometimes they have even been picked or harvested that same morning. For example, last week when I bought some local lettuce at my neighborhood farmer's market, I was so impressed by the tender, fresh leaves. We enjoyed the best salad ever that night as a result. Unlike farmer's markets, grocery stores often receive their produce from out of state. It may have been picked and refrigerated as much as a week before being placed on the shelves. Another reason for shopping at a farmer's market is that not only are the fruits and vegetables fresher than in stores but they are also higher quality. The farmers take pride in displaying their best produce on their stands. Many also sell organic produce, so these items have not been treated with chemicals in any way. At a grocery store, the prices for organic produce are higher, and they have fewer choices. A final reason for shopping at a farmer's market is the sheer variety of produce available at the stands. For instance, at most grocery stores one will find only a couple varieties of tomatoes. However, a good farmer's market will offer several varieties of tomatoes. For instance, last week I saw Roma tomatoes, cherry tomatoes, beefsteak tomatoes, and the most beautiful and colorful heirloom tomatoes I have ever seen. One of the heirloom varieties was a deep purple color, almost black. <u>In so many ways, shopping at the farmer's market for produce is the best way to ensure getting fresh, high quality, and diverse offerings of fruits and vegetables.</u>

Concluding sentence

Notice how the sentences in this paragraph build on each other to provide support (examples and details) and analysis and how transitional words and phrases help move the reader from one point to the next smoothly.

To help you remember to include all the elements that make a paragraph successful, use the following checklist to review your paragraph draft for all the basic building blocks.

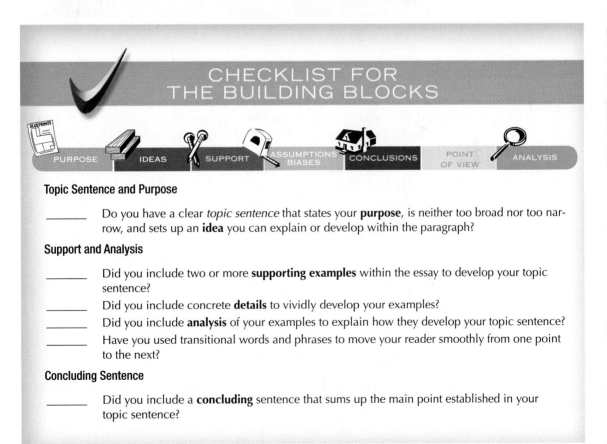

CHECKLIST FOR THE BUILDING BLOCKS

PURPOSE   IDEAS   SUPPORT   ASSUMPTIONS BIASES   CONCLUSIONS   POINT OF VIEW   ANALYSIS

Topic Sentence and Purpose

_____   Do you have a clear *topic sentence* that states your **purpose**, is neither too broad nor too narrow, and sets up an **idea** you can explain or develop within the paragraph?

Support and Analysis

_____   Did you include two or more **supporting examples** within the essay to develop your topic sentence?

_____   Did you include concrete **details** to vividly develop your examples?

_____   Did you include **analysis** of your examples to explain how they develop your topic sentence?

_____   Have you used transitional words and phrases to move your reader smoothly from one point to the next?

Concluding Sentence

_____   Did you include a **concluding** sentence that sums up the main point established in your topic sentence?

LO 4   ORDERING PARAGRAPHS

Just as the fruit in the produce section of the farmer's market pictured above is organized so that shoppers can find what they are looking for easily, you should plan your paragraph so that your reader can follow your train of thought without difficulty. The **order** in which you arrange your ideas is extremely important to the success of your paragraph, as it will be hard for your reader to understand the point you are trying to make if they are not logically organized. Making sure your paragraph has **coherence**—the ideas move smoothly from one to the next—and **unity**—contains only ideas that support your topic sentence—will help your reader successfully follow your ideas and arguments.

As paragraphs can be organized in several ways, choose the order of development that best suits your purpose and allows you to organize your paragraph so that your reader can follow your ideas and your support for them. Three common order patterns are time order, spatial order, and order of importance.

Time Order

Cross Reference

See Chapters 6 and 8 on narration and process.

Time order, also called **chronological order**, is most often used in narration and process writing. This order pattern is used to describe a series of events in the order they occurred (narration), or it is used to explain how something works or how to complete a step-by-step process.

Narration Time Order: Some of the best days happen when you just follow your instincts and do what suits you at the moment. Yesterday, I decided to wash my car. After I finished, I wanted to show off my handiwork, so I decided to drive to the beach. On the way, I stopped by my best friend's house to see if he could join me. He was free, and we stopped for a quick lunch before getting on the highway to Narragansett Beach.

Process Time Order: This is my method for washing a car. First, gather together all the equipment you need to do a good job: bucket, dish soap, cotton rags, a hose, and large dry towels or sheets. Next, park your car near the spigot, so the hose can reach easily. Then, fill the bucket with warm water mixed with dish soap, dip in the rags, and start washing the car.

Order of Importance

Writers use **order of importance** when they want to emphasize their ideas in *the most to least important* order or *the least to most important* order, depending on the point they are trying to make. Order of importance is most often used in description, narration, cause and effect, comparison and contrast, or argument writing.

Cross Reference

See modes Chapters 6, 7, 12, and 14.

Most to Least Important Order: When you plan a wedding, you need to make several important arrangements well in advance. First, you need to book the church several months before the scheduled date. Then, you have to book a place for the reception. Next, it is important to hire a caterer and work on the menu. You also have to pick out and order a cake. Finally, if you want music at the reception, you need to contact local DJs or bands that play weddings to see if they are available and book the one you like for the big day.

Least to Most Important Order: Preparing for a trip out of the country involves several key steps. Pack wisely, making sure to bring clothes for all occasions. Be sure to book your plane tickets and make other travel arrangements well in advance. It is very important to make sure that you have updated your immunizations and received any additional vaccinations recommended for the country you are visiting. Some countries will not allow you to enter without the appropriate immunizations. Finally, and most importantly, make sure you have applied for or updated your passport long before the day you travel. If you do not have a current passport, you will not be able to travel internationally.

▶ NOTE   Refer to the **Transitions** section later in this chapter (pp. 53–57) for more information on how to make your order flow more smoothly.

Spatial Order

Spatial order works well when you want to describe what a place (like a town, city, or room in your house) or an object (like a building or a vehicle) looks like: a messy room, a flower float in a parade, or a neighbor's well-organized vegetable garden. Using spatial order helps create a mental picture for your reader of a place or item. For instance, if you were describing your room, you could start from the front and work backwards, go from the bottom to the top, or move from one side to the other.

Spatial Order: The classroom is arranged in a way that helps students learn. The front of the room features a whiteboard that the teacher uses frequently. Above the whiteboard is a clock, so students can check the time, especially during timed writing assignments. On the ceiling above the whiteboard, there is a drop-down screen the instructor uses for educational DVDs or PowerPoint presentations. On the right side wall, tall windows provide natural light and fresh air on hot days. The back wall of the room is reserved for student work: posters, sample writing, and bright collages. In the middle of the room, student desks are arranged in the shape of a horseshoe, so students can see the front of the classroom and also see each other, which creates a sense of community.

ACTIVITY 3-5   Patterns of Order

Directions: *Which order pattern would you choose for each of the following paragraph topics? Some topics may work with more than one order pattern; if so, list all that apply.* Answers will vary. Sample answers provided.

1. A typical morning for you *time order*

2. How to get the most out of a class *most to least important or least to most*

3. Finding your way around your local grocery store. *spatial order*

4. Steps for learning to ride a bike. *time order*

5. Reasons we need a new park in our neighborhood *most to least important or least to most*

USING TRANSITIONS TO ACHIEVE UNITY AND COHERENCE

LO 5

Good writing flows smoothly from one point to the next with nothing out of place. When you write a paragraph, it's important to maintain both **unity** (every detail belongs) and **coherence** (smooth flow from one point to the next). **Transitional words, phrases, or sentences** provide the bridges needed to keep the flow smooth from sentence to sentence or from one idea to the next.

Unity

Unity means that each sentence you include in your paragraph helps develop the point you set out to make. In order to achieve unity, each sentence must support and develop your paragraph's topic sentence, the controlling idea of the paragraph. For example, which two sentences in this paragraph do not belong?

[1] Lip-syncing by modern bands and performers is becoming more and more common. [2] Lip-syncing is when an individual performer or band plays a supposedly live performance but is actually faking the music and singing, mouthing, and playing along to a prerecorded version of the song. [3] Several live performers have taken to lip-syncing as a way to guarantee that they sound good during TV performances. [4] For instance, in a now infamous guest performance on Saturday Night Live, Ashlee Simpson was caught lip-syncing when there was a technical difficulty during her performance and she stopped singing but the recording kept going. [5] She ended up walking off the stage in embarrassment. [6] Saturday Night Live has lots of other good performers that guest star though. [7] Another situation in which bands or individual performers frequently resort to lip-syncing is when they are performing elaborately choreographed dance routines as they sing. [8] Madonna, the Backstreet Boys, and Paula Abdul were all rumored to have lip-synced at their concerts in order to perform dance routines on stage. [9] Madonna is also known for her strange wardrobe choices on stage. [10] Without a doubt, lip-syncing is more common these days at live venues.

Did you spot the sentences that didn't belong in this paragraph? The sentences that do not support the topic sentence (and interfere with the unity of this paragraph) are sentence numbers 6 and 9. All of the sentences should be related to or be examples of lip-syncing. Not all unity errors will be this easy to spot. Sometimes, you will find you have changed direction or switched focus in a very subtle way during the process of writing your first draft.

ACTIVITY 3-6 Test for Unity

Directions: *Read the following paragraph and list the two sentences that do not belong. Then explain briefly, on the lines provided, why they don't belong in this paragraph.*

[1] Deciding on a career path is an important task during college. [2] Though some students already know exactly what career they want to pursue when they graduate, many students take classes as a way to figure out what jobs might interest them. [3] College courses provide the opportunity to find out more about specific subjects and learn useful skills. [4] Some people never go to college at all, though, and head straight to a job after high school. [5] Taking a variety of classes, especially in the first two years, is a great way for students to find out what subjects they find most interesting. [6] Based on this information, they can begin to explore what jobs are available in those fields. [7] Some students have to work while they are taking courses in order to pay their tuition. [8] Next, through the process of attending classes, meeting new people, and working on group projects they can discover what kind of people skills they have and the types of interaction they enjoy. [9] Using this information and taking into account the subjects they like and do well in, they can then begin to narrow down their job choices and start taking classes that will enable them to get a degree that will help them with their job goals. [10] Indeed, taking courses in college is an excellent way for a person to figure out a good career path.

Sentences that don't belong: _____ *4 and 7* _____

Explain why: _____ *They do not support the topic sentence.* _____

APPLYING CRITICAL THINKING

To check your writing for unity, go through the entire first draft and **analyze** each sentence to make sure it **supports** the **purpose** of your paragraph. To help you accomplish this task, ask yourself the following question for each sentence:

Does this sentence specifically support or develop the topic sentence? If you answer "no" to this question, revise or delete the sentence.

Coherence and Transitions

Coherence means that every sentence in your paragraph flows smoothly from one point to the next. Coherence relates to the **order of development** you choose for your paragraph and involves the use of transitions between key sentences and ideas. **Transitions** are words, phrases, or sometimes even complete sentences that help move the reader smoothly from one point to the next. They point the reader in the direction you want to take them. Transitions are necessary both *within* paragraphs and *between* them. When a transitional word, phrase, or sentence is used to connect one paragraph to the next, the transition can come at the end of the previous paragraph or at the beginning of the next, whichever works best for your purpose and organization.

Here is a partial list of transitional words or phrases categorized into tables by type for easy use in paragraphs and essays:

TRANSITIONS TO . . .

Show Addition of Another Point

again	but also	in addition	nor
also	equally important	last	plus the fact
and	finally	lastly	secondly
and then	first	likewise	then too
another	further	moreover	thirdly
besides	furthermore	next	too

Show Contrast or a Change in Ideas

although	even though	instead	on the other side
anyhow	for all that	nevertheless	otherwise
at the same time	however	notwithstanding	regardless
but	in any event	on the contrary	still
despite this	in contrast	on the other hand	yet

Show a Comparison

in like manner	in the same way	likewise	similarly

Show Summary or Repetition

as has been noted	in closing	in other words	on the whole
as I have said	in conclusion	in short	to conclude
in brief	in essence	in summary	to sum up

Continued ▶

TRANSITIONS TO . . .

Illustrate or Give Examples/Specifics

a few include	essentially	in particular	the following
an example	for example	let us consider	specifically
especially	for instance	the case of	you can see this in

Strengthen a Point

basically	indeed	truly	without a doubt
essentially	irrefutably	undeniably	without question

Show Results or Cause/Effect Relationships

accordingly	consequently	since	therefore
as a result	for this reason	so	thereupon
because	hence	then	thus

Indicate Purpose

all things considered	for this reason	to accomplish	with this in mind
for this purpose	in order to	to this end	with this objective

Indicate Place (Usually Prepositions)

above	beside	inside	outside
across	between	nearer	over
adjacent to	beyond	nearly	there
below	farther	next to	through
beneath	here	opposite	under

Show Time

after	before	in the meantime	not long after
afterwards	between	later	soon
at last	first	meanwhile	then
at length	immediately	next	while

Show Amount

a great deal	less than	most	smaller
few	many	over	some
greater	more than	several	under

ACTIVITY 3-7   Provide Transitions

Directions: *Choose transitions from the preceding tables, or use a transitional word or phrase of your own, to fill in the blanks below and make this paragraph flow more smoothly.* Answers will vary. Sample transitions provided.

The most famous landmark in St. Louis, Missouri, is the St. Louis Arch, an engineering marvel and a popular tourist attraction. The Arch was designed by Eric Saarinen and completed in 1947. ___To begin with/First___ , the Arch is the tallest national monument in the United States at 630 feet. At its base, the legs of the Arch are 630 feet apart. _Furthermore/In addition_ , the Arch weighs 17,246 tons. Nine hundred tons of stainless steel was used to build it, more than for any other project in history. It is ___also___ the tallest structure in St. Louis that people can enter. The legs of the Arch are hollow and contain a unique tram system for transporting visitors to an observation deck at the top. ___Also/In addition___ , it is a popular tourist attraction for several reasons. ___For example___ , visitors who ride to the top get spectacular views of St. Louis and the Mississippi River and can see for thirty miles on a clear day. Each year, approximately one million visitors ride the trams to the top of the Arch. ___Also/Furthermore___ , depending on whether they enter the Arch from the south or the north, they can learn about the construction of the Arch or the St. Louis waterfront during the nineteenth century. _To sum up/In conclusion_ , the St. Louis Arch is an important monument that displays engineering ingenuity and attracts numerous visitors each year.

LO 6 OUTLINING

One of the best ways to ensure a well-organized paragraph and an appropriate order of development is to write an outline of your ideas. Some writers begin with a rough outline of their paragraph before they've written a draft.

However, even if you didn't *start* with an outline, it is a powerful tool to use *after you have written your first draft* to check and revise the organization and structure of your ideas.

Outline Format

An **outline** helps you to order your thoughts, and it allows you to order your examples and details in the most logical way to develop the purpose of your paragraph.

Outlines have a consistent format. The main idea, the topic sentence, is placed closest to the left margin. Supporting examples and details used to develop this idea are indented, so the further right your ideas are placed, the more specific or detailed the support they provide. Here are some guidelines for writing an outline:

Guidelines for Writing an Outline for a Paragraph

1. Write your working **topic sentence** as your main idea labeled with the Roman numeral I.

2. List the **examples** you will use to support your topic sentence, using capital letters (A, B, C, and so on). Write a short phrase to explain each example, not a complete sentence. Think of these phrases as titles for each section of your paragraph. Indent each example one tab right from the margin.

3. List the **supporting details** you will use to support your examples using numbers such as 1 or 2. Use short phrases to explain each one. Indent each detail two tabs from the margin.

   ▶ NOTE   When you list examples and details, you must have at least two of each: if you have an "A," then you must have at least a "B," and if you have a 1, then you will need at least a 2. If you have only one detail, combine it with the example it supports or develop a second detail.

4. List commentary and/or **analysis** of your examples and details as lettered or numbered points below each example or detail.

5. Write your working **concluding sentence** at the end of your outline, aligned left.

   ▶ NOTE   Check your campus writing center for software that automatically creates outlines in the correct format.

Sample Outline

Kelli Petersen

Professor Hajib

English 090

3 March 2010

    I. **Topic sentence:** The most famous landmark in St. Louis, Missouri, is the St. Louis Arch, an engineering marvel and a popular tourist attraction.

       A. The physical marvels of the arch

          1. Tallest national monument in U.S.

          2. Width at its base

          3. Weight and amount of steel used

       B. Tourist Destination

          1. Spectacular views from the top

          2. Can learn about how Arch was built and local history

   II. **Concluding sentence:**   To sum up, the St. Louis Arch is an important monument that displays engineering ingenuity and attracts numerous visitors each year.

APPLYING CRITICAL THINKING

PURPOSE   IDEAS   SUPPORT   ASSUMPTIONS BIASES   CONCLUSIONS   POINT OF VIEW   ANALYSIS

Here are some questions you can ask to help you develop an effective outline.

1. What is the main point or **idea** I want to make about my topic? What is my **purpose** for writing this paragraph?

Continued ▶

2. What **support** (examples and details) will I use in my paragraph, and in what order do I want to present that support?

3. Do I have any examples that may need more support or **analysis** in order to convince my reader of my main point?

4. What is the best order of development to successfully make my point? Time order? Spatial order? Order of importance?

5. Are there any examples that should be deleted, expanded upon (through the addition of more details or analysis), or reordered?

Now use the Outline Critique Form below to self-review your outline or ask a peer to use it for peer review of your outline.

OUTLINE CRITIQUE FORM

1. Does the outline start with a topic sentence?
2. Is the topic sentence an idea or opinion that can be developed through examples and details? Does it make a clear point?
3. Is it in correct outline format?
4. Are the examples and details clear and each explained with a short phrase?
5. If there is an "A" after an example, is it followed by at least one more point "B" and so on?
6. Are there any examples or details that do not belong?
7. Is there a good working concluding sentence?

Comments and suggestions for revision:

_____

_____

_____

_____

_____

LEARNING OBJECTIVES REVIEW

LO1 What is an expository paragraph? What is its main purpose? (See p. 37)	An **expository paragraph** is a structured unit of writing that has a purpose or message. Expository paragraphs are designed to explain ideas or persuade a reader to support a specific idea.
LO2 How is a paragraph commonly structured? (See pp. 37–41)	A **common paragraph structure** starts with a topic sentence that states a point, an analytical idea, or an argument (although it can also appear in the middle or at the end) followed by support, and a concluding sentence that restates the main point.
LO3 What are the building blocks of a paragraph? (See pp. 41–49)	The **building blocks of a paragraph** are the *topic sentence*; *support*, which includes examples, details, analysis, and commentary; *transitional words and phrases*; and a *concluding sentence*.
LO4 What are three ways to logically order/organize information within a paragraph? (See pp. 50–52)	Three ways to logically organize a paragraph are **time order** (the order in which events happen), **order of importance** (most to least or least to most), and **spatial order** (front to back, top to bottom, left to right).
LO5 How can transitions help you achieve unity and coherence in a paragraph? (See pp. 53–57)	**Transitional words, phrases, or sentences** provide the bridges that maintain unity (ensuring that every detail belongs) and coherence (a smooth flow from sentence to sentence or from one idea to the next in a paragraph).
LO6 How do you outline information, and why are outlines useful? (See pp. 57–60)	You **outline a paragraph** by placing the main idea, the topic sentence, closest to the left margin. Supporting examples and details are indented; the further right they are placed, the more specific or detailed the support they provide. An outline helps you to organize your thoughts and order your examples and details in the most logical way to develop the purpose of your paragraph.

For support in meeting this chapter's objectives, log in to www.mywritinglab.com and select **Recognizing a Paragraph, The Topic Sentence,** and **Developing and Organizing a Paragraph**.

4 Paragraphs: Planning and Process

THINKING CRITICALLY

Answer the following questions about your usual writing process.

1. What are some writing habits (good or bad) that come into play when you write an assignment for a class?

   _____

   _____

2. What do you think you could do to strengthen your good habits and minimize your bad ones?

   _____

   _____

LO 1 PLANNING AND WRITING PARAGRAPHS

Paragraphs should have a clear purpose and a logical plan. To write effective expository paragraphs, use your critical thinking skills to develop your ideas in stages. Good writing depends on prewriting to generate ideas, organizing those ideas, writing a first draft, revising and rewriting, and editing. Some writers follow these steps in the writing process in the same order every time they write, and some do not. You want to develop a writing process that works best for you.

Here's an overview of the five major stages in the writing process.

The Writing Process

1. Prewriting   Generate ideas and your paragraph's purpose.

2. Organizing   Develop a plan for presenting the purpose and ideas.

3. Drafting   Create a first draft of the paragraph based on your plan; develop support for the paragraph's purpose.

4. Revising   Re-assess the draft for content, development, organization, and support (examples and details).

5. Editing   Check for sentence-level effectiveness, style, diction, grammar, and spelling errors.

▶ IMPORTANT NOTE   You can change the order of the above stages or delete stages if you don't need them—this process is a tool—decide what works best for you in each writing task.

Cross Reference

The five stages of the writing process will be explained in more detail and modeled later in this chapter (see "Ten Steps for Writing an Effective Paragraph," pp. 77–93).

Using the writing process outlined above ensures that your paragraphs are clear, thoughtful, well supported, well organized, and grammatically sound. As you become a more confident writer, you can customize the writing process by figuring out what works best for you in general and what are the best choices for a particular assignment.

Subject, Purpose, and Audience

Before you can begin the writing process, you must understand the goal of your writing assignment and determine your **subject**, **purpose**, and **audience**. Understanding these three elements allows you to identify a specific topic; write a clear, effective topic sentence; devise a plan for development, including examples; and decide on an appropriate tone and style for your paragraph.

The following chart outlines how to move from subject to topic, from purpose to topic sentence, and from audience to tone and approach.

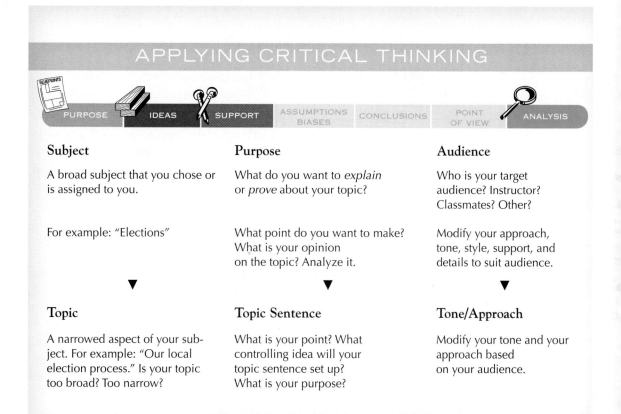

APPLYING CRITICAL THINKING

PURPOSE   IDEAS   SUPPORT   ASSUMPTIONS BIASES   CONCLUSIONS   POINT OF VIEW   ANALYSIS

Subject	**Purpose**	**Audience**
A broad subject that you chose or is assigned to you.	What do you want to *explain* or *prove* about your topic?	Who is your target audience? Instructor? Classmates? Other?
For example: "Elections"	What point do you want to make? What is your opinion on the topic? Analyze it.	Modify your approach, tone, style, support, and details to suit audience.
▼	▼	▼
Topic	**Topic Sentence**	**Tone/Approach**
A narrowed aspect of your subject. For example: "Our local election process." Is your topic too broad? Too narrow?	What is your point? What controlling idea will your topic sentence set up? What is your purpose?	Modify your tone and your approach based on your audience.

As you can see in the chart, before you start writing on an assigned subject or one you have chosen, you need to decide how you can narrow it down into a manageable topic. Then, you have to determine the purpose of your paragraph, the main idea you want to convey about your topic, and how you can communicate it in a topic sentence. Finally, you need to identify your audience and think about how you can adjust your tone and approach to best communicate your ideas to them.

Cross Reference

See Chapter 3, pp. 41–43 for more on topic sentences.

LO 2 SUBJECT AND PREWRITING

The **subject** of your paragraph is the broad topic or idea that you have been assigned or have chosen to write about. In writing assignments, instructors often provide you with a specific topic and a purpose for writing about it or a list of broad topics.

Cross Reference
See Chapter 15, p. 290, for examples of key words and what they mean.

If your instructor gives you a **specific writing assignment**, it may already contain a narrowed topic and indicate a specific purpose for writing about it. Also, you can look for key words, such as *explain* or *summarize*, that are clues to what your instructor wants you to accomplish in your paragraphs.

> **Writing prompt:** Write about your <u>local polling station</u>, and <u>explain</u> how the <u>voting process works</u> there. <u>Walk your readers through</u> the process.

With this prompt, you can tell exactly what the instructor wants you to do: Write about the local polling station and how the voting process works there. Focus on the key words in this prompt—*local polling station*, *explain*, *voting process works*, *walk your readers through*—to come up with a topic sentence and plan your writing.

If your instructor provides you with a list of **general or broad subjects**, or you choose a subject to write about, you will have to narrow the subject down into a specific topic you can discuss in the space of a paragraph. For example, your instructor might ask you to write a paragraph on the subject of elections, which is too broad to write a single paragraph about, so you would need to narrow it down into a manageable topic, a more specific aspect of elections like "my local election polling station," "getting out the local vote," or "recent local voting irregularities." Prewriting is a great way to generate ideas and narrow a broad subject to a manageable topic.

Prewriting and Generating Ideas

Several techniques can help you narrow your topic, generate ideas about it, determine your purpose, and organize your ideas. These techniques include thinking about your topic, freewriting, mapping, brainstorming, clustering, and journaling. Try these techniques and figure out which ones work best for you.

Some people prefer to do their prewriting on paper using a pen or pencil, and some prefer to use their computer to type brainstorm lists or rough outlines. Others like to use the columns function in their word processing program to create categories and brainstorm directly below the separate categories.

Thinking and Talking

Thinking about your subject and talking about it with someone is a great way to get started. As soon as you get your assignment or choose your subject, begin thinking about it. Some prewriting happens in your head before you even put pen to paper. Talk it out with a classmate or friend if you can. Ask yourself these questions:

- What do I already know about this subject?
- What are some questions I have about this subject?
- What aspect of this subject am I most interested in?
- What could I explain well about this subject to my readers?
- How could I narrow it down into a topic I could cover in a paragraph?
- What do I want to accomplish in this paragraph?

After you've thought up some ideas or worked some out with someone else, be sure to write them down so you don't forget them and will have a starting place for drafting.

ACTIVITY 4-1   Practice Thinking and Talking

Directions: *After you have thought about your subject for a day or so, sit down with a friend and discuss your ideas with him or her. After you've finished, you can jot down some notes.*

Freewriting

Freewriting is a popular technique for generating ideas and narrowing a subject down into a manageable topic. When you freewrite, you turn off your inner editor, put pen to paper, and just let the ideas flow out of you without worrying about spelling, grammar, or "dumb" ideas. Later, you can sort the good from the bad stuff.

Subject: Interesting places

Let me see.... There are so many cool things I could write about. Umm, for example, I like my local coffee shop, and there's a cool waterfront in my town, oh, and we have a great local art museum, and this morning I went to the local farmers' market.... I could write about it. hmmm I like going there because I can buy produce, fish, meat, flowers, plants, and even artwork and other handcrafted items. Also, everything is so beautiful in the stalls. There's so much good stuff to eat, and I can get free samples of stuff: tea, dried cherries, fruit, smoked salmon. It's a great way to spend a weekend morning.

This student's freewrite generated a couple of possible topics, but then she honed in on the one that caught her interest and imagination the most.

Possible Topics: Local coffee shop, waterfront, art museum, farmer's market

Topic: Farmer's market

ACTIVITY 4-2   Practice Freewriting

Directions: *On a separate sheet of paper, freewrite for 10 minutes on your subject. Use the freewrite above as a model. Do not worry about spelling or grammar.*

Mapping

Mapping is a way to literally map out your subject to find some topics for your paragraph. You can map using boxes and arrows, a flow chart, or whatever works best for your style.

Subject: Sports

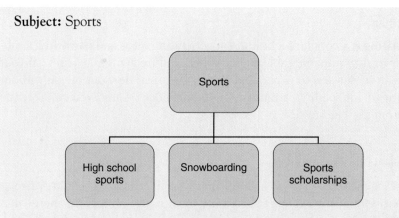

Possible Topics: High school sports, snowboarding, sports scholarships

Topic: Sports scholarships

▶ TIP   Computer software designed for generating ideas and mapping is available on most college campuses.

ACTIVITY 4-3   Practice Mapping

Directions: *Using the sample mapping graph as a guideline, on a separate sheet of paper, create a map of your own on your subject.*

Brainstorming

Storm your *brain* to generate ideas! **Brainstorming** is a free-flowing, free-association listing of words or ideas that you crank out on paper to get you thinking. As in freewriting, you need to turn off your inner editor and just write down as many ideas and details as you can related to your chosen subject or assigned writing prompt.

Subject: Violence

Brainstorm: Increased crime rate, violence in sports, violence on TV, kids and increased violence, violence in schools, violence in cartoons, violence in computer games

Possible Topics: Kids and increased violence, violence in schools, violence in cartoons, violence in computer games

Topic: Violence in computer games

ACTIVITY 4-4   Practice Brainstorming

Directions: *Using the sample brainstorm above as a guideline, on a separate sheet of paper, create a brainstorm of your own on your subject.*

Clustering

Clustering is another way to visually represent your ideas and narrow a broad subject into a narrow topic. To **cluster**, you draw a circle in the center of a piece of paper, write in your subject, and then draw lines and add circles containing related ideas. You can draw lines from each circle and add new circles with additional ideas, so that you form several related chains of ideas.

Subject: Hobbies

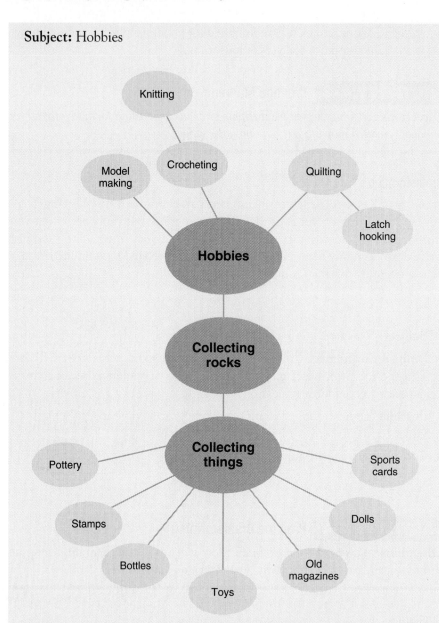

Possible Topics: Knitting, crocheting, quilting, collecting stamps, collecting sports cards, collecting rocks, collecting bottles, model-making, collecting pottery, collecting dolls, collecting toys, collecting old magazines

Topic: Collecting sports cards

ACTIVITY 4-5 Practice Clustering

Directions: *Using the sample cluster above as a guideline, on a separate sheet of paper, create a cluster of your own on your subject.*

Journaling

Journaling involves writing your thoughts down in a journal. Start a journal and use it to jot down ideas so you won't forget them. Include snippets of overheard conversations, ideas sparked by what you have been reading, interesting concepts you've discussed in other classes, or quotations from songs, poems, or books you are reading (make sure to note sources!). You can also use any of the prewriting techniques described above as you work out your topic ideas.

I like that line from John Lennon's song "Beautiful Boy" that says "Life is what happens when you're busy making other plans." Last week, I hardly enjoyed my free time because I was so worried about all the stuff I had coming up for school this next week. I'm thinking if I worked on some planning and time management techniques, I might be able to plan out my school work time and my play time better and therefore enjoy my play time better. I could use "time management" for the subject of my paragraph for English class because my instructor said she wants us to write an informative paragraph. Perfect.

Possible Topics: Song lyrics, planning, school stress, time management

Topic: Time management technique

ACTIVITY 4-6 Practice Journaling

Directions: *Begin a journal for your writing assignments this quarter. Do your first entry on your current assignment and subject. Write down any ideas in a casual tone for yourself. Do not worry about spelling, grammar, or "dumb ideas."*

Moving from a Broad Subject to a Narrowed Topic

It gets easier with practice to narrow a broad subject to a narrowed topic, and it is essential to perform this step before you attempt a first draft of your paragraph. You cannot write a focused paragraph with a clear purpose and topic sentence if you haven't narrowed down your subject. Here are some suggestions for narrowing your chosen or assigned subject to a focused topic, using the broad subject of "television." You can use some or all of the prewriting methods discussed above during this process.

1. **Prewrite.** Use a prewriting technique to generate a list of possible topics that come to mind when you think about the broad subject you have chosen to write about.

> **Subject:** Television
>
> **Brainstorming:** Sitcoms, reality shows, comedy shows, cartoons, nature channels, sports channels, news programming
>
> **Topic:** News programming

In this case, the student started with the broad subject of television and brainstormed some possible related topics. She focused in on news programming as the topic she was most interested in writing about.

2. **Think about the topic.** Ask yourself why you chose this topic after prewriting or, if it was assigned to you by your teacher, ask yourself why your teacher thought this was an interesting or important topic.

> What do I already know about this topic? Why does my teacher want us to write about it? What kind of paragraph can I produce, and what kinds of examples do I already know? I know that I watched news all through the last political campaign and it affected my views.
>
> **Narrowed Topic:** News programming and presidential campaigns

3. **Ask questions.** Generate a question or several questions you could ask about the narrowed topic.

> **Topic:** News programming
>
> - Who watches news programs?
> - What kinds of news programs are on TV?
> - Why are there channels dedicated exclusively to news?
> - Do news programs target specific audiences?
> - Do news programs ever show biases (such as political bias, liberal versus conservative)?
>
> **Narrowed Topic:** News programs and political coverage

4. Think of issues and ideas related to the topic.

> Specialized news programs, target audiences, political bias in newscasting, having a political agenda

ACTIVITY 4-7 Narrow Your Subject to a Topic

Directions: *Choose three of the subjects you did prewriting for in Activities 4-1 to 4-6 and list two possible narrowed topics for each.* Answers will vary.

Example

Subject: Camping

Narrowed Topic 1: *car camping versus tent camping*

Narrowed Topic 2: *foods that are best for campfire meals*

1. **Subject:** _____

   Narrowed Topic 1: _____

   Narrowed Topic 2: _____

2. **Subject:** _____

   Narrowed Topic 1: _____

   Narrowed Topic 2: _____

3. **Subject:** _____

   Narrowed Topic 1: _____

   Narrowed Topic 2: _____

LO 3 PURPOSE

The **purpose** of your paragraph is the main idea you are setting out to explain to your readers. Ask yourself what point you want to make to your readers about the topic you've chosen. For instance, in the example that started with the broad subject "TV," the student narrowed the topic down to "news programming." Through the process of freewriting, she could come up with a question like "Is there political bias (conservative versus liberal) in newscasting?" Asking and answering this question could become the purpose of her paragraph.

Look carefully at your prewriting to find a specific purpose for writing about your topic. Use the following questions from the Applying Critical Thinking box to help you develop a solid and thoughtful purpose for your paragraph.

To develop your **ideas** into a clear **purpose** for your paragraph, **analyze** the different parts of your topic and your reasons for writing about it.

1. What is my goal for writing about this topic?

2. Is there a problem that needs to be solved related to this topic? If so, what is it?

3. What do I want to say about the topic?

4. What do I already know about it?

5. What opinions do I have about it?

6. What is my **point of view**? From what perspective will I be writing?

ACTIVITY 4-8   Establish Your Purpose

Directions: *Choose one of the narrowed topics you came up with in Activity 4-7 and answer the five questions related to purpose from the Applying Critical Thinking Box.* Answers will vary.

1. What is my goal for writing about this topic? What do I want to say about it?

_____

_____

2. What is my point of view on the subject? From what perspective will I be writing?

_____

_____

3. Are there any questions about this topic that I want to address in my paragraph?

_____

_____

4. Is there a problem that needs to be solved related to this topic? If so, what is it?

_____

_____

5. What is my opinion on the topic, and what do I already know about it?

_____

_____

LO 4 AUDIENCE

Once you have established your topic and purpose, you need to consider your **audience**, the person or people who will read your writing. Are you writing for your instructor, your classmates, the general public, or a special interest group? There are three common types of audience:

General: All types of people

Academic: College students, your instructor, and possibly other faculty or administrators at your college

Specialized: An audience that is knowledgeable about a certain field such as nursing students or a political action group

Ask yourself which category above is the target audience for your paragraph. Think about what they already know about your topic, the point you want to convey about it, and what additional background information or explanation you may need to provide to make your point clear. Consider what level of vocabulary you will use and which specialized terms you will need to define. Then decide on what approach would work best for your topic and target audience, and how much evidence you will need to provide to convince your readers to support your point of view.

Finally, you will need to consider what kind of tone to use. **Tone** refers to the way you sound to your readers—formal, informal, informative, persuasive, humorous, and so on. It is important to match the tone you use to your topic, purpose, and audience, using language that will speak to your reader and make your point in the most effective way. For instance, if you were writing about the general subject "the rising cost of a college education" and you decided to focus on "increases in tuition," you would need to know who your target audience was before you could plan the best approach for your topic.

Cross Reference

See Chapter 3, pages 43–46, for more on how to provide support.

Topic: Rising cost of a college education

Purpose: Arguing against raising tuition

Audience 1: Other college students This audience is already familiar with the issues of rising college costs. As they are your peers, you might use a less formal tone and cite examples from your personal experience that would be familiar to them to make your points (having to work part time to pay tuition, having to apply for more loans, concern about accumulating debt). Your purpose would be to inform them, to provide information about what action they could take to lobby against rising tuition costs.

Audience 2: Parents of college students The people in this audience, many of whom are helping their children pay for college, are also familiar with the issues. However, you would probably choose to use a more formal tone in order to be taken seriously and choose examples that relate to their experience with rising costs (having to take on second jobs, cosigning for loans, concerns about how to pay for the education of their other children). Again, your purpose would be to inform, to provide information about what steps they could take to lobby against tuition increases. As they might not be familiar with some of the legislative bodies and agencies they would need to contact, you would probably spend some time explaining how these bodies work and defining any terms related to funding mechanisms that they would need to understand.

Audience 3: State legislators and administrators for the college Since state legislators and college administrators make the decisions about tuition increases and other college fees, this audience requires the most careful planning. Your purpose would be to persuade them not to increase college tuition. To achieve this goal, you would use a formal tone, cite statistics that show the negative impact of tuition increases on the ability of students to attend college, provide examples of the effect of higher costs on specific students, and present ways that money could be saved in other areas to offset tuition hikes.

After you have determined the topic, purpose, and audience for your paragraph, you are ready to start the process of writing a fully developed paragraph.

LO 5 TEN STEPS FOR WRITING AN EFFECTIVE PARAGRAPH

The following steps are designed to break down the five major stages of the writing process into manageable pieces. Feel free to change the order around and continually test what works best for you and your individual learning style. Each writing assignment may require you to modify your process. Remember, *all formulas and step-by-step processes are tools designed to help you write effective, well-organized paragraphs*. Don't let the tools control you: Use them, customize them, and abandon them if they don't work for you. As you go through these 10 steps, think critically and keep in mind your *purpose* for writing and the *information* you will need to develop and *support* that purpose.

Let's say you are assigned, or have chosen, to write a paragraph about a famous local landmark. You would need to narrow the subject down to a specific topic, a specific local landmark. You would then need to decide what point you wanted to make about that landmark. You could use the following steps to develop your ideas, outline an organizational plan, identify your target audience, and determine your purpose for writing.

Throughout the explanation of the steps that follow, the process is illustrated by a series of examples that show how a student would move from the broad subject of Disneyland in Anaheim, California, to a fully developed paragraph on why Disneyland is a good place for family vacations.

Prewrite

Step One: Generate Ideas

Prewriting helps you generate ideas about your subject (see pp. 66–71), narrow it down to a more focused topic, and identify possible examples and details you can use to support your topic sentence.

Student Example: Prewriting (Brainstorming)

Subject: Disneyland, in Anaheim, California

Let's see . . . I want to write about Disneyland, but I need to narrow the subject down to a more focused topic and get some ideas and details I can include in my paragraph . . . let me see . . . what comes to mind when I think of Disneyland. . . . Rides, Pirates of the Caribbean, The Haunted Mansion, Disney characters, Mickey Mouse and friends, my grandma and grandpa's visit to California when I was a kid, Tomorrowland, Fantasyland, the Castle, Finding Nemo, music, entertainment, the electric parade, Main Street, food, tourists, international fame, a place kids in America want to visit, family vacations to Disneyland, Disneyland hotels, my sister's fear of Mickey Mouse, California weather, other attractions near Disneyland . . .

Now, you try . . .

ACTIVITY 4-9   Generating Ideas

Directions: *On a separate paper, practice using two prewriting techniques (see pp. 66–71) to generate some narrowed topics for the general subjects listed below.*

relationships	roommates
manners	romantic places
water sports	memories

Once you have narrowed your subject down to a manageable topic, use prewriting to discover ideas and details related to it and to get an idea of the point you want to make about it.

Step Two: Ask Questions to Find Subject, Purpose, and Audience

Cross Reference
See Chapter 3, pp. 73–76, for more on purpose and audience.

Ask the following questions about your topic to determine your purpose, to identify your audience, and decide on your approach.

1. What is my *narrowed topic*?

2. What is my *purpose* for writing this paragraph? What do I intend to explain or prove to my audience about my topic? What specific question or idea will I be addressing?

3. Who is my intended *audience*? What background information or special information will they need to know? What approach and tone should I use to best address this audience?

Student Example: Asking Questions to Discover Subject, Purpose, and Audience

Let me try these questions on the subject of Disneyland.

1. What is my *narrowed topic*?

   Looking at my brainstorm and cluster, I will narrow my subject of Disneyland to the topic of Disneyland as a vacation destination.

2. What is my *purpose* for writing this paragraph? What do I intend to explain or prove to my audience about my topic? What specific question or idea will I be addressing?

   I want to explain to my readers why Disneyland is a good destination for a family vacation.

3. Who is my intended *audience*? What background information or special information will they need to know? What approach and tone should I use to best address this audience?

   My intended audience is American families with children. I will use an informative tone and provide lots of details about why Disneyland is family friendly to prove my point to people who have not visited before.

   Topic and Purpose: Disneyland is a great family vacation destination

Now, you try . . .

ACTIVITY 4-10   Topic, Purpose, and Audience

Directions: *Using one of the topics you generated in Activity 4-9, freewrite a bit more about it, and then answer the following questions.*

1. What is my *narrowed topic?*

_____

_____

2. What is my *purpose* for writing this paragraph? What do I intend to explain or prove to my audience about my topic? What specific question or idea will I be addressing?

_____

_____

3. Who is my intended *audience?* What background information or special information will they need to know? What approach and tone should I use to best address my audience?

_____

_____

Topic and Purpose: _____

_____

Develop Your Ideas

Now, you need to take the ideas and details you've generated in the prewriting stage and develop them by generating more examples and details to support your topic and purpose. Use the following steps:

1. Think again about your purpose. Ask yourself, What exactly do I want to explain or prove about my topic in this paragraph?

2. Assess the details and ideas you created in your prewriting. As you look at the material you generated, ask yourself which examples and details will be useful and which ones will not.

3. Delete ideas. Delete any ideas or details that don't fit your topic and purpose or seem off track.

4. Add ideas. As you review your prewriting materials, add new ideas or details that didn't occur to you before.

5. Re-brainstorm. Brainstorm more ideas now that your topic is more focused.

6. Re-freewrite. Freewrite again now that your ideas are more focused.

Student Example: Developing Topic and Purpose

Let's see, I have already figured out my purpose and generated some examples and details. Let me look at my brainstorm again, assess the examples and details, delete the ones that are off track, and add any new ideas that are related to my topic and purpose.

> **Previous brainstorm**
>
> Rides, Pirates of the Caribbean, The Haunted Mansion, Disney characters, Mickey Mouse and friends, ~~my grandma and grandpa's visit to California when I was a kid~~, Tomorrowland, Fantasyland, the Castle, Finding Nemo, music, entertainment, the electric parade, Main Street, food, tourists, international fame, a place kids in America want to visit, family vacations to Disneyland, Disneyland hotels, ~~my sister's fear of Mickey Mouse~~, California weather, ~~other attractions near Disneyland~~ . . .

I like most of the details I have here, but I think I should add some more and delete the ones about my grandma and grandpa's visit, my sister's fear of Mickey Mouse, and other attractions near Disneyland since they do not directly support my purpose.

Topic and Purpose: Disneyland as a great family vacation destination. Let me brainstorm a few more details about Disneyland that make it a great family vacation destination.

> Fun for all ages, variety of food and restaurant choices, people from all over the world to see, fun rides for every speed, roller coasters, Thunder Mountain, Mader horn, the Disneyland Train, the Monorail, It's a Small World, Jungle Cruise, Indiana Jones ride, Autotopia, Space Mountain, Main Street, shopping, clothing, accessories, music, live bands, good weather, warmer climate . . .

Organize

Step Three: Organize Your Ideas—Outline

Once you have focused your topic and have examples and details to support your purpose, an outline is a great way to figure out a "table of contents" for your paragraph. You can use it to create an organizational plan for your writing and to distinguish the main idea from the examples and details you will use to support it. The main idea should be aligned left and the examples and details indented, as in the following student example.

Cross Reference

See Chapter 3, pp. 57–60, for more on outlining.

Student Example: Outlining

Cross Reference

See Chapter 3, pp. 41–43, for more on topic sentences.

Now I am ready to create a rough outline of my ideas to see how they could be put together in a first draft of my paragraph. I will include my working topic sentence.

Rough Outline

Working topic sentence: Disneyland is a great family vacation destination.

    I. Entertaining rides for all ages

        A. Rollercoaster rides

        B. Themed rides

        C. Transportation rides

    II. Food and other entertainment options

        A. Casual restaurants and street vendor food

        B. Fancy restaurants

        C. Live music and shows

   III. Types of people and weather

        A. Famous cartoon characters

        B. Tourists from all over the world

        C. Mild California climate

▶ NOTE   Here the student could go back and brainstorm again to develop additional examples and details. She could also reorganize the outline to accommodate any new examples or ideas she decides to include. Check your campus writing center for software you can use to create outlines in correct format.

ACTIVITY 4-11   Creating a Rough Outline

Directions: *Using your answers to the questions in Activity 4-10, generate a working topic sentence. Then, on a separate sheet of paper, write a rough outline for a paragraph based on that sentence.*

Draft

Step Four: Write Your First Draft

Just dive in. Although this step is often the one where many students begin in their writing process, you shouldn't write an actual draft until you have accomplished the three steps above. Otherwise, you run the danger of wasting a lot of time and effort figuring out your purpose or rambling through the first part, or all, of your paragraph.

As you write your first draft, don't worry about spelling and grammar: You will only lose your *train* of thought and become *derailed* from the points you are making. Instead, check grammar and spelling later in the editing stage of the process.

Student Example: First Draft

Disneyland is a great family vacation destination. It has rides that are fun for all ages. There are great rollercoaster rides. There are themed rides such as Pirates of the Carribean. They don't have any rides for Batman or other superheroes though. If the family doesn't want to go on a fast ride, they can relax on a fun form of transportation like the Disneyland Train. All kinds of food is available at Disneyland. From burgers and hotdogs to fancy full corse meals. Also, the family can be entertained by live music and other kinds of shows. People from all over the world visit Disneyland. There's great people watching. The weather in Anaheim, California, where Disneyland is, is mild and usually it doesn't rain, which people enjoy when they visit. These are good reasons to go to Disneyland.

Now you try . . .

ACTIVITY 4-12   Write a First Draft

Directions: *On a separate sheet of paper, using the ideas you generated in Activity 4-10 and your rough outline from 4-11, write a first draft of your paragraph (5–10 sentences).*

Revise

Step Five: Reorganize for Order, Unity, Coherence, and Sentence Variety

Revision is the most crucial stage of the writing process. Few writers are such naturals that they can crank out perfect paragraphs and sentences in a first draft. Most need several drafts to accomplish a well-designed, well-written, and well-supported paragraph. Many students mistakenly confuse the term *revision* with the terms *edit* or *proofread*. **Revision** focuses on improving organization, style, and content. **Proofreading** and **editing**, which will be explained in the next stage, focus on fixing grammar and spelling errors.

Cross Reference
See Chapter 3, pp. 53–54, for a more detailed explanation of unity.

Revision is the key to excellence in content, support, and delivery. During revision, check the order of your paragraph and the examples provided, move sentences if necessary, and check for unity, deleting examples or details that don't belong. (Checking for **unity** means ensuring that each sentence helps develop the purpose stated in the topic sentence.) Make sure your paragraph has enough **support** in the form of examples and details to fully develop the topic sentence. Also, check that your paragraph has **coherence**—that it flows smoothly from sentence to sentence—by adding appropriate transitional words or phrases where needed. Finally, be sure that you have **sentence variety** (that you varied the length of your sentences and used a variety of sentence types).

Cross Reference

See Chapter 3 for more on order, coherence, transitions, and unity, and Chapter 20 for tips on achieving sentence variety.

REVISION CHECKLIST

PURPOSE   IDEAS   SUPPORT   ASSUMPTIONS BIASES   CONCLUSIONS   POINT OF VIEW   ANALYSIS

1. Check your topic sentence to ensure you have a focused topic and a clear **purpose** (**idea**, point, or opinion) for writing about it.

2. Reorganize your **support** (examples and details) if needed.

3. Add more **support**, if necessary, to fully develop your topic sentence.

4. Make sure you have provided **analysis** and commentary to explain how your examples support your topic sentence.

5. Check for unity and delete unnecessary words, sentences, ideas, or details.

6. Check for coherence and add transitions between sentences where needed. (See "Transitions and Coherence," Chapter 3.)

7. Make sure your **concluding** sentence restates the main point of the paragraph and does not introduce new or contradictory ideas.

8. Check for sentence variety (see Chapter 20).

9. Check for major sentence-level grammar errors (see Chapters 21–22).

Student Example: Revision

I'll use the revision checklist to make sure I check everything. (Added transitions are highlighted.)

Disneyland is a great family vacation destination. It has rides that are fun for all ages. There are great rollercoaster rides. Moreover, there are themed rides such as Pirates of the Caribbean. They don't have any rides for Batman or other superheroes though. If the family doesn't want to go on a fast ride, they can relax on a fun form of transportation like the Disneyland Train. In addition to great rides, also, all kinds of food is available at Disneyland. From burgers and hotdogs to fancy full corse meals, for example. Also, the family can be entertained by live music and other kinds of shows. Besides these things to do, people from all over the world visit Disneyland, so there's great people watching. Finally, the weather in Anaheim, California, where Disneyland is, is mild and usually it doesn't rain, which people enjoy when they visit. As you can see, these are good reasons to go to Disneyland.

ACTIVITY 4-13 Revision

Directions: *On a separate sheet of paper, revise your paragraph draft from Activity 4-12 using the Revision Checklist.*

Step Six: Fine-Tune Your Topic and Concluding Sentence

Cross Reference

See Chapter 3 for more on topic sentences and concluding sentences.

Check that your topic sentence has a clear purpose—an opinion or argument, not just a fact or detail—is neither too broad nor too narrow, and is worded well. Then make sure that your concluding sentence strongly reiterates the topic sentence without introducing a new idea.

Student Example: Fine-Tuning Topic and Concluding Sentences

OK, looking at my Disneyland paragraph draft, I can see that both my topic sentence and my concluding sentence could be improved. They are still too broad, so I should make them more specific.

Original Topic Sentence: Disneyland is a great family vacation destination.

Revision: Disneyland is a great family vacation destination choice because it offers entertainment for the whole family.

Original Concluding Sentence: As you can see, these are good reasons to go to Disneyland.

Revision: As you can see, Disneyland makes for a great vacation adventure that pleases the whole family.

ACTIVITY 4-14   Fine-Tuning Your Topic and Concluding Sentences

Directions: *Revise your topic sentence and concluding sentence from Activity 4-13 to make them clear and focused. If they are strong as they are already, just write "needs no revision" below.*

Original Topic Sentence: _____

_____

Revised Topic Sentence: _____

_____

Original Concluding Sentence: _____

_____

Revised Concluding Sentence: _____

_____

Step Seven: Provide Support—Add More Examples, Details, and Analysis

Make sure your paragraph has at least two statements of support for the idea set out in the topic sentence. Include examples to illustrate your point, as well as supporting details, and analysis of what these examples demonstrate in relation to your paragraph's purpose.

Student Example: Adding More Support, Examples, and Details

In this draft of my Disneyland paragraph, I'm going to add my new topic sentence and concluding sentence and see where I can provide more or better supporting examples and details.

Disneyland is a great family vacation destination choice because it offers entertainment for the whole family. It has rides that are fun for all ages. There are great rollercoaster rides. For example, three of my favorite rollercoaster rides ever are at Disneyland: the Maderhorn, Thunder Mountain, and Space Mountain. Moreover, there are themed rides such as Pirates of the Carribean. Two other famous theme rides at Disneyland are The Haunted Mansion, which lets you tour a house full of ghosts, and It's a Small World, which features singing doll-like puppets from around the world. If the family doesn't want to go on a fast ride, they can relax on a fun form of transportation like the Disneyland Train. The monorail is another popular form of transportation in the park. Even grandparents and toddlers enjoy these modes of transportation. In addition to great rides, all kinds of food is available at Disneyland. From burgers and hotdogs to fancy full corse meals, for example. In the French Quarter, you can get a Mint Julep and Cajun-style food. Also, the family can be entertained by live music and other kinds of shows. There are even marching bands and bands on stage. Besides these things to do, people from all over the world visit Disneyland, so there's great people watching. In one afternoon, you can see people from Japan, China, Europe, Africa, and many other places from around the world. Finally, the weather in Anaheim, California, where Disneyland is, is mild and usually it doesn't rain, which people enjoy when they visit. The average temperature in the fall is in the 70s. As you can see, Disneyland makes for a great vacation adventure that pleases the whole family.

ACTIVITY 4-15   Providing Supporting Examples and Details

Directions: *Come up with at least one new example to provide support for your topic sentence and then a detail to support that new example.*   *Answers will vary.*

Another Supporting Example

_____

_____

Supporting Detail for that example:

_____

_____

Proofread and Edit

After you have revised for style and content, you need to proofread your paragraph for grammar and spelling errors. It helps if you can put your final paragraph draft aside for a day before you complete the proofread and edit stage. That way you can spot simple errors and typos that are invisible to your brain for the first hours after writing (because you just wrote the sentences and know what they are *supposed* to say). Also, be sure to have your textbook and a dictionary handy as you go through your paragraph. Remember this rule of thumb as you proofread: When in doubt, look it up.

Step Eight: Check Word Choice, Tone, and Style

Check your vocabulary. If you are writing for an audience knowledgeable about a topic, you can use terms they would understand without providing definitions. However, if the topic is not familiar to your audience, avoid using jargon and provide definitions for any important terms. Identify words you overuse, and use a thesaurus to find synonyms to replace them. Also, check whether your tone is appropriate for your topic, purpose and audience. Is it too formal or informal?

Cross Reference
See Chapter 26 for help with tone.

Student Example: Checking for Word Choice and Tone

Cross Reference
See Chapter 22 for information on passive versus active voice.

Cross Reference
See Chapter 22 for information about point of view shifts.

OK, I have quite a few "There are" or "There is" statements or "is" and "has" verbs so I'll try and make them into more active verb constructions. I also switch point of view from third-person (they) to second-person (you). I will change the whole paragraph to third-person point of view. I use some informal language, so I'll take out any contractions and make sure I have a more formal tone. I also repeat the words "Disneyland" or "Disney" too often, so I'll see if I can replace or delete some of them.

Disneyland is a great family vacation destination choice because it offers entertainment for the whole family. This popular theme park boasts rides that are fun for all ages. Rollercoaster rides are one of the park's main attractions. For example, three of the most popular rollercoaster rides at Disneyland are the Matterhorn, Thunder Mountain, and Space Mountain. Moreover, there are themed rides such as Pirates of the Caribbean are a wonderful feature of this amusement park. Two other famous theme rides at Disneyland are The Haunted Mansion, which lets people tour a house full of ghosts, and It's a Small World, which features singing doll-like puppets from around the world. If the family doesn't want to go on a fast ride, they can relax on a fun form of transportation like the Disneyland Train. The monorail is another popular form of transportation in the park. Even grandparents and toddlers enjoy these transportation rides. In addition to great rides, all kinds of food are available. From burgers and hotdogs to fancy full-course meals, for example. In the French Quarter, shoppers can get Mint Juleps and Cajun-style food. Also, the family can be entertained by live music and other kinds of shows, even marching bands and bands on stage. Besides these activities, people from all over the world visit Disneyland, providing great people watching. In one afternoon, attendees can see visitors from Japan, China, Europe, Africa, and many other places. from around the world. Finally, the weather in Anaheim, California, is mild and usually it does not rain, which people enjoy when they visit. The average temperature in the fall is in the 70s. As anyone can see, Disneyland makes for a great vacation adventure that pleases the whole family.

ACTIVITY 4-16   Check Word Choice and Tone

Directions: *Go through your paragraph, and make sure you have used a consistent and appropriate tone throughout. Check your word choices and change any words that do not work well for your target audience. Eliminate contractions.*

Step Nine: Check for Sentence-Level Errors

1. **Check** for fragments, run-ons, and comma splices (see Chapter 21).
2. **Check** for incorrect comma usage, point of view shifts, pronoun agreement, subject–verb agreement, pronoun reference errors, semicolon and colon use, apostrophe use, faulty parallelism, dangling or misplaced modifiers, and unnecessary passive voice constructions (these common errors are covered in Chapters 21–24).

Student Example: Checking for Sentence-Level Errors

I checked my Disneyland paragraph, and I found one sentence fragment.

Fragment: From burgers and hotdogs to fancy full-course meals, for example.

Revised: From burgers and hotdogs to fancy full-course meals, there is food for every taste.

ACTIVITY 4-17   Grammar Review and Final Revision

Directions: *Go through your paragraph, and check for the common sentence-level grammar errors summarized in Step Ten. Revise any errors you find. Then, use the following Revision Checklist to evaluate the basic elements of your paragraph.*

Step Ten: Check for Spelling Errors

Cross Reference
See Chapter 25, p. 567, for more on commonly confused words.

Use a dictionary or "spell-check" to check the spelling of any words you are unsure about and also check for words that you might have used incorrectly.

Student Example: Checking for Spelling Errors

I'm a pretty good speller. But I've been burned by spell-check before. I'll just double-check the words I'm not one hundred percent sure of with a dictionary. Also, I'm going to glance through the Commonly Confused Words section of this text (Chapter 25) to see if I have misused any of those.

I found a couple spelling errors:

Maderhorn = Matterhorn   corse = course   Carribean = Caribbean

ACTIVITY 4-18   Check for Spelling Errors

Directions: *Check the Commonly Confused Words list on page 567 to see if you have made any of these common mistakes. Then, use a dictionary or spell-check to double-check your spelling of any words you are unsure about.*

Once you have completed the 10 steps above, use the following revision checklist to review your paragraph and make any final revisions.

REVISION CHECKLIST

BLUEPRINTS   PURPOSE   IDEAS   SUPPORT   ASSUMPTIONS BIASES   CONCLUSIONS   POINT OF VIEW   ANALYSIS

_____   Check that you have a clear topic sentence that states your **purpose**, the controlling **idea** of your paragraph.

_____   Check that you have used appropriate vocabulary, tone, and approach for your target audience.

_____   Check to make sure that you have organized your paragraph well with transitions when needed (coherence).

_____   Check to make sure you have maintained unity—all sentences help develop your topic sentence.

_____   Check to make sure you have included enough **support** in your paragraph to develop your purpose. Do you need more examples and details?

_____   Check to make sure you have framed **support**, your examples and details, with comments and **analysis** that show how these examples and details illustrate your topic sentence.

_____   Check to make sure that your sentence structure and your vocabulary choices are varied and interesting.

_____   Check for a strong **concluding** sentence that sums up the purpose established in your topic sentence.

_____   Check for complete sentences (no fragments, run-ons, or comma splices).

_____   Check for correct punctuation throughout the paragraph (commas, semicolons, colons, other punctuation marks).

_____   Check for conventional rules of mechanics (spelling, capitalization, underlining, italics, abbreviations, numbering) using the grammar section of this text and a dictionary.

Tips for Paragraph Success

Here are some tips to keep in mind when writing expository paragraphs.

Tip One: **Avoid awkward announcements.** Don't announce what you are going to write about: just say it.

Announcement: In this paragraph I will show that sports fans have different game-viewing habits.
Revised: Sports fans have different game-viewing habits.

Announcement: I will provide a list of "do's and don'ts" for registering for college courses.
Revised: Students need to learn the basic "do's and don'ts" of registering for college courses.

Tip Two: **Delete *It seems*, *I think*, or *I feel* statements in paragraphs.** They weaken your voice and argument. You can use first person and write "I" statements such as "When I feel tired, I usually take a nap." However, there is no need to add statements such as "I believe" or "I feel" or "I think" to a point you are making when it is already understood that you are presenting your own ideas.

***It seems* statement:** It seems that prices are rising.
Revised: Prices are rising.

***I think* statement:** I think local stores should be supported more than large corporations.
Revised: Local stores should be supported more than large corporations.

***I feel* or *I think* statement:** I feel (or I think) that our school should offer more online classes.
Revised: Our school should offer more online classes.

Tip Three: **Avoid introducing a new idea or contradicting yourself in the conclusion: the "shoot yourself in the foot" effect.**

Original topic sentence: Sports fans have different game-viewing habits.
"Shot in the foot" conclusion: Sports fans also have strange eating habits. (Here the writer added a whole new topic in the last line of the paragraph.)
Contradictory conclusion: However, in general, most sports fans have the same habits. (Here the writer contradicts the point of the topic sentence.)
Revised conclusion: The TV game-viewing habits of sports fans are as varied as the people themselves.

Tip Four: **Choose the appropriate paragraph length and amount of support and analysis needed, based on your topic and purpose.** The number of sentences in a paragraph varies depending on the topic sentence and its scope. Also, the length of a paragraph is affected by how many examples and details are included to support the topic sentence. On average, most paragraphs range from 4 to 15 sentences in length. Decide carefully how many examples you will need.

LO 6   SELF AND PEER ASSESSMENT

Self and peer assessment of your writing allows you to go through a draft step-by-step and look at the separate elements to ensure a well-thought-out and organized presentation of your point. Think of these elements *before* you begin to draft, and use the following self-assessment checklist to see if you have addressed them all well after you have written it. Then, ask a peer (classmate, friend, or tutor) to use the same checklist to critique your paragraph.

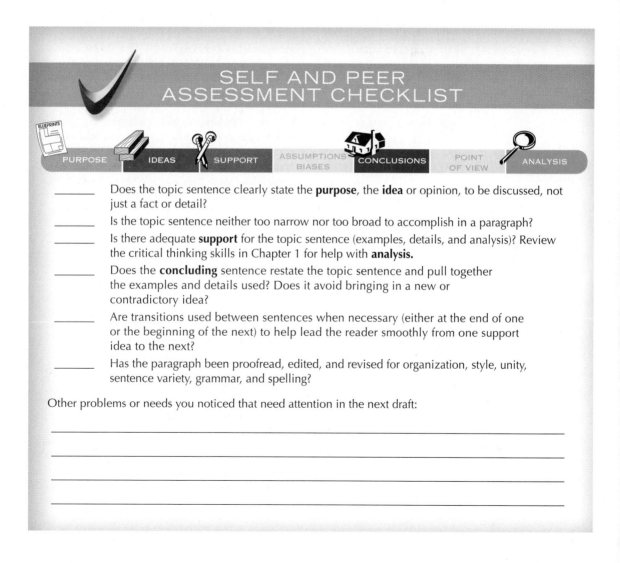

SELF AND PEER ASSESSMENT CHECKLIST

PURPOSE   IDEAS   SUPPORT   ASSUMPTIONS BIASES   CONCLUSIONS   POINT OF VIEW   ANALYSIS

_____   Does the topic sentence clearly state the **purpose**, the **idea** or opinion, to be discussed, not just a fact or detail?

_____   Is the topic sentence neither too narrow nor too broad to accomplish in a paragraph?

_____   Is there adequate **support** for the topic sentence (examples, details, and analysis)? Review the critical thinking skills in Chapter 1 for help with **analysis.**

_____   Does the **concluding** sentence restate the topic sentence and pull together the examples and details used? Does it avoid bringing in a new or contradictory idea?

_____   Are transitions used between sentences when necessary (either at the end of one or the beginning of the next) to help lead the reader smoothly from one support idea to the next?

_____   Has the paragraph been proofread, edited, and revised for organization, style, unity, sentence variety, grammar, and spelling?

Other problems or needs you noticed that need attention in the next draft:

_____

_____

_____

_____

LEARNING OBJECTIVES REVIEW

LO 1	What are the five major stages of the writing process? (See p. 64)	The **five major stages** of the writing process are *prewriting, organizing, drafting, revising,* and *proofreading and editing.*
LO 2	What prewriting techniques can you use to discover your subject and narrow your topic? (See pp. 66–73)	**Prewriting techniques** you can use to discover your subject and narrow your topic are *talking/thinking, freewriting, mapping, brainstorming, clustering,* and *journaling.*
LO 3	What are six questions you can ask yourself to help you figure out your paragraph's purpose? (See p. 74)	**Six questions** you can ask yourself to figure out your purpose are (1) What is my goal for writing about this topic? (2) Is there a problem that needs to be solved related to this topic? (3) What do I want to say about the topic? (4) What do I already know about it? (5) What opinions do I have about it? (6) What is my point of view?
LO 4	How do you determine your audience and the best approach to use? (See pp. 75–76)	In order to **determine your audience**, ask yourself which category of audience (general, academic, and specialized) you are targeting in your paragraph. To determine the **best approach** to use, think about what they already know about the topic, the point you want to convey about it, and what additional background information or explanation you may need to provide to make your point clear.
LO 5	What are the 10 steps for writing an effective paragraph? (See pp. 77–94)	The **10 steps for writing an effective paragraph** are (1) generate ideas; (2) ask questions to find subject, purpose, and audience; (3) organize your ideas; (4) write a first draft; (5) reorganize for order, unity, coherence, and sentence variety; (6) fine-tune topic sentence and concluding sentence; (7) add more support (examples and details); (8) check word choice and tone; (9) check for sentence-level errors; and (10) check for spelling errors.
LO 6	What is self and peer assessment, and why is it helpful? (See p. 95)	**Self and peer assessment** involves you, and later a peer, using a checklist to go through a draft step-by-step and looking at the separate elements to ensure a well-thought-out and organized presentation of your point.

For support in meeting this chapter's objectives, log in to www.mywritinglab.com and select **The Writing Process, Getting Started,** and **Prewriting.**

Essays: Structure and Process

LEARNING OBJECTIVES

In this chapter you will learn to

LO1 Structure essays

LO2 Recognize and use the building blocks of essays

LO3 Use 10 steps for writing effective essays

LO4 Use self and peer assessment

THINKING CRITICALLY

Moving from paragraphs to short essays is easier if you keep in mind the same basic principles you learned for writing good paragraphs: *subject*, *purpose*, and *audience*. Like the pieces of coral on lava, these principles are the same as for paragraphs but the ways in which they are used to create essays produces unique compositions. Before reading this chapter, what elements that you learned from writing paragraphs do you think you will need to include when writing essays too?

_____

_____

LO 1 ESSAY STRUCTURE

Good news! The basic structure of a paragraph translates into the structure for an essay. Both the paragraph and the essay start with a statement of purpose; use examples, details, and analysis to support and develop the purpose statement; and include a conclusion that reiterates the purpose.

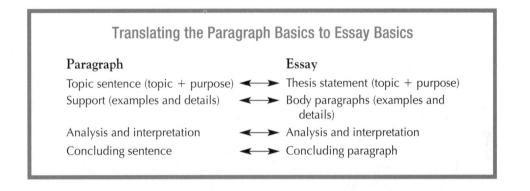

Translating the Paragraph Basics to Essay Basics

Paragraph	Essay
Topic sentence (topic + purpose) ⟷	Thesis statement (topic + purpose)
Support (examples and details) ⟷	Body paragraphs (examples and details)
Analysis and interpretation ⟷	Analysis and interpretation
Concluding sentence ⟷	Concluding paragraph

APPLYING CRITICAL THINKING

BLUEPRINTS PURPOSE   IDEAS   SUPPORT   ASSUMPTIONS BIASES   CONCLUSIONS   POINT OF VIEW   ANALYSIS

Paragraph to Essay: Pattern Similarities

Think critically about the basic structure and purpose of a good paragraph, and then transfer that knowledge to writing essays. Both begin with an introduction that sets up the topic, main **idea**, and **purpose**; include **support** in the form of examples, details, and **analysis** and interpretation of those examples and details; use transitions between major points to maintain flow and coherence; and have a **conclusion** that reiterates the statement of purpose and provides a closing remark or idea for further thought.

Expository Essays

The goal of an **expository essay** is to develop ideas and draw some conclusions about those ideas. Think of the introductory paragraph as the set up, the body paragraphs as the arena for developing your ideas, and the conclusion as your forum for summing up and driving home your ideas and purpose.

The number of paragraphs in an essay varies depending on the topic and the goal(s) of the thesis statement. Most essays have at least four paragraphs and six or more is common. Let your topic, goals, and the guidelines of your instructor's assignment set the length and the number of paragraphs you will need, rather than relying on a formula with a set number of paragraphs that might limit your ideas.

The **introductory paragraph** in an essay should draw in your audience and set up your subject and purpose, just as the topic sentence does in a paragraph. Include an attention-grabber to intrigue your reader, a general introduction and background information about your topic, and a thesis statement. The **thesis statement** is a sentence that explains your purpose for writing an essay. It should include *what* you are writing about, *how* you will explain your purpose, and the *so what?*—what you want your readers to understand about your chosen topic.

Body paragraphs follow the same basic principles you have learned about in previous chapters: a topic sentence, support through examples, details and analysis, and a concluding sentence. The only difference now is that you need to add transitions between paragraphs, as they are part of a greater whole, so use transitions at the end of one body paragraph or at the beginning of the next to make your essay flow smoothly. Transitions are discussed in depth on page 53–56.

The **concluding paragraph** should reiterate and sum up your thesis statement and include your closing comments. Be careful not to introduce any new or contradictory ideas in your conclusion.

Use the following chart as an essay writing guide.

THE ESSAY FORMAT

INTRODUCTORY PARAGRAPH

Opening Line/Attention-Grabber: Designed to draw in your readers

General Background for the Topic: The setup

Thesis Statement: States the purpose of your essay. It outlines what you plan to explain to your readers about your subject, the conclusion you have reached about the topic.

Ask yourself these questions to develop a strong thesis statement:

- **What** am I writing about?
- **How** will I demonstrate my purpose?
- **So What?** What is the main conclusion I have reached on the subject?

BODY PARAGRAPHS

Topic Sentence: Main idea for the paragraph and develops the thesis

Support: Backs up the topic sentence idea with a statement of support, fact, or opinion (one to three support statements per body paragraph)

- **Examples:** One or two examples to illustrate each idea
- **Details:** One or more details to illustrate and explain each example
- **Analysis/commentary:** Analysis and commentary on the importance of the supporting examples and details and how they illustrate the topic sentence
- **Concluding sentence:** sums up the main idea from the topic sentence and/or provides ideas for further thought, or serves as transition to next paragraph

Include these elements in each body paragraph in your essay. Use transitions at the end of one body paragraph or at the beginning of the next to make your essay flow smoothly.

CONCLUDING PARAGRAPH

Re-emphasizes your essay's thesis without restating it: Reminds your reader of your thesis and sums up your main points

- Sums up your analytical conclusions
- Ends with closing ideas for further thought

▶ NOTE   Be careful not to introduce a new or contradictory idea in the concluding paragraph.

LO 2 THE BUILDING BLOCKS OF AN ESSAY

Following is a description of the basic building blocks of an essay. Throughout, it uses examples from a model student essay (see p. 121) on the topic of the advantages of having a roommate in college.

Title

Though most paragraph assignments do not require a formal title, an essay does. The title for your essay is the key to introducing your topic and drawing in your reader. Try for titles that are clear, yet interesting, and will intrigue your reader.

The Case for Getting a Roommate

Cross Reference

See Chapter 17 for more on typing format.

The title should be centered, use the same font style and size as the rest of your essay, and not be in bold font or underlined.

Introductory Paragraph and Thesis Statement

The purpose of the introduction is to engage your reader's attention, introduce your topic and purpose for writing about it (your thesis), provide any necessary background information, and establish the style and tone of your essay. To create a successful introduction, include the following elements.

Opening Line(s)/Attention-Grabber

The first sentence or two of your essay should intrigue your readers, draw them in, and introduce the subject of your paper. Here are some tried and true techniques for accomplishing this goal:

1. **Begin with a rhetorical question.**

   > When you move out on your own, is it more important for you to save money or to have your own space?

   ▶ NOTE   Usually, it is best to avoid second-person (*you*) point of view in an essay, but opening an essay with a rhetorical question is a widely accepted exception.

2. **Begin with a declaration.**

   > Having a roommate in college saves money and helps ease the burden of college expenses.

3. **Begin with a definition, a statistic, or a quotation.** Define a key term, present a powerful statistic related to your topic, or use an intriguing quotation to engage your readers' attention.

   > Getting a roommate can cut one's monthly living expenses by as much as 50%.

4. **Begin with a topic detail or example.**

   > The thought of having a roommate may terrify you, but it builds communication and negotiation skills.

▶ NOTE   If you use a detail you learned through research, cite your source.

5. Begin with a creative scenario or an anecdote.

> The first month of living on my own, I could barely make ends meet and I was stressed by the bills and grocery prices. I remember going to the store and watching the total creep up while my stomach clenched.

▶ NOTE   Avoid using a generalized dramatic statement as your opening line. For instance, "All people feel a need to have their own space." You may be wrong, and it is just too broad. Also, avoid worn, formulaic introductory phrases like *In today's society* . . . , *Throughout history* . . . , *According to the dictionary* . . . , and so on.

General Background on the Topic

Provide some general information about your topic, and then begin narrowing down to your focused thesis statement. Sometimes you need to provide background information about the problem or subject or give a brief history of the issue in order to provide your audience with necessary context for the point you want to make. For instance, if you were writing about the advantages and disadvantages of having a college roommate, you might need to give a little background about the basic issues related to sharing a room.

Thesis Statement

A good **thesis statement** establishes your topic, provides at least one controlling idea or analytical purpose it will develop, and gives a basic "map" to let your readers know how you will structure and develop your ideas. A thesis statement has a message to convey; it is making a claim. Therefore, a thesis always involves your opinion (attitude or point of view on the subject) and not just facts or details.

Most thesis statements will be one sentence in length for essays that range from one to four pages in length. Generally a good thesis statement will address the following three questions:

1. *What* is the purpose of my essay?
2. *How* will I develop it?
3. So *what* is the main point I want to prove?

Asking and answering these questions forces you to create a specific and well-developed thesis statement. For example, here is a thesis statement that includes answers to what, how, and so what questions related to the topic of having a college roommate:

> [*What?*] Deciding whether to have a college roommate or not is a tough decision [*How?*] because there are many pros and cons to sharing a living space, [*So what?*] but, without a doubt, the benefits outweigh the drawbacks.

Remember, though, that your thesis statement should not be a question or a series of questions. Instead, it should be your *answers* to the questions you want to address on the topic. Also, avoid *awkward announcements* like "In this essay, I will attempt to show you the benefits of having a college roommate." Instead, take out the announcement part and jump right to your point: "Having a college roommate is a good idea for many reasons." In fact, throughout your essay, delete all statements that begin with *I believe* or *I feel* or *I think* or *I will explain* and weak statements like *It seems that . . .* You can use *I* in expository essays, but use *I* only when you are giving a personal example for support. For instance, "I didn't have a roommate my first month of college, and I really struggled with finances."

Finally, your thesis needs to be specific enough to be developed thoroughly. If it is too broad, it will be too big to cover within the scope of your essay; if it is too narrow, you will not have enough to write about. Review Chapter 4, pages 64–65, for a detailed discussion of topic, purpose, and audience and how they contribute to developing a strong topic sentence, much of which directly relates to writing a clear, effective thesis statement.

ACTIVITY 5-1   Thesis Practice

Directions: *Create a one-sentence thesis statement that is neither too broad nor too narrow and that provides an opinion and purpose (plan for development) to pull together the three supporting points listed for the following topics.*

Answers will vary. Sample answers provided.

Example

Thesis: *A rise in crimes on campus has made our college less safe.*

  a. We have experienced several car break-ins in the main campus parking lot.
  b. Student property is being stolen from the classrooms.
  c. Classroom equipment has been stolen.

1. Thesis: *There are several benefits to getting enough exercise.*

    a. Exercise helps maintain one's weight.

    b. Exercise helps reduce stress.

    c. Exercise helps keep the heart healthy.

2. Thesis: *Sports programs on college campuses provide many benefits to students.*

    a. Sports programs help students stay in college.

    b. Sports programs help teach collaboration and team skills.

    c. Sports programs increase college identity and spirit.

3. Thesis: *Colleges need to provide or search out scholarship opportunities for their students.*

    a. Many students would not be able to attend college without a scholarship.

    b. Scholarships allow for equal access to all students.

    c. Scholarships from the community and local businesses build community.

Body Paragraphs

The function of **body paragraphs** is to provide evidence that backs up the argument in your thesis. Each body paragraph develops and supports an idea that explains and develops the thesis of the essay. The number of sentences in a body paragraph varies depending on the topic sentence and its scope; on average, most body paragraphs range from 4 to 15 sentences in length. The number of body paragraphs in an essay varies based on the topic, your purpose, your plan for development, and the tasks and page requirements of your writing assignment.

Be sure that each body paragraph achieves the following:

- **Develops the thesis** of your essay
- **Provides a clear topic sentence** that states the topic of the paragraph and the main point you are making about that topic
- **Provides support for the topic sentence** through ample examples, evidence, and analysis

Cross Reference

See Chapter 3, pp. 37–47, for details on writing analytical paragraphs.

Cross Reference

See Chapter 3 for more on unity, development, coherence, and transitions.

- **Demonstrates unity,** with each sentence supporting the topic sentence
- **Demonstrates coherence,** with sentences and ideas flowing smoothly from one to the next in a logical order through the use of appropriate transitions

The **topic sentence** of each paragraph in an essay should state an opinion, argument, or analytical point that supports the thesis. Here's a topic sentence that supports the roommate thesis:

Cross Reference

See Chapter 3, pp. 41–43, for detailed coverage on writing topic sentences.

Thesis: Deciding whether to have a college roommate or not is a tough decision because there are many pros and cons to sharing a living space, but, without a doubt, the benefits outweigh the drawbacks.

Topic sentence: To begin with, having a roommate in college is a great idea since it cuts overall living expenses by as much as half.

ACTIVITY 5-2   Topic Sentence Practice

Directions: *Create three topic sentences for each of the thesis statements provided below. Answers will vary.*

Example

Thesis: Students need to take certain precautions when buying used textbooks online.

Topic Sentence 1 *First, make sure that the book you are buying is the right title, the right publisher, and it is the most current edition by doing some preliminary research online.*

Topic Sentence 2 *Also, make sure that the book you are buying is in good condition, is complete, and is not marked on or overly highlighted by another user.*

Topic Sentence 3 *Finally, be sure the source or person you are purchasing from is reliable and legitimate.*

1. **Thesis:** Getting along well with one's neighbors requires some conscious effort.

   Topic Sentence 1 _____

   _____

   Topic Sentence 2 _____

   _____

   Topic Sentence 3 _____

   _____

2. **Thesis:** There are several ways you can work on remembering important events.

   Topic Sentence 1 _____

   _____

   Topic Sentence 2 _____

   _____

   Topic Sentence 3 _____

   _____

3. **Thesis:** Limiting the amount of television children watch provides several benefits.

   Topic Sentence 1 _____

   _____

   Topic Sentence 2 _____

   _____

   Topic Sentence 3 _____

   _____

Provide **support** for topic sentences by using examples, details, and analysis. Do not assume that the facts will speak for themselves. Most readers need commentary from you that explains the significance of the examples and details you have provided and their relevance to your argument. You can use the Analytical Ice Cream Sandwich model described in Chapter 3 (see pp. 43–45). Here is an example:

Analytical Ice Cream Sandwich

Top cookie	A roommate can save you half of your rent expenses.
Ice cream filling	Every month, my roommate pays half of our apartment's rent, a $400 contribution.
Bottom cookie	Saving 50 percent of my rent allows me to pay for my textbooks and buy more groceries each month

---

ACTIVITY 5-3   Ice Cream Sandwich Practice

Directions: *Choose one of the topic sentences you created in Activity 5-2 and create a full Ice Cream Sandwich to support that topic sentence.*
Answers will vary.

Top cookie (topic sentence):_____

_____

Ice cream filling (example and detail(s)):_____

_____

Bottom cookie (concluding sentence—interpretation and analysis):_____

_____

_____

Concluding Paragraph

The concluding paragraph sums up the main purpose of your essay and re-emphasizes your thesis without repeating it word for word. Most concluding paragraphs are at least three sentences long, although they can be longer, depending on the scope of the thesis, and should be succinct and end with a "Ta da!"—an overall sense of wrapping up with a bang.

▶ NOTE   Be sure to avoid the common pitfalls of introducing a new idea or contradicting yourself in the conclusion: the "shoot yourself in the foot" effect.

As you can see, a roommate can help in college in many ways, *but it may be even better to move back in with one's parents.*

Ouch! You just shot yourself in the foot by introducing a whole new topic and opinion from the one you have discussed throughout the rest of your essay.

Once you are familiar with the building blocks of an expository essay, you can customize and develop them to best suit your purpose and audience. After you have written a complete draft of an essay, use the following checklist to make sure you have included the necessary building blocks.

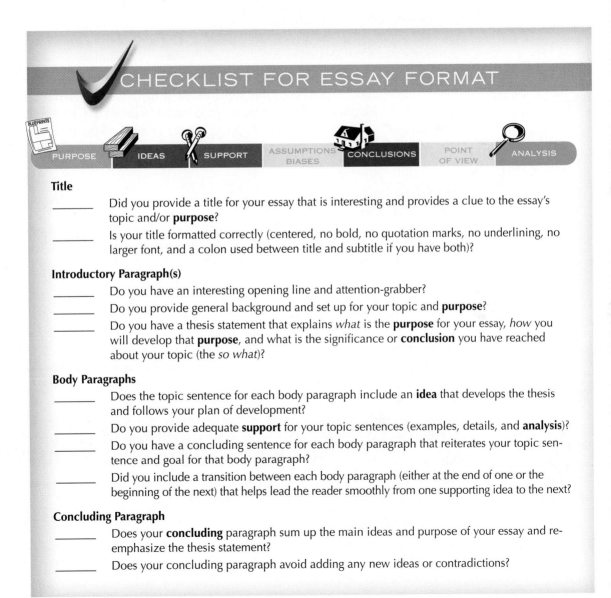

CHECKLIST FOR ESSAY FORMAT

PURPOSE   IDEAS   SUPPORT   ASSUMPTIONS BIASES   CONCLUSIONS   POINT OF VIEW   ANALYSIS

Title

_____ Did you provide a title for your essay that is interesting and provides a clue to the essay's topic and/or **purpose**?

_____ Is your title formatted correctly (centered, no bold, no quotation marks, no underlining, no larger font, and a colon used between title and subtitle if you have both)?

Introductory Paragraph(s)

_____ Do you have an interesting opening line and attention-grabber?

_____ Do you provide general background and set up for your topic and **purpose**?

_____ Do you have a thesis statement that explains *what* is the **purpose** for your essay, *how* you will develop that **purpose**, and what is the significance or **conclusion** you have reached about your topic (the *so what*)?

Body Paragraphs

_____ Does the topic sentence for each body paragraph include an **idea** that develops the thesis and follows your plan of development?

_____ Do you provide adequate **support** for your topic sentences (examples, details, and **analysis**)?

_____ Do you have a concluding sentence for each body paragraph that reiterates your topic sentence and goal for that body paragraph?

_____ Did you include a transition between each body paragraph (either at the end of one or the beginning of the next) that helps lead the reader smoothly from one supporting idea to the next?

Concluding Paragraph

_____ Does your **concluding** paragraph sum up the main ideas and purpose of your essay and re-emphasize the thesis statement?

_____ Does your concluding paragraph avoid adding any new ideas or contradictions?

(LO 3) TEN STEPS FOR WRITING AN EFFECTIVE ESSAY

These steps will help you break essay writing down into a manageable process. You might find some steps more useful than others. Try them in order first; then experiment to see what order works best for you.

Prewrite: Generate Ideas

Step One: Generate Ideas

It's essential to generate some ideas to work with for your essay and to narrow a broad subject to a manageable topic. Several methods for generating ideas that can help you with this process are covered in detail in Chapter 4: *thinking and writing, freewriting, mapping, brainstorming, clustering,* and *journaling.* (See Chapter 4, Step One, pages 66–71.)

ACTIVITY 5-5   Generating Ideas

Directions: *On a separate sheet of paper, pick one of the prewriting techniques covered in Chapter 4 and generate some ideas, subtopics, and details for the following five subjects:*

1. local one-day getaways
2. cartoons and comics
3. best places to dine in town
4. music and the Internet
5. best values in transportation
6. good jobs for students

Step Two: Ask Questions to Find Your Topic, Purpose, and Audience

Cross Reference
See Chapter 4, pp. 64–65, for more on purpose and audience.

Ask the following questions about your topic to determine your purpose, identify your audience, and decide on your approach.

1. What is my *narrowed topic*?
2. What is my *purpose* for writing this essay? What do I intend to explain or prove to my audience about my topic? What specific question or idea will I be addressing?

3. Who is my intended *audience?* What background information or special information will they need to know? What approach and tone should I use to best address this audience?

ACTIVITY 5-6   Topic, Purpose, and Audience

Directions: *Using one of the topics you generated in Activity 5-5, answer the following questions.* Answers will vary.

1. What is your narrowed topic, the narrowed subject you will address in your essay?

   _____

   _____

2. What is your purpose for writing this essay? What do you want to explain or prove to your readers?

   _____

   _____

3. Who is your target audience? To whom are you addressing this essay?

   _____

   _____

Now, you need to take the ideas and details from your initial prewriting and generate more examples and details to support your topic and purpose by doing the following:

- **Think again about your purpose.** Think about the ideas and details you have come up with in your prewriting, and ask questions about them that you could answer in your essay. What is it you will set out to explain or prove?
- **Re-brainstorm.** As you think about possible topics and reasons for writing about them, add new ideas and details.
- **Delete ideas.** As you refine your topic and purpose, delete ideas and details that don't fit.
- **Do a second round of prewriting.** Once you have a more focused topic and purpose, use freewriting to get more specific ideas and details.

Organize

Step Three: Organize Your Ideas: Outline

Cross Reference

Review Chapter 3, p. 57, for how to structure an outline.

An outline helps you to order your thoughts in the most logical and effective way and to create a plan for your essay's development. Here are some guidelines for writing an essay outline.

Guidelines for Writing an Essay Outline

1. **Write your thesis statement at the top of the outline,** but do not include the general introduction that will come before it.

2. **List the main ideas that will be developed as topic sentences in the body paragraphs** of your essay at the left margin, using Roman numerals (I, II, III, etc.). Use a brief phrase to explain each main idea.

3. **List the examples you will use to support the main idea (topic sentence) of each paragraph** using capital letters A, B, C, and so on. Use short phrases to describe each example. Indent examples one tab right from the left margin.

   ▶ NOTE   You must have at least two examples for each main idea: if you have an A then you must have a B. If you have only one example, then combine it with the main idea phrase or develop a second example.

4. **List the supporting details below each example.** Label details with numbers (1, 2, 3, and so on). If you have minor details to illustrate these details, label them with lowercase letters (a, b, c, and so on). Each level of detail progressively tabs right.

   ▶ NOTE   You must have at least two of each supporting level of detail, so if you have a 1 you need at least a 2. If you do not have a second detail at the same level, then create a second detail or wrap the detail into the previous one.

5. **Provide a brief conclusion.**

   ▶ NOTE   There is software available that automatically creates outlines in the correct format. However, although these tools and programs can make your job easier they are not always accurate. Consult a handbook if you have questions.

Sample Outline for "The Case for Getting a Roommate"

Alison Scott

Professor Navin

English 090

9 September 2010

Thesis: Deciding whether to have a college roommate or not is a tough decision because there are many pros and cons to sharing a living space, but, without a doubt, the benefits outweigh the drawbacks.

   I. Cuts overall living expenses by as much as half

      A. Splitting the cost of rent

         1. Rent for an apartment can be high

         2. Roommates can trade off each month or split the costs each month

      B. Splitting the bills

         1. Saves on utilities

         2. Saves on phone bills

      C. Splitting grocery costs

         1. Alternate shopping and costs

         2. Split food bills and assign cooking

  II. Having a roommate builds communication and negotiation skills

      A. Communication skills

         1. Builds social skills

         2. Nonverbal and verbal skills improved through living with roommate

      B. Negotiation skills

         1. Negotiating disagreements about money

         2. Negotiating personal space issues

III. Having a roommate can result in a lifelong friendship

    A. Talk out social and relationship issues together and get closer

        1. Confidante

        2. Problem solving

    B. Develop a lasting friendship and reminisce later about college years

        1. Develop a friendship

        2. Stay in touch over the years

Conclusion: The benefits of sharing a space with a roommate during your college years make the risks worthwhile.

Here are some questions to ask yourself as you develop your outline to ensure you have thought critically about what you want to say and how you want to say it:

CRITICAL THINKING QUESTIONS TO ASK AS YOU DESIGN YOUR OUTLINE

PURPOSE   IDEAS   SUPPORT   ASSUMPTIONS BIASES   CONCLUSIONS   POINT OF VIEW   ANALYSIS

1. What is my **purpose,** the main point or conclusion, I have reached about my topic?

2. How will I order my main **ideas** and body paragraphs? What is the *best order of development* to successfully argue my **conclusions** and present my *evidence*?

3. Do I have any claims that may need additional **support** (examples, details, and evidence) to convince my readers of their validity?

4. When I **analyze** my outline, do any parts need to be deleted, expanded upon, or reordered?

Finally, use the following Outline Critique Form for self or peer review of your outline.

OUTLINE CRITIQUE FORM

1. Does the outline start with a thesis statement?
2. Does the thesis statement clearly state the subject of the paper and the point being made about it?
3. Is the format correct?
4. Are the supporting examples clear and is each explained with a short phrase?
5. Are the supporting details specific enough to be clear but not overly detailed?
6. If there is an A or a 1 in a category, is it followed by at least one more point (B or 2 and so on)?
7. Based on the outline, is the overall organization plan for the essay effective?

Comments and suggestions for revision:

_____

_____

_____

_____

ACTIVITY 5-7   Creating an Outline

Directions: *On a separate sheet of paper, pick one of the topics you generated ideas for in Activity 5-5 and create an outline. Use the Critical Thinking Questions to Ask as You Design Your Outline box to help you create it, and then use the Outline Critique Form to check it once you are finished.*

Draft

Step Four: Write Your First Draft

You are now ready to write the first draft of your essay. Use your prewriting and outline to guide you. Focus on developing support for each body paragraph. At this stage, don't worry as much about spelling and grammar: just get your ideas on paper and work on building the draft. You will edit and proofread later.

ACTIVITY 5-8   Write a First Draft

Directions: *Using your prewriting and outline, write a first draft of your essay, and add a working title.*

Revise

Step Five: Revise for Order, Unity, Coherence, and Sentence Variety

Few writers, if any, are able to write a perfect first draft. Essay writing requires that you go back and rework what you have written in order to improve organization and support and ensure a smooth, logical flow of ideas. *Revision is the key to writing excellent essays.* Consider the following when revising for order, unity, coherence, and sentence variety:

- **Review organization.** Check to see if you need to reorganize the order of your paragraphs to make your essay more effective.
- **Delete unnecessary information.** Delete any unnecessary words, sentences, or even paragraphs. Cut anything that does not directly support your purpose and thesis.
- **Include transitions.** Add transitions between and within paragraphs where needed to maintain the flow of your ideas. (See Chapter 3, p. 53, for more on transitions and coherence.)
- **Vary sentence types.** Check that your sentences are varied and interesting. (See Chapter 20 for more on sentence variety.)

ACTIVITY 5-9   Revise Your Essay

Directions: Revise your essay using the guidelines above.

Step Six: Fine-Tune Thesis and Topic Sentences

Go through your revised essay and make sure that your thesis statement is strong and that your topic sentences clearly support it. The thesis and topic sentences are the skeleton of your essay: they need to be strong and well developed to hold the flesh of your ideas and details.

ACTIVITY 5-10   Revise Your Thesis and Topic Sentences

Directions: *Review your thesis and topic sentences. Ensure you have a clear thesis that states your purpose for writing about your topic and that each of your topic sentences supports your thesis.*

Step Seven: Provide Support—Add More Examples, Details, and Analysis

Check if you need more examples and details to thoroughly develop your thesis statement and topic sentences. Also, make sure you have analyzed the significance of your examples and details to help the reader see your purpose. Try using the analytical Ice Cream Sandwich technique to frame your examples.

ACTIVITY 5-11   Add More Support

Directions: *Review your essay and add examples, details, and analysis where necessary to provide additional support for topic sentences.*

Proofread and Edit

Step Eight: Check Word Choice, Tone, and Style

If you are writing for an audience knowledgeable about a topic, you can use terms they would understand without providing definitions. However, if you are discussing a topic not known to your audience, you want to avoid using jargon and provide definitions for any important terms. Check your essay and make sure the words you have chosen convey the meaning you intend. Use a dictionary to check meanings and a thesaurus to find replacement words, if necessary, that more effectively express what you want to say. Make sure you haven't used slang, clichés, or gender-biased language. (See Chapter 26, pp. 606–613, for help in identifying and correcting these kinds of errors.) Also, check whether your tone is appropriate for your topic, purpose (to inform, persuade, or entertain), and audience. Is your tone too formal or too informal?

ACTIVITY 5-12   Word Choice, Tone, and Style

Directions: *Revise your essay for word choice, tone, and style.*

Step Nine: Check for Sentence-Level Errors

Look for and correct the following sentence errors:

- Fragments, comma splices, and run-ons (Chapter 21)
- Incorrect use of commas, semicolons, or colons (see Chapter 23)
- Unnecessary point-of-view shifts (Chapter 22)
- Faulty pronoun agreement (Chapter 22)
- Incorrect subject–verb agreement (Chapter 22)
- Pronoun reference errors (Chapter 22)
- Parallelism errors (Chapter 22)
- Dangling or misplaced modifiers (Chapter 22)
- Incorrect apostrophe use (Chapter 24)
- Passive voice constructions (Chapter 22)

ACTIVITY 5-13   Revise Sentence-Level Errors

Directions: *Revise your essay for sentence errors. Use the chapters listed above to find additional information on how to identify and correct specific errors.*

Step Ten: Check for Spelling Errors

Cross Reference
See Chapter 25, p. 567, for more on commonly confused words.

Use a dictionary or spell-check to check the spelling of any words you are unsure about and also check for words that you might have used incorrectly.

ACTIVITY 5-14   Check for Spelling Errors

Directions: *Check the Commonly Confused Words list on page 567 to see if you have made any of these common mistakes. Then, use a dictionary or spell-check to double-check spelling of any words you are unsure about.*

Once you have completed the 10 steps above, use the following revision checklist to review your essay and make any final revisions.

ESSAY REVISION CHECKLIST

_____   Check for a clear and interesting title in correct format.

_____   Check for an interesting introductory paragraph that sets up the purpose and leads into the thesis.

_____   Check for a clear thesis statement that states the topic and purpose of the essay.

_____   Check that vocabulary, tone, and approach are appropriate for the target audience.

_____   Check that the paper is logically organized and the body paragraphs have clear topic sentences and transitions.

_____   Check for unity—all sentences and paragraphs should help develop the purpose and thesis.

_____   Check that there is enough support in the essay to develop its purpose. Does it need more examples and details?

_____   Check that the sentence structure and vocabulary choices are varied and interesting.

_____   Check for a strong concluding paragraph that sums up the purpose established in the thesis.

_____   Check for complete sentences (no fragments, run-ons, or comma splices).

_____   Check for correct punctuation usage throughout the paper (commas, semicolons, colons, other punctuation marks).

_____   Check for mechanics (correct spelling and use of capitalization, underlining, italics, abbreviations, and numbering) using the grammar section of this text and a dictionary.

LO 4 SELF AND PEER ASSESSMENT

Self and peer assessment of your writing allows you to go through a draft step-by-step and look at the separate elements to ensure a well-thought-out and organized presentation of your point.

If you can, it is best to wait at least one day before you critique your essay. By waiting a while before your final check, you will be able to see mistakes and places where you went astray more easily. Use the following Essay Revision Checklist to go through your final draft and make any final revisions. Then, exchange essays with one of your classmates, or see a tutor in your campus writing center and have that person go through your essay using the checklist as a guideline. It is important not to have anyone fix your mistakes for you. Instead, he or she should just check to see if there are problems using the checklist.

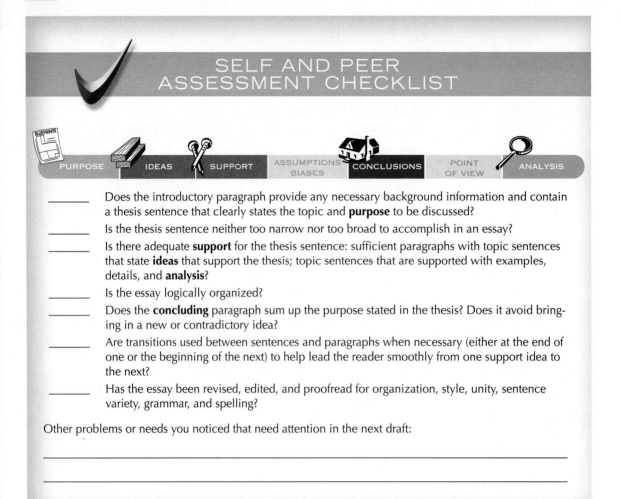

SELF AND PEER
ASSESSMENT CHECKLIST

PURPOSE   IDEAS   SUPPORT   ASSUMPTIONS   CONCLUSIONS   POINT   ANALYSIS
                                BIASES   OF VIEW

_____   Does the introductory paragraph provide any necessary background information and contain a thesis sentence that clearly states the topic and **purpose** to be discussed?

_____   Is the thesis sentence neither too narrow nor too broad to accomplish in an essay?

_____   Is there adequate **support** for the thesis sentence: sufficient paragraphs with topic sentences that state **ideas** that support the thesis; topic sentences that are supported with examples, details, and **analysis**?

_____   Is the essay logically organized?

_____   Does the **concluding** paragraph sum up the purpose stated in the thesis? Does it avoid bringing in a new or contradictory idea?

_____   Are transitions used between sentences and paragraphs when necessary (either at the end of one or the beginning of the next) to help lead the reader smoothly from one support idea to the next?

_____   Has the essay been revised, edited, and proofread for organization, style, unity, sentence variety, grammar, and spelling?

Other problems or needs you noticed that need attention in the next draft:

_____

_____

ACTIVITY 5-15   Self- and Peer-Review Your Essay

Directions: *Self- or peer-review your final essay draft using the checklist above. Make any needed changes to your final, polished essay draft.*

Here is the final essay Alison Scott wrote on the topic of roommates and the benefits of having one.

Sample Student Essay

Alison Scott

Professor Navin

English 090

9 September 2010

The Case for Getting a Roommate

Many students move out on their own when they begin college, and many of them choose to have a roommate. Having a roommate in college saves money and helps ease the burden of college expenses. Deciding whether to have a college roommate or not is a tough decision because there are many pros and cons to sharing a living space, but, without a doubt, the benefits outweigh the drawbacks.

To begin with, having a roommate in college is a great idea because it cuts overall living expenses by as much as half. Moving out on one's own is expensive. The biggest expenses are rent, utilities, and food. I did not have a roommate my first month of college, and I really struggled with finances. I could barely make ends meet, and I was stressed by the bills and grocery costs. I remember going to the store and watching the total creep up while my stomach clenched. After I got a roommate, however, everything got easier and more affordable. The monthly rent for my two-bedroom apartment is $1,000. Now that my roommate has taken the other bedroom, I only pay $500. When one looks at this savings alone, it is easy to see that the financial benefits of having a roommate add up quickly. Also, the utility bills are split and paid equally by both of us. With an average cost of $200 a month for heating and electricity bills, that immediately saves me another $100 a month.

Scott 2

Moreover, we both contribute to groceries. This month alone, I have saved about $150 in grocery costs. Clearly, the financial benefits of having a roommate are substantial.

In addition to saving money, having a roommate builds communication and negotiation skills. It is true that having a roommate requires some sacrifices. If one has a roommate, one no longer has complete privacy or the freedom to make decisions alone. However, there are benefits to giving up a certain amount of independence. One of the hidden benefits of a roommate is the socialization and people skills one gains from the experience. For example, if one person wants to have a party at the apartment, he or she has to work with his or her roommate to make it work. Communication is key. First, the roommates need to agree to have a party, and then when it will be held, how much money it will cost, who pays for what, and how the clean-up will be handled. It is possible that each element of this process will have to be negotiated so that there will be no hard feelings or tensions after the party. Also, roommates have to share the chores. It takes negotiation and compromise to develop a system that works for both roommates. Through this process of negotiation and communication, important life skills are practiced. These same types of communication and negotiation skills will come in handy later in romantic relationships and at work.

Finally, you might even gain a long-term friendship as a result of sharing an apartment. Some roommates remain good friends for many years after they graduate. Living together every day, roommates get to know each other very well. They may help each other work out problems from school and from other friendships or relationships. For example, roommates often socialize

Scott 3

when cooking and sharing meals together, a good time to share problems or news about what is going on in their lives. Before they know it, people begin to get to know each other on a much deeper level and a friendship forms. Often, that bond can last a lifetime. Some roommates become lifelong friends, helping each other through difficult times, celebrating successes, and reminiscing about shared memories.

Though one initially gives up some space, privacy, and decision-making freedom when taking a roommate, the benefits gained make it all worthwhile. Simply saving significant amounts of money each month is a strong argument in favor of a roommate. However, the communication and negotiation skills that one gets from learning to live with someone else and the potential for a lifelong friendship make it an excellent decision. A roommate is worth the risk.

Essay Assignments

1. Take one of the paragraphs you wrote for any of the activities in Chapter 3, and expand it into a full-length essay using the techniques explained in this chapter.

2. Write an essay that argues for or against requiring physical education classes in college.

3. Write an essay that describes one of the courses you took in high school or college that added to your life skills.

4. Write an essay on a subject related to culture or race based on your own experience. For example, write a personal narrative about your identity and how it has been shaped by your cultural and/or racial heritage.

5. Write an essay that argues for a change in the way your local grocery store runs its business. Argue for a change that would make it a better store for your community.

LEARNING OBJECTIVES REVIEW

LO 1	How do you structure an essay? (See pp. 99–101)	You **structure an essay** by writing an *introductory paragraph* with a clear *thesis statement* that states the purpose for your essay. You *support* the thesis using body paragraphs (four to six or more), each of which starts with a topic sentence that directly supports the thesis sentence and is supported in turn by specific examples, details, and analysis. A *concluding paragraph* sums up the main purpose of your essay, re-emphasizing your thesis without repeating it word for word.
LO 2	What are the building blocks of an essay? (See pp. 101–109)	The **building blocks** of an essay are the *title*, *introductory paragraph* and *thesis statement*, *body paragraphs*, and *concluding paragraph*.
LO 3	What are the 10 steps for writing essays? (See pp. 110–119)	The **10 steps for writing essays** are (1) prewrite to generate ideas; (2) ask questions to establish your topic, purpose, and audience; (3) organize your ideas (outline); (4) write a first draft; (5) revise for order, unity, coherence, and sentence variety; (6) fine-tune thesis and topic sentences; (7) provide additional support; (8) check word choice, tone, and style; (9) check for sentence-level errors; and (10) check for spelling errors.
LO 4	How do you use self and peer and assessment? (See pp. 119–120)	**Self and peer assessment** involves you, and later a peer, using a checklist to go through your essay step-by-step and looking at the separate elements to ensure a well-thought-out and organized presentation of your thesis.

For support in meeting this chapter's objectives, log in to www.mywritinglab.com and select **Recognizing the Essay, Essay Organization, Essay Introductions, Conclusions, and Titles** and **Thesis Statement.**

Cab Jumping Rocks   Steve Corvelo

THINKING CRITICALLY

Study the photograph above. Then, complete the following activities.

1. *Describe* what is going on in this photograph in your own words using as many specific descriptive words as possible.

   _____

   _____

2. *Narrate* a short, one-paragraph story about the action in this photograph.

   _____

   _____

PARAGRAPH MODES

You can use different **modes,** or *patterns of writing*, to write about the same topic. It all depends on your purpose and your intended audience. Use your critical thinking skills to figure out the best mode, or combination of modes, for the most effective paragraph for your purpose and audience. Which mode or modes you choose to use will be based on several key factors, which include the following:

1. Your instructor's assignment
2. The purpose of your paragraph
3. The most effective way to illustrate and develop your purpose
4. Your intended audience

CHOOSING THE RIGHT APPROACH

All paragraphs should have an **expository purpose:** a point they are designed to explain. Although each mode discussed in the following chapters has a distinct purpose and format, they can all be used to make an *argument* or *analytical point*. Many professional paragraphs and essays feature a dominant mode approach but also tap into one to three other modes to develop their purpose. You can do the same in your own writing.

The nine commonly used expository writing modes are listed in the following chart.

Expository Writing Modes

Narration	Tells a story using vivid details and description (see Chapter 6).
Description	Uses vivid details to paint a picture with words (see Chapter 7).
Process	Describes a step-by-step process, or a series of steps one must take to accomplish a task (see Chapter 8).
Classification	Categorizes people, things, or concepts into particular groups in order to draw conclusions about them (see Chapter 9).
Definition	Defines an item or a concept (see Chapter 10).
Example and illustration	Provides examples in order to illustrate an idea or set of ideas (see Chapter 11).
Cause and effect	Focuses on the relationship between causes (reasons) and effects (results) (see Chapter 12).

Comparison and contrast	Focuses on the similarities and differences between two subjects or among several subjects (see Chapter 13).
Argument or persuasion	Persuades an audience to agree with a particular viewpoint or arguing for a change in the way things work now (see Chapter 14).

All paragraphs written in a mode format follow a simple template for developing a purpose:

- They contain (often as the first sentence) a **topic sentence** that sets up the main, controlling **idea** and **purpose.**
- They develop the topic sentence using clear **supporting examples and details.**
- They end with a **concluding sentence** that restates or sums up the main purpose.

Cross Reference

Review Chapters 3 and 4 for details of paragraph structure.

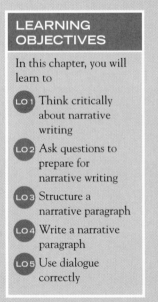

LEARNING OBJECTIVES

In this chapter, you will learn to

LO 1 Think critically about narrative writing

LO 2 Ask questions to prepare for narrative writing

LO 3 Structure a narrative paragraph

LO 4 Write a narrative paragraph

LO 5 Use dialogue correctly

Look at the photograph above. Then, on a separate piece of paper, write a brief story explaining what is going on in the picture. Use your imagination and include as many specific details about the situation and the people as you can. Then, answer the questions below.

THINKING CRITICALLY

1. What did you focus on when you wrote the story?

_____

_____

2. How did you organize your sentences and why?

_____

_____

Continued ▶

3. What effect did looking at a concrete image have on the way you wrote your story and the details you included?

_____

_____

LO 1 NARRATION PARAGRAPHS

In a **narrative paragraph,** you recount an event, story, or series of events in order to explain some insight or truth you gained from a specific experience. Good narration requires using specific sensory details related to touch, taste, smell, hearing, and sight.

Critical Thinking and Narration

Narration does not always have an analytical element. However, it is the *inclusion of a lesson,* implied or directly stated, with a specific point to convey that distinguishes a narrative paragraph from a mere description of events. This analytical purpose is stated in the *topic sentence* (or *purpose statement*), explained and illustrated in the body of the paragraph, and restated in the concluding sentence.

LO 2 PREPARING TO WRITE A NARRATIVE PARAGRAPH

Before you begin to write a narrative paragraph, start by asking yourself these questions:

1. What did I learn from the experience?
2. What do I want my readers to learn or understand after reading about the event I experienced or witnessed?
3. How can I recreate the event vividly in my readers' minds? What examples and details should I use to recreate the story?
4. How should I organize my sentences, and how can I move smoothly from one event or detail to the next?
5. How might I conclude my paragraph?

Answering these questions will lead you to develop a topic sentence that states a clear point, helps you decide which examples and details to include for support, and gives you a general idea of how you want to organize and conclude your paragraph.

APPLYING CRITICAL THINKING

To make sure you have an analytical purpose for your narration paragraph, think beforehand about the purpose of your story and what ideas will demonstrate it for your readers. Ask yourself these questions:

1. What is my **purpose** for telling this story?

2. What **ideas** do I want to explore in this narration?

3. What **supportive examples and details** can I include to develop the story?

4. What is my **analysis** of the significance of this story?

ACTIVITY 6-1   Outlining a Specific Event

Directions: *Think of an event you witnessed or a specific happy or sad event in your own life. Then, on a separate sheet of paper, answer the following questions about that event.* *Answers will vary.*

1. What happened?

2. What did you learn about yourself and/or others that day, and how did you learn it?

3. What would you want your readers to understand after reading about the event?

4. What specific details and examples could you use to recreate the event and vividly tell the story?

LO 3 STRUCTURING A NARRATIVE PARAGRAPH

Cross Reference
See Chapter 3, pp. 50–51, for more about time order.

The structure of a narrative paragraph is usually less formal than that of other types of paragraphs. Often, the paragraph tells a story about an event, or series of events, in chronological order, the order in which they occurred. When you recount an event in time order, be sure to include time order transitional words and phrases to move from one point in time to another:

"*After* we bought our new house, we had a great deal of work to do."

"*First*, we needed to move all of our belongings into the new house."

"*Next*, we needed to paint the outside of the house."

Cross Reference
See page 56 for more time transitions.

The *point of view* in narrative paragraphs is usually *first person*. Therefore, it is perfectly appropriate to use the word "I" throughout a narrative paragraph. For example:

Cross Reference
See p. 493 for more on point of view.

"When I arrived in America, I was amazed by the wide variety of food available in the grocery stores."

You should develop your narrative paragraph using *descriptive details*. Include specific details about the setting, and detailed descriptions of the people and their actions. Choose words that conjure up vivid images, not vague descriptors like "nice."

Vague descriptors: The beach was *nice* and looked *pretty*.

Revised: The beach had soft, white sand littered with colorful shells, and palm trees lined the shore, their lush, green fronds moving gently in the breeze.

Use real dialogue, as far as you can remember it from the event, to make a scene come alive on paper. Dialogue is a great way to provide supporting details to help develop the message or *purpose* of your paragraph. For information on how to use dialogue correctly, see page 138 later in this chapter.

Model Student Paragraph

Christina Dellisante

Professor Bahl

English 100

16 September 2010

Topic sentence indicates that writer will narrate an experience and what she learned from it

Writer uses time order to organize events

Inclusion of dialogue strengthens the narration

Sensory details bring the story to life

Specific descriptive details help the reader visualize what is being described

Concluding sentence reiterates purpose of the paragraph, what the writer learned

Growing up I was a real tomboy, and that sometimes caused me problems, but I knew how to stick up for myself. As a girl, I refused to wear pink, played in the dirt, and actually even looked a bit like a boy. The first time someone, a boy in fact, said something about my appearance was in fifth grade. "Hey Pinocchio!" he screamed across the playground. I knew without even looking away from my game of wall ball that he was talking to me. I could hear the giggles around me as this boy began taunting me. I should have said something back in my defense, screamed at the top of my lungs something about his knobby knees or uncombed blonde hair, but for some reason I could not bring myself to say anything. He kept calling me Pinocchio and saying I looked like a boy. I did nothing in the beginning, but the taunting became worse and worse. Soon he was saying that I wished I was a boy and was too ugly to be a girl. At that point I lost it, and I walked over to this boy and punched him square in the face. I was sent to the principal's office, and she called my mother, and I was sent home. I learned that day that my tomboy traits could cause me trouble from time to time, but I also knew that I could stand up for myself.

The chart on page 133 provides a brief overview of the structure of a narrative paragraph.

BASIC STRUCTURE FOR A NARRATION PARAGRAPH

TOPIC SENTENCE

State the main **idea** of your paragraph and describe your **purpose,** what you are trying to show, prove, or argue in your narrative paragraph, what you learned from the experience.

SUPPORT

Develop your idea using time order.

Use transitions to emphasize time changes and/or significant turns in the narrative.

Provide concrete details and description.

Use as many senses as possible in your description (sight, sound, smell, touch, and taste).

Add dialogue when appropriate.

ANALYSIS

Add analysis and commentary about the details and descriptions to help develop the purpose of the topic sentence.

Explain what you were thinking and feeling as the events took place.

CONCLUDING SENTENCE

Sum up and re-emphasize the topic sentence: the **lesson learned.**

ACTIVITY 6-2   Identifying the Elements of a Narration Paragraph

Directions: *Read the paragraph below. Then, perform the following tasks.*

1. *Underline the topic sentence.*

2. *Write an E above examples that support the topic sentence.*

3. *Write a D over any sentence that provides a specific detail to support or illustrate an example.*

4. *Highlight any word or phrase that serves as a transition from one part of the story to the next.*

5. *Double-underline any of the sentences that provide analysis of what the student learned from the event.*

Meshaela Benton

Ms. Vail

English 080

27 October 2010

When I was nine years old, I participated in a two-week summer camp and left my family for the first time. That trip taught me a powerful lesson about learning to be on my own. The first couple of days I was there I felt lonely and homesick. I thought about my mom and pictured her face at least six times a day. I missed her homemade meals. I even craved her infamous tuna fish casserole! At first I had trouble falling asleep at night. I would lie there thinking of my own bed at home and how much I wished I was in it. Then, I would picture my mom coming in to say, "Goodnight, Pumpkin," like she always did, and I felt even more sad. I also had trouble making friends at the camp at the beginning of my stay. Then, after a few days, things began to change. I started taking part in the activities that were offered such as hiking, horseback riding, Frisbee football, and crafts, and I started to make some friends too. Before I knew it, I was not thinking about home or my mother at all anymore. After that, each night I would fall asleep soon after my head hit the pillow, exhausted but happy. During my two-week stay at camp, I learned that I could survive and even thrive on my own, away from my home and family.

LO 4 WRITING A NARRATION PARAGRAPH

Topic

If you have been assigned a narrative topic, be sure to read the assignment carefully to make sure you understand what is being asked, so that you can create a strong topic sentence with a clear analytical **purpose**. If you are choosing your own topic, prewrite about possible events in order to decide which one you want to write about and what details to include. Focus on what happened and what you learned from the experience.

A Few Topic Possibilities

Your first day in the United States or a foreign country you traveled to

Your first date with your boyfriend, girlfriend, partner, or spouse

A traumatic event

The hardest day of your life

The happiest day of your life

A day you learned a lesson about trust

A surprising event

The death of someone

The birth of someone

A special celebration

The worst moment of your life

Topic Sentence

The topic sentence in a narrative paragraph contains the lesson learned from an event. If you have been assigned a specific topic, be sure to include key words from the assignment in your topic sentence. If you are generating your own topic and purpose, be sure to use the prewriting techniques from Chapter 3 to come up with ideas, details, and a purpose for telling a story about the event.

ACTIVITY 6-3 Creating Topic Sentences

Directions: *Create a topic sentence for each of the following topics. Make sure the topic sentence has a **clear message or lesson to convey** about what **you learned from the experience.*** *Answers will vary.*

1. My most traumatic memory: _____

_____

2. My first day at a new school: _____

_____

3. My first experience with loss: _____

_____

4. The scariest moment of my life: _____

_____

5. The happiest day of my life: _____

_____

Support

After you have come up with a strong controlling idea and written your topic sentence, you need to think of examples and details to support it. Use as many senses as possible to describe the event, the people involved, and what happened. For each example, provide concrete descriptive details that explain and illustrate it.

ACTIVITY 6-4   Providing Examples and Details

Directions: *Now, using **two** of the topic sentences you created in Activity 6-3, provide a specific example and a supporting detail to support each one.*
Answers will vary.

Topic sentence 1

Example: _____

_____

Supporting detail: _____

_____

Topic sentence 2

Example: _____

_____

Supporting detail: _____

_____

Specific details help make your narrative paragraphs more interesting and create a vivid picture of the event in your readers' heads. Be sure to avoid vague or abstract descriptions that do not create vivid images.

ACTIVITY 6-5   Abstract to Specific

Directions: *Replace the abstract descriptive word bolded in each sentence with concrete, specific descriptions of the thing or person in the sentence.*
Answers will vary.

Example: It was a beautiful dog.

Revised: *The dog had smooth and shiny honey-colored fur and*
large brown eyes that had an intelligent sparkle.

1. It was an **awesome** beach. _____

_____

2. The dessert was **unbelievable.** _____

_____

3. The car was **amazing.** _____

_____

4. It was a **strange-looking** clown. _____

_____

Concluding Sentence

The concluding sentence for a narration paragraph is quite basic. It restates the topic sentence using different words, and focuses on your purpose for recounting the event. Do not repeat the topic sentence.

> **Topic sentence:** Living in the South makes one aware of the importance of American history.
>
> **Concluding sentence:** The South's rich and controversial history makes it a interesting place to live.

Here, the concluding sentence echoes the topic sentence, but does not repeat it word for word.

ACTIVITY 6-6   Writing the Concluding Sentence

Directions: *Using the two topic sentences you wrote examples and details for in Activity 6-4, write a concluding sentence for each one as if you had written an entire paragraph.* *Answers will vary.*

Concluding sentence 1

_____

_____

Concluding sentence 2

_____

_____

_____

LO 5 Tips for Correct Use of Dialogue

Dialogue can play an important part in a narrative paragraph. Here are some helpful tips to keep in mind when you include dialogue in narrative writing.

1. **Use tags and quotation marks.** When you use dialogue, you need a tag to indicate who is speaking and quotation marks around the actual words that are spoken.

Cross Reference

See p. 325 for more about quotation marks.

> **Tag:** Jim asked,
>
> **Quotation Marks:** "Do you want to go get a cup of coffee?"
>
> **Used Together:** Jim asked, "Do you want to go get a cup of coffee?"

Tag placement can also come in the middle or at the end of dialogue:

> "Remember," **Brad said,** "there's no sense in worrying."
>
> "Remember, there's no sense in worrying," **Brad said.**

2. **Use correct punctuation.** Start sentences of dialogue within quotation marks and use a capital letter.

> Karen answered, "Yes, I will go to the movies with you."

Punctuation goes inside the quotation marks (except when using in-text citation in documented papers).

"The exact truth," Kelly said, "is something we'll have to dig for."

3. **Tab (indent five spaces) every time you switch speakers in dialogue.**

Trinh asked Munira, "Will you shop for groceries today?"

"Yes," Munira responded, "I will."

"And how will you afford to get all that you need?" Trinh asked, raising an eyebrow.

"I'll just get the basics for now," Munira responded, studying her list.

4. **Weave descriptions of the characters and their actions into your dialogue.** Create a "movie" of the scene by including details of what they were saying and what they were doing as they said it (see the dialogue exchange between Munira and Trinh above in tip number 3 for an example of weaving description into dialogue).

5. **Don't let the dialogue take over.** Use dialogue as a supporting detail in your paragraph, not as the main vehicle for imparting your story and your story's message. After you use dialogue in your narration paragraph, be sure to *explain* the realizations you came to and what you were feeling and thinking as the words were said during the incident—always re-emphasize your *purpose*.

She whispered, "No, I cannot marry you."

Until that moment, she hadn't realized how wrong he was for her, that they could never have a long-term relationship.

ACTIVITY 6-7 Writing Dialogue

Directions:

A. *On a separate sheet of paper, write a short dialogue between two people; each person should speak at least two times. You can use an actual dialogue that occurred between you and someone else (as best as you can remember it), or you can make up a dialogue between two fictional characters.*

B. *Be sure to include tags, start a new paragraph whenever you switch speakers, and include some physical motion or description of the characters as they speak. Review the tips on using dialogue for help.*

Revise and Edit

Remember to revise your paragraph draft for the best results. Use the following critique form to check for the basics in your narration paragraph draft.

NARRATION PARAGRAPH CRITIQUE FORM

| PURPOSE | IDEAS | SUPPORT | ASSUMPTIONS BIASES | CONCLUSIONS | POINT OF VIEW | ANALYSIS |

	Done well	Needs work
1. Does the paragraph tell a story using description that has a clear **purpose** (lesson(s) learned from the experience)?	_____	_____
2. Does the writer use time order in the paragraph?	_____	_____
3. Is there a clear topic sentence that explains the message of the story?	_____	_____
4. Do the events of the story flow smoothly?	_____	_____
5. Are time-order transitions used when needed?	_____	_____
6. Does the writer include **support**, **ideas**, descriptive examples, and details that enhance the story?	_____	_____
7. Does the writer use as many sensory details as possible in the description of what happened and how it made the writer feel?	_____	_____
8. Does the writer include some dialogue to bring the action to life?	_____	_____
9. Does the writer **analyze** the significance of the event—why it was important?	_____	_____
10. Does the **concluding** sentence sum up the story and re-emphasize the topic sentence without adding new ideas?	_____	_____

Editing

11. Circle the following errors in the draft: spelling, fragments, run-ons, comma splices, commas, semi-colon/colon use, pronoun agreement, reference fault errors, parallelism, apostrophe use, verb use/tense, and passive voice construction. (See Parts V and VI for help identifying and correcting these errors.)

12. Other types of grammar or sentence-level errors you noticed in this draft:

_____

_____

Comments:

_____

_____

ACTIVITY 6-8 Revising a Narration Paragraph

Directions: *Carefully read the student paragraph below. Then, use the critique form above to evaluate it. Finally, rewrite the paragraph on a separate sheet of paper and be sure to address the following revision tasks.*

1. Ensure there is a strong topic sentence that states the purpose of the paragraph.
2. Move any sentences that are not in the most effective order.
3. Add any details that would help explain the purpose of the narration and describe the experience more specifically.
4. Add transitional words or phrases where needed.
5. Revise informal language (including removing contractions).
6. Make sure the concluding sentence restates the main point of the story.

Hunter Thomas

Professor Lowe

English 080

18 November 2010

    I have some strong memories related to taking my driver's test. I didn't pass the driving test my first time trying. I didn't do a good job of following the instructor's directions. Sometimes, he would tell me to do things, and I would do the opposite. I was so bummed when I didn't pass the test. He asked me at one point in the driver's test to parallel park. It was very hard. I didn't understand another request he gave me. He asked me to do a "three-point turn." I just looked at him confused until he told me "never mind." Not passing my test was a bad experience.

PROFESSIONAL NARRATION PARAGRAPH

Excerpt from "Shooting an Elephant"

George Orwell

George Orwell, an English author born Eric Arthur Blair (1903–1950), was known for his focus on themes of social injustice and his passion for clarity in language. His most famous novels are *Animal Farm* (1945) and *Nineteen Eighty-Four* (1949). "Shooting an Elephant," written in 1936, is one of his most famous short stories and is based on his experiences working as a British soldier in India.

I did not want to shoot the elephant. I watched him beating his bunch of grass against his knees, with that preoccupied grandmotherly air that elephants have. It seemed to me that it would be murder to shoot him. At that age I was not squeamish about killing animals, but I had never shot an elephant and never wanted to. (Somehow it always seems worse to kill a large animal.) Besides, there was the beast's owner to be considered. Alive, the elephant was worth at least a hundred pounds; dead, he would only be worth the value of his tusks, five pounds, possibly. But I had to act quickly. I turned to some experienced-looking Burmans who had been there when we arrived, and asked them how the elephant had been behaving. They all said the same thing: he took no notice of you if you left him alone, but he might charge if you went too close to him.

Reading Reflection Questions   *Answers will vary. Sample answers provided.*

1. How is this excerpt an example of narration writing? What characteristics make it a narrative piece of writing?

   The author tells a story to make a point. It is written in the first person.

   It uses time order.

2. What is the narrator's main message in this paragraph?

   He had to make a difficult decision regarding what to do about the

   elephant.

3. Since this is an excerpt from a longer story, there is no concluding sentence for this paragraph. Write a sentence below that could work as the concluding sentence for this paragraph (be sure it connects to the topic sentence).

Though I did not want to kill the elephant, the situation was looking grim.

_____

Checking Vocabulary

List any words in this reading you did not know, and provide a dictionary definition for each one.

_____

_____

_____

Use the following Critical Thinking Checklist when you read narrative paragraphs by other authors or your peers.

CRITICAL THINKING CHECKLIST

1. What is the author's *purpose* or *goal* in this reading selection?

2. What are the *stated questions* being addressed?

3. What *specific details and examples* does the author use to develop his or her purpose or goal for the reading?

4. What *inferences* does the author include in this reading? (Inferences imply "if this, then this" types of cause/effect analysis.)

5. Who is the intended audience, and how did you reach that conclusion?

Paragraph Writing Assignments

1. Write a paragraph using one of the topic sentences you developed with examples and details in the activities in this chapter.

2. Write a paragraph about an incident that happened to you (or that you witnessed) that had a significant impact on you. What lesson did you learn that day (about yourself, others, our culture, other)?

   a. Start with a topic sentence that tells exactly what lesson(s) you learned from the experience.
   b. Use time order to organize your story. Use transitions to move from one point to the next, and include some dialogue to make the event come alive for your readers; follow the tips for correct dialogue usage on page 138.
   c. When describing the incident, include specific details and descriptions, using as many senses as possible (sight, sound, touch, smell, and taste). Review Chapters 3, 4, 5, and 6 for paragraph writing basics.
   d. In the concluding sentence, sum up the lesson(s) you learned and how you feel now about the incident.

After you finish your first draft of this paragraph, use the Narrative Paragraph Critique Form to check for the basics. You can also have a classmate or friend check your draft using the checklist.

Critical Thinking Journal Prompts

Write a journal reflection entry based on one of the following prompts.

1. What have you learned from this chapter about the makings of a good narration? What do you need to add to your writing to tell a story well?
2. In your opinion, what makes for the best kind of narration when you read others' writings? Give a specific example from something you have read recently.
3. Why would you need to **analyze** something that happened to you or that you witnessed? Give an example.

LEARNING OBJECTIVES REVIEW

LO 1 What do you want to achieve by thinking critically about writing a narration paragraph? (See p. 129)	**Thinking critically** helps you identify what you have learned, decide what message you want to convey to the reader, and determine what details to include and how to organize them.
LO 2 What questions should you ask before writing a narrative paragraph? (See pp. 129–130)	You should **ask the following questions:** (1) What did I learn from the experience? (2) What do I want my readers to learn or understand after reading about the event I experienced or witnessed? (3) How can I recreate the event vividly in my readers' minds, using examples and details? (4) How should I organize my sentences, and how can I move smoothly from one event or detail to the next? (5) How might I conclude my paragraph?
LO 3 How do you structure a narrative paragraph? (See pp. 130–133)	You **structure a narrative paragraph** by creating a topic sentence that contains the lesson learned from an event; support it with concrete, sensory details; and write a concluding sentence that restates the topic and focuses on the purpose of the paragraph.
LO 4 How do you write a narrative paragraph? (See pp. 135–141)	You **write a narrative paragraph** by telling a story that makes a point, organizing it using chronological order, developing your topic sentence using specific sensory details, and using real dialogue to add details and develop your purpose.
LO 5 What are five tips for correctly including dialogue in narrative? (See pp. 138–139)	**Five tips for correctly including dialog** are (1) use tags and quotation marks, (2) use correct punctuation, (3) start a new paragraph every time you switch speakers, (4) weave description into the dialogue, and (5) don't let dialogue take over.

PEARSON
mywritinglab

For support in meeting this chapter's objectives, log in to www.mywritinglab.com and select **Paragraph Development—Narration**.

Description

Annie Musselman

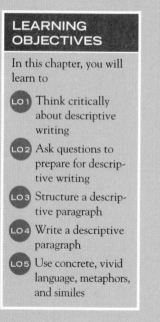

LEARNING OBJECTIVES

In this chapter, you will learn to

LO1 Think critically about descriptive writing

LO2 Ask questions to prepare for descriptive writing

LO3 Structure a descriptive paragraph

LO4 Write a descriptive paragraph

LO5 Use concrete, vivid language, metaphors, and similes

THINKING CRITICALLY

1. Describe what you see in the photograph above using **specific details** to create a verbal picture of the people, colors, shapes, lights, and contrasts.

_____

_____

_____

2. Do you think description is an important part of written communication skills? Why or why not?

_____

_____

Continued ▶

3. Provide some examples of when you would need to write specific descriptions in school- and career-related writing.

_____

_____

4. List some of the characteristics you would include in a description of a thing, place, or person (for example, shape, color, size, and so on).

_____

_____

LO 1 DESCRIPTION PARAGRAPHS

Description paragraphs describe people, places, things, or events using as many of _the senses_ as possible: _sight, sound, touch, smell,_ and _taste_. The key to writing good descriptive paragraphs is to use **concrete** language—words related to the senses that describe actual things, not abstract ideas—and to include specific details. For example, you could describe a tree in the following ways:

> The tree swayed in the wind.
>
> The tall maple tree was ablaze with color, each brilliant orange leaf, tipped with a candle-flame of yellow, rustling against its neighbor in the crisp breeze of a clear blue-sky fall day.

In the first example, you only know that a tree is moving in the wind. In the second you know that the tree is a maple, the leaves have changed color from green to orange and yellow, and it's a clear, breezy day in the fall.

Critical Thinking and Description

Like all expository paragraphs, descriptive paragraphs should have a clear purpose: to inform, to narrate, to convince your readers to do something or believe something. The key is to use description and details to demonstrate your purpose. For instance, you could describe a local coffee shop in detail in order to convince your readers that it is the best place to spend a quiet afternoon studying for a test.

LO 2 PREPARING TO WRITE A DESCRIPTIVE PARAGRAPH

Before you begin to write a descriptive paragraph, start by asking yourself these questions:

1. What do I want to describe and for what purpose?
2. What kind of language and details would best describe the object, place, or person?
3. How should I organize my paragraph?
4. What do I want my readers to learn or understand from reading this description?
5. How might I conclude the paragraph?

Answering these questions will lead you to an expository topic sentence, help you determine which language and details will provide vivid description and images for support, and give you a general idea of how you want to organize and develop your paragraph.

ACTIVITY 7-1   Practicing Description

Directions: *Briefly describe the following topics using concrete (vivid, sensory words) language and specific details. Then, provide a purpose for describing each one. Answers will vary.*

1. Briefly describe a close friend.

   _____

   _____

   Purpose: _____

   _____

2. Briefly describe your neighborhood.

   _____

   _____

   Purpose: _____

   _____

3. Briefly describe your car (or the car of someone you know).

   _____

   _____

Purpose: _____

_____

LO 3 STRUCTURING A DESCRIPTIVE PARAGRAPH

Organize your descriptive paragraph based on the physical characteristics of the object, place, or person you are describing and your purpose for writing about it. Common order patterns for descriptive paragraphs are spatial order and order of importance. For example, if you are describing a restaurant, you can use spatial order to explain how it is organized and decorated (going from front to back, bottom to top, or side to side), or you could use order of importance to focus on which particular elements are most important in creating an atmosphere or mood that attracts customers. Be sure to include transitional words and phrases as you move from one characteristic to another. For instance:

Cross Reference
See Chapter 3, pp. 51–52 for more on spatial order and order of importance.

> In the front of the coffee shop is a counter where employees take coffee orders and a large espresso machine sits that loudly cranks out espresso and steams milk, swooshing like a noisy wind tunnel. In the center of the shop are several round tables and high-backed, smooth maple chairs. On the back wall of the coffee shop, fliers for local events line the wall, including black and orange fliers for a local band called "Halloween Vacation" and light blue fliers with a pink butterfly announcing a ballet production of *Madame Bovary*.

APPLYING CRITICAL THINKING

PURPOSE | IDEAS | SUPPORT | ASSUMPTIONS BIASES | CONCLUSIONS | POINT OF VIEW | ANALYSIS

Use these tips to help you clarify your purpose and include effective descriptive details to support it:

1. **Be clear about why you are describing a particular person or thing.** What do you want your readers to understand about the subject through your description? What is your **purpose**?

Continued ▶

2. **Choose concrete, vivid, and sensory details to illustrate and support your topic sentence.** Use descriptive language to create a vibrant image in the reader's mind that will help convey your message.

3. **Organize your descriptive paragraph based on your purpose.** Make the best choice for the object, place, or person you are describing to make your point (spatial order or order of importance).

Model Student Paragraph

Beyla Geoffrey

Dr. deBaun

English 090

25 September 2010

Topic sentence sets up the purpose and indicates that writer will explain her impressions of the Statue of Liberty

Author uses order of importance

During my vacation to New York City a number of years ago, I saw the Statue of Liberty for the first time and was amazed by her appearance for several reasons. The first thing was her sheer size. Clothed in flowing robes, sandals on her feet, and a torch held aloft in her right hand, she towered high over the water on her star-shaped pedestal. She was almost as tall as some of the skyscrapers in Lower Manhattan. In fact, she is the tallest iron structure ever built and from the bottom of her foundation to the tip of her torch, she is over

Specific details help the reader visualize the statue

300 feet high. Another thing that surprised me about her was that she is green. I learned that she is green because the copper skin that covers her has oxidized over the years due to exposure to sun, rain, and salt winds. The greenish-white color looks a little like green

A simile is used to make a comparison description

marble or pistachio ice cream. Also, I thought it was incredible that people were allowed to climb the steep and winding steps inside the statue to the top. I climbed over 350 steps to reach her crown.

Author uses sensory details to enhance the description

I touched the cool metal plates and smelled their metallic odor. It was a windy day, and the statue swayed and creaked as I climbed. I could see through gaps between the metal plates to the water far below. Finally, I thought her face was beautiful. It was smooth and looked like the face of a marble statue from Greek or Roman times. Overall, the Statue of Liberty is one of the most incredible monuments I have ever visited, and I will always remember my visit with awe.

Concluding sentence reiterates purpose of the paragraph: her impressions of the Statue of Liberty

The chart below provides a brief overview of the structure of a description paragraph.

BASIC STRUCTURE FOR A DESCRIPTION PARAGRAPH

TOPIC SENTENCE

State the main **idea** of your paragraph and describe your **purpose,** what you are trying to explain, show, prove, or argue in your descriptive paragraph

SUPPORT

Develop the description using spatial order or order of importance

Use transitions to move from one example or detail to the next

Provide concrete examples and details

Use as many senses as possible in your description (sight, sound, smell, touch, and taste)

Use comparisons (similes and metaphors) to help describe the subject

ANALYSIS

Add commentary about the ex3amples and details to help develop the purpose of the topic sentence

CONCLUDING SENTENCE

Sum up and re-emphasize the topic sentence

ACTIVITY 7-2 Identifying the Elements of a Description Paragraph

Directions: *Read the paragraph below. Then, perform the following tasks.*

1. Underline the topic sentence.

2. *Write an E over each sentence that provides an example that adds description and supports the topic sentence.*

3. *Write a D over any sentence that provides a specific detail or use of the senses to further describe an example.*

4. *Highlight any word or phrase that serves as a transition from one part of the description to the next.*

5. *Double-underline any of the sentences that provide analysis of what is being described.*

Cindy Clarke

Professor Rhodes

English 089

28 March 2010

My aunt, Donna Harlow, is the warmest person I know. To begin with, she has a kind face. Her eyes are a soft, powder blue color, and they have fine lines at the corners that feather out like the leaves of a fern. Her cheeks are smooth and slightly rosy, like the blush color of a ripe peach. Her mouth is small, with pink-beige, bow-like lips. When she smiles, her cheeks rise into crescent circles below her eyes. She looks wise, maybe because of her fine lines, but also because there is something else in her eyes, a twinkle of knowledge that anyone can see. Furthermore, her voice is soothing and soft. It sounds like a wise and sweet kindergarten teacher whispering to get her young students to listen. She also dresses in lovely colors, lots of blues and greens and lavenders. It's comforting just to be around her when she is wearing those soft colors. For all these reasons and more, my Aunt Donna is the warmest person I know and a treat to be around.

WRITING A DESCRIPTIVE PARAGRAPH

Topic

If you have been assigned a descriptive topic, be sure to read the assignment carefully to ensure you understand what is being asked, and then prewrite to come up with descriptive details. If you are choosing your own topic, brainstorm for ideas about people, places, or things you might want to describe. Either way, come up with some **ideas** for a **purpose** for describing the topic. What do you want your readers to understand through your description? What can they learn from it?

A Few Topic Possibilities

Brainstorm a list of details and ideas about your topic or cluster to generate examples and details:

Describe your neighborhood, your house or room, a family member, a particular friend, your school, your classroom, your pet, your computer, your workplace, your favorite public place, an object in your home or town, or a work of art such as a painting or a photograph.

Cross Reference

See p. 66 for a review of prewriting techniques.

Topic Sentence

In a descriptive paragraph, you choose to describe something in detail in order to explain what is special about it, to critique it, or to inform your readers about it. To do this, you create a topic sentence that establishes the **purpose** of your description.

> **Topic:** A push mower
>
> **Purpose:** I want to describe my old push mower in detail to show what a great tool it is and to argue that the old-fashioned push mower is superior to a motorized lawnmower.
>
> **Topic sentence:** My old push mower is an amazing piece of machinery, and in many ways it is superior to a motorized lawnmower.

ACTIVITY 7-3   Creating Topic Sentences

Directions: *Now, create a possible **topic sentence** that you could use to develop a paragraph for each of the following subjects (you may have to do a brainstorm or freewrite on a separate page first to narrow your topic).* Answers will vary.

1. A close friend: _____

_____

2. Your neighborhood park: _____

_____

3. A favorite item of clothing: _____

_____

4. A relative: _____

_____

5. A particular tree: _____

_____

SUPPORT

LO 5 ## Support: Using Vivid Descriptive Details and Language

Once you have a solid topic sentence, you need to develop specific support that paints a picture of the person or object you are describing; for example:

> **Support statement:** A push mower lets you be a part of the mowing experience and get a physical workout.
>
> **Detail:** As you push the mower through the grass, you feel the process of the work you are doing as well as a burn in your upper arms from the workout.

Here are some suggestions for how to write a vivid, descriptive paragraph:

1. **Include as many details and specific images as possible.** Choose words that conjure up vivid images, not vague descriptors like "beautiful" or "good."

   > **Vague descriptors:** The sky was beautiful, and the sun felt good.
   >
   > **Revised:** The sky was clear and blue, except for some high, white streaks of cloud, and the sun warmed our heads and arms with a comforting heat.

2. **Use as many of the senses as possible when you describe something.** For instance, when describing a room, include visual details (furniture, windows), sounds (the buzz of florescent lights), taste (if possible—like a taste in the air), smells (of the cleaner used on the carpet), and touch (the smooth texture of a desk) to create the overall atmospheric feel.

3. Use *similes* (comparisons of one thing to another that begin with the words *like* or *as*) or *metaphors* (comparisons in which one thing is described as being another thing). For instance, you can use a simile to help someone get a better image of your car's paint by writing:

> My car's paint is peeling and rough, like paint chipping off an old fence.

Or you can use a metaphor to describe your car:

> My car is a dinosaur shedding patches of rough skin.

4. **Avoid using clichés.** Clichés do not create vivid images because they have been overused. For example:

> The car's paint was as black as coal.

Cross Reference
See page 607 for more about clichés.

Make sure the order of your examples and details makes sense and the paragraph flows smoothly from one detail to the next. Here are some transitions you could use in a descriptive paragraph.

Cross Reference
See pp. 55–56 for other transitional words and phrases.

TRANSITIONS TO . . .

Show a Comparison

in like manner	in the same way	likewise	similarly

Illustrate or Give Examples/Specifics

a few include	essentially	in particular	the following
an example	for example	let us consider	specifically
especially	for instance	the case of	you can see this in

Show Place (Usually Prepositions)

above	beside	inside	outside
across	between	nearer	over
adjacent to	beyond	nearly	there
below	farther	next to	through
beneath	here	opposite	under

Show Amount

a great deal	less than	most	smaller
few	many	over	some
greater	more than	several	under

ACTIVITY 7-4   Providing Details

Directions: *Now, provide at least three vivid, descriptive details you would use for the topic sentences you created in Activity 7-3.* Answers will vary.

1. A close friend: _____

   _____

2. Your neighborhood park: _____

   _____

3. A favorite item of clothing: _____

   _____

4. A relative: _____

   _____

5. A particular tree: _____

   _____

▶ TIP   Vivid description results from choosing words that are specific and concrete, not abstract or vague.

ACTIVITY 7-5   Abstract to Vivid Language

Directions: *Replace the abstract descriptive words that are bolded in each sentence into vivid, specific descriptions of the thing or person in the sentence. Try to include sensory description when possible (sight, touch, smell, sound, taste, and so on).* Answers will vary.

> **Example:** She looked **nice.**
> She looked lovely, her red hair blowing across her smiling face.

1. It is a **boring** outfit. _____

   _____

2. The bowl of fruit looked **good.** _____

   _____

3. The **dull-looking** car was slow. _____

   _____

4. That dog is **odd-looking.** _____

_____

5. The **beautiful** painting sat in the corner. _____

_____

▶ **TIP**   Another way to add specific description to your writing is to use comparisons like similes and metaphors. Be careful not to resort to clichés: Try to come up with a fresh simile or metaphor instead.

Cross Reference
See pp. 607–610 for more on similes, metaphors, and clichés.

ACTIVITY 7-6   Creating Comparisons (Similes and Metaphors)

Directions: *Come up with a simile or metaphor for each of the objects below to help your readers get a good visual or sensual image of it. Try not to use a clichéd, commonly used simile or metaphor.* Answers will vary.

Example: A dark night.

Simile: <u>A night as dark as black licorice</u> _____

Metaphor: <u>A black licorice sky</u> _____

1. Big mouth

Simile: _____

Metaphor: _____

2. Red hair

Simile: _____

Metaphor: _____

3. Smooth skin

Simile: _____

Metaphor: _____

4. A round body

Simile: _____

Metaphor: _____

5. The color black

Simile: _____

Metaphor: _____

Concluding Sentence

The concluding sentence for a descriptive paragraph should remind your readers what the purpose of your description was—why you described this person, place, or object.

ACTIVITY 7-7   Writing a Concluding Sentence

Directions: *Choose one of the topics you have been developing in the previous activities and write a concluding sentence for it.*   Answers will vary.

_____

_____

_____

ACTIVITY 7-8   Describe a Car

Directions: *This activity needs two people, so work with a partner. It is a fun way to practice using specific and concrete description and is a great way to increase your awareness of your reader and his or her need to visualize what you are describing.*   Answers will vary.

Step One   *On a separate sheet of paper, draw a car—be creative and enjoy yourself drawing any kind of car you want. Don't let anyone see your car drawing: turn it over on your desk.*

Step Two   *Now, on a separate sheet of paper, **write a one-paragraph description** of your car using **specific, concrete descriptive words**.*

Step Three   *Exchange the **written descriptions only** with your partner: keep your car drawings upside down so neither of you can see them.*

Step Four   *Read your partner's written description of his or her car. Then, on a separate sheet of paper, draw the car based on the description given.*

Step Five   *Compare the original drawings to the ones based on the written descriptions.*

Step Six   *Answer the following questions.*

1. Did the drawings look similar? Ignore any differences in drawing talent: focus on basic structure such as shape, details, and so on.

_____

_____

2. What problems arose as a result of missing details in the descriptions?

_____

_____

3. What would you do differently now if you were asked to rewrite your description of your car?

_____

_____

Revise and Edit

Remember to revise your paragraph draft for the best results. Use the following critique form to check for the basics in your description paragraph draft.

DESCRIPTION PARAGRAPH CRITIQUE FORM

Overall   Done well   Needs work

1. Is there a clear topic sentence that explains the purpose
for describing the topic (person, place, or thing)?   _____   _____

2. Does the writer use a logical order in the paragraph ?   _____   _____

3. Does the paragraph include descriptive details and concrete images?   _____   _____

4. Does the writer use as many senses as possible in the description?   _____   _____

5. If similes or metaphors are used, are they fresh and effective?   _____   _____

6. Are transitions used, when needed, within the paragraph?   _____   _____

7. Does the concluding sentence sum up the purpose of the description?   _____   _____

Editing

Circle the following errors you think you see in this draft: spelling, fragments, run-ons, comma splices, commas, semicolon/colon use, pronoun agreement, reference fault errors, parallelism, apostrophe use, verb use/tense, and passive voice construction. (See Parts V and VI for help identifying and correcting these errors.)

Other types of grammar or sentence-level errors you noticed in this draft:

_____

Comments:

_____

_____

ACTIVITY 7-9   Revising a Descriptive Paragraph

Directions: *Carefully read the student paragraph below. Then, use the critique form to evaluate it. Finally, rewrite the paragraph on a separate sheet of paper and be sure to address the following revision tasks.* Answers will vary.

1. *Underline the topic sentence. If there is not one, write a sentence that establishes the topic of the paragraph and the purpose for writing about it.*

2. *Be sure to include concrete, sensory description. Add examples and details that bring the subject to life.*

3. *Reorder sentences if necessary to improve the description and flow of the paragraph.*

4. *Add transitional words or phrases where needed.*

5. *Write a concluding sentence that restates the purpose of the paragraph.*

Anna Cruz

Mrs. Hernandez

English 080

22 April 2010

My cat is the ugliest cat on the block. He has ugly fur that always looks greasy. He has a big belly that hangs down. His face is the worst. It looks crooked. His fur is orange and black and white. He looks like a dirty Halloween nightmare. His eyes are green, but they are dull. His teeth are crooked. A couple are missing. His tail is short and stubby. He is so ugly. His whiskers look stubby too.

PROFESSIONAL DESCRIPTION PARAGRAPH

Excerpt from "A Clean, Well-Lighted Place"

Ernest Hemingway

Ernest Hemingway (1899–1961) was born in Oak Park, Illinois. He worked as a volunteer ambulance driver for the Italian army in World War I and was a reporter during the Spanish Civil War. Some of his best-known novels are *The Sun Also Rises, A Farewell to Arms, For Whom the Bell Tolls,* and *The Old Man and the Sea.*

It was very late and everyone had left the cafe except an old man who sat in the shadow the leaves of the tree made against the electric light. In the day time the street was dusty, but at night the dew settled the dust and the old man liked to sit late because he was deaf and now at night it was quiet and he felt the difference. The two waiters inside the cafe knew that the old man was a little drunk, and while he was a good client they knew that if he became too drunk he would leave without paying, so they kept watch on him.

"Last week he tried to commit suicide," one waiter said.

"Why?"

"He was in despair."

"What about?"

"Nothing."

"How do you know it was nothing?"

"He has plenty of money."

They sat together at a table that was close against the wall near the door of the cafe and looked at the terrace where the tables were all empty except where the old man sat in the shadow of the leaves of the tree that moved slightly in the wind. A girl and a soldier went by in the street. The street light shone on the brass number on his collar. The girl wore no head covering and hurried beside him.

Reading Reflection Questions   *Answers will vary. Sample answers provided.*

1. What and/or who is being described in this excerpt?

A café, the people in the café, and two people walking outside the café

2. List a couple of the descriptive details used in this passage.

The old man sat in the shadow of the leaves of the tree that moved slightly

in the wind. The street light shone on the brass number on his collar. The girl

wore no head covering.

3. How many people (characters) are featured in this excerpt?

five

Checking Vocabulary

List any words from this excerpt that you did not know; then provide a dictionary definition for each one. *Answers will vary.*

Use the following Critical Thinking Checklist to help you with this reading and for checking any other descriptive paragraph or writing.

CRITICAL THINKING CHECKLIST

1. What is the author's *purpose* or *goal* in this reading selection?

2. What are the *stated questions* being addressed?

3. What *specific details and examples* does the author use to develop his or her purpose or goal for the reading?

4. What *inferences* does the author include in this reading? (Inferences imply "if this, then this" types of cause/effect analysis.)

5. Who is the intended audience, and how did you reach that conclusion?

Paragraph Writing Assignments

1. Choose one of the topics you worked on in the activities for this chapter, and write a complete description paragraph about it.

2. Describe a classroom in your school using specific, concrete, and sensory details to paint a picture of the room. Then, come up with an expository purpose: a conclusion you've reached upon examining this room.

3. Describe a particular spot in your town. Pick a space no larger than 25′ × 25′ so you can include concrete, specific and sensory details. Then create a topic sentence that establishes a purpose for describing the atmosphere this place has and the mood it evokes.

4. Describe a person you know well using concrete, specific nouns and adjectives, including as many of the senses as possible. Avoid vague, abstract descriptions such as "beautiful," "handsome," and so on. Be sure the topic sentence states what you want to show or a conclusion you have reached about this person.

Critical Thinking Journal Prompts

Write a journal reflection entry based on one of the following prompts.

1. What makes for good descriptive writing? What should you include when you are describing something?

2. Why would you want to include as many senses as possible and **analyze** the parts and details of something in description writing?

3. Freewrite for 5 minutes describing yourself, how you look, using as many details and senses as possible. Next, freewrite for 5 more minutes on how you think someone else would describe you. Then, answer this question: How were the descriptions different or the same and why?

LEARNING OBJECTIVES REVIEW

LO1	What do you want to achieve by thinking critically about writing a description paragraph? (See p. 147)	**Thinking critically** helps you determine your purpose—to inform, to narrate, or to convince your readers to do something or believe something—and identify the descriptive details that will best illustrate your purpose.
LO2	What questions should you ask before writing a descriptive paragraph? (See p. 148)	You should ask the following **questions:** (1) What do I want to describe and why (purpose)? (2) What kind of language and details would best describe the object, place, or person? (3) How should I organize my paragraph? (4) What do I want my readers to learn from reading this description? (5) How might I conclude the paragraph?
LO3	How do you structure a descriptive paragraph? (See pp. 149–152)	You **structure a descriptive paragraph** by describing a person, place, thing, or event; organizing it using spatial order or order of importance; and developing your topic sentence using vivid language and sensory details.
LO4	How do you write a descriptive paragraph? (See pp. 153–160)	To **write a description paragraph,** create a topic sentence that explains your purpose for describing a specific object, person, place, or event; support it with vivid details and sensory language; and write a concluding sentence that reminds the reader of your purpose.
LO5	Why is concrete and vivid language important in descriptive writing? (See pp. 154–163)	Concrete and vivid language, as well as similes and metaphors (comparisons), are **important in descriptive writing** because they help paint a vivid picture of what you are describing.

For support in meeting this chapter's objectives, log in to www.mywritinglab.com and select **Paragraph Development— Describing.**

Process

LEARNING OBJECTIVES

In this chapter, you will learn to

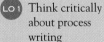 **LO 1** Think critically about process writing

LO 2 Ask questions to prepare for explaining a process

LO 3 Structure a process paragraph

LO 4 Write a process paragraph

THINKING CRITICALLY

Making a Fortune Teller Out of Paper

1. Fold the paper into fourths.
2. Unfold the paper.
3. Fold over the four corners evenly into the middle.
4. Fold into fourths again.
5. Flip over the paper.
6. Fold over the corners on the new side of the paper.
7. Fold into fourths one last time.
8. Fit your fingers into the slits.
9. Open.

Look at the directions above. Then translate them into a paragraph with a topic sentence and transitional words and phrases.

_____

_____

_____

_____

LO 1   PROCESS PARAGRAPHS

Process paragraphs describe how something works (like the Internet), explain how to do something (like register to vote), or analyze a process to see how efficient it is and/or to suggest a better way to do it (for example, the electoral-college system and an alternative to it). Process writing is very common in science and math classes and in careers that involve process-related tasks.

Critical Thinking and Process

Think critically about why you are writing a process paragraph. Is your purpose to describe a process to an audience, critique a process, or propose an alternative process after describing the current process? Read the following Applying Critical Thinking box for a list of questions you can ask to help you develop a purpose for your topic.

APPLYING CRITICAL THINKING

PURPOSE   IDEAS   SUPPORT   ASSUMPTIONS BIASES   CONCLUSIONS   POINT OF VIEW   ANALYSIS

To write an effective process paragraph, you need to consider the following questions:

1. Do I want to describe a process, critique a process, or propose an alternative to an existing process?

2. What do I already know about this process, and how can I use that information to form my **purpose**?

3. What additional information do I need to find out in order to clarify my **ideas** about it?

4. How will I **analyze** the process and break it down into its basic stages? How will I present them?

LO 2   PREPARING TO WRITE A PROCESS PARAGRAPH

Before you begin to write a process paragraph on an assigned topic, or one you have chosen, start by asking yourself these questions:

1. What process am I describing? What is my purpose for writing about it? Do I want to describe a process, critique a process, or propose an alternative to an existing process?

2. What do I want my readers to learn and understand after reading about this process, and will I need to define any terms?

3. Who is my intended audience and how much will they already know about my topic?

4. What specific steps, examples, and details should I use to describe the process?

5. How should I organize my paragraph, and how can I move smoothly from one step or detail to the next?

Answering these questions will lead you to an expository topic sentence, help you determine what examples to use, and give you a general idea of how you want to organize your paragraph.

ACTIVITY 8-1   Steps in a Process

Directions: *Briefly describe the major steps in each of the following common processes. Then, come up with a purpose for writing about each process (what you would want your readers to understand or learn through your description of it).* Answers will vary.

1. Hand washing: _____

_____

Purpose: _____

_____

2. Buying a car: _____

_____

Purpose: _____

_____

3. Buying textbooks: _____

_____

Purpose: _____

_____

4. Organizing a party: _____

_____

Purpose: _____

_____

5. Registering for college courses: _____

_____

Purpose: _____

_____

LO 3 STRUCTURING A PROCESS PARAGRAPH

The structure of a process paragraph is usually based on chronological order, describing one step at a time, in the order it happens (see the annotated student model below); however, it can also be organized by the order of importance of the individual steps if the process does not require a specific sequence of steps. For example, if you were describing the process of buying a used musical instrument, you might organize your paragraph based on which steps you thought were most important: how to use the Internet to search for particular brands or models, which online sites feature the best used instruments, how to bargain for the best price, and how to buy an item safely online. Whichever order you use, be sure to include *descriptive details* that explain and illustrate each step. Finally, make sure that your paragraph's concluding sentence reiterates the purpose of your process description or analysis.

Here is an annotated model paragraph that describes how to download a digital photo by following steps in a specific order.

Model Student Paragraph

Annabelle Caligrossi

Professor Mayes

English 100

28 September 2010

Topic sentence introduces the process and the purpose for discussing it

Both order of importance and time-order transitions are used to make the process clear

Downloading a digital photograph from your camera to your computer can be a very simple process. First, make sure that you have the directions that came with your digital camera handy in case you need to refer to them. If you do not have the directions, you should still be able to follow these basic steps to download your photo. Start by plugging one end of your cord adapter into your digital camera and the other end into a USB port on your computer. Next, you should see a pop-up box on your computer screen that first says it recognizes your camera in the USB port and then asks what you want to do, such as view the pictures, print the pictures, or download or copy the pictures to your computer. Click the option to copy/download the picture onto your computer. Also, designate where you want to save the picture (such as your "My Pictures" file). After you have downloaded and saved your photo to your chosen file, be sure to choose the "safely remove the USB mass storage device-Drive (E:)" option in the bottom toolbar of your computer (it usually looks like a little memory stick with a green arrow as the icon). Finally, as soon as a dialogue box that says "Safe to remove hardware" or "the USB device can now be safely removed" pops up, you can unplug your camera cord from the computer and turn off your camera. Congratulations, you have successfully downloaded a photograph from your digital camera to your computer.

> Second-person point of view is acceptable in a process paragraph to give step-by-step directions to your reader

> Specific details using exact terms help the reader follow the process

> Additional detail to help the reader find the correct icon as they follow the process

> Concluding sentence reiterates purpose of describing the process

The chart below provides a brief overview of the structure of a process paragraph.

BASIC STRUCTURE OF A PROCESS PARAGRAPH

TOPIC SENTENCE
State the main **idea** of your paragraph and describe your **purpose,** what you are trying to explain, show, prove, or argue through describing a process. Do you want to instruct someone in how to perform a specific task? Do you want to explain how a process works? Or do you want to critique a process and propose an alternative?

SUPPORT
Develop your description or explanation of a process using time order or order of importance.

Use transitions (time order or order of importance) to emphasize switching from one step to the next.

Include examples to illustrate the steps in the process.

Provide concrete details, facts, and description to describe and explain the examples.

Define terms when necessary, especially if the process involves parts or tools.

ANALYSIS

Add commentary and analysis about the steps, details, and descriptions to help develop the purpose of the topic sentence.

CONCLUDING SENTENCE

Sum up and re-emphasize the topic sentence: the **purpose** for describing the process.

ACTIVITY 8-2   Identifying the Elements of a Process Paragraph

Directions: *Read the paragraph below. Then, perform the following tasks.*

1. *Underline the topic sentence.*
2. *Double-underline each sentence that defines a step in the process.*
3. *Write a D over any sentence that provides a specific detail to support or illustrate a step.*
4. *Highlight any word or phrase that serves as a transition from one step to the next.*
5. *What order of organization is used in this paragraph? Is it effective?*

   time order
6. *Would another order pattern work better? Why?*

   order of importance

Karen Lucas

Professor Garcia

English 100

27 October 2011

   Buying a used car can be a risky venture, but as long as you follow some simple steps, you can get a great deal on a car that runs well.

First, do some online research before you even look at any cars in person. Research the kinds of cars you want, the average price for the years and models you are interested in, and the performance record for those cars. Then, check the *Kelly Blue Book* to find their current value. You can find a copy of the *Kelly Blue Book* at your local library or auto parts stores or find it online at http://www.kbb.com/. Once you have a clear idea of your top one or two choices and have researched both their value and average selling price, you are ready to start looking at cars for sale. Many people list their cars on places like Craig's List, but it is more difficult to negotiate test drives and financing when you are buying from an individual instead of a dealer. Therefore, be sure to have cash or a money order if you plan to buy from an individual, and know that you risk having no warranty on the vehicle. Still, if you are careful, you can get the best deal buying from a previous owner. One smart step is to bring your mechanic (or, if you are lucky, a friend who has a strong knowledge of cars) and have him or her check out the vehicle before you buy it. If you buy from a dealer, ask for a vehicle history report, which should be available on request. It will tell you if a car has been in any major accidents or had major work done. Also, ask for a money-back guarantee in case the car starts having problems soon after you buy it. You should feel comfortable negotiating about the price based on your research, whether you are buying from an individual or a dealer. What do you have to lose? Most sellers, including dealers, expect you to offer less than their asking price. Finally, have your car carefully inspected by your mechanic before you buy it to make sure it has no major mechanical or safety issues. Enjoy your purchase knowing that you have taken steps to ensure that you have paid the best price for a good used model of the vehicle you want to drive.

LO 4 WRITING A PROCESS PARAGRAPH

Topic

If you have been assigned a process topic, be sure to read the assignment carefully to make sure you understand what is being asked, and then prewrite to come up with examples and details related to the purpose for writing about the process. If you do not have a topic assigned by your instructor, brainstorm ideas for a process you might want to describe. Think of processes you are familiar with from your daily life (at school, work, home, or in your community). Then, write a list of the steps involved in the process you choose to write about.

It is also important to decide what your *purpose* is for writing a process description. Is it to evaluate a process? To teach or instruct? To propose an alternative process? Do not assume that your reader will know what you mean. For instance, if you are describing how to cut up an apple and say, "Start by cutting the apple in half," you may want to add "from the top near the stem to the bottom" or your readers could cut from the middle and not get the same wedge slices you are trying to help them achieve. Obviously, most people will know how to cut an apple correctly. However, for more complex processes, like changing a flat tire or getting seeds to germinate indoors, you will need to be very specific and even define the terms you use in the steps of the process in order for a general audience to understand you. For instance, even the term "germinate" used in the previous sentence could benefit from a simple definition so readers understand that it means "getting a seed to sprout initially."

A Few Topic Possibilities

There are many processes you are probably familiar with and could write about. Here are some suggestions you might find interesting:

- Write about any scientific or natural process you have learned about through other courses or through observations of your own.
- Write about a daily ritual such as getting ready for school, making your lunch, or studying for a test in order to show readers what you think is the best approach.

- Argue for the best way to accomplish a specific goal such as saving money for college or applying for a dream job.
- Explain how to set up a My Space or Facebook page or how to create a blog.
- Tell someone how to safely and successfully purchase something off the Internet.
- Tell someone how to open a checking or savings account.
- Tell someone how to apply for college or financial aid.

Topic Sentences

The topic sentence in a process paragraph establishes what process you are describing or analyzing and for what purpose. For instance, if you were writing a basic "how to" paragraph in order to explain how to do a task step-by-step, then the topic sentence would establish that very simply.

> Downloading a digital photograph from your camera to your computer is a very simple process.

If you were critiquing an existing process and proposing an alternative, you would state both of these goals in your topic sentence.

> Tuna fishers have used purse seine nets for many years to catch tuna; however, in the process they catch spotted and spinner dolphins, threatening their survival, so they should explore alternative options for catching their targeted species.

ACTIVITY 8-3   Creating Topic Sentences

Directions: *Create a topic sentence for each general topic. Make sure each topic sentence has a **clear purpose** and conveys the point you want to make in your description of the process.* Answers will vary.

1. Signing up for classes: _____

   _____

2. Taking an essay test: _____

   _____

3. Finding an apartment to rent: _____

   _____

4. Washing a car: _____

_____

5. Making a quick meal: _____

_____

SUPPORT

Support

The support for a process paragraph consists of examples, definitions, facts, or other information that illustrates or explains each step of the process. You can provide reasons for describing the process, analyze its significance, or analyze particular steps. The steps in the process can be presented in time order or order of importance, depending on which is the most effective method for your purpose. Use transitions to lead your readers from one step of the process to the next. Useful transitions include those that show time order or the addition of points.

TRANSITIONS TO . . .

Show Addition of Another Point

again	but also	in addition	nor
also	equally important	last	plus the fact
and	finally	lastly	secondly
and then	first	likewise	then too
another	further	moreover	thirdly
besides	furthermore	next	too

Show Time

after	before	in the meantime	not long after
afterwards	between	later	soon
at last	first	meanwhile	then
at length	immediately	next	while

ACTIVITY 8-4   Using Examples and Definitions

Directions: *Provide at least three examples and/or definitions you would include for each of the topic sentences you created in Activity 8-3.* *Answers will vary.*

1. Signing up for classes: _____

_____

_____

2. Taking an essay test: _____

_____

_____

3. Finding an apartment to rent: _____

_____

_____

4. Washing a car: _____

_____

_____

5. Making a quick meal: _____

_____

_____

Concluding Sentence

The concluding sentence in a process paragraph should restate both the process being described and the purpose for describing it.

ACTIVITY 8-5   Writing a Concluding Sentence

Directions: *Write a possible* **concluding sentence** *for two of the topic sentences you wrote in Activity 8-3. Be sure to reiterate the topic and purpose of each paragraph.*

Conclusion: _____

_____

Conclusion: _____

_____

Revise and Edit

Remember to revise your paragraph draft for the best results. Use the following critique form to check for the basics in your process paragraph draft.

PROCESS PARAGRAPH CRITIQUE FORM

Overall

	Done well	Needs work
1. Does the paragraph clearly describe a process and have a distinct purpose for doing so (e.g., to inform, critique, etc.)?	_____	_____
2. Is there a clear topic sentence that explains the purpose for describing the process?	_____	_____
3. Is the paragraph organized by time order or order of importance? Is the order used an effective choice?	_____	_____
4. Do the sentences develop the process logically and flow smoothly?	_____	_____
5. Are transitions used when needed within the paragraph?	_____	_____
6. Does the paragraph include examples and details that describe and explain the process?	_____	_____
7. Does the concluding sentence sum up the process and the purpose for describing it?	_____	_____

Editing

Circle the following errors you think you see in this draft: spelling, fragments, run-ons, comma splices, commas, semicolon/colon use, pronoun agreement, reference fault errors, parallelism, apostrophe use, verb use/tense, and passive voice construction. (See Parts V and VI for help identifying and correcting these errors.)

Other types of grammar or sentence-level errors you noticed in this draft:

_____

Comments:

_____

_____

_____

ACTIVITY 8-6 Revising the Paragraph

Directions: *Carefully read the following student paragraph. Next, use the critique form to evaluate it. Then, revise and rewrite the paragraph on a separate sheet of paper and be sure to address the following revision tasks.*

1. Make sure the topic sentence clearly states the purpose of the paragraph.

2. Reorder the sentences, if necessary, to make the explanation of the steps as clear and logical as possible.

3. Add examples and details that illustrate steps or suggestions in the paragraph, if needed.

4. *Add transitional words or phrases where needed to help the paragraph move smoothly. Use transitions appropriate to the organizational pattern (time order or order of importance).*

5. *Check that there is a strong concluding sentence.*

Carmen Hernandez

Professor Myers

English 100

15 November 2010

    In order to lose weight in a safe and permanent way, you should follow these three basic steps to success. Change your attitude to thinking that you are giving yourself a gift of better health. Losing weight takes discipline. You need a good attitude about losing weight. Try not to focus on not being able to eat what you want. After you have adjusted your attitude about losing weight, you will need to change your diet. Yo-yo diets and failed diets are the result of denying yourself too much. Having a positive outlook when you see tempting foods will help. Yes, everyone knows that losing weight involves a change in diet, but try not to go to extremes. Instead, eat sensibly. Try to have four to five smaller, healthier meals a day instead of three bigger, less healthy meals. Portion control is a big factor; eat smaller meals more often. Make sure that your food choices are good. You do not need to starve yourself. Just cut back and choose wisely. Safe weight loss involves exercise: You have to move. Weight loss is simple: Burn more calories than you consume to lose weight. So you need to increase your exercise to lose weight, even if you just add a 25-minute walk a day. Basically, the key to a good weight loss routine is to follow the three steps of changing your attitude, improving your diet, and increasing the amount of time you exercise.

PROFESSIONAL PROCESS PARAGRAPH

Excerpt from "A Few Words for Motherhood"

Wendell Berry

One of America's foremost essayists and social critics, Wendell Berry is a farmer in northeastern Kentucky and a writer in the tradition of Henry David Thoreau. In the following excerpt from his essay "A Few Words for Motherhood," Berry describes the process of assisting at the birth of a calf. This essay appears in the collection *The Gift of Good Land: Further Essays Cultural and Agricultural*, published by North Point Press, 1982.

My wife and son and I find the heifer in a far corner of the field. In maybe two hours of labor she has managed to give birth to one small foot. We know how it has been with her. Time and again she has lain down and heaved at her burden, and got up and turned and smelled the ground. She is a heifer—how does she know that something is supposed to *be* there? It takes some doing even for the three of us to get her into the barn. Her orders are to be alone, and she does all in her power to obey. But finally we shut the door behind her and get her into a stall. She isn't wild; once she is confined it isn't even necessary to tie her. I wash in a bucket of icy water and soap my right hand and forearm. She is quiet now. And so are we humans—worried, and excited, too, for if there is a chance for failure here, there is also a chance for success. I loop a bale string onto the calf's exposed foot, knot the string short around a stick which my son then holds. I press my hand gently into the birth canal until I find the second foot and then, a little further on, a nose. I loop a string around the second foot, fasten on another stick for a handhold. And then we pull. The heifer stands and pulls against us for a few seconds, then gives up and goes down. We brace ourselves the best we can into our work, pulling as the heifer pushes. Finally the head comes, and then, more easily, the rest. We clear the calf's nose, help him to breathe, and then, because the heifer has not yet stood up, we lay him on the bedding in front of her. And what always seems to me the miracle of it begins. She has never calved before. If she ever saw another cow calve, she paid little attention. She has, as we humans say, no education and no experience. And yet she recognizes the calf as her own, and knows what to do for it. Some heifers don't, but most do, as this one does. Even before she gets up, she begins to lick it about the nose and face with loud, vigorous swipes of her tongue. And all the while she utters a kind of moan, meant to comfort, encourage, and reassure—or so I understand it.

Reading Reflection Questions *Answers will vary. Sample answers provided.*

1. What is the **purpose** of this paragraph?

   To demonstrate the bond of motherhood between a cow and calf and how

   remarkable it is that the heifer knows instinctively what to do for her calf

2. What order pattern, transitions, support, and details distinguish this as a piece of *process* writing?

   Chronological order, step-by-step description of the birthing process, tran-

   sitions for steps such as "then" and "finally"

3. Does this paragraph have good transitions between steps? *yes*

   Where could you add transitions to make it smoother? *Answers will vary.*

Checking Vocabulary

List any words in this reading you did not know, and provide a dictionary definition for each.

CRITICAL THINKING CHECKLIST

1. What is the author's *purpose* or *goal* in this reading selection?

2. What are the *stated questions* being addressed?

3. What *specific details and examples* does the author use to develop his or her purpose or goal for the reading?

4. What *inferences* does the author include in this reading? (Inferences imply "if this, then this" types of cause/effect analysis.)

5. Who is the intended audience, and how did you reach that conclusion?

Paragraph Writing Assignments

1. Use one of the topics you developed in the activities in this chapter to write a process paragraph. Use the critique form to check your draft.

2. Write a process paragraph describing how to make your favorite recipe or sandwich. Include all the details you can, be very specific, and use the exact order for recreating the process that you go through when making this item.

3. Pick a routine you know well from everyday experience, and write a process paragraph that would show someone who has never done this activity how to accomplish it step by step. For example, you could tell them how to make a bed, change the oil in a car, or clean a bathroom.

4. Write a process description of how to apply or interview for a job.

Critical Thinking Journal Prompts

Write a journal reflection entry using one of the following prompts.

1. What are three strategies that you could use to write effectively about a process?

2. What task(s) can you think of in your own life that requires you to follow a process in order to complete it successfully?

3. In what situations—academic, work, or personal—would you need to **analyze** a process? Discuss an example.

LEARNING OBJECTIVES REVIEW

LO1 How can thinking critically help you write a process paragraph? (See p. 166)	**Thinking critically** helps you to decide your purpose for writing about a particular process—to evaluate it, instruct someone how to perform it, or critique an existing process and suggest how it can be improved—and determine what details to use to describe the steps and how to organize them.
LO2 What questions should you ask before writing a process paragraph? (See 166–167)	**You should ask the following questions:** (1) What process am I describing, and what is my purpose for writing about it? (2) What do I want my readers to learn from reading about this process, and will I need to define terms? (3) Who is my audience and how much do they already know? (4) What specific steps, examples, and details should I include? (5) How should I organize my paragraph, and how can I move smoothly from one step or detail to the next?
LO3 How do you structure a process paragraph? (See pp. 168–172)	You **structure a process paragraph** by describing and analyzing a process; using chronological order or order of importance; defining any terms your audience needs to know; and using facts, examples, and other details to describe the specific steps.
LO4 How do you write a process paragraph? (See pp. 172–179)	To **write a process paragraph,** create a topic sentence that states your purpose for describing and/or analyzing a process; support it with facts, examples, and definitions (if necessary) that describe, explain, and analyze the steps; and write a concluding sentence that sums up your main point.

PEARSON mywritinglab

For support in meeting this chapter's objectives, log in to www.mywritinglab.com and select **Paragraph Development—Process.**

Classification

Frederick L. Huston, Jr.

THINKING CRITICALLY

Classification is a great way to sort out the different categories within a group. For example, there are many different types of animals. They can be domestic pets or wild animals, herbivores or carnivores, land animals or sea animals, mammals or reptiles, and so on. How would you classify the animals in the photo above? What criteria did you use to make this classification?

_____

_____

LEARNING OBJECTIVES

In this chapter, you will learn to

LO1 Apply critical thinking to sort items into categories

LO2 Ask questions to prepare for classification writing

LO3 Structure a classification paragraph

LO4 Write a classification paragraph using examples

LO 1 CLASSIFICATION PARAGRAPHS

Classification, sometimes called "division," involves grouping, or dividing, items into categories based on common characteristics. In classes and at work, you might be asked to classify objects, tasks, or people into meaningful groups in order to analyze them. For instance, you might be asked to classify potential customers into groups depending on their age, gender, income, lifestyle, and education in order to decide how best to market a product to each group. In a biology class, you would study the systems that have been developed to classify animals or plants into families, orders, classes, phyla, and kingdoms.

When you classify, you need to think about the topic you have chosen, or been assigned, and the best way to subdivide it into categories. For example, if you were asked to write about the topic of music, you could decide to focus on contemporary popular music. There are a number of ways you could classify this topic: types of popular music (rock, alternative, indie pop, country and western), types of listeners (young, old, white collar, blue collar), or how the music is distributed (radio, iTunes, YouTube, CDs, vinyl). Once you decide on the criteria you are going to use, you can sort, or *classify*, items accordingly.

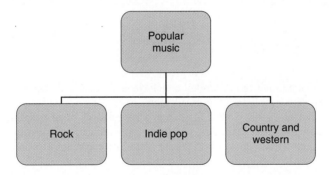

If these categories are too large for you to address within the scope of a paragraph, you can brainstorm again about one of them.

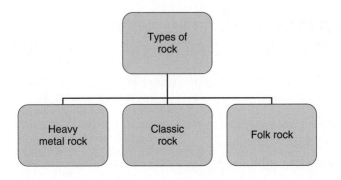

The classification mode is often used in argument writing and speeches and in analysis of written works (for instance categorizing, a novelist's techniques or characters).

Critical Thinking and Classification

One purpose of a classification paragraph is to sort a group into its specific parts in order to understand the whole better. Another is to *critique* the categories set out by someone else and to argue against the conclusions they have reached about particular people, items, places, or ideas.

Be careful to avoid biased classifications that do not fairly represent the members of subgroups or misrepresent the items, thoughts, or people within those groups. Also, do not oversimplify your topic group into subdivisions that do not fully represent its complexity.

APPLYING CRITICAL THINKING

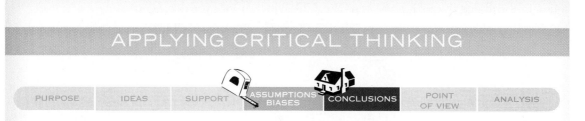

| PURPOSE | IDEAS | SUPPORT | ASSUMPTIONS BIASES | CONCLUSIONS | POINT OF VIEW | ANALYSIS |

It is easy to make the mistake of reaching unfair or unfounded **conclusions** about people based on stereotypes, such as "All women are less physically strong than all men" or "All men have more difficulty expressing their emotions than women do." Be aware that you may have **biases** or **assumptions** about people that are based on characteristics such as race, age, gender, or appearance, so ask yourself if the criteria—the standards you are using to classify people into groups—are legitimate before you use them. Check your reasoning to make sure you are being fair and even-minded.

LO 2   PREPARING TO WRITE A CLASSIFICATION PARAGRAPH

Before you begin to write a classification paragraph on an assigned topic, or one you have chosen, start by asking yourself these questions:

1. What do I want my readers to learn or understand about my topic after reading this paragraph?
2. What criteria will I use to classify the topic?

3. What categories can I break my topic into?

4. Have I unfairly or inaccurately classified the topic?

5. Have I oversimplified the categories?

Answering these questions will lead you to an expository topic sentence, help you determine which examples and details to include for support, and give you a general idea of how you want to organize your paragraph.

ACTIVITY 9-1 Practicing Classification

Directions: *For each topic, list two to three ways you could subdivide it into categories.* *Answers will vary.*

Example: Food

Categories: <u>**Mexican, Japanese, Indian**</u>

1. Plants

Categories: _____

2. Books

Categories: _____

3. Music

Categories: _____

4. Sports

Categories: _____

5. Animals

Categories: _____

LO 3 STRUCTURING A CLASSIFICATION PARAGRAPH

Classification paragraphs often involve a great deal of comparison and contrast, description, and narration, and are written to help a reader understand a topic through analyzing and discussing its parts or to argue against classifications made by others. In your **topic sentence,** identify your topic, your purpose for classifying it, and the categories you will discuss (the conclusion you reached through the process of subdividing the group). Then, develop your topic sentence with **supporting examples** and **specific details** that explain and illustrate the categories or subcategories involved, using transitions when needed. End with a **concluding sentence** that sums up the purpose set out in your topic sentence.

Here is an annotated model paragraph that classifies students by the ways they choose to relax.

Model Student Paragraph

Topic sentence indicates the paragraph will classify people based on how they relax

First category is gamers.

Specific details about gamers

Second category/example is readers

Specific details about readers

Third category is socializers

Specific examples about socializers

Concluding sentence reiterates the categories

Daniel Blake

Professor Moore

English 100

16 September 2010

In my dorm, I have noticed there are three distinct types of people in terms of how they choose to relax: gamers, readers, and socializers. The gamers are the ones who play video games in order to relax between studying and classes. You find the gamers on their X-Boxes or Game Cubes, no matter what time of day or night. You can distinguish them by their glazed-over eyes and their active thumbs, moving rapidly over the controls. The next type is the readers. They read novels, newspapers, magazines, graphic novels, even cereal boxes if there is nothing else available. You find them curled up in a chair, a single light overhead, and their noses pressed into a book for hours. The last category is the socializers. These people can only unwind if they have others around to help them. They chat their way into relaxation. Sometimes, they wander the halls, checking from room to room, until they find someone they can talk to and hang out with. Yes, it is true that there are many different ways to relax during free time in the dorm, but the people I live with fall into these categories: the gamers, the readers, and the socializers.

The following chart provides a brief overview of the structure of a classification paragraph.

BASIC STRUCTURE FOR A CLASSIFICATION PARAGRAPH

TOPIC SENTENCE

State the main **idea** of your paragraph and describe your **purpose,** what you are trying to explain, show, prove, or argue by using classification—and what conclusions you reached by subdividing your topic.

SUPPORT

Include examples to illustrate the categories.

Provide concrete details, facts, and description to describe and explain the examples.

Use transitions within the paragraph to make the sentences flow smoothly.

ANALYSIS

Add commentary and analysis about the categories, examples, and details to help develop the purpose of the topic sentence.

CONCLUDING SENTENCE

Sum up and re-emphasize the topic sentence: the **conclusions reached** by classifying your topic.

ACTIVITY 9-2   Identifying the Elements of a Classification Paragraph

Directions: *Read the paragraph below. Then, perform the following tasks.*

1. *Underline the topic sentence.*

2. *Double-underline each sentence that states a main category of the topic discussed in the paragraph.*

3. *Write a D over each sentence that provides a detail that supports or illustrates a category.*

4. *Highlight any word or phrase that serves as a transition from one category to the next.*

Hannah Shugrue

Professor Schaefer

English 081

8 September 2009

The perfect vacation spot depends on the people traveling and the type of vacation they desire. Three of the most common vacation categories are romantic getaways, trips for singles, and family holidays. For couples, whether it is a honeymoon trip or just a weekend getaway, they are usually looking for an atmosphere that is low-key and romantic. For that reason, beach vacations are ideal. For example, Hawaii and the Caribbean are perfect spots for this type of vacation. The combination of beautiful sandy beaches, warm weather and water, good food, and friendly people makes for a perfect experience. For single travelers hoping to meet other singles, beach vacations are also good, but they need to make sure that they pick a place that does not cater primarily to couples. For instance, the island of Oahu in Hawaii is great for singles because it has the most nightlife, including bars and dance clubs. Las Vegas and Atlantic City are also meccas for single vacationers due to the extensive nightlife opportunities and the high number of other singles looking to meet possible partners. Finally, family vacation spots can be very varied, but most families look for places that can entertain the whole family. For this reason, beach vacations are popular for families. Kids and parents alike can spend hours by the beach or pool and can hike or do water activities in the day and go out for good food in the evening. Many families also like to take camping vacations and stay in the woods or other rural areas. Some families "rough it" completely with tents and campfires, while others indulge themselves by renting a cabin to ensure they have the basic conveniences. In addition, families like to vacation in cities with theme or amusement parks such as Disneyland or Disney World. Orlando, Florida, is a city that consciously caters to traveling families for this very reason. What makes the perfect vacation spot depends on who the travelers are and what they are looking for as their ideal way to unwind.

LO 4 WRITING A CLASSIFICATION PARAGRAPH

Topic

If you have been assigned a topic that requires you to classify, be sure to read the assignment carefully to make sure you understand what is being asked, and then prewrite to come up with categories and subcategories that support your purpose for writing about it. If you do not have a specific classification assignment, come up with a topic idea through prewriting, and then use brainstorming to generate ideas about how you could classify it into groups.

For example, if you were going to write about the types of birds that live in the South, you would first need to come up with a list and then create some categories to classify them into (e.g., water fowl, tree birds, game birds, and so on). Next, you would need to freewrite or brainstorm for examples and details that would explain and illustrate each category. The point of your paragraph could be to explain that there are a variety of types of birds that live in the South or to briefly explain each type and show which ones are best adapted for living there.

A Few Topic Possibilities

There are many subjects that work well for a classification paragraph. Here are some suggestions:

- Write about a particular group of people you know (coworkers, church associates, classmates, etc.) and categorize them into particular groups based on their habits or personalities.

- Categorize the restaurants in your neighborhood.
- Categorize and classify movies.
- Classify Internet Web sites.
- Classify different types of singers.
- Classify different types of pets or animals.
- Classify colleges and universities in your state.

ACTIVITY 9-3   Breaking a Topic into Categories

Directions: *For each of the topics below, use one of the categories for classifying it that you chose in Activity 9-1 and come up with a list of subcategories.* Answers will vary.

> **Topic:** Cooking
>
> **Categories:** Mexican, Japanese, Indian
>
> **Category:** <u>Mexican</u>
>
> **Subcategories:** <u>Tacos, burritos, guacamole, enchiladas, tamales</u>

1. **Topic:** Plants

   Category: _____

   Subcategories: _____

2. **Topic:** Books

   Category: _____

   Subcategories: _____

3. **Topic:** Music

   Category: _____

   Subcategories: _____

4. **Topic:** Sports

   Category: _____

   Subcategories: _____

5. **Topic:** Animals

   Category: _____

   Subcategories: _____

Topic Sentence

If you have a specific classification assignment, customize your topic sentence using key words from the assignment to establish the controlling idea and purpose for your paragraph. If you have to come up with your own topic, brainstorm for one that can be broken down into categories, and then brainstorm or freewrite to come up with specific examples and details to illustrate those categories. Determine your purpose for writing about your topic by answering these questions: What point do I want to make about my classification of the topic? What conclusion have I reached about these categories? Then write a topic sentence that reflects your purpose and sets up the categories. For example,

Subject: Students' clothing styles

Topic sentence: Students on my campus showcase their personal identities and indicate their attitude toward how formal college dress should be through the style of clothing they wear.

ACTIVITY 9-4   Creating Topic Sentences

Directions: *Using the categories and subcategories you generated in Activities 9-1 and 9-3, create a topic sentence for each of the following topics. Make sure the topic sentence has a clear message or lesson to convey about the conclusion you reached using classification.* Answers will vary.

1. Plants: _____

   _____

2. Books: _____

   _____

3. Music: _____

   _____

4. Sports: _____

   _____

5. Animals: _____

   _____

Support

In your paragraph, develop and explain each category using specific examples and details. Useful transitions for classification paragraphs include those showing addition, comparison, and purpose.

TRANSITIONS TO . . .			
Show Addition of Another Point			
again	but also	in addition	nor
also	equally important	last	plus the fact
and	finally	lastly	secondly
and then	first	likewise	then too
another	further	moreover	thirdly
besides	furthermore	next	too
Show a Comparison			
in like manner	in the same way	likewise	similarly
Show Purpose			
all things considered	for this reason	to accomplish	with this in mind
for this purpose	in order to	to this end	with this objective

Definitions and Examples

Since you are discussing different categories in a classification paragraph, you need to provide clear definitions and examples to illustrate the differences and similarities between them. For instance, if you were taking a biology class, you might be asked to classify trees into groups. You might use *coniferous* and *deciduous* as two of your categories, and then you would need to both define these terms and provide examples of the types of trees they represent. For example, coniferous trees are evergreens that have needles all year round and bear cones. Deciduous trees have leaves, which they lose in the fall. Coniferous trees include pine, fir, and spruce, as well as yews and their allies that bear drupe-like seeds. Deciduous trees include maple, birch, aspen, and oak.

ACTIVITY 9-5   Providing Examples

Directions: *Now, provide at least three examples you could include for each of the topic sentences you created in Activity 9-4.*   *Answers will vary.*

1. Plants: _____

_____

2. Books: _____

_____

3. Music: _____

_____

4. Sports: _____

_____

5. Animals: _____

_____

Concluding Sentence

In your concluding sentence, restate your topic sentence emphasizing the conclusions you reached by classifying your topic and the overall purpose of the paragraph. Touch on the categories you used to classify your topic and the main point you want your readers to understand after they read your paragraph.

ACTIVITY 9-6   Writing a Concluding Sentence

Directions: *Choose one of the topics you have been developing in the preceding activities and write a **concluding sentence** that re-emphasizes the classification categories and the purpose for writing about them.*   *Answers will vary.*

_____

_____

Revise and Edit

Remember to revise your paragraph draft for the best results. Use the following critique form to check for the basics in your classification paragraph draft.

CLASSIFICATION PARAGRAPH CRITIQUE FORM

Overall

	Done well	Needs work
1. Does the paragraph classify a topic into two or more categories with similar characteristics?	_____	_____
2. Does the writer use these specific categories consistently and clearly?	_____	_____
3. Is there a clear topic sentence that explains the purpose of the classification being made?	_____	_____
4. Are transitions used when needed within the paragraph?	_____	_____
5. Does the paragraph include definitions, examples, and details that explain and illustrate the categories?	_____	_____
6. Does the concluding sentence sum up the categories with analysis and re-emphasize the purpose developed in the topic sentence without adding new ideas?	_____	_____

Editing

Circle the following errors you think you see in this draft: spelling, fragments, run-ons, comma splices, commas, semicolon/colon use, pronoun agreement, reference fault errors, parallelism, apostrophe use, verb use/tense, and passive voice construction. (See Parts V and VI for help identifying and correcting these errors.)

Other types of grammar or sentence-level errors you noticed in this draft:

_____

Comments:

_____

_____

_____

ACTIVITY 9-7   Revising the Paragraph

Directions: *Carefully read the following student paragraph. Then, use the critique form to evaluate it. Finally, revise and rewrite the paragraph on a separate sheet of paper and be sure to address the following revision tasks.* *Answers will vary.*

1. *Make sure the topic sentence clearly sets up the categories to be discussed and states the purpose for doing so.*

2. *If necessary, make the categories clearer or change or add categories.*

3. *If necessary, add any examples and details that help develop the purpose of the paragraph.*

4. *Move any sentences that are not in the most effective order, and add transitional words or phrases where needed.*

5. *Ensure there is a strong concluding sentence.*

Tom Clarke

Mr. Nelson

English 081

11 October 2011

     Sports spectators vary widely in the depth of their interest and support for their teams. The first category is the die-hard, thick or thin fan. These fans come to every game, rain or shine. The casual fan is different. Certainly the casual fan is not as dedicated. Then there are fans who fall in the middle ground. The die-hard fan would never miss a game even if it is pouring outside. The middle-ground fans might decide not to go to a game if it snows. The casual fan goes based on his or her mood that day as well as the weather. These three types of fans are certainly different when it comes to their levels of commitment to their teams.

PROFESSIONAL CLASSIFICATION PARAGRAPH

Diversity of Life

    There are millions of different types of individual organisms that inhabit the earth at any one time—some very similar to each other, some very different. Biologists classify organisms into a hierarchy of groups and subgroups on the basis of similarities and differences in their structure and behavior. One of the most general distinctions among organisms is between plants, which get their energy directly from sunlight, and animals, which consume the energy-rich foods initially synthesized by plants. But not all organisms are clearly one or the other. For example, there are single-celled organisms without organized nuclei (bacteria) that are classified as a distinct group. Animals and plants have a great variety of body plans, with different overall structures and arrangements of internal parts to perform the basic operations of making or finding food, deriving energy and materials from it, synthesizing new materials, and reproducing. When scientists classify organisms, they consider details of anatomy to be more relevant than behavior or general appearance. For example, because of such features as milk-producing glands and brain structure, whales and bats are classified as being more nearly alike than are whales and fish or bats and birds. At different degrees of relatedness, dogs are classified with fish as having backbones, with cows as having hair, and with cats as being meat eaters. The definition of species is not precise, however; at the boundaries it may be difficult to decide on the exact classification of a particular organism. Indeed, classification systems are not part of nature. Rather, they are frameworks created by biologists for describing the vast diversity of organisms, suggesting relationships among living things, and framing research questions.

Excerpt adapted from *Science for All Americans Online,* Chapter 5: The Living Organism.

Reading Reflection Questions   *Answers will vary. Sample answers provided.*

1. What are the direct or indirect (implied) messages in this paragraph?

   Living organisms are categorized into subgroups based on similarities and

   differences, but it's not an easy process to classify organisms.

2. What features distinguish this as a *classification* paragraph?

   Organisms are grouped and classified by their characteristics with

   categories/criteria and examples provided.

3. How are such classifications of living organisms helpful to biologists and students?

   They help them understand humans as well as other living organisms and

   how they are similar and/or different.

Checking Vocabulary

List any words in this reading that you did not know. Then provide a dictionary definition for those words.

Use the following Critical Thinking Checklist to help you with this reading and for checking any other classification paragraph or writing.

CRITICAL THINKING CHECKLIST

1. What is the author's *purpose* or *goal* in this reading selection?

2. What are the *stated questions* being addressed?

3. What *specific details and examples* does the author use to develop his or her purpose or goal for the reading?

4. What *inferences* does the author include in this reading? (Inferences imply "if this, then this" types of cause/effect analysis.)

5. Who is the intended *audience,* and how did you reach that conclusion?

Paragraph Writing Assignments

1. Write a classification paragraph using any of the topics you developed in the activities in this chapter.

2. Classify types of consumers into at least four categories (group them into particular *types* of consumers or customers). Then, come up with an analytical conclusion based on the categories or stereotypes.

3. Write a classification paragraph about three restaurants you go to regularly. First decide on two or three categories to use to classify them. Use specific examples and details to describe the categories. Then, come to an analytical conclusion related to the categories you used to discuss the restaurants.

4. Categorize members of your family based on criteria you choose. Then, come to an analytical conclusion as a result of your categories and criteria.

Critical Thinking Journal Reflection

Write a journal reflection entry based on one of the following prompts:

1. Describe a time when you had to use your classification skills in a job situation. What was the task? How did you determine the categories to use? What was your purpose? Was your classification successful?

2. Describe a time you had to use classification skills in a classroom situation. Explain what you were categorizing and how you determined how to divide and classify your subjects.

3. Classify your friends into three groups based on personality traits you establish first.

LEARNING OBJECTIVES REVIEW

LO 1 How can you use critical thinking to help you sort items into categories? (See pp. 183–184)	You can use **critical thinking** to decide what point you want to make about the topic and the best way to subdivide it into categories Once you decide on the criteria you are going to use, you can sort, or *classify*, items accordingly.
LO 2 What questions should you ask before writing a classification paragraph? (See pp. 184–185)	You should ask the following **questions:** (1) What do I want my readers to learn or understand about my topic? (2) What criteria will I use to classify the topic? (3) What categories can I break my topic into? (4) Have I unfairly or inaccurately classified the topic? (5) Have I oversimplified the categories?
LO 3 How do you structure a classification paragraph? (See pp. 185–189)	The purpose of a classification paragraph is to sort a group into its specific parts in order to better understand the whole. So you **structure a classification paragraph** by breaking a topic into categories in order to make a specific point, organize it by using compare and contrast and addition transitions, and use definitions and examples to support and explain the topic sentence.
LO 4 How do you write a classification paragraph? (See pp. 189–195)	To **write a classification paragraph,** create a topic sentence that states your purpose for classifying a topic and how you will divide it into categories; support it with specific examples and definitions that develop the categories or subcategories; use compare and contrast transitions when needed; and write a concluding sentence that sums up the purpose set out in your topic sentence.

For support in meeting this chapter's objectives, log in to www.mywritinglab.com and select **Paragraph Development—Classification.**

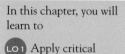

THINKING CRITICALLY

Define the insect in the photograph. Use the general name for it, and then add any information you know about this type of insect. Then, do a little research about butterflies on the Internet and add more details to your definition. Finally, to help define it, describe it in detail, as if your audience has no idea what this thing is and cannot see it for themselves.

_____

_____

_____

_____

_____

LO 1 DEFINITION PARAGRAPHS

Definition paragraphs describe, define, and clarify items, terms, and concepts. They are used to tell the reader what something is or what something means. When you define a term or object, don't just describe it: Explain what it is and what it means, including any implied meanings or associations it has.

Critical Thinking and Definition

The purpose of a definition paragraph can range from providing a straightforward definition of a term or concept to providing a definition that includes its symbolic meaning or cultural and historic relevance. For instance, you might define a "cross" as an object composed of two crossed lines or objects, but it is likely that you would also need to discuss the religious significance of the "cross" as a symbol in Christianity and earlier religions. Definition paragraphs are commonly used in reports to classmates and coworkers, to define specific terms or processes in a particular field or for a particular audience, and to give background and information on a subject.

LO 2 PREPARING TO WRITE A DEFINITION PARAGRAPH

Before you begin to write a definition paragraph on an assigned topic, or one you have chosen, start by asking yourself these questions:

1. What is my **purpose** for defining this object or concept?
2. Who is my target audience for this paragraph, and what do I want them to learn?
3. What general category does my subject fall into, and what distinguishing characteristics does it have?
4. Can I compare it to something similar to help define it, or can I explain it by saying what it is not?
5. What **support** can I use in my definition?
6. What is the most effective order of development for my paragraph (e.g., spatial, order of importance, etc.)?

Answering these questions will lead you to a topic sentence, will help you determine examples and details to include for support, and will give you a general idea of how you want to organize your paragraph.

ACTIVITY 10-1   Generate Terms for a Definition Paragraph

Directions: *Use prewriting to generate terms from class, your workplace, or home that could serve as a basis for a definition paragraph, and list them below.*

_____

_____

LO 3   STRUCTURING A DEFINITION PARAGRAPH

In your topic sentence, identify the term you will be defining and what your purpose is for defining it. You may need to use one of the prewriting techniques from Chapter 4 to generate ideas for your purpose, support, and overall definition.

In the body of your paragraph, define the item, term, or concept you have chosen by first discussing how it fits into a general category. Then, write about its distinguishing features in order to define it more specifically. For instance, if you had to define a socket wrench, you might first put it into the general category of tools. Then, you would get specific about the distinguishing qualities of the socket wrench: its shape, size, purpose, and so on.

In order to more precisely define your subject, you can also compare it to similar things. For instance, you could compare a narcissus to a daffodil, as they are similar kinds of flowers, but emphasize how they differ. Or you could compare something unfamiliar (the item you are defining) to something familiar to your audience. For example, you could explain that rugby is a popular British sport and then compare it to American football. You can also define a term by saying what it is not. For instance, you could define the term "obsession" by saying what it is not; it is not being "just a little concerned" about something.

If there are subcategories of a term, you should include those too. For instance, if you were defining the term *obsession*, you could include information about obsessive–compulsive disorder, obsession with weight, obsession with another person, and other types of obsessions. Conclude your definition paragraph by summing up what you have defined and why you have defined it, your purpose.

APPLYING CRITICAL THINKING

BLUEPRINTS

PURPOSE   IDEAS   SUPPORT   ASSUMPTIONS BIASES   CONCLUSIONS   POINT OF VIEW   ANALYSIS

1. What is my **purpose** for writing this definition paragraph? What is the main point, the main **idea** I want to convey to my audience?

2. How will I approach the subject? What is my prior knowledge about it? What is my **point of view?**

3. Have I thoroughly **analyzed** the term and chosen the most effective way to categorize and then define it? What general category does my subject belong to (e.g., a tulip is a bulb flower)?

4. What **support** do I need to include? What examples, descriptive details, and facts can I include to develop my definition?

Model Student Paragraph

Abigail Pundt

Professor Moreno

English 082

30 October 2009

    A "search engine" is a tool that allows people to search the Internet for information using a specific word or phrase. With a search engine, users can put in one word, get thousands of hits, then type in a more specific term or phrase to narrow their search to find the particular information they require. Search engines use a combination of approaches to achieve their task. First, they use "web crawlers," also called "spiders," which are programs that go through all searchable Web sites on the Internet looking for keywords from a

Topic sentence indicates that the paragraph will define the term "search engine"

The definition begins with a general explanation of a search engine

The general definition is followed with specific details about how search engines work

A specific example of a search engine process helps the reader understand how it works

Concrete details and specific names of search engines enhance the definition

Concluding sentence reiterates the term defined

search. They also use hyperlinks on each page they find to lead them to other related sites. For example, if a user puts the phrase "mitral valve prolapse" into the key word search box of a search engine, he or she will get a large number of "hits," or links, to Internet sites that provide definitions and information about this type of heart disorder. Search engines also automatically compile an index of links that is constantly being updated as more information becomes available on the Internet. Several search engines are available for use including Yahoo, Google, Lycos, and Alta Vista, so users can experiment to see which ones work best for them. Users usually find that particular search engines are better at certain types of searches or have visual features that work well for them, so they tend to go to them first. All in all, search engines are a valuable tool for finding information on the Internet on a specific topic as quickly as possible.

The chart below provides a brief overview of the structure of a definition paragraph.

BASIC STRUCTURE OF A DEFINITION PARAGRAPH

TOPIC SENTENCE
State the main **idea** of your paragraph and describe your **purpose**, what you are trying to explain, show, prove, or argue through your definition

SUPPORT
Develop your definition through identifying the group the item or concept belongs to and discussing its distinguishing characteristics. For example, a rose is a plant, specifically a type of flower, known for both its beauty and its scent. It is also distinguished as a flower that represents various emotional connections; for example, a red rose is associated with romance.

Provide concrete examples and details to illustrate and define your topic. Provide definitions of any unfamiliar terms you use in your explanation.

Use transitions within and between paragraphs to make the paragraphs flow smoothly

ANALYSIS

Add commentary and analysis about the definition, terms you may have used, examples, and details to help develop the purpose of the topic sentence

CONCLUDING SENTENCE

Sum up and re-emphasize the topic sentence: the **conclusions reached** through your definition of your topic

---

ACTIVITY 10-2 Identifying the Elements of a Definition Paragraph

Directions: *Read the paragraph below. Then, perform the following tasks.*

1. *Underline the topic sentence.*
2. *Double-underline each sentence or part of a sentence that provides an example that helps define the topic and supports the topic sentence.*
3. *Write a D over any sentence or part of a sentence that provides a specific detail that supports or illustrates an example for the definition.*
4. *Highlight over any word or phrase that serves as a transition from one step to the next.*

Malori Morley

Professor Whetham

English 090

17 November 2009

A "life coach" is someone trained to help individuals improve their lives and achieve their personal goals. Many people think that a life coach tells people what to do. In fact, what a life coach does is help people figure out a process for setting their own goals and create a plan for achieving them. Most life coaches see themselves as mentors or motivators, not as directors or armchair psychologists. Some of the skills that life coaches help their clients work on include time management, values assessment, and goal setting. For example, a life coach may help a person who has lost his or her job to identify new career goals. During that process, the life coach may help the client upgrade her computer skills, improve her oral and written communication skills, develop new work contacts, and write a new resume. A life coach helps people figure out how to make their lives better and provides the tools for doing so.

LO 4 WRITING A DEFINITION PARAGRAPH

Topic

If you have been assigned a definition topic, be sure to read the assignment carefully to make sure you understand what is being asked, and then prewrite to come up with examples and details related to the purpose for defining the specific term or concept.

If you do not have a topic assigned by your instructor, brainstorm ideas for things, places, people, or ideas you might want to define. Then, come up with some ideas for a purpose for defining your topic. What do you want your readers to understand through your definition? Your purpose may be simply to define an object or concept for an audience unfamiliar with it. Or it could be to establish a working definition of a term before making an argument about it (for example, you might want to define the term *racism* and then argue whether a certain behavior is or is not racist).

A Few Topic Possibilities

You can define a complex term or process you learned about in another class or a term, position, or item from your job. Some possibilities include the following:

- Defining a scientific term
- Defining a term used in a ritual or religion

- Defining a saying that comes from a particular culture or subculture
- Defining a term that is specific to a particular career
- Defining a visual symbol or icon

Topic Sentence

In your topic sentence, identify the term you will be defining. Then, based on your prewriting, establish how you will define the subject and your purpose for doing so.

> The term "international students" can be applied to several very diverse groups of students at our campus.

Sometimes, the purpose of a definition paragraph is to define something in order to reach a more complex conclusion related to the subject. For instance, in the "cross" example earlier in this chapter, the writer could first define what a *cross* is, and then explain the symbolic and religious associations of the cross.

> The cross is an important religious symbol and is associated with the Christian faith as well as other faiths, some even older than Christianity.

ACTIVITY 10-3   Creating Topic Sentences

Directions: *Choose three of the topics you generated in Activity 10-1 and create a one-sentence **topic sentence** for each. Make sure the topic sentence identifies the item, concept, or term being defined and your purpose for defining it.*

1. Item, concept, or term: _____

   Topic sentence: _____

   _____

2. Item, concept, or term: _____

   Topic sentence: _____

   _____

3. Item, concept, or term: _____

   Topic sentence: _____

   _____

Support and Analysis

After creating a strong topic sentence for your definition paragraph, you need to organize your **support,** presenting **examples, details,** and distinguishing characteristics in the most effective way to define your topic. For instance, using the cross example again, you could use the examples and details to further define the cross itself: its shape, the types of materials it can be made from, and so on. Then, you could define, explain, and **analyze** the cross's symbolic significance for Christians, explaining the religious history of the cross as a symbol of Christianity's sacrificial hero, Jesus. Use transitions between your examples and details to lead the reader smoothly from one characteristic, example, or comparison to the next. Useful transitions for definition paragraphs are listed below.

TRANSITIONS TO . . .

Show Addition of Another Point

again	but also	in addition	nor
also	equally important	last	plus the fact
and	finally	lastly	secondly
and then	first	likewise	then too
another	further	moreover	thirdly
besides	furthermore	next	too

Show a Comparison

in like manner	in the same way	likewise	similarly

Illustrate or Give Examples/Specifics

a few include	essentially	in particular	the following
an example	for example	let us consider	specifically
especially	for instance	the case of	you can see this in

Show Purpose

all things considered	for this reason	to accomplish	with this in mind
for this purpose	in order to	to this end	with this objective

ACTIVITY 10-4   Providing Supporting Examples and Details

Directions: *Now, list at least three possible examples you could use to support two of the topic sentences you created in Activity 10-3.*

1. Topic sentence: _____

_____

Example 1: _____

_____

Example 2: _____

_____

Example 3: _____

_____

2. Topic sentence: _____

_____

Example 1: _____

_____

Example 2: _____

_____

Example 3: _____

_____

Concluding Sentence

The concluding sentence in a definition paragraph should reiterate the definition of the object or concept briefly and sum up your purpose for defining it to your reader.

ACTIVITY 10-5 Concluding Sentences

Directions: *Choose one of the topics you've been developing in the preceding activities and write a **concluding sentence** that re-emphasizes the definition and the purpose you want to convey through your definition.*

_____

_____

Revise and Edit

Remember to revise your paragraph draft for the best results. Use the following critique form to check for the basics in your definition paragraph.

DEFINITION PARAGRAPH CRITIQUE FORM

Overall

	Done well	Needs work

1. Does the paragraph clearly define the term, concept, or object being discussed?

2. Is there a clear topic sentence that explains the purpose of the definition?

3. Is the paragraph developed well with examples and details?

4. Is the best order chosen for the organization of the definition?

5. Are transitions used when needed within the paragraph?

6. Does the concluding sentence sum up the definition and re-emphasize the purpose developed in the topic sentence?

Editing

Circle the following errors you think you see in this draft: spelling, fragments, run-ons, comma splices, commas, semicolon/colon use, pronoun agreement, reference fault errors, parallelism, apostrophe use, verb use/tense, and passive voice construction. (See Parts V and VI for help identifying and correcting these errors.) **Other types of grammar or sentence-level errors you noticed in this draft:**

_____

Comments:

_____

_____

ACTIVITY 10-6 Revising the Paragraph

Directions: *Carefully read the following student paragraph. Then, use the critique form to evaluate it. Finally, revise and rewrite the paragraph on a separate sheet of paper and be sure to address the following revision tasks.* *Answers will vary.*

1. *Make sure the topic sentence identifies the term being defined and establishes the purpose for doing so.*

2. *If necessary, add examples and details that will help develop the definition and purpose of the paragraph.*

3. *Move any sentences that are not in the best order to develop the definition in the most effective way.*

4. *Add transitional words or phrases where needed.*

5. *Ensure there is a strong concluding sentence.*

Lishai Goldstein

Professor Briggs

ENC 095

11 December 2010

A "blog," a contraction of the term "web log," is an online journal posted on a website, and it is written and maintained either by an individual or by a corporation or news media company. Blogs usually feature commentary and opinion by individual writers on either a dedicated subject or on various subjects. Some blogs also include video clips and images. Some newspapers have online blog sites too. Some blog sites allow outside contributors to post commentary or to "blog" on the site too. Some blog sites focus on one particular genre, such as Hollywood movies, and some are based on the writer him- or herself and his or her opinion on any subject. A blog is a way for individuals or corporations to inform people of comments and opinions on subjects via the Internet.

PROFESSIONAL DEFINITION PARAGRAPH

The following definition of the term "Addiction" is from the *Free Health Encyclopedia*.

Addiction

Addiction is a dependence on a substance, such as the drug heroin, or a type of behavior, such as gambling, that causes numerous problems for addicts, their families and friends, and society as a whole. At one time, the term "addiction" was used almost exclusively for substance addiction. That is, addicts were thought of as people who were totally dependent on drugs such as heroin, cocaine, nicotine, or alcohol. This form of addiction is now known as "substance addiction." Experts also recognize that people can become addicted to certain behaviors. Some individuals may develop a dependence on gambling, shopping, sexual activity, eating, or other activities. Addictions of this kind are sometimes called "process addictions." Addictions cause enormous personal harm to not only the addict, but to their families and friends as well. People who become addicted to drugs may develop any number of health problems. They may also experience personality changes and lose the ability to interact with other people socially. Addicts may have trouble staying in school or holding a job. If they do hold a job, they may pose a certain risk to their co-workers, to their customers, and to any individuals with whom they interact. For example, a truck driver who is addicted to alcohol may pose a serious safety threat to other drivers on the road. Addiction is also responsible for a host of societal problems. Because many addictions are very expensive, addicts may turn to crime in order to get the money they need.

From *Sick! V1* (http://www.faqs.org/health/Sick-V1/Addiction.html)

Reading Reflection Questions   *Answers will vary. Sample answers provided.*

1. In your own words, how would you define addiction in one sentence, based on the information in this paragraph?

   Answers will vary.
   _____

   _____

2. T/F ___*T*___ Eating can become an addiction.

3. T/F ___*F*___ Only the person who is addicted to something is harmed by that addiction.

4. T/F ___*T*___ Some people turn to crime as a result of addiction.

5. Summarize (in your own words) two of the worst possible effects of addiction.

   Answers will vary.
   _____

   _____

   _____

Checking Vocabulary

Define the following terms using your own words or provide a dictionary definition if you do not know the word.

1. dependence: *reliance upon, need* _____

2. substance: *physical matter of a certain chemical composition, in this* _____
   context an addictive material _____

3. societal: *related to the activities or functions of society* _____

Use the following Critical Thinking Checklist to help you with this reading and for checking any other classification paragraph or writing.

CRITICAL THINKING CHECKLIST

1. What is the author's *purpose* or *goal* in this reading selection?

2. What are the *stated questions* being addressed?

3. What *specific details and examples* does the author use to develop his or her purpose or goal for the reading?

4. What *inferences* does the author include in this reading? (Inferences imply "if this, then this" types of cause/effect analysis.)

5. Who is the intended audience, and how did you reach that conclusion?

Paragraph Writing Assignments

1. Write a definition paragraph using any of the topics you developed in the activities in this chapter.

2. Define a concept from one of your other classes (for instance, a term from economics, history, or biology).

3. Define a concept from your religion or from one of your cultural traditions.

Critical Thinking Journal Prompts

Write a journal reflection entry based on the following prompts:

1. Pick a term from one of your current or past classes and define it for a general audience.

2. Think of one of your family rituals. Freewrite about that ritual for five minutes and then come up with a plan for defining it for someone outside of your family.

3. Look up a term in a dictionary. Analyze the order, structure, and details provided for its definition. Is it effective? Why or why not?

LEARNING OBJECTIVES REVIEW

LO1 How can you use critical thinking to write meaningful definitions? (See p. 201)	**Thinking critically** helps you to determine your purpose, which can range from providing a straightforward definition of an item to providing a definition of a term or concept that includes its symbolic meaning or cultural and historical relevance.
LO2 What questions should you ask before writing a definition paragraph? (See p. 201)	You should ask the following **questions:** (1) What is my purpose for defining this object or concept? (2) Who is my target audience and what do I want them to learn? (3) What general category does my subject fall into and what distinguishing characteristics does it have? (4) Can I compare it to something similar, or can I explain it by saying what it is not? (5) What support can I use? (6) What is the most effective order of development for my paragraph?
LO3 How do you structure a definition paragraph? (See pp. 202–206)	You **structure a definition paragraph** by stating your purpose for defining an item, term, or concept; discussing the general category it fits into; and discussing its distinguishing characteristics by comparing it to similar things and/or by saying what it is not.
LO4 How do you write a definition paragraph? (See pp. 206–211)	To **write a definition paragraph,** create a topic sentence that explains your purpose for defining a specific item, concept, or term; describe the general category the item, term, or concept belongs in; use examples and comparisons to clarify your definition and support the point of your paragraph; and write a concluding sentence that sums up the purpose of your definition.

For support in meeting this chapter's objectives, log in to www.mywritinglab.com and select **Paragraph Development— Definition.**

Kids on a Fence   Tom Shugrue

LEARNING OBJECTIVES

In this chapter, you will learn to

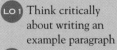 Think critically about writing an example paragraph

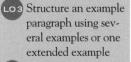 Ask questions to prepare to write using examples

LO3 Structure an example paragraph using several examples or one extended example

LO4 Write example and illustration paragraphs

THINKING CRITICALLY

1. Briefly describe the children in the picture above.

_____

_____

2. Based on these boys' facial expressions and body language, guess what type of personalities they have. Use their expressions and postures as **examples** to justify your assumptions about their personalities.

_____

_____

215

LO 1   EXAMPLE AND ILLUSTRATION PARAGRAPHS

Example and illustration paragraphs use examples to illustrate, clarify, explain, and support ideas. Examples are often facts or examples taken from personal experience. Several examples can be used in combination to support a topic sentence, or a single extended example can be used to develop a point.

Critical Thinking and Example and Illustration

In example paragraphs, use concrete examples (specific examples, not vague ideas) to illustrate the point you want to make about a topic. Before you begin generating examples, you need to have a clear idea of the point you want to illustrate and whether using an extended example or several related examples would be most effective.

APPLYING CRITICAL THINKING

PURPOSE   IDEAS   SUPPORT   ASSUMPTIONS BIASES   CONCLUSIONS   POINT OF VIEW   ANALYSIS

To write an effective example paragraph, you need to consider the following questions:

1. What is my **purpose** for writing this example/illustrative paragraph? What **idea** do I want to convey to my audience?

2. What **support** do I need to include? What **examples** (a series of examples to support your purpose or an extended example to illustrate your point) and **details** (descriptive details, facts, and sensory descriptions) can I include to develop my paragraph?

3. Have I thoroughly **analyzed** my purpose and chosen strong examples to develop it?

LO 2 PREPARING TO WRITE AN EXAMPLE PARAGRAPH

Before you begin to write an example paragraph on an assigned topic, or one you have chosen, start by asking yourself these questions:

1. What point am I trying to make?
2. What single, extended example or series of related example (facts, testimony, and experiences) can I include to illustrate my purpose?
3. What details should I provide to further illustrate my examples?
4. How should I organize this paragraph, and how should I conclude it?

Answering these questions will lead you to an expository topic sentence, help you determine which example or examples to include for support, and give you a general idea of how you want to organize and develop your paragraph.

ACTIVITY 11-1   Generating Examples

Directions: *For each of the following topics, brainstorm three examples you could use to develop it.*

1. Topic: Popular music

   Example 1: _____

   Example 2: _____

   Example 3: _____

2. Topic: Fast-food restaurants

   Example 1: _____

   Example 2: _____

   Example 3: _____

3. Topic: On-campus job opportunities

   Example 1: _____

   Example 2: _____

   Example 3: _____

LO 3   STRUCTURING AN EXAMPLE PARAGRAPH

All paragraphs depend on examples and illustrations to develop and support their topic sentences. Providing concrete examples for your readers is one of the best ways to convince them about the point you want to make. In your **topic sentence,** set up the overall purpose of your paragraph: the controlling idea your examples will illustrate. Then pick the most effective order to present your examples so that they powerfully illustrate your purpose. For instance, you might choose to provide your examples in a most to least important order or vice versa, or in chronological order.

Cross Reference

See Chapter 3 for more on choosing an effective order for your paragraph.

Next, use two to four examples or one extended example to illustrate and explain the purpose of your topic sentence. For instance, if you are explaining how important baseball players are as everyday heroes for kids, you can include several examples of current baseball stars, or one extended example of a baseball hero who embodies all the best role model qualities, such as Ichiro Suzuki. Your examples should be vivid and interesting, but not too unfamiliar to your readers. Most importantly, the examples should clearly demonstrate the point(s) your topic sentence sets out to make. Be sure to incorporate as many details and concrete images as possible into your examples, and use transitions to lead your reader smoothly from one example to the next. Transitional phrases such as "for example," "to illustrate," and "for instance" are useful for introducing the examples you provide to make your points. Finally, in the **concluding sentence** of your paragraph, re-emphasize the purpose you want to express to your readers through the examples you have chosen.

Cross Reference

See p. 225 for a list of transitional words and phrases.

Model Student Paragraph

Topic sentence introduces the topic that will be explained through examples

Order of importance, least to most, used in this paragraph

Example 1

Detail 1 for example 1

Example 2

Poker is a game that requires knowledge of what constitutes a winning hand. Lots of beginning card players love poker, but many people, unless they are poker regulars, do not know which hands are ranked the highest and in what order. However, specific rules for how to rank the value of hands do exist. First, the lowest hand a player can win with is the highest card. In this case, if no one even has a pair, then the player with the highest card, for instance an ace, wins. The next level winning hand is one pair, meaning two cards that are the same value, or a card with a wild card. If two or more players have a pair at the end, the pair with the highest value wins, for example, two kings would win over two eights. Similarly, the next highest winning hand is two pairs. Again, if more than one player has two pairs at the end, the highest value pairs wins. For example, if one player has two twos and two fours and another has two eights and two queens, the second player wins. The next level is three of a kind. After these hands, things get a little more complicated. For example, the next level hand is a straight: cards ordered in sequence, no matter what their suit (see diagram). Then, even higher, is a flush: in this hand, the cards are all the same suit, no matter their numbers (see diagram). Following the flush is a full house: three of a kind and a pair together in the same hand. After that comes four of a kind. Finally, there are the two highest and rarest hands. First, there is the straight flush, in which the cards are numbered in sequence and are all from the same suit (see diagram). Lastly, the highest winning hand in poker is the royal straight flush, where the cards are not only in sequence and from the same suit but are also all royal cards. As explained here, there is a clear hierarchy of winning hands, and knowing them increases a player's chances of doing well in poker.

Detail 1 for example 2

Example 3

Detail 1 and 2 for example 3

Example 4

Example 5

Example 6 and detail for example 6

Example 7

Example 8

Example 9 and supporting details

Examples 10 and supporting details

Concluding sentence reiterates topic sentence, restating the main point of the paragraph

The chart below provides a brief overview of the structure of an illustration/example paragraph.

Poker Winning Hands Diagram

Pair		
Two pairs		
Three of a kind		

Straight		3♦	4♦	5♣	6♣ 7♣
Flush		3♦	4♦	6♦	8♦ J♦
Full house		6♣	6♣	6♦	5♣ 5♦
Four of a kind		7♣	7♦	7♥	7♣
Straight flush		3♦	4♦	5♦	6♦ 7♦
Royal straight flush		10♣	J♣	Q♣	K♣ A♣

BASIC STRUCTURE FOR AN EXAMPLE PARAGRAPH

TOPIC SENTENCE

State the main **idea** of your paragraph and describe your **purpose**, what you are trying to explain, show, prove, or argue by using examples—and what conclusions you reached by developing your topic

SUPPORT

Include examples (one extended or several related ones)

Provide concrete details, facts, and descriptions to describe and explain the examples

Use transitions within the paragraph to make the sentences flow smoothly

ANALYSIS

Add commentary and analysis about the examples and details to help develop the purpose of the topic sentence

CONCLUDING SENTENCE

Sum up and re-emphasize the topic sentence: the **conclusions reached** by illustrating your topic through examples

ACTIVITY 11-2 Identifying the Elements of an Example Paragraph

Directions: *Read the paragraph below. Then, perform the following tasks.*

1. *Underline the topic sentence.*

2. *Double-underline each sentence that provides an example that supports the topic sentence.*

3. *Write a D over any sentence or part of a sentence that provides a specific detail that supports or illustrates an example.*

4. *Highlight any word or phrase that serves as a transition from one step to the next.*

Bayleigh Steinburg

Professor Jack

English 092

11 May 2010

Writing a successful resume for an entry-level job requires that you include specific information and use a commonly accepted format. It is important that the resume you send out is current and complete. Also, there is a standard format for presenting information that you should follow. First, list your contact information at the top of your resume. Include your full name, address, phone number, and email address. Next, include a section about your educational experience. Here you should list the colleges you attended, the degrees you attained, and any special awards and honors you earned. For example, if you won an award for Top Humanities Student, include that honor. In addition, if you graduated with honors, list that detail too. The next section of your resume should detail your work history. Here you should list the companies you have worked for, including dates of employment and the positions you held, as well as a bulleted list of your responsibilities and achievements. If you have completed internships, it's fine to include them in the experience section of your resume. You can also include summer jobs. In addition, list any skills you have learned, such as computer programming or office management, that would be useful for the job for which you are applying. Finally, provide references or a statement that references are available upon request. If you follow these basic guidelines, you should have a strong, clear resume.

LO 4 WRITING AN EXAMPLE PARAGRAPH

Topic

If you have been assigned an example paragraph, be sure to read the assignment carefully to make sure you understand what is being asked, and then prewrite to come up with relevant examples. If you do not have a topic assigned by your instructor, then brainstorm ideas for people, places, things, or events you might want to describe. Then, come up with some ideas for a purpose for describing the topic. What do you want your readers to understand through your use of examples?

A Few Topic Possibilities

Many topics work for writing an example paragraph. You could write an example paragraph that illustrates the kinds of cars you can buy in America, the variety of food and interesting cuisines available in your town or city, or the types of clothing currently popular on your campus. Here are some other possibilities:

- Types of hybrid cars
- Alternative energy sources
- New ways to access music

- Political groups on campus
- Volunteer work opportunities
- Good places for spring vacation

Topic Sentence

The **topic sentence** in an illustration paragraph states the purpose for writing about the topic. It must be an idea that needs to be demonstrated through the use of examples. It should not be just a fact or detail.

Fact or detail: Email is composed on the computer and sent through cyberspace. (While this information is true, there is no point here that needs development, just a statement of facts).

Converted to a topic sentence: There are several rules you can follow to ensure that workplace emails are efficient and professional.

Using this revised topic sentence, you could develop the idea with examples and also have a purpose: showing your readers how they should write when emailing from work.

ACTIVITY 11-3   Creating Topic Sentences

Directions: *Create a* ***topic sentence*** *for each of the following topics. Make sure that the point you want to make about the topic is something that needs to be demonstrated through examples.*

1. Music downloads: _____

_____

2. Green energy: _____

_____

3. Internet dating: _____

_____

Support

After you have created a topic sentence with a point you want to make, you need to come up with support for it by providing an extended single example or two to four related examples that illustrate your purpose. For instance, for the topic sentence, "There are several rules you can follow to ensure that workplace emails are efficient and professional," one possible supporting example would be "Do not write in capitals."

ACTIVITY 11-4   Providing Examples

Directions: *For each of the topic sentences you created in Activity 11-3, list one to three examples you could use to provide support for it.*

1. Music downloads: _____

   _____

2. Green energy: _____

   _____

3. Internet dating: _____

   _____

Next, you need to develop your examples using specific details. Details are like examples for your examples. You should provide a detail to further develop most examples. For instance, for the example, "Do not write in capitals," you could add the following detail: "If, for instance, you capitalize the words 'WRITE ME BACK,' the capital letters imply that you are yelling at the person, which he or she could find annoying or offensive."

ACTIVITY 11-5   Providing Details

Directions: *For each topic, provide one detail that supports one of the examples you listed in Activity 11-4 for that topic.*

1. Music downloads: _____

   _____

2. Green energy: _____

   _____

3. Internet dating: _____

   _____

Useful transitions to use in example paragraphs include transitions to show another point, to provide examples, and to show purpose.

TRANSITIONS TO . . .

Show Addition of Another Point

again	but also	in addition	nor
also	equally important	last	plus the fact
and	finally	lastly	secondly
and then	first	likewise	then too
another	further	moreover	thirdly
besides	furthermore	next	too

Illustrate or Give Examples/Specifics

a few include	essentially	in particular	the following
an example	for example	let us consider	specifically
especially	for instance	the case of	you can see this in

Show Purpose

all things considered	for this reason	to accomplish	with this in mind
for this purpose	in order to	to this end	with this objective

Concluding Sentence

The **concluding sentence** for your example paragraph should recap your purpose for writing the paragraph. For instance, for the topic sentence, "There are several rules you can follow to ensure that workplace emails are efficient and professional," a possible concluding sentence that would reiterate this point without repeating it word for word would be "In essence, there are specific guidelines people can use to ensure their workplace emails are concise, polite, and effective."

ACTIVITY 11-6   Writing a Concluding Sentence

Directions: *Based on your answers to Activities 11-3, 11-4, and 11-5, write a* ***concluding sentence*** *for each topic.*

1. Music downloads: _____

_____

2. Green energy: _____

_____

3. Internet dating: _____

_____

Revise and Edit

Remember to revise your paragraph draft for the best results. Use the following critique form to check for the basics in your example paragraph draft.

EXAMPLE PARAGRAPH CRITIQUE FORM

	Done well	Needs work
1. Is there a strong topic sentence that states the purpose of the paragraph?	_____	_____
2. Are there enough examples to explain and illustrate the main idea of the paragraph?	_____	_____
3. Are there enough details to develop the examples?	_____	_____
4. Are transitions used to help one example flow to the next?	_____	_____
5. Does the concluding sentence sum up the main point of the paragraph without repeating the topic sentence?	_____	_____

Editing

Circle the following errors you think you see in this draft: spelling, fragments, run-ons, comma splices, commas, semicolon/colon use, pronoun agreement, reference fault errors, parallelism, apostrophe use, verb use/tense, and passive voice construction. (See Parts V and VI for help identifying and correcting these errors.)

Other types of grammar or sentence-level errors you noticed in this draft:

_____

Comments:

_____

_____

ACTIVITY 11-7   Revising an Example Paragraph

Directions: *Carefully read the following student paragraph. Then, use the critique form to evaluate it. Finally, revise and rewrite the paragraph on a separate sheet of paper and be sure to address the following editing tasks.*   Answers will vary.

1. Check that the topic sentence clearly states the topic and purpose of the paragraph. Revise if necessary.

2. Move any sentences that are not in the most effective order, and revise them if they are vague or unclear.

3. Add transitional words or phrases where needed.

4. Add examples and details where necessary to help develop the purpose of the paragraph.

5. Check that the paragraph has an effective concluding sentence that restates the point of the paragraph.

Robynne Knight

Professor Hoene

ENC 0010

10 December 2010

  Naturopathic medicine focuses on natural health and on the body's ability to heal itself, and it features an interesting variety of methods and practices. Acupuncture is a practice that involves using tiny needles that are inserted into the body at key points to relieve pain. Reflexology focuses on applying pressure or rubbing particular spots in the feet or hands that correspond to internal organs or other parts of the body. Reflexologists believe that the life energy of the body must flow well to be healthy. Reflexology treatments help free the life flow again. Acupuncture is also related to the body's life energy. Herbalism is a traditional folk medicine practice based on the use of plants and plant extracts. Herbalism is also known as botanical medicine, and it is a regular aspect of naturopathic medicine. These various types of naturo-pathic treatments work with the natural healing powers of the body to help people.

Many professional authors use the example mode to convey messages. The following excerpt from Rachel Carson's *Silent Spring* uses specific examples to illustrate the deadly effects of DDT and other chemicals.

PROFESSIONAL EXAMPLE PARAGRAPH

Excerpt from *Silent Spring*

Rachel Carson

Rachel Carson (1907–1964) published *Silent Spring* in 1962, first as a series in *The New Yorker*, then as a book. In the 1950s Carson saw the rapid increase in artificial pesticide and herbicide spraying by farmers and government agencies and the negative effects on insects, birds, fish populations, and the overall food chain. Her work helped begin an investigation of the pesticide industry, which led ultimately to the Pesticide Control Act of 1972. Carson did not live to see this consequence of her work, dying of cancer in 1964.

Topic sentence

Soon after the spraying had ended there were unmistakable signs that all was not well. Within two days dead and dying fish, including many young salmon, were found along the banks of the stream. Brook trout also appeared among the dead fish, and along the roads and in the woods birds were dying. All the life of the stream was stilled. Before the spraying there had been a rich assortment of the water life that forms the food of salmon and trout—caddis fly larvae, living in loosely fitting protective cases of leaves, stems or gravel cemented together with saliva, stonefly nymphs clinging to rocks in the swirling currents, and the wormlike larvae of blackflies edging the stones under riffles or where the stream spills over steeply slanting rocks. But now the stream insects were dead, killed by DDT, and there was nothing for a young salmon to eat.

Reading Reflection Questions

1. Underline the topic sentence of the paragraph. Then explain briefly how it sets up a presentation of examples.

It indicates that there were signs that all was not well soon after the

spraying took place, which sets up a discussion of examples of these signs.

2. List two examples the author provides of the damage caused by spraying.

Answers will vary. 1. Within two days, dead and dying fish, including many

young salmon, were found along the banks of the stream. 2. All the life of

the stream was stilled.

3. List one detail the author gives to illustrate one of the examples she provides.

Answers will vary. "stonefly nymphs clinging to rocks in the swirling cur-

rents, and the wormlike larvae of blackflies edging the stones under riffles

or where the stream spills over steeply slanting rocks."

Checking Vocabulary

Define each of the following terms in your own words or provide a dictionary defi-nition if you don't know it.

4. larvae: *newly hatched, wingless form of insects, prior to adulthood*

5. DDT: *dichloro-diphenyl-trichloroethane, a synthetic pesticide*

CRITICAL THINKING CHECKLIST

1. What is the author's *purpose* or *goal* in this reading selection?

2. What are the *stated questions* being addressed?

3. What *specific details and examples* does the author use to develop his or her purpose or goal for the reading?

4. Are there any *implied messages* in this reading (hinted at but not directly stated)? If so, what are they? Also, is there a cause and effect relationship (if this happens, then this will follow)—direct or implied?

5. Who is the intended *audience,* and how did you reach that conclusion?

Paragraph Writing Assignments

1. Choose one of the topics you developed in the activities in this chapter and write a full example/illustration paragraph on that topic.
2. Write a paragraph about a genre of music (e.g., jazz, hip hop, rap, classical, rock, country, etc.) and provide several examples to illustrate your point about the genre.
3. Write a paragraph about types of fast food.
4. Write a paragraph about your best friend, using examples to explain and support why he or she is special to you.
5. Write a paragraph illustrating different kinds of rude behavior.

Critical Thinking Journal Prompts

Write a journal reflection entry based on one of the following prompts:

1. Brainstorm a list of examples of the kinds of writing you've had to do in the classroom and out of the classroom where you've needed to develop your points and ideas through examples. What did the examples do to develop your ideas?
2. Write a paragraph about friends and include three of your friends as examples of the types of friends you have.
3. Brainstorm a list of hobbies. Then, pick three and write about the benefits of pursuing each one.

LEARNING OBJECTIVES REVIEW

LO1 What do you want to achieve by thinking critically about writing an example paragraph? (See p. 216)	**Thinking critically** helps you determine the purpose of your example paragraph and decide whether one extended example or series of examples will best help develop and support that purpose.
LO2 What questions should you ask before writing an example paragraph? (See p. 217)	You should ask the following **questions:** (1) What point am I trying to make? (2) What single, extended example or series of related examples (facts, testimony, and experiences) can I include to clearly illustrate my purpose? (3) What details should I provide to further illustrate my examples? (4) How should I organize this paragraph, and how should I conclude it?
LO3 How do you structure an example paragraph? (See pp. 218–222)	You **structure an example paragraph** by clearly stating the point you want to illustrate using several vivid, interesting examples that clearly demonstrate your point, or one extended one that does so, and using time order or order of importance to organize your examples.
LO4 How do you write an example paragraph? (See pp. 222–226)	To **write an example paragraph,** create a topic sentence that identifies your topic and the point about it that you want to illustrate using a series of concrete, vivid examples, or one extended example, supported by details to illustrate your point, and conclude with a sentence that restates your purpose.

PEARSON
mywritinglab

For support in meeting this chapter's objectives, log in to www.mywritinglab.com and select **Paragraph Development— Illustrating.**

 **Cause and Effect**

LEARNING OBJECTIVES

In this chapter, you will learn to

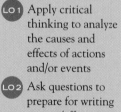

LO 1 Apply critical thinking to analyze the causes and effects of actions and/or events

LO 2 Ask questions to prepare for writing a cause/effect paragraph

LO 3 Structure a cause and effect paragraph

LO 4 Write a cause and effect paragraph

THINKING CRITICALLY

Look at the photo above from the March 11, 2011 Japanese tsunami. In the space below, list what the *cause(s)* (or reason(s)) was for this *effect* (or result).

Cause (reason): _____

_____

Effect (result):_____

_____

LO 1   CAUSE AND EFFECT PARAGRAPHS

A **cause and effect** paragraph looks at a cause(s), what led to a certain result or *why* something happens, and its effect(s), the consequences or the *results* of an action or event. Cause and effect analysis comes in handy in many aspects of college and career writing, including science and sociology classes, and careers that involve a great deal of causal analysis.

A cause and effect paragraph may focus on just a single cause and a single effect, or it may reflect a series of effects resulting from a single cause, or a series of causes that led to a particular effect. For instance, a friend could compliment you if you wear a new outfit (single cause, single effect), or not sleeping (single cause) could lead to several negative effects such as exhaustion, difficulty concentrating, irritability, and depression. Rainfall and dropping temperatures are two causes that lead to snow (a single effect), and so on.

Critical Thinking and Cause and Effect

Cause and effect analysis helps your readers understand complicated events. The careful examination of the *befores* and *afters* of a specific event, for instance, can help readers understand why it happened, its consequences, and how it could be avoided or maybe, if it was positive, repeated in the future. The analysis can also help you convince your readers of an argument you want to get across, for instance, that they should stop eating fast food due to the risks to their health.

APPLYING CRITICAL THINKING

PURPOSE   IDEAS   SUPPORT   ASSUMPTIONS BIASES   CONCLUSIONS   POINT OF VIEW   ANALYSIS

You see the causes and effects of actions and events every day. The sink blocks up and floods the kitchen because you poured fat into it, you get a ticket because you forgot to put money in the meter, or you get an A on a paper because you spent time researching and thinking about your topic. To write an effective cause and effect essay, you need to identify the event or action you want to discuss and then **analyze** the causes (reasons) for it occurring and the effects (results) of it happening. Based on your analysis, you can then determine your **purpose** for writing about the event or action.

LO 2 PREPARING TO WRITE A CAUSE AND EFFECT PARAGRAPH

Before you begin to write a cause and effect paragraph, start by asking yourself these questions:

1. What is the subject of my cause and effect analysis?

2. What was the cause(s) of the event or process?

3. What is the result(s), or effect, of this process or event?

4. What do I want my readers to learn from this cause and effect analysis?

Answering these questions will lead you to an expository topic sentence, help you determine the causes and effects you want to focus on, decide on the examples and details to include to support them, and give you a general idea of how you want to organize your paragraph.

ACTIVITY 12-1   Generating Cause and Effect Topics

Directions: *Brainstorm a list of possible causes and effects for the following broad subjects.*

1. Indigestion

Cause(s): _____   Effect(s): _____

_____   _____

2. Overfishing the oceans

Cause(s): _____   Effect(s): _____

_____   _____

3. Too much TV watching

Cause(s): _____   Effect(s): _____

_____   _____

LO 3 STRUCTURING A CAUSE AND EFFECT PARAGRAPH

The point of analyzing causes and effects is to look at the reasons why things happen and/or the results of them happening in order to understand them better and possibly to take action. For example, once it was understood that smoking causes many serious health conditions, labels were required on cigarette packages to warn consumers of the dangers of smoking.

When analyzing events, you first need to check for a causal relationship. Did one idea or event lead to another idea or event or is the apparent relationship coincidental? For example, if you see a shooting star and minutes later your TV has bad reception, it is most likely just a coincidence. However, if you are experiencing an electrical storm and after a particularly intense lightning strike your power goes out, most likely there is a causal relationship. If there is a causal relationship, ask yourself, what was the cause (or causes), and what was the effect (or effects)?

Once you determine there is a cause and effect relationship, you need to decide what you want to explain to your readers about it. Do you want to inform your readers of a process? Do you want to explain the process in order to critique its effects or causes or both? For example, if you were writing about health and exercise, you could explain the beneficial effects of exercise on one's health (weight loss, increased stamina, and an improved cardiovascular capacity) in order to convince your readers to engage in more exercise. Or, you could focus on the negative effects of too little exercise (weight gain, decreased strength and flexibility, and possible medical problems) to accomplish the same goal.

Next, you need to organize your paragraph in the best way to provide effective support for your topic sentence. When you look at the effects of one particular event or incident, it may help to think of the "domino effect" (see page 3): the dominos are lined up, then one is knocked over, and they fall over one by one and lead to an overall change in the structure. The initial push of the first domino would be the initial cause, and the dominos that fall one by one are the effects. It is a chain reaction: cause–effect–cause–effect, and so on.

Depending on your assignment and topic, you may analyze one cause and several effects, one effect and several causes, or several causes and several effects.

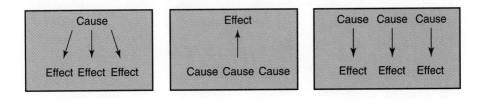

In each of the patterns diagrammed in the boxes, your paragraph would focus on the cause(s) and/or effect(s) you have established in your topic sentence. Use transitional words and phrases between the causes and/or effects you are providing as examples. Then, conclude your paragraph with a sentence that sums up and ties back in to your original topic sentence.

▶ NOTE   Use the word *effect* (a **noun**) when you are writing about results: The teacher could immediately see the *effect* of her lecture. Use the word *affect* (a **verb**) when you are writing about the action of the cause: The heat *affected* his mood.

Model Student Paragraph

David Nelson

Professor Moreno

English 082

24 November 2009

Topic sentence indicates that paragraph will discuss the negative effects of texting in classrooms

Example of effect 1

Order of importance, most to least important, used in this paragraph

Detail supporting effect 1

Example of effect 2

Detail supporting effect 2

Example of effect 3
Detail supporting effect 3

Concluding sentence reiterates topic sentence and purpose of paragraph

Cell phone texting in the classroom causes many negative effects, both for the people doing the texting and for others in the classroom. First of all, if students text while the professor is talking or a classroom activity is in progress, then they are not paying attention and therefore will not learn. For instance, if an instructor is discussing mathematical formulas that are crucial to solving certain problems, students risk not learning the tools they need to be successful in the class if they are texting under their desks. Texting can also be disruptive to classmates. It can be very distracting to have someone clicking away on his or her cell phone buttons when one is trying to listen, take notes, and understand complicated concepts. Finally, texting in the classroom is disrespectful to the instructor. Students who text during class send the message, intended or not, that what the instructor is saying or doing in the classroom is not important or worthy of full attention. For many reasons, texting in the classroom is a bad idea for all involved.

BASIC STRUCTURE FOR A CAUSE AND EFFECT PARAGRAPH

TOPIC SENTENCE

State the main **idea** of your paragraph and describe your **purpose**, what you are trying to explain, show, prove, or argue in your cause and effect paragraph

SUPPORT

Include examples to illustrate the purpose

Provide concrete details, facts, and description to describe and explain the examples

Use transitions within the paragraph to make the sentences flow smoothly

ANALYSIS

Add commentary and analysis about the examples and details to help develop the purpose of the topic sentence

CONCLUDING SENTENCE

Sum up and re-emphasize the topic sentence: the **conclusions reached** by illustrating your topic through cause and effect analysis

ACTIVITY 12-2 **Identifying the Elements of a Cause and Effect Paragraph**

Directions: *Read the paragraph below. Then, perform the following tasks.*

1. *Underline the topic sentence.*

2. *Write a C at the beginning of each sentence that states a cause for cheating on math exams.*

3. *Write an E at the beginning of each sentence that provides an effect of cheating on exams.*

4. *Highlight any word or phrase that serves as a transition from one cause or effect to the next.*

Aubrie Snieder

Professor Lear

English 082

22 May 2009

Students who cheat on math tests do so for a variety of rea-

sons, none of which are acceptable. The pressure to do well on tests

because math is a requirement for most majors leads some students

to cheat. Other students have struggled with math since elementary

school, never really understanding the basic concepts, and therefore

never able to confidently move on to the next level. For them, math

is a roadblock to their success and they cheat in an attempt to

overcome it. Another reason students cheat seems to be the format of

the tests: unlike essay or short-answer tests that require broad

knowledge of a subject, math relies heavily on formulas, theorems,

and equations that are easily written down and smuggled into class.

Furthermore, many students need to complete a sequence of math

courses as prerequisites for their majors, so they are more tempted

to do whatever it takes to move through the math "hoops" as quickly

and as easily as possible. However, no matter what the reason is for

cheating on a math test, it is never a good idea. Doing so can result

in not learning or understanding important information, experienc-

ing difficulty keeping up with subsequent material, and possibly

losing a grade or being disciplined by the college. Cheating is never

justified. As the saying goes, "Those who cheat only cheat themselves

out of learning."

WRITING A CAUSE AND EFFECT PARAGRAPH

Topic

If you have been assigned a cause and effect topic, be sure to read the assignment carefully to make sure you understand what is being asked, and then prewrite to come up with examples and details related to the purpose for writing about the topic. If you do not have a topic assigned by your instructor, brainstorm a list of events or processes you could discuss. Then, come up with some ideas for a purpose for looking at the causes and/or effects of these processes or events.

A Few Topic Possibilities

You can write a paragraph looking at the causes and/or effects of any of the following subjects:

- A medical condition
- A medical treatment
- Depression or another mental disorder
- A natural disaster

- Global warming
- Cuts in funding to a program or service personally important to you or someone you know
- Lying to a friend or partner

The key is to look at either what caused something to occur or what happened after something occurred, or both.

Topic Sentence

The topic sentence states the purpose of your cause and effect paragraph, what you are going to discuss and why. In it, you establish whether you are focusing on just causes, just effects, or both, and what you want your readers to understand. For example, if you were writing about how exercise helps with sleeping disorders, your topic sentence might establish both a causal relationship and an argument:

A regular exercise routine helps to alleviate sleeping problems for several reasons.

ACTIVITY 12-3   Creating Topic Sentences

Directions: *Create a **topic sentence** for each of the following topics. Make sure that the point you want to make about the topic is something that can be demonstrated through cause and effect analysis.* Answers will vary.

1. Technology in the classroom: _____

_____

2. Internet dating: _____

_____

3. Teenage pregnancy: _____

_____

Support

After you have written your topic sentence, think about what kind of examples and details would support it. For instance, a possible supporting example for the topic sentence, "A regular exercise routine helps alleviate sleeping problems for several reasons," could be the following:

> When a person exercises, endorphins—chemicals that transmit messages within the nervous system—are released in the brain and create a feeling of well-being that can help a person relax.

ACTIVITY 12-4   Providing Cause and Effect Supporting Examples

Directions: *For each of the topic sentences you wrote in Activity 12-3, provide **a cause or an effect example** that supports it.* Answers will vary.

1. Technology in the classroom: _____

_____

2. Internet dating: _____

_____

3. Teenage pregnancy: _____

_____

Next, you need to develop your examples by using specific details. For instance, in the paragraph about cheating on math tests, the example of smuggling in formulas could be elaborated on by providing a specific detail such as writing an algebraic formula on the palm of one's hand.

ACTIVITY 12-5   Providing Details

Directions: *For each of the examples you developed in Activity 12-4, provide one detail that supports it.*

1. Technology in the classroom: _____

   _____

2. Internet dating: _____

   _____

3. Teenage pregnancy: _____

   _____

Use transitional words and phrases to lead your readers from one cause or effect to the next. Here are some transitions that are useful in writing cause and effect paragraphs.

TRANSITIONS TO . . .

Illustrate or Give Examples/Specifics

a few include	essentially	in particular	the following
an example	for example	let us consider	specifically
especially	for instance	the case of	you can see this in

Result and/or Cause/Effect Relationships

accordingly	consequently	since	therefore
as a result	for this reason	so	thereupon
because	hence	then	thus

Show Purpose

all things considered	for this reason	to accomplish	with this in mind
for this purpose	in order to	to this end	with this objective

Concluding Sentence

Your concluding sentence should briefly recap your cause and effect analysis and the purpose of your paragraph. Re-emphasize what you want your readers to understand about the cause and effect connections you have discussed in your paragraph.

ACTIVITY 12-6   Concluding Sentences

Directions: *For each topic, write a **concluding sentence** based on your answers to Activities 12-3, 12-4, and 12-5.*   *Answers will vary.*

1. Technology in the classroom: _____

_____

2. Internet dating: _____

_____

3. Teenage pregnancy: _____

_____

Revise and Edit

Remember to revise your paragraph draft for the best results. Use the following critique form to check for the basics in your cause and effect paragraph draft.

CAUSE AND EFFECT PARAGRAPH CRITIQUE FORM

	Done well	Needs work
1. Is there a strong topic sentence that states the purpose of the paragraph?	_____	_____
2. Are there enough cause and effect examples to explain and illustrate the purpose of the paragraph?	_____	_____
3. Are there enough details to develop and elaborate on the examples?	_____	_____
4. Are transitions used to help one cause and effect example flow to the next?	_____	_____
5. Does the concluding sentence sum up the main point of the paragraph without repeating the topic sentence?	_____	_____

Editing

Circle the following errors you think you see in this draft: spelling, fragments, run-ons, comma splices, commas, semicolon/colon use, pronoun agreement, reference fault errors, parallelism, apostrophe use, verb use/tense, and passive voice construction. (See Parts V and VI for help identifying and correcting these errors.)

Other types of grammar or sentence-level errors you noticed in this draft:

_____

Comments:

_____

_____

ACTIVITY 12-7   Revising the Paragraph

Directions: *Carefully read the following student paragraph. Then, use the critique form to evaluate it. Finally, revise and rewrite the paragraph on a separate sheet of paper and be sure to address the following editing tasks.*   Answers will vary.

1. *Make sure the topic sentence clearly states the purpose for the cause and effect analysis and revise it if necessary.*

2. *Move any sentences that are not in the most effective order.*

3. *Review the examples and details that develop the cause and effect analysis in the paragraph. Add new ones or change existing ones if necessary.*

4. *Add transitional words or phrases where needed.*

5. *Check the concluding sentence to make sure it reiterates the purpose of the topic sentence, and revise or add to it if necessary.*

Terrill Harding

Professor Ball

English 90

3 April 2009

     Sleep deprivation can happen for a number of reasons and can lead to devastating physical and mental effects. When people are too stressed, it can affect their sleeping patterns. A lack of exercise can contribute to sleep problems. Stress can cause nighttime anxiety too. When someone doesn't get enough sleep, he or she can be sluggish mentally. People can become depressed when they go too long without enough sleep. A lack of sleep causes one's immune system to suffer. Stress and the immune system are directly related too. People who don't get enough sleep catch more colds and viruses than people who get enough sleep. The causes and the effects of not getting enough sleep are very serious.

PROFESSIONAL CAUSE AND EFFECT PARAGRAPH

Fundamental Causes of Air Pollution

www.tropical-rainforest-animals.com

In the last 200 years or so there appeared several fundamental trends which became the major forces behind the surge in levels of air pollution throughout the globe. *Industrialization* is the first fundamental pollution cause. Among other things, industrialization set in motion the widespread use of fossil fuels (oil, gas & coal) which are now *the* main pollution sources. *Population growth* is the second fundamental pollution cause. With population numbers literally exploding around the world, the demand for food and other goods goes up. This demand is met by expanded production and use of natural resources, which in its turn leads to higher levels of environmental pollution in general, and air pollution in particular. *Globalization* is the third major pollution cause. Globalization has become an effective facilitator of air pollution. Developing countries usually have much looser laws on environmental protection. With this "benefit" as well as the population growth and easy availability of cheap labor, big industry prefers to move its facilities to such "pollution havens" rather than work in more regulated markets. So we won't be wrong if we consider industrialization, population growth and globalization the fundamental drivers of pollution, the very roots of the gigantic pollution tree.

Reading Reflection Questions   *Answers will vary. Sample answers provided.*

1. List the three main causes of air pollution according to this paragraph.

   Industrialization, population growth, and globalization

2. T/F ___*T*___ According to this article, human activity has been a major factor in air pollution.

3. List some of the negative effects of the increasing growth of the human population.

   Higher demand for food and other goods, expanded production and use of

   natural resources, increased pollution and environmental damage

4. T/F ___*F*___ All countries have the same anti-pollution laws.

5. T/F ___*T*___ Dependency on fossil fuels contributes to air pollution.

Checking Vocabulary

Define the following words in your own words or provide a dictionary definition if you do not know the word.

6. industrialization: *move from agriculturally based society to one reliant on*

   development of large-scale industry, manufacturing, and marketing

7. globalization: *development of a world economy*

8. havens: *places offering favorable conditions*

CRITICAL THINKING CHECKLIST

1. What is the author's *purpose* or *goal* in this reading selection?
2. What are the *stated questions* being addressed?
3. What *specific details and examples* does the author use to develop his or her purpose or goal for the reading?
4. Are there any implied messages in this reading (hinted at but not directly stated)? If so, what are they? Also, is there a cause and effect relationship (if this happens, then this will follow)—direct or implied?
5. Who is the intended audience, and how did you reach that conclusion?

Paragraph Writing Assignments

1. Write a paragraph that illustrates the negative effects of eating too much.

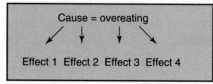

2. Write a paragraph that focuses on the potential causes of eating too much.

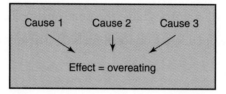

3. Write a paragraph that explores a chain reaction, or domino effect, where there is a sequence of one cause leading to an effect that starts a second cause that leads to a second effect, and so on.

4. Write a cause/effect paragraph on any of the subjects you worked on in the activities in this chapter.

Critical Thinking Journal Prompts

Write a journal reflection entry using one of the following prompts:

1. How does looking at the causes of an event improve your understanding of it? Write about an example from your own life. Trace the causes that led up to a situation, and explain what you learned as a result of examining those causes.

2. Now, write about the effects the above situation has had on your life or on people you know.

3. Freewrite for 10 minutes about the causes and/or effects of your choice to go to college.

LEARNING OBJECTIVES REVIEW

LO1 How can you use critical thinking to analyze causes and/or effects of actions or events? (See p. 233)	**Thinking critically** about what happened before and after a specific event allows you to analyze what caused it, the consequences of the event, how it could be avoided in the future, or, if it was a positive event, how to ensure it happens again.
LO2 What questions should you ask before writing a cause and effect paragraph? (See p. 234)	You should ask the following **questions:** (1) What is the subject of my cause and effect analysis? (2) What was the cause(s) of the event or process? (3) What is the result(s), or effect, of this process or event? (4) What do I want readers to learn from this cause and effect analysis?
LO3 How do you structure a cause and effect paragraph? (See pp. 234–238)	You **structure a cause and effect paragraph** by stating your purpose for analyzing the causes and/or effects of a process or event using examples and details to analyze one cause and several effects, several causes and one effect, or several causes and several effects.
LO4 How do you write a cause and effect paragraph? (See pp. 239–243)	To **write a cause and effect paragraph,** create a topic sentence that states your purpose for analyzing the cause(s) and/or effect(s) of an event or process; use examples and details to describe the cause(s) and/or effect(s) of the event or process; critique the cause and/or effect, possibly making suggestions for either preventing similar events or ensuring they continue to occur; and conclude with a sentence that restates your purpose.

PEARSON
mywritinglab

For support in meeting this chapter's objectives, log in to www.mywritinglab.com and select **Paragraph Development— Cause and Effect.**

Comparison and Contrast

THINKING CRITICALLY

Look at the two pictures of clowns above. List any similarities between these two photographs. Then, list any differences in subject, content, style, look, or feel.

Similarities: _____

_____

_____

_____

Differences: _____

_____

_____

_____

COMPARISON AND CONTRAST PARAGRAPHS

Comparison paragraphs look at the *similarities* between two subjects, and contrast paragraphs look at the *differences* between two subjects. A **comparison *and* contrast** paragraph looks at both the similarities *and* differences between two subjects. You use comparison and/or contrast as a way to figure things out or to communicate many times in your daily life, in college, and at work. You compare and contrast two houses for rent, two coworkers, two politicians running for office, two periods of history, two books, two theories, two speeches, two potential job opportunities—the possibilities are endless.

Critical Thinking and Comparison and Contrast

In order to compare and/or contrast two items, they usually need to have at least some similarities. Usually, they fall into the same general category (for instance, an apple and an orange are both in the general category of fruit), so you could start your comparison/contrast by stating that general category. Sometimes, you compare, or contrast, items that are in slightly different categories but still have a lot in common, for instance, a book and a movie based on the book. Even in this example, you need to sort out what basis for comparison and/or contrast you will use. For instance, looking at a book and a movie based on it, you can compare, or contrast, story lines, characters, and settings.

APPLYING CRITICAL THINKING

PURPOSE   IDEAS   SUPPORT   ASSUMPTIONS BIASES   CONCLUSIONS   POINT OF VIEW   ANALYSIS

Comparing is a way to find connections by looking at the similarities between things, and *contrasting* helps us to see the differences between things in order to better understand them. For example, if you were comparing attending high school versus starting college, it would be intriguing for your readers to see how you feel they are the same and how they are different. To write an effective comparison/contrast paragraph, you need to use your **analytical** skills to identify how things are similar and different. You also need to determine your **purpose** for writing about those similarities and differences, and decide what kind of **support** (examples and details) will best illustrate and explain the point (**main idea**) you want to make.

LO 2 PREPARING TO WRITE A COMPARISON/CONTRAST PARAGRAPH

Before you begin to write a comparison/contrast paragraph on an assigned topic, or one you have chosen, start by asking yourself these questions:

1. What two objects, people, or concepts am I going to compare/contrast?
2. Are they in the same general category?
3. Am I going to focus on similarities, differences, or both? Are the two subjects mostly alike, mostly different, or some of both?
4. How will I structure my paragraph?
5. What examples and details should I include for support?
6. What do I want my readers to learn or understand after reading this comparison and/or contrast paragraph?

Answering these questions will lead you to an expository topic sentence, help you develop examples and details to include for support, and give you a general idea of how you want to organize your paragraph.

LO 3 STRUCTURING A COMPARISON AND CONTRAST PARAGRAPH

When you are deciding which two subjects to compare and/or contrast, you need to find ones that are similar enough for a comparison to be useful, but also have enough differences to make your paragraph interesting and give it a purpose. Are your intended subjects in the same general group or category? Do they have both similarities and differences? Will you focus more on similarities? Differences? Both? Why? Brainstorming lists of the similarities and differences between your subjects will help you determine your purpose for comparing or contrasting them. Then, you need to choose an organizational plan to structure your paragraph.

There are two ways to organize comparison/contrast paragraphs: a subject-by-subject approach or a point-by-point approach.

Subject-by-Subject Organization Pattern

In a **subject-by-subject** organization pattern, you first identify the points of similarity or difference between two people, places, things, or ideas that you want to discuss. Then you address each point in terms of the first subject and then each point in terms of the second subject. For example, you might choose to compare soccer and football by looking at three main points:

> **Subject A: Soccer   Subject B: Football**
>> **Point 1** Objectives and rules
>>
>> **Point 2** Equipment and uniforms
>>
>> **Point 3** National versus international interest

An outline of the paragraph on soccer and football that you write using this method of organization might look like this:

> **Topic sentence:** Soccer and football have some general similarities when it comes to objectives and rules for the games, but they are quite different as far as equipment and uniforms as well as national versus international popularity.
>
> **Subject A: Soccer**
>> **Point 1:** Soccer's objectives and rules
>>
>> **Point 2:** Soccer's equipment needs and uniforms
>>
>> **Point 3:** Soccer's national versus international popularity
>
> **Subject B: Football**
>> **Point 1:** Football's objectives and rules
>>
>> **Point 2:** Football's equipment needs and uniforms
>>
>> **Point 3:** Football's national versus international popularity
>
> **Concluding sentence:** (Re-emphasizes the topic sentence) Though on the surface these two sports are very similar, they differ a great deal as far as equipment needed and national popularity.

Point-by-Point Organization Pattern

In a **point-by-point** organization pattern, you discuss one point at a time while looking at both subjects. An outline for a paragraph on soccer and football using this method might look like this:

Subject A: Soccer	**Subject B: Football**
Point 1 Objectives/rules	Objectives/rules
Point 2 Equipment/uniforms	Equipment/uniforms
Point 3 National versus international interest	National versus international interest

Topic sentence: Soccer and football have some general similarities when it comes to objectives and rules for the games, but they are quite different as far as equipment and uniforms as well as national versus international popularity.

Subject A: Soccer	**Subject B: Football**
Point One: Objectives and rules for soccer and football	**Point One:** Objectives and rules for soccer and football
Point Two: Equipment and uniforms for soccer and football	**Point Two:** Equipment and uniforms for soccer and football
Point Three: Popularity of soccer and football	**Point Three:** Popularity of soccer and football

Concluding sentence: (Re-emphasizes the topic sentence) Though on the surface these two sports are very similar, they differ a great deal as far as equipment needed and national popularity.

Pick the organizational pattern for your comparison/contrast paragraph that works best for your subject and purpose. Write a **topic sentence** that identifies the subjects you will compare or contrast and the points you want to make, and provide plenty of **examples and details** to illustrate these points in your paragraph.

Read both of the model paragraph versions below and see which pattern of organization you think worked best for the subject.

Model Student Paragraph (subject-by-subject)

Michelle Gillespie

Ms. Jensen

English 080

13 March 2009

Topic sentence states the subjects to be compared and contrasted and points to be discussed about each

Writer uses least to most important order within each category

   Soccer and football have some general similarities when it comes to objectives and rules for the games, but they are quite different as far as equipment and uniforms as well as national versus international popularity. The objectives and rules for soccer are pretty straightforward: get the ball into the goal and win points for the team. Soccer players have particular roles including goalkeeper, fullback, midfielder, and forward to allow for both offense and defense strategies. The equipment in soccer is basically a simple uniform of shirt, shorts, socks, and cleats, and a soccer ball. As far as popularity goes, soccer is an international phenomenon, played all over the world. Football, like soccer, has the simple objective of getting points from moving the ball over the end field. The ball can be thrown and caught or kicked for points depending on the situation. Also, like soccer, players have both offensive and defensive roles including quarterback, guard, tackle, fullback, and running back. However, football differs from soccer in its equipment needs and international renown. American football requires a uniform, but it also requires a lot of padding for protection and a helmet and faceguard to protect the face and head due to all the tackling in the sport. Finally, football is played mostly in America. Though it is played sometimes in other countries, it has nowhere near the popularity internationally as soccer does. Though on the surface these two sports are very similar, they differ a great deal as far as equipment needed and national popularity.

First category discussed is soccer. Example 1

Detail 1

Example 2

Example 3
Second category football. Example 1

Detail 1

Example 2

Detail 1

Example 3

Concluding sentence restates the purpose and conclusion of the paragraph

Model Student Paragraph (point-by-point)

Michelle Gillespie
Ms. Jensen
English 080
13 March 2009

   Soccer and football have some general similarities when it comes to objectives and rules for the games, but they are quite different as far as equipment and uniforms as well as national versus

Topic sentence states the subjects to be compared and contrasted and the points to be discussed

Example 1, soccer

Detail 1

Example 2, football

Example 3, soccer

Detail 1

Example 4, football

Detail 1

Example 5, soccer

Detail 1

Example 6, football

Detail 1

Example 7, soccer

Example 8, football,
Detail 1

Concluding sentence reiterates topic sentence and purpose of paragraph

international popularity. The objectives and rules for soccer are pretty straightforward: get the ball into the goal and win points for the team. Football, like soccer, has the simple objective of getting points from moving the ball over the end field. Next, soccer players have particular roles including goalkeeper, fullback, midfielder, and forward to allow for both offense and defense strategies. Similar to soccer players, football players have both offensive and defensive roles including quarterback, guard, tackle, fullback, and running back. The equipment in soccer is basically a simple uniform of shirt, shorts, socks, and cleats, and a soccer ball. In contrast, football requires a uniform, but it also requires a lot of padding for protection and a helmet and faceguard to protect the face and head due to all the tackling in the sport. As far as popularity goes, soccer is an international phenomenon, played all over the world. However, football is played mostly in America. Though it is played sometimes in other countries, it has nowhere near the popularity internationally as soccer does. Though on the surface these two sports are very similar, they differ a great deal as far as equipment needed and national popularity.

The chart below provides a brief overview of the structure of a comparison/contrast paragraph.

BASIC STRUCTURE FOR A COMPARISON/CONTRAST PARAGRAPH

TOPIC SENTENCE

State the main **idea** of your paragraph and also describe your **purpose,** what you are trying to explain, show, prove, or argue through comparing and/or contrasting two objects, ideas, places, people, and so on

SUPPORT

Organize using either a subject-by-subject or point-by- point organization pattern

Develop the comparisons and contrasts through examples and details

Use transitions within the paragraph to make it flow smoothly

ANALYSIS

Add commentary and analysis about the similarities, differences, and examples used to help develop the purpose of the topic sentence

CONCLUDING SENTENCE

Sum up and re-emphasize the purpose and topic sentence

ACTIVITY 13-1   Identifying the Elements of a Comparison/Contrast Paragraph

Directions: *Read the paragraph below. Then, perform the following tasks.*

1. *Underline the topic sentence.*

2. *Write C above each sentence, or part of a sentence, that provides a comparison (similarity between the two subjects).*

3. *Double-underline any sentence or part of a sentence that provides a contrast (difference between the two subjects).*

4. *Highlight any word or phrase that serves as a transition from one step to the next.*

5. *Note whether the paragraph is organized point-by-point or subject-by-subject:* <u>point by point</u>

Kate Atkinson

Professor Zhu

ENG 090

23 October 2010

   Pablo Picasso and Vincent Van Gogh are known for being innovative artists, and their painting styles have similarities and differences that make them both powerful and unique. Both Picasso and Van Gogh broke with previous artistic traditions in their paintings. Picasso was known for a style called "cubism," which featured using cube-like shapes for his subjects, even people. For example, Picasso's famous painting "Bust of a Woman" features a woman whose face is cube-like and appears to be further divided into two separate cubes or quadrants. Similarly, Van Gogh broke with the painters who preceded him, using thick blobs of paint and heavy brush strokes that created a textured look and feel to his paintings. For instance, Van Gogh's famous painting "Sunflowers" is thick with yellow and orange paint. The details of the painting blur together in one dramatic flow of color. In contrast, when it came to the subject matter these two artists chose to depict, they were quite different. Picasso focused on portraits or people and still-life compositions in his cubist paintings. Van Gogh, on the other hand, usually painted scenes in nature, though he also painted still life pictures and some portraits (usually self-portraits). He also often painted the same rural scenes or still life images over and over again. Though these two artists both pushed the boundaries of art of their time and are both remembered for that, they each had their own unique style and taste for subject matter.

LO 4 WRITING A COMPARISON AND CONTRAST PARAGRAPH

Topic

If you have been assigned a comparison/contrast topic, be sure to read the assignment carefully to make sure you understand what is being asked, and then prewrite to come up with examples and details related to the purpose for writing about the topic. If you do not have a topic assigned by your instructor, brainstorm ideas for things, places, people, or ideas that you could compare and contrast. Then, come up with ideas for a purpose for comparing/contrasting your subjects. What do you want your readers to learn or understand through your comparison/contrast?

A Few Topic Possibilities

Many subjects benefit from a comparison or contrast analysis; just make sure that the subjects have enough in common to make for a useful and effective paragraph. You could compare and contrast any of the following (as well as many other people places, things, or ideas):

- Two historical figures
- Two political figures
- Two people you know
- Two places you frequent
- Two restaurants
- Two musicians
- Two animals

- Two paintings
- Two photographs
- Two dwellings
- Two cities
- Two computers
- Two cameras

ACTIVITY 13-2   Generating Topics for a Comparison/Contrast Paragraph

Directions: *(1) Use prewriting to generate* **three** *pairs of items (people, places, things, or ideas) that could be usefully discussed in a comparison/contrast paragraph. (2) Then explain for each pair whether you would focus on similarities, differences, or both.*   Answers will vary.

1. Two subjects: _____

   Similarities, differences, or both: _____

   _____

2. Two subjects: _____

   Similarities, differences, or both: _____

   _____

3. Two subjects: _____

   Similarities, differences, or both: _____

   _____

Topic Sentence

The topic sentence in a compare/contrast paragraph states what subjects you will be analyzing, your purpose for doing so, and the points you will discuss. As you develop your topic sentence, ask yourself these questions: What conclusion did I reach by comparing and contrasting these subjects? What do I want my readers to learn or understand after reading this paragraph?

ACTIVITY 13-3   Creating Topic Sentences

Directions: *Create a topic sentence for each of the topics you generated in Activity 13-2.*

1. _____

   _____

2. _____

   _____

3. _____

   _____

Support

Structure your comparison/contrast paragraph using either a subject-by-subject or point-by-point organization pattern. Then, use specific examples and details to illustrate the comparisons and/or contrasts.

ACTIVITY 13-4   Providing Examples and Details

Directions: *Come up with at least **two examples** you could use to develop each of the topic sentences you wrote in Activity 13-3 and one detail to support each example. Answers will vary.*

1. _____

   _____

2. _____

   _____

3. _____

   _____

Useful transitions for comparison/contrast paragraphs include those that show comparison, contrast, addition of a point, examples, and purpose.

TRANSITIONS TO . . .

Show a Comparison

in like manner	in the same way	likewise	similarly

Show Contrast or a Change in Idea

although	even though	instead	on the other side
anyhow	for all that	nevertheless	otherwise
at the same time	however	notwithstanding	regardless
but	in any event	on the contrary	still
despite this	in contrast	on the other hand	yet

Show Addition of Another Point

again	but	in addition	plus
also	equally important	last	plus the fact
and	finally	lastly	secondly
and then	first	moreover	then
another	further	next	thirdly
besides	furthermore	nor	too

Illustrate or Give Examples/Specifics

a few include	essentially	in particular	the following
an example	for example	let us consider	specifically
especially	for instance	the case of	you can see this in

Show Purpose

all things considered	for this reason	to accomplish	with this in mind
for this purpose	in order to	to this end	with this objective

Concluding Sentence

The concluding sentence for a comparison/contrast paragraph should remind your readers of your purpose—why you compared and/or contrasted the subjects you chose.

ACTIVITY 13-5 | Writing a Concluding Sentence

Directions: *Now choose one of the topics you have been developing in the previous activities and write a **concluding sentence** that reflects back to the original topic sentence.*

_____

_____

_____

Revise and Edit

Remember to revise your paragraph draft for the best results. Use the following critique form to check for the basics in your comparison/contrast paragraph draft.

COMPARISON AND CONTRAST PARAGRAPH CRITIQUE FORM

	Done well	Needs work
1. Does the paragraph compare and/or contrast two subjects?	_____	_____
2. Is there a strong topic sentence that states the purpose of the comparison or contrast?	_____	_____
3. Does the writer use a clear order—subject-by-subject or point-by point—or an effective combination of the two?	_____	_____
4. Are there enough examples to explain and illustrate the purpose of the paragraph?	_____	_____
5. Are there enough details to develop and elaborate on the examples?		
6. Are transitions used to help one example flow to the next?	_____	_____
7. Does the concluding sentence sum up the main point of the paragraph without repeating the topic sentence?	_____	_____

Editing

Circle the following errors you think you see in this draft: spelling, fragments, run-ons, comma splices, commas, semicolon/colon use, pronoun agreement, reference fault errors, parallelism, apostrophe use, verb use/tense, and passive voice construction. (See Parts V and VI for help identifying and correcting these errors.)

Other types of grammar or sentence-level errors you noticed in this draft:

_____

Comments:

_____

_____

ACTIVITY 13-6   Revising a Paragraph

Directions: *Carefully read the following student paragraph. Then, use the critique form to evaluate it. Finally, revise and rewrite the paragraph on a separate sheet of paper and be sure to address the following revision tasks:* Answers will vary.

1. *Identify the pattern of organization used (subject-by-subject or point-by-point) and note whether it is effective. If it is not, decide whether to use a different pattern or improve the existing one.*

2. *Make sure the topic sentence clearly states the subject and purpose of the paragraph and whether a comparison, contrast, or both is being made.*

3. *Move any sentences that are not in the best order to develop the comparison and contrast in the most effective way, and add any examples and details that may help develop the purpose in the paragraph.*

4. *Add transitional words or phrases where needed.*

5. *Ensure there is a strong concluding sentence.*

L'Tanya Robinson

Ms. Lyman

Eng 99

3 September 2010

When deciding where to go on a first date, both comedy clubs and live music are exciting options; however, comedy clubs provide a couple of advantages that make them the best choice. Both live music and comedy clubs make an impressive venue for a first date. Most people would be impressed by their companion spending a little extra money to take them out for a lively evening. Both places win points for effort and originality too. After all, most people choose going out to dinner or to a movie, or maybe both, as the typical first date. Both date-night choices offer a fun night of being around people in a positive crowd atmosphere with the added excitement of live entertainment. However, there are more risks when it comes to live music shows than there are for comedy clubs. For example, most people have very specific musical tastes, and if a companion's taste doesn't match, it could pose an awkward situation. Most people enjoy most forms of comedy though, and it is less personalized when it comes to taste. Comedy helps create a good mood and makes people feel more at ease or comfortable. Music can be too loud, making it impossible to interact with each other on a date. Though both live music and live comedy make for a great first date, live comedy wins for the best odds.

PROFESSIONAL COMPARISON/CONTRAST PARAGRAPH

Excerpt from *Grant and Lee: A Study in Contrasts*

Bruce Catton

Grant and Lee were in complete contrast, representing two diametrically opposed elements in American life. Grant was the modern man emerging; beyond him, ready to come on the stage was the great age of steel and machinery, of crowded cities and a restless burgeoning vitality. Lee might have ridden down from the old age of chivalry, lance in hand, silken banner fluttering over his head. Each man was the perfect champion for his cause, drawing both his strengths and his weaknesses from the people he led. Yet it was not all contrast, after all. Different as they were—in background, in personality, in underlying aspiration—these two great soldiers had much in common. Under everything else, they were marvelous fighters. Furthermore, their fighting qualities were really very much alike. Each man had, to begin with, the great virtue of utter tenacity and fidelity. Grant fought his way down the Mississippi Valley in spite of acute personal discouragement and profound military handicaps. Lee hung on in the trench at Petersburg after hope itself had died. In each man there was an indomitable quality . . . the born fighter's refusal to give up as long as he can still remain on his feet and lift his two fists. Daring and resourcefulness they had, too: the ability to think faster and move faster than the enemy. These were the qualities which gave Lee the dazzling campaigns of Second Manassas and Chancellorsville and won Vicksburg for Grant. Lastly, and perhaps greatest of all, there was the ability, at the end, to turn quickly from war to peace once the fighting was over. Out of the way these two men behaved at Appomattox came the possibility of a peace, of reconciliation. It was a possibility not wholly realized, in the years to come, but which did, in the end, help the two sections to become one nation again . . . after a war whose bitterness might have seemed to make such a reunion wholly impossible. No part of either man's life became him more than the part he played in their brief meeting in the McLean house at Appomattox. Their behavior left all succeeding generations of Americans in their debt. Two great Americans, Grant and Lee—very different, yet under everything very much alike. Their encounter at Appomattox was one of the great moments of American history.

Catton, Bruce. "Grant and Lee: A Study in Contrasts." *The American Story*. Ed. Garet Garrett. Chicago, Regnery, 1955.

Reading Reflection Questions

1. Does this paragraph emphasize only the similarities or only the differences between Grant and Lee?

   No, it does both: although there are many differences, Grant and Lee also

   shared similarities

2. Is this paragraph arranged in a subject-by-subject pattern or a point-by-point pattern? *point-by-point*

3. T/F ___ *T* ___ Grant and Lee represented two different elements of American life according to Catton.

4. List two categories the author uses to compare the two generals.

   Answers will vary. They could include being champions for their causes, good

   fighters, and being daring and resourceful.

5. Does this paragraph focus more on comparison or on contrast? Why do you think the author chose this focus?

Comparison—to show how these two generals who fought on opposite

sides were actually quite alike

6. Do you think people would assume the two generals who led the North and the South in the Civil War were very different if they hadn't read about them? Why or why not?

Answers will vary.

7. How do these two generals illustrate "American" strengths?

Answers will vary. One possible answer is that even though they chose

opposing sides they were still representative of American pride, strength,

endurance, and intelligence.

Checking Vocabulary

Define the following words in your own words or provide a dictionary definition if you don't know the word.

8. diametrically: *in direct opposition, opposite extremes*

9. burgeoning: *growing, swelling*

10. reconciliation: *settling or resolving of differences*

CRITICAL THINKING CHECKLIST

1. What is the author's *purpose* or *goal* in this reading selection?

2. What are the *stated questions* being addressed?

3. What *specific details and examples* does the author use to develop his or her purpose or goal for the reading?

4. What *inferences* does the author include in this reading? (Inferences imply "if this, then this" types of cause/effect analysis.)

5. Who is the intended audience, and how did you reach that conclusion?

Paragraph Assignments

1. Choose one of the topics you worked on in the activities or one listed in this chapter for a comparison/contrast paragraph. Come up with an intriguing point that comes as a surprise when the two subjects are compared. Use the Applying Critical Thinking box on page 249 to help you get started.

2. For the following topics, determine at least three points you want to use for your comparison and/or contrast, and structure your paragraph using either subject-by-subject or point-by-point organization:

    a. Compare and contrast two places you have lived.

    b. Write a comparison/contrast paragraph on two teachers you have had.

Critical Thinking Journal Prompts

Write a journal reflection entry using one of the following prompts:

1. Think of two people in your life that would make for a good comparison. What categories would you use to compare them? What could you learn from comparing them that would be useful to you?

2. Compare and contrast your bedroom with the bedroom of a friend. What do your bedrooms say about who you are as people and how you are the same or different?

3. Compare and contrast two writing assignments you have already done for this class or another college class. How were they similar and different? What different skills did you learn from each?

LEARNING OBJECTIVES REVIEW

LO1	What do you want to achieve by thinking critically about writing a compare and contrast paragraph? (See p. 249)	**Thinking critically** helps you figure out how two people, places, ideas, or things are similar and how they are different; what conclusions you can draw from this information; and your purpose for writing about the similarities and/or differences.
LO2	What questions should you ask before writing a comparison/contrast paragraph? (See p. 250)	You should ask the following **questions:** (1) What two objects, people, or concepts am I going to compare/contrast? (2) Are they in the same category? (3) Am I going to focus on similarities, differences, or both? (4) How will I structure my paragraph? (5) What examples and details should I include? (6) What do I want my readers to learn from reading the paragraph?
LO3	How do you structure a comparison and/or contrast paragraph? (See pp. 250–256)	You can **structure a comparison/contrast paragraph** using either a *subject-by-subject organization* (addressing each point in terms of the first subject and then each point in terms of the second subject) or a *point-by-point organization* (addressing each point in terms of both subjects).
LO4	How do you write a comparison/ contrast paragraph? (See p. 256–262)	To **write a comparison/contrast paragraph,** create a topic sentence that states what subjects you will be analyzing, your purpose for doing so, and the points you will discuss; use a subject-by-subject or point-by-point organization pattern; include examples and details to illustrate the comparisons and/or contrasts; analyze the similarities and/or differences to make your point; and conclude with a sentence that reiterates your purpose.

PEARSON
mywritinglab

For support in meeting this chapter's objectives, log in to www.mywritinglab.com and select **Paragraph Development— Comparing and Contrasting.**

Super.
That's how milk makes
you feel. The calcium helps
bones grow strong,
so even if you're not from
Krypton™ you can have
bones of steel.

got milk?

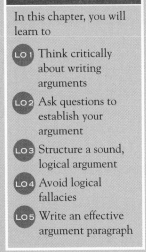

LEARNING OBJECTIVES

In this chapter, you will learn to

LO1 Think critically about writing arguments

LO2 Ask questions to establish your argument

LO3 Structure a sound, logical argument

LO4 Avoid logical fallacies

LO5 Write an effective argument paragraph

THINKING CRITICALLY

Most advertisements have embedded arguments within them: the most common argument, of course, is "Buy me!" Often other arguments are hinted at too, such as if you buy a certain car you will seem more good looking. Or, if you buy a drink of milk, you will be as strong as Superman. Choose a magazine, television, or billboard advertisement you've seen recently. Briefly describe the advertisement and what it is trying to persuade you to buy. Then, list any secondary arguments the ad is suggesting:

_____

_____

LO 1   ARGUMENT AND PERSUASION PARAGRAPHS

Whenever you are trying to convince someone to agree with your point of view about an issue, you are making an argument using persuasion, something you will do both in college classes and later in your career. Becoming skilled in clear, logical reasoning and argument will also help you to evaluate the arguments and logic of the writers of books, newspaper articles, political speeches, and other kinds of persuasive writing and help you to recognize faulty or misleading reasoning.

Critical Thinking and Argument

Making an **argument** involves stating a claim (a statement you believe to be true), supporting the claim with logical reasoning, providing valid evidence to support the reasoning, and, when needed, providing an even-handed presentation of counterarguments to a proposed solution. When writing arguments, or reading the arguments of others, check to make sure the reasons you, or another writer, provide are solid, reasonable, and well supported, and that counterarguments are presented in a fair and thorough way.

APPLYING CRITICAL THINKING

PURPOSE   IDEAS   SUPPORT   ASSUMPTIONS BIASES   CONCLUSIONS   POINT OF VIEW   ANALYSIS

To write an effective argument paragraph, you need to consider the following questions:

1. What is my **purpose** for writing this paragraph?

2. What **biases and assumptions** do I have? What are they based on? Are they logical?

3. What **biases or assumptions** might my audience have that I will need to address?

4. What is my **point of view** on the subject? Is it based on credible information?

5. Have I thoroughly **analyzed** my argument? How will I break it down into its basic parts, and how will I present them?

6. What **support** do I need to include? What reasons, **examples,** and **details** can I include to develop my argument?

7. What **conclusions** have I presented, and are they sound?

LO 2 PREPARING TO WRITE AN ARGUMENT PARAGRAPH

Before you begin to write an argumentative paragraph on an assigned topic, or one you have chosen, start by asking yourself these questions:

1. What is my position on this issue?
2. Is there a solution or plan of action I want to propose?
3. What examples and evidence can I provide to support my claim (my position)?
4. How will I organize my evidence?
5. Who would disagree with my stand or solution and why (counterarguments)?
6. How can I address these counterarguments?
7. How will I conclude my paragraph?

Answering these questions will lead you to an expository topic sentence, help you determine which examples and details will provide good support, and give you a general idea of how to organize your paragraph.

ACTIVITY 14-1   Brainstorming Potential Arguments

Directions: *On a separate sheet of paper, brainstorm a list of problems at your school, or in your neighborhood, that require action to resolve them.*

> **Example:** Campus bookstore does not have a book buyback program, not enough evening classes for working students, need more stoplights in my district, neighbors need to curb their dogs, need more recycling opportunities . . .

LO 3 STRUCTURING AN ARGUMENT PARAGRAPH

The purpose of an argument paragraph is to develop an *argument* or *claim* about a topic and support it with logical and valid reasons in order to persuade readers to agree with your position. Some writers focus on trying to persuade readers to believe a particular point of view about a debatable topic (such as whether or not smoking should be allowed on campus), but others go further and propose a solution to an existing problem. For example, they might argue that the most effective way to deal with secondhand smoke is to pass a regulation that bans smoking inside all campus buildings and within 25 feet of doors and windows on the outside. Often the topic sentence for an argumentative paragraph that proposes a plan of action to solve a problem includes the words *should, needs to, ought to,* or *must.*

Once you have stated your claim, you need to provide reasons to support your position and evidence that supports them. Evidence can include facts, statistics, detailed examples, firsthand accounts, interviews, or observations. Also, as an argument states your opinion about an issue, it can be biased, so make sure your supporting reasons are logical, accurate, and based in fact and that your tone is respectful and fair-minded.

Some argument assignments will ask you to argue for a proposed *solution* to a perceived *problem,* so you will also need to address possible counterarguments to both your position and the individual reasons you use to support it. Addressing **counterarguments**—what others would say in response to your arguments or suggest as alternative solutions to the problem—shows that you are being fair-minded and not presenting an issue in a biased way. Do not make the mistake of oversimplifying the counterarguments or underestimating your readers' position or knowledge of the issue: The stronger your logic, the stronger your chances of convincing someone else to agree with your stand. For instance, a counterargument to banning smoking outside is that smoking is legal, therefore smokers should not be banned from smoking near the entrances to buildings. To refute this, you might need to concede smokers' legal rights but point out that if nonsmokers are forced to breathe second-hand smoke as they enter a building then their rights have been violated.

When writing an argument paragraph, you need to adjust your approach, style, and support based on your target audience. If you were writing a position paragraph on the issue of premarital sex, for instance, you would need to modify your approach depending on whether you were presenting your views to a group of teachers and parents or to a group of teenagers.

It's easy when you are passionate about a subject to commit errors in logic (see "Most Common Errors in Logic" on page 271). Try not to use emotional appeals in your argument. Make sure that you are not using any misleading or inaccurate information. Check that you have not attacked people who might feel differently about the topic than you do (remember, you are trying to sway people to your point of view on the topic, not make them defensive). You might even try to point out any common ground that exists in a counterargument, or make a concession about an opposing point that is particularly good. For instance, if someone complains about the cost of a plan you have proposed, it is effective to concede that the idea will cost money, explain why it is worth the investment, and, if possible, suggest ways to pay for it.

Here are some guidelines you should keep in mind as you begin to write an argument paragraph.

Guidelines for Writing an Effective Argument

1. Define your position (claim).
2. Be aware of your audience and adjust your style and tone as needed; use tactful and fair language.
3. Provide evidence, examples, and support for your claim.
4. Check for logical errors and oversimplifications in your reasoning.
5. Acknowledge differing viewpoints and counterarguments.
6. Identify common ground and, when appropriate, point out the merits of another point of view.
7. Refute (address and disagree with) counterarguments using fair and respectful language.
8. Use the Critical Thinking Checklist from Chapter 1 to check for your own assumptions, biases, inferences, and overall point of view.
9. Use the critique form later in this chapter (see p. 279) to check the contents and organization of your paragraph.
10. Revise and proofread your argument paragraph carefully.

(LO 4) HOW TO AVOID COMMON ERRORS IN LOGIC

A **logical fallacy** is an error in reasoning. Logical fallacies often occur when you try to oversimplify an issue or do not really think through the consequences of your reasoning. Here are a few common logical fallacies you should strive to avoid:

Ad hominen (or attacking the man) fallacy. This involves personally attacking the person you are arguing against instead of their reasoning, thus avoiding addressing their argument head on.

> My right wing opponent, who everyone knows is in the pocket of big business, must be crazy if he thinks cutting taxes for the wealthy will solve the country's financial problems.

Post hoc (or unconnected occurrence) fallacy. This means that you state or imply that one event or idea led to another when there is no real cause and effect connection between them.

> The same day I found that dollar bill, my biology test was canceled; it was a lucky dollar bill.

Hasty generalization. This error involves jumping to a conclusion without having enough evidence to support it.

> He's guilty for sure. You can tell by the way he won't look you in the eye.

Either/or error (false dilemma fallacy). You are committing an either/or error when you suggest there are only two solutions to a problem, when in fact there may be several alternatives.

> Either you are for abortion or against it.

Slippery slope error. This is when you make an assumption that one event will automatically lead to a series of events that will eventually end in disaster and provide no evidence to support the steps in the process or the conclusion.

> Once they pass a health care bill including a single-payer option, we're on the road to becoming a socialist state.

Circular reasoning. Circular reasoning is when you make a claim and support it by restating the claim using different words.

> I believe we have the best government in the world because our government is better than any other government in the world.

Model Student Paragraph

Kristen Cabot

Professor Atkinson

English 092

9 March 2009

Topic sentence states claim.

    At least one student should serve on each hiring committee for new, full-time faculty members at our college. To begin with, students

First reason

are the ones who are the most affected by the new faculty members as they take classes with them. A teacher's academic credentials should not be the only factor considered. Personality and teaching style are also important. A new faculty member's knowledge of their subject, teaching experience, and ability to support student learning are all crucial to the students they teach. Therefore, students have a right to be involved in the hiring process since their learning and academic success is at stake. Secondly, full-time faculty members often teach for many years at the same institution. If a teacher typically teaches three to five classes a term, then 75–100 students a term will work with the faculty member. As student learning is strongly affected by the approach an instructor uses to impart information, these numbers are too large to overlook; at least one student should be on every committee to represent the voice of all the future students who will take classes with that person. Moreover, student tuition helps pay a significant percentage of faculty salaries at the college. As many students work to pay for their education, and most have to take out and repay loans in order to attend school, they should have a say in how their tuition money is spent. Many would argue that faculty members and administrators should make up the majority of the hiring committee since they are the experts in the field and are also able to conduct background checks. However, if only faculty members and administrators are involved in hiring new teachers, then the people who will most directly be affected by the hiring decision are left out. Some would also argue that students do not have enough knowledge of teaching techniques to be able to adequately assess potential candidates. However, responsible students are usually available who have taken a number of classes in a department and know what does and does not work in the classroom, and they can represent students on the hiring committees. Students should have a place and a voice on hiring

Details about teachers' effects on students provided to support first reason

Writer uses order of importance to present reasons to support it.

Second reason

Details provided to support the second reason

Third reason

Details provided to support it

Student outlines first counterargument to her position

Student refutes counterargument

Student presents counterargument 2

Student refutes argument

Concluding sentence strongly reiterates the argument, the two main support statements

committees for new faculty at this college because students are the best judge of good teaching and because students will be affected by the choice for years to come.

BASIC STRUCTURE FOR AN ARGUMENT PARAGRAPH

TOPIC SENTENCE

State the main **idea** of your paragraph and describe your topic and your **purpose** for writing about it, the point you are trying to argue or prove

SUPPORT

Develop your arguments with reasons, examples, and evidence

Use **transitions** between reasons or from one argument or part of an argument to the next

Provide specific **details** to develop your reasons and examples

Present **counterarguments** and provide answers to them

ANALYSIS

Add **commentary and analysis** about the examples and details used to develop your argument

CONCLUDING SENTENCE

Sum up and re-emphasize the topic sentence: your argument and the reasons that support it

---

ACTIVITY 14-2   Identifying the Elements of an Argument Paragraph

Directions: *Read the paragraph below. Then, perform the following tasks.*

1. Highlight the claim—the argument—that is being presented.

2. Write an E above each sentence, or part of a sentence, that provides a reason (example or detail) that supports the topic sentence.

3. *Double-underline the counterargument.*

4. *Highlight any word or phrase that serves as a transition from one reason to the next.*

Truc Nguyen

Professor Aquino

English 094

9 May 2010

Students should take a year off between high school and college to allow them a break to transition from high school and to give them an opportunity to gain some life experience before college, both of which will improve their overall success and satisfaction when they begin college. First, too many students come out of high school burned out and unready for the demands of college. After a year away, they will be refreshed and eager to learn due to having had a break and the opportunity to pursue new experiences. Second, many students who enter college directly after high school feel they are just extending their high school experience. However, if they spend a year out in the "real world" they have time to gain some perspective and develop a greater appreciation of the potential benefits of a college education. For example, if students work in low-level jobs they might be more motivated to get the skills they need for a higher-paying job. Also, they may take a job that allows them to get some experience in a field they are interested in before they commit to a particular degree. Moreover, during a year off students have the opportunity to travel and gain life skills and develop maturity that will benefit them in college courses. They will be more independent and able to relate to different types of people and cultural perspectives. Some educators or parents may argue that when students take a year off, they fall behind their peers, unnecessarily delay their graduation, and miss opportunities for good jobs. However, a year out of school working or traveling can pay off in ways that will make them stronger candidates than their peers due to their increased independence and responsibility, job experience, and improved ability to work and interact with others. Also, students who take a break can save more money for college and therefore have less chance of dropping out due to lack of funds. Overall, students would benefit in many ways from taking a one-year break between high school and college.

LO 5 WRITING AN ARGUMENT PARAGRAPH

Topic

The only real rule for a topic for an argumentative paragraph is that you must be trying to persuade your readers about something. You will usually be arguing for a change in the status quo (the way things currently are), so don't argue for something that already exists (though you could argue that an existing policy or situation is not effective and suggest an alternative to it).

A Few Topic Possibilities

Think about problems you see in your neighborhood, city, state, school, job, or society as a whole. What solution to a particular problem can you argue for? Think about a controversial issue, and then determine your stand on it. For example, what is your position on prayer in public school, on subsidized health care, subsidized child care, mandatory drug tests for athletes, or birth control education in high schools?

Topic Sentence

Once you have determined your subject and argument, you need to come up with the purpose for your paragraph: your **topic sentence.** What are you arguing for or against? Or, if you are solving a problem, what is your proposed change or plan of action? Try using either *should*, *must*, or *needs to* in your plan of action to indicate you are stating your argument.

ACTIVITY 14-3   Creating Topic Sentences

Directions: *Brainstorm on a separate sheet of paper about the following topics to get some ideas, and then create a **topic sentence** for each one.*

1. Subject 1: Mandatory drug testing for high school athletes

_____

_____

2. Subject 2: Birth control supplies being distributed in middle schools

_____

_____

3. Subject 3: Changing all college classes to optional attendance

_____

_____

Support

Use specific examples and details to illustrate the problem you are discussing and to explain your argument about or solution to the problem. You may need to predict, evaluate, and address what people might say *against* your plan (the **counterarguments**). Many counterarguments have to do with who will *pay* for the changes if the solution plan involves spending money. So, be sure to address *who* would pay and *how* the money would be raised. If the counterarguments are about something other than money, such as a moral concern or a political issue, make sure that you present the counterargument(s) fairly and thoroughly. If you discount valid counterarguments, your argument loses credibility.

ACTIVITY 14-4   Providing Support

Directions: *Provide one **specific reason to support** each topic sentence you created in Activity 14-3.*

1. Subject 1: _____

_____

2. Subject 2: _____

_____

3. Subject 3: _____

_____

Transitions

Useful transitions for argument paragraphs include transitions to strengthen a point, to show addition of another point, to provide examples, and to show purpose.

TRANSITIONS TO . . .

Strengthen a Point

basically	indeed	truly	without a doubt
essentially	irrefutably	undeniably	without question

Show Addition of Another Point

again	but also	in addition	nor
also	equally important	last	plus the fact
and	finally	lastly	secondly
and then	first	likewise	then too
another	further	moreover	thirdly
besides	furthermore	next	too

Illustrate or Give Examples/Specifics

a few include	essentially	in particular	the following
an example	for example	let us consider	specifically
especially	for instance	the case of	you can see this in

Show Purpose

all things considered	for this reason	to accomplish	with this in mind
for this purpose	in order to	to this end	with this objective

The Concluding Sentence

The concluding sentence should sum up your argument. Be sure not to introduce any new ideas, arguments, or evidence in the concluding sentence.

ACTIVITY 14-5   Writing a Concluding Sentence

Directions: *Now, choose one of the topics you have been developing in these activities and write a* **concluding sentence** *for it.*

_____

_____

Edit and Revise

Remember to revise your paragraph draft for the best results. Use the following critique form to check for the basics in your argument paragraph draft.

ARGUMENT PARAGRAPH CRITIQUE FORM

	Done well	Needs work
1. Is the topic sentence a brief and specific summary of the argument or for the plan for change—a solution?	_____	_____
2. Are the words *should, must,* or *needs to* used to help indicate the proposed plan of action?	_____	_____
3. Does the body of the paragraph develop reasons for your argument or claim and explain and elaborate the problem with examples and details?	_____	_____
4. Does the body of the paragraph provide one or more counterarguments and then address and/or refute them?	_____	_____
5. Are transitions used between reasons and support when needed?	_____	_____
6. Does the concluding sentence sum up well without adding new ideas?	_____	_____

Editing

Circle the following errors you think you see in this draft: spelling, fragments, run-ons, comma splices, commas, semicolon/colon use, pronoun agreement, reference fault errors, parallelism, apostrophe use, verb use/tense, and passive voice construction. (See Parts VII and VIII for help identifying and correcting these errors.)

Continued ▶

Other types of grammar or sentence-level errors you noticed in this draft:

_____

Comments:

_____

_____

ACTIVITY 14-6   Revising the Paragraph

Directions: *Carefully read the following student paragraph. Then, use the critique form to evaluate it. Finally, revise and rewrite the paragraph on a separate sheet of paper and be sure to address the following editing tasks.* *Answers will vary.*

1. *Does the topic sentence clearly state the writer's argument?*
2. *Does the paragraph include clear, logical reasons that support the argument?*
3. *Are the reasons presented in the most effective order?*
4. *Are there enough examples and details provided to explain and support the reasons?*
5. *Does the paragraph contain a counterargument and a reason(s) to refute it?*
6. *Are transitional words or phrases used where needed?*
7. *Is there a strong concluding sentence?*

Justin Sanders

Professor Han

ENC 0020

13 November 2010

   Learning a foreign language should be mandatory in public school starting as early as kindergarten. Too many American students don't speak a second language. In most other major countries around the world, most children speak at least one other language fluently by the time they begin high school. Many speak three or four languages by the time they are ready for college. In Sweden, students typically speak at least three languages well by the time they begin high school. However, in America, some students are just introduced to a second language in high school, or sometimes not until college, and in some cases not at all. American students will be at a disadvantage when it comes to our modern world and the international nature of business in the 21st century. American students should start learning a second language in grammar school.

PROFESSIONAL ARGUMENT PARAGRAPH

Metal Detectors and School Safety

Though many parents call for the installation of metal detectors in public high schools to protect their children from violence in schools, metal detectors are not the right choice for many reasons. Following high-profile incidents of school violence, such as school shootings or stabbing incidents, it is not uncommon for some parents, the media, and others in a school-community to call for metal detectors in response to such incidents. Parents understandably want some type of "guarantee" that these types of high-profile incidents will not occur again. Some falsely believe that metal detectors can provide that guarantee. Moreover, there is no single strategy, or even a combination of strategies, that can provide a 100% guarantee that there will not be a shooting or other act of violence at a school. School officials must therefore exercise caution to avoid overreaction, knee-jerk reactions and/or the temptation to throw up security equipment after a high-profile incident primarily for the purpose of appeasing parents and relieving parental, community, and media pressures. Doing so may very well create a false sense of security that will backfire on school officials in the long haul. In addition, school shootings and violence often occur outside of the school on school grounds. How will the metal detectors be deployed to prevent weapons offenses on those areas prior to students entering school? It is doubtful that any school district could accomplish this task even if it wanted to do so. Another question arises: Will all ground-level windows be permanently secured at all times so no one can pass a weapon through an open window to someone who already passed metal detector screening and is in the building? Would doing so even be allowed by local fire marshals? Also, the amount of time that would be required to get hundreds and in many cases thousands of students screened through the metal detectors and into their first classes on time without disrupting educational programs is too great. Even a well-run school metal detector program is not 100% foolproof. Any security technology is only as effective as the human element behind the equipment. We know that the first and best line of defense against school violence is a well-trained, highly-alert school staff and student body, and that the most common way we find out about weapons in schools is when students report such information to adults they have relationships with and trust. It is simply not an issue of buying the equipment and running the machines, and school safety threats will be eliminated. Too often the public does not see the complexities associated with operating a school metal detector program, nor do they understand that such a program will NOT provide the 100% guarantee of school safety they are openly or subliminally desiring or anticipating.

Modified from the National School Safety and Security Services website and facts provided by Ken Trump and colleagues at National School Safety and Security Services.

Reading Reflection Questions *Answers will vary. Sample answers provided.*

1. Do you think metal detectors should be installed in high schools? Why or why not?

   Answers will vary.

   _____

   _____

2. T/F ___F___ Metal detectors are a 100% guarantee against weapons being used in high schools.

3. T/F ___T___ According to this paragraph, people and their ability to be alert and responsible are the best defense against violence in schools.

4. What are two of the reasons given for not supporting the use of metal detectors (use your own words)?

   1. Weapons can still be used outside of the school. 2. The amount of time it would take all the students to pass through metal detectors would disrupt classes.

5. Summarize the overall claim or argument made in this paragraph regarding metal detectors in school.

   Metal detectors should not be installed in schools as they cannot guarantee safety, they can create a false sense of security, and they are not as effective as an alert staff and student body.

Checking Vocabulary

Define the following words in your own words or provide a dictionary definition if you don't know the word.

6. installation: *the act of putting something in place*

7. eliminated: *stopped, got rid of*

8. subliminally: *subconsciously, below the surface*

CRITICAL THINKING CHECKLIST

1. What is the author's *purpose* or *goal* in this reading selection?

2. What are the *stated questions* being addressed?

3. What *specific details and examples* does the author use to develop his or her purpose or goal for the reading?

4. Are there any implied messages in this reading (hinted at but not directly stated)? If so, what are they? Also, is there a cause and effect relationship (if this happens, then this will follow)—direct or implied?

5. Who is the intended audience, and how did you reach that conclusion?

Paragraph Writing Assignments

1. Choose one of the topics from this chapter, and narrow it down to a manageable topic. Then, decide where you stand on the issue (for or against or proposing a change) and write a paragraph that states and supports your position.

2. Choose a problem from the following list:

    a. A problem you see at your school (parking, bookstore prices, cafeteria prices and offerings, class scheduling, and so on)

    b. A problem where you work (parking, scheduling of shifts, coworker relationships, pay)

    c. A problem from your neighborhood that you would like to see fixed (a needed stop sign/stoplight, parking problems, a needed park)

    Now, think of a **plan for a solution** to this problem. After you finish your draft of this paragraph, use the Critique Form (p. 279) for self and peer review.

3. Take a stand on an issue related to one of these controversial topics:

Metal detectors in schools	Drug testing for high school athletes
Mandatory nutrition classes	Health care reform
Smoking laws	Same-sex marriage
Textbook prices	Grade exceptions for athletes
Tuition costs	Mandatory foreign language classes
Academic suspension for plagiarism	Jury and/or jury duty reform

Critical Thinking Journal Prompts

Write a journal entry based on one of the following prompts:

1. Brainstorm a list of 5–10 issues from your own life and/or experience that you think require action. Pick one of the issues you brainstormed and freewrite about it. What is the issue? What is the problem? Why are changes needed?

2. Think of an issue that you have changed your mind about in the past based on information you gained from reading, listening to others, or your life experience. Explain what the issue is and how and why you changed your mind about it.

3. Freewrite about one of the topics listed in the paragraph writing assignments above and come up with three issues related to it that you could write about.

LEARNING OBJECTIVES REVIEW

LO1 How can thinking critically help you develop your argument? (See p. 268)

Critical thinking helps you determine the *claim* you want to make (an argument for a specific position or suggestion for a solution to a perceived problem); identify any *biases or assumptions* you might have about the subject; examine and develop logical, valid *support;* and identify and address *counterarguments.*

LO2 What questions should you ask to prepare for writing an argument paragraph? (See p. 269)

You should **ask the following questions** when writing an argument paragraph: (1) What is my position on this issue? (2) Is there a solution or plan of action I want to propose? (3) What examples and evidence can I provide to support my claim? (4) How will I organize my evidence? (5) Who would disagree with my argument and why? (6) How can I address these counterarguments? (7) How will I conclude my paragraph?

LO3 How can you structure an effective, sound, and logical argument? (See pp. 269–271)

You structure an argument paragraph by stating your position (claim) about a subject; providing reasons and logical, valid evidence to support your claim; acknowledging differing viewpoints and refuting counterarguments; and, if appropriate, providing a solution to the problem you have identified.

LO4 What are logical fallacies, and why should you avoid them? (See pp. 271–272)

Logical fallacies are errors in reasoning and often result from oversimplifying an argument or not thinking through the consequences of a claim. Common logical fallacies are the ad hominen fallacy, post hoc fallacy, hasty generalization, either/or error fallacy, slippery slope error, and circular reasoning. **You should avoid these errors** as they will weaken or even invalidate your argument.

LO5 How do you write an argument paragraph? (See pp. 276–281)

When you write an argument paragraph, **start with a topic sentence that states what you are arguing for or against** (use s*hould, must,* or *needs to* to indicate you are stating an argument); **use examples and details** to illustrate the issue you are discussing; **predict, evaluate, and answer counterarguments;** and **sum up your argument** in your concluding sentence. You should **check for logical errors** and **oversimplifications** in your reasoning; **identify common ground** with those who disagree with you and when appropriate point out the merits of their point of view; and **adjust your style and tone to suit your audience.**

 For support in meeting this chapter's objectives, log in to www.mywritinglab.com and select **Paragraph Development— Argument.**

Short-Answer Exams and Timed Paragraphs

LEARNING OBJECTIVES

In this chapter, you will learn to

LO 1 Prepare for taking exams and writing timed paragraphs

LO 2 Use the writing process in exams

LO 3 Identify and use writing prompts

THINKING CRITICALLY

Answer the following questions related to writing under pressure.

1. How do you prepare for a timed or in-class essay?

_____

_____

2. Based on what you have learned about the writing process, how might you improve your current approach to generate ideas quickly and develop a strong focus?

_____

_____

STRATEGIES FOR TAKING SHORT-ANSWER EXAMS OR TIMED PARAGRAPHS

Paragraph exams and timed in-class paragraphs follow the same basic rules as take-home paragraphs. The added pressure, of course, is the time restriction and the nervousness factor. Timed paragraphs or in-class short-answer exams are great practice for writing under pressure in the real world and in your future career. Often prospective employers will ask you to write something for them during the interview process. For example, they might provide a couple of prompts for you to answer in paragraph form. Your paragraph(s) must be focused and thorough to address the prompt well and impress them. Also, in many jobs, you'll need to be able to crank out a memo or other important form of writing on the spot.

Like all paragraphs, a timed paragraph or a short-answer exam with a specific prompt requires you to stay focused and organized and to provide adequate support to illustrate your main point. The basic structure is the same too: a focused topic sentence that narrows the scope and purpose of your paragraph, examples and details that develop that focus, and a concluding sentence that wraps up your points in a concise way without introducing any new ideas or points.

LO 1 PREPARING TO TAKE SHORT-ANSWER EXAMS OR TIMED PARAGRAPHS

One of the best ways to improve your skills in writing timed paragraphs and/or short-answer exams is to reduce the panic factor. In order to alleviate that anxiety, you need to do some of the same things you do to perform well on a regular exam. First, be sure you are well prepared by reading any required materials before the day of the test. If you are asked to analyze an assigned reading, study it and prepare notes. If the paragraph prompt is one that requires no prereading, prepare by reviewing your writing textbook for the basics of paragraph writing.

Get a good night's sleep the night before a test. If you are exhausted, it is harder to concentrate and think clearly. Finally, be on time to class on test day, even arrive early if possible, since anxiety increases if you are running late and sometimes instructors provide crucial verbal directions right at the beginning of class.

Here is a list of what you need to bring to class.

1. **Pens or pencils** (even if you will be writing directly on a computer) for brainstorming or in case of printer or computer problems. Most instructors prefer black or blue ink. Avoid unusual-colored ink such as purple or green.

2. **Paper or a composition folder,** unless paper is provided by the instructor or you will be typing in a computer lab or classroom.

3. **A dictionary,** if it is allowed by the instructor. Check beforehand.

4. **A memory stick or disk** if you will be writing on a computer in class—always save a copy of your work, and save regularly as you type your paragraph—every 10 minutes or so.

5. **A watch** if there is no clock in your classroom, so you can monitor your time as you write.

LO 2 USING THE WRITING PROCESS DURING EXAMS

If you are particularly nervous before an exam, try some relaxation techniques such as deep breathing before you go into the classroom. Use positive thinking to tell yourself you are ready. After all, you've studied, right?

The same basic, five-step writing process outlined in Chapter 4 applies to writing in-class paragraphs and paragraph exams:

1. **Prewrite:** Generate ideas and your paragraph's purpose

2. **Organize:** Develop a plan for presenting your purpose and ideas

3. **Draft:** Create a first draft of your paragraph based on your plan and the pattern(s) of organization you have chosen; develop support for your paragraph's purpose

4. **Revise:** Reassess the draft for content, development, organization, and support

5. **Edit:** Check for sentence-level effectiveness, style, diction, grammar, and spelling errors

Remember to quickly assess your subject, purpose, and audience based on the writing prompt. Some assignments are specific enough that you can focus right away on your purpose. For instance, if your assignment reads "Argue for or against whether smoking should be allowed on our college campus," you can quickly decide your opinion and begin brainstorming your reasons. However, if the subject is very broad you will need to narrow it down first. For example, if your prompt reads, "Pick a problem on our campus that needs to be addressed, and then explain that problem and what you think should be done about it," you will need to narrow the subject down to one problem on campus (e.g., the negative effects of partying) that is a manageable **topic** for the length of your paragraph.

Your **purpose** is what you want to explain or prove related to the topic, so your **topic sentence** should be a statement of your overall goal. Your **audience** is the intended reader of your paragraph—who you are addressing—so you'll need to customize both your tone (such as casual/informal or more formal/academic) and the amount and types of information you include depending on the intended audience. Usually, in an in-class assignment, your audience will be the instructor, but sometimes the writing prompt will give you a specific audience. For instance, the prompt may say, "Your target audience is your fellow students."

LO 3 COMMON TERMS USED IN WRITING PROMPTS

As you review your writing prompt or question, check for words that indicate the specific tasks your instructor wants you to accomplish in the paragraph. Here are some of the common terms used in writing prompts that provide clues about the kind of information you are being asked to present:

Common Writing Prompt Terms and What They Mean

Analyze	Interpret the significance of something; divide the topic into individual components and analyze its parts. Look at cause and effect relationships; look for purpose, messages, or meanings.
Argue	Take a stand on an issue and develop your argument with reasoning and support.
Compare/contrast	Explore both similarities and differences among two or more subjects.
Defend	Provide evidence to support a stand or conclusion.
Define	Provide a definition (or set of definitions).
Discuss	Talk about (write!) the subject—be sure to focus on your purpose and not just randomly brainstorm on the topic.
Enumerate	Number off specific points, ways of doing something, steps in a process.

Examine	Analyze and explore an issue thoroughly.
Identify	Specifically list or identify what is required.
Illustrate	Show with examples, support, and analysis.
Interpret	Translate and analyze the significance of the material.
List/include	Provide a list of examples, support, and/or reasons.
Provide/support	Provide examples and details for support and explain them.
Summarize	Summarize, in your own words, the main ideas.
Trace	Detail in chronological order events or situations related to the subject.

ACTIVITY 15-1   Identifying Word Clues in Prompts

Directions: *In each of the following sample paragraph prompts, identify what the italicized words are asking the writer to do in his or her paragraph.*   Answers will vary.

1. Write a paragraph that *defines* romantic love.

   _____

2. Write a paragraph that *examines* a problem in your neighborhood.

   _____

3. *Analyze* the attached short article's main message.

   _____

4. *Summarize* the author's main points in the attached reading selection.

   _____

5. *Trace* the events that led to the recent stock market crash based on your readings this week.

   _____

6. *Interpret* the following lines from Keats's poem, "Ode on a Grecian Urn": "Beauty is Truth, Truth Beauty."

   _____

7. *List* the reasons that the North was drawn into the Civil War.

   _____

8. You have chosen to attend college. *Provide* your reasons and *support* your decision.

_____

9. Explain to other students why it is worthwhile to finish one's education. *Illustrate* your opinion through support.

_____

10. State a decision you have made recently about a political or social issue. *Defend* your reasons for this decision.

_____

11. Registering for classes is a complex process. *Enumerate* the necessary steps for a new student to follow.

_____

12. *Discuss* the issue of mandatory drug testing for athletes on our campus.

_____

13. *Compare and contrast* attending high school versus college.

_____

14. *Argue* for or against mandatory drug testing for college athletes.

_____

15. *Examine* the effects of overeating.

_____

APPLYING CRITICAL THINKING

The best way to make the most of your time in an exam situation is to do the following:

1. **Make sure you understand the prompt or question.** Read it carefully (see the list of Common Writing Prompt Terms). It helps to revise the given *question* into a topic sentence *answer* before you even start to prewrite, as you need to know your **purpose** for writing the paragraph before you begin.

2. **Allow at least five minutes for brainstorming** (on paper or using a computer) after you get your topic or prompt. It will help you generate **ideas** as well as **examples** and **details** to support them before you dive into writing.

3. Write a rough outline to organize your ideas.

4. **Focus more on ideas and details as you write,** and try not to obsess about spelling and style (though do use complete sentences and good paragraph structure). Strong **support** for and **analysis** of your ideas and topic sentence are the key to solid in-class writing.

5. **Allow at least five minutes for a quick review and flash revision** of glaring problems after you write your paragraph. Be sure to check for spelling or grammar mistakes, and check your tone and diction choices.

ACTIVITY 15-2   Adjusting Your Current Approach to Timed Writing

Directions: *Describe below what you have done in the past during a timed, in-class writing assignment (include a description of both your good and bad habits).*

_____

_____

_____

Now, based on what you have learned in this chapter, describe your ideas for what you plan to do the next time you have an in-class writing.

_____

_____

_____

ACTIVITY 15-3   Timed Paragraph Practice I

Directions: *Give yourself **30 minutes** to write this paragraph from start to finish.*

Prompt: *Write a paragraph about something you would like to see changed at your campus. Focus on what needs to happen and why.*

Complete the following steps:

1. *Brainstorm, prewrite, and outline for five minutes to generate ideas and support.*

2. *Begin with a strong topic sentence that addresses the prompt above.*

Cross Reference

All these techniques also work for in-class *essay* exams. See Chapter 17 for tips on applying them to essay writing.

3. *Develop your purpose with reasons, examples, and details. Structure your paragraph in a logical order to support your purpose such as order of importance or time order depending on your topic and support.*

4. *Write a concluding sentence that sums up your argument.*

5. *Do a quick review of organization and support; check quickly for spelling and grammar errors.*

ACTIVITY 15-4 Timed Paragraph Practice II

Directions: *Write for **30 minutes** on the following prompt.*

Prompt: *Do you think that junk food and sugar-based snacks should be sold in middle schools? Why or why not?*

Be sure to explain your reasons for your position and provide support and examples for your reasons.

ACTIVITY 15-5 Self-Assessment Paragraph

Use this exercise as an end of course assessment.

Directions: *Write a self-assessment paragraph. In the paragraph, address the following questions:*

1. *Assess your improvement over the span of this writing course in planning, drafting, and revising paragraphs. How exactly has your paragraph writing improved? Be specific.*

2. *What are your strengths in writing paragraphs?*

3. *What are your weaknesses in writing paragraphs? What do you need to work on in the future?*

4. *Is there anything else you would like to say about your writing journey during this course?*

LEARNING OBJECTIVES REVIEW

LO 1 How can you prepare for taking short-answer exams or writing timed paragraphs? (See pp. 288–289)	To **prepare for exams or writing timed paragraphs** you should do the following: read, study, and annotate relevant material, including your writing textbook, before the test; get a good night's sleep; arrive a little early; and bring everything you will need.
LO 2 How can you use the writing process to perform better in written exams? (See pp. 289–290)	You can **use the writing process in** exams to *prewrite* to generate ideas and purpose, *organize your ideas, draft* your paragraph, and *revise* and *edit* it. Be sure to quickly assess your subject, purpose, and audience based on the writing prompt before you start.
LO 3 Why is it helpful to be able to identify common writing prompts? (See pp. 290–292)	It is helpful to be able to **identify common writing prompts** because they indicate the specific tasks your instructor wants you to accomplish in a paragraph.

16 Summary, Paraphrase, and Writing About Fiction

Soul Senate   Wayne Buck

THINKING CRITICALLY

What is happening in this picture? Write a brief description of the scene and the people and what they are doing, just the most important information in the picture.

_____

_____

In answering the question above, you provided the most important points about the picture—there are two singers performing—and in doing so, you summarized the action in the picture.

Both summary and paraphrase are ways of briefly restating written information. In college, you will be asked to write summaries of longer pieces, paraphrases of short passages, or analyses of essays, articles, or short stories Use the assignment, this chapter, and your critical thinking to make the best choices for which technique to use when writing about someone else's work.

LO 1 PARAPHRASE

When you **paraphrase,** you use your own words to *restate* a sentence or two from a piece of writing. A paraphrase should be about the same length and contain about the same amount of detail as the original sentence(s). Make sure that you use different words and your own sentence structure when you paraphrase to avoid plagiarism, and always give the original author credit.

A paraphrase should be very short. If you paraphrase more than a few sentences, you are running dangerously close to plagiarizing an author's writing. Instead, summarize the main ideas of a piece of writing and only paraphrase (rephrase) the sentences that need to be given in detail. It is essential to be objective in your paraphrase of an author's ideas. Do not add your opinions or personal reactions to the material.

Five Steps for Paraphrasing Material

Here are five steps for writing a complete and accurate paraphrase.

Step One	**Read the sentences you want to paraphrase carefully before writing anything.** It is essential to understand the author's main point and supporting evidence before you can paraphrase it. You can use the T-KED method (p. 30).
Step Two	**Include the author's full name and the title of the work you are paraphrasing in your first sentence.** Place the title of a story, essay, or article in quotation marks, and use italics for the title of a book or play.
Step Three	**Paraphrase the sentence(s).** Write the paraphrase *using your own words*, not the words of the author (no direct quotations in a paraphrase) and use your own sentence structure and style.
Step Four	**Stay objective.** Do not offer your opinion or interpretation in the paraphrase itself. Check that you presented the author's ideas accurately without adding your own thoughts on the topic.
Step Five	**Include a page citation and/or publication information when needed**—even paraphrased references to a text in an essay need citations; otherwise you are guilty of plagiarism (not giving credit to the original author).

Cross Reference

See Chapter 17 for more on avoiding plagiarism and correct MLA citation format.

▶ TIP   In order to avoid using the same words or style as the author, write your paraphrase without looking at the original text. Then check to make sure you have included all of the author's main ideas and major supporting details. It can also help to explain an author's ideas and support to a friend before you write a paraphrase in order to be sure you understand them.

Sample Paraphrase

Original: Paragraph 8 from "Last Rites for Indian Dead," by Suzan Shown Harjo

One unusually well-publicized example of Indian grave desecration occurred two years ago in a western Kentucky field known as Slack Farm, the site of an Indian village five centuries ago. Ten men—one with a business card stating "Have Shovel, Will Travel"—paid the landowner $10,000 to lease digging rights between planting seasons. They dug extensively on the 40-acre farm, rummaging through an estimated 650 graves, collecting burial goods, tools and ceremonial items. Skeletons were strewn about like litter.

Paraphrase

In her article "Last Rites for Indian Dead," Suzan Shown Harjo tells how, two years ago, the violation of an Indian gravesite in Kentucky at a place called Slack Farm was extensively covered in the media. Ten men leased between-season digging rights for $10,000 from the owner, and then dug up an area that had been the site of an Indian village 500 years earlier. The men ransacked approximately 650 graves and took a variety of things including tools and burial and ceremonial items. Bones from the graves were scattered around like trash (2).

Notice that the paraphrase has the same number of sentences and the same basic information as the original two sentences, but it is worded differently and has a different sentence structure than the original: it is rephrased or *paraphrased*.

Use the following checklist to ensure that you have accurately paraphrased short passages.

Checklist for an Accurate Paraphrase

To ensure you have written an accurate paraphrase, check that you have done the following:

1. **Paraphrased the ideas in the original sentence(s) in the same order** they were presented in the original text.

2. **Included all of the main ideas and main examples** for support from the original sentence(s).

3. **Used your own words** and did not include any significant phrases that were in the original sentence(s) (no direct or even partial quotes).

4. **Checked that the paraphrase is accurate** in its restatement of the original material and that you have not added any reaction to or opinion about the material (the restatement should be objective).

5. **Included the author's name and the title of the original piece** at the beginning of your paraphrase and included a page citation at the end.

ACTIVITY 16-1   Paraphrasing

Directions: *Pick a reading from Chapter 18 (or your instructor might assign a passage) and write a paraphrase of one to three sentences from it on a separate sheet of paper, using the Five Steps for Paraphrasing Material. Use the T-KED method to gain a thorough understanding of the passage. Then, explain below what effect following this process had on the way you read the paragraph in preparation for writing your paraphrase and your overall understanding of the ideas it contained. Answers will vary.*

_____

_____

_____

_____

LO 2 SUMMARY

A **summary** is an objective, condensed statement of the main points, and the major support for them, of an original work (an article, text chapter, story, etc.) written in your own words. It should not include direct quotations or your opinions or personal reactions to the material. Here are seven steps for writing a complete and effective summary.

Seven Steps for Writing a Summary

Be sure to read all seven steps before you begin since some of these steps overlap.

Step One

Read the entire work (article, essay, short story), using the Six Steps to Active Reading and the T-KED method, at least twice before you write your summary. It is essential to thoroughly understand the author's main ideas and support *before* you start to summarize them. Explaining the author's ideas and support to a friend before you write can also be helpful.

Step Two

Be brief. Usually a summary contains about one paragraph for each two to three pages of original text. A good rule of thumb is that a summary should be about one quarter the length of the original work.

Step Three

Write the summary in your own words. You should not use direct quotations. In order to avoid using the same words or style as the author, re-read one section of the work at a time (a couple of paragraphs to a page or so), and then, without looking back at the page, write a summary of the section. Then, look at the text again, and be sure your summary includes all the author's main ideas from that section. Be sure to provide in-text citations after summarized text to avoid plagiarism.

Cross Reference
See Chapter 17, p. 334, for information on in-text citation.

Step Four

Stay objective. Do not offer your opinion or add interpretation: just summarize objectively. Read over your summary and check for accuracy. Did you represent the author's main ideas without adding your own opinions?

Step Five

State the author's main idea (the thesis), his or her full name, and the title of the work in the first sentence. You can identify the thesis by answering the question, What is the main message of this work? (Place the titles of stories, essays, articles, and poems in quotation marks and italicize the titles of books or plays.)

Step Six   **Divide summaries longer than 200 words into two or more paragraphs.** Use a natural break or change of main idea focus to decide where paragraph breaks should occur.

Step Seven   **Evaluate, revise, and edit.** Go back and reread the original work and double-check your summary for accuracy. Make sure you have included all the main ideas and major supporting details, used your own words, and not offered any personal opinions. Finally, check for grammar or spelling errors, overall sentence variety, and transitions.

> ▶ TIP   Try putting your summary away for a day or two; then, come back to it and *read it aloud*. Listen to make sure that it flows smoothly and captures the author's main ideas in a clear and accurate way.

Here is a sample summary of Suzan Shown Harjo's "Last Rites for Indian Dead" from Chapter 18, page 374. Read the selection carefully before reading the summary. Then notice how the summary keeps the same order of ideas as the article, provides the major ideas and the examples used for support of those ideas, remains objective in its presentation of the ideas, and uses transitions to flow smoothly from one idea to the next.

Sample Summary

Suzan Shown Harjo's essay, "Last Rites for Indian Dead," argues that Indian remains being held in American museums since the 1800s need to be reburied. Harjo first explains how these remains were collected by the U.S. Army in the 1800s as part of an Indian cranial study and how they ended up at the Smithsonian Museum. According to her essay, the heads were originally collected so that the army could do what she called pseudo-research, measuring the skulls and weighing the brains for research that ended up in a report with no findings or conclusions drawn. She says that the Smithsonian Museum alone houses 19,000 Indian remains and that there might be a total of over 1.5 million remains housed in American museums. She questions the use of Indian remains for scientific studies then and now. She points out that some universities have already returned the remains they possessed for burial and that other museums should do the same. She also emphasizes that the desecration of Indian graves is still going on. Today, though, the graves are desecrated by relic hunters, hoping to find ceremonial tools, jewelry, or other artifacts that can be sold for money. Some of the remains are still collected for supposedly scientific studies that might benefit living Native Americans, but Harjo doesn't agree. Harjo also points out that Congress and many state lawmakers are beginning to enact legislation that will protect the remains. Essentially, though, throughout her essay, she argues that Indian remains are not artifacts to be studied or collector's items; instead, they are the remains of relatives and ancestors that living Indians want returned so they can bury them with the dignity and respect they deserve.

Use the following checklist to ensure that you have accurately summarized an article, essay, or textbook chapter.

Checklist for an Accurate Summary

To ensure you written an accurate summary, check that you have done the following:

1. **Summarized the ideas in the same order** they were presented in the original work.

2. **Included all the main ideas and supporting examples.**

3. **Used your own words,** and not included any significant phrases that were in the original passage (no direct or even partial quotes).

4. **Checked that the summary is accurate** and you have not added any personal reactions to or opinions about the material.

5. **Included the author's name and the title of the piece** and an in-text citation at the end of your summary.

ACTIVITY 16-2 Summarizing

Directions: *Pick a reading from Chapter 18 (or your instructor might assign a reading for you to summarize) and write a summary of it following the Seven Steps for Writing a Summary. Use the T-KED method (p. 30) or the Six Steps for Active Reading (p. 22) to ensure you understand the material so you can accurately summarize it. Then, explain below what effect following this process had on the way you read the piece in preparation for writing the summary and your overall understanding of the original work.*   Answers will vary.

_____

_____

_____

_____

LO 3 COMBINING SUMMARY AND ANALYSIS

A **summary** explains *what* the author is saying; an **analysis** explains *what he or she means*.

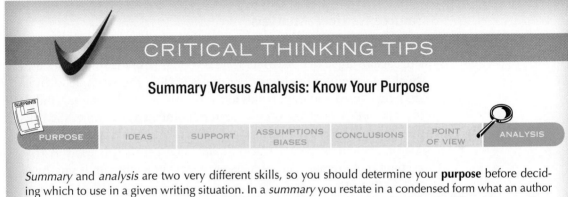

CRITICAL THINKING TIPS

Summary Versus Analysis: Know Your Purpose

PURPOSE | IDEAS | SUPPORT | ASSUMPTIONS BIASES | CONCLUSIONS | POINT OF VIEW | ANALYSIS

Summary and *analysis* are two very different skills, so you should determine your **purpose** before deciding which to use in a given writing situation. In a *summary* you restate in a condensed form what an author says in an article, essay, or other piece of writing using your own words without adding interpretation, commentary, or opinions on the material. **Analysis** involves using your critical thinking skills to *interpret* the important ideas in a piece of writing and to critique the techniques an author uses to present them.

To analyze a work well, you need to include a summary of the original ideas and arguments in an unbiased (fair) way. Then you use your analysis skills to interpret the direct and implied messages of the piece and to critique the author's techniques and style choices, adding your own opinions about both. You learned how to write an unbiased summary using the Seven Steps for Writing a Summary (p. 300). Here are two additional steps that you would use in order to add analysis to your summary.

Cross Reference
Review Chapter 1 for more on *summary, analysis, inference,* and *interpretation.*

Steps Eight and Nine for Writing Critical Analysis

Step Eight   **Interpret the language and techniques used by the author to make his or her point.** Use specific examples from the text to illustrate your interpretation or to demonstrate the writing or style choices the author has made and what effect those have on the reader and the delivery of the message. See "The Ice Cream Sandwich: Framing Facts and Sources" on page 304 for information on how to integrate paraphrases, summaries, or quotations into your analysis.

Step Nine **Analyze the author's purpose.** What are his or her main messages? What are the direct messages or points made, and what indirect messages are implied? What are his or her biases?

Here is the critical analysis (Steps Eight and Nine) for the summary of Suzan Shown Harjo's essay that appears on pages 301–02. Reread that summary and then read this analysis.

Sample Critical Analysis

Throughout the essay, Harjo uses strong examples, details, and language to argue her case. Her tone is serious, and she sometimes uses shocking examples to convey her message (like the example of Indians being killed and their heads instantly cut off for the cranial study). She also uses a sarcastic tone at certain points. For example, she calls the doctor who conducted the cranial study in the 1800s the "good doctor," which is ironic. Harjo's main message in this essay is that keeping these remains as artifacts or objects in a museum is unethical and disrespectful.

To help you create in-depth interpretation and analysis of lines from sources, use the Ice Cream Sandwich technique (introduced in Chapter 3, pp. 43–44) in a modified way as demonstrated below.

LO 4 The Ice Cream Sandwich: Framing Facts and Sources

First, introduce the point you want to make or critique, next provide support for it from the text, and then provide your interpretation of what the author is saying (directly and indirectly) and your analysis of its significance. You should also critique the author's technique (style, writing, tone, and language) in terms of how well he or she develops a point.

The Ice Cream Sandwich at a Glance

Top Cookie: A sentence or two to introduce the point you want to make or critique.

Ice Cream Filling: The text reference (summary, paraphrase, or quotation) that supports your point. Be sure to put the text reference into a sentence of your own:
- Summary
- Paraphrase ▶ plus page number (in parentheses)
- Direct quote

> **Bottom Cookie:**   Interpretation and analysis
> - Interpretation (what is being said—define key terms when necessary)
> - Analysis (what the messages are and a critique of the author's ideas, writing style, or techniques)

Top Cookie (introduction): Start with a sentence or two that introduces the point you want to make, using the author for support, or a point you want to critique, using an example from the author.

> Valerie Montoya argues that parents need to enforce strict limits when it comes to the amount of time their children spend in front of a computer screen (4).

Ice Cream Filling (paraphrase, summary, or quotation): After introducing the point you want to make, include a specific idea or example from the author that supports it, using a paraphrase, summary, or direct quote. A paraphrased line or a summarized idea can be integrated into your own sentence, but you need to put a page number citation after this material. If you use a direct quotation from the reading, you need to attach it to what you are saying. There are three ways to *weave* a quote into your sentence correctly.

1. **Use a tag line:**

> Valerie Montoya claims, "Children who spend more than two hours a day in front of a computer screen are spending too much time on the computer" (5).

2. **Weave the quotation into a sentence of your own:**

> Children who "spend more than two hours a day in front of a computer screen" (Montoya 5) can suffer negative effects.

3. **Set up the quote with an analytical sentence followed by a colon and the quotation that illustrates your point:**

> The negative effects of children under 12 spending too much time in front of a computer are numerous: "Some children's eyes were affected, some lost an interest in outdoor sports, and some had trouble interacting with their peers" (Montoya 6).

Cross Reference
See Chapter 17 for an
explanation of MLA
documentation format.

Then, be sure to add a *citation* in the assigned documentation format.

▶ NOTE   In MLA, the end punctuation goes after the parenthetical citation, as shown above.

Bottom Cookie (analysis): Analyze what the author is saying, defining terms when needed. Then, give an *analytical response* to the idea the quotation is expressing: that is, agree with, disagree with, elaborate on, or critique the ideas or the logic of the author's argument.

Analytical interpretation: Montoya is saying that if we do not set limits on the amount of time children spend on the computer now, they will form negative habits and suffer physical and social consequences.

Analytical response: As Montoya suggests, it is the parents' responsibility to set limits on screen time for children and to help their children learn to exercise self-control.

ACTIVITY 16-3   Analytical Ice Cream Sandwich Exercise

Directions: *Pick a one to two sentence quotation from one of the readings included in this text and use it to write a full analytical Ice Cream Sandwich.* Answers will vary.

Top Cookie (introduction): _____

_____

Ice Cream Filling (the quote): _____

_____

Add the page number citation: (_____).

Bottom Cookie (analytical interpretation): _____

_____

_____

Analytical reaction and/or critique: _____

_____

_____

ACTIVITY 16-4   Summary and Analysis

Directions: *Choose one of the readings from Chapter 18, and write a two-paragraph critique of it that includes both a summary of the main ideas and specific analysis and critical responses to the ideas in the reading (the Seven Steps PLUS Steps Eight and Nine—summary plus critical analysis). After you have finished, describe below what effect the process of summarizing and analyzing this reading had on your overall comprehension of the author's ideas.* Answers will vary.

_____

_____

ACTIVITY 16-5   Adding Analysis

Directions: *Review the summary you wrote for either Activity 16-3 or 16-4 and add Steps Nine and Ten to make it a summary with critical analysis. After you finish, describe below how your thinking process was different than it was when you were only writing a summary. How did you have to think differently in order to add analysis?* Answers will vary.

_____

_____

(LO 5) WRITING ANALYSIS PARAGRAPHS AND ESSAYS ABOUT FICTION

In an analysis paragraph or essay, you interpret (explain) and analyze an author's messages and the techniques he or she uses to communicate them to the reader. If you are writing an analysis of a selection you have read for class, then you usually do not need to summarize it, since your audience has already read it. Instead, you should focus on explaining the meaning of the story, identifying the author's main messages, and analyzing the techniques the author uses to convey them and discussing whether they are effective.

However, if your analysis is written for a broader audience who may not have read the original work, you may need to include a brief summary of the story first (see Seven Steps for Writing a Summary on pp. 300–301).

APPLYING CRITICAL THINKING

PURPOSE IDEAS SUPPORT ASSUMPTIONS BIASES CONCLUSIONS POINT OF VIEW ANALYSIS

Questions to Ask if You are Analyzing an Essay or Story

Before you begin writing your analysis of an essay or article, ask yourself the following questions:

1. What is the most important message the author wants to get across to the reader? What is his or her **purpose?**

2. What are some secondary messages or **ideas** developed in this piece?

3. Are there any implied messages or **ideas?** If so, what are they?

4. How does the author's tone affect the overall effectiveness of the essay or story?

5. What specific writing techniques does the author use?

6. **Analyze** the author's style and specific writing techniques in the piece and ask yourself, Are they effective? Why or why not?

Further questions to ask if you are analyzing short fiction:

7. What is the plot—what happens and how does the action build and resolve, or not?

8. Who is the main character (protagonist)? Is there something he or she wants?

9. Is the setting (physical place and/or historical setting) of the story significant?

10. Is there any symbolism in the language or in the action of the story?

Structuring an Analysis Paragraph

Cross Reference

Review pages 297–302 for paraphrase and summary techniques.

Begin your analysis paragraph with a topic sentence that states the main message of the article or story and the point(s) you want to make about it. Use summary, paraphrase, or specific quotations from the article or story to develop your topic sentence. Include specific scenes, events, or parts of the essay or story as examples to illustrate the point you stated in your topic sentence. Be sure to comment on the significance of the examples (parts or scenes) you include. Use the Ice Cream Sandwich technique (pp. 304–306) for framing quotations. End your paragraph with a concluding sentence that ties back to the main point you made in your topic sentence and reiterates the purpose of your analysis.

Sample Student Paragraph

▶ NOTE *Read the original essay "Shame," by Dick Gregory, on pages 388–392 first, so that you fully understand this student's analysis of the story.*

Robynne Knight

Professor Hoene

English 081

20 May 2010

In Dick Gregory's story, "Shame," young Richard experiences an embarrassing episode in his classroom that changes his life and his perception of himself: he learns to feel shame and spends many years trying to get back his self-worth. One day in his childhood, he is shamed by his teacher in front of the whole class and in front of the girl he has a big crush on, Helene. He writes, "Helene was sitting in that classroom when I learned to be ashamed of myself" (2). The teacher is asking each student what his or her father is going to contribute to a charity fundraiser. However, the teacher asks every student except Richard. When he raises his hand and says she forgot him and that "My daddy said he'd give . . . fifteen dollars," she replies, "We are collecting this money for you and your kind, Richard Gregory" (3). Then, to make things even worse, when he continues to try to say what his daddy would contribute, she gets annoyed and adds, "We know you don't have a daddy" (4). Richard notices now that Helene is crying, that she feels sorry for him, and he is so ashamed that he cries too. Then, he leaves and doesn't return to school much after that. He has been shamed so deeply that it stays with him until he is an adult. Gregory writes, "I guess I would have

Topic sentence (top cookie for entire paragraph, sets up examples and analysis to come)

Top cookie for an ice cream sandwich sets up the point of the quotation

Ice cream filling (quotation)

Bottom cookie (interpretation and analysis)

Top cookie for an ice cream sandwich sets up the point of the quotation

Ice cream filling (quotations)

Bottom cookie (interpretation and analysis)

Top cookie for an ice cream sandwich sets up the point of the quotation

Ice cream filling (quotation)

Bottom cookie of last
sandwich and of paragraph
(interpretation and
analysis)

gotten over Helene by summertime, but something happened in that classroom that made her face hang in front of me for the next twenty-two years" (1). This incident taught him to feel shame for the first time, and he spent the next twenty-two years learning how to get his self-respect back and prove himself.

Use the following critique form for self or peer review to check that all the important elements of a good analytical paragraph are included.

ANALYTICAL PARAGRAPH CRITIQUE FORM

	Done well	Needs work
1. Does the paragraph have a clear topic sentence?	_____	_____
2. Does the paragraph include support, examples, and quotations from the story or essay? (two to four quotations)	_____	_____
3. Is each quotation tagged or woven into a sentence?	_____	_____
4. Is each quotation framed with analysis—set up and then interpreted? The full ice cream sandwich?	_____	_____
5. Are quotation marks and punctuation handled correctly?	_____	_____
6. Is there a concluding analytical sentence?	_____	_____
7. Are transitions used when needed?	_____	_____
8. Does the paragraph have unity (all the sentences support the topic sentence)?	_____	_____
9. Are the tone and style (language choices) appropriate?	_____	_____
10. Is the spelling and grammar correct?	_____	_____

ACTIVITY 16-6   Story Analysis Paragraph Assignment

Directions: *Choose one of the stories or essays from Chapter 18 (or use a story you have been assigned or chosen). Read it, using the Six Steps for Active Reading (p. 22). Then, write a one- to two-paragraph analysis, using the suggestions above. Use the Analytical Paragraph Critique Form for self and peer review of your draft.*

Structuring an Analysis Essay

The first paragraph of your essay should begin with a general introduction (one to three sentences) to the ideas or themes of the story, essay, or article you are going to discuss. This should be followed by an analytical thesis statement that presents your opinion of what the main messages of the piece are and what can be learned from reading it.

Each body paragraph should start with an analytical topic sentence that directly supports the thesis. For instance, if you decided to focus on analyzing the characters in a story, the topic sentence for each paragraph would focus on one of the main characters. Or, if you wrote an analysis of a story that used time order and focused on the progression of events, your topic sentences would relate to how the author leads the reader to his or her final message step by step.

In the body of each paragraph, you should support the topic sentence with examples from the essay or story and analysis of their purpose and effect. Each example should be interpreted (translated by you to explain what it illustrates in relation to the story) and analyzed for its meaning (direct and implied). In general, you will need about two quotations from the essay or story for each body paragraph in order to provide adequate support for your topic sentence. Every time you use a quotation, structure it using the Ice Cream Sandwich technique.

Cross Reference

See Chapter 1, pages 3–9, for help writing a strong analytical paper.

Finish your essay with a concluding paragraph that restates your thesis (not the same words though; say it a different way) and sums up your essay's main points. Then use the following critique form for self or peer review to check that all the important elements of a good analytical essay are included.

ANALYTICAL ESSAY CRITIQUE FORM

Overall	Done well	Needs work
1. Is the essay analytical? Does it include interpretation, commentary, and analysis of the message(s)?	_____	_____
2. Does the essay avoid merely summarizing the story or essay?	_____	_____
3. Does the essay stay focused on proving the thesis?	_____	_____
Introduction		
4. Is the title interesting, appropriate, and typed in correct format?	_____	_____
5. Does the general introduction lead smoothly into the thesis?	_____	_____

Continued ▶

6. Is the thesis statement clear? (Is it a clear presentation of the story or essay's message?)   _____ _____

7. Is a plan of development included in the thesis (e.g., Does it indicate that body paragraphs will be organized by themes/ideas, characters, the author's style and writing techniques, and so on)?   _____ _____

Body

8. Do the body paragraphs have clear topic sentences?   _____ _____

9. Does each body paragraph include support, examples, and quotations from the story/essay (about two quotations per body paragraph)?   _____ _____

10. Is each quotation tagged or woven into a sentence?   _____ _____

11. Is each quotation framed with analysis—set up and then interpreted? (Ice Cream Sandwich approach)   _____ _____

12. Are quotation marks and punctuation handled correctly?   _____ _____

13. Is there a concluding analytical sentence in each body paragraph?   _____ _____

14. Are transitions used well, both within and between paragraphs?   _____ _____

Conclusion

15. Does the concluding paragraph sum up your points well without introducing new ideas or analysis?   _____ _____

Grammar/Spelling/Citation Format (MLA)

16. Citation format: Every time a quotation is used, is it followed by parentheses containing the page number and/or the author's name followed by a period?   _____ _____

17. Grammar: *Circle errors you think you see in this paper:* spelling, fragments, run-ons, comma splices, commas, semicolon/colon use, pronoun agreement, reference fault errors, parallelism, apostrophe use, verb use/tense, and passive voice construction.

18. Other types of grammar or sentence-level errors you noticed in this draft:

_____

Comments:

_____

_____

Sample Student Story Analysis Essay

▶ NOTE   Be sure to read the original essay "Shame" by Dick Gregory on pages 388–392 to get a full understanding of this student's analysis of this story.

Robynne Knight

Professor Hoene

English 081

20 May 2010

Overcoming Shame

Most of us have had childhood experiences that helped shape who we became as adults. Some of these experiences were positive, and some were negative. Sometimes the hardest experiences make us grow the most. In Richard Gregory's story, "Shame," young Richard has a hard experience related to his extreme poverty through which he learns to feel shame, and the grown-up Gregory wants his readers to learn how shame can be devastating and how important it is for all of us to respect all human beings because people want to feel pride instead of shame.

In the beginning of the story, Gregory establishes the young Richard's poverty through a powerful series of examples. For instance, he shows how Richard did not have more than one set of clothes and that he sometimes did not even have running water. He had to collect ice from a local store to melt in order to clean his clothes. He writes, "By evening the ice melted to water for washing. I got sick a lot that winter because the fire would go out at night before the clothes were dry. In the morning I'd put them on, wet or dry, because they were the only clothes I had" (1). Even though he only had one set of clothes, he was determined to keep them clean and feel dignity instead of shame. He was poor but proud and determined. He also gives examples of being embarrassed when the relief truck would come to his house, and he tells how he threw away the warm jacket (mackinaw) that welfare had given him because he was too embar-rassed to wear it. Furthermore, in the story he also explains how

Introduction

Thesis statement—sets up the author's purpose/ message in the story

Top cookie ice cream sandwich—sets up the quotation's message
Ice cream filling: a quotation

Bottom cookie: interpreta-tion and analysis

Knight 2

Top cookie ice cream sandwich—sets up the quotation's message

Ice cream filling: a quotation

Bottom cookie: interpretation and analysis

Ice-cream sandwich sets up message, includes quotation (filling), and ends with interpretation and analysis.

Ice-cream sandwich sets up message, includes quotation (filling), and ends with interpretation and analysis.

Ice-cream sandwich sets up message, includes quotation (filling), and ends with interpretation and analysis.

hungry he was. One powerful example of this is when he explains that he sometimes snuck spoonfuls of paste in class. He says, "Paste doesn't taste too bad when you're hungry," and he adds, "Pregnant people get strange tastes. I was pregnant with poverty" (2). He is making the point that when you are very poor and hungry, when you have no other options, you will eat anything, even paste in a classroom. The words and examples he uses to express his hunger and poverty throughout the story make the reader feel what he felt in a powerful way.

Young Richard also wanted to impress the girl he had a crush on, Helene Tucker. She was important to him on many levels. He says, "Everybody's got a Helene Tucker, a symbol of everything you want" (1). Helene represents a higher level, a goal, for him. He wants to impress her because she gives him something to aspire for. He tries to impress her mother and aunts, leaves money for her on her stoop, and he feels better about himself when she acknowledges him. When she would walk near his home, his siblings would call out to him that she was coming and he would "run out on the street. If I knew my place and didn't come too close, she'd wink at me and say hello. That was a good feeling" (1). She makes him feel good, and she makes him feel worthy when she notices him.

Unfortunately, young Richard experiences an embarrassing episode in his classroom that changes his life for many years as well as his perception of himself. He is shamed by his teacher in front of the whole class and in front of Helene. He writes, "Helene was sitting in that classroom when I learned to be ashamed of myself" (2). The teacher is asking each student what his or her father is going to contribute to a charity fundraiser. However, the teacher asks each student except Richard. When he raises his hand and says she forgot him, he adds, "My daddy said he'd give . . . fifteen dollars," and she replies, "We are collecting this money for you and your kind, Richard Gregory" (3). Then, to make things even worse, when he continues to try to say what his daddy would contribute, she gets annoyed and adds, "We know you don't have a daddy" (4). Richard notices now that Helene is crying, that she feels sorry for him, and he is so ashamed that he cries too. Then, he leaves and doesn't return to school much after that. He has been shamed so deeply that it stays with him until he is an adult. Gregory writes, "I guess I would have gotten over Helene by summertime, but something happened in that classroom that made her face hang in front of me for the next twenty-two years" (1). This incident taught him to feel shame for the first time, and he spent the next twenty-two years learning how to get his self-respect back and to prove himself.

Ice-cream sandwich sets up message, includes quotation (filling), and ends with interpretation and analysis.

Richard Gregory's story "Shame" explores the pain of poverty, but more importantly, it explains the devastating effects of experiencing shame. It took Gregory many years to overcome one childhood experience that made him lose his pride and, through his story, he wants his readers to see the importance of respecting others and the need to work hard to overcome being shamed by another.

Conclusion—reiterates the thesis and the author's message

ACTIVITY 16-7   Analysis Essay Assignment

Directions: *Choose one of the stories or essays from this text, and write a full analysis essay. Then, use the Analysis Essay Critique Form from this chapter to revise your draft.*

LEARNING OBJECTIVES REVIEW

LO1	What is a paraphrase, and how do you write one? (See pp. 297–299)	A **paraphrase** is a *restatement in your own words* of a sentence or two from a piece of writing. It should be about the same length and contain about the same amount of detail as the original. You can write an accurate paraphrase, and avoid plagiarism, by (1) carefully reading the material you want to paraphrase, (2) including the author's full name and the title of the work in the first sentence, (3) rephrasing the material using your own words, (4) not offering your opinion, and (5) including an in-text citation when needed.
LO2	What is a summary, and how do you write an accurate one? (See pp. 300–302)	A **summary** is an objective, condensed statement (usually a quarter the length of the original) written *in your own words* of the main points of an original work. It should include the author's *main ideas* and support for them in the order they appear in the original and no direct quotations. To write an accurate summary and avoid plagiarism, you should (1) read the entire work at least twice before you start; (2) be concise; (3) use your own words; (4) avoid offering your opinion, (5) state the author's main idea (the thesis) and support using your own words in the first sentence, as well as the author's name, and the title of the work; (6) divide summaries longer than 200 words into two or more paragraphs; and (7) evaluate, revise, and edit.
LO3	How can you combine summary and analysis, and why would you do so? (See pp. 303–304)	A **summary** explains *what* the author is saying: an **analysis** explains what he or she *means*. Some assignments require you to use a synthesis of both skills to thoroughly cover an assigned reading.
LO4	What are the three main components of the "Ice Cream Sandwich" method for framing material? (See pp. 304–306)	The three main components of the **Ice Cream Sandwich** are (1) the top cookie, a sentence or two that introduces the point you want to make; (2) the ice cream filling, which is a direct quotation, paraphrase, or summary with a page citation; and (3) the bottom cookie, which provides interpretation and analysis.
LO5	What is the purpose for writing an analytical paragraph or essay about a piece of fiction? (See pp. 307–315)	The purpose for writing an analysis paragraph or essay about a piece of fiction is to interpret (explain) and analyze an author's messages and the techniques he or she uses to communicate them to the reader.

For support in meeting this chapter's objectives, log in to www.mywritinglab.com and select **Summary Writing** and **Quotations.**

17 Researching and Documenting Sources

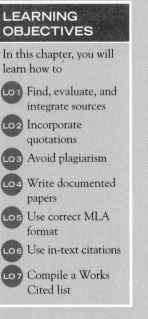
THINKING CRITICALLY

1. Do you think using sources in your writing can make your ideas have more power?

_____

_____

_____

2. What do you think you need to do to use sources well and to give proper credit for others' ideas?

_____

_____

_____

TYPES OF SOURCES

When you research a paper, you need to look for sources of information about your subject that will provide relevant and credible support for your ideas. Three general sources of information are

- **Reference sources,** such as dictionary or encyclopedia entries that you can use to explain or develop a term or concept in your paper.
- **Primary sources,** which are original materials such as journals, essays, novels, poems, stories, historical accounts, blogs, and so on.
- **Secondary sources,** which are materials that are written about or in response to primary sources such as summaries, bibliographies, critical analyses, and reviews.

Take care when using information from other writers to evaluate what you find and be alert to signs of author bias. Use your critical thinking skills to evaluate the credibility of their interpretations and evaluations.

Cross Reference
See page 323 for more on evaluating sources.

Documented Papers

A **documented paper** requires you to use sources to strengthen and support your own ideas. You first determine your argument, the point you want to make, and then research sources to find evidence to explain and support it. Before you begin to write, you should also spend some examining any assumptions or biases you might have on the subject.

> **Documented Paper:** write your own arguments/conclusion on a topic of your choice → research for support → integrate sources → document sources

Ask yourself the following questions before you begin your research.

APPLYING CRITICAL THINKING

PURPOSE   IDEAS   SUPPORT   ASSUMPTIONS BIASES   CONCLUSIONS   POINT OF VIEW   ANALYSIS

When you look for sources to support your argument in a paper, ask yourself the following questions:

1. What do I want to explain, show, or prove related to my topic? What is my **purpose?**

2. What information—**ideas**—do I need to research to develop my argument?

3. What **support** (information, facts, and data) will I need to explain and illustrate my ideas?

4. What concepts or principles will I need to include and define?

5. Where should I look for the kinds of information I need, and how will I know if these sources are reliable? How do I evaluate and **analyze** them?

6. What is my **point of view** about the topic?

7. What are my **biases and assumptions** about the topic? Are they fair?

LO 1   FINDING, EVALUATING, AND INTEGRATING SOURCES

When you conduct research, you should decide which sources would be most useful and how and where to find them; evaluate whether the sources are reliable and credible; and then integrate the information from the sources into your paper and correctly document it.

Finding Sources

These days, students are fortunate to have easy access, at home or on campus, to the most amazing source of information since the beginning of civilization: the Internet. However, don't forget that some of the old-fashioned techniques for finding sources still have their merit. Your campus or local library, databases, and personal interviews are all excellent resources too.

Libraries

Books and reference texts (such as specialized dictionaries and encyclopedias), as well as periodicals, magazines, and newspapers, are treasures that you'll find in any library, but libraries these days also hold valuable collections of DVD, CD-ROM, print, and database resources. Moreover, libraries pay for access to online databases that you might not be able to access from your home computer or would be charged for doing so. Libraries offer two major options that can make your research easier.

1. **Web sites designed to help you efficiently search all their holdings (print, CD-ROM, database, online subscriptions, and so on).** Often, you can access your college library's Web site from home, using your student ID and password. College library Web sites also include helpful links to other online resources that you might not have found on your own. Both college and local library Web sites have search engines designed to help you customize a search through their holdings (and even the holdings of other local libraries in your area) for the topic you are writing about. Another common feature on a library Web site is an "Ask a Librarian" link that will allow you to post questions to the librarian on duty who will get back to you with help.

2. **Helpful staff and trained research librarians who are whizzes at customized searches and can help you find exactly what you are looking for in a fraction of the time it would take you on your own.** It's not cheating to get help from librarians: that's what they're there for and most of the time they are eager, like detectives hot for a case, to help you dig for the perfect sources for your topic. They can even help you narrow and fine-tune the scope of your topic and the purpose for your research. Therefore, it helps to have a preliminary outline of the main ideas for your paper ready before you visit your local or college librarian. Remember, you can also check to see if your college or local libraries have online access to librarians so you can email questions from home.

Databases

Databases are collections of information. They are available as CD-ROMs stored in libraries or as online databases (like **Infotrac, ProQuest, EbscoHost,** and **CQ Researcher**) accessible through your library's subscription service. Go to your local or college library to check which databases they subscribe to (or check their Web site). The value of databases is that they are field- or subject-specialized and have search functions that allow for quick and easy access to reliable and credible sources. For instance, Infotrac is a database that provides articles on academic subjects either by a subject search or by author name.

Interviews with Experts

You can conduct interviews with experts on the subject you are writing about in person, by telephone, or via email. Be sure to check with your instructor first to see if interviews from experts are allowed as a source in your paper. Also, be sure that the person interviewed is a credible expert in the field or subject. Evaluate the expertise of an interviewee by finding out if he or she has the right credentials for the subject you are writing about. What degree does he or she hold? What has he or she published in relation to the subject? Is he or she a known authority on the subject?

The Internet and Search Engines

The World Wide Web has changed the way we conduct research and opened up possibilities we never dreamed possible. The easiest way to navigate the Web and find sources related to your subject is to use a search engine. A **search engine** allows you to use key words to search a database or the Web for information on specific topics. Some of the more prominent search engines include the following:

Google (www.google.com)

Google Scholar (www.scholar.google.com)

Yahoo (www.yahoo.com)

AltaVista (www.altavista.com)

Ask.com (www.ask.com)

Dictionary.com (www.dictionary.com)

You can do either a basic search using a key word or phrase, or you can do an **advanced search** that allows you to target more specific articles for your paper. All of the sites above, as well as more specialized discipline-specific databases, provide information on how to most effectively search their sites. If you get over 500 "hits" (articles or entries related to the key word or phrase you entered) when you do a basic search on your topic, do an advanced search to narrow the scope of the search to articles that more specifically address your topic.

The Internet is a gold mine of legitimate, up-to-date, and easily accessible sources for your paper. However, there are many Web sites and online articles and studies that contain inaccurate or even false information. You must be on guard particularly when evaluating a source or research study online (see the questions on page 323 for evaluating your sources).

Sample Google Page for a Search on the Subject of "Plagiarism"

Web <u>Images</u> <u>Videos</u> <u>Maps</u> <u>News</u> <u>Shopping</u> <u>Gmail</u> <u>more</u> ▼   I <u>Web History</u> I <u>Settings</u> ▼ I <u>Sign out</u>

Google | plagiarism | **Search** |

About 12,600,000 results (0.03 seconds)   Go to Google.com   Advanced search

<u>**Plagiarism.org**</u>
Welcome to **Plagiarism.org**, the online resource for people concerned with the
growing problem of internet **plagiarism**. This site is designed to provide the . . .
www.**plagiarism**.org/ - <u>Cached</u> - <u>Similar</u>

<u>**Plagiarism**- Wikipedia, the free encyclopedia</u>
Plagiarism, as defined in the 1995 Random House Compact Unabridged Dictionary,
is the "use or close imitation of the language and thoughts of another author . . .
en.wikipedia.org/wiki/**Plagiarism** - <u>Cached</u> - <u>Similar pages</u>

<u>Avoiding **Plagiarism** - The OWL at Purdue</u>
Sep 30, 2008 . . . Designed to help writers develop strategies for knowing how to
avoid accidental **plagiarism**. Available in printer friendly html and pdf . . .
owl.english.purdue.edu/owl/resource/589/01/ - <u>Cached</u> - <u>Similar pages</u>

<u>Plagiarism</u>
Apr 27, 2004 . . . To help you recognize what **plagiarism** looks like and what
strategies you can use to avoid it, select one of the following links or scroll . . .
www.indiana.edu/~wts/pamphlets/**plagiarism**.shtml - <u>Cached</u> - <u>Similar pages</u>

<u>Plagiarism</u>
You may have heard so many different definitions of plagiarism that you feel confused about exactly what it is. Despite all this variation, you can avoid . . .
www.unc.edu/depts/wcweb/handouts/**plagiarism**.html - <u>Cached</u> - <u>Similar pages</u>

Evaluating Potential Sources

Whenever you do research for a paper, you need to be very careful that the
sources you use are legitimate. Inaccurate, biased, or even false information
is available in all forms of print or electronic material. Here is a set of questions to use as guidelines for evaluating whether to include specific sources
in your documented paper. If you answer "no" to any of them, you may want
to decide against using the source, or at least check with a librarian to see if
it is legitimate.

Questions to Ask When Checking the Reliability of a Source

1. **Is the source completely up-to-date?** It is essential to use the most up-
   to-date and legitimate sources in your paper to support your ideas. If
   your sources don't have credibility, then neither do you.

2. **Is this a scholarly or academic resource?** Check the origin of your source
   and make sure the information is objective and not slanted in order to sell

a product or a particular point of view on a controversial issue. Is the source privately or publicly funded? In general, you are better off using sites that end in ".edu" (education sites), ".gov" (government sites), or ".org" (sites run by reputable companies or non-profit organizations) rather than for-profit ".com" sites.

3. **Does the author have the correct credentials to write knowledgeably on the subject?** Do not to assume that having an MD or PhD automatically gives a person credibility. Check an author's degree to make sure he or she is writing about his or her field of expertise. You can also see what job an expert holds to see if it relates to the subject and even conduct a Google or Yahoo! search to check his or her background. If the author's background seems unrelated to the subject, then he or she is probably not an expert for your subject.

4. **If statistics and numbers are included in a source, who commissioned the study or conducted the research?** For instance, if you are researching the effects of tobacco industry advertising on middle school students, you should look for unbiased sources of information and carefully evaluate the accuracy of studies commissioned by the tobacco industry itself.

5. **Can you verify the information contained in a source?** If numbers and statistics are involved, double-check the facts using one or more other sources.

6. **Does the author provide secondary research to support his or her ideas and claims?** Are these sources credible? Choose a few key facts and run a Google search to test them against what other sources say.

7. **Does the author present different sides of an issue even if strongly advocating a particular stance?** Check your source against other sources that come up in an Internet search on the subject. Many authors do have a particular bias on a subject and if they oversimplify an issue or do not address counterarguments, using them could hurt your credibility.

Again, if you answered "no" to any of these questions about a source, you may want to reject it or at least look at other sources. You do not want the sources you use in your paper to damage your credibility: You are using them to support and strengthen your claims.

Once you have determined a source is reliable, you want to ask specific questions in order to evaluate whether it provides unbiased information.

Questions to Ask When Evaluating the Content of a Source

1. What **assumptions** does the author make in his or her arguments?
2. What **point of view** is the author putting forward?

3. What **biases** are evident in the author's argument and point of view?

4. Who paid for or sponsored the author's research?

5. Has the author included the major counterarguments and objections to the claims he or she is making?

Integrating Sources into Your Paper

As you begin to incorporate sources into your writing, be sure that they serve as backup for your own ideas and the purpose of your essay. You want expert opinion, statistics, and other valuable nuggets of information you gleaned from your research to work for you: Don't let your voice, your purpose, your ideas, or your argument get lost in the background. The research is support; it should not speak for you.

When you incorporate ideas from other sources into your paper, you should smoothly weave them together with your own ideas. An effective way to do this is to use the concept of the analytical ice cream sandwich (see Chapter 3, p. 43 and Chapter 16, p. 304): Each time you include a piece of information from a source, first introduce it and then follow it with your critical analysis of what it means and how it supports your point. You can also use this tool to critique the techniques (style, writing, tone, and language) an author uses to develop his or her point(s).

Cross Reference
See Chapter 16 for more on summary and paraphrase.

Cross Reference
See the sample documented paper with integrated sources at the end of this chapter.

LO 2 Incorporating Quotations

All quotations must be cited. This means you need to include the name of the author and the page number(s) of the work the quoted information comes from in parentheses immediately after the quote. In general, end punctuation goes *after* the parenthetical citation, except in the case of a block (see "In-Text Citations" on p. 334 for further details).

Quotations from Prose or Text

Four lines or less: If a quotation is four lines or less in length, include the lines within the body of the text, surrounded by double quotation marks and followed by a parenthetical citation before the period. For quotations within a quotation, use single quotation marks.

Single quotation

Ivan Doig, in *The Sea Runners*, writes, "In a time and place earlier, Melander would have been the fellow you wanted to set a spire on a cathedral" (7).

Quotation within a quotation

According to Suzan Shown Harjo, "There is doubt as to whether permanent curation of our dead really benefits Indians. Dr. Emery A. Johnson, former assistant surgeon general, recently observed, 'I am not aware of any current medical diagnostic or treatment procedure that has been derived from research on such skeletal remains. Nor am I aware of any during the 34 years that I have been involved in American Indian . . . health care' " (2).

More than four lines (block quotation): If a quotation runs more than four lines in length, set it off from the main body of the text in an indented block form 1 inch, or 10 spaces, from the regular margin, double-spaced, and do not use quotation marks. Place the parenthetical citation after the period at the end of a long quotation.

Block quotation

Ernest Hemingway explores emptiness in the following passage from "A Clean, Well-Lighted Place":

> Turning off the electric light he continued the conversation with himself. It was the light of course but it is necessary that the place be clean and pleasant. You do not want music. Certainly you do not want music. Nor can you stand before a bar with dignity although that is all that is provided for these hours. What did he fear? It was not a fear or dread. It was a nothing that he knew too well. It was all a nothing and a man was a nothing too. It was only that and light was all it needed and a certain cleanness and order (2).

Quotations from Poetry

Three lines or less: If you are quoting three lines or less from a poem, include the lines within the body of the text, with each line break indicated by a slash with a space on either side of it, and place the parenthetical citation *before* the final period. In the citation include the line numbers for the lines you are quoting. The first time you do this, include the word *line* or *lines* before the number(s). For subsequent citations, just include the line number(s).

In Suzanne Paola's poem "Genesis," she writes, "First, there was nothing. / In that, a severe beauty" (lines 1–2).

Three lines or more: If you are quoting three lines or more from a poem, set the quotation off from the main text in an indented block form 1 inch or 10 spaces from the regular margin, double-spaced, and do not use quotation marks. The parenthetical citation should follow the final period or word of the poem you are quoting.

In Suzanne Paola's poem "Genesis," she writes about life and alludes to the Bible:

First, there was nothing.

In that, a severe beauty—

Then

The geometry of being,

Circle & angle, thorax

& horn.

The Word,

Life after life (lines 1–8)

Indicating Editorial Information

Sometimes when you are quoting writers and citing information, you need to insert notes to explain some of the information or to note existing errors within the quoted material. Certain conventions for doing this are outlined below.

1. **Indicating errors in an original source:** If there is an error in a quotation you are using from a source (grammar, spelling, etc.), indicate you are aware of the error by placing the word "sic" (Latin for "thus") in brackets immediately after it, so your readers will know it is not your error.

2. **Omitting words, phrases, or sentences from a direct quotation:** Make sure that the word(s), phrase(s), or sentence(s) you are omitting from the direct quotation does not change the author's intended meaning, and use the following guidelines to indicate what information has been omitted or changed.

   ■ **To omit one or more words or a part of a sentence from an original quotation,** use an ellipsis (a series of three spaced periods). So the following passage,

> "The tension between them had started to grow even more intense. They knew that money was tight and that the rent was due, bills were waiting, the kids were hungry. However, now he had lost his job too, and they didn't speak of it, but their eyes met with a stressful exchange whenever they stopped for a moment."

minus parts of two sentences, *becomes*

> "The tension between them had started to grow even more intense. They knew that money was tight and that the rent was due . . . now he had lost his job too, and they didn't speak of it, but their eyes met with a stressful exchange whenever they stopped for a moment."

- **To omit one or more sentences from a quotation,** use an ellipsis with an extra period (a total of four periods):

> "The tension between them had started to grow even more intense. . . . However, now he had lost his job too, and they didn't speak of it, but their eyes met with a stressful exchange whenever they stopped for a moment."

- **To insert clarifying words or information.** Use brackets around words, phrases, or needed tense changes that must be added within a quotation to provide clarification for the reader or make the tense or form consistent.

> "They had not seen [his daughter] in three years."
> "She want[ed] a new life."

LO 3 PLAGIARISM

Plagiarism is taking someone else's words, ideas, or concepts and using them as if they were your own without giving credit to the original source. Some people are tempted to cheat when they find information, even full papers, on the Internet; others set out to intentionally use someone else's work as if it were their own. Either way, these people are committing plagiarism, the most serious and damaging act possible in an academic career. Even if they are not caught cheating immediately, the plagiarized work can be discovered later in their academic or professional career, with very damaging consequences.

How to Avoid Plagiarism

You can avoid plagiarism by being aware of what it is and then taking precautions to accurately document and cite all sources. Here are some guidelines for accurately recording the sources of print, online, and other media sources in your notes.

Guidelines for Accurately Recording Source Information

1. **Write a summary of the information you want to use, with specific sections that are particularly relevant paraphrased in more detail.** Make sure that you use your own words and sentence construction when you paraphrase or summarize the ideas of others and that you clearly credit the original source.

2. **Enclose any quotations you may want to use in your paper in quotation marks followed by page numbers.**

3. **Record all relevant source information as listed below.**

   - **Book:** author name(s), title (and edition if relevant), city of publication, publisher, year of publication, page number(s)

   - **Journal article:** author name(s), title, journal name, volume and issue numbers, year of publication, and page number(s)

   - **Magazine article:** author name(s); title; magazine name; day, month, and year of publication; and page number(s)

   - **Newspaper article:** author name(s); title; newspaper name; day, month, and year of publication; section letter or number; and page number(s)

   - **Online sources:** name(s) of author if credited, title of article, name of Web site, version or edition number, if provided, publisher or sponsor of the site, date of publication, URL, date you accessed the site

   ▶ NOTE   As you search for sources online, remember to consult the checklist earlier in this chapter in order to evaluate their credibility.

How to Avoid "Accidental" Plagiarism

Some people commit "accidental" plagiarism by not correctly documenting and citing the source(s) from which they obtained information. Even if they do not intend to cheat, this sloppy scholarship can seriously damage their academic credibility and lead to serious consequences. Not knowing the rules for citing sources correctly is not an acceptable excuse: Always give credit for others' ideas or words. To avoid accidental plagiarism, follow these guidelines:

1. **Do not use the annotated instructor's edition of a course textbook.** It will have answers to most of the exercises in the book and insights for teaching that are meant for your instructors only. Reading the sample answers before you write your own answers, or rewriting the answers in your own words, is plagiarizing. If you are caught using an instructor's edition, you are subject to disciplinary action by the college.

2. **Do not use phrases, passages, or visuals from a source—print or electronic—without citing it.** Whether you quote, paraphrase, or summarize content, always cite its source.

3. **Do not use *ideas or concepts* from a source—print or electronic—without citing it.** Except for ideas you came up with on your own *before* you read anything about a subject, you need to cite the source of every idea you use in a paper—even if you phrase the ideas in your own words. Instead of having to defend the fact that you just "coincidentally" came up with the same idea as a noted scholar, cite the scholar and add credibility to your claim.

   Be careful, too, that the brilliant idea you put in your paper didn't come from something you read a while back. Research to find the original source, and give credit where credit is due. The only exception is when you include a "common knowledge" fact, information that most people know. For example, if you mention that George Washington was our first president and his home was in Mt. Vernon, you wouldn't have to cite a source. Rule of thumb: When in doubt, always cite the source.

4. **Be very careful when you paraphrase, even when you cite your source.** When you paraphrase too much content from a source, and/or your overall writing style and use of words and phrases is too close to the original (without using quotation marks), **you are plagiarizing,** *even if you cite the source.* Be careful not to rely too much in your paper on other people's words or ideas.

ACTIVITY 17-1 Avoiding Plagiarism

Directions: *Go to your library either in person or online and find an academic article or essay. Use the Guidelines for Accurately Recording Source Information above and write in the correct source documentation below.*

_____

_____

Then, on a separate sheet of paper, either summarize the article in one to two paragraphs, using your own words, or paraphrase one paragraph of it. After you have summarized or paraphrased, go back over your draft and make sure that you have used your own words, style, and sentence constructions, not those of the original author. Answers will vary.

 ## LO 4   TEN STEPS FOR WRITING A DOCUMENTED PAPER

The following guidelines will help you work through the process of writing a documented paper.

Step One   **Select your subject and prewrite to narrow it down to a manageable topic.** Unless your topic is assigned, pick a subject that interests you and can be researched with relative ease. Then narrow it down by prewriting and thinking about it.

▶ NOTE   If you do not know a great deal about your chosen subject, you may have to complete Step Two before you can adequately prewrite.

Step Two   **Get an overview of your topic.** Read background articles and get a sense of the issues and subtopics related to it. You may find you need to narrow your topic and the scope of your paper still further after you have done some preliminary research.

Step Three **Brainstorm, freewrite, and organize your ideas to develop a preliminary thesis statement.** This is a chance to think about *how* you will structure your paper and *what* kind of information you will need to find to support your thesis statement.

Step Four   **Prepare a working outline.** Take the ideas you generated in Step Three, create a rough outline and determine the main subheadings for your paper. Ask yourself, *What do I want to say? How will I develop my arguments? What support will I provide?* Be sure to put your preliminary thesis at the top of your outline.

Cross Reference

See a sample outline on pages 113–14.

Step Five   **Conduct research and take notes.** Be sure to record all bibliographical information in your notes for each source you locate and decide to use. You can use 3×5 cards, a research notebook, or a thumb drive to record ongoing source ideas and notes. (See page 325 for guidelines on how to accurately record source information.)

▶ TIP   Keep your notes sorted alphabetically by the authors' last names to make it easier to create your bibliography or Works Cited page later.

Step Six   **Review your notes carefully to see if there are any information gaps.** Use your preliminary thesis and your rough outline to assess whether you need to look for further support. If you do, go back and continue to research your topic.

Step Seven   **Re-outline your paper, fine-tuning the structure and organization and modifying your arguments and your thesis (if necessary) based on any newly discovered information.** Add more details to your outline if necessary, noting carefully which sources you will use in which sections of your paper.

Step Eight   **Write the first draft of your documented paper.** Your introduction should lead into and then present your thesis (argument). The body of your paper should develop and support your thesis using the sources you have identified. Be sure to cite all your sources, using the documentation format required by your instructor, to avoid plagiarism (see "Avoiding Plagiarism" on page 329.) Your conclusion should sum up and reiterate your thesis.

Step Nine   **Prepare your Works Cited page.** Follow the instructions for the documentation format assigned. See "Using Modern Language Association Format" on the next page for MLA format; for other styles, use a handbook.

Step Ten   **Revise, edit, and proofread your paper.** Check for unity, coherence, organization, support, and details, and then fine-tune your introduction, thesis, and conclusion. Double-check format and accuracy in all references (summary, paraphrase, or direct quotes). Check especially for punctuation errors within your citations. Use a dictionary and spell-check and consult a thesaurus to find synonyms for words you have overused. Add transitions where needed within and between paragraphs.

▶ TIP   If you can put your draft away for at least two days before completing Step Ten, you will see errors you did not see before and get a clearer and more accurate assessment of your paper. Also, you may want to visit your college's tutoring or writing center to get some objective feedback on your ideas, organization, and use of sources.

LO 5 USING MODERN LANGUAGE ASSOCIATION (MLA) FORMAT

MLA style is the standard documentation format used in the United States for writing in the humanities (literature, philosophy, history, art, etc.). For a more detailed and complete description of MLA style, consult the *MLA Handbook for Writers of Research Papers* (7th ed., 2009), or a current writer's handbook that includes a full section on MLA documentation format. You can also access information on MLA format online at **www.mla.org**.

Two main principles of MLA format include the use of in-text citations and a Works Cited list that provides detailed publishing information for each source cited in the body of the paper, both of which will be discussed in more detail. First, here are some guidelines for formatting your paper using the MLA style:

Formatting Your Paper

Here are guidelines for formatting a paper using MLA style:

Paper	8½ × 11-inch white paper.
Line Spacing	Use double-spacing through the entire paper, including the heading and title—with no extra spaces between them or between paragraphs.
Margins	Leave one-inch margins on all sides, and justify left margins.
Page Numbering	Number every page, including the first page and the Works Cited page. Numbers should be in the upper, right corner one-half inch from the top of the page and flush with the right margin. Include your last name, a space, and then the page number. Do not use a comma or *p* or *page* between your name and the number.
Font	Use an easy to read font and font size, for example, 12 point Times Roman (check with your instructor).
Title page	Do not create a separate title page unless your instructor requests one, in which case get specific formatting directions.
First page	In the top left corner, 1 inch from the top of the page, type your full name, your instructor's name, the course name, and the date, each on a separate line. Double-space these lines. Double-space again, and then center your paper's title (see sample paper on p. 345).

Title	Capitalize the first, last, and all significant words in the title. Do not italicize the title; only use italics or quotation marks if you are including the name of another published work in your title. Double-space all titles longer than one line. If you have a title and a subtitle, separate the title from the subtitle with a colon.
Italics	Italicize the titles of books. For shorter works such as short stories or magazine articles, uses quotation marks around the titles.
Clarifying words or information	Use brackets around words, phrases, or tense changes that must be made within a quotation to clarify meaning or make verb tense or form consistent.

LO 6 IN-TEXT CITATIONS

For every piece of information, idea, or reference used in your paper that comes from someone else, you must include a parenthetical citation. This means providing the name of the author(s) and/or the title of the work and the relevant page number(s) in parentheses immediately after the information you are using. This brief citation refers to a Works Cited list at the end of the paper, which provides the reader with detailed information on each source. Here is an overview of the most common in-text citations.

Print Sources

Text by one author

- **Author named in text:** If you name the author in your introduction to a quotation, paraphrase, or summary, include both his or her first and last names the first time you mention him or her, and include only the page number(s) in the parenthetical citation:

> Michael Dorris, in his novel *A Yellow Raft in Blue Water*, writes "My school in Seattle was better than the Mission, and I know more than anyone expects" (46).

If you use the author's name again in the body of the text, use only his or her last name.

▶ NOTE   If you use more than one work by the same author, include an abbreviated version of the title in your citation.

> When the character first realizes she's in love, she struggles with the emotion: "Your love is newly born, the first page in a blank notebook" (Allende, *Paula*, 77).

- **Author not named in text:** If you do not name the author in your introductory sentence, list the last name of the author and the page number(s) of the source in your citation:

> The character is very self-aware: "My school in Seattle was better than the Mission, and I know more than anyone expects" (Dorris 46).

Text by two or three authors

If a text is by two or three authors, you can either include their names in the body of the text

> Julie Moore, Lori Vail, and Amanda Schaefer write that the "students in composition classes at our university are looking for solid information and explicit examples" (51).

or include them in the citation.

> In contrast, the "students in composition classes at our university are looking for solid information and explicit examples" (Moore, Vail, and Schaefer 51).

Text by three or more authors

Either list the authors' names in your introductory sentence before the quotation or include the first author's last name followed by the Latin words "et al." (meaning "and others") and the page number(s) in the parenthetical citation:

> In contrast, the "students in composition classes at our university are looking for solid information and explicit examples" (Moore et al. 51).

Two different authors with the same last name

Distinguish between two authors with the same last name by using their first initials, or by using their whole first names if they share the same first initial:

> (B. Smith 22) or (Brenda Smith 22)

Works with no author listed

Include the first one to three words of the title (or the whole title if it is short enough) in the parentheses followed by the page number(s):

> Many people "learn by getting involved, by putting their hands in and engaging in a task with another" ("Learning by Touch" 38).

Work from an anthology

When you quote a selection from an anthology, cite the name of the author, not the name of the editor of the anthology; you will provide the editor and anthology information in the Works Cited list. For example, if you were quoting the short story "In Roseau" by Jamaica Kincaid from the *Best American Short Stories* anthology, your citation would look like this:

> She writes, "My father had inherited the ghostly paleness of his own father" (Kincaid 196).

Works by a corporation, government agency, or other group author

If you mention the name of an organization in your introductory sentence, only include the page number(s) in parentheses:

> According to a study conducted in 2007 by the Department of Transportation, "Most people who carpool do so less than four times a week" (4).

If you do not mention the organization in your sentence, include its name and the page number in your parenthetical citation:

> In fact, "Most people who carpool do so less than four times a week" (Department of Transportation 4).

Verse dramas/plays

Provide the title of the play in the sentence, and then cite the act, scene, and line number(s), separated by periods, in the parenthetical citation. Do not use Roman numerals.

> In Sam Shepard's play, *Action*, one of the main characters, Jeep, starts the play with an intriguing statement: "I'm looking forward to my life. I'm looking forward to uh—me. The way I picture me" (1.1.1–2).

Poetry

If you use the name of the poet in your introductory sentence, list the line number(s) in the citation:

> In Sylvia Plath's poem "Daddy," she writes these powerful lines: "Daddy, I have had to kill you. / You died before I had time—" (lines 6–7).

If you do not mention the author in your introductory sentence, then cite the author's last name and the line number(s) in your citation:

> The narrator in the poem says, "Daddy, I have had to kill you. / You died before I had time—" (Plath 6–7).

Indirect citations

If you quote someone quoting someone else, use the abbreviation "qtd. in" to indicate that it is an indirect quote. Use the full name of the person you are quoting in the body of the sentence before the quote and place the name of the author of the source in the parenthetical citation, preceded by "qtd. in":

> Connor Murphy asserts, "One must always portray pride in his or her heritage, no matter what happened in the past" (qtd. in Kennedy 228).

Reference entry from a dictionary or encyclopedia

If the entry does not credit a specific author, use the title of the entry in your citation:

> Bioluminescence is "light produced by a chemical reaction within an organism" ("Bioluminescence" 203).

Sacred/religious texts

When you quote from a religious text, use the title of the book in your introductory sentence or in the citation the first time you refer to it. Identify specifically where a quotation came from using book, verse, and line numbers. For example, if you quote from the Bible, include the name of the book and the chapter and verse number(s) in the citation: (Revelation 10:14). It is also acceptable to include an abbreviated code for the version of the Bible you are citing, for instance, *KJV* stands for King James Version:

> (KJV, Genesis 1:1–5)

Electronic Sources

Information found in databases, CD-ROMs, or on the Internet must be cited in your paper. Give the author's name(s) if provided; if not, give the title of the material. If the electronic source is paginated, then provide a page number.

Author named in source

If the work has an author and uses page numbers, then use the standard rules for parenthetical citations outlined above:

> In fact, "The housing market is so dismal that sellers are desperate for any halfway decent offer" (Cranston 1).

Author not named in source

If the work has no author but does have a title and page numbers, then use a shortened version of the title in the citation:

> In fact, "The housing market is so dismal that sellers are desperate for any halfway decent offer" ("Hostile Housing Market" 1).

Page numbers not included in source

If the source does not include page numbers but does use paragraph numbers, include the relevant paragraph number(s) in your parenthetical citation. If there are no page or paragraph numbers, just use the author's name in the citation:

> In fact, "The housing market is so dismal that sellers are desperate for any halfway decent offer" ("Hostile Housing Market" para. 5).

No information available

If there is no article name, no author, and no page numbers or other information and you are using just a fact or statistic from a Web site, then include the address of the Web site in your parenthetical citation:

> In fact, "The housing market is so dismal that sellers are desperate for any halfway decent offer" (www.housingfactsonline.com).

LO 7 COMPILING A WORKS CITED LIST

Every work or idea that you cite parenthetically in your paper must also be included in the Works Cited section at the end of your paper. Here are some guidelines for formatting your Works Cited page.

Formatting Your Works Cited Page

1. **Start your list on a new page at the end of your paper.** Center the title Works Cited 1 inch below the top of the page (but be sure to have your last name and the page number in the right-hand corner as in the other pages of your paper). Do not bold the Works Cited title, put it in quotation marks, or make it a larger font.

2. **Double-space everything.** Double space between the title and the first entry and between and within all subsequent entries.

3. **Align and indent entries.** Align the first line of each entry flush with the left margin of the page, and indent each subsequent line of the entry five spaces (one tab) from the margin (sometimes called the "hanging indent format"). Do not number the entries.

4. **Alphabetize the Works Cited list by authors' last names.** If a work has a corporate or group author, list it alphabetically by the first word of the name of the organization. If a work does not have an author, alphabetize by the first word of the title (but ignore *A*, *An*, or *The*).

5. **If you have two or more works by the same author,** use three hyphens "---." in place of the author's name in the second and subsequent entries by the same author.

6. **If a work has an editor or translator, be sure to include that information.** If a work has a named author, list that name first, then the title, followed by either the abbreviation "Ed." for editor or "Trans." for translator and then that person's first and last name, followed by a period.

> Ibsen, Henrik. *Three Plays: The Pillars of the Community, The Wild Duck, Hedda Gabler.* Trans. Una Ellis-Fermor. London: Penguin, 1950. Print.

If there is no author, list the name of the editor or translator first, followed by either the abbreviation "ed." or "trans." then the title and the publication information.

> Galmish, Hank, ed. *White Whale Symbolism.* Auburn: Green River P, 2009. Print.

Common Works Cited Entries for Print Sources

Print sources such as books, magazines, journals, and newspapers usually provide thorough publication information. Use the following the guidelines listed below for Works Cited entries. For sources not included here, check the *MLA Handbook,* MLA Web site, or a composition handbook with a comprehensive MLA section.

Books

There are six basic units of information to include for book entries: (1) name of author(s), last name first; (2) full title (italicized; if there is a subtitle include it after a colon); (3) city of publication; (4) name of publisher; (5) year of publication; (6) medium of publication.

Book by one author

> Erdrich, Louise. *Love Medicine*. New York: Bantam, 1984. Print.

> ▶ NOTE   If you have two or more works by the same author, use three hyphens (---) in place of the author's name for the second and subsequent books. Alphabetize by the title.

> Erdrich, Louise. *Love Medicine*. New York: Bantam, 1984. Print.
>
> ---. *Tracks*. New York: Harper, 1989. Print.

Book by two or three authors: Reverse the name of the first author only:

> Moore, Julie, and Pamela Dusenberry. *Crossroads*. New York: Pearson, 2010. Print.

Book by four or more authors: Name only the first author listed and then add "et al." or you may choose to list all the authors in the order they appear in the original source:

> Moore, Julie, et al. *Outcomes Assessment in the Community College*. New York: Pearson, 2009. Print.

Book with no author (alphabetize by the work's title):

> *A Complete Concordance to Shakespeare*. New York: Macmillan, 1969. Print.

Articles from Scholarly Journals

There are seven basic units of information needed for journal articles: (1) name of the author(s), last name first; (2) full title of the article in quotation marks; (3) full name of the journal in italics; (4) volume and issue number; (5) year of publication; (6) page number(s) of the article; (7) medium of publication.

> Martin, Joann. "Teens in College." *Community College News* 18.5 (2009): 22–34. Print.

Magazine Articles

There are six basic units of information needed for magazine articles: (1) name of the author(s), last name first; (2) full title of the article in quotation marks; (3) full title of magazine name in italics; (4) day, month, and year of publication with no punctuation between them (abbreviate all months except for May, June, and July); (5) page number(s) of the article; (6) medium of publication.

> Perkins, Connor. "The Dynamics of Macho-ism." *Gendered Times* 24 May 2008: 48–63. Print.

Articles, Editorials, and Letters from Newspapers

There are six basic units of information needed for newspaper articles: (1) name of author(s), last name first; (2) full title of the article in quotation marks; (3) full title of newspaper in italics; (4) day, month, and year of publication with no punctuation between them (abbreviate all months except for May, June, and July); (5) section letter or number and page number(s) of the article; (6) medium of publication.

> Musselmann, Rachel. "A New Park for Dogs." *The Monrovia Times* 12 May 2009: A5. Print.

▶ NOTE   If the entry from the newspaper is an editorial, type the word "Editorial" after the name of the article followed by a period and a space. If it is a letter to the editor, type the word "Letter" after the author's name, followed by a period and a space.

Selection from an Anthology

A selection from an anthology (a poem, story, play, essay, or article) must include the original work's author and title as well as the name of the anthology and the editor(s) of that anthology.

Sample Entry

> Shelley, Percy Bysshe. "Ozymandias." *The Longman Anthology of British Literature, Volume 2A.* Eds. David Damrosch and Keven J. H. Dettmar. New York: Pearson Longman, 2006. 823. Print.

Articles in Reference Books

Use the following guidelines for citing articles in reference books.

- **Author named in text:** If the author's name is given, provide that first, then the title of the article in quotation marks, followed by the title of the work it came from (in italics). If the entries are arranged alphabetically, do not list the volume or page numbers. For commonly used reference works, particularly ones that are regularly revised, just provide the edition number and years of publication followed by the medium, *Print*.

> Wells, Cathy. "Chinese Civil War." *Encyclopædia Britannica.* 15th ed. 2010. Print.

- **Author not named in text:** If the author is not named, begin the entry with the article title.

> "Chinese Civil War." *Encyclopædia Britannica.* 15th ed. 2010. Print.

Common Works Cited Entries for Electronic Sources

Three different kinds of electronic sources are databases supplied on CD-ROM or DVD, databases accessed online, and Web sites accessed through search engines like Google.

CD-ROM and DVD-ROM Databases

Use the following guidelines for citing information accessed from CD-ROM or DVD-ROM databases:

- **Nonperiodical CD-ROM or DVD databases.** Information accessed from a single-issue CD-ROM (one that is only produced once, like a print version dictionary, book, or encyclopedia) should be cited in the same way as a book, with the medium "Print" replaced by "CD-ROM" or "DVD-ROM." If the disc is produced by a vendor other than the publisher of the material, provide the vendor's name and the date of electronic publication after the medium.

"Aristotle." *The Complete Works of Aristotle: The Revised Oxford Translation*. Ed. Jonathan Barnes. 2 vols. Princeton: Princeton UP, 1984. CD-ROM. Auburn: Proquest, 2010.

■ **Periodical CD-ROM or DVD databases.** Information accessed from a periodical CD-ROM (one that contains newspaper, journal, and other articles and is issued once or twice a year) should be cited the same way as the equivalent print version, but "Print" should be replaced by CD-ROM or DVD-ROM, followed by the title of the database (in italics), the vendor's name, and the date of publication (month and year).

Marshall, Patrick. "Cybersecurity: Are US Military and Civilian Computer Systems Safe?" *CQ Press*. Feb. 2010: 16+ CD-ROM. *GRCC-CQ Researcher Online*. Feb. 2010.

Online Databases

When you cite sources from online databases, include as many of the following elements as possible:

1. **Name of author(s):** If the name of the author (or authors) is provided, start the citation with it, last name first.

2. **Name of article or entry:** Provide the title of the piece. If no author is listed for an article, alphabetize the entry by the material's title.

3. **Name of source:** Include the name of the source—magazine, newspaper, etc. Next list the date the material was first published in print using the format day month year.

4. **Page numbers:** If the page numbers of the source are given, place them after the source name and a colon. If pages are all in one sequence of numbers, give them all: for example, 1–10. If page numbers aren't in sequence, give the first page number followed by a plus sign. No space comes between the two: 2+ If no page numbers are listed, use the abbreviation *n. pag.*

5. **Name of database and medium of publication:** Provide the name of the database in italics. Then list the medium of publication: Web.

6. **Date the source was accessed:** Include the date you accessed the source, for example, 7 Dec. 2008. Abbreviate the names of all months except May, June, and July.

Barrera, Rebeca María. "A Case for Bilingual Education." *Scholastic Parent and Child* 12.3 (2004): 72–73. *EBSCOhost*. Web. 1 Feb. 2009.

Common Work Cited Entry for an Internet Source

Give as much information as necessary to direct the reader to the original online source. Include all of the following information that is available:

1. **Names of the author(s):** If there is an author credited (or authors), start the citation with it, last name first.

2. **Title of the article:** Provide the full title. If there is no author listed for the material, alphabetize the Works Cited entry under this title.

3. **Name of Web site:** Provide the name of the Web site, in italics, if it is different from the title of the article.

4. **Version or edition number:** If such a number is given, provide it. Rev. ed., for instance, means "revised edition."

5. **Publisher or sponsor of the Web site:** If not given, use the abbreviation n.p. for "no publisher."

6. **Date of electronic publication:** If not given, use the abbreviation n.d. for "no date."

7. **Medium of publication:** Web.

8. **Date of access:** Give the date you accessed the site. Use the day month year format.

9. **URL:** Only provide the URL for sources that readers won't be able to find using the information provided in the citation. For example, if you type the name of the Web site you are citing in the Google search box, you can go to that site, then use the site search feature to find the particular page you are citing. If you can find the source using a method like this, you don't need to include the URL in your citation.

Bernstein, Mark. "10 Tips on Writing the Living Web." *A List Apart: For People Who Make Websites.* A List Apart Magazine, 16 Aug. 2002. Web. 4 May 2009.

Many professional Web sites and nonprofessional, private Web sites do not provide all the information listed above. The key is to include as many of the nine elements as possible in the same order as they are listed. For complicated or difficult-to-access online sources, go to www.mla.org for more information on citing online and Internet-based sources.

Documented Student Paper

Acacia Willey   Willey 1

Professor Moore

English 100

11 May 2009

Students or Objects?

When was the last time you walked into a school and didn't see a soda machine? Six years ago, the first soda machine was installed on my middle school campus. Kids from every building raced to the cafeteria the second the recess bell rang. They were all waiting for the same thing: to pay a dollar for a twenty-ounce sugar drink. Kids darted to the cafeteria as if their clothes were on fire. Teachers rewarded good behavior by allowing kids to go to recess early, letting them get a better spot in line. Forget the "no running indoors rule." All that mattered was getting in that line. Michael Moore, a filmmaker and author, wrote *Stupid White Men* to criticize the hold corporations have on the young people of this country. Another man, John Gatto, who has been named New York City teacher of the year three times, quit teaching recently, claiming that he didn't want to hurt children anymore. After quitting, he became a public speaker on school reform. Since then, he has expressed his opinions on the school system through books and media appearances. One thing that Gatto and Moore agree on is that corporations should not be allowed to play such a big role in children's education.

Michael Moore points out the huge role of corporations, starting with one of the biggest corporate involvements, the agreements made

Continued ▶

Willey 2

between schools and the three biggest soda companies. He writes, "Two hundred and forty school districts in thirty-one states have sold exclusive rights to one of the big three soda companies (Coca Cola, Pepsi, Dr. Pepper) to push their product in schools" (Moore 165). By making these agreements, schools are obligated to sell a certain amount of soda. In return, the soda company is selling their product at higher prices, but more importantly, they are heavily promoting their product to students. Many students will drink whatever is available, regardless of whether they really enjoy it, but after drinking the soda everyday they start to like it, get addicted to the sugar, and begin to crave it. Moore continues, explaining how Pizza Hut got involved in targeting students: "When students meet the monthly reading goal, they are rewarded with a certificate for a Pizza Hut personal pan pizza" (165). At least Pizza Hut gives a little to the students by encouraging them to read, but they are far from good. They reward students with a pizza. Like soda, the introduction to pizza hooks students to the product and their company, and soon they will spend their own money (or their parents') for Pizza Hut pizzas.

Like Moore, Gatto agrees that corporations play too big of a role in education. He writes, "The experts make all the important choices; only I, the teacher, can determine what my kids must study, or rather, only the people who pay me can make those decisions" (176). Therefore, if the principal encourages the selling of soda, then that is what the teachers teach, encouraging their students to purchase it. The soda companies pay the schools to teach their students to drink their product. Schools are buying into these agreements with soda companies and other corporations because they get great deals for free or for a low price. They just don't think about how badly it affects their students in terms of their long-term eating habits and health.

Willey 3

Moore also explains how schools force their students to support the corporation. He writes, "When Mike Cameron wore a Pepsi shirt on 'Coke Day' . . . he was suspended for a day. . . . Cameron was suspended for 'being disruptive and trying to ruin a school photo' . . . the shirt was visible all day, but he didn't get in trouble until posing for the picture" (166). The school officials explained that his suspension was due to his disruption and ruining a photo of students spelling out the word "Coke." It seems more like the school had all these students who did exactly as they were told, supported Coca Cola, but felt there was one bad seed who did not. This occurrence made the school look bad in front of their "boss," also known as the Coca Cola Company. Companies like Coca Cola are "the boss" because they often donate money to schools for supplies or become a "corporate sponsor" for a school, as long as the school is visibly promoting their product. In this case, to prevent bad feelings between their school and Coca Cola, officials suspended the student who expressed a different, but non-harmful opinion.

Gatto also discusses in his article how students are forced to believe what they are told. He writes, "I teach kids to surrender their will to the predestined chain of command. Rights may be granted or withheld by any authority without appeal because rights do not exist inside a school" (178). Gatto feels that students are not allowed the right to form their own opinions. The school teachers explain exactly what they want the students to know. In this case, it is that Coca Cola, Pepsi, or Dr. Pepper are the best soft drinks, and they should drink whichever is approved by the school. Failure to agree results in the student being labeled as "the bad kid" by their classmates and teachers. Rejection of these brands can also possibly result in trips to the principal's office.

Continued ▶

Corporations have been involved with children's education for too long. As the years go by, children become adults who believe it is necessary to buy from corporate companies. Why do you think "The Astrodome," home of the Houston Astros, was renamed "Minute Made Park"? The point of education is to teach children to be successful in life by giving them the skills they need, including the ability to think for themselves. Being told that one company is better because it gives you the most money is not a skill children should learn or a skill they need. Schools need to find other sources for funds for supplies. Parents can get more involved in fundraising, or companies can sponsor schools anonymously, without expecting their products to be visible on campus. Students' opinions and tastes should not be for sale.

Willey 5

Works Cited

Gotto, John Taylor. *Dumbing Us Down.* New York: New Society Publishers, 1992. Print.

Moore, Michael. *Stupid White Men.* Los Angeles: Regan Books, 2001. Print.

LEARNING OBJECTIVES REVIEW

LO1	How do you find, evaluate, and integrate sources? (See pp. 320–325.)	You can **find sources** through *libraries, databases,* and the *Internet* and **integrate them** using *paraphrasing, summary,* and *quotation,* as well as the ice-cream sandwich format. **Evaluate** sources by asking questions about their reliability and content.
LO2	How do you incorporate and cite quotations? (See pp. 325–328.)	You **incorporate quotations** by including short ones enclosed in quotations marks in the body of your text and longer ones in an indented block format, without quotation marks. All quotations should be followed by in-text citations.
LO3	What is plagiarism, and how can you avoid it? (See pp. 328–331.)	**Plagiarism** is taking someone else's words, ideas, or concepts and using them as if they are your own. You can **avoid plagiarism** by carefully documenting all sources of information in your notes (enclose direct quotes in quotation marks and note page numbers); citing your sources every time you quote, paraphrase, summarize, or discuss another person's ideas in your papers; using your own words and style when you paraphrase; and providing a complete Works Cited list.
LO4	What are the ten steps for writing a strong documented paper? (See pp. 331–332)	The **10 steps for writing a documented paper** are (1) select a subject and narrow it to a manageable topic; (2) do preliminary reading; (3) write a preliminary thesis; (4) prepare a working outline; (5) research and take notes; (6) check notes for information gaps; (7) fine-tune, structure, organization and thesis if necessary; (8) write a first draft; (9) prepare the Works Cited page; and (10) revise, edit, and proofread.

(LO5) What is the MLA documentation format? (See pp. 333–334.)	**MLA** (Modern Language Association) format is a documentation style used in the humanities that provides specific guidelines for formatting papers. It is based on two main principles: the use of in-text citations and a Works Cited list that provides detailed information for each source used in a paper.
(LO6) What are in-text citations? (See pp. 334–338.)	**In-text, or parenthetical, citations** include the page number(s) of the source being quoted or cited and, if appropriate, the author's name and/or title of the work. They are placed before the period at the end of short quotations and after the period at the end of block quotations.
(LO7) How do you create a Works Cited list? (See pp. 339–349.)	A **Works Cited** page is an alphabetical listing that provides detailed information on all sources referenced in in-text citations. It starts on a separate page and is double-spaced throughout. The first line of each entry is aligned flush left and subsequent lines are indented five spaces.

For support in meeting this chapter's objectives, log in to www.mywritinglab.com and select **Research Process.**

Father and son fishing   Jeb Wyman

THINKING CRITICALLY

Reading an essay or story involves thinking critically about what an author is saying both on the surface and below the surface. Think of the words as conveying the surface messages, and think of what the author is saying beyond the words, between the words, behind the words, and through his or her choice of words, style, and symbolism as the implied messages—like an iceberg, what appears on the surface is often smaller than what is under the water. On a separate sheet of paper, write a literal description of the photograph above, and then write what feelings or ideas this picture evokes when you look at it.

Ask yourself the following questions as you read to help you think critically about what an author is saying:

APPLYING CRITICAL THINKING

PURPOSE   IDEAS   SUPPORT   ASSUMPTIONS BIASES   CONCLUSIONS   POINT OF VIEW   ANALYSIS

1. What is the author's **purpose** or goal? What does he or she set out to explain, argue, or prove?

2. What are the implied or stated questions being addressed?

3. What **ideas** and **support** (evidence, data, experience, or facts) does the author use to develop his or her purpose? Is the support adequate? Convincing?

4. Does the author present alternative **points of view** when needed?

5. What **assumptions** does the author make in this reading selection? Are the assumptions valid?

6. What are the implications and **conclusions** of the author's reasoning and/or ideas and arguments (direct or implied)? What cause and effect connections are made? Use your **analysis** skills to evaluate them.

Also, refer to the strategies for active reading in Chapter 2 as needed.

Packing for America

Frank McCourt

Frank McCourt (1930–2009) was an American author born in Brooklyn, New York, of Irish parents. The family returned to Ireland in 1934, when he was 4 years old, and lived in desperately poor conditions. McCourt returned to the United States at the age of 19, was drafted into the army, and after his discharge used the GI bill to obtain a degree. He went on to teach in the New York City school system for 27 years. He is best known for his autobiographical works, the most famous being the novel *Angela's Ashes*. He won numerous awards for his writing, including the Pulitzer Prize, one of the most prestigious awards for a novelist.

1   . . . . there are thirteen faces. There are no smiles. Why should there be? They haven't learned yet the value of the American smile. But there is the look. It's the look of people just arrived. It is tentative, hopeful, yearning, a look that says "We're here. It's America. We're safe. We don't have to check over our shoulders. We'll sleep well tonight. No one will crash through our door with gun or machete. Our children are safe." [Three families] arrived in the United States in August 2004: the Banguras from Sierra Leone; the Mostoslavskyys from Ukraine; the Jahanyars from Afghanistan. . . . Of the three families, the Mostoslavskyys are probably the most fortunate. They have relatives in the U.S., in New York, Los Angeles, and Boston. Oleksandr, 49, will join his 77-year-old father in Boston. Joining his father was a major reason for coming here. Oleksandr brings with him his wife, Yuliya, 46, and their son, Anatoliv, 13. He also has a cousin in Boston who will give him a job in his auto-repair shop. The cousin worked at the shop for a while and then managed to buy it out.

2   Look what they've packed: sheets, if you don't mind, sheets, pillows, blankets. Some know-it-all Ukrainian assured them these items were tremendously expensive in America and (here, Americans should stand and protest) of inferior quality. There are other precious items in the bags: bottles of vodka, ceramic mugs, photographs. What will Yuliya think when she sees her first white sale in Boston?

3   The Banguras of Sierra Leone traveled lightly, not by choice: They simply have nothing. They have scars. They have memories: In 1999, Mohammed, 35, was beaten so badly his hearing is damaged forever; his wife, Kadiatu Kamara, 32, was stabbed in the chest; their son, Ibrahim, 9, was stabbed in the groin. There are two other children: a girl, 11; a boy, 6. The family fled Sierra Leone to Liberia, then to Ghana. In their bags they carry a few items of clothing, Kadiatu's X-ray, Mohammed's medical evaluations. It will be a while before they realize, in Gretna, Louisiana, that they're not living on the edge of life and death anymore.

4   Centerpiece in any picture of the Jahanyars is the Koran, the book that sustained Ahmad, 37, and his family since they first fled Kabul in 1993. He worked in Mazar-e Sharif till 1998, when the approach of the Taliban forced another move, this time to Moscow. He and his wife, Rona, 39, grabbed their children, the Koran, some jewelry and photos, and that is all they have left from their native land. They will live in San Diego, where, they hope, they can pray in peace.

5   The look. They will carry the look a long time, but in a few weeks if you stroll by certain schools in Boston, Gretna, San Diego, you'll see any or all of these seven children chattering away on playgrounds while their parents, at home or at work, banish horror with hope. They may still be tentative about their new lives, but these families consider themselves lucky.

6   We may not understand their feelings, or we may not try to. We haven't been hungry lately, or ever. No one has threatened to stab our wives and children. We notice these people, or we don't. Books are cheap here, but if you can't afford them the public library is down the road. Education is available here, and if you don't take advantage of it, well, your loss. What do we have to concern ourselves with? The expanding waistline, the shrinking imagination, our favorite program, the team we root for.

7   And so will they, someday.

8   If I were still teaching in the high schools of New York City I'd take my students to Kennedy Airport so they could observe the faces of people landing here, people fleeing tyranny, hunger, religious persecution, despair. I'd like my students to be able to recognize the look that passes over those faces, ranging from fear to ecstasy. My students might say "Oh, what's the big deal?" and if they did I'd have to be patient. They don't know any better, and that's strange because no generation has been endowed with so much information. They've seen the starving African babies, flies in their eyes, bellies swollen, sucking at breasts dried forever. They may be aware of the horrors of Bosnia, Rwanda, Sudan, but, like, you know, that's television, man. The Mostoslavskyys, the Banguras, the Jahanyars are among us. Their brothers and sisters are sneaking across the border from Mexico. The snakes are packing the holds of ships with dreaming Chinese, Vietnamese, Cambodians.

9   They are among us. The adults are slow to adjust, but the children take up the bat and the baseball, the football, the basketball, and watch out, the pen. There will be a poetry, a literature, we cannot even imagine. And there will be music. Jazz, rap, hip-hop will be old stuff. Make way for those American-Ukranians, American-Sierra Leoneans, American-Afghans.

10   We may demand that "something be done about those people sneaking in here."

11   What?

12   This cry is now heard everywhere. Ireland, long-suffering Ireland, now prosperous Ireland, recently held a referendum on immigration. Ireland has been invaded (if you choose to call it that) by Romanians, Nigerians, Chinese. There was talk of the country being swamped, so, in the referendum, nearly 80 percent of the voting Irish said, "Close the borders. Just because you have a baby here doesn't mean you have a right to stay. Out!" You hear the cry here, of course. And why? These people, these Romanians, Nigerians, Chinese, Vietnamese, Cambodian, Mexicans, Ukrainians—they flatter us. In this time of Paris hating Washington, of Abu Ghraib, and of all manner of American-bashing, they want to join us. They need it—they need America—like they need food, water, air. To them, America is still the light of the world. It is free. It is still the dream.

13   There is a lurking sadness in the 13 faces . . . , the faces of people jolted, pushed, threatened, bullied. The Mostoslavskyys, the Jahanyars, the Banguras. There are millions behind them, and they are dreaming, too, of the day they'll arrive at Kennedy Airport with light baggage and the look.

Reading Reflection Questions   *Sample answers provided.*

1. **What is Frank McCourt's main message (his thesis) in this essay? Explain in your own words.** *Many immigrants who come to America have suffered greatly and are deeply relieved to get to America. Many Americans have no idea what it was like for these new immigrants in their homelands.*

2. **Who is McCourt's target audience for this essay, and what does he want them to realize?** *Americans who are not immigrants; he wants them to have empathy for these arrivals and what they have gone through.*

3. **Which of the three families he gives as examples suffered the hardest circumstances before they came to America? List specific examples of their hardships.** *The Sierra Leone family—stabbing of the mother and 9-year-old son and beating of father.*

4. **In your own words, explain what McCourt means by "the look" that he says some immigrants have when they arrive in America.**
   A combination of past fears and current hope and relief

5. **T/ F ___F___ McCourt thinks these immigrants take entry into America for granted, as their right.**

6. **___C___ Which of the following best describes McCourt's feelings about these immigrant families?**
   a. They should find other countries to inhabit.
   b. They put too much strain on the American economy.
   c. They are appreciative and deserve to be here.
   d. They are bitter and angry.

Checking Vocabulary

Define each of the following words by figuring out its meaning using context clues in the reading selection (see Chapter 27 for how to use context clues). If you cannot work out the meaning of a word, use a dictionary.

7. **the Koran (paragraph 4):** *religious text of the Muslim religion*

8. **banish (paragraph 5):** *get rid of, cast out*

   9. tentative (paragraph 5): _uncertain, hesitant_

   10. persecution (paragraph 8): _oppression or harassment, often because of_
   race, religious practices, etc.

READING CRITICALLY

Answer the following questions on a separate sheet of paper.

   1. What is the author's **purpose** or goal in this reading selection?

   2. What are the implied or stated questions or **ideas** being addressed?

   3. What specific **support** (details and examples) does the author use to develop his purpose or goal for the reading?

   4. What **conclusions or arguments** does the author reach based on what is happening or **inferences** (inferences imply "if this, then this" types of cause and effect analysis) he draws in the reading?

   5. Who is the intended audience, and how did you reach that conclusion?

Relate to the Reading

Form a group of three to five students from your class. Sit facing each other or in a circle. One at a time, share information about your heritage or family background. Choose one person to take notes. Then, discuss what message you think McCourt wants to convey to his American readers regarding heritage and identity.

Writing Assignments

   1. Write a one-paragraph summary of this reading (see p. 300).
   2. Write a narration paragraph that describes a personal travel experience that was scary or uncomfortable (see Chapter 6).
   3. Write an example paragraph or essay that describes and provides examples of diverse families, including recent immigrants, in your city or neighborhood (see Chapter 11).
   4. Write a cause and effect paragraph or essay that explores the causes for and effects of people deciding to emigrate from their home countries (see Chapter 12).
   5. Write an argument/persuasion paragraph or essay that presents support for or argues against allowing more immigrants into the United States (see Chapter 14).

A Chinese Kitchen

Eileen Yin-Fei Lo

Eileen Yin-Fei Lo is an educator, chef, and author. She is best known for her books on Chinese cooking. Born in Sun Tak, in Canton, China, she later moved to Hong Kong, and, in 1959, to the United States, where she started teaching Chinese cookery in the 1970s.

1   Food is not only life-giving but also a source of familial or societal leanings. Our food is inextricably linked with manner, with form, with tradition, with history. I grew up with these beliefs. I remember my father, Lo Pak Wan, my first cooking teacher, telling me that we must eat our food with our eyes, then with our minds, then with our noses, and finally with our mouths. He believed this. He taught this to my brother and me.

2   He would say, only partly joking, that fine vegetables should be chosen with as much care as one would a son-in-law. He would show me the correct way to prepare rice, telling me that if our rice was old then perhaps more water than customary might be needed to give our congee its fine and silky finish. "Keep an open mind," he would say. "Cook the way it has been written, but keep an open mind. If you keep walking only in a straight line, you will go into a wall. You must learn to make a turn if necessary. Do not be narrow." Or he would tell me, "*Tau mei haw yantiu, mo mei haw yan tin,*" an aphorism that translates as "If you don't have a tail, you cannot imitate the monkey; if you do have a tail, then do not imitate the monkey." By this he was telling me to follow the classical manner but not to be a simple, mindless imitator.

3   My mother, Lo Chan Miu Hau, encouraged me to cook as well. I recall her saying to me, "If you are wealthy and know how to cook, then servants cannot take advantage of you. If you are poor and know how to cook, you will be able to create wonderful meals with few resources." Cooking and its ramifications were that important to her, as well as to my father, when I was young and growing up in Sun Tak, a suburb of Canton, now Guangzhou.

4   They and my Ah Paw, my mother's mother, insisted that I be involved in our family table. Ah Paw, despite her household of servants, despite the presence of a family cook, made certain whenever I visited her, which was every opportunity I had, every school holiday, that I was in her kitchen.

5   My Ah Paw knew instinctively, without ever having had to personally put a spatula into a wok, how things ought to be cooked, what foods wedded in combination, and what clashed. I am tempted to suggest that she was a brilliant, instinctive kitchen chemist. I will say it. Brilliant she was indeed, her knowledge about foods was encyclopedic, and she was never wrong about cooking, then or now, in my memory. I spent much of the Lunar New Year at her house. I liked her home, I liked her kitchen, and she spoiled me. Except when it came to imparting cookery lessons.

6   When we ate raw fish, *yue sahng,* she taught, one had to prepare the fish in the proper manner. You hit the fish at the front of its head to stun it, then, when it was still nominally alive, you scaled it, gutted and cleaned it, then sliced it for eating. This special dish, which we ate on important birthdays, and on the eves of family weddings, had to be prepared this way, only this way. Ah Paw said.

7   When we steamed a fish, she taught me to softly lay the fish atop a bed of rice at the precise moment that the rice was in the final state of its absorption of water. It would then be perfectly prepared.

8   Once I steamed a fish, quite well, I thought, and proudly carried it to her at the family table. She sniffed. I had forgotten to pour boiled peanut oil over it just before serving. "Take it back to the kitchen and add the oil," she ordered. My grandmother's kitchen always had a crock of boiled peanut oil near the stove. To pour it over fish was to give the fish fragrance and to dispel any unpleasant odors. It does, even if the oil is not warm.

9   She would eat no vegetables that were older than two hours out of the ground, which necessitated repeated trips to the markets by her servants, a lesson of the importance of freshness that was not lost on me.

10   She cautioned me to eat every kernel of rice in my bowl, for if I did not, she warned, the man I married would have a pockmarked face, one mark for each uneaten rice kernel. I did as she cautioned, and I must have eaten well, for my husband's face is clear.

11   Do not shout in the kitchen. Ah Paw would insist. Do not use improper words in the kitchen. Do not show shortness of temper in the kitchen by, for example, banging chopsticks on a wok. All of these would reflect badly on us as a family, she would say, when done in front of Jo Kwan, the Kitchen God, whose image hung on the wall over the oven. For just before the Lunar New Year the image of Jo Kwan, his lips smeared with honey, was always burned so that he would go up to heaven and report only nice things about our family.

12   Ah Paw would consult her Tung Sing, an astrological book, for propitious days on which to begin preparing the special dumplings we made and ate during the New Year festival. She would specify to the second time to make the dough, heat the oven, add the oil, in what we called "*hoi yau wok,*" or literally translated, "begin the oil in the wok." So admired was

she for her knowledge that young married couples, not even of our family, would consult with her. A memory I have is of pumping the pedal of the iron and stone-grinding mill in our town square, at her orders, to get the flour we would use for our dumplings.

13   She was an observant Buddhist who declined to eat either fish or meat on the first and the fifteenth of each month and for the first fifteen days of the New Year, and our family ate similarly out of deference to her. She was happy that my mother always encouraged me to cook, happy that my father brought kitchen discipline to me as well. She nodded with pleasure, in support of my father, I remember—not in sympathy with me—when I complained how boring it was when my father gave me the task of snapping off the ends of individual mung bean sprouts. "If you wish to learn how to make spring rolls well, learn the beginning of the spring roll. It must be done," Ah Paw said.

14   We had no grinders. We chopped meats and other seafood with the cleaver on a chopping board. "Clean it," Ah Paw would say when I was finished. "If you do not, the food you chop next will not stick together. It will fall apart. There will be no texture. If it falls apart, I will know that you did not listen."

15   All of this she conferred on me without ever setting foot in the kitchen of her house. As a further example of her vision I should note in passing that Ah Paw, a most independent woman, as is evident, refused to have bound the feet of my mother, her daughter, much the practice of high born women. This despite the fact that her own feet had been bound since babyhood and were no more than four inches long. This extraordinary woman, never more than seventy-five pounds, who could not totter more than a few hundred feet and was usually carried by servants, brought my mother and then me into modern times in her own way. I wanted nothing more than to be with her, and I would listen, wide-eyed and receptive, to her talk about food and its meanings . . .

Reading Reflection Questions *Sample answers provided.*

1. What is Eileen Yin-Fei Lo's main message (her thesis) in this essay? Explain in your own words. *That she learned a lot about cooking and her*

   own culture and history in her grandmother's kitchen

2. In your opinion, why does Lo end the essay with the details about her grandmother's foot binding? *To show how her grandmother helped bring*

   her mother and herself into modern society and her grandmother's personal

   strength and belief in her convictions

3. What lesson does Lo say she learned from her father in regards to food and cooking? *"We must eat our food with our eyes, then with our minds,* *then with our noses, and finally with our mouths."*

4. Which particular dish or lesson about cooking affected you the most when you read this essay and why? *Answers will vary.*

_____

5. T/ F ____*F*____ The grandmother cooked the meals for the family herself.

6. Explain how the grandmother's cooking lessons were about more than cooking and food. *Answers will vary.*

_____

Checking Vocabulary

Define each of the following words by figuring out its meaning using context clues in the reading selection (see Chapter 27 for how to use context clues). If you cannot work out the meaning of a word, use a dictionary.

7. aphorism (paragraph 2): *brief statement of truth or opinion*

8. ramifications (paragraph 3): *results, effects*

9. instinctive (paragraph 5): *natural, unlearned*

10. pockmarked (paragraph 10): *blemished, scarred by acne*

READING CRITICALLY

1. What is the author's **purpose** or goal in this reading selection?

2. What are the implied or stated questions or **ideas** being addressed?

3. What specific **support** (details and examples) does the author use to develop her purpose or goal for the reading?

4. What **conclusions or arguments** does the author reach based on what is happening or **inferences** (inferences imply "if this, then this" types of cause and effect analysis) she draws in the reading?

5. Who is the intended audience, and how did you reach that conclusion?

Discussion Questions

Form a group of three to five students from your class. Sit facing each other or in a circle. Choose one person to take notes during the discussion. One at a time, share your personal experiences with cooking or family recipes. Who cooks in your household? How is food part of your family's routine or heritage? Then, discuss together what lessons you think Yin-Fei Lo learned besides how to cook in those sessions in the kitchen.

Writing Assignments

1. Write an argument/persuasion paragraph or essay (Chapter 14) arguing for or against all children in a household learning to cook.

2. Write a narration paragraph or essay (Chapter 6) about a family member who passed important information on to you: how it was taught and what you learned.

3. Using the Seven Steps to Writing a Summary (p. 300), write a one-paragraph summary of this reading.

4. Write a descriptive/process paragraph or essay (Chapter 7) that describes step-by-step how to make a certain food dish.

5. Write an example paragraph or essay (Chapter 11) related to how food reflects history or culture. Include specific examples from your own culture.

Shooting an Elephant

George Orwell

George Orwell (1903–1950), born Eric Arthur Blair, was born in India but grew up in England. He served in the Indian Imperial Police in Burma (hence his firsthand knowledge of British imperialism, the heart of this story), and fought in the Spanish Civil War. He wrote many essays and novels that focused on the need for social and political democracy, the potential and actual abuse of people by their governments, and the power of language. He is best known for his novels *Animal Farm* and *1984*.

Burma
currently the country
Myanmar

1   In Moulmein, in lower **Burma,** I was hated by large numbers of people—the only time in my life that I have been important enough for this to happen to me. I was a sub-divisional police officer of the town, and in an aimless, petty kind of way anti-European feeling was very bitter. No one had the guts to raise a riot, but if a European woman went through the bazaars alone somebody would probably spit betel juice over her dress. As a police officer I was an obvious target and was baited whenever it seemed safe to do so. When a nimble Burman tripped me up on the football field and the referee (another Burman) looked the other way, the crowd yelled with hideous laughter. This happened more than once. In the end the sneering yellow faces of young men that met me everywhere, the insults hooted after me when I was at a safe distance, got badly on my nerves. The young Buddhist priests were the worst of all. There were several thousands of them in the town and none of them seemed to have anything to do except stand on street corners and jeer at Europeans.

2   All this was perplexing and upsetting. For at that time I had already made up my mind that imperialism was an evil thing and the sooner I chucked up my job and got out of it the better. Theoretically—and secretly, of course—I was all for the Burmese and all against their oppressors, the British. As for the job I was doing, I hated it more bitterly than I can perhaps make clear. In a job like that you see the dirty work of Empire at close quarters. The wretched prisoners huddling in the stinking cages of the lock-ups, the grey, cowed faces of the long-term convicts, the scarred buttocks of the men who had been flogged with bamboos—all these oppressed me with an intolerable sense of guilt. But I could get nothing into perspective. I was young and ill-educated and I had had to think out my problems in the utter silence that is imposed on every Englishman in the East. I did not even know that the British Empire is dying, still less did I know that it is a great deal better than the younger empires that are going

to supplant it. All I knew was that I was stuck between my hatred of the empire I served and my rage against the evil-spirited little beasts who tried to make my job impossible. With one part of my mind I thought of the British Raj as an unbreakable tyranny, as something clamped down, in **sæcula sæculorum,** upon the will of prostrate peoples; with another part I thought that the greatest joy in the world would be to drive a bayonet into a Buddhist priest's guts. Feelings like these are the normal by-products of imperialism; ask any Anglo-Indian official, if you can catch him off duty.

sæcula sæculorum
forever, for ages

3   One day something happened which in a roundabout way was enlightening. It was a tiny incident in itself, but it gave me a better glimpse than I had had before of the real nature of imperialism—the real motives for which **despotic** governments act. Early one morning the sub-inspector at a police station the other end of the town rang me up on the phone and said that an elephant was ravaging the bazaar. Would I please come and do something about it? I did not know what I could do, but I wanted to see what was happening and I got on to a pony and started out. I took my rifle, an old .44 Winchester and much too small to kill an elephant, but I thought the noise might be useful **in terrorem.** Various Burmans stopped me on the way and told me about the elephant's doings. It was not, of course, a wild elephant, but a tame one which had gone **"must."** It had been chained up, as tame elephants always are when their attack of "must" is due, but on the previous night it had broken its chain and escaped. Its **mahout,** the only person who could manage it when it was in that state, had set out in pursuit, but had taken the wrong direction and was now twelve hours' journey away, and in the morning the elephant had suddenly reappeared in the town. The Burmese population had no weapons and were quite helpless against it. It had already destroyed somebody's bamboo hut, killed a cow and raided some fruit-stalls and devoured the stock; also it had met the municipal rubbish van and, when the driver jumped out and took to his heels, had turned the van over and inflicted violences upon it.

despotic
absolute or tyrannical use of power

in terrorem
to serve as a threat, to intimidate

must
state of frenzied sexual excitement

mahout
the keeper or driver of an elephant

4   The Burmese sub-inspector and some Indian constables were waiting for me in the quarter where the elephant had been seen. It was a very poor quarter, a labyrinth of squalid bamboo huts, thatched with palmleaf, winding all over a steep hillside. I remember that it was a cloudy, stuffy morning at the beginning of the rains. We began questioning the people as to where the elephant had gone and, as usual, failed to get any definite information. That is invariably the case in the East; a story always sounds clear enough at a distance, but the nearer you get to the scene of events the vaguer it becomes. Some of the people said that the elephant had gone in one direction, some said that he had gone in another, some professed not even to have heard of any elephant. I had almost made up my mind that the whole story was a pack of lies, when we heard yells a little distance away. There

was a loud, scandalized cry of "Go away, child! Go away this instant!" and an old woman with a switch in her hand came round the corner of a hut, violently shooing away a crowd of naked children. Some more women followed, clicking their tongues and exclaiming; evidently there was something that the children ought not to have seen. I rounded the hut and saw a man's dead body sprawling in the mud. He was an Indian, a black **Dravidian** coolie, almost naked, and he could not have been dead many minutes. The people said that the elephant had come suddenly upon him round the corner of the hut, caught him with its trunk, put its foot on his back and ground him into the earth. This was the rainy season and the ground was soft, and his face had scored a trench a foot deep and a couple of yards long. He was lying on his belly with arms crucified and head sharply twisted to one side. His face was coated with mud, the eyes wide open, the teeth bared and grinning with an expression of unendurable agony. (Never tell me, by the way, that the dead look peaceful. Most of the corpses I have seen looked devilish.) The friction of the great beast's foot had stripped the skin from his back as neatly as one skins a rabbit. As soon as I saw the dead man I sent an orderly to a friend's house nearby to borrow an elephant rifle. I had already sent back the pony, not wanting it to go mad with fright and throw me if it smelt the elephant.

Dravidian

member of native population of Southern India

5   The orderly came back in a few minutes with a rifle and five cartridges, and meanwhile some Burmans had arrived and told us that the elephant was in the paddy fields below, only a few hundred yards away. As I started forward practically the whole population of the quarter flocked out of the houses and followed me. They had seen the rifle and were all shouting excitedly that I was going to shoot the elephant. They had not shown much interest in the elephant when he was merely ravaging their homes, but it was different now that he was going to be shot. It was a bit of fun to them, as it would be to an English crowd; besides they wanted the meat. It made me vaguely uneasy. I had no intention of shooting the elephant—I had merely sent for the rifle to defend myself if necessary—and it is always unnerving to have a crowd following you. I marched down the hill, looking and feeling a fool, with the rifle over my shoulder and an ever-growing army of people jostling at my heels. At the bottom, when you got away from the huts, there was a metalled road and beyond that a miry waste of paddy fields a thousand yards across, not yet ploughed but soggy from the first rains and dotted with coarse grass. The elephant was standing eight yards from the road, his left side towards us. He took not the slightest notice of the crowd's approach. He was tearing up bunches of grass, beating them against his knees to clean them and stuffing them into his mouth.

6   I had halted on the road. As soon as I saw the elephant I knew with perfect certainty that I ought not to shoot him. It is a serious matter to

shoot a working elephant—it is comparable to destroying a huge and costly piece of machinery—and obviously one ought not to do it if it can possibly be avoided. And at that distance, peacefully eating, the elephant looked no more dangerous than a cow. I thought then and I think now that his attack of "must" was already passing off; in which case he would merely wander harmlessly about until the mahout came back and caught him. Moreover, I did not in the least want to shoot him. I decided that I would watch him for a little while to make sure that he did not turn savage again, and then go home.

7   But at that moment I glanced round at the crowd that had followed me. It was an immense crowd, two thousand at the least and growing every minute. It blocked the road for a long distance on either side. I looked at the sea of yellow faces above the garish clothes—faces all happy and excited over this bit of fun, all certain that the elephant was going to be shot. They were watching me as they would watch a conjurer about to perform a trick. They did not like me, but with the magical rifle in my hands I was momentarily worth watching. And suddenly I realized that I should have to shoot the elephant after all. The people expected it of me and I had got to do it; I could feel their two thousand wills pressing me forward, irresistibly. And it was at this moment, as I stood there with the rifle in my hands, that I first grasped the hollowness, the futility of the white man's dominion in the East. Here was I, the white man with his gun, standing in front of the unarmed native crowd—seemingly the leading actor of the piece; but in reality I was only an absurd puppet pushed to and fro by the will of those yellow faces behind. I perceived in this moment that when the white man turns tyrant it is his own freedom that he destroys. He becomes a sort of hollow, posing dummy, the conventionalized figure of a **sahib**. For it is the condition of his rule that he shall spend his life in trying to impress the "natives," and so in every crisis he has got to do what the "natives" expect of him. He wears a mask, and his face grows to fit it. I had got to shoot the elephant. I had committed myself to doing it when I sent for the rifle. A sahib has got to act like a sahib; he has got to appear resolute, to know his own mind and do definite things. To come all that way, rifle in hand, with two thousand people marching at my heels, and then to trail feebly away, having done nothing—no, that was impossible. The crowd would laugh at me. And my whole life, every white man's life in the East, was one long struggle not to be laughed at.

sahib

an Indian term of respect, similar to "sir," used in addressing Europeans

8   But I did not want to shoot the elephant. I watched him beating his bunch of grass against his knees, with that preoccupied grandmotherly air that elephants have. It seemed to me that it would be murder to shoot him. At that age I was not squeamish about killing animals, but I had never shot an elephant and never wanted to. (Somehow it always seems worse to kill

a *large* animal.) Besides, there was the beast's owner to be considered. Alive, the elephant was worth at least a hundred pounds; dead, he would only be worth the value of his tusks, five pounds, possibly. But I had got to act quickly. I turned to some experienced-looking Burmans who had been there when we arrived, and asked them how the elephant had been behaving. They all said the same thing: he took no notice of you if you left him alone, but he might charge if you went too close to him.

9   It was perfectly clear to me what I ought to do. I ought to walk up to within, say, twenty-five yards of the elephant and test his behavior. If he charged, I could shoot; if he took no notice of me, it would be safe to leave him until the mahout came back. But also I knew that I was going to do no such thing. I was a poor shot with a rifle and the ground was soft mud into which one would sink at every step. If the elephant charged and I missed him, I should have about as much chance as a toad under a steam-roller. But even then I was not thinking particularly of my own skin, only of the watchful yellow faces behind. For at that moment, with the crowd watching me, I was not afraid in the ordinary sense, as I would have been if I had been alone. A white man mustn't be frightened in front of "natives"; and so, in general, he isn't frightened. The sole thought in my mind was that if anything went wrong those two thousand Burmans would see me pursued, caught, trampled on and reduced to a grinning corpse like that Indian up the hill. And if that happened it was quite probable that some of them would laugh. That would never do.

10   There was only one alternative. I shoved the cartridges into the magazine and lay down on the road to get a better aim. The crowd grew very still, and a deep, low, happy sigh, as of people who see the theatre curtain go up at last, breathed from innumerable throats. They were going to have their bit of fun after all. The rifle was a beautiful German thing with cross-hair sights. I did not then know that in shooting an elephant one would shoot to cut an imaginary bar running from ear-hole to ear-hole. I ought, therefore, as the elephant was sideways on, to have aimed straight at his ear-hole, actually I aimed several inches in front of this, thinking the brain would be further forward.

11   When I pulled the trigger I did not hear the bang or feel the kick—one never does when a shot goes home—but I heard the devilish roar of glee that went up from the crowd. In that instant, in too short a time, one would have thought, even for the bullet to get there, a mysterious, terrible change had come over the elephant. He neither stirred nor fell, but every line of his body had altered. He looked suddenly stricken, shrunken, immensely old, as though the frightful impact of the bullet had paralysed him without knocking him down. At last, after what seemed a long time—it might have been five seconds, I dare say—he sagged flabbily to his knees. His mouth slobbered. An enormous senility seemed to have settled upon him. One

could have imagined him thousands of years old. I fired again into the same spot. At the second shot he did not collapse but climbed with desperate slowness to his feet and stood weakly upright, with legs sagging and head drooping. I fired a third time. That was the shot that did for him. You could see the agony of it jolt his whole body and knock the last remnant of strength from his legs. But in falling he seemed for a moment to rise, for as his hind legs collapsed beneath him he seemed to tower upward like a huge rock toppling, his trunk reaching skyward like a tree. He trumpeted, for the first and only time. And then down he came, his belly towards me, with a crash that seemed to shake the ground even where I lay.

12   I got up. The Burmans were already racing past me across the mud. It was obvious that the elephant would never rise again, but he was not dead. He was breathing very rhythmically with long rattling gasps, his great mound of a side painfully rising and falling. His mouth was wide open—I could see far down into caverns of pale pink throat. I waited a long time for him to die, but his breathing did not weaken. Finally I fired my two remaining shots into the spot where I thought his heart must be. The thick blood welled out of him like red velvet, but still he did not die. His body did not even jerk when the shots hit him, the tortured breathing continued without a pause. He was dying, very slowly and in great agony, but in some world remote from me where not even a bullet could damage him further. I felt that I had got to put an end to that dreadful noise. It seemed dreadful to see the great beast lying there, powerless to move and yet powerless to die, and not even to be able to finish him. I sent back for my small rifle and poured shot after shot into his heart and down his throat. They seemed to make no impression. The tortured gasps continued as steadily as the ticking of a clock.

13   In the end I could not stand it any longer and went away. I heard later that it took him half an hour to die. Burmans were bringing dahs and baskets even before I left, and I was told they had stripped his body almost to the bones by the afternoon.

14   Afterwards, of course, there were endless discussions about the shooting of the elephant. The owner was furious, but he was only an Indian and could do nothing. Besides, legally I had done the right thing, for a mad elephant has to be killed, like a mad dog, if its owner fails to control it. Among the Europeans opinion was divided. The older men said I was right, the younger men said it was a damn shame to shoot an elephant for killing a coolie, because an elephant was worth more than any damn **Coringhee coolie.** And afterwards I was very glad that the coolie had been killed; it put me legally in the right and it gave me a sufficient pretext for shooting the elephant. I often wondered whether any of the others grasped that I had done it solely to avoid looking a fool.

Coringhee coolie
Coringhee person from town of Coringo, India

coolie
unskilled worker

Reading Reflection Questions   *Sample answers provided.*

1. What is George Orwell's main message (his thesis) in this essay? Explain in your own words. <u>*That imperialism is not good and that the ele-*</u> <u>*phant that was killed when it shouldn't have been represents the injustices*</u> <u>*of British rule in then Burma.*</u>

2. What does Orwell want his readers to realize after reading this story? <u>*That the officer didn't want to kill the elephant but felt he had to perform in*</u> <u>*a certain way to maintain his role with the Burmans . . . that sometimes*</u> <u>*situations affect decisions in a negative way.*</u>

3. Why do you think Orwell includes so many graphic details in this essay? What effect do they have? <u>*We are shocked and feel more sympathy*</u> <u>*for the elephant and the officer and how wrong the act was.*</u>

4. In your own words, explain what Orwell means when he writes, "And it was at this moment, as I stood there with the rifle in my hands, that I first grasped the hollowness, the futility of the white man's dominion in the East" (p. 5). <u>*Shooting the elephant made him realize the fundamental*</u> <u>*problem with imperialistic rule.*</u>

5. T/ F ____<u>*F*</u>____ The officer had intended to shoot the elephant as soon as he asked for the rifle.

6. T/F ____<u>*T*</u>____ The elephant had killed a man.

Checking Vocabulary

Define each of the following words by figuring out its meaning using context clues in the reading selection (see Chapter 27 for how to use context clues). If you cannot work out the meaning of a word, use a dictionary.

7. perplexing (paragraph 2): <u>*confusing, bothersome*</u>

8. tyranny (paragraph 2): <u>*unjust government, arbitrary imposed government*</u>

9. squeamish (paragraph 8): <u>*easily disgusted or made nauseous*</u>

10. senility (paragraph 11): <u>*the mental and physical deterioration of old age*</u>

READING CRITICALLY

Answer the following questions on a separate sheet of paper.

1. What is the author's **purpose** or goal in this reading selection?

2. What are the implied or stated questions or **ideas** being addressed?

3. What specific **support** (details and examples) does the author use to develop purpose or goal for the reading?

4. What **conclusions or arguments** does the author reach based on what is happening or **inferences** (inferences imply "if this, then this" types of cause and effect analysis) he draws in the reading?

5. Who is the intended audience, and how did you reach that conclusion?

Group Activity

Form a group of three to five students from your class, and choose one person to take notes during the discussion. This essay contains many vocabulary words and concepts that can make it difficult to understand. As a group, go through the essay and write down any words that you do not understand. Then use a dictionary to look up the words and write down their definitions. Afterwards, discuss how this process helped your overall understanding of this complex reading.

Writing Assignments

1. Write a one-paragraph summary of this reading (see p. 300).

2. Write a description paragraph about the elephant and his behavior based on the details Orwell provides in this reading (see Chapter 7).

3. Write a narration paragraph or essay that describes an event you witnessed that you knew was wrong but were powerless to stop (see Chapter 6).

4. Write an argument/persuasion paragraph or essay that argues for or against animal protection rights (see Chapter 14).

5. Write a cause and effect paragraph or essay that explores the causes of and effects on people who are governed by a power from outside their country (see Chapter 12).

Chocolate Equals Love

Diane Ackerman

Diane Ackerman (1948–) is best known for her essays and books on natural history, the most famous being A *Natural History of the Senses*, which was made into a TV miniseries for Nova. Her writing weaves science, history, and contemporary culture in a style that is literary and sometimes poetic.

1   What food do you crave? Add a hint of mischief to your desire, and the answer is bound to be chocolate. Dark, divine, sense-bludgeoning chocolate. A wooer's gift. A child's reward. A jilted lover's solace. A cozy mug of slumber. Halloween manna. A gimme-more that tantalizes young and old alike. Almost every candy bar. Chocolate.

2   We can thank the Indians of Central and South America for chocolate's bewitching lusciousness. As the Spanish explorer Hernán Cortés found, the Aztecs worshiped chocolate (which they named *cacahuatl*) as a gift from their wise god Quetzalcoatl. Aztec soldiers and male members of court drank as many as 2000 pitchers of chocolate every day. They spiked their drink with vanilla beans and spices, they drank it bubbly thick from golden cups. Adding chili peppers gave it bite. The Aztec leader Montezuma required a chocolate ice, made from pouring syrup over snow that runners brought to him from the nearest mountain.

sublime
supreme or outstanding

3   Invigorating and dangerously **sublime,** chocolate dominated every facet of Aztec life, from sexuality to the economy. Cocoa beans even served as currency: You could buy a rabbit for 10 beans, a slave for 100 beans.

pungent
penetrating and biting
smell or taste

4   At first, Cortés hated chocolate's shocking taste, which mingled bitter, spicy, **pungent,** silky, dank and dusty flavors. But in time its magic seduced him, and it is said that he introduced it to Spain, flavoring it with sugar instead of hot chili peppers.

5   By the 17th century, chocolate was thrilling Europeans with its sensory jolt—less devilish than liquor but still stimulating, luxurious and pleasantly addictive. Those who could afford it drank it thick and hot, as the Indians did, sometimes adding orange, vanilla or spices. Society ladies sipped several cups a day and even insisted on drinking it during church services. Doctors prescribed chocolate as a flesh-and-bone rejuve-

libido
sex drive

nator that could lift the spirits, hasten healing and raise a flagging **libido.**

6   Forget Viagra. Think bonbons.

7   Casanova, it is said, swore by chocolate and ate it as a prelude to lovemaking. The French King Louis XV's principal mistress, Madame du Barry, served exquisitely refined but essentially drug-level chocolate to her various suitors. Unknowingly, they were following the custom of Montezuma, who was believed to have consumed extra chocolate before visiting his harem.

8   A liquid treasure until the 19th century, chocolate suddenly changed shape and personality when a Dutch chemist discovered how to separate cocoa butter, leaving powdered cocoa. The public clamored for portable, ever-ready chocolate, and confectioners obliged with pyramids of chocolate bars. Joining the chocolamania, the Cadbury brothers introduced chocolate in heart-shaped boxes in 1868. Milk chocolate appeared in Switzerland in 1875, thanks to Peter Daniel and Henri Nestlé. Then American mass-production provided cheap chocolates for the multitudes, thanks to the foresight of Milton Hershey. And the rest is history.

9   Is chocolate a health food? Chocolate is chemically active—a mind-altering drug that's good for you in moderation. The higher the cocoa content, the more antioxidants and other nutritious bonuses. Cocoa powder contains the most antioxidants, followed by dark chocolate and milk chocolate.

10   What delivers the chocolate buzz? Chocolate contains more than 300 chemicals, including tiny amounts of anandamide, which mimics the active ingredient in marijuana, plus such stimulants as theobromine and phenylethylamine. A 1.4-ounce bar of chocolate also can provide 20 milligrams of caffeine. That's jitters away from the 140 milligrams of an average cup of coffee, not to mention a thimbleful of espresso. But it's rousing enough, combined with the rest of chocolate's chemical bag of tricks. And the full sensory and nostalgic saga of eating chocolate—the mouth feel, the aroma, the taste, the memories—can calm the brain or lighten one's thoughts, for a while anyway.

11   If we luxuriate in a memory framed by the heaven of chocolate—say, eating s'mores around a campfire with a giggling Girl Scout Troup or receiving a box of chocolates from a sappy beau and then sampling them with him—a small constellation of pleasure will attach itself to the idea of chocolate lifelong. That happens early on to nearly everyone.

12   For example, when I was a child, each year my mother and I would choose a colossal chocolate Easter rabbit with pink candy dot eyes. Together, we would sit on the floor of the aptly named "den" and devour most of the hollow rabbit—always starting with the ears and working our way down—until we went way beyond sated and started to feel a little sick. We would laugh with shared delight as we gobbled and afterward lounged about in a chocolate haze.

visceral

instinctive as opposed to
intellectual

13   It was a cherished bonding ritual more **visceral** than verbal, reminding me how much we adore our senses. They're our house-guests, our explorers, our pets—and we love to give them treats. So how do you reward the sense of taste? For ages, the delicacy of choice has been rich, sensuously inviting chocolate.

Reading Reflection Questions *Sample answers provided.*

1. What is Diane Ackerman's main message (her thesis) in this essay? Explain in your own words. *Why we crave chocolate and how it becomes*

   part of our daily life

2. Do you have any special memories associated with eating chocolate? If so, list at least one. *Answers will vary.*

   _____

3. In what form (bars, food, liquid) did the Aztecs drink their chocolate?

   As a thick liquid with spices and sometimes chili peppers added

4. List at least two benefits the author says chocolate provides. *Answers*

   will vary. A "lift" in mood, increased sex drive, antioxidant properties

5. T/ F _____F_____ Chocolate has more caffeine than coffee.

6. T/F _____T_____ Chocolate contains antioxidants that are good for you.

Checking Vocabulary

Define each of the following words by figuring out its meaning using context clues in the reading selection (see Chapter 27 for how to use context clues). If you cannot work out the meaning of a word, use a dictionary.

7. manna (paragraph 1): *spiritual food*

8. currency (paragraph 3): *money*

9. rejuvenator (paragraph 5): *something that re-energizes, makes youthful*

10. nostalgic (paragraph 10): *sentimental, wistful for old time*

READING CRITICALLY

Answer the following questions on a separate sheet of paper.

1. What is the author's **purpose** or goal in this reading selection?

2. What are the implied or stated questions or **ideas** being addressed?

3. What specific **support** (details and examples) does the author use to develop her purpose or goal for the reading?

4. What **conclusions or arguments** does the author reach based on what is happening or **inferences** (inferences imply "if this, then this" types of cause and effect analysis) she draws in the reading?

5. Who is the intended audience, and how did you reach that conclusion?

Group Activity

Form a group of three to five students from your class, and choose one person to take notes during the discussion. Discuss and record answers for the following questions:

- What surprised you most about the history of chocolate consumption as outlined in this essay?
- What traditions and associations can you think of in your own family or your larger social group that revolve around the eating or sharing of chocolate?

Writing Assignments

1. Write a one-paragraph summary of this reading (see p. 300).

2. Write a narration paragraph that describes an event or memory from your own life regarding chocolate (see Chapter 6) .

3. Write a cause and effect paragraph or essay that explores the causes and/or effects of indulging in too much of a good thing such as chocolate or another food or substance (see Chapter 12).

4. Write an argument/persuasion paragraph or essay arguing for or against suitors using chocolate to woo their intended loves (see Chapter 14).

5. Write a comparison and contrast paragraph or essay that compares rewarding children with treats versus rewarding them with praise or non-food-related prizes (see Chapter 13). Decide which is better and explain why.

Rites for Indian Dead

Suzan Shown Harjo

Suzan Shown Harjo (1945–) is a Native American activist and author. She has been a political activist since 1960 and has helped make the U.S. government return both land and artifacts to Native Americans. She writes essays and poetry and is a curator as well as a lecturer specializing in Native American issues.

1   What if museums, universities, and government agencies could put your dead relatives on display or keep them in boxes to be cut up and otherwise studied? What if you believed that the spirits of the dead could not rest until their human remains were placed in a sacred area?

2   The ordinary American would say there ought to be a law—and there is, for ordinary Americans. The problem for American Indians is that there are too many laws of the kind that make us the archaeological property of the United States and too few of the kind that protect us from such insults.

3   Some of my own Cheyenne relatives' skulls are in the Smithsonian Institution today, along with those of at least 4500 other Indian people who were violated in the 1800s by the U.S. Army for an "Indian Cranial Study." It wasn't enough that these unarmed Cheyenne people were mowed down by the cavalry at the infamous Sand Creek massacre; many were decapitated and their heads shipped to Washington as freight. (The Army Medical Museum's collection is now in the Smithsonian.) Some had been exhumed only hours after being buried. Imagine their grieving families' reaction on finding their loved ones disinterred and headless.

4   Some targets of the Army's study were killed in noncombat situations and beheaded immediately. The officer's account of the decapitation of the Apache chief Mangas Colorada in 1863 shows the pseudoscientific nature of the exercise. "I weighed the brain and measured the skull," the good doctor wrote, "and found that while the skull was smaller, the brain was larger than that of Daniel Webster."

5   These journal accounts exist in excruciating detail, yet missing are any records of overall comparisons, conclusions or final reports of the Army study. Since it is unlike the Army not to leave a paper trail, one must wonder about the motive for its collection.

6   The total Indian body count in the Smithsonian collection is more than 19,000, and it is not the largest in the country. It is not inconceivable that the 1.5 million of us living today are outnumbered by our dead stored in museums, educational institutions, federal agencies, state historical societies

and private collections. The Indian people are further dehumanized by being exhibited alongside the **mastodons** and dinosaurs and other extinct creatures.

mastodons
massive, elephant-like mammals, now extinct

7   Where we have buried our dead in peace, more often than not the sites have been desecrated. For more than 200 years, relic hunting has been a poplar pursuit. Lately, the market in Indian artifacts has brought this **abhorrent** activity to a fever pitch in some areas. And when scavengers come upon Indian burial sites, everything found becomes fair game, including sacred burial offerings, teeth and skeletal remains.

abhorrent
repugnant; detestable

8   One unusually well-publicized example of Indian grave desecration occurred two years ago in a western Kentucky field known as Slack Farm, the site of an Indian village five centuries ago. Ten men—one with a business card stating "Have Shovel, Will Travel"—paid the landowner $10,000 to lease digging rights between planting seasons. They dug extensively on the 40-acre farm, rummaging through an estimated 650 graves, collecting burial goods, tools and ceremonial items. Skeletons were strewn about like litter.

9   What motivates people to do something like this? Financial gain is the first answer. Indian relic-collecting has become a multimillion-dollar industry. The price tag on a bead necklace can easily top $1000; rare pieces fetch tens of thousands.

10   And it is not just collectors of the macabre who pay for skeletal remains. Scientists say that these deceased Indians are needed for research that someday could benefit the health and welfare of living Indians. But just how many dead Indians must they examine? Nineteen thousand?

11   There is doubt as to whether permanent **curation** of our dead really benefits Indians. Dr. Emery A. Johnson, former assistant surgeon general, recently observed, "I am not aware of any current medical diagnostic or treatment procedure that has been derived from research on such skeletal remains. Nor am I aware of any during the 34 years that I have been involved in American Indian . . . health care."

curation
keeping of items in museums or collections

12   Indian remains are still being collected for racial biological studies. While the intentions may be honorable, the ethics of using human remains this way without full consent of relatives must be questioned.

13   Some relief for Indian people has come on the state level. Almost half of the states, including California, have passed laws protecting Indian burial sites and restricting the sale of Indian bones, burial offerings and other sacred items. Representative Charles E. Bennett (D-Fla.) and Sen. John McCain (R-Ariz.) have introduced bills that are a good start in invoking the federal government's protection. However, no legislation has attacked the problem head-on by imposing stiff penalties at the marketplace, or by changing laws that make dead Indians the nations' property.

14   Some universities—notably Stanford, Nebraska, Minnesota and Seattle—have returned, or agreed to return, Indian human remains; it is fitting that institutions of higher education should lead the way.

funerary
relating to funerals

15   Congress is now deciding what to do with the government's extensive collection of Indian human remains and associated **funerary** objects. The secretary of the Smithsonian, Robert McAdams, has been valiantly attempting to apply modern ethics to yesterday's excesses. This week, he announced that the Smithsonian would conduct an inventory and return all Indian skeletal remains that could be identified with specific tribes or living kin.

16   But there remains a reluctance generally among collectors of Indian remains to take action of a scope that would have a quantitative impact and a healing quality. If they will not act on their own—and it is highly unlikely that they will—then Congress must act.

artifacts
items created by humans
and/or human remains

17   The country must recognize that the bodies of dead American Indian people are not **artifacts** to be bought and sold as collectors' items. It is not appropriate to store tens of thousands of our ancestors for possible future research. They are our family. They deserve to be returned to their sacred burial grounds and given a chance to rest.

18   The plunder of our people's graves has gone on too long. Let us rebury our dead and remove this shameful past from America's future.

Reading Reflection Questions   *Sample answers provided.*

1. What is Suzan Shown Harjo's main message (her thesis) in this essay? Explain in your own words. *The country must recognize that the bodies of dead American Indian people are not artifacts to be bought and sold as collectors' items.*

2. What distinguishes this writing as an argument/persuasion essay? *The writer argues for the return of all Indian remains and gives specific reasons for why this must happen.*

3. What reasons do the collectors of these "artifacts" give for collecting them, according to Harjo? *For conducting medical research for the benefit of living American Indians and for profit (from the sale of artifacts such as beads)*

4. According to Harjo, why is it important that her Indian ancestors be buried? *As a sign of respect and so their souls can rest as according to their beliefs*

5. T/ F _____T_____At the time of this essay, at least 19,000 Indian remains were kept in the Smithsonian Institute for research purposes.

6. T/ F _____T_____Some universities and museums have voluntarily begun to return the remains to families and tribes.

Checking Vocabulary

Define each of the following words by figuring out its meaning using context clues in the reading selection (see Chapter 27 for how to use context clues). If you cannot work out the meaning of a word, use a dictionary.

7. decapitated (paragraph 3): _beheaded_

8. exhumed/disinterred (paragraph 3): _dug up, unearthed_

9. pseudoscientific (paragraph 4): _related to a theory without a scientific basis_

10. desecrated (paragraph 8): _destroyed/violated sacred sites and/or items_

READING CRITICALLY

Answer the following questions on a separate sheet of paper.

1. What is the author's **purpose** or goal in this reading selection?

2. What are the implied or stated questions or **ideas** being addressed?

3. What specific **support** (details and examples) does the author use to develop her purpose or goal for the reading?

4. What **conclusions or arguments** does the author reach based on what is happening or **inferences** (inferences imply "if this, then this" types of cause and effect analysis) she draws in the reading?

5. Who is the intended audience, and how did you reach that conclusion?

Group Activity

Form a group of three to five students from your class, and choose one person to take notes during the discussion. Answer the following questions:

- Did any of you know that this type of desecration was going on?
- What do you think about it personally?

- What do you think should be done? Argue against Harjo, in support of her arguments, or even go beyond her argument. Together, create a thesis statement that could be used for an argument essay on the topic of the treatment of Native American remains.

Writing Assignments

1. Write a one-paragraph summary of this reading (see p. 300).

2. Write a narration paragraph about a time you visited a museum. Use as many senses as possible to describe the visit (see Chapter 6).

3. Write a cause and effect paragraph or essay that explores the causes and effects of being disrespectful of a particular group of people (Chapter 12).

4. Write an argument paragraph or essay about whether you think all the American Indian remains should be returned. Explain the reasons for your point of view (Chapter 14).

5. Write a comparison and contrast paragraph or essay about museums collecting art versus collecting human artifacts (Chapter 13).

Retreat into the iWorld

Andrew Sullivan

Andrew Sullivan (1963–) is a journalist and gay-rights activist who has written for many major papers, including *The New York Times*. Beginning in 2000, Sullivan became one of the first mainstream journalists to experiment with blogging, and has a famous daily blogging site called Daily Dish (andrewsullivan.com's Daily Dish) in the *The Atlantic Online*.

1   I was visiting New York last week and noticed something I'd never thought I'd say about the city. Yes, nightlife is pretty much dead (and I'm in no way the first to notice that). But daylife—the insane mishmash of yells, chatter, clatter, hustle and **chutzpah** that makes New York the urban equivalent of methamphetamine—was also a little different. It was quieter.

chutzpah
Yiddish slang for nerve, audacity, gall

2   Manhattan's downtown is now a Disney-like string of malls, riverside parks and pretty upper-middle-class villages. But there was something else. And as I looked across the throngs on the pavement, I began to see why.

3   There were little white wires hanging down from their ears, or tucked into pockets, purses or jackets. The eyes were a little vacant. Each was in his or her own musical world, walking to their soundtrack, stars in their

own music video, almost **oblivious** to the world around them. These are the iPod people.

4   Even without the white wires you can tell who they are. They walk down the street in their own MP3 cocoon, bumping into others, dead to small social cues, shutting out anyone not in their bubble.

5   Every now and again some start unconsciously emitting strange tuneless squawks, like a badly tuned radio, and their fingers snap or their arms twitch to some strange soundless rhythm. When others say "Excuse me" there's no response. "Hi," ditto. It's strange to be among so many people and hear so little. Except that each one is hearing so much.

6   Yes, I might as well own up. I'm one of them. I witnessed the glazed New York looks through my own glazed pupils, my white wires peeping out of my ears. I joined the cult a few years ago: the sect of the little white box worshippers.

7   Every now and again I go to church—those huge, luminous Apple stores, pews in the rear, the **clerics** in their **monastic** uniforms all bustling around or sitting behind the "Genius Bars," like priests waiting to hear confessions.

8   Others began, as I did, with a Walkman—and then a kind of clunkier MP3 player. But the sleekness of the iPod won me over. Unlike other models it gave me my entire music collection to rearrange as I saw fit—on the fly, in my pocket.

9   What was once an occasional musical diversion became a compulsive obsession. Now I have my iTunes in my iMac for my iPod in my iWorld. It's **Narcissus** heaven: we've finally put the "i" into Me.

10   And, like all addictive cults, it's spreading. There are now 22m iPod owners in the United States and Apple is becoming a mass-market company for the first time.

11   Walk through any airport in the United States these days and you will see person after person gliding through the social ether as if on autopilot. Get on a subway and you're surrounded by a bunch of **Stepford** commuters staring into mid-space as if anaesthetized by technology. Don't ask, don't tell, don't overhear, don't observe. Just tune in and tune out.

12   It wouldn't be so worrying if it weren't part of something even bigger. Americans are beginning to narrow their lives.

13   You get your news from your favourite blogs, the ones that won't challenge your view of the world. You tune into a satellite radio service which aims directly at a small market—for new age fanatics, liberal talk or Christian rock. Television is all cable. Culture is all subculture. Your cell phones can receive e-mail feeds of your favourite blogger's latest thoughts— seconds after he has posted them—get sports scores for your team or stock quotes of your portfolio.

oblivious
unaware, not conscious

clerics
members or leaders in a church

monastic
related to a monastery or monks

Narcissus
mythical figure who stared at his own reflection

Stepford
refers to the novel *The Stepford Wives*, by Ira Levin, in which women in a small town are replaced by docile, thoughtless, lookalike robots

serendipity

good luck or fortune, a
lucky discovery or
happening

atomisation

reducing something to fine
particles or atoms

14   Technology has given us a universe entirely for ourselves—where the **serendipity** of meeting a new stranger, hearing a piece of music we would never choose for ourselves or an opinion that might force us to change our mind about something are all effectively banished.

15   **Atomisation** by little white boxes and cell phones. Society without the social. Others who are chosen—not met at random. Human beings have never lived like this before. Yes, we have always had homes, retreats or places where we went to relax, unwind or shut out the world.

16   But we didn't walk around the world like hermit crabs with our isolation surgically attached.

17   Music was once the preserve of the living room or the concert hall. It was sometimes solitary but it was primarily a shared experience, something that brought people together, gave them the comfort of knowing that others too understood the pleasure of a Brahms symphony or that Beatles album.

18   But music is atomised now as living is. And it's secret. That bloke next to you on the bus could be listening to heavy metal or a Gregorian chant. You'll never know. And so, bit by bit, you'll never really know him. And by his white wires, he is indicating he doesn't really want to know you.

19   What do we get from this? The awareness of more music, more often. The chance to slip away for a while from everydayness, to give our lives its own soundtrack, to still the monotony of the commute, to listen more closely and carefully to music that can lift us up and keep us going.

20   We become masters of our own interests, more connected to people like us over the Internet, more instantly in touch with anything we want, need or think we want and think we need. Ever tried a Stairmaster in silence? But what are we missing? That hilarious shard of overheard conversation that stays with you all day; the child whose chatter on the pavement takes you back to your early memories; birdsong; weather; accents; the laughter of others. And those thoughts that come not by filling your head with selected diversion, but by allowing your mind to wander aimlessly through the regular background noise of human and mechanical life.

21   External stimulation can crowd out the interior mind. Even the boredom that we flee has its uses. We are forced to find our own means to overcome it.

22   And so we enrich our life from within, rather than from white wires. It's hard to give up, though, isn't it.

23   Not so long ago I was on a trip and realized I had left my iPod behind. Panic. But then something else. I noticed the rhythms of others again, the sound of the airplane, the opinions of the taxi driver, the small

social cues that had been obscured before. I noticed again how others related to each other. And I felt just a little bit connected again and a little more aware.

24   Try it. There's a world out there. And it has a soundtrack all its own.

Reading Reflection Questions   *Sample answers provided.*

1. What is Andrew Sullivan's main message (his thesis) in this essay? Explain in your own words. *To explore the negative effects of a technology*

   that isolates us from each other and to argue for us to reconnect with the

   world

2. According to Sullivan, what happens when so many people are listening to headphones in public—what are the results? *They miss social*

   clues and interactions and the natural soundtrack of life.

3. Provide two examples of what Sullivan argues people can miss by walking around tuned-in to their iPods or other electronic devices.
   "That hilarious shard of overheard conversation that stays with you all day;

   the child whose chatter on the pavement takes you back to your early mem-

   ories; birdsong; weather; accents; the laughter of others." "Thoughts that

   come not by filling your head with selected diversion, but by allowing your

   mind to wander aimlessly through the regular background noise of human

   and mechanical life."

4. In what way are you guilty of some of the technological tuning-out that Sullivan describes in this essay?

   Answers will vary.

5. T/ F ____*F*____ According to Sullivan, technological advances in music have brought people closer together in regards to music appreciation.

6. T/ F ____*F*____ The author never uses this kind of technology himself.

Checking Vocabulary

Define each of the following words by figuring out its meaning using context clues in the reading selection (see Chapter 27 for how to use context clues). If you cannot work out the meaning of a word, use a dictionary.

7. anaesthetized (paragraph 11): *sedated, drugged*

8. ether (paragraph 11): *clear space*

9. atomized (paragraph 18): *individualized, segregated*

10. shard (paragraph 20): *fragment*

READING CRITICALLY

Answer the following questions on a separate sheet of paper.

1. What is the author's **purpose** or goal in this reading selection?

2. What are the implied or stated questions or **ideas** being addressed?

3. What specific **support** (details and examples) does the author use to develop his purpose or goal for the reading?

4. What **conclusions or arguments** does the author reach based on what is happening or **inferences** (inferences imply "if this, then this" types of cause and effect analysis) he draws in the reading?

5. Who is the intended audience, and how did you reach that conclusion?

Group Activity

Form a group of three to five students from your class, and choose one person to take notes during the discussion. Discuss what you have seen when it comes to technology interfering with social interaction. Then, share a couple of personal experiences where you were treated rudely by someone tuned into technology, or when you were treated as if you were being rude for being engrossed in technology. Predict the changes you think will occur in the future related to technology and social interaction.

Writing Assignments

1. Write a one-paragraph summary of this reading (see p. 300).

2. Write a narration paragraph about a time you were treated rudely by someone because of his or her focus on or addiction to technology (see Chapter 6).

3. Write an example paragraph or essay of various types of modern technology that contribute to social isolation (see Chapter 11).

4. Write a cause and effect paragraph or essay about the increase in the number of technological gadgets used by Americans on a regular basis (see Chapter 12).

5. Write an argument paragraph or essay that supports or opposes banning the use of personal music devices in public spaces (see Chapter 14).

A Clean Well-Lighted Place

Ernest Hemingway

Ernest Hemingway (1899–1961) is considered one of America's most important authors. He wrote numerous essays and many novels including *The Old Man and the Sea*, *The Sun Also Rises*, and *For Whom the Bell Tolls*. He won the Pulitzer Prize for *The Old Man and the Sea* and he won the prestigious Nobel Prize in Literature in 1954. He was a veteran of World War I and a famous adventurer.

1   It was very late and everyone had left the café except an old man who sat in the shadow the leaves of the tree made against the electric light. In the daytime the street was dusty, but at night the dew settled the dust and the old man liked to sit late because he was deaf and now at night it was quiet and he felt the difference. The two waiters inside the cafe knew that the old man was a little drunk, and while he was a good client they knew that if he became too drunk he would leave without paying, so they kept watch on him.

2   "Last week he tried to commit suicide," one waiter said.

3   "Why?"

4   "He was in despair."

5   "What about?"

6   "Nothing."

7   "How do you know it was nothing?"

8   "He has plenty of money."

9   They sat together at a table that was close against the wall near the door of the café and looked at the terrace where the tables were all empty except where the old man sat in the shadow of the leaves of the tree that moved slightly in the wind. A girl and a soldier went by in the street. The street light shone on the brass number on his collar. The girl wore no head covering and hurried beside him.

10   "The guard will pick him up," one waiter said.

11   "What does it matter if he gets what he's after?"

12   "He had better get off the street now. The guard will get him. They went by five minutes ago."

13   The old man sitting in the shadow rapped on his saucer with his glass. The younger waiter went over to him.

14   "What do you want?"

15   The old man looked at him. "Another brandy," he said.

16   "You'll be drunk," the waiter said. The old man looked at him. The waiter went away.

17   "He'll stay all night," he said to his colleague. "I'm sleepy now. I never get into bed before three o'clock. He should have killed himself last week."

18   The waiter took the brandy bottle and another saucer from the counter inside the café and marched out to the old man's table. He put down the saucer and poured the glass full of brandy.

19   "You should have killed yourself last week," he said to the deaf man. The old man motioned with his finger. "A little more," he said. The waiter poured on into the glass so that the brandy slopped over and ran down the stem into the top saucer of the pile. "Thank you," the old man said. The waiter took the bottle back inside the café. He sat down at the table with his colleague again.

20   "He's drunk now," he said.

21   "He's drunk every night."

22   "What did he want to kill himself for?"

23   "How should I know."

24   "How did he do it?"

25   "He hung himself with a rope."

26   "Who cut him down?"

27   "His niece."

28   "Why did they do it?"

29   "Fear for his soul."

30   "How much money has he got?"

31   "He's got plenty."

32   "He must be eighty years old."

33   "Anyway I should say he was eighty."

34   "I wish he would go home. I never get to bed before three o'clock. What kind of hour is that to go to bed?"

35   "He stays up because he likes it."

36   "He's lonely. I'm not lonely. I have a wife waiting in bed for me."

37   "He had a wife once too."

38   "A wife would be no good to him now."

39   "You can't tell. He might be better with a wife."

40   "His niece looks after him. You said she cut him down."

41   "I know."

42   "I wouldn't want to be that old. An old man is a nasty thing."

43   "Not always. This old man is clean. He drinks without spilling. Even now, drunk. Look at him."

44   "I don't want to look at him. I wish he would go home. He has no regard for those who must work."

45   The old man looked from his glass across the square, then over at the waiters.

46   "Another brandy," he said, pointing to his glass. The waiter who was in a hurry came over.

47   "Finished," he said, speaking with that omission of syntax stupid people employ when talking to drunken people or foreigners. "No more tonight. Close now."

48   "Another," said the old man.

49   "No. Finished." The waiter wiped the edge of the table with a towel and shook his head.

50   The old man stood up, slowly counted the saucers, took a leather coin purse from his pocket and paid for the drinks, leaving half a peseta tip. The waiter watched him go down the street, a very old man walking unsteadily but with dignity.

51   "Why didn't you let him stay and drink?" the unhurried waiter asked. They were putting up the shutters. "It is not half-past two."

52   "I want to go home to bed."

53   "What is an hour?"

54   "More to me than to him."

55   "An hour is the same."

56   "You talk like an old man yourself. He can buy a bottle and drink at home."

57   "It's not the same."

58   "No, it is not," agreed the waiter with a wife. He did not wish to be unjust. He was only in a hurry.

59   "And you? You have no fear of going home before your usual hour?"

60   "Are you trying to insult me?"

61   "No, hombre, only to make a joke."

62   "No," the waiter who was in a hurry said, rising from pulling down the metal shutters. "I have confidence. I am all confidence."

63   "You have youth, confidence, and a job," the older waiter said. "You have everything."

64   "And what do you lack?"

65   "Everything but work."

66   "You have everything I have."

67   "No. I have never had confidence and I am not young."

68   "Come on. Stop talking nonsense and lock up."

69   "I am of those who like to stay late at the café," the older waiter said. "With all those who do not want to go to bed. With all those who need a light for the night."

70   "I want to go home and into bed."

71   "We are of two different kinds," the older waiter said. He was now dressed to go home. "It is not only a question of youth and confidence although those things are very beautiful. Each night I am reluctant to close up because there may be someone who needs the café."

72   "Hombre, there are bodegas open all night long."

73   "You do not understand. This is a clean and pleasant café. It is well lighted. The light is very good and also, now, there are shadows of the leaves."

74   "Good night," said the younger waiter.

75   "Good night," the other said. Turning off the electric light he continued the conversation with himself. It was the light of course but it is necessary that the place be clean and pleasant. You do not want music. Certainly you do not want music. Nor can you stand before a bar with dignity although that is all that is provided for these hours. What did he fear? It was not a fear or dread. It was a nothing that he knew too well. It was all a nothing and a man was a nothing too. It was only that and light was all it needed and a certain cleanness and order. Some lived in it and never felt it but he knew it all was **nada y pues** nada y nada y pues nada. Our nada who art in nada, nada be thy name thy kingdom nada thy will be nada in nada as it is in nada. Give us this nada our daily nada and nada us our nada as we nada our nadas and nada us not into nada but deliver us from nada; pues nada. Hail nothing full of nothing, nothing is with thee. He smiled and stood before a bar with a shining steam pressure coffee machine.

76   "What's yours?" asked the barman.

77   "Nada."

78   "**Otro loco mas**," said the barman and turned away.

79   "A little cup," said the waiter.

80   The barman poured it for him.

81   "The light is very bright and pleasant but the bar is unpolished," the waiter said. The barman looked at him but did not answer. It was too late at night for conversation.

82   "You want another **copita**?" the barman asked.

83   "No, thank you," said the waiter and went out. He disliked bars and bodegas. A clean, well-lighted café was a very different thing. Now, without thinking further, he would go home to his room. He would lie in the bed and finally, with daylight, he would go to sleep. After all, he said to himself, it's probably only insomnia. Many must have it.

nada
nothing
y pues
and therefore

Otro loco mas
another crazy person

copita
glass

Reading Reflection Questions *Sample answers provided.*

1. What is Ernest Hemingway's main message (his thesis) in this story? Explain in your own words. *To give a glimpse into loneliness and to explain*

   that people just need a safe place to be in public sometimes

2. In your own words, what is meant by this statement from paragraph 74 "It was all a nothing and a man was a nothing too"? *Life has little meaning.*

   _____

3. Provide two examples of description from this story (description of the setting or people).

   Answers will vary.

   _____

   _____

4. Do you think the waiter should have kept giving the man more to drink? Why or why not?
   Answers will vary.

   _____

5. T/ F _____*T*_____ The old man is alone in the world with no wife.

6. T/ F _____*T*_____ The old man had attempted suicide.

Checking Vocabulary

Define each of the following words by figuring out its meaning using context clues in the reading selection (see Chapter 27 for how to use context clues). If you cannot work out the meaning of a word, use a dictionary.

7. colleague (paragraph 17): *coworker*

8. omission (paragraph 47): *left out*

9. peseta (paragraph 50): *Spanish coin*

10. bodegas (paragraph 83): *bars with music*

READING CRITICALLY

Answer the following questions on a separate sheet of paper.

1. What is the author's **purpose** or goal in this reading selection?

2. What are the implied or stated questions or **ideas** being addressed?

3. What specific **support** (details and examples) does the author use to develop his purpose or goal for the reading?

4. What **conclusions or arguments** does the author reach based on what is happening or **inferences** (inferences imply "if this, then this" types of cause and effect analysis) he draws in the reading?

5. Who is the intended audience, and how did you reach that conclusion?

Group Activity

Form a group of three to five students from your class, and choose one person to take notes during the discussion. Discuss the following questions:

- Do you think that restaurants should have limits on how long a person can stay?
- Do you think restaurants should be responsible for how much alcohol person consumes while in their establishment? Why or why not?

Writing Assignments

1. Write a one-paragraph summary of this reading (See p. 300).

2. Write a description or example paragraph about someone you see on a weekly basis in a public place that you do not know (see Chapters 7 and 11).

3. Write a narration paragraph or essay about a time you were treated rudely by someone who was suppose to be serving you such as a waiter. (see Chapter 6).

4. Write a cause and effect paragraph or essay that explores the causes and effects of loneliness and isolation (Chapter 12).

5. Write an argument paragraph or essay about the dangers of drinking and driving (Chapter 14).

Shame

Dick Gregory

Dick Gregory (Richard Claxton Gregory) (1932–) is a civil rights activist, a comedian, and an author. He has written several essays and books, some autobiographical, and has made many comedy recordings, videos, and TV appearances.

1   I never learned hate at home, or shame. I had to go to school for that. I was about seven years old when I got my first big lesson. I was in love with a little girl named Helene Tucker, a light-**complexioned** girl with pigtails and nice manners. She was always clean and she was smart in school. I think I went to school then mostly to look at her. I brushed my hair and even got me a little old handkerchief. It was a lady's handkerchief, but I didn't want Helene to see me wipe my nose on my hand.

complexioned
related to color and appearance of skin

2   The pipes were frozen again, there was no water in the house, but I washed my socks and shirt every night. I'd get a pot, and go over to Mister Ben's grocery store, and stick my pot down into his soda machine and scoop out some chopped ice. By evening the ice melted to water for washing. I got sick a lot that winter because the fire would go out at night before the clothes were dry. In the morning I'd put them on, wet or dry, because they were the only clothes I had.

3   Everybody's got a Helene Tucker, a symbol of everything you want. I loved her for her goodness, her cleanness, her popularity. She'd walk down my street and my brothers and sisters would yell, "Here comes Helene," and I'd rub my tennis sneakers on the back of my pants and wish my hair wasn't so nappy and the white folks' shirt fit me better. I'd run out on the street. If I knew my place and didn't come too close, she'd wink at me and say hello. That was a good feeling. Sometimes I'd follow her all the way home, and shovel the snow off her walk and try to make friends with her momma and her aunts. I'd drop money on her stoop late at night on my way back from shining shoes in the taverns. And she had a daddy, and he had a good job. He was a paperhanger.

4   I guess I would have gotten over Helene by summertime, but something happened in that classroom that made her face hang in front of me for the next twenty-two years. When I played the drums in high school, it was for Helene, and when I broke track records in college, it was for Helene, and when I started standing behind microphones and heard applause, I wished Helene could hear it too. It wasn't until I was twenty-nine years old and married and making money that I finally got her out of my system. Helene was sitting in that classroom when I learned to be ashamed of myself.

5   It was on a Thursday. I was sitting in the back of the room, in a seat with a chalk circle drawn around it. The idiot's seat, the troublemaker's seat.

6   The teacher thought I was stupid. Couldn't spell, couldn't read, couldn't do arithmetic. Just stupid. Teachers were never interested in finding out that you couldn't concentrate because you were so hungry, because you hadn't had any breakfast. All you could think about was noontime; would it ever come? Maybe you could sneak into the cloakroom and steal a bite of some kid's lunch out of a coat pocket. A bite of something.

Paste. You can't really make a meal of paste, or put it on bread for a sandwich, but sometimes I'd scoop a few spoonfuls out of the big paste jar in the back of the room. Pregnant people get strange tastes. I was pregnant with poverty. Pregnant with dirt and pregnant with smells that made people turn away. Pregnant with cold and pregnant with shoes that were never bought for me. Pregnant with five other people in my bed and no daddy in the next room, and pregnant with hunger. Paste doesn't taste too bad when you're hungry.

7   The teacher thought I was a troublemaker. All she saw from the front of the room was a little black boy who squirmed in his idiot's seat and made noises and poked the kids around him. I guess she couldn't see a kid who made noises because he wanted someone to know he was there.

8   It was on a Thursday, the day before the Negro payday. The eagle always flew on Friday. The teacher was asking each student how much his father would give to the Community Chest. On Friday night, each kid would get the money from his father, and on Monday he would bring it to the school. I decided I was going to buy a daddy right then. I had money in my pocket from shining shoes and selling papers, and whatever Helene Tucker pledged for her daddy I was going to top it. And I'd hand the money right in. I wasn't going to wait until Monday to buy me a daddy.

9   I was shaking, scared to death. The teacher opened her book and started calling out names alphabetically: "Helene Tucker?"

10   "My Daddy said he'd give two dollars and fifty cents."

11   "That's very nice, Helene. Very, very nice indeed."

12   That made me feel pretty good. It wouldn't take too much to top that. I had almost three dollars in dimes and quarters in my pocket. I stuck my hand in my pocket and held on to the money, waiting for her to call my name. But the teacher closed her book after she called everybody else in the class.

13   I stood up and raised my hand. "What is it now?"

14   "You forgot me."

15   She turned toward the blackboard. "I don't have time to be playing with you, Richard."

16   "My daddy said he'd . . ."

17   "Sit down, Richard, you're disturbing the class."

18   "My daddy said he'd give . . . fifteen dollars."

19   She turned around and looked mad. "We are collecting this money for you and your kind, Richard Gregory. If your daddy can give fifteen dollars you have no business being on relief."

20   "I got it right now, I got it right now, my Daddy gave it to me to turn in today, my daddy said . . ."

21   "And furthermore," she said, looking right at me, her nostrils getting big and her lips getting thin and her eyes opening wide, "We know you don't have a daddy."

22   Helene Tucker turned around, her eyes full of tears. She felt sorry for me. Then I couldn't see her too well because I was crying, too.

23   "Sit down, Richard." And I always thought the teacher kind of liked me. She always picked me to wash the blackboard on Friday, after school. That was a big thrill; it made me feel important. If I didn't wash it, come Monday the school might not function right.

24   "Where are you going, Richard!"

25   I walked out of school that day, and for a long time I didn't go back very often.

26   There was shame there. Now there was shame everywhere. It seemed like the whole world had been inside that classroom, everyone had heard what the teacher had said, everyone had turned around and felt sorry for me. There was shame in going to the Worthy Boys Annual Christmas Dinner for you and your kind, because everybody knew what a worthy boy was. Why couldn't they just call it the Boys Annual Dinner—why'd they have to give it a name? There was shame in wearing the brown and orange and white plaid mackinaw the welfare gave to three thousand boys. Why'd it have to be the same for everybody so when you walked down the street the people could see you were on relief? It was a nice warm mackinaw and it had a hood, and my momma beat me and called me a little rat when she found out I stuffed it in the bottom of a pail full of garbage way over on Cottage Street. There was shame in running over to Mister Ben's at the end of the day and asking for his rotten peaches, there was shame in asking Mrs. Simmons for a spoonful of sugar, there was shame in running out to meet the relief truck. I hated that truck, full of food for you and your kind. I ran into the house and hid when it came. And then I started to sneak through alleys, to take the long way home so the people going into White's Eat Shop wouldn't see me. Yeah, the whole world heard the teacher that day—we all know you don't have a Daddy.

27   It lasted for a while, this kind of numbness. I spent a lot of time feeling sorry for myself. And then one day I met this wino in a restaurant. I'd been out hustling all day, shining shoes, selling newspapers, and I had googobs of money in my pocket. Bought me a bowl of chili for fifteen cents, and a cheese-burger for fifteen cents, and a Pepsi for five cents, and a piece of chocolate cake for ten cents. That was a good meal. I was eating when this old wino came in. I love winos because they never hurt anyone but themselves.

28   The old wino sat down at the counter and ordered twenty-six cents worth of food. He ate it like he really enjoyed it. When the owner, Mister

Williams, asked him to pay the check, the old wino didn't lie or go through his pocket like he suddenly found a hole.

29   He just said: "Don't have no money."

30   The owner yelled: "Why in hell did you come in here and eat my food if you don't have no money? That food cost me money."

31   Mister Williams jumped over the counter and knocked the wino off his stool and beat him over the head with a pop bottle. Then he stepped back and watched the wino bleed. Then he kicked him. And he kicked him again.

32   I looked at the wino with blood all over his face and I went over.

33   "Leave him alone, Mister Williams. I'll pay the twenty-six cents."

34   The wino got up, slowly, pulling himself up to the stool, then up to the counter, holding on for a minute until his legs stopped shaking so bad. He looked at me with pure hate.

35   "Keep your twenty-six cents. You don't have to pay, not now. I just finished paying for it."

36   He started to walk out, and as he passed me, he reached down and touched my shoulder. "Thanks, sonny, but it's too late now. Why didn't you pay it before?"

37   I was pretty sick about that. I waited too long to help another man.

Reading Reflection Questions   *Sample answers provided.*

1. What is Dick Gregory's main message (his thesis) in this essay? Explain in your own words. *That people have pride and can be shamed by others*

   and that poverty can bring shame and cause a person to be labeled or

   pitied (like young Richard and the wino)

2. Do you have any memories from your own childhood where you felt shamed by someone else? Describe one briefly.

   Answers will vary.

3. Do you think Richard's teacher was a mean or cruel woman? Explain your answer.

   Answers will vary.

4. Why do you think the story ends with the example of the old wino who gets beaten? What does Richard learn from this experience?

   That he too could help another person and that even a wino has pride and

   can feel shame, paralleling Richard's own experience.

5. T/ F _____*T*_____ Helene Tucker felt sorry for Richard.

6. T/F _____*F*_____ Richard never had any money.

Checking Vocabulary

Define each of the following words by figuring out its meaning using context clues in the reading selection (see Chapter 27 for how to use context clues). If you cannot work out the meaning of a word, use a dictionary.

7. squirmed (paragraph 7): *wriggled around* _____

8. relief (paragraph 19): *state help or welfare* _____

9. mackinaw (paragraph 26): *a coat* _____

10. wino (paragraph 27): *a drunk* _____

READING CRITICALLY

Answer the following questions on a separate sheet of paper.

1. What is the author's **purpose** or goal in this reading selection?

2. What are the implied or stated questions or **ideas** being addressed?

3. What specific **support** (details and examples) does the author use to develop his purpose or goal for the reading?

4. What **conclusions or arguments** does the author reach based on what is happening or **inferences** (inferences imply "if this, then this" types of cause and effect analysis) he draws in the reading?

5. Who is the intended audience, and how did you reach that conclusion?

Group Activity

Form a group of three to five students from your class, and choose one person to take notes during the discussion. One at a time, share an experience where either you felt shame, or a time when you inadvertently made another person feel ashamed. What kinds of situations can cause people to feel ashamed? Do you think feeling shame can ever have a positive effect? Explain.

Writing Assignments

1. Write a one-paragraph summary with critical analysis of this reading (see p. 300–01).

2. Use description to write a paragraph about a classroom you were a student in during elementary school (see Chapter 7).

3. Write a narration paragraph or essay about a time you were treated differently based on your appearance and felt ashamed (see Chapter 6).

4. Write a cause and effect paragraph or essay of how one's economic situation can affect self-esteem positively or negatively (see Chapter 12).

5. Write an argument/persuasion paragraph or essay (Chapter 14) arguing for or against welfare (see Chapter 14).

Raising the Sash for a View of the City's Daily Ballet

Andy Newman and Cassi Feldman

From *The New York Times,* August 18, 2007

Andy Newman and Cassi Feldman are both journalists who write for *The New York Times*. Newman is also the religion reporter for the Metro Section of *The New York Times*, and Feldman specializes in travel pieces and hosts a blog for *NY Times Online* called *The Empire Zone*.

1   Edna Ford starts early, at 6:30 a.m., sometimes 5. She showers, takes her medication, settles into the wheelchair by her window in the Bronx, then looks out at the courtyard.

2   In East Harlem, Marcelina Figueroa sits at her broad windowsill, one hand curled around a cafecito, the other dangling a cigarette, feeling the breeze and watching the procession: passers-by, parking-spot seekers, pecking sparrows. In Little Italy, Kenneth Marino chats into a cordless phone from his perch above Mulberry Street, casting a wary eye on the day's first tourists gawking up at him.

3   All across the city, the watchers take up their posts, pillow or towel spread across windowsill, Bible or remote close at hand. The white-haired woman leaning on a golden cushion above Nostrand Avenue in Crown Heights, Brooklyn. The retired pizza maker on the Upper East Side of Manhattan in his undershirt and khakis. The tragic-looking woman with pulled-back hair over the Drama Cafe in Park Slope, Brooklyn, and the long-sideburned deaf man two windows down.

4   And they sit there. And they look out at nothing; and at everything.

Marcelina Figueroa at her window in East Harlem.   Oscar Hidalgo/*New York Times*

5   From the city sidewalk, there are few summer sights more archetypically urban than the face glimpsed in an open window, gazing silently out at the street. In a world where entertainment is delivered via modem and iPod, the very idea of someone drinking deep from the well of unmediated, nonvirtual reality exerts a strange pull. It also taps into our own voyeurism: to see someone inside a home, after all, is to witness a private moment.

6   The view from the other side of the window frame turns out to be no less engrossing. For the committed window gazer, there is no better place than the exact **juncture** of the public and private **realms.**

7   "Instead of going outside," said Willie Taylor, 69, who holds court over his block in Harlem, "you sit at the window and you are outside. It's better than being outside."

8   The sociologist and window-gazer extraordinaire Jane Jacobs, in her 1961 **polemical** valentine "The Death and Life of Great American Cities," championed "the ballet of the good city sidewalk," an intricate dance which, she wrote, "never repeats itself from place to place, and in any one place is always **replete** with new improvisations."

9   Outside Edna Ford's apartment in the Boston Secor housing project in the Eastchester section of the Bronx, the dance is often sinister, involving indiscreet handoffs and bouts of violence. A cluster of teenagers—Ms. Ford calls them "2-cent drug dealers"—mills beneath her window.

10   "They talk all their business right here," said Ms. Ford, 70, a retired nurse's aide, "who they're going to rob, who they're going to stick up." She has witnessed more shootings than she cares to recall.

juncture
the place at which two things join

realms
domains, regions

polemical
controversial argument

replete
filled with

Kenneth Marino of Little Italy likes the morning scene.   Oscar Hidalgo/*New York Times*
"You see the day start progressing."

11   The action along Frank Baiardi's stretch of Second Avenue on the Upper East Side is a little tamer. "Yesterday, there was a big truck out there on fire," Mr. Baiardi, the former pizza maker, said the other day. "Usually, there's not too much trouble over here."

12   It makes no difference. The dance is hypnotic, addictive.

13   "I look in the morning," Mr. Marino, 52, said in the cluttered kitchen of the Mulberry Street tenement apartment that has been in his family for five generations. "It's nice and quiet. I see everybody cleaning their restaurants, like they're doing right now. You see the day start progressing."

14   When things heat up at the Boston Secor houses, Ms. Ford finds herself unable to tear herself from the window until the bullets actually start flying. "When I see all these things," she said, I think, 'Oh my God, why do I see all this stuff?' But I've got to look and see what's going on."

15   Over the course of a day, a season, a decade, the details accrete like the discarded furniture piling up against the wrought-iron fence beneath a "No Garbage Is to Be Placed Outside the Building" sign in Ms. Ford's courtyard.

16   To witness the flow of life itself, though, requires a considerable investment of time, something that window gazers tend to be rolling in: most are retired or disabled, or both.

17   Mr. Baiardi, 66, knows that his kind is vanishing. He gestured across Second Avenue to a modern high-rise. "Those people there, they never look out the window," he said. "I don't know why. Maybe they're not used to it."

18   But window gazing has its younger practitioners, too. Artemis Karotseri-Vermeulen is 14, and at night, after her father declares lights out, she stares out her window on Fifth Avenue in Park Slope until sleep comes calling. "Once I saw a car accident, and I was like, 'Whoa, cool,' " she said. "I saw this guy back into another guy and they were cursing at each other. I see a lot of yelling."

19   Many window gazers treat the window, against all evidence, as if it were, or at least should be, a one-way glass.

20   "My cousin sits at the window all the time, and every time he does the tourists take his picture," Mr. Marino said. "They go, 'Look at them sitting by the window.' What's wrong with sitting by the window? They'll look up and point at you. I just stare at them. They keep walking."

21   On East 107th Street in East Harlem, a square-jawed woman in a sleeveless T-shirt answered a request for an interview with a cigarette butt flicked from the third floor.

22   Mr. Taylor, who in his day worked as a waiter, a construction worker, a record-company executive and a cocaine dealer, trades heavily in neighborhood gossip across his sill. But if he sits in the window long enough, he said, "People start coming by and begging. 'It's my birthday, can you get me a meal?' "

23   That lets him know it is time for a break.

24   Then there are the rare likes of Ms. Figueroa, 71, who treats her ground-floor roost at the corner of East 117th Street and Park Avenue like a combination takeout counter and dispensary. Anyone who looks hungry or thirsty gets a glass of ice water, a coffee, a sandwich, a plate of her pernil and rice and beans. To the wounded, she hands out Band-Aids, Tylenol, peroxide.

25   "They call me the nurse," she said. In her spare time, she campaigns for her favorite City Council candidate.

26   And once in a lifetime, perhaps, something absolutely unexpected comes through the window.

27   Long ago, Mr. Taylor rented a room in a **labyrinthine** ground-floor apartment in Graham Court, the jewel box built by the Astor family at West 117th Street and Seventh Avenue. His landlady was Evelyn Moore, who liked to sit in her magnificent nine-foot-high bedroom window and feed the sparrows.

labyrinthine
winding, maze-like

28   Eventually, Mr. Taylor moved around the corner. A few years later, Ms. Moore's husband died. Mr. Taylor sensed an opportunity. "I'd come by every day, pick at her, talk junk, tell her my troubles; she'd tell me hers," he said. "We courted in the window."

29   Twenty-something years ago, Mr. Taylor moved back in. Now he and Ms. Moore take turns in the catbird seat by the radiator in the bedroom.

Evelyn Moore has a prime view of Harlem from
Graham Court, built by the Astor family.

Oscar Hidalgo/*New York Times*

30   "Sometimes I'll be looking out one window, and she'll be in the
kitchen looking out that window," Mr. Taylor said. "She talks to somebody,
I can hear."

31   Ms. Moore still marvels at the framework of their union. "It's a complicated story, but it's the truth," she said. "You can't get around the truth. It
was a strange meeting. Don't you think so?"

Reading Reflection Questions   *Sample answers provided.*

1. What is the main message (thesis) in Newman and Feldman's article?
Explain in your own words. *There are a wide variety of people, young and*

old, who spend a lot of time watching what happens outside their windows.

2. Which window watcher's description or story in this article did you like
best and why? *Answers will vary.*

3. What did the authors mean by "nonvirtual reality" (paragraph 5)?

It is an ironic statement about watching "real" life and not a video or digi-

tally created world.

4. What is the usual tourist reaction to the window watchers?

They stare up at them and point.

5. T/ F _____*F*_____ Every window watcher described in this article is an older person (over age 50).

6. T/ F _____*F*_____ The window watchers never interact with the people going by on the street.

Checking Vocabulary

Define each of the following words by figuring out its meaning using context clues in the reading selection (see Chapter 27 for how to use context clues). If you cannot work out the meaning of a word, use a dictionary.

7. procession (paragraph 2): *people moving along in an orderly way*

8. archetypically (paragraph 5): *typically*

9. voyeurism (paragraph 5): *desire to secretly look at or watch others*

10. engrossing (paragraph 6): *fascinating*

READING CRITICALLY

Answer the following questions on a separate sheet of paper.

1. What is the authors' **purpose** or goal in this reading selection?

2. What are the implied or stated questions or **ideas** being addressed?

3. What specific **support** (details and examples) do the authors use to develop thier purpose or goal for the reading?

4. What **conclusions or arguments** do the authors reach based on what is happening or **inferences** (inferences imply "if this, then this" types of cause and effect analysis) they draw in the reading?

5. Who is the intended audience, and how did you reach that conclusion?

Group Activity

Form a group of three to five students from your class. Sit facing each other or in a circle. Choose one person to record notes of the discussion. One at a time, share what you would see on a typical day looking out of a window of your home. What could you learn from spending a day people watching from that window? Be as specific as you can be in drawing conclusions about what you could learn from observing the people in your neighborhood for a full day.

Writing Assignments

1. Write a one-paragraph summary of this reading (see p. 300).

2. Write a paragraph that defines the word voyeurism as it is used in paragraph 5 (see Chapter 10).

3. Write a description paragraph about one of the pictures from this article (see Chapter 7).

4. Write a narration paragraph or essay about a time you did some people watching (see Chapter 6).

5. Write a paragraph or essay that compares living in the city with living in the suburbs (see Chapter 13).

For Some, the Blogging Never Stops

Katie Hafner and Tim Gnatek

Katie Hafner writes articles, essays, and books on topics ranging from history to Internet phenomena. She is currently a technology reporter for *The New York Times* and a contributing editor for *Newsweek*. In 2004, she won the Wired Magazine Award for New Media Journalism. Tim Gnatek is a journalist who also specializes in online and Internet topics.

1   To celebrate four years of marriage, Richard Wiggins and his wife, Judy Matthews, recently spent a week in Key West, Fla. Early on the morning of their anniversary, Ms. Matthews heard her husband get up and go into the bathroom. He stayed there for a long time.

2   "I didn't hear any water running, so I wondered what was going on," Ms. Matthews said. When she knocked on the door, she found him seated with his laptop balanced on his knees, typing into his Web log, a collection of observations about the technical world, over a wireless link.

3   Blogging is a pastime for many, even a livelihood for a few. For some, it becomes an obsession. Such bloggers often feel compelled to write several times daily and feel anxious if they don't keep up. As they spend more time hunkered over their computers, they neglect family, friends and jobs. They blog at home, at work and on the road. They blog openly or sometimes, like Mr. Wiggins, quietly so as not to call attention to their habit.

4 "It seems as if his laptop is glued to his legs 24/7," Ms. Matthews said of her husband.

5 The number of bloggers has grown quickly, thanks to sites like blogger.com, which makes it easy to set up a blog. Technorati, a blogtracking service, has counted some 2.5 million blogs.

6 Of course, most of those millions are abandoned or, at best, maintained infrequently. For many bloggers, the novelty soon wears off and their persistence fades.

7 Sometimes, too, the realization that no one is reading sets in. A few blogs have thousands of readers, but never have so many people written so much to be read by so few. By Jupiter Research's estimate, only 4 percent of online users read blogs.

8 Indeed, if a blog is likened to a conversation between a writer and readers, bloggers like Mr. Wiggins are having conversations largely with themselves.

9 Mr. Wiggins, 48, a senior information technologist at Michigan State University in East Lansing, does not know how many readers he has; he suspects it's not many. But that does not seem to bother him.

10 "I'm just getting something off my chest," he said.

11 Nor is he deterred by the fact that he toils for hours at a time on his blog for no money. He gets satisfaction in other ways. "Sometimes there's an 'I told you so' aspect to it," he said. Recent ruminations on wigblog.blogspot.com have focused on Gmail, Google's new e-mail service. Mr. Wiggins points with pride to Wigblog posts that voiced early privacy concerns about Gmail.

12 Perhaps a chronically small audience is a blessing. For it seems that the more popular a blog becomes, the more some bloggers feel the need to post.

13 Tony Pierce started his blog three years ago while in search of a distraction after breaking up with a girlfriend. "In three years, I don't think I've missed a day," he said. Now Mr. Pierce's blog (www.tonypierce.com/blog/bloggy.htm), a chatty diary of Hollywood, writing and women in which truth sometimes mingles with fiction, averages 1,000 visitors a day.

14 Where some frequent bloggers might label themselves merely **ardent**, Mr. Pierce is more realistic. "I wouldn't call it dedicated, I would call it a problem," he said. "If this were beer, I'd be an alcoholic."

ardent
intense, passionate

15 Mr. Pierce, who lives in Hollywood and works as a scheduler in the entertainment industry, said blogging began to feel like an addiction when he noticed that he would rather be with his computer than with his girlfriend— for technical reasons.

16 "She's got an iMac, and I don't like her computer," Mr. Pierce said. When he is at his girlfriend's house, he feels "antsy." "We have little fights because I want to go home and write my thing," he said.

gratification

pleasure or satisfaction

17   Mr. Pierce described the rush he gets from what he called "the fix" provided by his blog. "The pleasure response is twofold," he said. "You can have instant **gratification**; you're going to hear about something really good or bad instantly. And if I feel like I've written something good, it's enjoyable to go back and read it."

18   "And," he said, "like most addictions, those feelings go away quickly. So I have to do it again and again."

19   Joseph Lorenzo Hall, 26, a graduate student at the School of Information Management and Systems at the University of California at Berkeley who has studied bloggers, said that for some people blogging has supplanted e-mail as a way to procrastinate at work.

20   People like Mr. Pierce, who devote much of their free time to the care and feeding of their own blogs and posting to other blogs, do so largely because it makes them feel productive even if it is not a paying job.

21   The procrastination, said Scott Lederer, 31, a fellow graduate student with Mr. Hall, has a collective feel to it. "You feel like you're participating in something important, because we're all doing it together," he said.

22   Jeff Jarvis, president of Advance.net, a company that builds Web sites for newspapers and magazines, and a blogging enthusiast, defended what he called one's "obligation to the blog."

23   "The addictive part is not so much extreme narcissism," Mr. Jarvis said. "It's that you're involved in a conversation. You have a connection to people through the blog."

24   Some compulsive bloggers take their obligation to extremes, blogging at the expense of more financially rewarding tasks.

25   Mr. Wiggins has missed deadline after deadline at *Searcher*, an online periodical for which he is a paid contributor.

26   Barbara Quint, the editor of the magazine, said she did all she could to get him to deliver his columns on time. Then she discovered that Mr. Wiggins was busily posting articles to his blog instead of sending her the ones he had promised, she said. "Here he is working all night on something read by five second cousins and a dog, and I'm willing to pay him," she said.

27   Ms. Quint has grown more understanding of his reasons, if not entirely sympathetic. "The Web's illusion of immortality is sometimes more attractive than actual cash," she said.

28   Jocelyn Wang, a 27-year-old marketing manager in Los Angeles, started her blog, a chronicle of whatever happens to pop into her head (www.jozjozjoz.com), 18 months ago as an outlet for boredom.

29   Now she spends at least four hours a day posting to her blog and reading other blogs. Ms. Wang's online journal is now her life. And the people she has met through the blog are a large part of her core of friends.

30   "There is no real separation in my life," she said. Like Mr. Wiggins, Ms. Wang blogs while on vacation. She stays on floors at the Hotel Nikko in San Francisco with access to a free Internet connection. ("So I can blog," she explains.)

31   Others find they are distracted to the point of neglectfulness. Tom Lewis, 35, a project manager for a software firm in western Massachusetts who has a photo blog (tomdog.buzznet.com/user), has occasionally shown up "considerably late" for events and has put off more than a few work-related calls to tend to his blog.

32   Mr. Jarvis characterizes the blogging way of life as a routine rather than an obsession. "It's a habit," he said. "What you're really doing is telling people about something that they might find interesting. When that becomes part of your life, when you start thinking in blog, it becomes part of you."

33   The constant search for bloggable moments is what led Gregor J. Rothfuss, a programmer in Zurich, to blog to the point of near despair. Bored by his job, Mr. Rothfuss, 27, started a blog that focused on technical topics.

34   "I was trying to record all thoughts and speculations I deemed interesting," he said. "Sort of creating a digital alter ego. The obsession came from trying to capture as much as possible of the good stuff in my head in as high fidelity as possible."

35   For months, Mr. Rothfuss said, he blogged at work, at home, late into the night, day in and day out until it all became a blur—all the while knowing, he added, "that no one was necessarily reading it, except for myself."

36   When traffic to the blog, greg.abstract.ch, started to rise, he began devoting half a day every day and much of the weekend to it. Mr. Rothfuss said he has few memories of that period in his life aside from the compulsive blogging.

37   He was saved from the rut of his online chronicle when he traveled to Asia. The blog became more of a travelogue. Then Mr. Rothfuss switched jobs, finding one he enjoyed, and his blogging grew more moderate.

38   He still has the blog, but posts to it just twice a week, he said, "as opposed to twice an hour." He feels healthier now. "It's part of what I do now, it's not what I do," he said.

39   Suffering from a similar form of "blog fatigue," Bill Barol, a freelance writer in Santa Monica, Calif., simply stopped altogether after four years of nearly constant blogging.

40   "It was starting to feel like work, and it was never supposed to be a job," Mr. Barol said. "It was supposed to be an anti-job."

41   Even with some 200 visitors to his blog each day, he has not posted to his blog since returning from a month of travel.

42   Still, Mr. Barol said, he does not rule out a return to blogging someday.

43   "There is this seductive thing that happens, this kind of snowball-rolling-down-a-hill thing, where the sheer momentum of several years' posting becomes very keenly felt," he said. "And the absence of posting feels like—I don't know, laziness or something."

Reading Reflection Questions   *Sample answers provided.*

1. What is Hafner and Gnatek's main message (thesis) in this essay? Explain in your own words. *Blogging can become a habit, even an unsatis-fying addiction.*

2. Using your own words, explain what the tern "blogging" means, as it is used in this article. *Answers will vary.*

3. Provide two examples of how blogging could be an unhealthy habit according to this article. *Answers will vary, but some possibilities include being obsessive about blogging, compulsively adding to a blog hour-by-hour, allowing blogging to draw one's focus away from real work.*

4. Do you think blogging is good for the advancement of writing as an art form? Why or why not? *Answers will vary.*

5. T/ F ____*F*____ Most of the bloggers in this article have a large audience of readers.

6. T/ F ____*T*____ For some of the bloggers in this article, the pressure to write became another form of stress, like work.

Checking Vocabulary

Define each of the following words by figuring out its meaning using context clues in the reading selection (see Chapter 27 for how to use context clues). If you cannot work out the meaning of a word, use a dictionary.

7. blogging (paragraph 3): *Web logging or journaling*

8. chronically (paragraph 12): *constantly, habitually*

9. procrastination (paragraph 21): *putting things off, delaying*

10. travelogue (paragraph 37): *writing about travelling*

READING CRITICALLY

1. What is the authors' **purpose** or goal in this reading selection?

2. What are the implied or stated questions or **ideas** being addressed?

3. What specific **support** (details and examples) do the authors use to develop their purpose or goal for the reading?

4. What **conclusions or arguments** do the authors reach based on what is happening or **inferences** (inferences imply "if this, then this" types of cause and effect analysis) they draw in the reading?

5. Who is the intended audience, and how did you reach that conclusion?

Group Activity

Form a group of three to five students from your class. Sit facing each other or in a circle. Choose one person to record notes of the discussion. Have any of you ever written a blog entry? Have any of you ever read a blog entry? How are they different from other forms of writing? What do you think the increase of blogging sites on the Internet says about our relationship to technology? Explain.

Writing Assignments

1. Write a narration paragraph or essay (Chapter 6) that describes an event or memory where you let a hobby get out of hand.

2. Write a cause and effect paragraph or essay (Chapter 12) that explores the causes and effects of a habit that can turn into an unhealthy addiction.

3. Write an argument/persuasion paragraph or essay (Chapter 14) arguing for or against bloggers getting paid for their work.

4. Write a one-paragraph summary of this reading (p. 300).

5. Write a paragraph in which you define the word *blogging*.

Death of a Homeless Man

Scott Russell Sanders

Scott Russell Sanders (1945–) was born in Memphis, Tennessee, attended Brown University, earned a PhD from Cambridge University in England, and taught at Indiana University from 1971 until his retirement in 2009. He has written novels, essays, and nonfiction including *Hunting for Hope, Staying Put,* and *Writing from the Center*. His book *A Private History of Awe* was nominated for a Pulitzer Prize. He has focused on the place of humans in nature, social justice, the interaction between geography and culture, and spirituality. His writing is detailed and descriptive, and he is famous for his attention to detail.

1   This past winter, not long after Christmas, a man named John Griffin burned to death in South Boston. He was fifty-five, a veteran of the Korean War, an alcoholic, well-known and liked by his neighbors, who remembered him as a streetwise philosopher, a genial storyteller, gracious and kindly and full of song. His body, from which all the clothing had been burned away except for tatters at ankles and wrists, was found twenty feet from Dorchester Bay. Evidently Griffin had collapsed on his way to the water, for staggery footprints marked a trail back over the sand to his plywood hovel. No one knows what set his clothes alight, whether a cigarette or the fire of twigs and cardboard he'd been using to keep warm.

2   So there you have it, the death of a homeless man. At this point a good journalist would tell you how many hundreds of thousands, even how many millions, of souls go to sleep cold and hungry and roofless each night in this rich land. Although I am thankful for those conscientious reporters, I am not any sort of journalist, good or bad; I am a novelist, snagged on particulars. I cannot get beyond that charred body of John Griffin, those wristlets and anklets of cloth, those eloquent footprints in the sand, the quenching waters only a few paces beyond his outstretched arms. Instead of brooding on statistics about poverty, I keep seeing his little shanty cobbled together out of scavenged plywood, the cigarette butts and empty vodka bottles strewn on the ground.

3   As it happens, one of those who passed by John Griffin's homestead almost daily (while jogging) was Boston Mayor Raymond Flynn. Another who saw him regularly was a minister, Leonard Coopenwrath. Both men described Griffin as a friend, and both attended his funeral, along with a cardinal, the police commissioner, the state secretary for human affairs, and other dignitaries. No one could figure out what to do with Griffin alive, but they turned out in force to bury him.

4   Mayor Flynn was quoted in the papers as saying, "It goes to show you that this country is not meeting the needs of people with physical and mental problems." Indeed, indeed. The mayor seems to be a compassionate man, and so I respect his grief as genuine, although it occurs to me that the city of Boston, as the local portion of "this country," ought to shoulder part of the blame for Griffin's suffering.

5   As if in counterpoint, the Reverend Coopenwrath observed, "I don't think the system failed him. He wanted to live basically apart from shelters and we must respect that." I'm all for respecting a man's desires, but if those include a preference for spending the Boston winter in a plywood lean-to instead of a public shelter, I think I would take a hard look at the shelter. I would ask what sort of help this Korean War veteran received for his alcoholism, where he last worked, what agency last trained him for a job, what doctors last examined him; what relatives or neighbors or church ever thought of taking him in.

6   When I reflect on what my nation is up to, what it is achieving with all its huffing and puffing, I do not think about the Gross National Product or the Dow Jones Industrial Average; I think about John Griffin. The GNP, as everyone knows, or should know, is gross indeed, including the price of Griffin's funeral and vodka while ignoring the value of his stories and songs. The stock market see-saws wildly at news of a polyp on the President's colon, but does not so much as tremble over the incineration of John Griffin, would not tremble even if the suffering of all the jobless, homeless, futureless people in America could be added together by some **calculus** into a Gross Misery Product.

calculus
mathematical method of calculating

7   There is no such calculus, for the simple reason that suffering, like death, is personal. Each of us meets it, or avoids it, inside the arena of his or her own skin. You can tote up dollars or tons or kilowatts or spectators, and arrive thereby at a number that might be cause for boasting or lamenting; but you cannot work arithmetic on pain. So much should be obvious in a country that lights candles at the shrine of individualism. We brag to the world about valuing the **sovereignty** of self. What we actually value is the right of (selected) individuals to accumulate wealth and power at the expense of community and planet.

sovereignty
power or rule over

8   On the night of his death, John Griffin was cold, abandoned, most likely drunk, and, in the last few minutes, wrapped in flames. He dwelt at the center of an utterly private agony. I can share in it only faintly, through imagination. That is where the drive for change begins, unshielded by statistics or mansions, in **empathy** with those who suffer.

empathy

feeling for another, sympathy and understanding

Reading Reflection Questions   *Sample answers provided.*

1. What is Sanders's main message (thesis) in this essay? Explain in your own words. *That it is a tragedy that this homeless man didn't get the kind of help he needed before his death; that we are more focused on accumulating personal wealth than caring for those less fortunate.*

2. List a few of the specific, graphic details included in this essay that make it powerful. *Answers will vary.*

3. How does he describe this homeless man who died?

Answers will vary, "He was fifty-five, a veteran of the Korean War, an alcoholic, well-known and liked by his neighbors, who remembered him as a streetwise philosopher, a genial storyteller, gracious and kindly and full of song."

4. Why do you think the author doesn't include statistics or facts about homelessness in this essay?

Answers will vary. Mostly to make this a more human and powerful story— one real case instead of facts and statistics.

5. T/ F _____*F*_____ No one in the town knew that the homeless man was on his own and in poverty before his death.

6. T/ F _____*T*_____ Even the town mayor knew this man and knew he lived the way he did.

Checking Vocabulary

Define each of the following words by figuring out its meaning using context clues in the reading selection (see Chapter 27 for how to use context clues). If you cannot work out the meaning of a word, use a dictionary.

7. genial (paragraph 1): *friendly, pleasant*

8. conscientious (paragraph 2): *thoughtful, dedicated*

9. eloquent (paragraph 2): *expressive, speaking of*

10. incineration (paragraph 6): *burn completely, burn to ashes*

READING CRITICALLY

Answer the following questions on a separate sheet of paper.

1. What is the author's **purpose** or goal in this reading selection?

2. What are the implied or stated questions or **ideas** being addressed?

3. What specific **support** (details and examples) does the author use to develop his purpose or goal for the reading?

4. What **conclusions or arguments** does the author reach based on what is happening or **inferences** (inferences imply "if this, then this" types of cause and effect analysis) he draws in the reading?

5. Who is the intended audience, and how did you reach that conclusion?

Group Activity

Form a group of three to five students from your class, and choose one person to record notes of the discussion. Do you see homeless people where you live or have you seen them in cities you have visited? What did you do (be honest)? How do you think our culture reacts to homeless people in general? Why do you think we act that way?

Writing Assignments

1. Write a one-paragraph summary, including critical analysis, of this reading (see pp. 300 and 303).

2. Write a description paragraph or about someone you have seen or know who is poor or even homeless but proud (see Chapter 7).

3. Write a narration paragraph or essay that describes a time when you experienced or witnessed the effects of poverty (see Chapters 6 and 12).

4. Write a cause and effect paragraph or essay that explores poverty or homelessness (see Chapter 12).

5. Write an argument/persuasion paragraph or essay (Chapter 14) arguing for mandatory outreach to the homeless who refuse to use city shelters (see Chapter 14).

Friends, Good Friends—and Such Good Friends

Judith Viorst

Judith Viorst (1936–) is an editor and columnist at Redbook magazine, where the following essay originally appeared in 1977. In addition, she has written a number of books, including *Alexander and the Terrible, Horrible, No Good, Very Bad Day* (1982); *Sad Underwear and Other Complications* (1995); *It's Hard to Be Hip Over Thirty and Other Tragedies of Modern Life* (1970); and *How Did I Get to Be Forty and Other Atrocities* (1984). Her writing is humorous and very accessible.

1   Women are friends, I once would have said, when they totally love and support and trust each other, and bare to each other the secrets of their souls, and run—no questions asked—to help each other, and tell harsh truths to each other (no, you can't wear that dress unless you lose ten pounds first) when harsh truths must be told.

2   Women are friends, I once would have said, when they share the same affection for Ingmar Bergman, plus train rides, cats, warm rain, charades, Camus, and hate with equal ardor Newark and Brussels sprouts and Lawrence Welk and camping.

3   In other words, I once would have said that a friend is a friend all the way, but now I believe that's a narrow point of view. For the friendships I have and the friendships I see are conducted at many levels of intensity, serve many different functions, meet different needs and range from those as all-the-way as the friendship of the soul sisters mentioned above to that of the most nonchalant and casual playmates.

Consider these varieties of friendship

4   **1. Convenience friends.** These are women with whom, if our paths weren't crossing all the time, we'd have no particular reason to be friends: a next-door neighbor, a woman in our car pool, the mother of one of our children's closest friends or maybe some mommy with whom we serve juice and cookies each week at the Glenwood Co-op Nursery.

5   Convenience friends are convenient indeed. They'll lend us their cups and silverware for a party. They'll drive our kids to soccer when we're sick. They'll take us to pick up our car when we need a lift to the garage. They'll even take our cats when we go on vacation. As we will for them.

6   But we don't, with convenience friends, ever come too close or tell too much; we maintain our public face and emotional distance. "Which means," says Elaine, "that I'll talk about being overweight but not about being depressed. Which means I'll admit being mad but not blind with rage. Which means that I might say that we're pinched this month but never that I'm worried sick over money."

7   But which doesn't mean that there isn't sufficient value to be found in these friendships of mutual aid, in convenience friends.

8   **2. Special-interest friends.** These friendships aren't intimate, and they needn't involve kids or silverware or cats. Their value lies in some interest jointly shared. And so we may have an office friend or a yoga friend or a tennis friend or a friend from the Women's Democratic Club.

9   "I've got one woman friend," says Joyce, "who likes, as I do, to take psychology courses. Which makes it nice for me—and nice for her. It's fun to go with someone you know and it's fun to discuss what you've learned, driving back from the classes." And for the most part, she says, that's all they discuss.

10   "I'd say that what we're doing is *doing* together, not being together," Suzanne says of her Tuesday-doubles friends. "It's mainly a tennis relationship, but we play together well. And I guess we all need to have a couple of playmates."

11   I agree.

12   My playmate is a shopping friend, a woman of marvelous taste, a woman who knows exactly *where* to buy *what,* and furthermore is a woman who always knows beyond a doubt what one ought to be buying. I don't have the time to keep up with what's new in eyeshadow, hemlines and shoes and whether the smock look is in or finished already. But since (oh, shame!) I care a lot about eyeshadow, hemlines and shoes, and since I don't *want* to wear smocks if the smock look is finished, I'm very glad to have a shopping friend.

13   **3. Historical friends.** We all have a friend who knew us when . . . maybe way back in Miss Meltzer's second grade, when our family lived in that three-room flat in Brooklyn, when our dad was out of work for seven months, when our brother Allie got in that fight where they had to call the police, when our sister married the endodontist from Yonkers and when, the morning after we lost our virginity, she was the first, the only, friend we told.

14   The years have gone by and we've gone separate ways and we've little in common now, but we're still an intimate part of each other's past. And so whenever we go to Detroit we always go to visit this friend of our girlhood. Who knows how we looked before our teeth were

straightened. Who knows how we talked before our voice got un-Brooklyned. Who knows what we ate before we learned about artichokes. And who, by her presence, puts us in touch with an earlier part of ourself, a part of ourself it's important never to lose.

15   "What this friend means to me and what I mean to her," says Grace, "is having a sister without sibling rivalry. We know the texture of each other's lives. She remembers my grandmother's cabbage soup. I remember the way her uncle played the piano. There's simply no other friend who remembers those things."

16   **4. Crossroads friends.** Like historical friends, our crossroads friends are important for *what was*—for the friendship we shared at a crucial, now past, time of life. A time, perhaps, when we roomed in college together; or worked as eager young singles in the Big City together; or went together, as my friend Elizabeth and I did, through pregnancy, birth and that scary first year of new motherhood.

17   Crossroads friends forge powerful links, links strong enough to endure with not much more contact than once-a-year letters at Christmas. And out of respect for those crossroads years, for those dramas and dreams we once shared, we will always be friends.

18   **5. Cross-generational friends.** Historical friends and crossroads friends seem to maintain a special kind of intimacy—dormant but always ready to be revived—and though we may rarely meet, whenever we do connect, it's personal and intense. Another kind of intimacy exists in the friendships that form across generations in what one woman calls her daughter–mother and her mother–daughter relationships.

19   Evelyn's friend is her mother's age—"but I share so much more than I ever could with my mother"—a woman she talks to of music, of books and of life. "What I get from her is the benefit of her experience. What she gets—and enjoys—from me is a youthful perspective. It's a pleasure for both of us."

20   I have in my own life a precious friend, a woman of 65 who has lived very hard, who is wise, who listens well; who has been where I am and can help me understand it; and who represents not only an ultimate ideal mother to me but also the person I'd like to be when I grow up.

21   In our daughter role we tend to do more than our share of self revelation; in our mother role we tend to receive what's revealed. It's another kind of pleasure—playing wise mother to a questing younger person. It's another very lovely kind of friendship.

22   **6. Part-of-a-couple friends.** Some of the women we call our friends we never see alone—we see them as part of a couple at couples' parties.

And though we share interests in many things and respect each other's views, we aren't moved to deepen the relationship. Whatever the reason, a lack of time or—and this is more likely—a lack of chemistry, our friendship remains in the context of a group. But the fact that our feeling on seeing each other is always, "I'm *so* glad she's here" and the fact that we spend half the evening talking together says that this too, in its own way, counts as a friendship.

23   (Other part-of-a-couple friends are the friends that came with the marriage, and some of these are friends we could live without. But sometimes, alas, she married our husband's best friend; and sometimes, alas, she *is* our husband's best friend. And so we find ourself dealing with her, somewhat against our will, in a spirit of what I'll call *reluctant* friendship.)

24 **7. Men who are friends.** I wanted to write just of women friends, but the women I've talked to won't let me—they say I must mention man–woman friendships too. For these friendships can be just as close and as dear as those that we form with women. Listen to Lucy's description of one such friendship:

25   "We've found we have things to talk about that are different from what he talks about with my husband and different from what I talk about with his wife. So sometimes we call on the phone or meet for lunch. There are similar intellectual interests—we always pass on to each other the books that we love—but there's also something tender and caring too."

26   In a couple of crises, Lucy says, "he offered himself for talking and for helping. And when someone died in his family he wanted me there. The sexual, flirty part of our friendship is very small, but *some*—just enough to make it fun and different." She thinks—and I agree—that the sexual part, though small, is always *some,* is always there when a man and a woman are friends.

27   It's only in the past few years that I've made friends with men, in the sense of a friendship that's *mine,* not just part of two couples. And achieving with them the ease and the trust I've found with women friends has value indeed. Under the dryer at home last week, putting on mascara and rouge, I comfortably sat and talked with a fellow named Peter. Peter, I finally decided, could handle the shock of me minus mascara under the dryer. Because we care for each other. Because we're friends.

28 **8.** There are medium friends, and pretty good friends, and very good friends indeed, and these friendships are defined by their level of intimacy. And what we'll reveal at each of these levels of intimacy is **calibrated** with care. We might tell a medium friend, for example, that yesterday we had a fight with our husband. And we might tell a pretty good friend that this fight with our husband made us so mad that we slept on the couch. And

calibrated

checked, adjusted

we might tell a very good friend that the reason we got so mad in that fight that we slept on the couch had something to do with that girl who works in his office. But it's only to our very best friends that we're willing to tell all, to tell what's going on with that girl in his office.

29   The best of friends, I still believe, totally love and support and trust each other, and bare to each other the secrets of their souls, and run— no questions asked—to help each other, and tell harsh truths to each other when they must be told.

30   But we needn't agree about everything (only 12-year-old girl friends agree about *everything*) to tolerate each other's point of view. To accept without judgment. To give and to take without ever keeping score. And to *be* there, as I am for them and as they are for me, to comfort our sorrows, to celebrate our joys.

Reading Reflection Questions *Sample answers provided.*

1. What is Judith Viorst's main message (thesis) in this essay? Explain in your own words. *That women forge many different types of friendships,*

   which serve different needs

2. Do you as a male or female have different categories of friends? If so, list two of those categories. *Answers will vary.*

   _____

3. Do you agree that it is necessary to have different levels of friendship from casual to more serious? Why or why not? *Answers will vary.*

   _____

4. List at least two qualities you look for in a friend. *Answers will vary.*

   _____

5. T/ F ___T___ Viorst thinks the best kind of friends accept us without judgment.

6. T/F ___T___ Male–female friendships are discussed in this article.

Checking Vocabulary

Define each of the following words by figuring out its meaning using context clues in the reading selection (see Chapter 27 for how to use context clues). If you cannot work out the meaning of a word, use a dictionary.

7. ardor (paragraph 2): *passion*

8. nonchalant (paragraph 3): *unconcerned, casual*

9. dormant (paragraph 18): _asleep, inactive_ _____

10. revelation (paragraph 21): _disclosure_ _____

READING CRITICALLY

Answer the following questions on a separate sheet of paper.

1. What is the author's **purpose** or goal in this reading selection?

2. What are the implied or stated questions or **ideas** being addressed?

3. What specific **support** (details and examples) does the author use to develop her purpose or goal for the reading?

4. What **conclusions or arguments** does the author reach based on what is happening or **inferences** (inferences imply "if this, then this" types of cause/effect analysis) she draws in the reading?

5. Who is the intended audience, and how did you reach that conclusion?

Group Activity

Form a group of three to five students from your class, and choose one person to record notes of the discussion. Brainstorm the type of friendships you think men form in response to Viorst's analysis of female friendships. After you have come up with some categories, compare how they compare or contrast with Viorst's categories of female friendship. What conclusions can you draw from these comparisons about male versus female friendships? Be specific.

Writing Assignments

1. Write a one-paragraph summary of this reading (see p. 300).

2. Write a narration paragraph that describes an event or memory that is related to a good friend helping you out when you were in need (see Chapter 6).

3. Write a cause and effect paragraph or essay that explores how a good friend of yours became a close friend (see Chapter 12).

4. Write a paragraph or essay that compares and/or contrasts two of your closest friends (see Chapter 13).

5. Write an argument/persuasion paragraph or essay arguing for or against developing male–female friendships (see Chapter 14).

I'm a Banana and Proud of It

Wayson Choy

Wayson Choy (1939–) was born in Vancouver and now lives in Toronto, where he teaches at Humber College. His first novel, *The Jade Peony* (written in 1995), was awarded the Trillium Award for best book of 1996. He has also published other books and essays, many of which are autobiographical.

1   Because both my parents came from China, I took Chinese. But I cannot read or write Chinese and barely speak it. I love my North American citizenship. I don't mind being called a "banana," yellow on the outside and white inside. I'm proud I'm a banana.

2   After all, in Canada and the United States, native Indians are "apples" (red outside, white inside); blacks are "Oreo cookies" (black and white); and Chinese are "bananas." These metaphors assume, both rightly and wrongly, that the culture here has been primarily anglo-white. Cultural history made me a banana.

3   History: My father and mother arrived separately to the B.C. coast in the early part of the century. They came as unwanted "aliens." Better to be an alien here than to be dead of starvation in China. But after the Chinese Exclusion laws were passed in North America (late 1800s, early 1900s), no Chinese immigrants were granted citizenship in either Canada or the United States.

4   Like those Old China village men from *Toi San* who, in the 1850s, laid down cliff-edge train tracks through the Rockies and the Sierras, or like those first women who came as mail-order wives or concubines and who as bond-slaves were turned into cheaper labourers or even prostitutes—like many of those men and women, my father and mother survived ugly, unjust times. In 1917, two hours after he got off the boat from Hong Kong, my father was called "chink" and told to go back to China. "Chink" is a hateful racist term, stereotyping the shape of Asian eyes: "a chink in the armour," an undesirable slit. For the Elders, the past was humiliating. Eventually, the Second World War changed hostile attitudes toward the Chinese.

5   During the war, Chinese men volunteered and lost their lives as members of the American and Canadian military. When hostilities ended, many more were proudly in uniform waiting to go overseas. Record Chinatown dollars were raised to buy War Bonds. After 1945, challenged by such money and ultimate sacrifices, the Exclusion laws in both Canada and the

United States were revoked. Chinatown residents claimed their citizenship and sent for their families.

6   By 1949, after the Communists took over China, those of us who arrived here as young children, or were born here, stayed. No longer "aliens," we became legal citizens of North America. Many of us also became "bananas."

7   Historically, "banana" is not a racist term. Although it clumsily stereo-types many of the children and grandchildren of the Old Chinatowns, the term actually follows the old Chinese tendency to assign endearing nick-names to replace formal names, semicomic names to keep one humble. Thus, "banana" describes the generations who assimilated so well into North American life.

8   In fact, our families encouraged members of my generation in the 1950s and sixties to "get ahead," to get an English education, to get a job with good pay and prestige. "Don't work like me," Chinatown parents said. "Work in an office!" The *lao wahkiu* (the Chinatown old-timers) also warned, "Never forget—you still be Chinese!"

9   None of us ever forgot. The mirror never lied.

10   Many Chinatown teen-agers felt we didn't quite belong in any one world. We looked Chinese, but thought and behaved North American. Impatient Chinatown parents wanted the best of both worlds for us, but they bluntly labelled their children and grandchildren "*juk-sing* " or even "*mo no.*" Not that we were totally "shallow bamboo butt-heads" or entirely "no brain," but we had less and less understanding of Old China traditions, and less and less interest in their village histories. Father used to say we lacked **Taoist** ritual, Taoist manners. We were, he said, "*mo li.*"

11   This was true. Chinatown's younger brains, like everyone else's of whatever race, were being colonized by "white bread" U.S. family televi-sion programs. We began to feel Chinese home life was inferior. We co-operated with English-language magazines that showed us how to act and what to buy. Seductive Hollywood movies made some of us secretly weep that we did not have movie star faces. American music made Chinese music sound like noise.

12   By the 1970s and eighties, many of us had consciously or uncon-sciously distanced ourselves from our Chinatown histories. We became bananas.

13   Finally, for me, in my 40s or 50s, with the death first of my mother, then my father, I realized I did not belong anywhere unless I could under-stand the past. I needed to find the foundation of my Chinese-ness. I needed roots.

14   I spent my college holidays researching the past. I read Chinatown oral histories, located documents, searched out early articles. Those early

Taoist

follower of the philosophi-cal system evolved by Lao-tzu and Chuang-tzu that advocates a life of complete simplicity and naturalness

citizens came back to life for me. Their long toil and blood sacrifices, the proud record of their patient, legal challenges, gave us all our present rights as citizens. Canadian and American Chinatowns set aside their family tongue differences and encouraged each other to fight injustice. There were no borders. "After all," they affirmed, "*Daaih ga tohng yahn . . .* We are all Chinese!"

15   In my book, *The Jade Peony,* I tried to recreate this past, to explore the beginnings of the conflicts trapped within myself, the struggle between being Chinese and being North American. I discovered a truth: these "between world" struggles are universal.

16   In every human being, there is "the Other"—something that makes each of us feel how different we are to everyone else, even to family members. Yet, ironically, we are all the same, wanting the same security and happiness. I know this now.

17   I think the early Chinese pioneers actually started "going bananas" from the moment they first settled upon the West Coast. They had no choice. They adapted. They initiated assimilation. If they had not, they and their family would have starved to death. I might even suggest that all surviving Chinatown citizens eventually became bananas. Only some, of course, were more ripe than others.

18   That's why I'm proudly a banana: I accept the paradox of being both Chinese and not Chinese.

19   Now at last, whenever I look in the mirror or hear ghost voices shouting, "You still Chinese!," I smile.

20   I know another truth: In immigrant North America, we are all Chinese.

Reading Reflection Questions   *Sample answers provided.*

1. What is Wayson Choy's main message (thesis) in this essay? Explain in your own words. *He accepts, embraces, the label "banana" as one that truly*

   represents him as both a Chinese person and Chinese-American citizen.

2. Have you ever been labeled based on some physical characteristic? If so, what was it and how did it make you feel? *Answers will vary.*

3. What does the term "banana" mean in this essay?

   Yellow on the outside, white on the inside, a term Choy has heard used to

   describe assimilated Chinese Americans

4. Explain why the author ends up embracing this term and why he uses the metaphor of a banana throughout this piece to impart his message.

   Answers will vary. He is proud of his Chinese American heritage and the

   term sums up his personal combination of Chinese heritage and Western

   identity.

5. T/ F _____ *F* _____ Choy has an angry tone in this essay.

6. T/ F _____ *T* _____ Choy thinks that blending into a culture can be positive.

Checking Vocabulary

Define each of the following words by figuring out its meaning using context clues in the reading selection (see Chapter 27 for how to use context clues). If you cannot work out the meaning of a word, use a dictionary.

7. metaphors (paragraph 2): *comparisons*

8. concubines (paragraph 4): *prostitutes/mistresses*

9. revoked (paragraph 5): *took back, reversed*

10. assimilated (paragraph 7): *adapted, adjusted*

READING CRITICALLY

Answer the following questions on a separate sheet of paper.

1. What is the author's **purpose** or goal in this reading selection?

2. What are the implied or stated questions or **ideas** being addressed?

3. What specific **support** (details and examples) does the author use to develop his purpose or goal for the reading?

4. What **conclusions or arguments** does the author reach based on what is happening or **inferences** (inferences imply "if this, then this" types of cause/effect analysis) he draws in the reading?

5. Who is the intended audience, and how did you reach that conclusion?

Group Activity

Form a group of three to five students from your class. Sit facing each other or in a circle. Choose one person to record notes of the discussion. Taking turns, share a time that you were judged or stereotyped by your race, age, physical size (weight or height), or gender. How did it make you feel? What are some habits or mindsets you have formed in reaction to these judgments?

Writing Assignments

1. Write a one-paragraph summary of this reading (see p. 300)

2. Write a paragraph defining the the term *heritage* (see Chapter 10).

3. Write an argument/persuasion paragraph or essay arguing for or against a required diversity course in college (see Chapter 14).

4. Write a narration paragraph or essay that describes an event or memory from your own life when you were judged by your race or gender (see Chapter 6).

5. Write a cause and/or effect paragraph or essay (Chapter 12) about judging people based on their appearance.

That Lean and Hungry Look

Suzanne Britt Jordan

Suzanne Britt Jordan was born in Winston-Salem, North Carolina, and is a professor of English at Meredith College. Her poems have been published in a number of literary magazines and her essays have appeared in the *New York Times*, the *Boston Globe*, *Newsweek*, and other publications, as well as in collections like *Skinny People Are Dull and Crunchy Like Carrots* (1982) and *Show and Tell* (1983).

Caesar

A famous Roman leader

1   **Caesar** was right. Thin people need watching. I've been watching them for most of my adult life, and I don't like what I see. When these narrow fellows spring at me, I quiver to my toes. Thin people come in all personalities, most of them menacing. You've got your "together" thin person, your mechanical thin person, your condescending thin person, your tsk-tsk thin person, your efficiency expert thin person. All of them are dangerous.

2   In the first place, thin people aren't fun. They don't know how to goof off, at least in the best, fat sense of the word. They've always got to be doing. Give them a coffee break, and they'll jog around the block. Supply them with a quiet evening at home, and they'll fix the screen door and lick S&H green stamps. They say things like "there aren't enough hours in the day." Fat people never say that. Fat people think the day is too damn long already.

3   Thin people make me tired. They've got speedy little metabolisms that cause them to bustle briskly. They're forever rubbing their bony hands together and eyeing new problems to "tackle." I like to surround myself with sluggish, **inert,** easygoing fat people, the kind who believe that if you clean it up today, it'll just get dirty again tomorrow.

inert
inactive

4   Some people say the business about the jolly fat person is a myth, that all of us chubbies are neurotic, sick, sad people. I disagree. Fat people may not be chortling all day long, but they're a hell of a lot *nicer* than the wizened and shriveled. Thin people turn surly, mean, and hard at a young age because they never learn the value of a hot fudge sundae for easing tension. Thin people don't like gooey soft things because they themselves are neither gooey nor soft. They are crunchy and dull, like carrots. They go straight to the heart of the matter while fat people let things stay all blurry and hazy and vague, the way things actually are. Thin people want to face the truth. Fat people know there is no truth. One of my thin friends is always staring at complex, unsolvable problems and saying, "The key thing is. . . ." Fat people never say that. They know there isn't any such thing as the key thing about anything.

5   Thin people believe in logic. Fat people see all sides. The sides fat people see are rounded blobs, usually gray, always **nebulous** and truly not worth worrying about. But the thin person persists. "If you consume more calories than you burn," says one of my thin friends, "you will gain weight. It's that simple." Fat people always grin when they hear statements like that. They know better.

nebulous
hazy, indistinct

6   Fat people realize that life is illogical and unfair. They know very well that God is not in his heaven and all is not right with the world. If God is up there, fat people could have two doughnuts and a big orange drink anytime they wanted it.

7   Thin people have a long list of logical things they are always spouting off to me. They hold up one finger at a time as they reel off these things, so I won't lose track. They speak slowly as if to a young child. The list is long and full of holes. It contains tidbits like "get a grip on yourself," "cigarettes kill," "cholesterol clogs," "fit as a fiddle," "ducks in a row," "organize," and "sound fiscal management." Phrases like that.

8   They think these 2,000-point plans lead to happiness. Fat people know happiness is elusive at best and even if they could get the kind thin people talk about, they wouldn't want it. Wisely, fat people see that such programs are too dull, too hard, too off the mark. They are never better than a whole cheesecake.

9   Fat people know all about the mystery of life. They are the ones acquainted with the night, with luck, with fate, with playing it by ear. One thin person I know once suggested that we arrange all the parts of a jigsaw

puzzle into groups according to size, shape, and color. He figured this would cut the time needed to complete the puzzle by at least 50 percent. I said I wouldn't do it. One, I like to muddle through. Two, what good would it do to finish early? Three, the jigsaw puzzle isn't the important thing. The important thing is the fun of four people (one thin person included) sitting around a card table, working a jigsaw puzzle. My thin friend had no use for my list. Instead of joining us, he went outside and mulched the boxwoods. The three remaining fat people finished the puzzle and made chocolate, double-fudge brownies to celebrate.

cerebral machinations
crafty thinking

10   The main problem with thin people is they oppress. Their good intentions, bony torsos, tight ships, neat corners, **cerebral machinations,** and pat solutions loom like dark clouds over the loose, comfortable, spread-out, soft world of the fat. Long after fat people have removed their coats and shoes and put their feet up on the coffee table, thin people are still sitting on the edge of the sofa, looking neat as a pin, discussing rutabagas. Fat people are heavily into fits of laughter, slapping their thighs and whooping it up, while thin people are still politely waiting for the punch line.

expound
explain in detail

prognose
to figure out, diagnose

11   Thin people are downers. They like math and morality and reasoned evaluation of the limitations of human beings. They have their skinny little acts together. They **expound, prognose,** probe, and prick.

convivial
friendly, agreeable

12   Fat people are **convivial.** They will like you even if you're irregular and have acne. They will come up with a good reason why you never wrote the great American novel. They will cry in your beer with you. They will put your name in the pot. They will let you off the hook. Fat people will gab, giggle, **guffaw, galumph, gyrate,** and gossip. They are generous, giving, and gallant. They are gluttonous and goodly and great. What you want when you're down is soft and jiggly, not muscled and stable. Fat people know this. Fat people have plenty of room. Fat people will take you in.

guffaw
laugh loudly

galumph
move around heavily, clumsily

gyrate
move in a circle or whirl

Reading Reflection Questions   *Sample answers provided.*

1. What is Suzanne Britt Jordan's main message (her thesis) in this essay? Explain in your own words. *She is being humorous and using the body types of fat and skinny to make fun of stereotyping and to show two opposite personality types.*

2. What kind of tone is the author using, and how do you know? *A humorous, witty, or sarcastic tone*

3. Do you think the author really believes that fat people and thin people behave in specific ways based on their weight? Explain your answer.

Answers will vary, but no, she is stereotyping to be funny and to say the

opposite—people don't behave in certain ways based on their body weight.

4. How does the content and style of this sentence reflect the tone of the essay: "Fat people will gab, giggle, guffaw, galumph, gyrate, and gossip" (paragraph 12)? _Answers will vary. It is humorous, like the rest of the essay_

and the use of alliteration is playful.

5. T/ F ____F____ All fat people are jolly, and all thin people are uptight.

6. T/ F ____T____ The author does touch on some legitimate personality types, though they are not necessarily related to weight.

Checking Vocabulary

Define each of the following words by figuring out its meaning using context clues in the reading selection (see Chapter 27 for how to use context clues). If you cannot work out the meaning of a word, use a dictionary.

7. menacing (paragraph 1): _threatening_

8. metabolism (paragraph 3): _chemical process in body that supports life_

9. neurotic (paragraph 4): _disturbed, poorly adjusted_

10. fiscal (paragraph 7): _financial, pertaining to money_

READING CRITICALLY

Answer the following questions on a separate sheet of paper.

1. What is the author's **purpose** or goal in this reading selection?

2. What are the implied or stated questions or **ideas** being addressed?

3. What specific **support** (details and examples) does the author use to develop her purpose or goal for the reading?

4. What **conclusions or arguments** does the author reach based on what is happening or **inferences** (inferences imply "if this, then this" types of cause/effect analysis) she draws in the reading?

5. Who is the intended audience, and how did you reach that conclusion?

Group Activity

Form a group of three to five students from your class, and choose one person to record notes of the discussion. Do you know any thin people that fit Jordan's descriptions? Do you know any thin people that are not at all like Jordan's descriptions? Discuss the same questions with regard to heavy people. Do you think that someone's physical size can dictate his or her personality traits? Why or why not?

Writing Assignments

1. Write a one-paragraph summary of this reading (see p. 300).

2. Write a narration paragraph that describes an event or memory from your life that related to your own body image (see Chapter 6).

3. Write a cause and effect paragraph or essay about judging others by their body type (see Chapter 12).

4. Write an argument/persuasion paragraph or essay that is for or against mandatory nutrition classes in high school (see Chapter 14).

5. Write a paragraph or essay that compares and/or contrasts people based on a different physical attribute than weight, using the same style as Jordan does in this essay (see Chapter 13).

PEARSON
mywritinglab

For support in meeting this chapter's objectives, log in to www.mywritinglab.com and select **Critical Thinking** and **Reading Skills.**

19   Sentence Parts

Cluster One   Paul Metivier

In this chapter, you will
learn to

 Identify subjects
and predicates

 Recognize and use
different types of
phrases

 Use articles and
noun determiners
correctly

LO 4 Use conjunctions
to connect
sentences

THINKING CRITICALLY

Sentence parts are like individual parts of a sculpture: individual pieces
come together to make a coherent whole and create an overall message, with each piece adding to the meaning. What sentence parts do
you already know before reading this chapter? List all the sentence
parts you can think of here. *Answers will vary.*

_____

_____

_____

_____

_____

425

THE BUILDING BLOCKS OF SENTENCES

The building blocks are the individual components of sentences. All sentences must have at least a **subject** (the *what* or *who* the sentence is about) and a **verb** (the *action* of the sentence) and convey a complete thought. However, there are many other parts to a sentence—phrases, articles, noun determiners, coordinating and subordinating conjunctions, and conjunctive adverbs—which can be fitted together to express what you want to say.

APPLYING CRITICAL THINKING

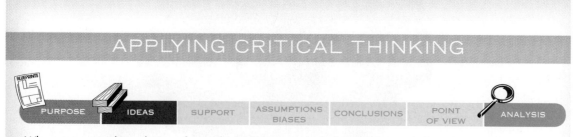

When you are making choices about which elements to include when **constructing a sentence,** you need to ask yourself the following questions:

1. What is my **purpose** for this particular sentence? What do I want to say?

2. What **ideas** and information do I need to include in this sentence?

3. Who is my target audience? How can I best put the parts of the sentence together to convey my ideas to this audience?

Then, use your **analysis** skills to break the sentence back down into its parts and make sure that you have constructed it correctly. Check that the sentence contains a verb and a subject, expresses a complete thought, and is written in the correct tense.

LO 1 SUBJECTS AND PREDICATES

A **sentence** is a group of words that expresses a complete thought. Every sentence contains at least a subject (a noun or a noun plus its modifiers) and a predicate (a verb or a verb plus its modifiers). When the modifiers are stripped from the subject and predicate, leaving only the noun and verb, the noun is called the **simple subject** and the verb is called the **simple predicate**.

The simple subject and simple predicate are the two most basic building blocks of the sentence.

SUBJECT	PREDICATE
The gray-haired **dog** / *limped* slowly to its dog bed.	
SIMPLE SUBJECT	SIMPLE PREDICATE
dog	*limped*

The Subject: The main, simple subject of the sentence is *dog. Gray-haired* describes the dog. *The* describes the rest of the words in the subject. When a word describes another word, it is called a modifier. *The gray-haired dog* is the complete subject.

The Predicate: What did the dog do? It *limped*. That action is the verb, the simple predicate. How did it limp? *Slowly.* This word describes how the dog limped; it modifies the verb. The verb plus the modifier and the other words that complete the meaning of the verb make up the complete predicate: *limped slowly to its bed.*

ACTIVITY 19-1   Simple Subjects and Predicates

Directions: *Underline the simple subject in each sentence and mark it with an S. Then double-underline the simple predicate (the verb) in each sentence and mark it with a V.*

1. A typical breakfast was served at the inn.

2. Karen practiced until she had a perfect serve.

3. The towels were washed with lavender.

4. On Saturday, Lilia won the cooking contest.

5. With determination, Miyuki finished the marathon.

Subjects

The **subject** is the word or words that indicate *who* or *what* is doing the action of the verb. The subject can be a noun or noun phrase, a pronoun, a gerund phrase, or the implied *you* of a command. In the following sentences, the subjects are in **bold** and the verbs are in *italics.*

> **Kenneth** *called* the fire department last night. (noun as subject)
>
> **She** *didn't use* a recipe for the cake. (pronoun as subject)
>
> **The old theater building** *created* an old-fashioned feel to the neighborhood. (noun phrase as subject)
>
> **Its stubby legs** *took* it slowly across the room. (noun phrase as subject)
>
> *Grab* the keys. (implied you as subject)
>
> **Knowing she could change** *kept* her motivated. (gerund phrase as subject)

1. **The subject can be a noun, a noun phrase, or an infinitive.**
   - **Noun as subject.** A **noun** can be a person, place, thing, idea, or state of existence.

Nouns at a Glance

Common nouns	name general categories or types: *object, person, navy, tornado*
Proper nouns	name specific people or items: *Lincoln Memorial, Sherman Alexie*
Abstract nouns	are not related to specific details: *love, fear, faith, happiness, beauty*
Concrete nouns	are related to specific sensory details: *brittle, soft, sweet, whistling, stone*
Singular nouns	name one of something: *child, Tom, Columbia River*
Plural nouns	name more than one of something: *children, tables, clouds, movies*
Collective nouns	name several items grouped as one collective item: *team, family, group*
Count nouns	can be counted as individual units: *girl, friend, dog, couch*
Non-count (mass) nouns	cannot be counted as individual units in English: *sand, vegetation, education, flour, biology, anger, blood*

   - **Noun phrase as subject.** A **noun phrase** is a noun plus its modifiers, the words that describe it.

> **Most people** *sleep* at night.
>
> (The noun is *people*. The word that describes it is *Most*.)

   - **Infinitive as subject.** Phrases beginning with *to* can be subjects.

> *To be happy* is something most people want.

- **Nouns and noun phrases can be joined to form a *compound subject*.** A **compound subject** is made of two or more nouns or noun phrases joined with the words *and* or *or*.

> **Clara and Soroa** *caught* the morning train. (Compound subject)
> **Clara's cousins**, Jerith and Mathew, *arrived* on the late train. (Subject)
> **Either the eastbound train or the westbound train** *will arrive* first. (Compound subject)

2. The subject can be a pronoun.

A **pronoun** is a word that replaces a noun that was mentioned previously: *I, you, he, she, it, we, they, this, that, these,* and *those* are pronouns. Pronouns can also be indefinite or refer to one or more unspecified beings, objects, or places, for example, *everyone, someone, anybody, both, few,* and *many.*

> The couple were married in Hawaii. **They** *planned* the wedding a full year in advance.
> (The pronoun *They* replaces *the couple* from the first sentence.)

3. The subject can be a gerund phrase (an -ing phrase that serves as the subject of the sentence).

> **Taking the test early** *is* sometimes a bad idea.
> (*Taking the test early* is the subject, a gerund phrase; *is* is the main verb of the sentence.)

4. All sentences must have a subject, but in commands the subject *you* is implied.

The subject *you* is implied in a command or request directly stated to someone.

> **(You)** *Run!* (*You* is implied; *Run* is the verb)
> **(You)** *Eat* the cake. (*You* is implied; *Eat* is the verb.)

▶ NOTE   The subject doesn't always come first in the sentence. Sometimes other words come before the subject of a sentence. For instance, the second sentence in the following example starts with a **transition,** that is, a word that shows the relationship between the two sentences. The subject follows it. To find the subject, look for the verb and then ask who or what performed the action of the verb.

> *The* **laundry** *waited* to be washed. Next to the basket, **the washing machine** *sat waiting*.

ACTIVITY 19-2   Identifying Subjects

Directions: *Underline the subjects in the following sentences. Be careful not to underline all the nouns—only the noun functioning as the subject. If the subject is implied, write "implied" at the end of the sentence.*

1. Pei Pei organized a shopping trip.
2. Trang bought a new dress at the boutique.
3. Trang's friends, Khue and Heidi, also bought new dresses.
4. However, Kim decided to wait for the next sale.
5. Buy clothes on sale if you can. *Implied (you)*

Predicates

All sentences must have at least one verb or verb phrase. A **verb** is the action of a sentence—it can be a physical action, a mental action, or a state of being.

> **Physical Action**
> Hannah *kicked* the ball.
> (*Kicked* is the simple predicate; *the ball* describes what she kicked. The complete predicate is *kicked the ball*.)
> Hannah *kicked* the ball and *ran* behind it.
> (Compound predicate; the two verbs are in italics. The complete compound predicate is *kicked the ball and ran behind it*.)
>
> **Mental Action**
> I *thought* about taking a trip. (*Thought* is the simple predicate.)
>
> **State of Being**
> I *am*. (Simple predicate)

Verbs function in different ways depending on their role in a particular sentence:

1. **Some verbs can stand on their own as the main verb of a sentence.**

> **My dog** *eats* three times a day. (Simple present tense verb)
> **Clara's sisters** *called* all their friends to invite them to the party. (Simple past tense verb)

2. Some verb forms need auxiliary, or helping, verbs to complete them.

A **verb phrase** is two or more words working together to create the action (verb) for the sentence.

> The new campaign *was created* today.
> (*Created* can't be a main verb on its own in this sentence.)
> She *has been waiting* for a new mission.
> (*Waiting* can't be a main verb on its own.)
> When *will* he *arrive?*
> (*Will* adds the meaning of "the future" to the verb *arrive*.)

There are three verb forms that can't be the main verb of a sentence without some helping verbs. They are the *to* form, the *-ed* form in certain cases, and the *-ing* form:

- **to + Verb (Infinitives)** In an infinitive, the word *to* comes before the plain form of the verb: *to walk, to run, to eat.* The infinitive can't be used alone as the main verb of a sentence—you couldn't write, *The child to eat cake.* Infinitives don't give enough information about when something is happening to be used as the main verb. In predicates, they normally follow the main verb.

> Emily **had promised to cook** dinner for Kyle.
> (*Had promised to cook* is the whole verb phrase.)
> The meeting **was scheduled to occur** at noon on Tuesday.

> ▶ NOTE   To avoid splitting an infinitive, do not place a word between the "to" and the verb it relates to:

> **Incorrect:** Phoebe wanted *to boldly go* where no woman had gone before.
> **Correct:** Phoebe wanted *to go boldly* where no woman had gone before.

To verbs can also act as the subject of a sentence:

> *To run a marathon* **takes** true determination.

- **-ed Verbs (Past Participles)** To indicate the past tense of most verbs, *-ed* or *-d* is added to the plain form. If there is no helping verb (such as *is, was, has,* or *had*), then the verb is in simple past tense form. A verb in the simple past can act as the main verb of a sentence. In other cases, the *-ed* form of a verb must be helped by an auxiliary verb. A helping verb plus an *-ed* verb forms a perfect tense.

> **Simple past tense:** She *cooked* lasagna. She also *made* a nice salad.
>
> **Present perfect:** She *has wanted* to have a party for all her friends for years. (*Has* adds the meaning of "the present" to *wanted*.)
>
> **Past perfect:** She *had planned* to throw a party for her colleagues too. (*Had* adds the meaning of "the past" to *planned*.)

- ***-ing* Verbs (Gerunds)** Verbs that end with *-ing* are called gerunds. An *-ing* form is never a complete verb by itself—you wouldn't say *My boyfriend washing his car.* In predicates, a form of the verb *to be* is needed before the gerund to indicate an action that *was*, *is*, or *will be* continuing. An *-ing* word can also serve as a subject, without the auxiliary verb.

> He **is** *having* a hard time understanding.
> (*Is* adds the meaning of "the present" to the gerund.)
> Yesterday, he *was hoping* to take the test.
> (*Was* adds the meaning of "the past.")
> He *will be studying* for the test all night long. (*Will be* adds the meaning of "the future.")

▶ REMEMBER   Gerunds can also serve as the subject of the sentence—see subjects above.

3. **Verb tense indicates time—past, present, and future.** (See "Verb Tense at a Glance," below, for more information.)

Verb Tense at a Glance

Think of tense as a timeline that starts on the left, in the past, and moves to the right, in the future.

Past	Present	Future
◀——I walked.	I am walking.	I will walk.——▶
X-----present progressive----------Y----------future progressive-----Z		

Here's a chart that shows the past, present, and future tenses of the verb *walk*:

Tense	Past	Present	Future
Simple	She walked.	She walks.	She will walk.
Perfect	She was walking.	She has walked.	She will be walking.
Progressive	She was walking.	She is walking.	She will be walking.
Perfect Progressive	She had been walking.	She has been walking.	She will have been walking.

▶ NOTE   Most verbs in the present tense use the base form (as found in the dictionary) for the first-person subjects *I* and *we*, the second-person subject *you*, and the third-person plural subject *they*. For third-person singular subjects *he*, *she*, and *it*, add *-s* or *-es*.

Example: base form: *walk*

First-person, second-person, third-person plural: I walk. You walk. They walk.

Third-person singular: He walk**s**. She walk**s**. It walk**s**.

Base Forms: *To Be* Verbs

Since there are many irregular verbs in English that don't follow this pattern, be sure to consult a dictionary and/or grammar handbook for correct verb forms. Here are the three irregular verbs that are most common and a chart showing how they change tenses.

Base Verb	Past Singular	Present Plural	Present Singular	Past Plural
Be	I am	We are	I was	We were
	You are	You are	You were	You were
	He/she/it is	They are	He/she/it was	They were
Have	I have	We have	I had	We had
	You have	You have	You had	You had
	He/she/it has	They have	He/she/it had	They had
Do	I do	We do	I did	We did
	You do	You do	You did	You did
	He/she/it does	They do	He/she/it did	They did

Irregular Verbs

Here is a list of some of the most common irregular verbs in English.

Base Form	Simple Past Tense	Past Participle
awake	awoke	awoken
be	was, were	been
bear	bore	born
beat	beat	beat
become	became	become
begin	began	begun
bend	bent	bent
beset	beset	beset
bet	bet	bet
bid	bid/bade	bid/bidden
bind	bound	bound
bite	bit	bitten
bleed	bled	bled
blow	blew	blown
break	broke	broken
breed	bred	bred
bring	brought	brought
broadcast	broadcast	broadcast
build	built	built
burn	burned/burnt	burned/burnt
burst	burst	burst
buy	bought	bought
cast	cast	cast
catch	caught	caught
choose	chose	chosen
cling	clung	clung
come	came	come
cost	cost	cost
creep	crept	crept
cut	cut	cut
deal	dealt	dealt
dig	dug	dug
dive	dived/dove	dived

Base Form	Simple Past Tense	Past Participle
do	did	done
draw	drew	drawn
dream	dreamed/dreamt	dreamed/dreamt
drive	drove	driven
drink	drank	drunk
eat	ate	eaten
fall	fell	fallen
feed	fed	fed
feel	felt	felt
fight	fought	fought
find	found	found
fit	fit	fit
flee	fled	fled
fling	flung	flung
fly	flew	flown
forbid	forbade	forbidden
forget	forgot	forgotten
forgive	forgave	forgiven
forsake	forsook	forsaken
freeze	froze	frozen
get	got	gotten
give	gave	given
go	went	gone
grind	ground	ground
grow	grew	grown
hang	hung	hung
hear	heard	heard
hide	hid	hidden
hit	hit	hit
hold	held	held
hurt	hurt	hurt
keep	kept	kept
kneel	knelt	knelt
knit	knit	knit
know	knew	know

Continued ▶

Base Form	Simple Past Tense	Past Participle
lay	laid	laid
lead	led	led
leap	leaped/leapt	leaped/leapt
learn	learned/learnt	learned/learnt
leave	left	left
lend	lent	lent
let	let	let
lie	lay	lain
light	lighted/lit	lighted
lose	lost	lost
make	made	made
mean	meant	meant
meet	met	met
misspell	misspelled/misspelt	misspelled/misspelt
mistake	mistook	mistaken
mow	mowed	mowed/mown
overcome	overcame	overcome
overdo	overdid	overdone
overtake	overtook	overtaken
overthrow	overthrew	overthrown
pay	paid	paid
plead	pled	pled
prove	proved	proved/proven
put	put	put
quit	quit	quit
read	read	read
rid	rid	rid
ride	rode	ridden
ring	rang	rung
rise	rose	risen
run	ran	run
saw	sawed	sawed/sawn
say	said	said
see	saw	seen
seek	sought	sought

Base Form	Simple Past Tense	Past Participle
sell	sold	sold
send	sent	sent
set	set	set
sew	sewed	sewed/sewn
shake	shook	shaken
shave	shaved	shaved/shaven
shear	shore	shorn
shed	shed	shed
shine	shone	shone
shoe	shoed	shoed/shod
shoot	shot	shot
show	showed	showed/shown
shrink	shrank	shrunk
shut	shut	shut
sing	sang	sung
sink	sank	sunk
sit	sat	sat
sleep	slept	slept
slay	slew	slain
slide	slid	slid
sling	slung	slung
slit	slit	slit
smite	smote	smitten
sow	sowed	sowed/sown
speak	spoke	spoken
speed	sped	sped
spend	spent	spent
spill	spilled/spilt	spilled/spilt
spin	spun	spun
spit	spit/spat	spit
split	split	split
spread	spread	spread
spring	sprang/sprung	sprung
stand	stood	stood
steal	stole	stolen

Continued ▶

Base Form	Simple Past Tense	Past Participle
stick	stuck	stuck
sting	stung	stung
stink	stank	stunk
stride	strod	stridden
strike	struck	struck
string	strung	strung
strive	strove	striven
swear	swore	sworn
sweep	swept	swept
swell	swelled	swelled/swollen
swim	swam	swum
swing	swung	swung
take	took	taken
teach	taught	taught
tear	tore	torn
tell	told	told
think	thought	thought
thrive	thrived/throve	thrived
throw	threw	thrown
thrust	thrust	thrust
tread	trod	trodden
understand	understood	understood
uphold	upheld	upheld
upset	upset	upset
wake	woke	woken
wear	wore	worn
weave	weaved/wove	weaved/woven
wed	wed	wed
weep	wept	wept
wind	wound	wound
win	won	won
withhold	withheld	withheld
withstand	withstood	withstood
wring	wrung	wrung
write	wrote	written

ACTIVITY 19-3   Identifying Verbs

Directions: *Underline the verbs in the following sentences. If there is an auxiliary verb, be sure to underline that as well.*

1. Pei Pei <u>organized</u> a shopping trip.
2. Trang <u>bought</u> a new dress at the boutique.
3. Trang's friends, Khue and Heidi, also <u>bought</u> new dresses.
4. However, Kim <u>decided</u> to wait for the next sale.
5. She <u>thought</u> they <u>had jumped</u> into hasty decisions.

APPLYING CRITICAL THINKING

PURPOSE · IDEAS · SUPPORT · ASSUMPTIONS BIASES · CONCLUSIONS · POINT OF VIEW · ANALYSIS

Analysis involves breaking down an **idea** and working out the meaning of the individual parts and how they relate to the whole. Use your analysis skills to help you choose the correct tense to use as you write. Ask the following questions to determine *when* the action of the sentence is taking place, and then check that you have used the correct tense.

1. Am I writing about something that happened in the past and then stopped? If so, use the **simple past:**

   Manny **went to** the store yesterday.

2. Am I writing about something that happened and stopped before another past event? If so, use the **past perfect:**

   Although he **had brought** a grocery list, he still **forgot** to buy milk.

3. Am I writing about something that started before but still happens? If so, use **the present perfect tense:**

   She **has wondered** for a long time what it would be liked to be married.

4. Am I writing about something that is happening now?

   If so, use the present or present progressive tense. She **is leaving** now.

Continued ▶

5. Am I writing about something that hasn't happened yet but will happen in the future? If so, use the **future tense:**

> By tomorrow, I **will know** how it feels to be married!

6. Am I writing about something that will start in the future, continue, and then stop at a particular time? If so, use the **future perfect:**

> According to her grand plan, she **will have been married** for a couple of years before she has children.

ACTIVITY 19-4   Correct Verb Forms and Tenses

Directions: *Choose the correct verb form and tense of the verb in brackets to fill each space in the following paragraph.*

Last Sunday, we [to go] _____*went*_____ to my local farmer's market. The fresh vegetables we saw [to be] _____*were*_____ beautiful. We [to buy] _____*bought*_____ fresh lettuce, tomatoes, and carrots. We [to be] _____*were*_____ so excited to find local produce for good prices. We [to be] _____*are*_____ big fans of fresh produce. When we got to the flower stand, we [to see] _____*saw*_____ all sorts of fresh flowers. One vendor [to have] _____*had*_____ fresh-cut dahlias and roses. However, our favorite flowers were the sunflowers. They [to rise] _____*rose*_____ almost two feet out of the buckets, and they [to dazzle] _____*dazzled*_____ our eyes with their colors. We [to visit] _____*visited*_____ every flower stand at the market.

Inside the Predicate: Objects

An **object** in grammar is usually part of the predicate, and it is the object of the action, the receiver of the action. A **direct object** is the receiver of the action within a sentence, as in "He hit the ball." Therefore, the direct object refers to the person or thing receiving the action of a transitive verb.

The **indirect object** identifies to or for whom or what the action of the verb is performed. In the sentence, "She sent Anders the letter," "letter" is the *direct object* as it is directly affected by the action, and "Anders" is the *indirect object* as he receives the letter.

Here are some additional things to keep in mind about objects:

1. Some verbs describe an action that doesn't include a receiver:

   > The sun **rises.** The moon **sets.**

2. Other verbs do require (or can have) a receiver:

   > The potential employer **took** new applications once a month.

   The verb *took* needs a receiver, which is called the **object of the verb.** What did the potential employer take? New applications. *Applications* is the object of the verb *took*.

3. Pronouns can take the place of nouns. Therefore, a pronoun can be the object of a verb.

   > The company **will take** more applications soon. It **will advertise** next month.

   In the second sentence, *it* replaces *the company*.

4. Sometimes the subject acts on an object *to* or *for* someone or something else. That someone or something else is called the **indirect object.**

   > Too much exercise *can cause* **problems** for one's back.

   To find the direct object, you would ask "What can too much exercise cause?" The direct object is *problems*. To find the indirect object, ask "Problems to or for whom?" In this case, the word *for* is in the sentence. The indirect object is *one's back*.

ACTIVITY 19-5   Identifying Direct and Indirect Objects

Directions: *Underline the direct objects and indirect objects in the following sentences. Mark DO over the direct objects and IO over the indirect objects.*

1. Barb gave Jess [IO] a new uniform. [DO]

2. Stan cashed the check [DO] quickly.

3. She tossed the pencil [DO] to Baraka. [IO]

4. Henry finished the crossword puzzle. [DO]

5. Ricardo passed the book [DO] to Esteban. [IO]

LO 2 PHRASES

A **phrase** is a group of related words without a subject and a predicate. You saw at the beginning of the chapter that a subject can be a noun phrase, which includes a noun and all its modifiers:

> *The sparkling ocean* stretched for miles in every direction.

A noun phrase can also act as the object of a verb:

> She wanted to swim in *the blue green sea.*

Two of the **verbals** (forms of verbs that function as another part of speech such as a gerund or infinitive and are usually part of a phrase) that you studied earlier can also be considered noun phrases: one is the gerund phrase

> *Swimming in the ocean* is refreshing.

and the other is the infinitive phrase

> *To swim in the ocean* takes strength and skill.

A noun phrase can also be the object of a preposition, which is discussed in the next section.

Prepositions and Prepositional Phrases

Prepositions are words that connect nouns and pronouns to other parts of a sentence. Prepositions indicate relationships in time, place, and direction, as well as signal connections such as cause and effect or addition: *before, after, above, below, across, because of,* and *in addition to.* A **prepositional phrase** begins with a preposition (see chart on p. 443) and ends with a noun, pronoun, gerund, or clause, the "object" of the preposition.

> The **subject** of the film *is* the problem of child labor in some countries.

The prepositional phrases underlined above help guide you through the meaning of the sentence. (The subject of the sentence above is in bold and the verb is in italics.)

▶ VISUALIZATION/MEMORY TIP   Think of a cat and a set of two large tubes or pipes: prepositions are anything the cat can do in relation to those two tubes (for instance, the cat can go *around* the tubes, *toward* the tubes, *over* the tubes, *on* the tubes, *in* the tubes, *between* the tubes, and so on). Of course, there are many prepositions that don't work with the

cat/tubes example; for instance, a cat cannot be "of" the tubes. This is just a memory trick (mnemonic device) to help you recognize many common prepositions.

The Most Common Prepositions in English		
about	down	outside
above	during	over
according to	except	past
across	except for	plus
after	excepting	regarding
against	for	respecting
along	from	round
along with	in	since
among	in addition to	than
apart from	in case of	through
around	inside	throughout
as	in spite of	till
at	instead of	to
because of	into	toward
before	like	under
behind	near	underneath
below	next	unlike
beneath	of	until
beside(s)	off	unto
between	on	up
beyond	onto	upon
by	on top of	up to
concerning	opposite	with
considering	out	within
despite	out of	without

You should try not to end your sentences with a preposition.

> **Example:** Cara is who Steve is having dinner with.
>
> **Rearranged:** Cara is the one with whom Steve is having dinner.
>
> **Or even better:** Steve is having dinner with Cara.

However, there are cases where there is no other way to rearrange the sentence.

> It was something he couldn't stop thinking *about*.
>
> The cat wants to come *in*.

Prepositional phrases include a preposition, the object of the preposition, and any modifiers of the object. The entire prepositional phrase functions as a modifier in the sentence.

> That mean mother *of hers* is always looking *for more to be mad about*.

Of hers modifies *mother* and so is part of the subject. Put another way, *of hers* modifies a noun, so it is an adjective. *For more to be mad about* modifies a verb, so it is an adverb. Adjectives and adverbs are discussed later in the chapter.

ACTIVITY 19-6   Finding Prepositional Phrases

Directions: *Underline the prepositional phrases in the following sentences.*

1. The trip to the sea took longer with all the unexpected stops.
2. She left the note on the table with an apple beside it.
3. Because of the weather, the trip to the beach was canceled.
4. She decided to choose between the lesser of two evils.
5. Guarav preferred to read the paper at a certain time each day.

Participles and Participial Phrases

Participles are verb forms that can either be part of the main verb or can function as adjectives or adverbs. Present participles end in *-ing*: *leaving, heaving, ringing*. Past participles usually end in *-ed* or *-d*: *hated, performed, laid*. However, some participles are formed irregularly with endings such as *-n* and *-t*: *forgiven, taken, spent, brought*.

Part of main verb: Chester *was having* second thoughts.

Daniel *was defeated* in the tennis match.

As adjective: The *defeated* player shook hands graciously with his opponent.

As adverb: I saw JoAnn *looking at* Tim with a playful expression.

Participial phrases use the *-ing* form for present participle, and *-ed*, *-d*, *-n*, or *-t* for the past participle phrase—as in elec*ted*, delete*d*, chose*n*, and sen*t*.

I saw Daniel *trying to hit* her serve.

The *elected* official will take her office in the fall.

ACTIVITY 19-7   Identifying Participles and Participial Phrases

Directions: *Underline the participles and participial phrases in the following sentences.*

1. Walking both ways to the store, she was now tired.
2. The neglected dog looked anxious.
3. Hoping to get ahead, Tori studied all night.
4. Laughing, she had to catch her breath.
5. Disconnected from the lecture, Harold was daydreaming.

Adjectives and Adjective Phrases

Adjectives are words that modify nouns and pronouns (the adjectives below are italicized; the nouns they modify are in bold).

Modifying nouns: The *skinny* **dog** looked thin and scared.

Modifying pronouns: **They** were very *thin*.

Descriptive adjectives can take three forms:

1. **The positive form,** used to express simple descriptions like *red, heavy, tiny, flat, beautiful:*

The *new* **car** looked good.

2. **The comparative form,** used to compare two things such as *lower, smarter, more functional, less useful:*

> Trina has a *newer* **car** than her boyfriend.

3. **The superlative form,** used to compare three or more things such as *largest, dirtiest, most functional, least useful:*

> She had the *newest* **car** on the block: newer than any of her neighbors' cars.

An **adjective phrase** is a phrase that modifies a noun or pronoun:

> The **woman** *parking the car* is my mother.

The adjective phrase describes *woman,* a noun.

ACTIVITY 19-8   Identifying Adjectives and Adjective Phrases

Directions: *Underline all the adjectives and adjective phrases in the following sentences.* **Tip:** *It might help to circle all the nouns first.*

1. The complicated language on the economics test made it harder.
2. The savory spices in Jen's pantry filled the tiny space with a wonderful aroma.
3. The large modern house being built at the end of the street looked expensive.
4. The local street band was playing a melancholy tune for the mellow crowd.
5. The lady handing out the hotdogs gave them to the hungriest people first.

Adverbs and Adverb Phrases

Adverbs are words that modify verbs, verb forms, adjectives, and other adverbs to indicate *how, where, when,* or *how much.* Many adverbs end with *-ly,* but not all. The adverbs below are in italics; what they are modifying is in bold.

Modifying verbs: Lori **spoke** *loudly.*

Modifying verb forms: Troy had *barely* **noticed** the child hiding in the back.

Modifying adjectives: It was a *very* **fancy** dinner.

Modifying other adverbs: The dog ran *very* **quickly.** Who knew he could run *this far?*

Like adjectives, adverbs have three forms. The adverbs below are in italics; what they are modifying is in bold.

1. **Positive:** *quietly, smoothly, slow, awkward/ly, intensely*

   She **limped** *awkwardly.*

2. **Comparative:** *quieter, smoother, slower, more awkwardly, more intensely*

   She **limped** even *more awkwardly* when she noticed she was being watched.

3. **Superlative:** *quietest, smoothest, slowest, most awkwardly, most intensely*

   She **limped** the *most awkwardly* after a few people laughed.

An **adverb phrase** is a phrase that begins with a preposition and functions as an adverb:

   The casserole was **full** *of vegetables from her garden.*

The adverb phrase *of vegetables from her garden* modifies *full,* an adjective.

ACTIVITY 19-9   Identifying Adverbs and Adverb Phrases

Directions: *Underline the adverbs and adverb phrases in the following sentences.*

1. The car was loaded with camping gear.
2. The cat stalked stealthily toward the trees.

3. The child ran <u>quicker</u> than the parents.

4. In fact, she ran the <u>quickest</u> of all the visitors.

5. The canoe was weighted down <u>by too much luggage and fishing gear.</u>

ACTIVITY 19-10   Identifying Adjectives and Adverbs

Directions: *Underline the adjectives and adverbs in the following sentences. Then circle the nouns, verbs, verb forms, or adverbs they are modifying.*

1. The <u>bright red</u> and <u>blue</u> (parrots squawked) <u>noisily</u> in the <u>lush</u> (canopy) of trees.

2. <u>Clumsily,</u> she (stumbled) down the <u>rocky hiking</u> (trail.)

3. The <u>fire-engine red</u> (house stood out) <u>garishly</u> on the block.

4. The woman <u>with the orange-red</u> (hair was laughing) <u>annoyingly</u> during the concert.

5. The <u>variously colored</u> (fruit) were (laid out) <u>neatly</u> in rows on the <u>farmer's market</u> (stand.)

LO 3 ## ARTICLES AND OTHER NOUN DETERMINERS

The **articles** *a, an,* and *the* are a type of **noun determiner**—a word that signals a noun is to follow—and knowing which one to use is determined by the context and the type of noun that follows.

1. A and *an* are indefinite articles used for general description nouns.

- Use *a* when the noun that follows starts with a consonant or a consonant sound: *a car, a sheep, a place, a united front* (the *u* sounds like a consonant, *y*, so use *a*).

- Use *an* when the noun that follows has a vowel or a vowel sound: *an Englishman, an orange, an elevator, an honor* (the *h* is silent; the word begins with a vowel sound of *o*, so use *an*).

Cross Reference

See Chapter 28 for more about when to use an article.

2. *The* is a definite article.

Use *the* when the word that follows is a specific noun (not a general descriptor): **the** *best place to shop,* **the** *champion racehorse,* **the** *movie to watch.*

3. Other noun determiners include the following:

- **Demonstratives:** *this, that, these, those*

- **Possessives:** *my, our, your, his, her, their, its*
- **Cardinal numbers:** *one, two, three,* etc.
- **Miscellaneous noun determiners:** *all, another, each, every, much,* etc.

ACTIVITY 19-11   Identifying Articles and Noun Determiners

Directions: *Underline the articles and noun determiners in the following sentences.*

1. The teacher asked each student in class his or her name.
2. Ticking loudly, the clock on the wall was a distraction in class.
3. Every afternoon, I drink a cup of tea.
4. An annual trip to the mountains is a tradition in our family.
5. That direction said to fill in every answer box completely.

LO 4 CONJUNCTIONS

Conjunctions are words or phrases used to link together words, phrases, or clauses in sentences. *Coordinating conjunctions, subordinating conjunctions,* and *conjunctive adverbs* help correctly join two clauses. If the clauses are both independent (two complete sentences, each with its own subject and verb), use a coordinating conjunction with a comma or a conjunctive adverb with a semicolon. If one of the clauses is dependent on the other, use a subordinating conjunction.

Coordinating Conjunctions

Coordinating conjunctions connect two independent clauses using a comma and a coordinating word. The **seven words** that can be used along with a comma to connect two independent clauses are the following coordinating conjunctions:

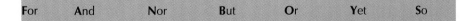

For	And	Nor	But	Or	Yet	So

A simple mnemonic device for remembering these seven words is the acronym **FANBOYS,** which consists of the first letter of each.

▶ NOTE   Be careful not to assume that whenever you use one of these seven words in a sentence they are serving as a coordinating conjunction. You may be using the word "and," for instance, in a list of items such as *bread, cheese,* **and** *mustard,* in which case the word "and" is not coordinating two independent clauses.

ACTIVITY 19-12 Identifying Coordinating Conjunctions

Directions: *Underline the coordinating conjunctions in the following sentences. Check to make sure that the word is functioning as a coordinating conjunction: (1) it must be one of the seven words listed on page 449; (2) it must be preceded by a comma; and (3) it must be between two independent clauses. If the word is one of the seven words listed above, but does not fulfill one of the other two criteria needed to be a coordinating conjunction, do not underline it.*

1. My best friend was moving, <u>so</u> I helped her load the moving truck.
2. The smell of smoke and the smell of the ocean filled the air.   *Correct*
3. I decided to let him go to the concert, <u>for</u> I knew his heart was set on it.
4. The new deck looked great, <u>and</u> so did the fresh coat of house paint.
5. She had a feeling it was a bad idea, <u>yet</u> she did it anyway.

Subordinating Conjunctions

Subordinating conjunctions connect dependent (or subordinating) clauses to independent clauses. If the dependent clause is first, be sure to use a comma after it. If it follows the independent clause, do not use a comma.

> **Dependent clause first:** *Because* she always supported her students, Jaeney decided to contribute to the scholarship fund.
>
> **Dependent clause second:** Jaeney decide to contribute to the scholarship fund *because* she always supported her students.

The twenty most common subordinating conjunctions are listed below.

TWENTY MOST COMMON COORDINATING CONJUNCTIONS			
after	before	though	whether
although	if	unless	which
as	once	until	while
as though	since	when	who
because	that	whereas	whose

Conjunctive Adverbs

Conjunctive adverbs are words that can also connect two independent clauses, but they are not coordinating conjunctions: they are adverb transitions. Conjunctive adverbs are also used at the beginning of a sentence to help connect it to a preceding sentence or paragraph. Here is a list of the most common conjunctive adverbs:

CONJUNCTIVE ADVERBS		
consequently	moreover	therefore
furthermore	nevertheless	thus
however	otherwise	

When a conjunctive adverb appears between two clauses, a semicolon sets it off from the clause that comes before it, and a comma sets it off from the clause that comes after it.

Kathleen wanted to win the race; *consequently*, she trained for weeks.

Ty wanted to compete too; *however*, he injured his knee.

ACTIVITY 19-13   Identifying Subordinating Conjunctions and Conjunctive Adverbs

Directions: *Underline the subordinating conjunctions and/or conjunctive adverbs in the following sentences.*

1. Cassie wanted a vacation; however, her boss said no.

2. When she asked him the first time, he said no sharply without even looking up.

3. The next day, she wrote a follow-up request in a note; moreover, she sent an email with her justifications for the vacation time she'd earned.

4. By email, he replied that it was a bad time since the company was in a crisis.

5. Although she understood his response, Cassie still thought she deserved to take her vacation.

ACTIVITY 19-14   Identifying Coordinating and Subordinating Conjunctions and Conjunctive Adverbs

Directions: *On the lines provided, label the word bolded in each sentence as either a coordinating conjunction (CC), a subordinating conjunction (SC), or a conjunctive adverb (CA).*

__*SC*__   **1.** **Since** barbeque is considered a fine art in Texas, I knew I had to try it.

__*CC*__   **2.** I love ribs, **but** I had never tried ribs like these.

__*CA*__   **3.** I like spicy sauce; **however,** this sauce was both spicy and delightfully sweet.

__*CC*__   **4.** I loved it right away, **so** next I tried the chicken.

__*CA*__   **5.** The chicken was golden brown; **however,** the inside was white and tender.

ACTIVITY 19-15   Identifying Parts of Speech

Directions: *In the following excerpt (paragraph 8) from Frank McCourt's "Packing for America" from Chapter 18, mark the various parts of speech or connecting words in the following way: Find the independent clause in each sentence, and then circle the subject, underline the verb, and double-underline all prepositions or prepositional phrases in the independent clauses.*

If I were still teaching in the high schools of New York City I'd take my students to Kennedy Airport so they could observe the faces of people landing here, people fleeing tyranny, hunger, religious persecution, despair. I'd like my students to be able to recognize the look that passes over those faces, ranging from fear to ecstasy. My students might say "Oh, what's the big deal?" and if they did I'd have to be patient. They don't know any better, and that's strange because no generation has been endowed with so much information. They've seen the starving African babies, flies in their eyes, bellies swollen, sucking at breasts dried forever. They may be aware of the horrors of Bosnia, Rwanda, Sudan, but, like, you know, that's television, man. The Mostoslavskyys, the Banguras, the Jahanyars are among us. Their brothers and sisters are sneaking across the border from Mexico. The snakes are packing the holds of ships with dreaming Chinese, Vietnamese, Cambodians.

LEARNING OBJECTIVES REVIEW

LO 1 What are the primary components of a sentence? (See pp. 426–441)	The primary components of a sentence are the **subject** (the *who* or *what* that is doing the action) and the **predicate** (verb), the action of the sentence. All sentences must have at least a subject and a verb and convey a complete thought.
LO 2 What is a phrase, and what are some specific types of phrases? (See pp. 442–448)	A **phrase** is a group of related words without a subject and a predicate. There are several types of phrases: *prepositional phrases, participial phrases, adjective* and *adverb phrases*.
LO 3 What are noun determiners, and how are they used? (See pp. 448–449)	**Noun determiners** are words that signal a noun is to follow (the **articles** *a*, *an*, and *the* are examples), and knowing which one to use is determined by the context and the type of noun that is used.
LO 4 What are conjunctions, and how are they used to combine dependent and independent clauses in sentences? (See pp. 449–453)	**Conjunctions** are words or phrases used to link together words, phrases, or clauses in sentences. Clauses can be **dependent** (they cannot stand on their own as a complete sentence) or **independent**, which means they are complete sentences. If both clauses are independent, use a *coordinating conjunction* with a comma or a *conjunctive adverb* with a semicolon. If one of the clauses is dependent on the other, use a *subordinating conjunction*.

For support in meeting this chapter's objectives, log in to www.mywritinglab.com and select **Parts of Speech, Phrases and Clauses,** and **Sentence Structure.**

20 Sentence Variety

Dancers in Orange and Gold

LEARNING OBJECTIVES

In this chapter, you will learn to

 Use coordination and subordination

 Write sentences that have specific purposes

 Write sentences using the four basic structures

LO4 Revise sentences to increase sentence variety

THINKING CRITICALLY

Just as the individual dancers above contribute to create different combinations and images, the parts of a sentence can be arranged to create different sentence structures and achieve sentence variety, which keeps writing interesting. Once you know the parts, you can arrange them in different ways in order to get your desired effect. List any sentence parts that you can remember besides **subject** and **verb:**

Answers will vary.

_____

_____

455

LO 1 COORDINATION AND SUBORDINATION

A **clause** is a group of words containing a finite verb. A clause can be *dependent*, which means it cannot stand on its own as a complete sentence, or *independent*, which means it is a complete sentence. Coordination and subordination are crucial, because they allow you to combine dependent and independent clauses in different ways so as to make sentences more effective and interesting.

Coordination

Coordination is when two independent clauses of equal importance are joined to form a **coordinate sentence.** They can be joined in two ways:

1. **Coordinating conjunctions:** Use one of the **FANBOYS** (*for, and, nor, but, or, yet, so*) and a **comma** to combine the two independent clauses.

> The news report said the weather was turning blustery, *so* Hannah went back for her hat and gloves.

2. **Conjunctive adverbs:** Use one of the conjunctive adverbs (followed by a comma) after a semicolon to combine two independent clauses. Some commonly used conjunctive adverbs include *however, therefore, thus, moreover, furthermore, otherwise, nevertheless,* and *consequently.*

> Mahmoud slammed the oven door; *consequently,* the cake fell.

Subordination

Subordination is when one clause is less important (needs less emphasis) and is made into a dependent or *subordinate* clause, a clause *dependent* on the independent clause. Use subordinating conjunctions to mark the beginning of the dependent or subordinate clause. Some of the most common subordinating conjunctions are *because, since, if, after, although, until, while, as, as though, before, once, that, who, whose, which,* and *whereas.*

The map indicated we were getting close, *although* we couldn't see a sign of civilization.

Even though we were starving, we decided to keep driving to the next town.

Since Trinh ate all the eggs, we couldn't have pancakes this morning.

ACTIVITY 20-1 Sentence Combining Using Coordination and Subordination

Directions: *Combine each of the following pairs of sentences into one grammatically correct sentence using either coordination or subordination as indicated.* Answers will vary. Sample answers provided.

> **Example:** Good eating habits are part of a long-term health plan. It is important to teach children about nutrition early.
>
> **Coordination:** Good eating habits are part of a long-term health plan, so it is important to teach children about nutrition early.
>
> (*coordinating conjunction*)
>
> **Subordination:** Good nutrition, which is an important part of a long-term health plan, should be taught early to children.
>
> (*subordinating conjunction*)

1. Sewing by hand has become a lost art. Children, especially young women, used to be taught how to sew by their mothers but aren't anymore.

   Sewing by hand has become a lost art since children, especially young women, used to be taught by their mothers but aren't anymore.

2. Windsurfing and kite surfing are similar sports. They are different in a few ways.

   Windsurfing and kite surfing are similar sports; however, they are different in a few ways.

3. The Tour de France takes place in July. It is watched internationally by millions.

   The Tour de France takes place in July, and it is watched internationally by millions.

4. Some people prefer to drink iced tea in the summer. Others favor soft drinks.

While some people prefer to drink iced tea in the summer, others favor soft drinks.

5. Hummingbirds are amazing flyers. They can hover and zoom faster than any other bird.

Hummingbirds are amazing flyers, for they can hover and zoom faster than any other bird.

6. New Orleans is a historical city. The food, coffee, and music are unique and flavorful.

New Orleans is a historical city; moreover, the food, coffee, and music are unique and flavorful.

7. I used to drink five cups of coffee a day. I have had to cut down to one cup in the morning.

I used to drink five cups of coffee a day, but I have had to cut down to one cup in the morning.

8. Tom likes to row when the water is clear and calm. Tom begins rowing at five in the morning.

Because he likes to row when the water is clear and calm, Tom begins rowing at five in the morning.

9. Miyuki trained every day for two months. She was determined to run a marathon.

Because she was determined to run a marathon, Miyuki trained every day for two months.

10. The World Cup was exciting to watch this year. Italy was knocked out early.

The World Cup was exciting to watch this year, but Italy was knocked out early.

LO 2 SENTENCE PURPOSES

A **sentence** is a group of words that expresses a complete thought and contains at least one independent clause. An independent clause includes, at a minimum, an implied or stated subject and a main verb; it expresses a complete thought.

There are four main types of sentences, each with a different purpose (the verbs are in italics and the subjects are in bold in the sample sentences below):

1. Declarative: They make a statement or declaration.

> The new hybrid **cars** *are* better than ever.
> Both the hybrid **sedans** and the **SUVs** *drive* well and *get* good mileage.

2. Interrogative: They ask a question.

> Will **you** *buy* a hybrid car?

3. Imperative: They give a command.

> *Try* a test drive of one of the new models. (subject is the implied **you**)

4. Exclamatory: They express a strong emotion or sentiment.

> The newest **hybrids** *are* spectacular!

ACTIVITY 20-2 Practicing Sentence Types

Directions: *Write one sentence of your own for each of the sentence types below:* Answers will vary.

Declarative:_____

Interrogative:_____

Imperative:_____

Exclamatory:_____

LO 3 SENTENCE STRUCTURES

There are four basic sentence structures. The subjects in the sample sentences on the next page are in bold, and the verbs are in italics.

1. **Simple Sentences:** Simple sentences have one independent clause.

> The **banks** *are* lowering the interest rate.

2. **Compound Sentences:** Compound sentences have two or more independent clauses.

> The **banks** *are* lowering the interest rate, and **people** *are* beginning to buy new houses again.

3. **Complex Sentences:** Complex sentences have at least one independent clause and at least one dependent clause (in any order and number).

> The housing **market** *is* staring to get busy again since the interest rate dropped.

4. **Compound-Complex Sentences:** Compound-complex sentences have at least two independent clauses and at least one dependent clause (in any order).

> The **realtors** in my neighborhood *have* jumped on the bandwagon, and **they** *are pushing* for even more sales because the rates will surely rise again soon.

ACTIVITY 20-3   Practicing with Sentence Structures

Directions: *Create a sentence using each of the following sentence structures:*
Answers will vary.

Simple Sentence:_____

Compound Sentence:_____

_____

Complex Sentence:_____

_____

Compound-Complex Sentence:_____

_____

    To vary your writing, you can combine dependent clauses with independent clauses (coordination and subordination) in various patterns to achieve a variety of sentence types, connecting them with the appropriate coordination or subordination hook.

Engage your critical thinking skills to decide on the best sentence type to express your ideas in the context of your writing assignment. The types of sentences you use will depend on what you are discussing and who you are writing for. Here are a few possible combinations (DC = dependent clause, IC = independent clause).

1. Two independent clauses (joined by a coordinating conjunction)

IC	+	IC

Selling a home is stressful, *but* it helps to hire a realtor.

2. A dependent clause in front of an independent clause

DC	+	IC

When I sold my home, I tried doing it on my own at first.

3. Independent clause followed by a dependent clause

IC	+	DC

The stress of waiting for an offer was intense when I first advertised the sale of my house.

4. A dependent clause followed by an independent clause and a dependent clause

DC	+	IC	+	DC

When I didn't get an offer for over a month, I finally hired a realtor *because* I needed some professional help.

See how many types of sentences you can create as you experiment with coordination and subordination (review Chapter 19 for more on coordination and subordination).

ACTIVITY 20-4   Sentence Combining Practice

Directions: *On a separate sheet of paper:* **Step One:** *Write a paragraph that describes one specific spot on your campus or in your neighborhood using 8–15 simple sentences.* **Step Two:** *Go back and revise your original paragraph, and combine some of your sentences using coordination and subordination to achieve sentence variety.*

LO 4   SENTENCE VARIETY

When writing paragraphs and essays, you should vary your sentences in length, type, and rhythm. Readers get tired of short, choppy sentences, so use a variety of sentence lengths to keep your reader interested. Similarly, change the structure of your sentences to avoid a monotonous style, tone, and rhythm.

One way to achieve sentence variety is to add more details and examples. For instance, if you had a sentence that read *I like to snorkel*, you could vary it in length and style by simply adding more details: *I like to snorkel because of the intense connection it provides me with nature through the many sea plants and animals I get to see firsthand.*

Another way is to combine sentences through coordination and subordination to create more complex sentences, as you have been practicing in this chapter, for example:

Before: I like to snorkel. Sea turtles are the most exciting creatures to see while snorkeling.

Revised with coordination: I like to snorkel, and sea turtles are the most exciting creatures to see underwater.

Revised with subordination: Though I like to see all kinds of plants and animals when I snorkel, sea turtles are my favorite.

You can also achieve more sentence variety by varying your sentences so that they are *declarative, interrogative, imperative,* or *exclamatory.*

I really enjoy snorkeling. Have you ever tried it? You have to try snorkeling in Hawaii. It is the best spot to snorkel by far!

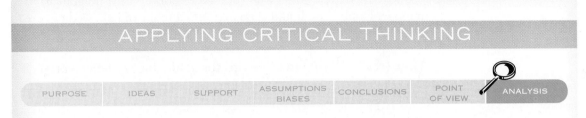

APPLYING CRITICAL THINKING

PURPOSE   IDEAS   SUPPORT   ASSUMPTIONS BIASES   CONCLUSIONS   POINT OF VIEW   ANALYSIS

In order to achieve sentence variety in the revision stage of your writing, engage your **analysis** skills. Go back through your draft and read each sentence carefully. Make sure you have expressed your thoughts clearly, using correct grammar, and that all the parts of each sentence work together to express what you want to say. Then see if you can incorporate some of the following suggestions for making your sentences more interesting and expressive.

Five Tips for Achieving Sentence Variety

1. Double-check to make sure you have a good balance of sentence lengths and types.

2. Add additional details to shorter, simpler sentences.

3. Use different types of sentences: statements (declarative), questions (interrogative), commands (imperative), and exclamations.

4. Combine some of your sentences to create compound, complex, or even compound-complex sentences using coordination and subordination.

5. Vary the style and rhythm of your sentences. Read them aloud to check whether they sound interesting or could benefit from some of the changes listed above.

Here is an example of a first draft paragraph and how it was revised, using the tips above, to improve sentence variety:

Before (no variety)

Making soap at home is a fun hobby and can be used to make beautiful gifts. Soap making involves following a step-by-step process and caution. Most soap is made by combining fats with lye. Some soaps use animal fat and some use vegetable fat. Also, some soap is cold processed, some hot processed. In the cold process, lye is dissolved in water, and then fatty oils are stirred in. However, the cold process requires very exact measurements for the lye and oils. In the hot process, the lye and the oils are boiled together to a temperature of 80–100 degrees Celsius. The measurements don't have to be as exact in the hot process because the heat will adjust the balance until saponification occurs (the fat changes into soap). Next, the soap starts to thicken. At that point, one can add essential oils or fragrances to the soap. Finally, the liquid is poured into a mold and allowed to cure for a day to up to a month, depending on the process used.

After (revised using the five tips for achieving sentence variety)

Change in sentence type
for variety
Use of coordination to
combine two sentences

Use of subordination to
combine two sentences

Subordination

Subordination

Use of coordination to
combine two sentences

Have you ever thought of making your own soap? Making soap at home is a fun hobby and can be used to make beautiful gifts. Soap making involves following a step-by-step process, and one needs to use extreme caution when working with harsh ingredients such as lye. In fact, most soap is made by combining fats, animal fats or vegetable fats such as olive oil, with lye. Also, some soap is cold processed, while some is hot processed. In the cold process, lye is dissolved in water, and then fatty oils are stirred in; however, the cold process requires very exact measurements for the lye and oils. In the hot process, the lye and the oils are boiled together to a temperature of 80–100 degrees Celsius, and the measurements don't have to be as exact because the heat will adjust the balance until saponification occurs (the soap sets up). Next, the soap starts to thicken and, at that point, one can add other essential oils, such as moisturizing jojoba oil or fragranced oils such as peppermint oil, to the soap. Finally, the liquid is poured into a mold, and the soap is allowed to cure for a day to up to a month depending on the process used. Try making your own soap today! Beautiful, handmade soap makes a perfect gift.

ACTIVITY 20-5   Practicing Sentence Variety

Directions: *On a separate sheet of paper, use the five tips on page 463 to revise the following paragraph to achieve greater sentence variety. Answers will vary.*

Last summer I took my niece and nephew camping and learned a couple lessons. I got all the equipment I thought we would need. I brought a tent, sleeping bags, and a cooking stove. We loaded up on food before we left too. We brought hot dogs, chips, sodas, granola bars, orange juice, bottles of water, and all the makings for smores. What I didn't know was that it was going to rain the whole time we were there. It rained all day and all night for two days. We were miserable. No one wants to make smores in the rain. Also, I didn't think to bring umbrellas or rain jackets. We got soaked. Finally, we decide to go hiking in the rain. It was wet but not cold. We started having fun just hiking around in the rain. We got back to camp. We were so wet. We decided to stay in our wet clothes and play Frisbee. We played Frisbee football. We ran through puddles. We laughed and got muddy. It was so much fun. So, I learned to prepare for all kinds of weather and to find ways to have fun even if we get hit with bad weather.

ACTIVITY 20-6   More Practice with Sentence Variety

Directions: *On a separate sheet of paper, write a short paragraph about your family. Create at least 10 simple sentences. Then, revise the paragraph using a combination of the Five Tips for Achieving Sentence Variety (p. 463) to vary the sentence types and lengths.* Answers will vary.

LEARNING OBJECTIVES REVIEW

LO1 What are coordination and subordination, and why are they important in creating sentences? (See pp. 456–458)	**Coordination** means combining independent clauses using a comma and a coordinating conjunction (*for, and, nor, but, or, yet, so*—FANBOYS) or a semicolon and a conjunctive adverb (*however, therefore, consequently,* etc.) followed by a comma. **Subordination** involves making an independent clause into a dependent clause using a subordinating conjunction (*because, since, if, after,* etc.) They are important because they allow you to combine dependent and independent clauses in different ways to make sentences more effective and interesting.
LO2 What are the four main types of sentences and what are their purposes? (See pp. 458–459)	The four main types of sentences are (1) **declarative** (they make a statement); (2) **interrogative** (they ask a question); (3) **imperative** (they give a command); and (4) **ex**clamatory (they express a strong emotion or sentiment).
LO3 What are the four basic sentence structures? (See pp. 459–461)	The four basic sentence structures are (1) the **simple sentence** (one independent clause); (2) the **compound sentence** (two or more independent clauses); (3) the **complex sentence** (has at least one independent clause and one dependent clause); and (4) the **compound-complex sentence** (has at least two independent clauses and one dependent clause, in any order).
LO4 What are five tips for achieving greater sentence variety? (See p. 463)	The **five tips** for achieving sentence variety are (1) ensure you have a good balance of sentence lengths and types; (2) add details to shorter, simpler sentences; (3) use different types of sentences; (4) combine sentences using coordination or subordination to create compound, complex, or compound-complex sentences; and (5) vary the style and rhythm of your sentences.

For support in meeting this chapter's objectives, log in to **www.mywritinglab.com** and select **Varying Sentence Structure** and **Sentence Structure.**

Correcting Major Sentence Errors

Mosaic Reflection

LEARNING OBJECTIVES

In this chapter, you will learn to

 LO1 Recognize and correct sentence fragments

LO2 Recognize and correct run-ons and comma splices

THINKING CRITICALLY

You can't just put the parts of a sentence together randomly; they should form a meaningful combination, like the individual parts of the mosaic in the picture above. If you don't have all the necessary parts and/or use incorrect punctuation, you can end up with a major construction error, sentence fragment, comma splice, or run-on.

Based on what you learned in Chapter 19, what are the two main sentence parts that will determine if you have a complete sentence?

subject and verb

LO 1 FRAGMENTS

A **sentence fragment** is a piece of a sentence posing as a complete sentence. It starts with a capital letter and ends with a period, but it does not express a complete thought. Though we often use fragments in everyday speech and in written dialogue, college essays require the use of grammatically complete sentences.

See the following box for a list of errors that can cause fragments.

Common Errors That Create Fragments

1. **Missing subject:** leaving out the *subject* of the sentence

2. **Missing, incomplete, or incorrect form of verb:** leaving out the *verb,* using an *incomplete verb,* or using the *wrong form of a verb.*

3. **Including a subordinating word or phrase before the subject and verb:** adding a word or phrase that makes a clause *dependent* on another clause for meaning.

Check your writing carefully for these three common errors that lead to sentence fragments:

1. Missing a subject

> Forgot to close the car door.

[Subject missing: *Who* forgot to close the car door?]

> *Mahad* forgot to close the car door.

2. Missing the verb, using an incomplete verb, or using the wrong form of a verb

> A good variety of dining options in the cafeteria.

[No verb. Add one to make the complete sentence.]

> A good variety of dining options *is* available in the cafeteria.

Margaret studying for the test.

[Incomplete verb: add the helping verb *is* or *was* before *studying*.

Margaret *is studying* for the test.
Margaret *was studying* for the test.

The machine running the elevator.

[Wrong form of verb: change to *runs* or *ran*.]

The machine *runs* the elevator.
The machine *ran* the elevator.

3. **Including a subordinate word or phrase before the subject and verb (makes the word group a dependent clause)**

Since she travels every spring.

[Since is a subordinating word, making this a dependent clause. Either delete the word *Since*, or add an independent clause before or after it.]

~~Since~~ She travels every spring.
Since she travels every spring, she has accrued a great deal of frequent flyer miles.

Identifying Sentence Fragments

A complete sentence contains a subject and a verb and does not have a subordinating word or phrase before the subject. Here are three steps you can use to identify sentence fragments:

Three Steps for Identifying Sentence Fragments

1. Find the verb
2. Find the subject
3. Check for a subordinating word or phrase

Cross Reference

See p. 430 for more on verbs.

1. **Find the verb.** If there is no verb (or an auxiliary verb is needed), then you have a sentence fragment. Ask yourself, "What is happening in this sentence?" For example:

> The kitten in the living room.

[What is the kitten doing in the living room? The sentence needs a verb.]

> The kitten is sleeping in the living room.

If the verb is an *-ing* form (verbal), make sure there is an auxiliary or helping verb (a *to be* verb such as *is*, *was*, *are*, or *were*) in front of it. For instance:

> Tom *taking* a nap.

[The above sentence needs a helping verb.]

> Tom *is taking* a nap.

OR, change the *-ing* form to a regular verb:

> Tom *takes (or took)* a nap.

Cross Reference

See p. 427–30 for more on subjects.

2. **Find the subject.** Ask yourself, "*Who* or *what* is the subject of the action/verb I found?" If there isn't a noun that serves as the subject, then the word group is a sentence fragment. For example:

> Takes the bus almost every day.

[Who is taking the bus? Who is the subject of this sentence?]

> *Lori* takes the bus almost every day.

▶ EXCEPTION   The one exception is when the subject is implied, as in the word *you* in a command. For example:

> Don't drop that glass.

[Although not stated, the subject of this sentence is the implied "You"]

(You) Don't drop that glass.

Cross Reference

See p. 429 for more on the "implied you" subject.

3. **Check for a subordinating word or phrase that creates a dependent clause.** If there is a subordinating conjunction such as *whenever* in front of the subject, a clause is dependent. It is incomplete because it depends on the addition of more information to make sense, for example:

Whenever she works on weekends.

[The word *whenever* makes this a dependent phrase. Either delete the subordinating word *whenever*, or add an independent clause before or after the phrase.]

Cross Reference

See Chapter 20, p. 456 for a more complete list of subordinating words and explanation of using subordination.

~~Whenever~~ She works on weekends.

Her partner complains whenever she works on weekends.

Whenever she works on weekends, *her kids don't get to see much of her.*

Here are a few of the most common words that indicate the beginning of a dependent clause or subordinate phrase:

because, since, when, whenever, if, as, on, in, every time, knowing that, believing that, hoping that, and *especially*

Correcting Sentence Fragments

When you have spotted a fragment caused by one or more of the errors listed above, use that error or set of errors as a key to fixing the problem.

1. **Missing verb**

Fragment: Rainfall on the streets. [Missing a verb, so add one]

Revised: Rainfall *puddles* on the streets.

Fragment: The kids playing on the lawn.

[Not a complete verb, so add an auxiliary verb or change the verb form]

Revised: The kids are playing on the lawn.

The kids play on the lawn.

2. Missing subject

> **Fragment:** Needs to find a good career. [Missing a subject, so add one]
>
> **Revised:** *Clay* needs to find a good career.

3. Dependent clause

> **Fragment:** Because I rowed yesterday.
>
> [Dependent clause due to the word *because*—delete the word *because*, follow it with a comma and an independent clause, or precede it with an independent clause followed by a comma]
>
> **Revised:** ~~Because~~ I rowed yesterday.
>
> Because I rowed yesterday, *I will rest today.*
>
> *I will rest today* because I rowed yesterday.

ACTIVITY 21-1   Identifying and Correcting Fragments I

Directions: *Using the three-step test for fragments, look at the fragments below and list which type or types of error created each fragment. Some items may have more than one error.*

   1. *Missing a subject*

   2. *A missing, incomplete, or incorrect form of verb*

   3. *Subordinate word or phrase before the subject and verb*

Then, add or delete words to fix the fragment and rewrite it as a complete sentence. You may need to add more information for the sentence to make sense.

Answers may vary; sample answers provided.

> **Example:** Ate the salad.   Error Type(s) _____*1*_____
>
> Corrected: *Cameron ate the salad.* _____

   1. My grandmother making homemade bread.   Error Type(s) _____2_____
   Corrected: *My grandmother was making homemade bread.* _____

   2. Feeling like she had made a bad decision.   Error Type(s) _____1_____
   Corrected: *Yumi was feeling like she had made a bad decision.* _____

3. Because he had his own boat.   Error Type(s) _____ *3* _____

   Corrected: *He had his own boat.* _____

4. Good sleep necessary before a race.   Error Type(s) _____ *2* _____

   Corrected: *Good sleep is necessary before a race.* _____

5. Breathing in too much air.   Error Type(s) _____ *1, 2* _____

   Corrected: *Feeling stressed, she was breathing in too much air.* ___

ACTIVITY 21-2   **Identifying and Correcting Fragments II**

Directions: *Review the following word groups. If a word group is a complete sentence, write S on the line provided. If it is a fragment, write F, and then revise it to make it into a complete sentence. You may add or delete words to fix the fragments.*   Answers may vary; sample answers provided

_____ *S* _____   **1.**   The St. Louis Gateway Arch is located on the banks of the Mississippi River.

_____

_____ *F* _____   **2.**   The monument, built in the 1960s, honoring westward expansion.

   The monument, built in the 1960s, is meant to honor west-

   ward expansion.

_____ *S* _____   **3.**   The arch stands out high above the St. Louis skyline.

_____

_____ *F* _____   **4.**   Costing over $13 million in the 1960s to build.

   It cost over $13 million to build in the 1960s.

_____ *F* _____   **5.**   People visiting from all over the world to see this marvel of engineering.

   People visit from all other the world to see this marvel of

   engineering.

ACTIVITY 21-3   **Identifying and Correcting Fragments III**

Directions: *In the spaces provided after the paragraph, mark F for a fragment and S for a complete sentence. You should find eight fragments. After you have marked each word group, complete the second part of the exercise.*

[1]The amazing St. Louis Gateway Arch. [2]It is a symbol of our pioneers and westward expansion. [3]The monument was finished in 1965. [4]Designed as a result of a contest. [5]Winning the contest, the architect Eero Saarinen. [6]The arch stands 630 feet high. [7]It is also 630 feet wide at the base. [8]Made completely of stainless steel. [9]Impressive as it towers over the St. Louis skyline. [10]The shape of the arch is a stable structure called a "catenary curve." [11]Each leg of the arch contains 1,076 steps. [12]Moreover, a tram traveling to the top. [13]The tram takes about 4 minutes to get to the top of the arch. [14]The foundation going 60 feet into the ground. [15]The St. Louis Gateway Arch is a testament to our history and to great engineering.

1. ___F___	5. ___F___	9. ___F___	13. ___S___
2. ___S___	6. ___S___	10. ___S___	14. ___F___
3. ___S___	7. ___F___	11. ___S___	15. ___S___
4. ___F___	8. ___F___	12. ___F___	

Now, pick five of the fragments you found above and rewrite them on a separate sheet of paper, making them into complete sentences by adding the needed subject, fixing or adding the needed verb, or by removing the word that makes them a dependent clause. Answers may vary.

ACTIVITY 21-4 Identifying and Correcting Fragments IV

Directions: *Add the needed words or even a complete additional independent clause to the following fragments to make them into complete sentences. You may also need to change the tense of a word to correct a sentence.*

Answers will vary; sample answers provided.

1. To live life fully.

   To live life fully, one has to take risks.

2. Taking a week-long vacation.

   Carly was taking a week-long vacation.

3. To learn as much as possible.

   To learn as much as possible was Carmelo's goal.

4. Leaning against the table.

   Leaning against the table, Vanessa felt dizzy.

5. Cheating on his diet.

   Cheating on his diet, Jarrod inhaled the burger.

Cross Reference
See Chapter 19, Sentence Parts, for more about independent clauses.

LO 2 RUN-ONS AND COMMA SPLICES

A **run-on,** sometimes called a *fused sentence*, occurs when you combine two or more independent clauses (complete sentences) with no punctuation to separate them. Use your analysis skills to check for the necessary parts of a sentence and to make sure you don't have two or more independent clauses that need stronger punctuation to join them.

Example run-on/fused sentence

Rain brings flowers spring is stunning.

[This group of words is a run-on because it includes two full sentences, each with a subject and verb.]

Rain	brings	flowers	spring	is	stunning.
(subj)	(verb)	(obj)	(subj)	(verb)	(obj)

A **comma splice** is a particular type of run-on that occurs when you combine two or more independent clauses with just a comma.

Example comma splice

Rain brings flowers, spring is stunning.

[This word group is a comma splice because it contains a full sentence, with its own subject and verb, on both sides of the comma.]

Correcting Run-ons and Comma Splices

Here are four ways to fix run-ons and comma splices:

Four Ways to Fix Run-ons and Comma Splices

1. Add a comma followed by a coordinating conjunction, FANBOYS (, + conjunction)

2. Add a final punctuation mark (a . or a ! or a ?)

3. Add a semicolon (;) or a colon (:)

4. Make one a sentence into a dependent clause by adding a subordinating conjunction.

1. **Add a coordinating conjunction** (FANBOYS—*for, and, nor, but, or, yet, so*) after a comma. A comma with a coordinating conjunction is equal to a period.

   > Rain brings flowers, and spring is stunning.

2. **Change the comma into a period** (or an exclamation point, or a question mark if the first independent clause is a question).

   > Rain brings flowers. Spring is stunning.

3. **Change the comma into a semicolon or a colon.** A semicolon can be used to combine two independent clauses that have a strong content connection, but use semicolons sparingly to indicate a powerful a connection between two complete thoughts.

   > Rain brings flowers; spring is stunning.

Cross Reference

See Chapter 23 for more on using semicolons and colons.

   A colon can also be used between two independent clauses if the second clause *answers* or *explains* the first one.

   > I like spring rain for one reason: it brings flowers.

4. **Turn one of the independent clauses into a dependent clause by adding a subordinating conjunction.** See page 456 for more on subordination.

   > Since it rains a great deal in the spring, we get stunning flowers.

ACTIVITY 21-5   Correcting Run-ons

Directions: *Fix the following run-on (fused) sentences by (1) adding a comma and a coordinating conjunction (For And Nor But Or Yet So), (2) adding a period, or (3) adding a semicolon or colon.*   Answers will vary. Sample answers provided

1. Matt is performing in the play it is set to open in July.

   Matt is performing in the play, and it is set to open in July.

2. It was 90 degrees outside Megan decided to stay inside.

   It was 90 degrees outside. Megan decided to stay inside.

3. Vegetarian options for all-American favorites are available veggie burgers are delicious.

   Vegetarian options for all-American favorites are available; veggie burgers

   are delicious.

4. Kate wanted to dance. Her muscles were sore.

   Kate wanted to dance, but her muscles were sore.

5. Vic has a passion for one particular hobby. He loves motorcycles.

   Vic has a passion for one particular hobby: he loves motorcycles.

ACTIVITY 21-6   Correcting Comma Splices

Directions: *Fix the following comma splices by (1) adding a coordinating conjunction after the comma (**For And Nor But Or Yet So**), (2) changing the comma to a period, or (3) changing the comma to a semicolon or colon.*
Answers will vary. Sample answers provided.

1. The Texas temperatures soared to over 100 degrees, the people suffered.

   The Texas temperatures soared to over 100 degrees, and the people

   suffered.

2. Florida gets so humid in the summer, the ocean is a great escape from the heat.

   Florida gets so humid in the summer; the ocean is a great escape from

   the heat.

3. The Internet has changed the music business, anyone can become a star.

   The Internet has changed the music business. Anyone can become a star.

4. Melody quit her job, she was fed up.

   Melody quit her job; she was fed up.

5. She wanted to pursue a new career, she wanted to work at the zoo.

   She wanted to pursue a new career: she wanted to work at the zoo.

The Alamo

ACTIVITY 21-7   Run-ons and Comma Splices I

Directions: *Mark each sentence RO for run-on (no punctuation between two independent clauses), CS for a comma splice (two independent clauses joined with only a comma), or C if the sentence is correct. Then fix run-ons and comma splices using one of the methods listed in the Four Ways to Fix a Run-on or Comma Splice box on page 475. Answers will vary. Sample revisions provided.*

_____C_____ **1.** The Alamo is considered hallowed ground by most Texans, and it is a symbol of freedom to most Americans.

_____

_____

_____CS_____ **2.** The Alamo became a symbolic reminder of the men who fought bravely for the Texas Revolution, their sacrifice inspired all Texans.

The Alamo became a symbolic reminder of the men who

fought bravely for the Texas Revolution; their sacrifice

inspired all Texans.

_CS_   **3.** The men who died in the Alamo had vowed to fight to the death, they held out longer than seemed humanly possible.

The men who died in the Alamo had vowed to fight to the

death; they held out longer than seemed humanly possible.

_CS_   **4.** During the actual battle of the Alamo, Texas formally declared its independence from Spain on March 2, 1836, the men who were fighting in the Alamo died without knowing this had happened.

During the actual battle of the Alamo, Texas formally

declared its independence from Spain on March 2, 1836.

The men who were fighting in the Alamo died without know-

ing this had happened.

_C_   **5.** General Sam Houston led a relief expedition to San Antonio.

_CS_   **6.** Houston's army arrived in San Antonio on March 11, the Alamo had already fallen, so it was too late.

Houston's relief army arrived in San Antonio on March 11,

but the Alamo had already fallen, so it was too late.

_RO_   **7.** The Alamo is one of the most famous sites in Texas hundreds of visitors come to the Alamo daily.

The Alamo is one of the most famous sites in Texas:

hundreds of visitors come to the Alamo daily.

_C_   **8.** There are still many myths and legends attached to the site of the Alamo.

_CS_   **9.** Souvenirs from the Alamo include miniature versions of the old mission, another popular item is a Davy Crockett–style hat.

Souvenirs from the Alamo include miniature versions of the old

mission; another popular item is a Davy Crockett–style hat.

____RO____ **10.**   Most of the men who defended the Alamo were lost in this bloody battle their legends will live on in American history and folklore.

Most of the men who defended the Alamo were lost in this

bloody battle, but their legends will live on in American

history and folklore.

Franklin Delano Roosevelt Memorial, final room and statue

ACTIVITY 21-8   Run-ons and Comma Splices II

Directions: *In the spaces provided below the paragraph, mark RO for run-ons, CS for comma splices, and C for correct sentences. You should find five comma splices and six run-ons. After you have marked each word group, complete the second part of this exercise.*

[1]Another aspect of the Franklin Delano Roosevelt Memorial that makes it special is artwork within it. [2]The bronze statues and reliefs in the memorial are incredible there are also pillars with artwork and bronze reliefs in the last section of the memorial. [3]It's an amazing design. [4]The designer of the memorial was Lawrence Halprin, the bronze sculptures are an integral part of the overall design. [5]The

sculptures appear in every room, they are also at the entrance and exit of the memorial. [6]Many of the sculptures are of FDR himself, however, not all of them are. [7]The sculptures also feature his wife Eleanor and even his favorite dog, moreover, some of the sculptures feature everyday people from the Depression era. [8]Each of the sculptures is a separate work of art most of them are very detailed, especially in terms of the characters' faces. [9]Moreover, the memorial invites people to touch the sculptures, many of the sculptures have areas that are gleaming gold, made shiny by the touch of so many hands. [10]The memorial and the artwork inside inspire interaction people are drawn to touch sculptures or take part in rituals. [11]One ritual involves the sculpture of people standing in a breadline, the ritual is to get one's picture taken at the end of the breadline. [12]Also, people ritualistically touch Roosevelt's knee and his beloved dog's ears in the final sculpture. [13]One sculpture that is included in the memorial was a controversial choice it features FDR in his wheelchair. [14]It caused an outcry because FDR had worked so hard to keep his disability hidden from the public, he suffered from polio. [15]Without a doubt, the FDR Memorial and all of the stunning sculptures and artwork within it are worth seeing on a trip to Washington, DC.

1. _____C_____	5. _____RO_____	9. _____CS_____	13. _____RO_____
2. _____RO_____	6. _____CS_____	10. _____RO_____	14. _____CS_____
3. _____C_____	7. _____CS_____	11. _____RO_____	15. _____C_____
4. _____CS_____	8. _____RO_____	12. _____C_____	

Now, pick five of the run-ons and/or comma splices you found above and revise them on a separate sheet of paper by adding the needed punctuation or joining word. Answers will vary.

LEARNING OBJECTIVES REVIEW

LO 1 What are sentence fragments, and how can recognize and correct them? (See pp. 468–474)	**Sentence fragments** start with a capital letter and end with a period but do not express a complete thought. **Three common errors** that create fragments are (1) a missing subject; (2) a missing, incorrect, or incomplete form of the verb; and (3) the inclusion of a subordinating word that makes a clause dependent. You can **correct fragments** by adding a subject, adding a verb, or deleting a subordinating conjunction and following it with a comma and an independent clause or preceding it with an independent clause followed by a comma.
LO 2 What is a run-on versus a comma splice, and what are the four ways to fix these errors? (See pp. 475–481)	A **run-on** occurs when you combine two or more independent clauses with no punctuation to separate them. A **comma splice** is a type of run-on that occurs when you combine two or more independent clauses with just a comma. The **four ways to fix run-ons and comma splices** are (1) add a comma followed by a coordinating conjunction; (2) change a comma to a final punctuation mark; (3) change a comma to a semicolon or colon; and (4) make one sentence into a dependent clause by adding a subordinating conjunction.

For support in meeting this chapter's objectives, log in to www.mywritinglab.com and select **Fragments** and **Run-Ons.**

22 Common Shift and Constructions Errors

LEARNING OBJECTIVES

In this chapter, you will learn to

 LO 1 Identify and correct subject–verb agreement errors

LO 2 Ensure pronouns agree with their antecedents

LO 3 Identify and correct pronoun reference errors

 LO 4 Identify and correct point-of-view shifts

LO 5 Identify and correct faulty parallelism

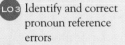 **LO 6** Identify and correct dangling and misplaced modifiers

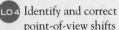 **LO 7** Avoid unnecessary passive voice constructions

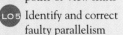

THINKING CRITICALLY

Look at the picture above. How would this scene be different if it was seen from an alternative point of view? Someone flying low overhead? A person standing on the shore? Another windsurfer?

_____

_____

_____

_____

What you see depends on who you are and your relationship to what you are viewing. In writing, a sudden change in the structure of your sentences or a shift in point of view can interfere with your readers' ability to understand your point or change the meaning of the sentence completely.

This chapter explains some of the most common construction and shift errors people make when writing and shows how to fix them.

483

LO 1 SUBJECT–VERB AGREEMENT

A verb must agree with its subject in number. A singular subject requires a singular verb, and a plural subject requires a plural verb.

> **Singular subject:** The *restaurant* **is** open until 10:00 P.M.
>
> **Plural subject:** Most *restaurants* **are** open until 10:00 P.M.

Subjects composed of collective nouns, singular nouns ending in s, or certain nouns that refer to measurements require singular verbs.

- **Collective nouns** (words that include a group but can act as a singular noun) take singular verbs:

  > The *band* **plays** during halftime.

- **Singular nouns** ending in *s* still take singular verbs:

  > *Physics* **is** a field that demands skills in math.
  >
  > *Measles* **is** an awful illness for children.

- **Nouns referring to measurements,** such as time, weight, and money usually take singular verbs:

  > The twenty *dollars* **goes** to Beth.
  >
  > The extra five *pounds* **looks** good on her.

Correcting Subject–Verb Agreement Errors

For a subject and verb to "agree," both must be in singular or plural form. A **subject–verb agreement** error occurs when a writer uses a singular noun with a plural verb or a plural noun with a singular verb. Errors often occur in subject–verb agreement in the following situations:

- When the verb comes before the subject
- When words come between the subject and the verb
- When the subject is an indefinite pronoun
- When a sentence has a compound subject

Here's how to avoid these errors:

1. Verb before the subject (verb is in bold and subject is in italics).

> **Incorrect:** There **is** many *birds* in our yard.
>
> **Corrected:** There **are** many *birds* in our yard.

2. **Words that come between the subject and the verb** (often prepositional phrases).

> **Incorrect:** *One* of the students **were** in the bookstore this morning.
>
> **Corrected:** *One* of the students **was** in the bookstore this morning.

The subject of the sentence is the word *one* and, since the subject *one* is singular, the verb should also be singular. The subject is not *students*, which would require the verb *were*. A noun at the end of a prepositional phrase, such as *students*, can never be the subject of a sentence.

> ▶ TIP: To avoid mistaking part of a prepositional phrase for the subject, try crossing out all the prepositional phrases in a sentence to help you find the subject and check if the verb agrees with it. For example, you could cross out the prepositional phrase "of the students" in the incorrect example shown above.

> One ~~of the students~~ **were** in the bookstore this morning.

Doing this clearly shows the disagreement between the singular subject *one* and the plural verb *were*, letting you know that you should correct the sentence by changing *were* to *was*.

3. **Subjects that are indefinite pronouns take singular or plural verbs.**

Indefinite pronouns function as general nouns rather than as substitutes for specific nouns. Some indefinite pronouns take singular verbs, and other indefinite pronouns take plural verbs. Listed below are some of the most common indefinite pronouns that require singular verbs.

> *another, anybody, each, either, everybody, everyone, everything, neither, no one, nothing, one, something*

> **Example:** *Everybody* **is** going to the concert.

Here are some of the most common indefinite pronouns that require plural verbs:

> *all, both, few, many, most, some*

> **Example:** *All* **are** welcome to attend the reception.

Writers often make the mistake of using plural verbs with singular indefinite pronouns.

> **Incorrect:** *Everyone* **like** to eat good food.
>
> *Each* of the customers **order** food from the menu.
>
> **Corrected:** *Everyone* **likes** to eat good food.
>
> *Each* of the customers **orders** food from the menu.

4. Compound subjects take plural or singular verbs.

Compound subjects can take either singular or plural verbs, depending on the subject. Subjects joined by *and* generally take a plural verb:

> **Incorrect:** *Fruit and cheese* **tastes** good together
>
> **Corrected:** *Fruit and cheese* **taste** good together.

When subjects are joined by *either . . . or, neither . . . nor,* or *not only . . . but also,* the verb agrees with the subject closer to the verb:

> **Incorrect:** Neither Rob nor *Jim* **want** to wash the dishes.
>
> Neither the kids nor *Jim* **want** to wash the dishes.
>
> Neither Jim nor the *kids* **wants** to wash the dishes.
>
> **Corrected:** Neither Rob nor *Jim* **wants** to wash the dishes.
>
> Neither the kids nor *Jim* **wants** to wash the dishes.

ACTIVITY 22-1   Subject–Verb Agreement, Part I

Directions: *Correct the error in subject–verb agreement in each of the following sentences. Cross out the incorrect word(s), and write the correction above the word(s) you deleted.* Answers will vary.

1. Home for a unique herd of wild horses ~~are~~ *is* Assateague Island, a barrier island off the coasts of Virginia and Maryland.

2. According to local folklore, the horses survived a shipwreck more than 300 years ago, but a more likely explanation for the presence of the wild horses ~~are~~ *is* that 17th century farmers moved their horses to the island to avoid paying livestock taxes.

3. The wild horses form family groups; each of the groups, known as
   "bands," ~~consist~~ *consists* of a stallion, 2–10 mares, and their offspring.

4. Marshes on the island ~~furnishes~~ *furnish* saltmarsh cordgrass, saltmeadow hay,
   and beach grass that the horses graze on during the spring and summer
   months.

5. During the summer, the horses escape pesky mosquitoes by spending
   time at the beach; in the fall, cooler temperatures and lower humidity
   ~~reduces~~ *reduce* the insect count.

ACTIVITY 22-2   Subject–Verb Agreement, Part II

Directions: *Correct subject–verb agreement errors in the following passage.*
Cross out the errors and write the corrections above the line.

Many of the birds in my neighborhood ~~is~~ *are* loud in the morning.

One of my neighbors ~~say~~ *says* that she regularly ~~get~~ *gets* woken up at 5:00 A.M.

daily. I love the birds, though. Each of them ~~are~~ *is* special in ~~their~~ *its* own

way. Last week I saw a glorious blue jay. He was squawking at the cat

in the next yard. One of his buddies ~~were~~ *was* helping him. Maybe there

~~was~~ *were* baby birds in that nest.

(LO 2) PRONOUN–ANTECEDENT AGREEMENT

A **pronoun** (*he, she, it, we, they,* or *our*) takes the place of another noun or
pronoun used earlier in a sentence or in a preceding sentence. The noun or
pronoun to which it refers is called the **antecedent.**

> My *boss* communicates well, and *she* is always fair.

In this example, the pronoun *she* refers to the noun *boss; boss* is the
antecedent of *she.* A pronoun must agree with its antecedent in **number**
(singular/plural), **gender** (male/female), and **person** (first, second, or
third).

My *great-grandfathers* were farmers, and *they* both raised dairy cattle.

The plural, third-person pronoun *they* agrees with its antecedent, the plural noun *great-grandfathers*.

My *great-grandfather* was a farmer, and *he* raised dairy cattle.

In this example, the singular, third-person, masculine pronoun *he* agrees with its antecedent, the singular noun *great-grandfather*.

Correcting Pronoun–Antecedent Agreement Errors

Pronoun agreement errors occur when a pronoun "disagrees" with its antecedent. Often writers create pronoun agreement errors in an attempt to avoid using gender-specific language. However, the rules of pronoun usage relate to the logic of singular and plural balance. If the noun is singular, then the pronoun that refers to that noun must be singular. If the noun is plural, then the pronoun must be plural.

Incorrect: A *student* can get *their* books at the campus bookstore.

The subject *student* is singular; therefore, using the pronoun *their* (which is plural) creates a pronoun error. There are two ways to fix this error:

1. Make the pronoun singular:

A *student* can get *his or her* books at the campus bookstore.

2. Make the subject plural:

Students can get *their* books at the campus bookstore.

Cross Reference
See Chapter 26, "Avoiding
Sexist Language."

Making the subject plural helps avoid two problems related to sexist language: using unnecessarily gender-specific language, and using the split pronoun *his/her*.

▶ NOTE   If the singular subject *is* gender-specific, then be sure to use a gender-specific pronoun.

> A *boy scout* must keep *his* uniform clean.
>
> A *ballerina* must have *her* shoes custom-made.

It's a matter of logic: when gender *is* specific, use a gender-specific pronoun. When gender *is not* specific, don't use a gender-specific pronoun.

ACTIVITY 22-3   Pronoun Agreement, Part I

Directions: *Fix the pronoun agreement error in each of the following sentences. Cross out the error and write the correction over it. If you change a pronoun or antecedent, remember that you may have to change the verb too.* *Answers will vary.*

1. Gardening can allow children to slow down and spend some quality
   time with ~~his or her~~ [*their*] parents/guardians.

2. The teamwork skills involved in gardening can enhance family life;
   ~~it also promotes~~ [*they also promote*] academic achievement, helping students collaborate
   on group projects.

3. Unlike computer games, gardening is a physical activity, and ~~they provide~~ [*it provides*]
   plenty of exercise, such as walking, bending, stretching, and carrying.

4. Growing his or her own fruits and vegetables can motivate ~~children~~ [*a child*] to
   try new foods, learn about nutrition, and make healthier food choices.

5. Gardening can also encourage scientific curiosity, as the child observes
   how a plant grows and learns about ~~their~~ [*its*] requirements for water, sun-
   light, and soil.

ACTIVITY 22-4   Pronoun Agreement, Part II

Directions: *Fix the pronoun agreement errors in the following passage. Cross out the error and write the correction over it. When changing a pronoun or antecedent, remember that you may have to change other words (such as the verb) as well.* *Answers will vary.*

Students must be careful about food to stay healthy during ~~his or~~ [*their*]
her college years. Stressed by the demands of school and work, a

student may slip into unhealthy eating habits that end up making

his or her life

~~their lives~~ even more difficult. All too often a student will just grab a

        it   *produces*

donut for breakfast, but ~~they~~ only ~~produce~~ a temporary spike in

energy rather than fueling the day's activities. Even worse, both male

and female students sometimes fall prey to peer pressure to be thin:

students   *themselves*

~~a student~~ in this situation can find ~~herself~~ suffering from an eating dis-

order. Many healthy foods are widely available or easy to prepare,

     they

and ~~it~~ can be tasty as well as nutritious. For example, a chef's salad

containing mixed greens, chicken strips, and cherry tomatoes tastes

         it

delicious, and ~~they~~ can be ordered at many fast-food restaurants.

(LO 3) PRONOUN REFERENCE

A pronoun should clearly refer to its antecedent, the noun it is replacing.

Correcting Pronoun Reference Errors

Pronoun reference errors occur when a pronoun does not have a clear connection to its antecedent (the noun it refers to). The antecedent can be *ambiguous* (it is unclear which noun is the antecedent), *vague* (the antecedent is often completely missing), or *too broad* (there is no specific antecedent).

1. **Ambiguous pronoun reference errors** occur when there are two or more possible antecedents for the pronoun. To fix this type of reference error, revise the sentence to distinguish which antecedent you meant to refer to.

   > **Example:**   Julie told Mayra that she needed to take her test at the Testing Center. [Who is taking the test, Julie or Mayra?]
   >
   > **Corrected:** Julie told Mayra that she *was planning* to take *the* test at the Testing Center.

2. **Vague pronoun reference errors** occur when the antecedent for the pronoun is completely missing. To fix this type of reference error, you need to fill in the missing noun or subject.

Example: At this coffee shop, *they* never provide enough free coffee refills.

[Who does *they* refer to? *Coffee shops* is not the antecedent.]

Corrected: At this coffee shop, *the servers* are always very busy, and *they* never provide enough free coffee refills.

3. **Broad pronoun reference errors** occur when a relative pronoun (most commonly *who, whom, whose, which, these, those, that,* and *this*) is used without a clear noun to refer to. The relative pronoun may refer to a whole group of words, or even a whole sentence, instead of referring back to one clear noun antecedent. To fix this type of pronoun reference error, supply the missing noun or replace the relative pronoun with a noun.

Incorrect: The landlord did not allow pets, which many tenants did not like.

[The relative pronoun *which* refers to the entire situation of pets being prohibited, which creates ambiguity. Do the tenants referred to not like pets or not like the policy prohibiting pets? In order to correct this broad pronoun reference error, an antecedent for *which* must be supplied or the sentence restructured to indicate a clear subject.]

Corrected: The landlord did not allow pets, a policy that many tenants did not like.

OR

The landlord did not allow pets because many tenants objected to them.

The pronouns *this, that, these,* or *those* can cause pronoun reference errors when they are used to refer to a whole sentence or a situation described in a previous sentence. The error occurs because the pronoun has no clear, specific noun antecedent. Usually, this type of reference error requires you to insert a noun or a noun phrase after the pronoun.

Examples

This is the reason for our trouble.

[*What* is the reason for our trouble?]

That is the one I want.

[What is the *that*?]

These (or *those*) are the ones I want.

[What are the *these*?]

Corrected

This **lack of funding** is the reason for our trouble.

That **puppy** is the one I want.

These (or *those*) **puppies** are the ones I want.

▶ TIP   When a reference error is caused by using a pronoun like *this* or *that*, think of adding a "fill in the blank" answer after it. Answer the question, "This *what?*" or "That *what?*"

ACTIVITY 22-5   Correcting Pronoun Reference Errors

Directions: *Rewrite the sentences below to correct pronoun reference errors. You may need to add nouns or rewrite sentences completely to fix the errors.* Answers will vary. Sample answers provided.

1. Before adding the egg to the batter, he beat it with an electric mixer.

   He beat the batter with an electric mixer before adding the egg.

   _____

2. The landlord didn't inform me that the rent was about to go up, and that was unfair.

   It was unfair of the landlord not to inform me that the rent was about

   to go up.

3. When I realized that the cream that I'd put in my coffee was sour, I poured it down the sink.

   When I realized that the cream I'd put in my coffee was sour, I poured my

   coffee down the sink.

4. Tyrone was planning on going fishing with his father, but he got sick and had to stay home.

   Tyrone was planning on going fishing with his father, but Tyrone got sick and

   had to stay home.

5. I used to worry that coffee was bad for me, but now they say that coffee, in moderation, may actually protect against various diseases.

I used to worry that coffee was bad for me, but recently I've learned that

coffee, in moderation, may actually protect against various diseases.

LO 4 POINT-OF-VIEW SHIFTS

In Chapter 1, the term *point of view* was used to refer to a writer's perspective on a subject. In grammar, however, **point of view** determines the pronouns you use in essay writing. While it is possible to switch among points of view within an essay, you generally use personal pronouns associated with a single point of view: *first person, second person,* or *third person.*

1. First person

> **Singular:** *I, me, my, mine, myself*
> **Plural:** *we, us, our, ours, ourselves*

First-person point of view is most commonly used in narrative writing.

> *I* went on a vacation with *my* family this summer. *We* took *our* favorite car, but two days into the trip, *our* car broke down.

2. Second person

> **Singular and plural:** *You, yours,* or *implied you/imperative* (command form)

Second-person point of view is most commonly used for rhetorical questions (a question you ask to interest your readers) in an essay introduction. In general, avoid using second-person point of view when writing essays, and be careful not to use the pronoun *you* to refer to people in general. Use the second person only when specifically addressing the reader. For example

> Do you think you pay too much for your college textbooks?

3. Third person

> **Singular:** *He, she, him, her, his, hers, himself, herself, it, its*
>
> **Plural:** *They, them, their, theirs, themselves*

Third person is the preferred point of view for most essays.

> Author Alice Walker met Martin Luther King, Jr. during the early 1960s. *He* inspired *her* to become active in the Civil Rights Movement, and *she* participated in the 1963 March on Washington.

Indefinite Pronouns

See page 485 for a list of the most common indefinite pronouns. For all indefinite pronouns except *one*, third-person personal pronouns may be used with the indefinite pronoun to maintain a consistent point of view.

> *Anyone* who wants to use a gym locker is required to bring *his or her* own padlock.
>
> Michael and Janine joined the other musicians for a jam session; *both* brought *their* own guitars.

The indefinite pronoun *one* can refer to the writer or the average person. For example:

> *One* would think that the library would stay open all night during finals.

This sentence suggests that the writer thinks the library should stay open all night. The sentence also implies that other people are likely to agree.

The possessive form of one is *one's*. For example: "One should be attentive to *one's* personal hygiene." (Note that one's—unlike *hers, ours,* or *theirs*—includes an apostrophe.) Do not mix the indefinite pronoun *one* with personal pronouns or general nouns such as "a person," especially in the same sentence.

> **Incorrect:** *One* should not neglect *his or her* studies.
>
> *One* should not neglect *their* studies.
>
> A *person* should not neglect *one's* studies.
>
> **Correct:** *One* should not neglect *one's* studies.

Avoiding Incorrect Point-of-View Shifts

If you choose to employ more than one point of view in an essay, be sure that the switch is logical and needed grammatically. The most common point-of-view shift error involves switching to the second-person pronoun *you*. In casual speech, people often use the generic *you* to mean "people in general." However, in formal writing, this substitution is not acceptable.

Incorrect: *I* had a wonderful time collecting shells on the beach. When *a person* looks carefully at low tide, *you* could see many different kinds of shells.

Correct: *I* had a wonderful time collecting shells on the beach. When *I* looked carefully at low tide, *I* could see many different kinds of shells.

▶ **NOTE**   Many teachers suggest using third-person plural point of view in most college writing to avoid both point-of-view (POV) shifts and other agreement errors, for example:

POV shift error (indefinite pronoun shift to second person):

One can get *your* classes paid for by financial aid.

Pronoun agreement error (plural pronoun for singular noun):

A student can get *their* classes paid for by financial aid.

Both errors fixed by substituting a plural noun for the subject and using a third-person personal pronoun:

Students can get *their* classes paid for by financial aid.

ACTIVITY 22-6   Correcting POV Shifts

Directions: *Fix any incorrect point-of-view shifts in the following passage. Keep the point of view in* **third person** *throughout. Cross out the word(s) that are in the first or second person, and write corrections above the crossed-out POV errors.*

Answers will vary.

All cooks   they
~~We all~~ like to experiment in the kitchen, but ~~you~~ should never

experiment with fruits or vegetables that are of poor quality. Even the

the cook cuts   *his or her*

best recipes can end in disaster if ~~you cut~~ corners with ~~your~~ ingredients. At

shoppers   *their*

the grocery store, ~~you~~ need to make ~~your~~ selections carefully, keeping in

mind that fresh or frozen fruits and vegetables are almost always prefer-

able to canned. When selecting fresh vegetables, people should check for

they

firmness; ~~you~~ also need to consider color. Firm, bright-orange carrots, for

shoppers

example, taste better than limp, faded ones. For fresh fruit and herbs, ~~you~~

their

can use ~~your~~ sense of smell too, making sure that the peaches smell sweet

and the basil smells pungent. If aspiring cooks follow these simple guide-

they

lines, ~~I know you~~ will be pleased with the results in the kitchen.

ACTIVITY 22-7   Correcting Subject–Verb and Pronoun
Agreement Errors and Point-of-View Shifts

Directions: *Fix errors in subject–verb agreement, pronoun agreement, and point of view in the following passage. Cross out the errors and write corrections above them. You will find a total of six errors.* Answers will vary.

Why do people dream? Nobody knows for sure, but a recent study sug-

is

gests that one purpose of dreams ~~are~~ to solve problems. According to

Harvard psychologist Deirdre Barrett, dreaming is just a particular type

a person

of thinking, so ~~you~~ can actually solve problems while sound asleep.

offers

Scientific and historical literature ~~offer~~ many examples of people solv-

their

ing problems, ranging from the mathematical to the artistic, in ~~his or~~

~~her~~ dreams. Barrett says that dreaming seems to be particularly well

defy

suited to solving problems that require visualization or that ~~defies~~ con-

ventional wisdom. One of Barrett's experiments involved a group of stu-

dents. Each student focused on an unsolved homework assignment

he or she

every night before ~~they~~ fell asleep. After a week, about a quarter of the

students had dreams that revealed the solution to the problem.

Source for factual information: http://www.livescience.com/health/dream-
problem-solving-100627.html

LO 5 PARALLELISM

Parallelism (or parallel structure) involves using a consistent grammatical form or word form in sentences that have a series of verbals or phrases in order to keep them in balance.

Correcting Faulty Parallelism

Faulty parallelism occurs when the same grammatical form or structure is not used throughout. When this happens, the form changes and the sentence becomes unbalanced.

> **Incorrect:** When we're on vacation, we *swim* in the ocean, *run* on the beach, and *hiking* in the mountains.

The last verb in this list of three verbs is *hiking,* which uses an *-ing* form of the verb, while the first and second verbs use the base forms. To correct this error, simply change *hiking* to *hike.* Or, if you prefer to use *-ing* verbs, then change *swim* and *run* to *-ing* verb forms by restructuring the sentence.

> **Corrected:** When we're on vacation, we *swim* in the ocean, *run* on the beach, and *hike* in the mountains.

OR

> When we're on vacation, we like *swimming* in the ocean, *running* on the beach, and *hiking* in the mountains.

Sometimes, problems with parallelism occur with whole phrases, especially when comparisons are being made.

> **Incorrect:** Page didn't know *whether to give* Jacob her new toy or *if she should keep* it for herself.

The phrases *whether to . . .* and *if she should . . .* are not parallel constructions. Choose one or the other to create the comparison. Here is one way to correct the sentence:

> **Corrected:** Page didn't know *whether to give* Jacob her new toy or *keep* it for herself.

Notice that when there are two infinitive phrases (*to give, to keep*), the "to" does not need to be repeated.

Here are two other ways to correct the parallelism error in the original sentence:

> **Corrected:** Page didn't know *if she should give* Jacob her new toy or *if she should keep* it for herself.

OR

> Page didn't know if she should *give* Jacob her new toy or *keep* it for herself.

ACTIVITY 22-8   Correcting Faulty Parallelism

Directions: *Rewrite the following sentences to correct errors in parallelism.*
Answers will vary. Sample answers provided.

> **Example:** Each morning I make a pot of coffee, eat some cereal, and reading the paper.
>
> **Revised:** Each morning I make a pot of coffee, eat some cereal, and read the paper.

1. If you love the idea of surfing but are worrying that it might be too hard, you should try boogie boarding.

   If you love the idea of surfing but worry that it might be too hard, you should try boogie boarding.

2. Boogie boarding is less challenging and the expenses are lower than surfing.

   Boogie boarding is less challenging and less expensive than surfing.

3. Unlike surfers, who stand on their boards, boogie boarders are lying belly-down on their boards, which makes the boards easier to control.

   Unlike surfers, who stand on their boards, boogie boarders lie belly-down on their boards, which makes the boards easier to control.

4. A boogie board is cheaper, lighter, and not as long as a surfboard.

   A boogie board is cheaper, lighter, and shorter than a surfboard.

5. Whether you want to become an expert boogie boarder or just having fun, boogie boarding is a great way to spend a day at the beach.

Whether you want to become an expert boogie boarder or just have fun,

boogie boarding is a great way to spend a day at the beach.

LO 6 DANGLING AND MISPLACED MODIFIERS

A **modifier** is a word or word group that *refers to* or *modifies* a nearby word or word group. Errors in modifiers occur when the nearby word or word group is not directly stated (so the modifier is "dangling" without anything to connect to) or the modifier is in the wrong place and therefore isn't close enough to the word or word group it is supposed to modify (a misplaced modifier).

Correcting Dangling Modifiers

Dangling modifiers are missing a home base: The word they intend to modify is missing in action. As a result, dangling modifiers are often unintentionally funny. This example illustrates the dangers, and the humor, of dangling modifiers:

Galloping across the finish line, the crowd cheered loudly.

Clearly, the writer meant to describe race horses galloping across the finish line, but by failing to include the noun *horses*, the sentence unintentionally creates the humorous image of people ("the crowd") galloping across a finish line.

Revised: The crowd cheered loudly as the horses galloped across the finish line.

OR

As the horses galloped across the finish line, the crowd cheered loudly.

▶ NOTE   Dangling modifiers often occur due to an introductory phrase not being followed by a needed subject. A possessive noun does not count as such as a subject. For example:

> **Incorrect:** After examining the patient, the doctor's recommendation was to continue the prescribed treatment.
>
> **Correct:** After examining the patient, the doctor recommended continuation of the prescribed treatment.

ACTIVITY 22-9   Correcting Dangling Modifiers

Directions: *Edit the following sentences to correct dangling modifiers. You may need to add a subject, change words, or rearrange the sentence.*
Answers will vary. Sample answers provided.

1. Learning to drive, the hardest part was parallel parking.

   When I was learning to drive, the hardest part was parallel parking.

2. Hearing that the tickets had already sold out, it was pointless for us to continue standing in line.

   Hearing that the tickets had already sold out, we realized it was pointless to continue standing in line.

3. Arriving home late, there was no time to prepare a home-cooked meal.

   Arriving home late, he had no time to prepare a home-cooked meal.

4. Having caught up on emails, several phone calls needed to be made.

   Having caught up on emails, she needed to make several phone calls.

5. Canoeing down the river, a majestic blue heron waded through shallow water near the shore.

   Canoeing down the river, they observed a majestic blue heron wading through shallow water near the shore.

6. Lost in a maze of side streets, the restaurant described in the guidebook could not be found.

   Lost in a maze of side streets, the tourists could not find the restaurant described in the guidebook.

7. Splashing happily in a puddle, the toddler's hair was covered with mud.

The toddler was splashing happily in a puddle, and her hair was covered with

mud.

8. Seeing the look on his face, it was obvious that the meeting had not gone well.

It was obvious from the look on his face that the meeting had not gone well.

9. After talking with the professor, the assignment no longer seemed so daunting.

After I talked with the professor about the assignment, it no longer

seemed so daunting.

10. When searching for an apartment, referrals from friends were particularly helpful.

When we were searching for an apartment, referrals from friends were

particularly helpful.

Correcting Misplaced Modifiers

A **misplaced modifier** is in the wrong place in a sentence, so the reader thinks it modifies the wrong word or cannot figure out what it is modifying.

> **Example:** I was chased by a dog wearing my pajamas.

Okay, it's bad enough to be chased by a dog, but it adds insult to injury if he's wearing my pajamas! The modifier *wearing my pajamas* is in the wrong spot: it is closer to *dog* than to *I*.

> **Revised:** Wearing my pajamas, I was chased by a dog.

Single-word modifiers, such as *often* and *almost*, are often misplaced:

> **Example:** I almost made $200 for the lawn-mowing job.

So did the job not happen? If the writer means that he or she made almost $200 for the job, then the modifier needs to be placed immediately before the word (or words) being modified:

> **Revised:** I made almost $200 for the lawn-mowing job.

ACTIVITY 22-10 Correcting Misplaced Modifiers

Directions: *Rewrite each of the following sentences to correct the misplaced modifier. You may need to completely restructure the sentence.*

Answers will vary. Sample answers provided.

1. The irate customer was referred to a manager with complaints about the product.

   The irate customer who had complaints about the product was referred to

   a manager.

2. Wrapped in a baby blanket, the proud father took a picture of his infant daughter.

   The proud father took a picture of his infant daughter wrapped in a baby

   blanket.

3. Gnawing on a bamboo stalk, they saw a giant panda at the zoo.

   At the zoo, they saw a giant panda gnawing on a bamboo stalk.

4. The weightlifter was 6'5" with huge biceps and a shaved head weighing 230 pounds.

   Weighing 230 pounds, the 6'5" weightlifter had huge biceps and a shaved

   head.

5. Covered with chocolate sauce, my kids love any kind of ice cream.

   My kids love any kind of ice cream when it's covered with chocolate sauce.

6. When exercising outside on a hot day, sports drinks can help replace the electrolytes that athletes lose through sweating.

   When athletes exercise outside on a hot day, sports drinks can help replace

   the electrolytes that the athletes lose through sweating.

7. Fascinated by dinosaurs, he decided he wanted to be a paleontologist when he was nine years old.

   When he was nine years old, he was fascinated by dinosaurs and decided he

   wanted to be a paleontologist.

8. Giving off a delightful fragrance, he carefully arranged the flowers in a vase.

The flowers gave off a delightful fragrance as he carefully arranged them in a

vase.

9. A professor in the psychology department is teaching a course on maladaptive behaviors at Springfield College.

At Springfield College, a professor in the psychology department is teach-

ing a course on maladaptive behaviors.

10. Enclosed in a protective chrysalis, the teacher explained that the caterpillar undergoes metamorphosis and is transformed into a butterfly.

The teacher explained that the caterpillar, enclosed in a protective chrysalis,

undergoes metamorphosis and is transformed into a butterfly.

ACTIVITY 22-11 Correcting Dangling and Misplaced Modifiers, Part I

Directions: _On the line before each sentence, write DM if the sentence includes a dangling modifier and MM if it includes a misplaced modifier. Then revise the sentences to correct the errors._   _Answers will vary. Sample answers provided._

___MM___   **1.** Many shirts were on sale, but he only found one in his size, and it was an ugly color.

Many shirts were on sale, but he found only one in his size,

and it was an ugly color.

___DM___   **2.** Researching the topic on the Internet, one site in particular was very helpful.

Researching the topic on the Internet, she found that one

site in particular was very helpful.

___DM___   **3.** Thrilled to have front-row seats for the concert, the band's live performance was even better than their CD.

Thrilled to have front-row seats for the concert, we thought

the band's live performance was even better than their CD.

_____ MM _____   **4.**   The applicants were rejected by the company without any prior job-related experience.

The applicants without any prior job-related experience were

rejected by the company.

_____ MM _____   **5.**   The pastry chef made a wedding cake for the bride covered with pink roses made of frosting.

For the bride, the pastry chef made a wedding cake covered

with pink roses made of frosting.

ACTIVITY 22-12   Correcting Dangling and Misplaced Modifiers, Part II

Directions: *Underline misplaced and dangling modifiers in the following paragraph. Then write MM over the underlined word or phrase if it is a misplaced modifier or DM over the phrase if it is a dangling modifier. You should find seven modifier errors.*

Born on a Wisconsin farm in 1887, the paintings [MM] of Georgia O'Keeffe made her one of the most celebrated artists of the 20th century, and her works remain enormously popular. After studying at the Art Institute of Chicago, opportunities [MM] arose for O'Keeffe to work as a commercial artist and art educator. In 1916 Alfred Stieglitz exhibited some of O'Keeffe's drawings. A prominent New York photographer, they [DM] were married in 1924. Shown in dramatic close-up, O'Keeffe [MM] depicted oversized details of flowers and other plants in her early paintings, developing a unique abstract style. Fascinated by the landscape of the American Southwest, desert-inspired images [DM], such as weathered animal skulls, began to dominate her paintings during the 1930s. Moving to New Mexico after her husband's death in 1946, details [DM] of her adobe house, transformed into abstract blocks of color, were featured in many paintings. Still painting until a few weeks before her death at the age of 99, many [DM] of her most memorable works are now on display at the Georgia O'Keeffe Museum in Santa Fe.

LO 7 PASSIVE VOICE CONSTRUCTION

As a grammatical term, "voice" refers to verbs. Verbs can be in the active or passive voice. When a verb is in the **active voice,** the subject performs the action. When a verb is in the **passive voice,** the subject experiences the effect of the action. Passive voice includes a form of the verb "to be" and a past participle.

Avoiding Unnecessary Passive Voice Constructions

Whenever possible, avoid using *passive* voice construction and opt for *active* construction to write clear, powerful sentences. An active verb construction is easier for readers to understand because the active voice places the emphasis on *who* is doing the action:

> **Passive voice:** The ball *was thrown by* Thomas.
>
> **Revised to active voice:** Thomas *threw* the ball.

Not only does the active voice construction sound cleaner, it is also clearer since the "doer" of the action (Thomas) is emphasized and not buried at the end of the sentence. Here is another example of passive voice construction:

> **Passive:** The puppy that was selected by the children was wagging its tail.
>
> **Changed to active:** The children selected the puppy that was wagging its tail.

ACTIVITY 22-13   Changing Passive Voice to Active Voice, Part I

Directions: *Rewrite each of the following sentences in the space provided, changing the sentence from the passive voice to the active voice.* Answers will vary.

1. The editorial in the campus newspaper was written by Tanisha.

   Tanisha wrote the editorial in the campus newspaper.

   _____

2. In the college production of *Hamlet,* the lead role was played by Juan.

Juan played the lead role in the college production of Hamlet.

3. At the barbecue, the hamburgers and veggie burgers were grilled by Chloe.

Chloe grilled the hamburgers and veggie burgers at the barbecue.

4. When Diego arrived home, he was greeted by Celia, his younger sister.

Diego's younger sister Celia greeted him when he arrived home.

5. The syllabus prepared by the professor was read by students on the first day of class.

On the first day of class, students read the syllabus that the professor had prepared.

6. A persuasive argument in support of the proposal was presented by the speaker.

The speaker presented a persuasive argument in support of the proposal.

7. The main route to campus was blocked by a tree that had fallen across the road.

A tree had fallen across the road, blocking the main route to campus.

8. The computer printer was purchased by Huang at a local office supply store.

Huang purchased the computer printer at a local office supply store.

9. The patio was illuminated by citronella candles that repelled mosquitoes.

Citronella candles illuminated the patio, repelling mosquitoes.

10. Every summer, a great block party is organized by the family that lives next door to us.

Every summer, the family that lives next door to us organizes a great block party.

ACTIVITY 22-14 Changing Passive Voice to Active Voice, Part II

Directions: *On a separate sheet of paper, rewrite the following passage in the space provided, changing each sentence from the passive to the active voice.* *Answers will vary.*

A wind instrument of the indigenous Australians, the didgeridoo is sometimes called a "drone pipe," but it is classified by musicologists as an aerophone. Possibly the world's oldest wind instrument, the didgeridoo appears in ancient cave and rock art in Australia's Northern Territory, suggesting that the instrument has been used by Aboriginal people for as long as 2,000 years. The didgeridoo continues to play an important role in the ceremonial life of Aboriginal groups; ritual singing and dancing are often accompanied by the music of the didgeridoo.

A special breathing technique known as circular breathing is employed by skilled didgeridoo players. Simultaneously, air is drawn in through the nose and expelled through the mouth, allowing the player to sustain unbroken tones for as long as 40 minutes. When the player vocalizes into the instrument while blowing it, tones known as "screeches" can be produced, which evoke the sounds of Australian animals such as the dingo or kookaburra.

Source for factual information: http://www.newworldencyclopedia.org/entry/ Didgeridoo

APPLYING CRITICAL THINKING

| PURPOSE | IDEAS | SUPPORT | ASSUMPTIONS BIASES | CONCLUSIONS | POINT OF VIEW | ANALYSIS |

Once you have drafted and revised your work, use your **analysis** skills to break your sentences down into their particular parts to make sure you have constructed them correctly and haven't made any of the errors discussed in this chapter. Ask yourself the following questions:

- **Have I switched point of view when I shouldn't have** (from first person—*I, me, us;* to second person—*you;* or to third person—*he, she, they*)?
- **Does each verb agree with its subject** (are the verb and the subject both singular or both plural)?
- **Do pronouns agree with their subjects** (are the pronoun and the subject both singular or both plural)?

- **Are pronoun references clear** (is it clear to which noun a pronoun refers)?
- **Are my sentence structures parallel** (do they stay consistent throughout the sentence)?
- **Are my modifiers attached and in the right place** (are the words they modify included in the sentence)?
- **Did I avoid passive voice construction?**

LEARNING OBJECTIVES REVIEW

LO1 What is subject–verb agreement, and how do you correct subject–verb agreement errors? (See pp. 484–487)	**Subject–verb agreement** means that a verb agrees with its subject in number: a singular subject requires a singular verb, and a plural subject requires a plural verb. A **subject–verb agreement error** occurs when a singular noun is used with a plural verb or a plural noun with a singular verb. **Correct** subject–verb agreement errors by (1) ensuring the verb and subject are both singular or plural; (2) if the pronoun is indefinite, checking if it takes a singular or plural verb; and (3) if there is a compound subject joined by *and,* using a plural verb, and if it is joined by *either/or, neither/nor,* or *not only . . . but also,* making it agree with the closest verb.
LO2 What is pronoun antecedent agreement? (See pp. 487–490)	A **pronoun** (*he, she, it, we, they,* or *our*) takes the place of another noun or pronoun (the **antecedent**) used earlier in a sentence or in a preceding sentence. A pronoun must agree with its antecedent in **number** (singular/plural), **gender** (male/female), and **person** (first, second, or third).
LO3 What are pronoun reference errors, and how can you correct them? (See pp. 490–493)	**Pronoun reference errors** occur when a pronoun does not have a clear connection to its antecedent: 1. The antecedent can be **ambiguous** (it is unclear which noun is the antecedent). **Correct** by revising to clarify which antecedent is being referred to. 2. The antecedent can be **vague** (the antecedent is often completely missing). **Correct** by adding the missing noun or subject. 3. The antecedent can be **too broad** (there is no specific antecedent). **Correct** by adding a noun or replacing a relative pronoun with a noun.
LO4 What is point of view, and how can you avoid point-of-view errors? (See pp. 493–496)	**Point of view** is the perspective from which you are writing. In an essay, you generally use personal pronouns associated with a single point of view: *first, second,* or *third person.* Be sure that your use of pronouns is consistent with the point of view you are using; making pronouns plural can help.

LO5 What is parallelism and how can you correct faulty parallelism? (See pp. 497–499)	**Parallelism** involves using a consistent grammatical form in sentences that contain a series of related words, phrases, or clauses. **Faulty parallelism** occurs when the same grammatical form or structure is not used throughout a sentence. **Correct** it by making all the elements have the same grammatical structure.
LO6 What is a modifier, and how can you correct a dangling or misplaced modifier? (See pp. 499–504)	A **modifier** is a word or word group that *refers to* or *modifies* a nearby word or word group. In a **dangling modifier** the word it is intended to modify is missing. **Correct** it by adding the missing subject to the main clause or revising the dangling modifier to include the missing subject and a verb. A **misplaced modifier** is in the wrong place in a sentence, so the reader thinks it modifies the wrong word or cannot figure out what it is modifying. **Correct** it by moving the modifier closer to the word or words it modifies.
LO7 What is passive voice construction, and why should you avoid it? (See pp. 505–507)	**Passive voice** construction is when the subject of a sentence *experiences* the effect of the action. **Active verb construction** is easier for readers to understand because it places the emphasis on *who* is doing the action.

For support in meeting this chapter's objectives, log in to www.mywritinglab.com and select **Subject-Verb Agreement, Pronoun-Antecedent Agreement, Pronoun Reference and Point of View, Parallelism, Misplaced or Dangling Modifiers,** and **Tense.**

23 Commas, Semicolons, and Colons

Frank and Ernest

© 1998 Thaves. Reprinted with permission. Newspaper dist. by UFS, Inc.

THINKING CRITICALLY

Punctuation is essential to imparting meaning. What do you think it would be like to read a paragraph with no punctuation marks? Why?

_____

_____

_____

_____

_____

_____

_____

_____

(LO 1) COMMAS

Commas (,) are the most common form of punctuation. They serve several functions in writing and help your readers understand your ideas and sentences. **Commas** clarify, make distinctions, or create the pauses needed to let your readers follow your sentences and ideas.

Five Comma Rules

There are five basic rules of comma use, and if you keep them in mind, the mystery of comma usage will be solved. Do not use the "comma by instinct" approach. When you are editing your writing, check to see if the commas you have used are covered by one of these rules, and if they are not, then remember the old comma saying: "When in doubt, leave it out." A comma where it doesn't belong usually causes more problems than leaving it out does.

Rule 1 Use a comma before a coordinating conjunction in order to combine two independent clauses to create a compound sentence.

Here are the seven coordinating conjunctions: **F**or **A**nd **N**or **B**ut **O**r **Y**et **S**o.

Independent clause +, + FANBOYS + independent clause

▼

(Coordinating conjunctions)

Use the mnemonic device (memory trick) of FANBOYS to recall them. They are the only seven words in English that can be used after a comma to combine two independent clauses (use any other word and you have a comma splice).

> The computer graphics course is fun, and the professor is excellent.
>
> Many students want to take the course, but it is already full.

▶ **TIP**   The comma comes *before* the coordinating conjunction. Also, be careful not to put a comma in automatically as soon as you see one of the FANBOYS. These words need to have an independent clause (with a subject and a verb) on *both* sides in order to use the comma.

Otherwise, they are part of a compound subject or compound predicate, and you don't use a comma:

> Maya took the course last year and said it was great.

There is only one subject in this sentence: *Maya*. There are two verbs that both relate to the subject: *took* and *said*. The word *and* links two parts of a compound predicate, and no comma is needed.

Rule 2 Use a comma to separate the items in a series (a list of three or more items) or a list of coordinate adjectives.

1. **Using commas with items in a series.** Commas help separate distinct items within a list of items:

> Item **+** , item **+** , item **+** , and item

> Maya has taken several other computer courses, including Computer Programming, Software Tools, and Web Site Development.

Placing the last comma before the *and* is one of the comma rules currently in debate. Some people argue that a comma replaces the word *and* so the last comma isn't necessary. However, there are cases when a reader could get confused, so it's usually a good idea to put it in. For example:

> I went to the movie with my cousins, Marco, and Sofia.

Without the second comma, the reader would not know whether Marco and Sofia are the names of the speaker's cousins or the names of two other people who went to the movie.

2. **Coordinate adjectives versus cumulative or compound adjectives**

   A. **Coordinate adjectives:** If two or more adjectives before a noun indicate separate qualities, use a comma between them:

   > Marco thought it was a poignant, thought-provoking, inspiring movie.

▶ TIP   If you can change the order of the adjectives and replace each comma with the word *and*, then you are dealing with coordinate adjectives:

> Marco thought it was a thought-provoking and inspiring and poignant movie.

B. Cumulative adjectives: If the adjectives are working together in order to describe something or modify each other in stages, then *do not* use commas:

> Author Betty Friedan pointed out the inequities of traditional gender roles.

No comma should come between *traditional* and *gender* because the words function as cumulative adjectives. "Gender roles" functions as a single unit, and "traditional" describes that unit.

▶ TIP   Try adding *and* between the adjectives or reversing their position. If the sentence changes meaning or sounds wrong, the adjectives are cumulative adjectives and should not be separated by a comma. For example:

> Author Betty Friedan pointed out the inequities of traditional and gender roles.
> Author Betty Friedan pointed out the inequities of gender traditional roles.

Inserting *and* between *traditional* and *gender* changes the meaning of the sentence, and "gender traditional roles" sounds wrong. Here is another example of a sentence containing cumulative adjectives:

> Even today an impenetrable glass ceiling blocks career advancement for women in certain professions.

Again, you wouldn't want to change the order of *impenetrable* and *glass* in this sentence. Cumulative adjectives should sound right in the particular order they are in—they are not interchangeable. You wouldn't say "glass impenetrable ceiling."

C. Compound adjectives: If two adjectives are used together to make one descriptor, then they become a compound adjective, and you should use a hyphen between them instead of a comma.

> **Coordinate adjectives:** The lilac bushes were covered with lavender, blue, and pink blossoms. [Three separate qualities/colors: Use commas.]
>
> **Compound adjective:** The lilac bushes were covered with lavender-blue and pink blossoms. [Lavender-blue is one color: Use a hyphen, not a comma.]

> **Coordinate adjectives:** The small, modern hospital provides excellent care for patients. [Small and modern are two separate qualities: Use a comma.]
>
> **Compound adjective:** The small-animal hospital provides excellent care for dogs and cats. [Small-animal is one quality: Use a hyphen.]

Rule 3 Use a comma after introductory material (an introductory dependent clause, an introductory prepositional or participial phrase, or an introductory single word for emphasis or transition).

> **Dependent clause + , + remainder of sentence**
>
> **Introductory phrase + , + remainder of sentence**
>
> **Introductory word + , + remainder of sentence**

A comma sets off the introductory word, phrase, or clause from the rest of the sentence. To find introductory material, look for the main subject and verb and see what comes before them.

1. Introductory dependent clause

Use a comma between the end of an introductory dependent clause and the remainder of the sentence. A dependent clause begins with a subordinating word, such as *though*, *because*, *since*, *when*, or *if*.

Cross Reference

See page 456 for more about subordinating words.

> *If the weather is good,* I go jogging in the park.

However, if a dependent clause comes after an independent clause, then a comma is not required:

> I go jogging in the park *if the weather is good.*

2. Introductory prepositional phrase

Use a comma after a prepositional phrase that comes at the beginning of the sentence. A prepositional phrase begins with a preposition such as *on, in, before,* or *after:*

> *Before heading out to jog,* I do some warm-up exercises.

If, however, a prepositional phrase comes after an independent clause, then *do not* use a comma:

> I do some warm-up exercises *before heading out to jog.*

3. Introductory participial phrase

Use a comma after a participial phrase that comes at the beginning of the sentence. A participial phrase begins with a word ending in *-ing:*

> *Jogging through the park,* I feel a little creaky at first.

4. Introductory word for emphasis or transition

Use a comma after a transitional or emphatic word that comes at the beginning of the sentence:

> *Eventually,* I hit my stride and feel totally energized.

5. Direct address

When you begin a sentence by directly addressing someone by name or title, use a comma after the name or title:

> *Daniel,* have you ever served on a jury?

▶ TIP   If the direct address comes at the end of the sentence, you will need a comma before the name or title. If the direct address comes in the middle of the sentence, use two commas, one before and one after the name or title:

> Have you ever served on a jury, *Daniel?*
>
> With all due respect, *Your Honor,* the prosecution objects.
>
> *Dear Ashley,* I hope you win the case. [Also used in an informal letter greeting]

6. Yes and no statements

Use a comma after a *yes* or *no* that begins a sentence:

> *Yes,* I was proud to serve as a juror.

7. Tag lines for dialogue or quotations

Use a comma after a tag word or phrase that comes before a quotation or dialogue in your sentence:

> *The lawyer asked,* "What caused you to trip and fall?"
>
> *Walt Whitman wrote,* "Justice is always in jeopardy."

▶ NOTE   Sometimes the comma can be omitted after introductory material if there is a short clause or a phrase that causes no danger of misreading.

> *Without a doubt* jury duty is a solemn responsibility.

However, it's acceptable to use the comma there too.

> *Without a doubt,* jury duty is a solemn responsibility.

Rule 4 Use a comma to set off interrupters—words, phrases, or clauses that "interrupt" a sentence between the beginning and end of an independent clause (IC).

> **Beginning of IC + , + interrupter + , + end of IC**

1. Dependent clause interrupter

Use commas before and after a dependent clause that interrupts an independent clause:

Mary decided, *after she discovered the high cost of housing,* to share an apartment.

> ▶ TIP   Imagine taking the middle clause out of the sentence, using the two commas like two handles you can grab to remove the interrupting clause. The sentence should still make sense if you removed the interrupting clause.

Mary decided to share an apartment.

2. Transitional words and phrases or parenthetical interrupters

Use commas before and after transitional words or parenthetical interrupters.

Most of her friends, *however,* had already made other housing arrangements.

> ▶ TIP   You can also imagine these commas as handles you can use to remove the transitional word or phrase or the parenthetical interrupter. Test to make sure your sentence still makes sense without the deleted word(s).

Most of her friends had already made other housing arrangements.

> ▶ NOTE   Use commas around parenthetical or side information instead of using parentheses when the information is important to the sense and purpose of the sentence.

3. Appositive interrupters

Use commas before and after appositive interrupters (nouns or phrases that rename or categorize nearby nouns):

Mary heard that Brianna, *a friend from college,* was looking for an apartment mate.

4. Nonrestrictive clauses

A nonrestrictive adjective clause starts with a relative pronoun (*who, whom, whose,* or *which*) or with a relative adverb (*where* or *when*). The information conveyed by this type of clause is not essential for identifying the subject of the sentence. That is, the clause doesn't *restrict* the subject.

> Mary, *who had always enjoyed Brianna,* was delighted to learn that she was interested in sharing an apartment.

In this instance, the relative pronoun *who* introduces a nonrestrictive clause; you do not need the information in this clause to identify the subject, Mary. The clause provides extra, nonrestrictive information.

> ▶ NOTE   Restrictive clauses. When the information in the relative pronoun statement or adverb statement is necessary in order to *restrict* or identify the noun/subject, then *do not* use commas:

> The friend *whom Brianna had been sharing an apartment with* was moving to a different town.

The clause "whom Brianna had been sharing an apartment with" *restricts* the noun.

5. Tag lines that interrupt dialogue or quotations

Two commas are used to set off tag lines that interrupt dialogue or quotations in the middle of the sentence.

> "My friend is leaving next month," *Brianna explained,* "so you could move in then, if you like."

> ▶ TIP   You even need a comma if the tag comes at the end:

> "That should work out perfectly," *Mary said.*

> ▶ NOTE   Notice the comma comes *inside* the quotation marks in both cases.

> ▶ NOTE   Do not use quotation marks or a comma with an indirect quotation:

> Brianna *said that* she was looking forward to sharing the apartment with Mary.

Rule 5 Use commas according to conventions for dates, locations, numbers, titles, and to avoid confusion. Here are some examples of commas used to indicate date, location, number, and title.

1. Dates

> Abraham Lincoln was born *February 12, 1809.*
>
> Charles Darwin was born *February 12, 1809,* the same day Abraham Lincoln was born.

[Notice the comma is required after the year, as well, if more information follows, as in the second example.]

2. Addresses/locations

> Darwin grew up in a large, comfortable home in *Shrewsbury, England.*
>
> Lincoln grew up in *Hardin County, Kentucky,* in a one-room log cabin.

[Notice the required comma after *Kentucky.*]

3. Numbers

> There are more than 230,000 dollars in his bank account.

4. Formal titles

> Don Kroodsma, *Ph.D.*, analyzes how and why birds sing.

Use commas to prevent confusion and to distinguish between repeated words or phrases:

> The recent oil spill can only be described as *a disaster, a disaster* that seriously damaged the environment and cost the lives of many birds.
>
> Because of bird-rescue efforts after the oil spill, some oil-coated birds that were not expected to *survive, survived.*

When Not to Use a Comma

Here is a list of when not to use a comma:

- **Do not use a comma** to separate a subject from its verb.

- **Do not use a comma** to separate verbs that share the same subject.
- **Do not automatically put a comma** before every *and* or *but*. Check to be sure that they have a subject and verb on both sides (in other words, that they link two independent clauses).
- **Do not put a comma** between the verb and the direct object.
- **Do not put a comma** before a dependent clause that follows an independent clause (unless the comma is necessary for reading clarity).
- **Do not put a comma** after *especially* or *such as*.

ACTIVITY 23-1   Correcting Misused Commas

Directions: *Delete the misused or unnecessary commas in the following sentences.*

1. Food can be expensive, but it is possible to trim your grocery bill, if you follow a few simple guidelines.
2. First, make a habit of collecting grocery coupons from a variety of sources, such as, the local newspaper, store circulars, and supermarket Web sites.
3. Before heading out to the store, you need to plan your meals for the week, and make a grocery list consisting only of necessary items.
4. Try to cook from scratch whenever possible, as processed foods are typically more expensive, and less healthy than recipes you make yourself.
5. People who shop when they are hungry, are more likely to make unplanned purchases, so have a snack before you leave for the store!

ACTIVITY 23-2   Adding Commas and Comma Rules

Directions: *Each of the 10 sentences below needs one or more commas. Place the commas where they belong in the sentences. Then write the number of the rule that applies for each added comma or commas.*

1. Petrified Forest National Park, which is located near Navajo, Arizona, has one of the largest displays of petrified wood in the world.

Rule(s) _____4_____

2. Covering about 50,620 acres, the area was designated a National Park on December 9, 1962.

Rule(s) _____3, 5_____

3. Composed mostly of quartz, the petrified logs are the remains of coniferous trees that flourished during the Late Triassic period 225 million years ago.

Rule(s) _____3_____

4. The original trees were killed by fire, insects, or other natural causes.

Rule(s) _____2_____

5. Washed into river channels by seasonal flooding, the decaying logs were buried under mud and sand containing volcanic ash.

Rule(s) _____3_____

6. Eventually, silica from the volcanic ash gradually replaced the wood cells, and the logs became petrified when the silica hardened into quartz.

Rule(s) _____3, 1_____

7. Quartz breaks cleanly, so the petrified logs look like someone cut them with a saw.

Rule(s) _____1_____

8. Iron, manganese, carbon, and other minerals are responsible for the varied hues of the petrified wood.

Rule(s) _____2_____

9. Because petrified wood is very hard as well as beautiful, it is prized as a semi-precious gemstone.

Rule(s) _____3_____

10. Part of the park's desert-like ecosystem, the petrified logs have holes that provide secure, sturdy homes for birds, mice, insects, and other wildlife.

Rule(s) _____3, 2_____

ACTIVITY 23-3 **Adding Commas**

Directions: *Add commas to the following paragraphs where needed.*

The Vietnam Memorial is located on the National Mall in Washington, DC. The monument was dedicated on November 13, 1982. The design was chosen through an open competition, and the winning design was submitted by a 21-year-old amateur architect named Maya Lin.

The monument, a long V-shaped wall, is sunk into the ground, and visitors walk along a path that follows the course of the monument. The wall is made of black marble, and the names of the soldiers who died or who are still missing in action are carved into it. The shiny, highly polished marble highlights the names of those lost during the war, and the surface reflects the images of the visitors who stop and gaze at the names. This reflection, the image of the viewer's own face superimposed, on the names heightens the powerful effect of the memorial.

Besides the interactive quality of the reflection, the memorial has become interactive in other ways over the years. People leave mementos and offerings at the memorial, placing flowers, notes, artwork, flags, photographs, and other personal items along the base of the wall. These artifacts, collected on a daily basis, are stored (except for the live flowers and plants) and archived for historical purposes.

ACTIVITY 23-4   Add, Delete, and Move Commas

Directions: *Add, delete, and move commas as necessary in each sentence. If you add or move a comma, write the rule that applies in the space provided. If you delete a comma, briefly explain why in the space provided.*

1. I love pets but am allergic to dogs and cats, so I became the proud owner of a pot-bellied pig named Harriet.

   Reason for change: _Rule 1_

2. Originating in Vietnam and China, pot-bellied pigs were introduced to the United States in the 1980s and have become very popular as pets.

   Reason for change: _Rule 3 (introductory participial phrase)_

3. Harriet, who is about the size of a cocker spaniel, has black and white markings.

   Reason for change: _Rule 4 (nonrestrictive clause)_

4. When I adopted Harriet from an animal shelter, I knew immediately that she was the pet for me.

   Reason for change: _Rule 3 (introductory dependent clause)_

5. My best friend asked, "Are you sure about this?"

   Reason for change: _Rule 3 (tagline for quotation)_

6. "Yes, I'm sure," I responded. "I've read that pot-bellied pigs make excellent pets."

   Reason for change: *Rule 3 ("yes" statement)*

7. Living up to all my expectations, Harriet has proven to be a smart, affectionate, and often hilarious companion.

   Reason for change: *Rule 2 (series)*

8. Pot-bellied pigs are like all other pets in their need for firm consistent discipline.

   Reason for change: *Rule 2 (coordinate adjectives)*

9. Harriet spends much of her time indoors, but also enjoys rooting in a fenced-in area of the backyard.

   Reason for change: *Misuse of Rule 1: "But" does not link two independent clauses, so comma is not needed.*

10. Harriet and I look forward to a long and happy future together, because pot-bellied pigs can live up to twenty years.

    Reason for change: *Misuse of Rule 3: Dependent clause does not begin the sentence, so comma is not needed.*

APPLYING CRITICAL THINKING

| PURPOSE | IDEAS | SUPPORT | ASSUMPTIONS BIASES | CONCLUSIONS | POINT OF VIEW | ANALYSIS |

When you are constructing sentences and making choices about using commas, ask yourself the following questions:

- What is my **purpose** for this particular sentence, and how can I best construct my sentence and use commas to achieve my purpose?
- How can commas make my meaning clearer?

Then *break down the particular parts* of the sentence, using your **analysis** skills to make sure that you have constructed the sentence correctly and used comma(s) correctly.

SEMICOLONS AND COLONS

Semicolons and colons are stronger marks of punctuation than commas. Semicolons and colons are used to separate clauses, clarify meaning, or provide emphasis.

LO 2 The Semicolon

The **semicolon** (;) is used to separate related clauses and phrases that are of equal importance, and when used correctly, it functions as a specific and powerful punctuation mark.

There are only two rules for using the semicolon:

Rule 1 Use a semicolon between two independent clauses when the second clause has a strong connection to the first, and they are equally important.

Use a semicolon instead of a comma with a coordinating conjunction when you want to emphasize to your reader the connection between the two independent clauses.

> Independent clause   +   ;   +   independent clause

> **Angel Falls** *is* a scenic wonder; from the top of a mountain in
>   (SUBJ) (VERB)
>
> Venezuela the **waterfall** *plunges* more than 2,640 feet.
>   (SUBJ)   (VERB)

Notice that each of the two independent clauses in the example could function as a complete sentence with a subject and verb; however, the semicolon emphasizes the connection between the two clauses more than a period or coordinating conjunction would. Here is another example:

> The remote **location** of Angel Falls *enhances* its mystique; the **waterfall** *is hidden* deep in the jungle.

Sometimes a student will mistakenly use a comma alone to link two independent clauses in a sentence, creating a comma splice. To correct the comma splice, the student can either add a coordinating conjunction after the comma or replace the comma with a semicolon.

Often, semicolons are followed either by a transitional expression or word (see p. 55 for a list of common transitional words or expressions) or by a conjunctive adverb followed by a comma.

Cross Reference

See page 475 for more about comma splices.

> Angel Falls is the tallest waterfall in the world; however, Victoria Falls in Zimbabwe is known as the world's largest waterfall.

CONJUNCTIVE ADVERBS OFTEN USED AFTER A SEMICOLON (AND FOLLOWED BY A COMMA)

also	conversely	indeed	next	subsequently
besides	finally	likewise	otherwise	then
certainly	furthermore	meanwhile	similarly	therefore
consequently	however	moreover	specifically	thus

> ▶ TIP   The semicolon should be used sparingly for maximum effect. It is a gem, so use it when it is the perfect punctuation mark, not when a period would do.

Rule 2 Use a semicolon to separate complex items in a series.

When items in a list already have commas in them, use semicolons to separate the items.

> **Item 1, with internal punctuation ; item 2, with internal punctuation ; and item 3, with internal punctuation.**

Remember Rule 2 for commas separating items in a series (see p. 514)? This semicolon rule is very similar except that you use semicolons when the items you are listing have subcomponents separated by commas:

> In the United States, travelers can observe impressive waterfalls in Yosemite National Park, California; Colonial Peak, Washington; Glacier National Park, Montana; and Niagara Falls, New York.

If only commas had been used, a reader might become confused and think the sentence was identifying the locations of eight waterfalls instead of four.

> ▶ TIP 1   Notice that you include a semicolon before the "and" that comes before the final item listed.

▶ **TIP 2**   If the sentence had not included the states in which the waterfalls are located, you would use only commas: Yosemite National Park, Colonial Peak, Glacier National Park, and Niagara Falls.

Here's another example:

> Other dramatic waterfalls include Dettifoss, a glacier-fed waterfall in Iceland; Kaieteur Falls, a broad waterfall in the rainforest of Guyana; and Iguazu Falls, a cascading waterfall in Argentina.

When Not to Use a Semicolon

You should not use a semicolon in the following situations:

- **Do not use a semicolon** after the phrases *especially* or *such as*.
- **Do not use a semicolon** after a coordinating conjunction (FANBOYS).
- **Do not use a semicolon** before the words *because* or *since* if they introduce a dependent clause at the end of a sentence.
- **Do not use a semicolon** before a list of words or items that follows an independent clause (use a colon).

ACTIVITY 23-5   Adding Semicolons

Directions: *Add semicolons where they belong in the following sentences.*

1. My book club has read *Pillars of the Earth*, by Ken Follett;*Hot, Flat, and Crowded*, by Thomas Friedman;and *Olive Kittredge*, by Elizabeth Strout.

2. Whipped cream is delicious served with fresh strawberries;however, it's loaded with calories.

3. The baseball team is not performing well;several key players are out with injuries.

4. I have to avoid drinking coffee after 2:00 in the afternoon;otherwise, the caffeine would keep me up most of the night.

5. Elroy is a committed environmentalist;he recycles religiously and rides a bike to work.

6. Our team for the project includes Emma, who is responsible for background research;Kenji, who is assembling the necessary materials;and Terence, who will produce a first draft of the report.

7. My friends know that I hate horror movies;specifically, I refuse to see slasher films.

8. Autumn is Yuan's favorite season;he loves the cool weather and fall colors.

9. When I arrive home after work, the first thing I do is change into jeans;
then I take my dog for a walk.

10. Ethan started mopping the kitchen floor;meanwhile, his roommate finished vacuuming the living room.

ACTIVITY 23-6   Adding or Deleting Semicolons

Directions: *In each of the following sentences, add or delete a semicolon or
change a semicolon to a comma.*

1. When I was growing up, my siblings and I had daily chores;even as toddlers, we were expected to make our beds, put away our toys, and help
set the dinner table.

2. Some chores were on a rotating schedule;for example, one week I
would be responsible for helping cook dinner, but the next week that
would be my brother's chore.

3. Depending on the season, we also had outdoor chores; in summer we
helped weed the garden, and in winter we helped shovel snow.

4. It was fun doing chores with my older sister; because she would always
make a game of it.

5. I must admit, however, that I always hated washing dishes; and I still do!

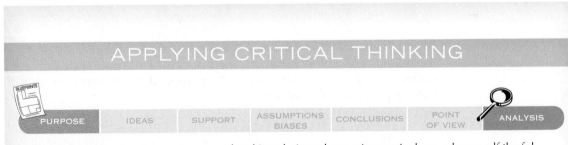

APPLYING CRITICAL THINKING

| BLUEPRINTS | | | | | | |
| PURPOSE | IDEAS | SUPPORT | ASSUMPTIONS BIASES | CONCLUSIONS | POINT OF VIEW | ANALYSIS |

When you are constructing sentences and making choices about using semicolons, ask yourself the following critical thinking questions:

- What is my **purpose** for this particular sentence, and how can I best construct my sentence and use a
  semicolon to achieve my purpose?
- Will a semicolon make my meaning clearer or add emphasis to a cause and effect relationship
  between two clauses?

  Then *break down the particular parts* of the sentence using your **analysis** skills to make sure that you
have constructed the sentence correctly and used a semicolon correctly.

LO 3 The Colon

Colons (:) are used to clarify meaning, provide emphasis, or introduce information. There are several rules for using a colon, but it basically indicates that a list or explanation is to follow.

Rule 1 Use a colon between two independent clauses when the second clause explains, summarizes, or answers the first one.

> The **contestants** in the singing contest all *had* the same dream: **They**
> (SUBJ)   (VERB)   (SUBJ)
>
> *wanted* to become famous.
> (VERB)

Each independent clause in the example could function as a complete sentence. The second clause explains the first one. Although a period, a comma followed by a coordinating conjunction, or even a semicolon would work here, a colon is the *best choice* because it helps the reader see the explanation relationship between the two clauses. Here's another example:

> The contestant had two choices: She could sing a popular song or perform a song she had composed herself.

▶ NOTE   When a colon separates two independent clauses, the second independent clause usually begins with a capital letter.

Rule 2 Use a colon after an independent clause that is followed by a word or phrase that answers or explains the idea set up in the independent clause.

> The contestants in the singing contest all had the same dream: becoming famous.

[Colon followed by a phrase]

> The contestants in the singing contest all had the same dream: fame.

[Colon followed by a single word]

The contestant had two choices: to sing a popular song or perform her own song.

[Colon followed by a phrase]

Rule 3 Use a colon after an independent clause that introduces a list of items.

When planning our trip to Montana, I started a list of items to take on hikes: water, energy bars, first-aid kit, rain gear, insect repellent, and sunscreen.

▶ TIP 1   Be sure that the clause that comes before the colon and the list is independent. It should have both a subject and a verb and not be introduced by a subordinating conjunction.

Incorrect: Several mountains to climb in Montana: Blue Mountain, Heaven's Peak, and Rising Wolf Mountain.

Correct: We wanted to climb several mountains in Montana: Blue Mountain, Heaven's Peak, and Rising Wolf Mountain.

▶ TIP 2   Don't use a colon after words and phrases such as *for example, such as,* and *including.* Think of these words as replacements for a colon; they serve the same function.

Incorrect: We also scheduled other activities, such as: fishing excursions, horseback riding, and museum visits.

Correct: We also scheduled other activities, such as fishing excursions, horseback riding, and museum visits

Rule 4 Use a colon before a quotation if an independent clause is used to set up the quotation.

In *Travels with Charley,* John Steinbeck wrote the following line: "Montana is a great splash of grandeur."

Miscellaneous Uses

There are several miscellaneous uses for colons.

- **In greetings:**

  To Whom It May Concern:
  Dear Mr. Ortiz:

- **To show hours and minutes:**

  6:05 PM

- **In titles and subtitles:**

  Angels and Ages: A Short Book about Darwin, Lincoln, and Modern Life

- **To show ratios:**

  The odds were 4:1 that the new drug would be effective.

Cross Reference
See Chapter 19 for information on documenting sources.

- **In bibliography or works cited formats:**

  Upper Saddle River: Pearson, 2010.

When Not to Use a Colon

- **Do not use a colon** after *especially, such as, consisted of, including,* and other words or phrases that indicate a list will follow.
- **Do not use a colon** after a verb that sets up a list of objects.
- **Do not use a colon** between book and verse or act and scene (in MLA style). Use periods instead:

Correct: Genesis 4.2

Incorrect: Genesis 4:2

Correct: *Phantom of the Opera,* 1.3 (or I.III)

Incorrect: *Phantom of the Opera,* 1:3 (or I:III)

ACTIVITY 23-7   Adding Colons

Directions: *Add colons where they belong in the following sentences.*

1. There are two good ways to prepare salmon: cooking it on the grill or poaching it in white wine.

2. In 1813, John Jay Audubon described a flock of passenger pigeons, a species that later was hunted to extinction: "The air was literally filled with Pigeons, and the noon-day light was obscured as by an eclipse."

3. This semester I'm taking three courses: Physics, African-American Literature, and Computer Animation.

4. I spent two hours shopping for clothes but only bought one item: a new pair of jeans.

5. My friend has a clear career goal: to become a children's librarian.

ACTIVITY 23-8   Adding or Deleting Colons

Directions: *Add or delete colons where needed in the following sentences.*

1. I asked my friend to recommend a good nonfiction book, and she suggested *The Glass Castle: A Memoir*, by Jeannette Walls.

2. An outstanding athlete, Shandra enjoys playing: basketball, baseball, and soccer.

3. The final grade for the course is based on three assessments: a mid-term exam, a research paper, and a final exam.

4. When I'm stressed out, I crave junk food, especially: French fries, donuts, and brownies.

5. Julio has already begun his job search: monitoring employment Web sites, sending out resumes, and networking in his field.

ACTIVITY 23-9   Adding Semicolons and Colons

Directions: *Add colons or semicolons to the following sentences where needed. Choose the best, most specific choice for each.*

1. If you are thinking about buying a car, there are three good reasons to consider buying a motorcycle instead: Motorcycles are affordable, environmentally friendly, and enjoyable.

2. Motorcycles cost considerably less than automobiles; in fact, a new or used motorcycle costs, on average, about half as much as a comparable car.

3. Motorcycles are also less expensive to operate, due to their fuel efficiency; a medium-sized motorcycle averages between 35 and 60 miles per gallon.

4. Like cars, motorcycles obviously incur maintenance costs; however, motorcycles are easier to repair, and owners can save money by taking a class to learn how to make repairs themselves.

5. Motorcyclists also save on insurance; the annual cost of auto insurance can exceed $1,000, but the average cost of motorcycle insurance is just a few hundred dollars.

6. Switching from a car to a motorcycle can help the environment: Motorcycles use less oil than cars do and produce lower carbon emissions.

7. For many people, the sheer pleasure of operating a motorcycle is the deciding factor; they love the freedom and excitement of roaring down the open road.

8. Motorcycle riding can be a social activity: There are many motorcycle clubs that sponsor rallies, road trips, and other social events.

9. For some people, half the fun is buying motorcycle apparel and accessories; the classic black leather jacket remains a popular item.

10. Here are three enjoyable books about motorcycling: Savvy Guide to Motorcycles, by Shirley Duglin Kennedy; Zen and the Art of Motorcycle Maintenance, by Robert M. Pirsig; and Street Strategies: A Survival Guide for Motorcyclists, by David L. Hough.

ACTIVITY 23-10   Adding Commas, Semicolons, and Colons

Directions: *Commas, semicolons, and colons are three punctuation marks that are often confused. For each sentence of the passage, insert the correct punctuation mark—comma, semicolon, or colon—in the appropriate blank. Review the rules if you get stumped.*

, (comma) ; (semicolon) : (colon)

When I was three years old ___,___ I had a bad experience at the beach that made me afraid of the water. As a result ___,___ I refused to take swimming lessons ___,___ so I never learned how to swim. Many years later, when I had a child of my own ___,___ I wanted my son to be happy and safe in the water ___;___ however ___,___ I worried that my fear of the water might cause him to feel afraid too. I realized the time had come for me to face my fear ___:___ It was now or never.

I discovered that the local Parks and Recreation Department offered adult swim lessons ____;____ one instructor specialized in helping adults overcome fear of the water. I bravely signed up for the instructor's class ____,____ but I had to force myself to show up for the first lesson. Fortunately ____,____ the instructor was very reassuring ____;____ she explained that this initial lesson would focus on helping me feel more relaxed and comfortable in the water. For the next half hour ____,____ I just moved through the water in the shallow end of the pool ____:____ walking back and forth ____,____ swishing my arms and legs ____,____ jumping up and down. When it was time to leave ____,____ I could honestly say that much of my fear had melted away!

APPLYING CRITICAL THINKING

When you are constructing sentences and making choices about using colons, ask yourself the following critical thinking questions:

- What is my **purpose** for this particular sentence, and how can I best construct my sentence and use a colon to achieve my purpose?
- Am I using a colon after an independent clause to list items? Am I using a colon to separate two independent clauses, where the second clause answers the first?

Then, *break down the particular parts* of the sentence using your **analysis** skills to make sure that you have constructed the sentence correctly and used a colon correctly.

LEARNING OBJECTIVES REVIEW

LO1 What are commas used for, and what are five rules for using them correctly? (See pp. 511–523)	**Commas** (,) are used to clarify, make distinctions, or create the pauses that help readers follow your ideas. **Five rules for correctly using commas include the following:** use a comma (1) before a coordinating conjunction to combine two independent clauses and create a compound sentence; (2) to separate the items in a series or a list of coordinate adjectives; (3) after introductory material; (4) to set off interrupters; and (5) according to conventions for dates, locations, numbers, and titles.
LO2 What are semicolons used for, and what are two rules for using them correctly? (See pp. 524–527)	**Semicolons** (:) are used to separate related clauses and phrases that are of equal importance. **Two rules for using semicolons** are (1) use a semicolon between two independent clauses when the second clause has a strong connection to the first, and they are equally important, and (2) to separate complex items in a series.
LO3 What are colons used for, and what are four rules for using them correctly? (See pp. 528–533)	**Colons** (:) are used inside sentences to clarify meaning, provide emphasis, or introduce information. **Four rules for using colons include the following:** use a colon (1) between two independent clauses when the second clause explains, summarizes, or answers the first one; (2) after an independent clause that is followed by a word or phrase that answers or explains the idea set up in the independent clause; (3) after an independent clause that introduces a list of items; and (4) before a quotation if an independent clause is used to set up the quotation.

For support in meeting this chapter's objectives, log in to www.mywritinglab.com and select **Commas, Semicolons, Colons, Dashes and Parentheses.**

Frank and Ernest

THE CAT RAN UP THE TREE TO GET AWAY FROM THE DOG WHO STARTED CHASING THE CAT WHEN THE OWNER OF THE DOG DROPPED THE LEAS BECAUSE SHE WAS SCARED WHEN A DRIVER HONKED BECAUSE A CAR STOPPED A

ARE YOU SURE?-- I THINK PUNCTUATION MIGHT BREAK THE MOMENTUM.

© 2002 Thaves. Reprinted with permission. Newspaper dist. by UFS, Inc.

LEARNING OBJECTIVES

In this chapter, you will learn to

 LO 1 Use end punctuation correctly

LO 2 Use apostrophes correctly

LO 3 Use quotation marks correctly

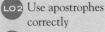 **LO 4** Use other punctuation to set off information, separate words, and show omissions

THINKING CRITICALLY

Do you think punctuation is important? Why or why not? What function does it serve for the reader?

_____

_____

_____

_____

_____

_____

_____

_____

LO 1 END PUNCTUATION

As its name implies, end punctuation comes at the end of a sentence. There are three types of end punctuation: the period, the question mark, and the exclamation point.

Period

A **period** (.) is used to end a statement. You should use a period under the following circumstances:

1. **Use a period at the end of a complete sentence (independent clause).**

    The sentence can be a statement or an indirect question:

    > Coldplay is his favorite band. [Statement]
    >
    > He asked me if I'd like to go to the Coldplay concert. [Indirect question]

2. **Use periods with some abbreviations (not all abbreviations require periods; check a dictionary if you are unsure).**

Mr.	Ms.	etc.	e.g.	R.S.V.P.	B.C.	A.D.
A.M. (or a.m.)	P.M. (or p.m.)	Dr.	Ph.D.			

    ▶ NOTE   Some of these abbreviations are acceptable without the periods: AM, PM, BC or BCE, AD or ACE.

ACTIVITY 24-1   Period Practice

Directions: *Add periods where needed in the following passage.*

Dr. Whitney Smith, a beloved professor in the college's history department, is retiring at the end of this academic year, and I'm helping organize a retirement party for her Dr. Smith's credentials are impressive; she received her PhD from Columbia University, and she has written several important books. Students consistently rate her teaching as excellent, and the department's administrative assistant, Ms. Jenkins, says that Professor Smith is popular with other faculty and staff as well as students. I'm responsible for sending out invitations for the party and keeping track of the RSVP's. I'll also help out with the refreshments (ordering the cake, buying sodas, etc).

Question Mark

A **question mark** (?) is used at the end of a sentence to indicate that a question is being asked. Use a question mark when a sentence is a direct question.

> Do you think Coldplay is better than Radiohead?

> Do not use a question mark if the sentence is an indirect question:

> I asked my friend if she liked Coldplay better than Radiohead. [Period, not a question mark]

Using Question Marks with Quotations or Dialogue

Be sure to check if a question mark is part of a quotation or a piece of dialogue (whether you are quoting a question or a person is asking a question) or if you are asking a question about a quotation. If it is part of a quotation or a piece of dialogue, the question mark goes inside the quotation marks.

> She asked, "Are the Radiohead tickets already sold out?"

If you are asking a question about a quotation, the question mark comes after the closing quotation marks:

> Who was it that said, "Music is the universal language"?

ACTIVITY 24-2   Question Mark Practice

Directions: *Add question marks, move question marks, or change question marks to another form of punctuation as necessary in the following passage.*

Elena asked Anthony if he knew what salsa is ? "Of course I do," he replied. "Doesn't everyone? It's that spicy tomato sauce you eat with tortilla chips."

Elena smiled and said, "No, I mean the other kind of salsa."

"Like salsa verde, that green salsa?" asked Anthony.

"I'm talking about salsa dancing," Elena laughed.

"Oh, I get it," said Anthony. "But why are you asking me about salsa dancing?"

"I was wondering if you might be interested in taking salsa lessons ?" Elena said.

Exclamation Point

Use an **exclamation point** (!) to show emphasis, to express strong emotion—excitement, surprise, disbelief—or to indicate a strong command.

> I'm starving, and that stew smells delicious!
>
> You scared me to death!
>
> I can't believe he gave us a pop quiz the day before spring break!
>
> Stop—it's a red light!

▶ NOTE   Try not to overuse exclamation points or they will lose their power! See what I mean?! Too much!

ACTIVITY 24-3   Exclamation Point Practice

Directions: *Add exclamation points or replace exclamation points with a different type of punctuation mark as needed in the following passage.*

"Please pass the syrup," said Mario. Anna reached for the pitcher of syrup, but it slipped out of her hand and spilled onto the table!

"Oh, no!" she cried as the syrup quickly spread toward the table's edge! "Quick, hand me some napkins!"

"Don't worry—we can clean it up!" Mario said calmly.

"You've got syrup on your blouse!" said Anna's friend Nina.

"This blouse isn't even mine!" moaned Anna, scrubbing the spot with another napkin. "I borrowed it from my sister. If it's ruined, she's going to kill me!"

LO 2   APOSTROPHES

Apostrophes (') are used to indicate contractions (words in which certain letters have been omitted) and to show possession (who or what owns something).

Apostrophes and Contractions

Use an apostrophe to indicate the omission of one or more letters when words are combined to form a contraction. Put the apostrophe where the missing letter(s) would be: *it's (it is)* or *haven't (have not)* or *would've (would have)*. Contractions may not be appropriate for formal, academic writing. See Chapter 26 for more about tone and word choice.

Common Contractions	
aren't	are not
can't	cannot
could've	could have
couldn't	could not
didn't	did not
doesn't	does not
don't	do not
hadn't	had not
hasn't	has not
haven't	have not
he'd	he had/he would
he'll	he will
he's	he is
I'm	I am
isn't	is not
it'd	it had/it would
it'll	it will
it's	it is
let's	let us
mightn't	might not
might've	might have
mustn't	must not
she'd	she had/she would
she'll	she will
she's	she is
shouldn't	should not
should've	should have
there'd	there had/there would
there'll	there will
they're	they are
'twas	it was

Common Contractions	
wasn't	was not
we'll	we will
we're	we are
weren't	were not
what'd	what had/what would
what's	what is
won't	will not
wouldn't	would not
would've	would have
you'll	you will
you're	you are

▶ NOTE   Be careful when you use the following contractions. They sound like other words that have different meanings (see "Commonly Confused Words," p. 567).

they're	(they are)	vs.	there	(adverb)
you're	(you are)		your	(possessive pronoun)
who's	(who is)		whose	(possessive pronoun)
it's	(it is)		its	(possessive pronoun)

▶ SIMPLE TEST   If the word can be said aloud as two words, then it is probably the contraction you want.

Correct: The car needs new tires, and *it's* not getting good mileage. [The car needs new tires, and *it is* not getting good mileage.]

Incorrect: The car needs new brake pads, and *it's* windshield is cracked.

[The car needs new brake pads, and *it is* windshield—oops, wrong word; use "its," a possessive pronoun, instead—*its* windshield is cracked.]

Apostrophes and Possession

Add an apostrophe to a noun or indefinite pronoun to indicate possession. (But don't add an apostrophe to a pronoun that is already possessive, such as *his, hers,* or *its.*)

Sam's essay about her most embarrassing moment was hilarious.

[The apostrophe indicates the essay belongs to Sam.]

Someone's dirty dishes are in the sink.

[The apostrophe indicates that dirty dishes belonging to someone are in the sink.]

1. **Singular possession** Use an apostrophe before the added *s* to indicate possession.

> The hummingbird's wings can beat up to 78 times per second.
>
> [The apostrophe indicates that the wings of the hummingbird can beat up to 78 times per second.]
>
> *History's* lessons are always being relearned.
>
> [The apostrophe indicates that the lessons of history are always being relearned.]
>
> Dr. Ortega is *everyone's* favorite professor.
>
> [The apostrophe indicates that the favorite professor of everyone is Dr. Ortega.]

If the singular noun already ends with the letter *s*, then add an apostrophe and another *s*.

> Each of the *octopus's* eight arms has two rows of suction cups.
>
> [The singular noun *octopus* ends with an *s*, so add an apostrophe and another *s*.]

> ▶ NOTE   Don't use apostrophes with pronouns that are already possessive.

> **Correct:** Is this textbook yours or mine? Its cover is torn.
>
> **Incorrect:** Is this textbook *your's* or mine? *It's* cover is torn.

2. **Plural possession** Use an apostrophe after the *s* that indicates a plural, possessive noun.

> Many of the *trees'* branches broke during the ice storm.
>
> [Refers to two or more trees—the only way to know this is by the placement of the apostrophe.]

The *artists'* paintings are on display in the main gallery.

[The placement of the apostrophe indicates there is more than one artist.]

▶ NOTE   If the form of the noun is already plural, add an apostrophe and an *s*.

The *women's* locker rooms are on your right.

▶ NOTE   Don't use an apostrophe to make nouns plural.

Correct: There are several news Web sites that I check every day.

Incorrect: There are several news Web site's that I check every day.

3. **Possessive and compound nouns**   Place apostrophes at the end of compound nouns in order to indicate possession.

My *brother-in-law's* jokes are pretty lame.

[Apostrophe goes at the end of the compound noun; you do not write *brother's-in-law*.]

With two brothers-in-law, you make the word "brother" plural by adding an *s*; then just use apostrophe and an *s* after "law" (only one law but two brothers).

My *brothers-in-law's* favorite joke is so lame that they are the only ones who laugh.

4. **Possession and proper names**   Add an apostrophe and an *s* to single proper names to show possession.

Shanika's job interview went very well.

[There is only one Shanika, so the apostrophe goes before the *s*.]

Professor Wang's letter of recommendation helped Shanika get the job.

If a proper name ends in *s*, usually you show possession by adding an apostrophe and another *s*.

> *Chris's* dream is to become a marine biologist.
>
> [The name *Chris* already ends with an *s*, so add an apostrophe and another *s*.]
>
> *Henry James's* novels are psychologically complex.

However, if the pronunciation would be awkward with the added *s*, it is acceptable to omit the extra *s*.

> The New Testament includes descriptions of *Jesus'* [or *Jesus's*] disciples.

If the proper name is plural, put the apostrophe after the *s*.

> *The Steinbergs'* house is always full of neighborhood kids.
>
> [Adding the *s* makes the name *Steinberg* plural to indicate a whole family, not one person, and the apostrophe after it indicates their joint possession of the house.]

5. **Joint possession** If two or more people share a possession, then add an apostrophe and an *s* only after the last name.

> Are you riding in *Lamont* and *Whitney's* car?
>
> [The car belongs to both of them, so the apostrophe goes after *Whitney*.]

If people individually (separately) possess things, use an apostrophe and an *s* for each one.

> Are you riding in *Lola's* car, *Ethan's* car, or *Kenji's* car?
>
> [There are three separate cars, so the apostrophes are used to indicate individual possession.]

Apostrophes and Plurals

Use an apostrophe to indicate plural numbers, letters, and symbols and to indicate the plurals of words used as an item. (Due to the dynamic nature of grammar, it is now often acceptable to use an apostrophe or to omit the apostrophe in many of these cases. You may choose to do either, but be consistent).

The Federal Aviation Association announced that mechanical defects on two *747's* had been corrected. [It's okay to use *747s*.]

The two *A's* I got last semester raised my GPA.

For the arithmetic worksheet, the kindergarten teacher printed the *+'* and *−'s* in different colors.

When making an oral presentation, try to avoid using *uh's*, *um's*, and *you know's*.

Apostrophes and Missing Letters or Numbers

You can use apostrophes to indicate letters or numbers that are missing from words in dialogue, slang, or colloquial speech. Remember, you should only include slang or colloquial words like this in dialogue; these words are inappropriate in academic writing.

"*Y'all* come in now. I'm *fixin'* to serve up some three-alarm chili."

My grandmother said, "We went through some tough times during the *30's*, but we never doubted that things would get better."

When Not to Use an Apostrophe

- Do not use an apostrophe with possessive pronouns (*his, hers, its, ours, yours, theirs, whose*).
- Do not use an apostrophe to form plurals that do not indicate possession.

ACTIVITY 24-4   Apostrophe Practice, Part I

Directions: *Add, delete, or move apostrophes in the following sentences as needed. Change in an apostrophe may also require a spelling correction. Write C for correct if the use of apostrophes is correct.*

_____ 1. The professor does'nt accept any late papers without a doctor's note.

_____ 2. Lack of sleep can undermine your'e ability to analyze and retain information.

_____ 3. My kids used to hate flossing their teeth, but then I bought some mint floss; the flosse's pleasant flavor is a good motivator.

_____ 4. Arctic foxes' fur changes color with the seasons.

_____ **5.** Many companies now rely on office email rather than hardcopy memo's.

___C___ **6.** Recently, my two mothers-in-law and my brother's mother-in-law met for the first time; the mothers-in-law's reaction was to give each other a big hug.

_____ **7.** Tess's psychology experiment uses white mice and requires weeks of careful monitoring.

___C___ **8.** The Strokes' "Is This It" CD brought garage rock back into popular music culture.

_____ **9.** Taj's and Zahra's wedding took place at the beach.

_____ **10.** I let my sister borrow my car when her's wouldn't start.

ACTIVITY 24-5   **Apostrophe Practice, Part II**

Directions: *Add, delete, and move apostrophes as needed in the following passage. Change in an apostrophe may also require a spelling correction. There are 16 apostrophe-related errors.*

My friend Jenny and I recently moved into an apartment. The apartment's furnishings didn't include a dining table, but we found a great antique table for $20 at a yard sale. The table was just the right size, though it's ugly green paint was not very appealing. Mr. and Mrs. Grant, who live in the apartment next to our's, admired the table. The Grants' apartment is furnished with some beautiful antiques. Mrs. Grant asked if we were planning to refinish our table. We hadn't considered it, but Mrs. Grant's enthusiasm was contagious, so we decided to take on the project. We began by printing out various Web sites' instructions for refinishing furniture. In a local store's home improvement section we found all the supplies we needed.

Applying paint stripper was the first task. The chemical's odor bothered me at first, but we opened all the windows and put on disposable face masks to protect us from the toxic fumes. Using large paintbrushes, Jenny and I covered the table's surface with paint stripper. Mrs. Grant had told us that it ~~would'nt~~ *wouldn't* take long for the stripper to work, and we only had to wait half an hour.

Scraping and sanding were next. Using putty knives, we gently scraped off the ugly green paint, uncovering the wood's natural beauty. After the table was dry, we spent a long time sanding it; to keep our spirits up, we competed to see ~~who's~~ *whose* part of the table was smoother.

The refinishing process' last step—applying stain to the wood—was the most fun. Using fine-bristle paintbrushes, we coated the table with stain, taking special care to stain the decorative carvings' swirls and crevices. We were delighted with the results! The next day, the Grants' helped us celebrate by giving us some homemade lasagna to eat at our beautifully refinished dining table.

LO 3 QUOTATION MARKS

Quotation marks (" ") are used to indicate direct quotations or dialogue (written or spoken), to indicate some types of titles, and to define words or to use them ironically.

1. **Use quotation marks around direct quotations.** Enclose all words that are quoted directly from another source in a pair of **double quotation marks,** and remember to include a page citation:

   > John Sawhill said, "In the end, our society will be defined not only by what we create but by what we refuse to destroy" (56).

   Cross Reference
   See Chapter 17 for correct MLA citation format.

   When there is a quotation within a quotation, use **single quotation marks** around the internal quotation:

   > Describing her rival, writer Lillian Hellman, Mary McCarthy said, "Every word she writes is a lie, including 'and' and 'the.'"

2. **Use quotation marks to quote prose or poetry.** Use the following information to help you use quotation marks correctly:

   • **Introducing quotations.** If you quote a complete sentence, use a tag to introduce the quotation followed by a comma.

> **Tag:** James Baldwin said, "The challenge is in the moment; the time is always now" (83).

If you introduce a quotation using a complete sentence of your own, use a colon, and start the quotation with a capital letter.

> **Introductory sentence:** James Baldwin said it best: "The challenge is in the moment; the time is always now" (83).

- **Quoting partial sentences.** If you quote only part of a sentence, don't start the quotation with a capital letter.

> James Baldwin said that "the time is always now" (83).

- **Leaving words out of a quotation.** If you leave out part of a quotation, use an ellipsis (three spaced dots) to indicate where the omitted word or words were deleted.

> Frederico García Lorca wrote, "There is nothing more poetic and terrible than the skyscrapers' battle with the heavens that cover them. Snow, rain, and mist highlight, drench, or conceal the vast towers, but those towers . . . shine their three thousand swords through the soft swan of the fog."

- **Adding words and phrases.** If you add a word or phrase for clarification within a direct quotation, put brackets around the insertion.

> Tom Paine wrote, "What we obtain too cheap, we esteem too lightly; it is dearness [high cost] only that gives everything its value."

- **Quoting lines of poetry.** If you quote lines of poetry within your own sentence, use slashes to indicate where the original line breaks were.

> Poet Maya Angelou wrote, "The caged bird sings with a fearful trill / Of things unknown but longed for still" (1).

- **Quoting four or more lines of poetry.** If you quote four or more lines of poetry or prose, set the quotation off in a block by indenting 10 spaces from the left margin and omit quotation marks.

> Maya Angelou wrote the following lines:
>> The caged bird sings with a fearful trill
>> Of things unknown but longed for still
>> And his tune is heard on the distant hill for
>> The caged bird sings of freedom. (1)

3. **Use quotation marks with dialogue.** Here are some tips for using quotation marks with dialogue:

- Put the actual words spoken by the person in quotation marks.
- Use commas to set off tags at the beginning, middle, or end of the dialogue.
- Start a new paragraph whenever you switch speakers or characters in dialogue, even if the line is only one word long.

> "So what did you think?" she asked.
>
> "The special effects were sick!" he said. "I was surprised the 3-D glasses worked so well."
>
> "I know," she said. "The visuals were amazing, but the plot was lame."
>
> "You're right," he said. "It's been done before."

4. **Use quotation marks for specific types of titles.** Use quotation marks around the titles of short stories and poems (not book-length epic poems, though), chapter titles, essay titles, magazine article titles, television episodes from series, and song titles.

> **Story title:** "What You Pawn I Will Redeem" by Sherman Alexie
>
> **Poem title:** "Where the Sidewalk Ends" by Shel Silverstein
>
> **Magazine article title:** "Four Ways of Looking at Breakfast" by Thomas Fuller
>
> **Television episode title:** "No More Mister Nice Guy"
>
> **Song title:** "Not a Robot, But a Ghost" by Andrew Bird

▶ NOTE   Titles of books, epic poems, plays, movies, CD/albums, TV shows, and magazines are all italicized.

5. Use quotation marks around words that are being singled out for definition or to indicate irony.

> The word "miscreant" refers to a person who is dishonest or unkind.
>
> School and work leave little time for anything else: My "free time" is used for running errands and doing chores.

Punctuation and Quotation Marks

Place commas and periods inside quotation marks if you do not include a page citation.

> "Wildwood," a short story by Junot Díaz, won the O'Henry Award.
>
> William Strunk said, "Omit needless words."

If you do include a citation, the punctuation goes after the citation.

> In his eulogy for Eleanor Roosevelt, Adlai Stevenson said, "She would rather light candles than curse the darkness, and her glow has warmed the world" (McCarthy 63).

> ▶ NOTE   When you use semicolons and colons in your writing, they should come after quotation marks. For instance:

> The ad described the apartment as "dirt cheap": It turned out to be more dirty than cheap.

ACTIVITY 24-6   Quotation Marks Practice

Directions: *Put quotation marks where needed in the following sentences. Write a C if the sentence is correct as written.*

_____C_____ **1.** Our host announced there was plenty of cake left if anyone wanted seconds.

_____ **2.** "Poker Face" is one of Lady GaGa's most popular songs.

_____ **3.** Mathematicians often use the word "elegant" to describe a mathematical proof that is especially concise, surprising, or original.

_____ **4.** "Everything is funny," said Will Rogers, "as long as it is happening to somebody else."

_____ **5.** "The Highwayman," a long, melodramatic narrative poem by Alfred Noyes, is fun to read aloud.

ACTIVITY 24-7   Adding Quotations Marks

Directions: *Add quotation marks where needed in the following passage.*

My housemate Frank is a great guy, but he's always late for everything. Recently he got engaged, and he volunteered to pick up his girlfriend's parents, who he'd never met, at the airport at 9:30 A.M. The day before, I talked the situation over with my other housemate, Ben.

"No way Frank's going to make it on time," said Ben.

"But he's got to," I said. "Caity's father is in the military. Being late is simply not allowed."

"I'm just sayin'," shrugged Ben.

"We've got to do something," I mused. "We have to save him from himself."

"Save him how?" asked Ben.

"By tricking him, of course," I said.

"How do you trick someone into being on time?" scoffed Ben. "No way that'll work."

"Hey, dude," I said. "It's worth a try. You know—like that old saying, 'Nothing ventured, nothing gained.'" Ben looked blank. "Never mind," I said. "Here's the deal. After he goes to sleep tonight, we'll reset all the clocks an hour ahead. So he'll think it's 9:00 A.M. when it's actually 8:00 A.M.—get it? So instead of being a half hour late, he'll be a half hour early."

The plan worked beautifully.

⒧ OTHER PUNCTUATION

Various other forms of punctuations are used to set off information (parentheses, dashes, and brackets), combine or divide words (hyphens), indicate choice between two words or breaks in lines of poetry (slashes), and show that information has been omitted (ellipses).

Parentheses

Parentheses (()) are used for setting off information or citations. Parentheses can be used in a number of ways:

1. **Use parentheses to set off nonessential information or side comments in the middle of sentence.**

> The school's science teacher (who also coaches the soccer team) has really gotten the kids excited about science.

If the information in a side comment is relatively important, it is preferable to use parenthetical commas to set it off (see Chapter 23, "Commas" section, Rule 4, p. 516).

> The storm, which included high winds and hail, caused widespread power outages.

▶ **TIP**   You can test to see if parentheses or commas work best around a word or phrase by reading the sentence without them to see if it still makes sense.

2. Use parentheses to set off numbers or letters in a list or series.

> If your clothes catch on fire, follow these three simple steps: (1) stop moving, (2) drop to the ground, and (3) roll to extinguish the flames.
>
> When administering CPR, remember your ABC's: (A) **A**irway (check the airway), (B) **B**reathing (provide rescue breathing), and (C) **C**irculation (check pulse to determine if chest compressions are needed).

▶ **NOTE**   Only certain style formats, for instance, writing for business or science, encourage the use of numbers or letters with parentheses. Writing in the humanities usually involves using full words to list items (such as "first," "second," "next," and so on).

3. Use parentheses to indicate formal citations (see Chapter 17).

> As H. L. Mencken observed, "The cure for the evils of democracy is more democracy" (36).

4. Use parentheses to indicate abbreviations. Use the full name and follow it with the abbreviation in parentheses at first mention, so readers know what the initials stand for when you use them again:

> The Federal Drug Administration (FDA) has not yet approved the new medication.

ACTIVITY 24-8   Parentheses Practice

Directions: *Add or delete parentheses as needed in the following paragraph.*

Founded in 1876, the American Library Association(ALA)seeks to promote library service (and librarianship). The organization's motto (adopted in 1892)is, "The best reading, for the largest number, at the least cost." ALA identifies seven key action areas:(1)Diversity, (2)Equitable Access to Information and Library Services,(3)Education and Lifelong Learning,(4)Intellectual Freedom,(5)Advocacy for Libraries and the Profession,(6)Literacy, and(7)Organizational Excellence. ALA presents itself as "an incredibly rich and varied organization" that "offers something for everyone"(ALA Handbook of Organization, "Great Ways to Get Involved in ALA").

Hyphens

Hyphens (-) are used to combine or divide words. Here are some examples of the uses for hyphens.

1. **Use hyphens (-) to form compound words.** Check your dictionary to be sure that the compound word you're using is usually hyphenated. Some are not. Here are some commonly hyphenated compound words:

   Fractions such as *one-third, two-thirds, one-fourth*

   Numbers that are spelled out between twenty-one and ninety-nine

   Compound nouns such as *mother-in-law* or *brother-in-law*

2. **Use hyphens with compound modifiers.** Use hyphens with compound modifiers, usually adjectives, which are used together as one descriptor before a noun.

   The bank approved the store owners' application for a *short-term* loan.

   [Here *short-term*—a compound adjective—modifies the word *loan.*]

   The *well-liked* professor was awarded tenure.

> ▶ NOTE   If a compound modifier is not followed by a noun, then omit the hyphens.

> The bank loan would enable them to keep the store open in the *short term*.
>
> The tenured professor was *well liked*.

3. **Use hyphens to join letters, prefixes, and suffixes to a word.** Here are some examples of common prefixes that require hyphens:

> **Letters before words:** T-shirt, B-team, A-frame, J-bar, C-note
>
> ***Self-* before words:** self-addressed, self-control
>
> ***All-* before words:** all-knowing, all-seeing
>
> ***Ex-* before words:** ex-husband, ex-mayor

Usually the prefixes *anti-, pro-, pre-, co-, non-,* and *re-* do not require hyphens (*antitrust, propel, premodern, nonresponsive, cosponsor, retrace*). However, there are exceptions, for example, *non-union, re-cover* (to cover again). A hyphen may also be required if the prefix ends in a vowel and so does the root word, for example, *anti-inflammatory, co-owner, de-emphasize,* and *co-ed*.

4. **Use a hyphen when dividing words at the end of a line.** It is preferable not to divide words at all, but if you do, be sure to follow these guidelines:

- Divide words at syllable breaks.
- Don't leave less than three letters at the end of a sentence before the hyphen or have two or less letters on the next line.

   Dividing words is rare these days since computers automatically wrap words over to the next line. Some textbooks still divide words at the end of a line, but in your papers, you should avoid dividing words and let the computer format them for you.

ACTIVITY 24-9   Hyphen Practice

Directions: *Add hyphens where needed in the following sentences. If the sentence is correct, then write C on the line provided.*

_____   1.   My twenty four year old friend is frustrated that car insurance rates do not decrease until a driver is twenty five years old.

_____ **2.** Three quarters of a pound of fish should be enough to serve three people.

_____ **3.** The high powered group makes me feel like a nobody.

_____ **4.** My son's favorite activity at the playground is to ride the merry go round.

___C___ **5.** Though college can be expensive, students who get a college degree have higher earnings in the long run.

_____ **6.** My roommate is addicted to self help books.

_____ **7.** When roads are icy, maneuvering the S curves on that mountain pass can be totally hair raising.

_____ **8.** During the 1970s, the federal government implemented antiinflation policies.

___C___ **9.** When they get together, my brother and his buddies act like they are ten years old.

_____**10.** The only medications I take are over the counter cold remedies.

Dashes

Dashes (—) are used to help information stand out, to add emphasis, and can be used around a phrase in the middle of a sentence or at the end of a sentence. At the end of a sentence, a dash can work much like a colon, but it is more informal.

> Generally speaking, I'm a great supporter of tradition, but I draw the line—and I suspect I'm not alone in this—at the tradition of spring cleaning.
>
> Early autumn is my favorite time of year—the morning air is crisp, and the first red leaves appear.

▶ NOTE   Material enclosed by dashes can be removed, and the sentence will still make sense.

▶ NOTE   Dashes are considered an informal punctuation mark. In more formal writing, use commas or colons instead of a dash.

ACTIVITY 24-10 Dashes Practice

Directions: *Add or delete dashes in the following passage.*

Last month, when I was attempting to cram some papers into an overstuffed file drawer, I had an important insight I have too much stuff! I'm not a pathological hoarder or anything I've thrown out plenty of items over the years but the clutter in my apartment was definitely starting to get to me. I decided it was time to take charge.

At the local hardware store I purchased the most important weapon in my battle against stuff large plastic trash bags. These weren't just any plastic bags wimpy kitchen trash bags wouldn't do for this job. No way, I went for the type of heavy-duty plastic trash bags that construction crews use that's how serious I was!

Using masking tape and an indelible marker, I made four labels Keep, Sell, Give Away, Throw Away and fixed them to four of the trash bags. That was the easy part! The thought of sorting through all my stuff books, CDs, DVDs, clothes, shoes, toiletries, kitchen gadgets, whoopee cushions, plastic flamingos made me feel a little faint, and I almost gave up then and there. But then my mother's favorite phrase "one step at a time" popped into my mind. Step by step or, better yet, room by room this job would get done!

Slashes

A **slash** (/) is a diagonal line slanting from right to left that is used to indicate a choice between words or line breaks in quoted excerpts from poems.

1. Use slashes between two words to indicate there is a choice of using either.

yes/no	and/or	either/or

2. Use slashes to indicate line breaks when you quote two or three lines of poetry within your own sentence.

> The first three lines of "Juke Box Love Song," a poem by Langston Hughes are: "I could take the Harlem night / and wrap around you, / Take the neon lights and make a crown" (24).

ACTIVITY 24-11   Slashes Practice

Directions: *On a separate sheet of paper, write three sentences that use words that are sometimes combined with slashes to show that either could be used.*
Answers will vary.

Ellipses

An **ellipsis** (. . .) is used to indicate that words, phrases, or even complete sentences have been omitted. An ellipsis consists of three spaced periods with a space before the first period and a space after the last one.

1. **Use an ellipsis to signify where words have been omitted in a quotation.** Be careful not to change the author's intent when omitting a word or words in the middle of a phrase or sentence. An ellipsis is not needed at the beginning or end of a quotation if you are quoting part of a sentence or a phrase. For example, here is an excerpt from Amy Tan's novel *Joy Luck Club:*

> My mother believed you could be anything you wanted to be in America. You could open a restaurant. You could work for the government and get good retirement. You could buy a house with almost no money down. You could become rich. You could become instantly famous.

Here is the same passage with some of the text removed as indicated by the use of an ellipsis (note the ellipsis follows the period at the end of the sentence immediately preceding the deleted material):

> My mother believed you could be anything you wanted to be in America. You could open a restaurant. You could work for the government and get good retirement. . . . You could become instantly famous.

2. **Use an ellipsis to indicate a cutting off or trailing off of a sentence in dialogue.**

> Noticing her frown, he hastily added, "Oh, never mind . . ."
>
> OR
>
> "Hold on a minute . . .," Eliot interrupted. "That doesn't make sense!"

ACTIVITY 24-12   Ellipses Practice

Directions: *Choose one of the readings from Chapter 18, and, on a separate sheet of paper copy five sentences from it. Then remove at least five words from one of the sentences using an ellipsis and without changing the original meaning of the passage.* Answers will vary.

Brackets

Brackets ([ ]) are similar to parentheses, only square as opposed to curved, and they are used to set off information.

1. Use brackets to add a word or comments to a direct quotation.

> In the words of Thomas Wolfe, "It [New York City] was a cruel city, but it was a lovely one."
>
> One of the goals stated in the first sentence of the U.S. Constitution is to "provide for the common defence [sic]."

> ▶ NOTE   The word *sic* (Latin for "as is") in brackets is used to show that a word in a quotation has been quoted exactly, even if it is incorrect or misspelled.

2. Use brackets when you need to translate a word or phrase.

> The conductor reminded the orchestra to play *sotto voce* [quietly] during the vocalist's solo.

3. Use brackets when you need to set off material that is already in parentheses.

> (Herman Melville [1819–1891] worked for nineteen years as a customs inspector for the City of New York.)

ACTIVITY 24-13 Brackets Practice

Directions: *Choose one of the reading selections from Chapter 18 and, on a separate sheet of paper, quote two sentences from it, adding a word or phrase of your own in brackets.* *Answers will vary.*

ACTIVITY 24-14 Practicing Punctuation

Directions: *In the paragraph below, choose the appropriate punctuation mark from the list below to fill in each of the blanks.*

, comma	**'** apostrophe	**__** dash
; semicolon	**" "** quotation mark	**/** slash
: colon	**( )** parentheses	**[ ]** brackets
? question mark	**-** hyphen	

Are you feeling stressed out ____?____ Are daily worries and obligations crowding out your *joie de vivre* ____[____ joy of living ____]____ ____?____ Perhaps you should consider meditating. If you are not familiar with meditation ____,____ you may be thinking ____,____ _____" Meditate ____?____ Me ____?____ No way ____!____ _____" Even if you _____'____ re curious about meditation ____,____ you may think that you just don _____'____ t have enough time for it. But the simple truth is that anyone can benefit from meditation ____;____ even a few minutes of meditating each day can ease the effects of stress and create an oasis of calm in your busy life.

There are many different ways to meditate _____,____ but all of them involve focusing your attention in a way that helps quiet your anxious thoughts. Beginners often choose among three methods of meditation _____:____ mindfulness meditation _____,____ mantra meditation _____,____ and guided meditation. In mindfulness meditation, you focus on being mindful _____—____ fully engaged in the present moment _____—____ rather than preoccupied with the past or future. Mantra meditation is based on silent repetition of a calming word _____,_____

thought _____,_____ or phrase. The goal of transcendental meditation

_____(_____TM _____)_____ _____,_____ a type of mantra meditation

_____,_____ is to achieve a state of restful alertness called _____" pure

awareness. _____" Guided meditation _____,_____ also called guided

imagery or visualization _____,_____ guides you to form mental images of

relaxing places or situations.

   In meditation _____,_____ nothing is forced _____;_____ you are gentle

to yourself. Rather than fighting distracting thoughts _____,_____ you

gently recall your attention to your point of focus. Thich Nhat Hahn

_____—_____ a well-known Buddhist monk _____—_____ describes this

process in his poem _____" To Meditate _____" _____:_____

_____" To meditate does not mean to fight with a problem._____/_____

To meditate means to observe. _____/_____ Your smile proves it. _____"

APPLYING CRITICAL THINKING

| PURPOSE | IDEAS | SUPPORT | ASSUMPTIONS BIASES | CONCLUSIONS | POINT OF VIEW | ANALYSIS |

When you are constructing sentences and making choices about punctuation, ask yourself the following critical thinking questions:

- How can punctuation make my meaning and **purpose** clearer?
- What are the best choices I can make for punctuation in this sentence? A period? An apostrophe? Quotation marks? A colon or semicolon?
- Am I sure I've used this punctuation correctly?

Then, *break down the particular parts* of the sentences using your **analysis** skills to make sure that you have constructed the sentence correctly.

LEARNING OBJECTIVES REVIEW

LO1 What is end punctuation, and how is it used? (See pp. 535–537)	There are three types of **end punctuation: Periods** (.) are used to end a statement or indicate an abbreviation; **question marks** (?) are used to indicate a direct question is being asked; and **exclamation points** (!) are used to provide emphasis or express strong emotion, excitement, or disbelief.
LO2 What are the main uses of apostrophes? (See pp. 537–545)	**Apostrophes** (') are used (1) to indicate the omission of one or more letters and numbers; (2) after nouns or indefinite nouns to show possession; and (3) to indicate plural numbers, titles, symbols, and the plurals of words used as an item.
LO3 What are the main uses of quotation marks? (See pp. 545–549)	**Quotation marks** (" ") are used to indicate (1) direct quotations from prose or poetry; (2) dialogue; (3) titles of stories, poems, articles, songs, and television episodes; and (4) words that are being defined or used ironically.
LO4 What are the six other punctuation marks discussed in this chapter, and how are they used? (See pp. 549–558)	The six other punctuation marks are **parentheses** (( )), used to set off information or citations; **hyphens** (-), used to combine or divide words; **dashes** (—), used to help information stand out or to add emphasis; **slashes** (/), used to indicate a choice between words or line breaks in quoted excerpts from poems; **ellipses** (. . .), used to indicate that words, phrases, or even complete sentences have been omitted; and **brackets** ([ ]), similar to parentheses, only square as opposed to curved, and also used to set off information.

For support in meeting this chapter's objectives, log in to www.mywritinglab.com and select **Final Punctuation, Apostrophes, and Quotation Marks.**

25 Spelling and Mechanics

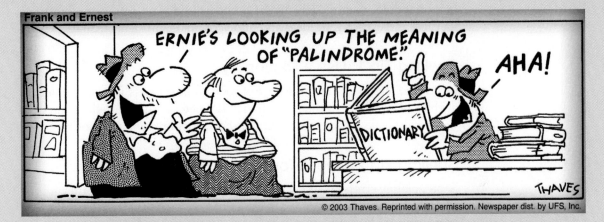

Frank and Ernest

ERNIE'S LOOKING UP THE MEANING OF "PALINDROME."

AHA!

DICTIONARY

THAVES

© 2003 Thaves. Reprinted with permission. Newspaper dist. by UFS, Inc.

LEARNING OBJECTIVES

In this chapter you will learn to

LO1 Improve your spelling

LO2 Distinguish between commonly confused words

LO3 Use a dictionary

LO4 Use a thesaurus

LO5 Capitalize correctly

LO6 Use numbers correctly

LO7 Use abbreviations correctly

THINKING CRITICALLY

Explain what this comic is about. What is funny about it? (Use a dictionary if necessary.)

_____

_____

_____

_____

_____

This chapter gives you tips on how to choose the right word and how to use a dictionary or thesaurus for help in spelling the word correctly. It will also provide tips for how to abbreviate words and how to use numbers and capitalization correctly in your writing.

LO 1 TEN TIPS FOR SPELLING IMPROVEMENT

Correct spelling is important in your writing. If you make spelling mistakes in a final draft, your readers may still understand what you mean, but they may lose respect for your ideas and find your arguments less credible.

Spelling Tip 1: Use a Dictionary

During the revision and editing stage of your writing process, use a dictionary to double-check any word that you are not 100 percent sure is spelled correctly. *When in doubt, look it up.*(See pages 583–84 for tips on using a dictionary.)

Spelling Tip 2: Check for Correct Pronunciation

Some spelling errors occur because words are not spelled the way they sound or are pronounced. Here are a few examples of words that are commonly mispronounced and, consequently, misspelled: *accidentally* (not "accidently"), *athletics* (not "atheletics"), *disastrous* (not "disasterous"), *February* (not "Febuary"), *government* (not "goverment"), *mathematics* (not "mathmatics"), *publicly* (not "publically"), *temperament* (not "temperment"), and *wondrous* (not "wonderous").

Spelling Tip 3: Do Not Confuse Homophones

Some spelling mistakes occur as the result of confusing two **homophones,** words that sound the same, or nearly the same, but have different meanings and sometimes are spelled differently. Here are some examples:

affect/effect   complement/compliment   break/brake   right/write/rite

See "Commonly Confused Words" later in this chapter (p. 567) for a more complete list of homophones, and use it to help you avoid spelling errors.

Spelling Tip 4: Use Rules for Making Words Plural

Some plural forms of words are commonly misspelled. Watch for them. Here are a few rules to help you spell plurals correctly:

1. **Most nouns are made plural by adding a final s:** *cat/cats, dog/dogs,* and *apple/apples*.
2. **Nouns ending with s, x, ch, or sh need an es to form the plural:** *boss/bosses, ax/axes, crutch/crutches,* and *dish/dishes*.

3. **If a noun ends in *y* with a consonant in front of it, then change the *y* to an *i* and add *es* to form the plural:** *beauty/beauties* and *city/cities*. However, always keep the *y* when you are making a family's name plural: *the Murphys*.

4. **If a noun ends in *y* with a vowel in front of it, then keep the *y* and add an *s* to form the plural:** *boy/boys* and *ray/rays*.

5. **If the noun ends in *o*, add either an *s* or an *es*.** It's best to check a dictionary if you're not sure whether the word you're spelling ends in *s* or *es*: *solo/solos, piano/pianos, hero/heroes*, and *tomato/tomatoes*.

6. **If a noun ends in *f* or an *f* followed by a silent *e*, then change the *f* to a *v* and add *es* (for words ending in f) or s (for words ending in f followed by a silent e):** *leaf/leaves, self/selves, wife/wives,* and *knife/knives*. However, for some words ending in *f*, the plural is formed just by adding *s*: *chief/chiefs* and *proof/proofs*. Use a dictionary if you are not sure which ending is correct.

7. **There are many irregular plurals in English, and most of them are well known from regular usage.** Here are a few examples: *child/children, man/men, woman/women, tooth/teeth, mouse/mice, deer/deer, moose/moose, sheep/sheep, datum/data,* and *medium/media*. When in doubt, consult a dictionary.

Spelling Tip 5: Distinguish Between *ei* and *ie*

Learn the correct spelling of words containing *ei* or *ie*. Pay attention to the previous letter and the sound of the word to figure out whether *i* goes before *e* or vice versa. There are some simple rules you can follow:

1. **When the sound you want to make is *ee* as in *see*, then use *i* before *e*:** *believe, chief, grief,* and *yield*.

2. **When the combination is preceded by a *c*, the spelling is almost always *ei*:** *receive, deceiving, ceiling,* and *conceit*.

3. **When the word has an *ay* sound, as in *bay* or *way*, then the spelling is almost always *ei*:** *neigh, neighborhood, weigh,* and *weight*.

> ▶ TIP   Remember the famous saying taught in grammar school: "*i* before *e* except after *c* or when it sounds like an *a* as in *weigh* or *neighborhood*."

Even this rule has exceptions: *caffeine* and *seize*, for example. So remember to consult the dictionary when you have any doubts.

Spelling Tip 6: Learn the Rules for Adding Suffixes and Prefixes

Adding Suffixes

1. **When adding the *-ing* suffix, in general drop the silent *e* at the end of a word:** *become/becoming, come/coming, hope/hoping, scare/scaring,* and *surprise/surprising.* However, there are a few exceptions, such as *dye/dyeing* and *shoe/shoeing.*

   When the word ends with a *y*, then retain the *y*: *cry/crying, enjoy/enjoying, lay/laying,* and *study/studying.*

2. **When adding the *-ible* suffix, drop the silent *e*:** *force/forcible.*

3. **When adding the *-able* suffix, sometimes you drop the silent *e* and sometimes you keep it, so check a dictionary if you are unsure:** *advise/advisable, argue/arguable, manage/manageable,* and *change/changeable.*

4. **A final silent *e* that is preceded by another vowel is always dropped when adding any suffix:** *argue/arguable* and *true/truly.*

5. **When a word ends with a *y* that is preceded by a consonant (and the suffix added is not *-ing*), then change the *y* to an *i* before adding the suffix:** *happy/happiest/happier, pity/pitiful,* and *ugly/uglier/ugliest.* However, when the *y* is preceded by a vowel, keep the *y* and add an *s*: *delay/delays, enjoy/enjoys, toy/toys,* and *valley/valleys.*

6. **When you are adding a suffix to a word that ends in a consonant, you often need to double the consonant first:** *cancel/cancelled, grip/gripping, grip/gripped, sad/saddest, occur/occurrence, refer/referred,* and *scar/scarring.* But there are exceptions (such as *deep/deepened, cancel/canceling,* and *crawl/crawler*), so check your dictionary when in doubt.

Adding Prefixes

Adding a prefix to a word does not typically require a change in the spelling of the base word, but if the base word starts with a vowel, a hyphen may be needed. Again, when in doubt, consult your dictionary.

appear/disappear	eminent/preeminent	operate/cooperate
educate/re-educate	spell/misspell	emphasize/re-emphasize
usual/unusual		

Spelling Tip 7: Keep a List of Your Errors

Keep a list of your own repeat offenders—frequently misspelled words—in a spelling log or journal. Just being aware of your most frequent errors will help you eradicate them.

Spelling Tip 8: Be Familiar with Some of the Most Commonly Misspelled Words

Consult the following list for some of the most commonly misspelled words in college essays: *believe, conceive, curiosity, definitely, disastrous, environment, forty, friend, interrupt, irrelevant, license, mathematics, medieval, necessary, occasion, precede, professor, receive, tendency, themselves, thorough, tomorrow,* and *weird.*

Spelling Tip 9: Be Aware of Common Letter Groupings

Be aware of common letter groupings, such as *qu, ei, ie, au, ch, ou, th, sh,* and *gh.* Notice patterns and remain aware of them: *quiet, quite, receive, diet, launch, those, should,* and *tough.* Use those patterns as spelling tips.

Spelling Tip 10: Use Spell-Check

Use the spell-check function on your computer, but be careful. See "The Rewards and Dangers of Spell-Check" on the next page.

ACTIVITY 25-1 Trying Out the Spelling Tips

Directions: *Correct the spelling errors in the following paragraph. Refer to the 10 spelling tips above for help. You should find 11 spelling errors in this paragraph.*

The ~~mideval~~ *medieval* legend of King Arthur has held enduring fascination for generations of readers. Though the legend was once ~~beleived~~ *believed* to be based on historical fact, most historians now consider the story of Arthur to be ~~largly~~ *largely*, if not totally, fictional. The roots of the legend reach back to a ninth-century manuscript penned by the Welsh monk Nennius, who ~~refered~~ *referred* to Arthur as a great warrior. But it was Geoffrey of Monmouth, a twelfth-century Welsh cleric, who first developed the story of King Arthur as the most beloved of ~~heros~~ *heroes*.

The popularity of Arthurian legend is not ~~surpriseing~~ *surprising*, given its dramatic elements, which include adventure, magic, romance, and chivalry. Some versions of the legend describe Arthur's ~~wonderous~~ *wondrous* childhood, presided over by Merlin the magician, as well as Arthur's adult reign as king. After pulling a magical sword from a stone, Arthur assumes the

government
throne and establishes his ~~goverment~~ at Camelot, rallying his knights of

the Round Table to defeat the invading Saxons. A love affair between

Arthur's beautiful wife, Queen Guinevere, and the valiant knight

disastrous effect
Lancelot has a ~~disasterous affect~~ on the kingdom, which descends into

Deceived
civil war. ~~Decieved~~ by his wicked nephew Mordred, Arthur is mortally

wounded in battle; placed on a boat, his body floats down the river to

the isle of Avalon, where three mysterious maidens await.

The Rewards and Dangers of Spell-Check

Spell-check is certainly a gift to writers, but it is not always right. Spell-check will always suggest a correctly spelled word, but it might not be the word you intended, and may even mean something completely different. Many spell-check programs automatically indicate a misspelled word as soon as you've finished typing it (indicated by a red underline). You can use your computer mouse to right-click the word, and spell-check will offer possible correct spellings. When in doubt, though, use your dictionary to double-check.

The Rewards of Spell-Check

1. **Spell-check can help you spot many of your spelling errors.**
2. **Spell-check is convenient,** requiring just the click of an icon. In some word processing programs or computer systems, spell-check operates automatically.
3. **Spell-check offers a fairly extensive collection of correctly spelled words.**

The Dangers of Spell-Check

1. **Spell-check may not point out words in your essay that are spelled correctly but not used correctly.** For example, spell-check would not identify these two errors:

> **Incorrect:** My brother suggested that we play Monopoly, but I get *board* with *bored* games.

These two italicized words should be reversed.

> **Corrected:** My brother suggested that we play Monopoly, but I get *bored* with *board* games.

2. **Spell-check may suggest words that are correctly spelled but do not fit the context of your sentence:**

> **Example:** I'm not sure whether to take a biology course, but I'm *definnately* taking physics.
>
> **Spell-check suggestion:** I'm not sure whether to take a biology course, but I'm *defiantly* taking physics.
>
> **Intended correct spelling:** I'm not sure whether to take a biology course, but I'm *definitely* taking physics.

In this example, the writer misspelled the word *definitely*, meaning "without a doubt," but spell-check incorrectly substituted the word *defiantly*, meaning "in a challenging or disobedient manner."

> ▶ NOTE   Be careful not to automatically click "Replace" for words suggested by spell-check. Look carefully and, when in doubt, use a dictionary to make sure you are choosing the right word based on context.

3. **Spell-check does not include every word you might use.** Sometimes spell-check improperly indicates that correctly spelled words (such as proper names with unusual spellings) are not spelled correctly. Check a dictionary or other resource, as needed.

   Students often rely too heavily on spell-check and run into trouble. Use it with caution: Apply critical thinking, and have a good dictionary handy as a backup.

LO 2 COMMONLY CONFUSED WORDS

Often, spelling mistakes result from writers confusing one word with another that sounds like it (a homonym). Some confusion also results from using the wrong form of a word, using slang, or misusing a word that is spelled correctly.

Here is a list of some of the commonly confused words that most often show up in student writing. Consult this list to make sure that you haven't used a word that sounds like the word you want but is incorrectly spelled.

a/an

Both of these words are indefinite articles (see p. 448 for more on articles). Use **a** when the word following it starts with a consonant sound, and use **an** when the word following it starts with a vowel sound (*a*, *e*, *i*, *o*, *u*) or a silent *h*. When the *h* is not silent, use **a.** Sometimes an initial vowel has a consonant sound; when this is the case, use **a.**

> Lil ate *an* apple from Hallie's fruit bowl, and Hallie thought it was *an* honor to provide her with a treat. Neither was interested in eating *a* banana.
>
> The author is currently writing *a* history of the Iditarod, *a* unique dog sled race that began in 1973.

a lot/allot/alot (misspelling)

a lot is two words (an article and a noun) that mean "a great deal" or "many." It is best to use them only in informal writing.

allot is a transitive verb meaning "to divide something up" or "to portion" or "to allow."

alot is a common misspelling of "a lot." It is not a word.

> Marge didn't want *a lot* from life: She just wanted what was *allotted* to her.

accept/except

accept is a transitive verb that means "to agree" or "to receive."

except is either a verb meaning "to exclude" or "leave out" or a preposition meaning "other than" or "apart from."

> Sandy decided to *accept* all the gifts from Sam *except* the new pet lizard.

adapt/adopt

adapt is a verb meaning "to adjust" or "to fit or make suitable."

adopt is a verb meaning "to make something or someone one's own."

> Martin had to *adapt* his viewpoint to match his wife's state of mind so they could *adopt* the newborn kittens.

advice/advise

advice is a noun meaning "a suggestion or recommendation."

advise is a verb meaning "to suggest, give a recommendation."

> I *advise* you not to listen to all of your parents' *advice* when you have a new baby.

affect/effect

affect is a verb meaning "influence" (think "a" for action).

effect is a noun meaning "a result" (think "e" for ending), or it can be a verb if used to mean "to bring about."

> Monique's strong academic goals *affected* her success and created long-lasting, positive career *effects*. The new rules *effected* a change in policy.

afraid/frightened

afraid is an adjective, usually followed by the preposition *of* or the word *that*; *afraid* means "filled with fear, regret, or concern."

> As a child, I was *afraid of* the dark.
>
> He was *afraid that* he would not have enough time to study.

frightened can be an adjective, meaning "filled with fear" or "alarmed"; *frightened* can also function as a verb, meaning "made afraid."

> The *frightened* dog hid under the bed.
>
> The loud crack of thunder *frightened* the dog.

aggravate/irritate

aggravate is a verb meaning "to make worse."

irritate is a verb meaning "to annoy, anger, inflame, or to chafe."

> Winston was *irritated* by the rash on his arm, but he *aggravated* the rash by constantly scratching it.

all ready/already

> **all ready** is an adjective phrase meaning "prepared."
> **already** is an adverb used in expressions of time.

> We were *all ready* to leave for the airport, but we realized that our ride had *already* left.

all right/alright (misspelling)

> **all right** is an adjective or an adverb, depending on the context, and means "agreeable, satisfactory."
> **alright** is a misspelling of "all right" and should not be used.

> Kelly was *all right* after she found out that many students confused words and their spellings.

allude/refer

> **allude** is a verb meaning "to call attention to something *indirectly*."
> **refer** is a verb meaning "to describe something in a particular way."

> In her speech, Susan didn't *refer* directly to the Bible, but she *alluded* to it.

allusion/illusion

> **allusion** is a noun meaning "an indirect or casual reference" or "a specific reference to a well-known artistic or literary work."
> **illusion** is a noun meaning "an unreal perception" or a "visual trick."

> Houdini often included *allusions* to famous lines from Shakespeare before he performed one of his famous *illusions*.

among/between

> **among** is a preposition used for referring to *more than two* people or things.
> **between** is a preposition used for referring to *two people or things*.

> The money was divided *among* the nieces and nephews, but the furniture was divided equally *between* the son and the daughter.

bad/badly

bad is an adjective used to describe a negative attribute of a person or a thing.

badly is an adverb used to describe a verb or action in a negative light. A descriptive linking verb—such as *look, seem, smell, sound,* or a form of the verb *to be* (am, is, were, etc.)—uses *bad* instead of *badly*, but other verbs require the adverb *badly*.

> It was a *bad* idea to act *badly* on the first day at my new job. I felt *bad* about complaining, but the office refrigerator smelled *bad*, and something needed to be done about it.

beside/besides

beside is a preposition meaning "by the side of" or "next to."

besides is an adverb meaning "in addition to."

> *Besides* waiting for him for over two hours, she had to stand *beside* a smelly dumpster.

board/bored

board is a noun meaning "a wooden plank."

bored is a verb meaning "a disengaged mindset, uninterested."

> Sharif was so *bored* by the lecture that he wanted to hit his head against a *board*.

brake/break

brake is a noun meaning "an instrument for stopping a vehicle" or a verb meaning "to stop a vehicle."

break is a noun meaning either "a rest period" or "a fractured bone or object," or a verb meaning "to separate something(s) into two or more pieces" or "to exceed a record or violate a rule."

> Mohammad decided to *brake* suddenly so he didn't damage the bumper on his car or *break* any of his bones.

can/may

can is a verb meaning "to be able to."

may is a verb meaning "permission to do" or "possible to do."

> Since Valery *can* eat anything he wants, he *may* ask you if he *may* have more cookies.

cannot/can not/can't

cannot is the correct spelling of the negative form of "can."

can not is a common misspelling of "cannot."

can't is a contraction—less formal—for "cannot."

> Marisela *cannot* believe her ears whenever her daughter Soroa says, "I *can't* do it, Mom."

capital/capitol

capital is a noun meaning "the location or seat of a government (states and countries)"; the word also can refer to wealth, an uppercase letter, or the death penalty (capital punishment).

capitol means the actual building where the state or country's government meets.

> When Jane visited an elementary school in Washington, D.C., she learned that students had taken a tour of the U.S. *Capitol* building and had also memorized all of the *capital* cities of the United States.

coarse/course

coarse is an adjective meaning "rough" either in texture or attitude.

course is a noun that can mean "a class," "a curriculum," "a direction for a journey," or "one part of a several-part meal."

> Lee didn't accept *coarse* language in his workshop. He did let people work with *coarse* material like sandpaper though.
>
> Ilona took a special *course* on French cooking and learned to make a full five-*course* meal. She now wants to continue on her *course* to receive a full culinary degree.

complement/compliment

complement is a noun meaning "something that completes or coordinates with something else" or a verb meaning "to complete."

compliment is a noun meaning "a positive statement about something or someone" or a verb meaning "to give a positive statement about something or someone."

> Craig gave Joan a *compliment* about the way her aqua-colored blouse *complemented* her eyes.

conscious/consciousness/conscience/conscientious

conscious is an adjective meaning "able to feel, think, or be aware."

consciousness is the noun form meaning "awareness" or "knowledge."

conscience is a noun meaning "a person's sense of right or wrong, morals."

conscientious is the adjective form of "conscience" used to describe a person.

> Lily had a guilty *conscience* about what she had done, but Shima wasn't even *conscious* of her inappropriate behavior.
>
> Mikhail's acute *consciousness* allowed for him to become a more *conscientious* student.

could have/could've/could of

could have is the helping verb *could*, meaning either "might" or "having the ability to," plus the main verb *have*.

could've is the correct contraction form of "could have"—use in informal writing only.

could of is a misuse/misspelling of "could have"—do not use.

> Kate decided her students needed a reminder not to use *could of* in their papers instead of *could have*. After class, Marta declared, "I *could've* done without that lesson!"

desert/dessert

desert can be a noun meaning "a dry, arid place, usually with sand and little vegetation"; as a verb, desert means "to leave or abandon."

dessert is a noun meaning "the last course in a meal, usually sweet."

The Mojave *Desert* is probably the most prominently featured *desert* in Hollywood movies. Often, the hero is *deserted*—wounded and horseless—in the *desert* by the enemy.

Bev remembered the memory trick for how to spell *dessert:* It's the one you want two helpings of after dinner, so remember to include *s* twice when you spell it.

device/devise

device is a noun that means "an object, usually high-tech."

devise is a verb meaning "to create a plan or think up something."

The spy *devised* a way to escape that involved creating a *device* that would blow up the lock on his cell door.

effect/affect (see affect/effect)

either/neither

either can be an adjective or pronoun meaning "one of two people, things, or concepts"; *either* can also be an adverb introducing "the first of two alternatives."

neither is the negative version of "either": "not one of . . . "

Nguyen planned to order *either* a taco or a burrito for lunch but later decided to have *neither*, asking instead for a hamburger.

▶ NOTE   If more than two things or people are involved, use *any* instead of *either*: Nguyen wasn't sure she liked *any* of the choices on the menu.

except/accept (see accept/except)

explicit/implicit

explicit is an adjective meaning "directly expressed."

implicit is an adjective meaning "implied but not directly expressed."

The rules of board games are usually *explicit,* but the rules of life tend to be *implicit.*

farther/further

farther is an adjective, adverb, or noun meaning "more distance."

further is an adjective or noun meaning "more."

> Francisca needed *further* proof that walking improves heart health before she would commit to walking a little bit *farther* every day.

fewer/less

fewer is an adjective or noun meaning "less" and is used only for things that can be counted.

less is an adjective or noun that refers to an "amount" or "specific value or degree." It is used with nouns that cannot be counted.

> To diet successfully, it helps to consume *fewer* calories and take in *less* fat.

good/well

good can be an adjective that is used to describe a person or thing in a positive way; *good* can also be a noun meaning "positive."

well is an adverb, noun, or adjective used to describe positive attributes. When used to describe a person, "well" focuses on health or state of being and feelings, while "good" focuses on character or personality.

> Sibyl is a *good* person. She is feeling *well* now, after her long bout with pneumonia. She can dance almost as *well* as she used to before her illness.

hanged/hung

Both *hanged* and *hung* are past tense forms of *hang*.

Use **hanged** only as a past tense of the verb *hang* when referring to an execution.

Use **hung** for all other past tense forms of "hang."

> In the novel, the prisoner was *hanged* and, afterwards, a sign was *hung* over the gallows that stated his crimes.

hear/here

> **hear** is a verb meaning the physiological act of *hearing*.
>
> **here** is a noun that indicates a physical or symbolic place.

> Eduardo, did you *hear* that loud noise? I think it is coming from behind *here*.

> ▶ TIP   Remember that the word *hear* has the word *ear* in it.

hole/whole

> **hole** is a noun that means "an opening."
>
> **whole** is a noun or an adjective that means "complete."

> Pedro, there must be a *hole* in Napoleon's stomach because I can't believe he ate the *whole* pie.

imply/infer

> **imply** is a verb meaning "to suggest a secondary meaning, to suggest indirectly."
>
> **infer** is a verb meaning "to deduce, or to draw a conclusion."

> I didn't mean to *imply* that he was stingy, but I did *infer* from his comments that he won't be joining us on the trip.

its/it's

> **its** is a possessive pronoun indicating ownership.
>
> **it's** is a contraction for the words "it is."

> *It's* a fact that that dog loves *its* bone.

lay/lie

> **lay** is a transitive verb meaning "to put or place." It is followed by a direct object. *Lay* is the present-tense form of the verb. *Laid* is the past tense form and the past participle.
>
> **lie** can be a noun meaning "false statement," but it also can be an intransitive verb meaning "to recline or rest." *Lie* is the present tense form of the verb. *Lay* is the past tense form, and *lain* is the past participle.

The robber *had laid* his gun on the floor of the car, but he grabbed the gun out of the car when the police officer approached. The officer ordered the robber to *lay* down the gun and *lie* on the ground with his hands behind his back. He warned him not to *lie* about the stolen goods in his car.

lead/led

lead has two pronunciations and two meanings: (1) pronounced *led*, it is a noun meaning a "type of metal" and (2) pronounced *leed*, it is a noun or verb meaning to "show the way" or "to make follow."

led (rhymes with *bed*) is a verb and is the past tense form of definition (2) of *lead*, above.

David asked Traci to *lead* the way to the kitchen so he could inspect the *lead* pipes, so Traci *led* him there.

loose/lose

loose (pronounced *loohs*, with a final s sound) is a noun or adjective meaning "not attached," "roomy, unbinding," or "not exact."

lose (pronounced *loohz*, with a final z sound) is a verb meaning "to fail" or "to not be able to keep or to find something."

We knew we would *lose* the match since Iliana managed to *lose* her lucky socks and her confidence the day before the match.

She must have a *loose* interpretation of sports fashion to wear such *loose* shorts.

passed/past

passed is a past tense verb meaning "to go by" or "to have achieved," such as a goal or test.

past is a noun or adjective used with time meaning "in a previous time, not current."

Sophia *passed* Brad on the way to take her last test. Later, she told him that she had *passed* the exam. Now her *past* fears related to passing the test have been laid to rest.

precede/proceed

precede is a verb or adjective meaning "something that comes before."
proceed is a noun or a verb meaning "to go forward" (action).

> The winter *precedes* the spring, but when spring arrives, we will *proceed* with wearing lighter clothing.

principal/principle

principal is a noun meaning "the head position of a school" or an adjective meaning "first, most important."
principle is a noun meaning "a basic truth, moral law, or assumption."

> Andy always acts on the *principles* he learned from his parents. Because of his good moral sense, he would make a great *principal* for my son's elementary school.

▶ TIP   The princi*pal* is the one with whom you hope to be "pals."

quiet/quit/quite

quiet is a noun, verb, adjective, or adverb meaning "silent, or with little or no sound."
quit is a verb meaning "to stop or give up."
quite is an adverb meaning "very, entirely, completely."

> The crowd suddenly went *quiet* as the band walked onstage. Saito *quit* talking to Dolly and turned toward the stage, and it was all *quite* magical.

raise/rise

raise is a noun or a verb. The noun *raise* means "an increase in salary." The transitive verb *raise* means "to move or lift something up to a higher position."
rise is a noun meaning "an increase," and it is an intransitive verb meaning "to go (or come) up."

> After Val decided to *raise* her expectations and work her hardest, she finally got her *raise*.
>
> We *rise* at sunrise and hope not to see another *rise* in gas prices.

right/rite/write

right is a noun meaning "a moral," "guaranteed condition," or "the opposite of left"; it can also be an adjective meaning "appropriate" or "correct"; it can even be a verb meaning "to make something correct, fix."

rite is a noun for a "ritual or ceremonial act, literal or symbolic."

write is a verb meaning "the creation of words or symbols on a surface."

> Lisa knew she had the *right* to make the *right* choice for her own life and to set things *right* with Sam, so she made a sharp *right* turn onto back streets to go talk with him yet again.
>
> In California, learning to surf is a *rite* of passage for many teens.
>
> The textbook title *The Write Stuff* is a pun on the idea of being "right" when one *writes* an essay.

than/then

than is a conjunction used for comparison of two or more unequal items.

then is an adverb related to a particular period in time or a conjunction meaning "therefore."

> My three-year-old daughter first asked if I was older *than* Daddy; *then* she asked if I was older *than* Grandma.

that/which/who

See the discussions of restrictive versus nonrestrictive clauses on p. 518 and pronouns on p. 429 for more help on these.

that can function as a relative pronoun that introduces a restrictive clause—a clause that limits or restricts the meaning of the words that are modified. The clause is essential to the meaning of the sentence.

> Did you try the new restaurant *that* Will told us about?

which can function as a relative pronoun that introduces a nonrestrictive clause, a clause that is not essential to the meaning of the sentence.

> Washington, D.C., *which* is lovely in the fall, is not really a state or a city: It's a district.

who is a relative pronoun used to refer to a person; *who* is used to convey both essential (restrictive) and nonessential (nonrestrictive) information.

> **Restrictive:** Maria is the one *who* knows how to make perfect Mexican wedding cookies from scratch.
>
> **Nonrestrictive:** Maria, *who* grew up in Mexico, knows how to make perfect Mexican wedding cookies from scratch.

their/there/they're

their is a plural possessive pronoun.

there is a noun, an adverb, or an impersonal pronoun. Use it to indicate a place or direction and as a pronoun to start sentences.

they're is a contraction for the words "they are."

> Did Anna and Liz finish *their* paperwork so we can go to lunch?
>
> Do you want to go *there* for lunch? *There* is an excellent lunch menu.
>
> Cindy and Allen are my cousins; *they're* the ones who live in Virginia.

threw/through/thru

threw is the past tense form of the verb "throw."

through is a preposition indicating passage or movement, often from one side to another; and it is also an adverb meaning "finished" or "done."

thru is a common misspelling of "through," and it should not be used in formal writing.

> Heather *threw* the pen to Abby.
>
> Sothera is *through* with love since she has gone *through* the rocky passage of heartbreak too many times.

to/too/two

to is a preposition used to indicate direction or movement.

too is an adverb meaning "also," "in addition," or "very."

two is a noun or adjective used to indicate the number that comes after one and before three.

> After Emma and Dominic moved *to* Arizona, Ann and Dale moved there, *too*. Carlene and John were *too* happy to complain about them all coming at once.

> Becky was lucky *to* get *two* weeks of vacation during the busiest season ever.

waist/waste

waist is a noun meaning the middle part of a person's body.

waste can function as a noun or a verb. The noun can refer to a failure to use something wisely; the verb can mean "to squander something."

> Juliette, even though she has had two children, has a tiny *waist*.
>
> It is a *waste* of time to watch television.
>
> I ordered the gift online because I didn't want to *waste* my energy by checking a bunch of different stores.

weather/whether

weather is a noun used to indicate climate conditions.

whether is a conjunctive adverb, similar to "if," used in clauses to indicate conditions.

> The *weather* conditions for the Labor Day weekend in Lake Chelan were favorable.
>
> *Whether* he liked it or not, Josh's parents made him stick with his piano lessons.

were/we're/where

were is a past tense form of the verb *to be* (the plural form of *was*).

we're is a contraction for the words "we are" or "we were."

where is a noun indicating a direction or a place.

> The kindergarteners *were* eager for snack time.
>
> *We're* ready to serve the milk and cookies now.
>
> *Where* do you want us to set the cookies?
>
> Home is *where* the heart is.

who/whom

Both *who* and *whom* are used to refer to people. Use **who** as the subject of a sentence (subjective case) and **whom** as the object (objective case).

To test whether **who** or **whom** should begin a question, try answering the question by using a personal pronoun.

> *Who* was William Shakespeare? [*He* was a playwright.]

The pronoun *he* is in the subjective case, so *who* is correct.

> *Whom* did you invite to the party? [I invited *him*.]

The pronoun *him* is in the objective case, so *whom* is correct.

> ▶ TIP   Remember the *m* in *whom* like the *m* in *him*.

who's/whose

who's is a contraction for "who is" or "who has," and **whose** is used to indicate possession.

> *Who's* ready to read *Hamlet? Whose* book is this?

would have/would of (misuse)

would have is the correct spelling for this verb tense phrase and **would of** is an incorrect usage of the verb tense.

> Caroline *would have* been sad if she had missed the concert.

your/you're

your is a second-person possessive pronoun.
you're is the contraction for the words "you are."

> Did you take *your* medicine yet?
> *You're* not looking too well.
> *You're* welcome.

ACTIVITY 25-2   Commonly Confused Words

Directions: *Underline the correct word for each bracketed choice below.*

A French term meaning "fools the eye," trompe l'oeil (pronounced tromp loy) [alludes, refers] to a style of art that produces an [effect, affect] of almost photographic realism. The trompe l'oeil artist "tricks" viewers into confusing art and reality by creating optical [illusions, allusions] that make two-dimensional objects appear three-dimensional.

The trompe l'oeil style dates back [too, to] ancient times. According to a Roman historian, [there, they're] was a competition [between, among] two Greek artists in 400 BCE to see who could create the most realistic painting. Clusters of grapes depicted in the first artist's painting [where, were] so realistic that birds tried to peck at them. The second artist's painting was reportedly hidden behind some closed curtains, but an observer [who, which] tried to pull them back discovered they were only a painted image.

As the Roman Empire declined, [fewer, less] trompe l'oeil works were produced, but the style was revived periodically [through, threw] the centuries that followed. During the Renaissance, the discovery of mathematical perspective—an artistic technique used to suggest space and depth—[complimented, complemented] trompe l'oeil techniques and [lead, led] to renewed interest in the genre. Painters [then, than] began designing murals for windowless areas in churches; the murals often depicted open archways that appeared to offer expansive views of the outdoors.

In the eighteenth and nineteenth centuries, American artists [further, farther] [adopted, adapted] the genre of trompe l'oeil. According to one account, George Washington once [past, passed] a staircase on which two boys appeared to be standing, so Washington [proceeded, preceded] to greet the boys. Moments later he was [quiet, quite] startled to realize the boys were part of a life-size trompe l'oeil painting that the artist had [hanged, hung] inside [a, an] actual doorframe. In the nineteenth century, perhaps the most popular trompe l'oeil artist in the United States was William Harnett, [who's, whose] still-life paintings included objects such as newspapers, pipes, guns, and musical instruments.

LO3 TIPS FOR USING A DICTIONARY

A **dictionary** is a reference tool that gives the pronunciation and definitions of words. It is a good idea to buy a comprehensive college dictionary and/or to use an online version. Be sure that your dictionary is no more than five years old and that it features American spellings and usage. There are also specialized dictionaries available in hard copy and online for subjects such as biology, history, or psychology, as well as foreign language dictionaries that give a word in one language and then the word in another language (be careful not to depend on these for accurate translations).

Wait until you are ready to revise and edit your paper to use a dictionary. (If you keep stopping to look up words, you may lose your train of thought.) Once you have written your first full draft, go back and use a dictionary to check that the words you are using are appropriate in terms of their denotations (exact meanings) and connotations (associated meanings), spelling, tone and style, and context.

Anatomy of a Dictionary Entry

A dictionary entry has several parts: the word's pronunciation, part(s) of speech, meaning(s), origin(s) (etymology), related forms, synonyms, and antonyms. Here is an example of a typical dictionary entry from *dictionary .com* for the word *formidable*:

for·mi·da·ble [fawr-mi-*duh-buhl*]
–adjective
1. causing fear, apprehension, or dread: *a formidable opponent.*
2. of discouraging or awesome strength, size, difficulty, etc.; intimidating: *a formidable problem.*
3. arousing feelings of awe or admiration because of grandeur, strength, etc.
4. of great strength; forceful; powerful: *formidable opposition to the proposal.*

Origin:
1400–50; late ME < F < L *formīdābilis* causing fear, equiv. to *formīd-* (s. of *formīdāre* to fear) + *-ābilis* -able

—Related forms
for·mi·da·ble·ness, for·mi·da·bil·i·ty, *noun*
for·mi·da·bly, *adverb*
non·for·mi·da·bil·i·ty, *noun*

—Can be confused: formative, **formidable.**

—Synonyms
1. dreadful, appalling, threatening, menacing, fearful, frightful, horrible.

—Antonyms
1. pleasant.

LO4 TIPS FOR USING A THESAURUS

If you find that you have used certain words too often in an essay or that you need a better, more precise, or just more interesting word than the one you have used, a thesaurus can be a great help. A **thesaurus** provides **synonyms** (words that have very similar meanings) and sometimes **antonyms** (words that have opposite meanings) for words. You can buy a hard copy or use an online version.

When using a thesaurus, you have to be particularly careful to check the connotations of a word to make sure you have used the *best* word for your intended meaning. It's a good idea to use a dictionary in tandem with a thesaurus to check the synonyms listed and make sure the one you choose has the right meaning.

Anatomy of a Thesaurus Entry

A thesaurus entry lists the word in bold, names its part of speech, and then lists its synonyms and sometimes its antonyms. Here is an example of a typical thesaurus entry:

Main Entry:	formidable
Part of Speech:	*adjective*
Definition:	horrible, terrifying
Synonyms:	appalling, awful, dangerous, daunting, dire, dismaying, dreadful, fearful, fierce, frightful, horrific, imposing, impregnable, intimidating, menacing, redoubtable, shocking, terrible, terrific, threatening

Sometimes a thesaurus will list words that are not clear synonyms or antonyms of the target word but have related or contrasting meanings. If you are not sure how to interpret an entry, make sure to check the key provided in the thesaurus. A thesaurus can come in very handy on those days when you are writing your essay draft and several of the same words come up again and again. For instance, consider the following synonyms for the word *said:*

acknowledged	advocated	answered
added	affirmed	argued
addressed	agreed	asserted
admitted	alleged	assured
advised	announced	attested

avowed	indicated	related
began	inferred	repeated
called	implied	replied
claimed	instructed	responded
commented	lectured	resumed
complained	maintained	retorted
confided	mentioned	returned
cried	moaned	reveal
debated	mumbled	snapped
decided	murmured	sneered
declared	muttered	solicited
denounced	narrated	specified
described	noted	spoke
dictated	objected	stated
directed	observed	stressed
disclosed	petitioned	suggested
divulged	pleaded	thought
droned	pled	threatened
elaborated	pointed out	told
emphasized	predicted	urged
entreated	proclaimed	uttered
exclaimed	professed	vowed
explained	ranted	whispered
exposed	reassured	yelled
expressed	refuted	

Each of these words imparts a particular connotation for *how* a person *said* something.

ACTIVITY 25-3   Using Synonyms

Directions: *Fill in each blank using the most appropriate synonym for said listed above.* Answers will vary. Sample answers provided.

1. "That apartment is the best one we've seen so far!" __exclaimed__ Celia.

2. "But it's also more expensive than the others," __complained__ Emily.

3. "That's true," __acknowledged__ Keisha, "but it's within walking distance of campus, so we'd save on transportation costs."

4. "Before we decide, let's just check out a few more apartments,"
   ___pleaded___ Emily. "Maybe we'll find one that's just as good for less money."

5. "If we wait too long to make up our minds, someone else is sure to snap up that apartment," ___predicted___ Celia.

ACTIVITY 25-4 Using a Dictionary and Thesaurus in Combination

Directions: *Use a thesaurus to look for an alternative word for each of the words listed below. Then, use a dictionary to provide the meaning for the new word you chose. Write your findings on a separate sheet of paper.* Answers will vary.

1. association
2. consume
3. deny
4. essential

5. harmony
6. light
7. power
8. recover

9. sassy
10. treacherous

LO 5 CAPITALIZATION

Capital letters are used for the first word of a sentence and proper nouns (words that describe a specific person, place, or thing). Words that describe a general object or category are not capitalized. Here are some specific rules for when to capitalize.

Cross Reference

For a review of nouns, see p. 428.

Rules for Correct Capitalization

1. **Capitalize the first word of a sentence and the first word of a sentence used in a direct quotation.**

   > In *The Waste Land*, T. S. Eliot described April as the "cruelest month."
   >
   > Edna St. Vincent Millay said, "April comes like an idiot, babbling and strewing flowers."

   ■ *Do not capitalize* the first word of the second part of an interrupted or continuing quotation.

   > "April," said Edna St. Vincent Millay, "comes like an idiot, babbling and strewing flowers."

2. Capitalize the pronoun *I* and the names of specific people.

> Here are some famous people I'd love to meet: Toni Morrison, Jimmy Page, Mae C. Jemison, Bill Gates, Sandra Day O'Connor, and Stephen Hawking.

3. Capitalize the names of nationalities, cultural or ethnic groups, and languages.

> Cambodian, Italian, Canadian, Mexican American, Nigerian, Hebrew, Asian American, Swahili, Japanese, Portuguese, African American, Greek, Russian

If a prefix comes in front of a word that is usually capitalized, keep the formal name capitalized: *un-American, anti-American,* and so on.

4. Capitalize formal and informal titles for specific persons or positions.

> Chancellor Merkel, Uncle Robert, Senator Feinstein, United Nations Secretary-General Ban Ki-moon

- Do *not capitalize* a title if it follows a proper name—Angela Merkel, chancellor; Robert, my uncle; Dianne Feinstein, senator.
- *Do not capitalize* nouns that refer to family relationships—for example, mother, father, mom, dad, grandfather, grandmother, aunt, and uncle—unless they are being used as proper names:

> My *grandfather* was a real character. He used to play tricks on *Grandmother* to make her laugh. My *father* was their only child. I love to hear *Dad* tell stories about his childhood. I also love the story of how my mom and dad met. He says it was love at first sight, but *Mom* said it took awhile. My *mother's* sister, *Aunt Rose,* claims my *mother* had a crush on my *father* before he even noticed her. My *uncle,* Ed, says it took months for *Dad* to get up his courage to ask her out.

5. **Capitalize names of specific places (including continents, countries, regions, states, counties, cities, parks, and streets).**

> Antarctica, Europe, Ghana, Brazil, the Middle East, New England, North Dakota, Oregon, Boone County, Hong Kong, Seville, Tampa, Forest Park, Hollywood Boulevard, Bourbon Street

6. **Capitalize the names of days, months, and holidays.**

> Tuesday, August, Thanksgiving, Valentine's Day, Memorial Day, Mother's Day, Veterans Day, Presidents Day

- In general, *do not* capitalize the seasons (summer, winter, spring, and fall). However, if they are part of a specific event or title, they are capitalized: *Spring Fling, Winter Festival,* and so on.

7. **Capitalize the names of religions, religious titles used for specific individuals, holy texts, and holy days.**

> Buddhism/Buddhists, Christianity/Christians, Hinduism/Hindus, Islam/Muslims, Judaism/Jews, Taoism/Taoists, the Dalai Lama, Father Morris, Reverend Adams, Rabbi Hirshfeld, Tipitaka, Holy Bible, New Testament, Rig Veda, Qur'an, Talmud, Tao-te-Ching, Easter, Ramadan, Yom Kippur

8. **Capitalize the names of specific organizations (including businesses, government institutions, political groups, and academic or cultural institutions).**

> General Motors, Whole Foods, Cub Scouts, Boys and Girls Clubs of America, National Endowment for the Humanities (NEH), Democratic Party, Republican Party, Amnesty International, Parent Teacher Association (PTA), Association of Higher Education, Library of Congress

Capitalize abbreviations (or acronyms) for companies, institutions, and organizations: NBC, AARP, NATO, FDA, UPS, and so on (see "Abbreviations" later in this section for more examples).

9. **Capitalize the names of historical periods, events, or historical documents and holy texts.**

> Iron Age, Italian Renaissance, Industrial Revolution, Age of Enlightenment, World War I, Cold War, Battle of Waterloo, Reformation, Fall of Constantinople, Norman Invasion, Treaty of Versailles, New Deal, Code of Hammurabi, Emancipation Proclamation, Gutenberg Bible, Bill of Rights

- Do not capitalize *centuries:* the *seventeenth century,* etc.
- *Lord* and *God* are usually capitalized and so are pronouns that go with particular supreme beings: the *Lord* and *His* teachings, the *Goddess* and *Her* ways.

10. **Capitalize the names of monuments, buildings, and famous objects.**

> Eiffel Tower, St. Louis Arch, Stonehenge, Empire State Building, Taj Mahal, Alhambra, Rockbridge High School, Crown Jewels

- *High school, middle school,* and *elementary school* are not capitalized if they are not part of the name of a specific school:

> Next year my brother will be a senior at Rockbridge *High School.* The year after next, he will graduate from *high school.*

11. **Capitalize the names of specific brands or trademarks.**

> Levi's, Mercedes-Benz, Dunkin' Donuts, Betty Crocker, Black & Decker, Disneyland, Apple Inc., Google

12. **Capitalize the titles of books, magazines, articles, stories, poems, plays, films, TV shows, albums, CDs, songs, and works of art.**

In titles, capitalize the first and last word and all significant words in between except articles (*the, a,* and *an*) and prepositions (*of, in, on,* and so on):

> *The Brief Wondrous Life of Oscar Wao, US Weekly,* "Three Quick and Easy Meals," "The Tell-Tale Heart," "The Road Not Taken," *Streetcar Named Desire, Avatar, Survivor, Led Zeppelin IV,* "We Are the World," *The Scream*

ACTIVITY 25-5   Capitalization Practice, Part I

Directions: *Underline the letters in the following paragraph that should be capitalized. Refer to the rules above for help.*

President James Madison was not a physically imposing person; standing only 5'4" and weighing only 100 pounds. Yet he was arguably a giant in american history, taking the lead role in writing the U.S. constitution and the bill of rights.

Born in 1751, Madison grew up at montpelier, his father's plantation in orange county, virginia. Madison quickly proved himself an excellent student and a capable leader in the years leading up to the american revolution. Attending the college of new jersey, which later became princeton university, he studied history, government, and law. He then embarked on a career of public service, helping draft the virginia constitution and serving in the continental congress. At the constitutional convention, he distinguished himself as an eloquent and persuasive debater. Later in his career, he served as secretary of state in Thomas Jefferson's administration. He was the first to use the term republican party and is considered a co-founder of the Jeffersonian-republican party.

ACTIVITY 25-6   Capitalization Practice, Part II

Directions: *Correct the capitalization errors in the following sentences. Underline the error(s) in each sentence, and then write the correct form(s) in the space provided. If the sentence has no capitalization errors, write "Correct."*

1. My family lives in New York city, and it's always fun to go sightseeing with visitors.

   City

2. When I was a senior in high school, my family hosted an exchange student from France.

   Correct

3. Therese spoke fluent English, which was fortunate, because I was just learning to speak french.

   French

4. Therese arrived shortly before labor day and stayed until the start of the Winter break.

   Labor Day, winter

5. She attended classes with me at Martin Luther King high school.

High School

6. Sometimes we would walk through central park and watch children jumping in piles of Autumn leaves.

Central Park, autumn

7. At the Guggenheim museum, Therese admired the painting *woman with yellow hair* by Pablo Picasso.

Museum, Woman with Yellow Hair

8. One weekend mom drove us through the catskill mountains.

Mom, Catskill Mountains

9. Another weekend my Grandparents took us to see *phantom of the opera,* a broadway musical.

grandparents, Phantom of the Opera, Broadway

10. Therese enjoyed all of our sightseeing, but she said that her favorite experience was seeing the statue of liberty.

Statue of Liberty

LO 6 NUMBERS

Rules for using the correct format for numbers vary according to context. The following standards will work for most academic writing.

1. **Spell out numbers zero through ten and numbers that can be written using one or two words.**

> We had to choose among ten different kinds of cookies and eight kinds of cake.
>
> So far, twelve hundred citizens have signed the petition.

▶ NOTE   For business or technical writing, use numbers for all numerals above ten.

2. **Spell out numbers that begin a sentence, no matter how large the number.**

If possible, however, revise the sentence so you don't need to start with a number. Make sure to use commas correctly in numbers over 1,000.

> Twenty-seven hundred fans clapped and cheered loudly for the band. When the band came onstage, 2,700 fans clapped and cheered loudly.

3. For extremely large numbers, use a combination of figures and words.

> The national debt now stands at $12.4 trillion.

However, if it is not a round number, you'll have to use all figures.

> If the national debt were divided equally among all U.S. citizens, each person's share would be $40,315.65.

4. Use figures for dates, years, and times.

> July 6, 2002   11:25 AM

5. Use figures in addresses.

> The White House, 1600 Pennsylvania Avenue NW, Washington, D.C. 20500

6. Use figures for exact measurements and specific identifications.

> The football player is 6'5" tall and weighs 265 pounds.
>
> Room 274, Interstate 91, Channel 22, Chapter 12, page 74, Act 3, Scene 2, 1:3, 65% (or 65 percent), 3.7 GPA, 30°, $32.35, 40 hours, 1/3, 1,395

ACTIVITY 25-7   **Numbers Practice**

Directions: *Correct the errors in numbers usage in the following sentences. Underline the error(s) in each sentence, and then write the correct form(s) in the space provided. If the sentence has no errors, write "correct."*

1. Last year I saw the DVD of *Shakespeare in Love*, a film that was released nearly <u>15</u> years ago.

fifteen

2. The film was an enormously popular romantic comedy that reportedly grossed about <u>one hundred million dollars</u>.

   $100 million

3. Though the film is fictional, it contains many allusions to the <u>37</u> plays written by Shakespeare.

   thirty-seven

4. After watching the film, I decided to sign up for a lecture class on Shakespeare; it met <u>3</u> times a week at <u>ten o'clock</u> for <u>45</u> minutes in Room <u>one sixty-five</u> of the Humanities Building.

   three, 10:00, forty-five, 165

5. <u>326</u> students enrolled for the course.

   Three hundred and twenty-six

6. Shakespeare was only eighteen years old when he married Anne Hathaway, but she was twenty-six.

   Correct

7. In Shakespeare's lifetime an epidemic called the Black Death swept through England, killing over <u>33,000</u> people in London during the outbreak of 1603.

   thirty-three thousand

8. The professor suggested that students watch the 1968 film adaptation of *Romeo and Juliet*, which was being shown on Channel <u>fifty-seven</u>.

   57

9. The film was great, especially the balcony scene, which takes place in Act <u>two</u>, Scene <u>two</u> of the play.

   2, 2

10. I really enjoyed the course, and I even got an A, which raised my GPA to <u>three point two</u>.

    3.2

LO 7 ABBREVIATIONS

Although abbreviations are common in casual writing, they are less acceptable in academic writing. These are the most commonly accepted categories of abbreviations.

1. Titles or Academic Degrees

- **Mr./Mrs./Ms.** These abbreviations are acceptable when used as titles before a person's last name.

- **Academic titles/degrees.** Abbreviated academic titles and/or degrees are used *after* a person's name:

> B.A. (Bachelor of Arts), M.A. (Master of Arts), B.S. (Bachelor of Science), M.F.A. (Master of Fine Arts), Ph.D. (Doctor of Philosophy), R.N. (Registered Nurse), M.D. (Doctor of Medicine), C.P.A (Certified Public Accountant)
>
> W. E. B. DuBois, Ph.D.; Shan Shan Sheng, M.F.A.; Christiaan Barnard, M.D.

> ▶ NOTE   The title *Professor* is usually spelled out: Professor George C. Gross.

- **Government/military/religious titles.** Abbreviate governmental, military, and religious titles when they are used *in front* of someone's complete name. If only a person's last name is given, then use his or her full title.

> Sen. Daniel Inoue of Hawaii has served eight terms in the U.S. Senate. Senator Inoue serves as Chairman of the U.S. Senate Committee on Appropriations.
>
> Rev. Martin Luther King, Jr. said: "Nonviolence is a powerful and just weapon." Reverend King went on to describe nonviolence as "a sword that heals."

2. Countries, States, or Cities

In addresses, abbreviate the state and country. In sentences, spell out the names of cities and states.

> Johnson Space Center, 2101 NASA Parkway, Houston, TX 77058 U.S.A. Astronauts are trained at the Johnson Space Center in Houston, Texas.

> ▶ NOTE   Abbreviate United States only when used in an address or used as an adjective.

> In the United States, astronauts are trained at the Johnson Space Center.

> NASA, the National Aeronautics and Space Administration, manages the U.S. Space Program.

3. Common Acronyms

Acronyms are composed of the first letter of each word of a name that includes two or more words. Acronyms designating agencies, businesses, or institutions are commonly used in writing and speech. These types of acronyms do not require periods between the letters.

> AAA (American Automobile Association), AP (Associated Press), ASAP (as soon as possible), CEO (Chief Executive Officer), CIA (Central Intelligence Agency), CPR (cardiopulmonary resuscitation), DOD (Department of Defense), EST (Eastern Standard Time), FDA (Federal Drug Administration)

Use these abbreviations when using the following terms with **numbers:**

> A.M. or a.m. (ante meridian), P.M. or p.m. (post meridian), and MPH or mph (miles per hour).

4. Latin Terms

The following Latin terms are abbreviated only when they appear inside parentheses.

> c. or ca. (approximately), cf. (compare), e.g. (for example), etc. (and so forth), et al. (and all others), i.e. (that is), re (concerning), and vs. or v. (versus)
>
> Many items are now on sale (clothes, linens, kitchenware, etc.)

In the main body of a sentence, use complete words and/or their English equivalents.

> Many items are on sale now: clothes, linens, kitchenware, furniture, and more.

5. Documentation Formats Such as MLA or APA

The following abbreviations are commonly used in documenting sources using MLA, APA, or other styles. (See Chapter 17 for specific MLA documentation information.)

> vol. for "volume," vols. for "volumes," trans. for "translator" or "translated by"

ACTIVITY 25-8   Abbreviation Practice, Part I

Directions: *Underline the correct word(s) or abbreviation for each bracketed choice. Refer to the rules above for help.*

1. As Chair of the Senate Select Committee on Intelligence, [Senator, Sen.] Dianne Feinstein of California oversees the nation's sixteen intelligence agencies.

2. All of the counselors who work at the camp are required to participate in [cardiopulmonary resuscitation, CPR] training.

3. Rock musician John Mayer grew up in Fairfield, [Connecticut, CT] and attended the Berklee College of Music in Boston.

4. The Bugatti Veyron SuperSport automobile can attain speeds of up to 268 [MPH, miles per hour].

5. If you are a first-time applicant for a [U.S., United States] Passport, you must apply in person at an official Acceptance Facility or Passport Agency.

EXERCISE ACTIVITY 25-9   Abbreviation Practice, Part II

Directions: *Underline any mistakes in the use of abbreviations in the following paragraph. You should find five errors. Refer to the rules above for help.*

During the 1940s and 1950s, Benjamin Spock, Medical Doctor became the most famous pediatrician in the U.S. His popular parenting books emphasized respect for infants and children. In 1967, Prof. Spock became a controversial figure when he resigned his university post to campaign against the Vietnam War. Some critics claimed that his overly permissive parenting philosophy had helped create a generation of narcissists—i.e., self-centered, irresponsible dropouts and draft-dodgers. However, after his death, an associated press article praised his humane approach to parenting, which effectively countered many oppressive child-raising theories and practices from the past.

LEARNING OBJECTIVES REVIEW

LO1	Why is correct spelling important, and how can you improve your spelling? (See pp. 562–567)	**Correct spelling** is important, as spelling mistakes can cause your readers to lose respect for your ideas and find your arguments less credible. Improve your spelling, using the Ten Tips for Spelling Improvement: (1) use a dictionary; (2) check pronunciation; (3) do not confuse homophones; (4) pluralize correctly; (5) distinguish between *ei* and *ie;* (6) learn the rules for adding suffixes and prefixes; (7) keep an error list; (8) become familiar with commonly misspelled words; (9) be aware of common letter groups; and (10) use spell-check.
LO2	Why are some words commonly confused? (See pp. 567–583)	Often, **spelling mistakes result** from writers confusing one word with another that sounds like it (a homonym), using the wrong form of a word, using slang, or misusing a word that is spelled correctly.
LO3	What information does a dictionary contain, and when should you use it? (See pp. 583–584)	A **dictionary entry** has several parts: the word's pronunciation, part(s) of speech, meaning(s), origin(s) (etymology), related forms, synonyms, and antonyms. **Wait until the revision stage** to use a dictionary to check spelling, tone, and context and whether the words you are using are appropriate in terms of their denotation and connotations.
LO4	What is a thesaurus, how do you use it, and what information does an entry contain? (See pp. 585–587)	A **thesaurus** is a text that provides **synonyms** (words that have very similar meanings) and sometimes **antonyms** (words that have opposite meanings) for a word. A **thesaurus entry** lists the word in bold, names its part of speech, and then lists its synonyms and antonyms. A thesaurus can help you find better, more precise or expressive words when you are writing.
LO5	What is the most general rule for capitalization? (See pp. 587–592)	The **general rule** is that you should capitalize proper nouns (words naming a specific person, place, or thing) and not capitalize common nouns (words describing a general object or category).
LO6	What are the six rules for writing numbers as numbers or spelling them out? (See pp. 592–594)	The **six rules** for how you write numbers are (1) spell out the numbers zero through ten and numbers that can be written using one or two words; (2) spell out numbers that begin a sentence; (3) use a combination of figures and words for very large numbers; (4) use numbers for dates, years, and time; (5) use numbers for addresses; and (6) use numbers for exact measurements.

LO 7 What are the most commonly accepted categories of abbreviations? (See pp. 594–597)	The **most commonly accepted categories of abbreviations** are (1) titles or academic degrees; (2) countries, states, or cities; (3) common acronyms; (4) Latin terms; and (5) documentation formats such as MLA or APA.

For support in meeting this chapter's objectives, log in to www.mywritinglab.com and select **Spelling.**

LEARNING OBJECTIVES

In this chapter, you will learn to

LO 1 Modify your tone and style to suit your audience

LO 2 Choose the words that best express your thoughts

LO 3 Avoid sexist language

LO 4 Avoid common ESL usage errors.

THINKING CRITICALLY

Look at the cartoon above. Word choice has a powerful effect on how readers understand ideas. Explain the different meanings the phrases "half truth" and "whole lie" have and what effect those two different terms have on your understanding of the cartoon and of what advertisers sometimes do with language.

_____

_____

_____

_____

_____

_____

When you write, you should choose your words wisely, use the right tone for your audience, and be careful to avoid usage mistakes.

LO 1   THINKING CRITICALLY ABOUT TONE AND STYLE

Tone and style are important elements in writing essays. Tone and style together create your writing "voice." **Tone** reflects your manner or attitude, and **style** includes the choices you make about language, diction, and sentence structure. The tone and style choices you make affect the way a reader hears or responds to your ideas and the credibility and effectiveness of your ideas. Some writers create style, tone, and voice patterns in their essays unconsciously. However, it's important to become aware of these choices and *evaluate critically* whether they are the best choices for your assignment and audience.

Tone

When deciding on a particular tone for an assignment, remember that the tone you use reflects your attitude toward the subject and the arguments you are making. Also, be sure to think about your audience when choosing the most effective and appropriate tone for your essay. Your tone may be formal, serious, informative, playful, persuasive, sarcastic, or impartial. For instance, the tone that Suzan Shown Harjo uses in "Last Rites for

APPLYING CRITICAL THINKING

PURPOSE   IDEAS   SUPPORT   ASSUMPTIONS BIASES   CONCLUSIONS   POINT OF VIEW   ANALYSIS

Consider the following questions before you begin writing and then make conscious choices about tone and language as you write your drafts. Use **analysis** to determine the best choices.

1. What is my topic, and what kind of tone would be most appropriate for the subject matter, **ideas**, and arguments that I want to make?

2. What attitude do I want to portray in this essay (for example, informative/impartial, playful/informal, persuasive/formal, etc.)?

3. What tone and style choices would be most effective for conveying my **purpose?**

Indian Dead" in Chapter 18 is quite formal and works well for her argument and the serious nature of her topic. However, the tone in Diane Ackerman's "Chocolate Equals Love" is more informal, even playful, which suits the subject, the joy that chocolate brings. Both authors made these style and tone choices consciously based on their subject matter and their intended audience.

As you revise your essay draft, check to make sure that the style and tone of your writing is appropriate and is the most effective choice for your topic, your audience, and your arguments and conclusions. Here is an example of inappropriate tone in an academic paper that evaluates Diane Ackerman's essay:

> Diane's essay talked about how awesome chocolate is.

Revised:

> Diane Ackerman's essay "Chocolate Equals Love" explores the benefits, the pleasures, and the history of chocolate.

ACTIVITY 26-1   Tone

Directions: *The following sentences are from a student's draft essay about the life of poet Emily Dickinson. Rewrite each sentence to change the overly informal tone to a tone that is more appropriate for an academic paper.*   Answers will vary. Sample answers provided.

1. Emily Dickinson's father was a big-time politician, and he had plenty of money.

   Emily Dickinson's father was a prosperous, prominent political figure.

2. He was a real controlling father, and there were some books he wouldn't let Emily read because he thought they were bad for her.

   He was a strict parent and screened Emily's reading materials, censoring

   books he considered inappropriate.

3. Emily lived kind of a weird life when she got older because she wanted to stay home most of the time and didn't get out and see people.

   In her later years, Emily chose an unusual life of social seclusion.

4. After Emily died, her family was looking through her stuff and found more than 1,700 poems that were in her own handwriting.

   After Emily died, her family discovered more than 1,700 handwritten poems among her possessions.

5. The poems have a whole bunch of short and long dashes instead of normal commas and periods.

   The poems use varied, unconventional dashes instead of traditional punctuation.

Formal Style and Tone Versus Academese

Even when you are writing a more formal academic paper, avoid **academese**: writing that uses pompous multisyllabic words and unnecessarily complicated sentence structures. Academese is filled with passive voice constructions (see page 505 for more on passive construction) and contains overly complex language or jargon. Here is an example:

> Facilitation of the deliberations of the collaborative, strategic-planning body was assumed by individuals possessing requisite levels of professional expertise and relevant experience.

Translation into a more reasonable tone and style:

> Senior staff led the meetings of the planning committee.

The bottom line is that academese doesn't make you sound smarter if your audience doesn't understand what you are trying to say—and sometimes even when they do. Successful writing communicates ideas clearly.

> ▶ NOTE   Using a complex vocabulary word in and of itself is not a bad idea. Just be sure that the word you choose is the best one to convey your intended meaning and that overall the passage is not too complex for your intended audience. See the vocabulary-building section in Chapter 27 for more on using complex words and expanding your vocabulary.

Doublespeak is a kind of language that deliberately distorts or disguises meaning. It typically contains *euphemisms*, deliberately vague or indirect words used in place of words that might be considered overly direct, unpleasant, or offensive. For example:

Corporate downsizing and outsourcing have resulted in job flexibility or termination. (Employees have been fired or have lost their job security because the management is restructuring the business or using cheaper labor.)

The mission to neutralize the target resulted in some collateral damage. (A government operation to kill an enemy agent caused unintended deaths or injuries of innocent bystanders.)

ACTIVITY 26-2   Revising to Eliminate Academese

Directions: *Read the following paragraph, and in the space provided, rewrite it to eliminate academese and make the passage readable for a general audience. You may need to look up some of the words in a dictionary in order to translate them.* Answers will vary. Sample revision provided.

During periods of financial austerity, intergenerational initiatives in early childhood education have demonstrated that optimal utilization of volunteer resources includes integration of older adults on a volunteer basis. A familial dimension is established in the educational environment through the nurturing assistance of the elder volunteers. The instructional services of professional staff are complemented by the targeted assistance provided to individual students by elder volunteers. Development of prosocial behaviors among students can be accelerated through flexible, spontaneous intergenerational activities with elder volunteers in the classroom community. Enhancement of productive aging for volunteers through successful application of existing skills and strengths is a supplemental outcome of intergenerational, classroom-based early childhood initiatives.

When budgets are tight, older adult volunteers can be especially helpful in

preschool classrooms. The caring volunteers create a more homelike atmos-

phere. The volunteers help teachers by giving each child more individual atten-

tion. Playing with the volunteers helps children learn to share and cooperate.

The adult volunteers also find the experience rewarding.

LO 2   WORD CHOICE

Word choice, sometimes referred to as **diction,** is exactly that: You make a conscious *choice* and pick the best word for the idea you are expressing based on the content of the sentence and where the word will appear. Think about your intended audience as you choose your words. Will you need a formal or informal word? Will you need to use language that a general audience can understand or should you use discipline-specific terms for a specialized audience? Is your tone academic or more casual? How should that affect your word choices? For example:

> **Intended audience:** Local school board
>
> **Inappropriate diction:** The school board is crazy to even think about cutting art classes. There are lots of better ways to solve our money problems.
>
> **Revised:** I urge the school board to preserve the arts program and to seek alternative strategies for balancing the budget.

Many words have both literal and implied meanings. Primary or literal meanings are called **denotations**, and secondary or implied meanings are called **connotations**. Think of the denotation of a word as its exact or surface meaning; think of connotations as the "baggage" or associations that come with that word. The denotation of a word is like the tip of an iceberg that shows above the surface of the water, and the connotations, which often impart the most meaning, are the base of the iceberg under the water's surface. Some words have very few connotations, while others are rich with connotative associations. For instance, consider the following two signs:

Which language is more effective? Both signs advertise a residence for sale, but *house* is a more denotative word while *home* is full of connotations. *Home* is where the heart is; it's apple pie, mom, comfort, and everything we associate with the bigger concept of *home*. So make word choices carefully in order to get the maximum effect and be sure the words you choose are conveying (both on the surface and more subtly) exactly what you mean to say.

Slang

Slang is casual language consisting of informal words that are not listed as "real" words in the dictionary (though they might be listed as slang). The old saying "*Ain't* ain't a word 'cause it ain't in the dictionary" is partially true: It isn't a real word, but it is listed in most dictionaries—as slang. It's fine to use slang in casual social speech or emails between friends, or even in dialogue in narration essays. However, in most cases in essay writing, you should convert slang into more conventional word choices.

> **Slang:** The author's first novel was a bust, and the critics were cold, but her next novel was kickin', and the critics were blown away.
>
> **Revised:** The author's first novel was unsuccessful, and the critics judged it harshly, but her next novel was excellent, and the critics were impressed.

Jargon

Jargon is the language used in a specific field. If one is writing for an audience familiar with the jargon in a distinct field, then it's fine to use it. Otherwise, it needs to be translated into more general language. For instance, if you worked in a computer repair store, you could leave a list of instructions for your coworkers that would be filled with jargon that they would understand but a new computer owner would not.

> **Jargon:** The search engine allowed him to download jpegs loaded with megapixels onto his hard drive.
>
> **Revised:** The Internet search engine he used allowed him to save extremely large picture files onto his computer.

Dialect

Dialect is language that reflects the speech (word choice and accent) of a certain region or a particular economic group or cultural heritage.

> **Dialect:** I reckon the dogs are fussin' at a critter down yonder.
>
> **Revised:** I think the dogs are barking at some animal over there.

Although you would not use dialect in an academic paper, it would certainly be appropriate to use it in dialogue to communicate information about a person or character speaking.

Foreign Words

Foreign words that are used without a specific purpose can be confusing. If you decide to use a foreign term in your sentence, be sure it is one your intended audience will recognize. Otherwise, use the English version of the term, or define it in parentheses:

> **Foreign term:** When he saw her reaction to his remark, he realized he had made a *faux pas*.
>
> **Revised:** When he saw her reaction to his remark, he realized he had made a *social blunder*.
>
> **With definition:** When he saw her reaction to his remark, he realized he had made a *faux pas* (social blunder).

There are times when it is appropriate to use slang, dialect, technical jargon, and foreign words in dialogue or in direct quotations, but in general, you should not use them in formal academic writing.

ACTIVITY 26-3   Slang, Dialect, Foreign Words, and Tone

Directions: *Read the following entry from a student's journal for a writing class. On a separate sheet of paper, rewrite the paragraph to make it understandable for a general audience. Eliminate slang, and translate foreign words. If necessary, consult a slang dictionary or online resources.* Answers will vary. Sample revision provided in IM.

> Friday evening I went to hang out with my amigo Tito. When I got to his place, he killed the DVD. "Sup, dawg?" I asked. He said he was straight chillin'. I asked him why the TV face, and he said he'd been powerdisking *Survivor*. I thought that was fresh and asked if he bought the box set. He said yeah but said he had sticker shock. When I asked cuánto es, he just said it was mondo bucks and looked bummed. I said, "I feel you, Dude."

Clichés

Clichés are expressions that once effectively conveyed a powerful image or idea to readers, but through extensive use have become stale, no longer communicating their intended meaning.

Most clichés are metaphors or similes that make implied or direct comparisons between two things in order to convey an idea. **Metaphors** are implied comparisons to other things.

> Emily Dickinson wrote, " 'Hope' is the thing with feathers— / That perches in the soul."

In this example, the metaphor implicitly compares hope to a bird.

Similes are comparisons that use the specific words *like* or *as*:

> Anna Akhmatova wrote, "Summer's ardent rustling / Is like a festival outside my window."

This simile uses *like* to compare the rustling of summer leaves to the sounds of a festival.

> In "Names of Horses," Donald Hall describes how a horse's neck "rubbed the windowsill / of the stall, smoothing the wood as the sea smoothes glass."

This simile uses *as* to compare the repetitive action of the horse's neck to the repetitive action of ocean currents; the simile also compares the smoothness of the wooden sill to the smoothness of sea glass.

Often, famous metaphors and similes from literature pop up in student writing. However, many have lost their power and should be avoided. Instead, create a fresh comparison of your own. Who knows, maybe it will be so good that everyone will want to use it, and it too will become a cliché one day. Here are some of the most overused clichés.

> I've been *busy as a bee* preparing for the party.
>
> For a moment, he didn't respond to the insult, but it was the *calm before the storm*.
>
> She never gets stage fright; she's always *cool as a cucumber*.
>
> My grandmother exercises every day, so she's *fit as a fiddle*.
>
> After his girlfriend broke up with him, he was *sadder but wiser*.
>
> Wearing old jeans, he *stuck out like a sore thumb* at the fancy reception.
>
> Sitting close to the cozy fire, I was *snug as a bug in a rug*.

He describes his volunteer work at the shelter as a *labor of love*.

She reached down to pick up her briefcase, but it had *vanished into thin air*.

I checked once again to make sure I had my car keys: *better safe than sorry!*

The high school reunion was a real *trip down memory lane*.

As a lawyer, she's *tough as nails* and *drives a hard bargain*.

The plant he had forgotten to water was *dead as a doornail*.

My husband *slept like a log*, but I *didn't sleep a wink*.

In the revision stage of your writing process, check to make sure that clichés haven't crept into your writing—they can be automatic and hard to spot. Here is a list of some of the most common clichéd phrases in English—be sure to look again at the very common clichés used in the sentences above, too.

Common Clichés

add(ing) insult to injury	green with envy	rise to the occasion
better half	heavy as lead	sharp as a tack
beyond a shadow of a doubt	hit the nail on the head	sink or swim
bottom line	in this day and age	smart as a whip
brave as a lion	last but not least	sneaking suspicion
cold, hard facts	light as a feather	straight and narrow
come to grips with	nose to the grindstone	tears streamed down
crazy as a loon	paint the town red	tried and true
crying over spilled milk	pale as a ghost	untimely death
deep, dark secret	pass the buck	walk the line
drunk as a lord	pretty as a picture	wax eloquent
face the music	quick as a flash	white as a sheet
few and far between	red as a rose	work like a dog
flat as a pancake	right as rain	worth its weight in gold
	rise and shine	

ACTIVITY 26-4 Revising Clichés

Directions: *On a separate sheet of paper, rewrite each of the following sentences to eliminate the cliché, replacing it with fresh imagery.* Answers will vary.

Example: After she agreed to go out with him, he was *grinning from ear to ear*.

Revised: After she agreed to go out with him, his smile was wide as a Texas morning.

1. I pestered my friend to tell me the secret, but his *lips were sealed.*

2. Last week Jayden had a cold, but now he's *hale and hearty* again.

3. When properly cared for, African gray parrots can live to *the ripe old age* of 50 or more.

4. My friend is in the *depths of despair* about her grade on the midterm exam.

5. I knew *beyond a shadow of a doubt* that he was the right man for me.

6. As Keiko prepared to skydive for the first time, her *heart was in her throat.*

7. The joys of parenthood outweigh all the *trials and tribulations.*

8. After a 10-hour shift at work, it was a relief to *rest my weary bones.*

9. The film was pretty lame, but we stuck it out to the *bitter end.*

10. I hate public speaking, so I was *sweating bullets* before my oral presentation.

LO 3   AVOIDING SEXIST LANGUAGE

Language is dynamic: It evolves with culture. It used to be acceptable to use gender-specific terms such as *man* or *mankind* to stand for all people, but due to political and societal changes of the last 30 to 40 years, the use of such language is now considered sexist.

Use Gender-Specific Terms Only When Appropriate

Gender-specific terms are words that refer to a specific gender. The key to avoiding sexist language is to use logic: Use gender-specific terms only when the subject really is gender specific. For instance, the terms *men* and *he* refer to males, and the terms *women* and *her* refer to females.

> Each member of the women's basketball team put on *her* uniform.
>
> The man with the clipboard raised a whistle to *his* lips.

If your subject is not gender specific, use inclusive (non-gender-specific) language.

Fans roared *their* approval as the home team scored another point.

Non-gender-specific terms are neutral and therefore include both sexes: *people, one, humanity,* and *humankind.* Plural pronouns such as *they, them,* or *their* are also gender neutral. When you use terms like *people* or *humans,* you can use the plural pronoun *their.*

If you use singular terms such as *a person* or *one* as your subject, then you'll need to use *he or she* instead of *they* to avoid a pronoun agreement error (see p. 487 for more on pronoun agreement). In general, the easiest way to avoid a pronoun agreement error is to use the plural forms of non-gender-specific terms and the corresponding plural pronouns.

> **Singular:** Any student who wishes to change majors should consult his or her faculty advisor.
>
> **Plural:** Students who wish to change majors should consult their faculty advisors.

Don't Assume an Occupation Is Exclusively Male or Female

Another kind of sexist language arises from stereotyping certain occupations as being primarily for women or for men. Consider the following examples:

> **Sexist language:** Demand for qualified nurses remains high, and a student who graduates with an R.N. degree can be optimistic about *her* job prospects.
>
> **Revised:** Demand for qualified nurses remains high, and students who graduate with an R.N. degree can be optimistic about *their* job prospects.

> **Sexist language:** When discussing treatment options with a physician, make sure that *he* answers all of your questions about possible side effects.
>
> **Revised:** When discussing treatment options with a physician, make sure that *he or she* answers all of your questions about possible side effects.

Both original sentences stereotype men and women. Of course, men can be nurses and women can be doctors. Careers are not limited to a single gender.

Along the same lines, be careful not to write *male nurse* or *woman doctor*—just say *nurses* or *doctors*, and then use the plural pronoun *their*.

Use Parallel Terms for Men and Women

Be careful not to have double standards. For instance, if you are writing about high school students, don't call the males *men* and the females *girls*. Instead, call them *boys and girls* or *men and women*. Be consistent and fair in your use of terms.

Here are some gender-specific terms that are already obsolete and some non-gender-specific terms that can be used to replace them.

Gender-Specific Term	Inclusive Term
man or mankind	humans, humanity, people, humankind, human beings
fireman	firefighter
policeman	police officer
mailman	mail carrier, postal carrier
weatherman	meteorologist, weather forecaster
salesman	sales associate
congressman	representative, senator, legislator
foreman	supervisor
chairman	chairperson, chair
businessman	business person or exact title (e.g., sales manager)
manpower	staff, personnel, workers
to man	to operate, to staff
man-made	handcrafted, human-made
male nurse	nurse
female doctor	doctor

ACTIVITY 26-5   Revising Sexist Language

Directions: *Rewrite each of the following sentences to eliminate sexist or inappropriately gender-specific terms.* Answers will vary. Sample answers provided.

1. When retail businesses lay off employees, customers often notice a difference, as stores may lack the manpower needed to provide high-quality customer service.

   When retail businesses lay off employees, customers often notice a difference, as stores may lack the staff needed to provide high-quality customer service.

2. For example, a single salesman in a busy electronics store cannot be expected to serve all customers in a timely manner during peak shopping hours.

For example, a single sales associate in a busy electronics store cannot be expected to serve all customers in a timely manner during peak shopping hours.

3. This fall the college bookstore was woefully understaffed; during the first week of classes, if a student wanted to buy a textbook, he typically had to wait in line for a half hour.

This fall the college bookstore was woefully understaffed; during the first week of classes, if a student wanted to buy a textbook, he or she typically had to wait in line for a half hour.

4. At a local copy center, I recently saw a man complaining to the girl behind the counter about the poor customer service, but it clearly wasn't her fault—there weren't enough staff.

At a local copy center, I recently saw a man complaining to the woman behind the counter about the poor customer service, but it clearly wasn't her fault—there weren't enough staff.

5. Cutting municipal services can create safety issues, as there may not be enough policemen to serve and protect the community.

Cutting municipal services can create safety issues, as there may not be enough police officers to serve and protect the community.

LO 4   USAGE ERRORS

Non-native speakers often make errors in usage due to their unfamiliarity with Standard English, idioms, and grammar rules that are different from those of their native language. Below are ten tips for avoiding the most common errors non-native speakers make when writing in English.

TEN USEFUL TIPS FOR NON-NATIVE SPEAKERS

Here are 10 grammar tips that are useful for both non-native speakers and those students who need to brush up on their grammar usage.

Tip 1: Check for Count Versus Noncount Nouns

Count nouns name items that can be counted as individual units:

> *dog/dogs, cat/cats, boy/boys, girl/girls, flower/flowers, window/windows, cracker/crackers, street/streets, nut/nuts*

Noncount (or mass) nouns name items that cannot be counted as individual units:

> *food, rice, flour, water, sugar, peace, life, death, furniture, milk, wood, cotton, leather, beauty, chess, evidence*

Tip 2: Check for Article Use and Definite Versus Indefinite Articles

Articles (sometimes called determiners) are divided into two categories: **definite**, or specific (*the*) and **indefinite**, or nonspecific (*a* or *an*, *some*, or no article at all).

1. **Definite articles:** Use *the* to refer to particular or specific common nouns (singular or plural) and noncount nouns that are specific because the noun was previously identified:

> *The* sandwiches we ordered were delicious.

> Let me pay for *the* food this time.

Or, because the noun is identified by a modifier:

> *The* best vegetarian pizza has caramelized onions on it.

The is also used with some proper nouns:

> *The* Smiths just moved to New Mexico.
> They used to live in *the* Midwest.
> We took a riverboat cruise on *the* Mississippi.
> *The Columbia Tribune* is known for its lively editorials.

2. Indefinite articles: Use *a* or *an* with singular countable nouns that are generic or are nonspecific because the noun was not mentioned previously:

> She asked if he would like to get *a* cup of coffee sometime.

Or, because the noun's identity is not important to the context:

> He scribbled his phone number on *a* scrap of paper and handed it to her.

Or, because the noun has no restricting modifier:

> A few days later, they went to *a* movie together.

Use *some* with plural nouns or noncount nouns that refer to a particular or specifiable quantity:

> *Some* roses are very fragrant, but others have no fragrance at all.
> The orchids need *some* water, but not too much.

Do not use any articles with noncount common nouns that are generic and nonspecific and have no particular quantity or identity:

> She sprinkled *sugar* on the cookies while they were still warm.

Tip 3: Choose the Right Preposition or Prepositional Phrase

Getting prepositions right is difficult since many are learned through use and familiarity with a language, but some logical rules do apply for using some prepositions. The most easily confused prepositions are those related to *space* and *time*.

1. Space: Think location versus direction.

Location: Use *at*, *on*, or *in*

> They had a picnic *at* [location] the park.
>
> They sat *on* [surface] a blanket because the grass was damp.
>
> He put the leftover food *in* [enclosed] the basket.

Direction: Use *to, onto,* or *into*

> They ran *to* [direction] the car when it started to rain.
>
> Muddy water splashed *onto* [surface] her new jeans when she got out of the car.
>
> They carried the picnic basket and other gear *into* [enclosed] the house.

2. **Time:** Use *at* for an exact point in time, *on* for a particular day or date, and *in* for months, years, centuries, and longer periods.

> The baby was born *at* 1:30 AM *on* Sunday.
>
> My parents were married *in* 1974.
>
> The play is a period drama set *in* the nineteenth century.

3. **Prepositional phrases:** A prepositional phrase cannot be used as the subject of a sentence. Instead, use a noun or add a subject pronoun after the prepositional phrase.

> **Incorrect:** *In my apartment complex* has a nice community room.
>
> **Correct:** My apartment complex has a nice community room.
>
> *In my apartment complex,* there is a nice community room.

Tip 4: Avoid Mixing Subordination and Coordination

Use a subordinating clause with a comma, or connect two clauses with a coordinating conjunction, but do not use both (see Chapter 23 for more on sentence combining).

> **Incorrect:** *Although* I went to bed early, *but* I was still tired in the morning.
>
> **Correct:** *Although* I went to bed early, I was still tired in the morning.
>
> I went to bed early, *but* I was still tired in the morning.

Tip 5: Be Sure to Use Subject Pronouns

If you have used a noun subject in a sentence and don't want to repeat the subject in the next sentence, be sure to use a pronoun to represent the original noun in your second sentence.

> **Incorrect:** I'm taking upper-level physics this semester. *Is* a challenging course. [no subject pronoun]
>
> **Correct:** I'm taking upper-level physics this semester. *It is* a challenging course. [subject pronoun added]

Tip 6: Use *It* or *There* Correctly with Deferred Subjects

In English, when a subject is deferred (placed later in the sentence than is usual), the usual subject spot has to be filled with *it* or *there*.

> **Incorrect:** *Is* not good to use a cell phone while driving.
>
> **Correct:** *It is* not good to use a cell phone while driving.

> **Incorrect:** *Are* risks even when drivers use hands-free cell phones.
>
> **Correct:** *There are* risks even when drivers use hands-free cell phones.

Tip 7: Be Familiar with Idioms

Idioms reflect the customary speech patterns of a given language. They are particular ways of saying things that develop in a specific region or language that do not translate directly or easily into another language. Idioms are learned over time through immersion in a language, and the incorrect use of an idiom is often an indicator that the writer is not a native speaker. Many mistakes in idiom usage come from the misuse of prepositions (see Tip 3) or verbal phrases.

Verbal phrases are formed when a verb is combined with an adverb or preposition to create a new meaning. Most verbal phrases are idioms, and they are used more in informal conversation or informal writing than in formal essays. However, even when used in informal writing, verbal phrases are written in a particular order.

Here's a list of verbal phrases that form some of the most common idioms in English:

Common English Idioms

ask out	figure out	pass out
break down	fill in	pick out/up
break up (with)	fill out	put away/back/off/on/out/up
bring up	fill up	quiet down
burn down	find out	run across/into/out
burn out	get along (with)	show off/up
burn up	get away (from or with)	shut off/up
call back	get back in/on	speak out/up
call off	get out/over/up	stand up (for)
call up	give back/in/up	stay in/off/up
catch up (with)	go out (with)	stop up
check in	go over	take after/in/off/out/over
check out	grow up	take care (of)
check up (on)	hand in/out	tear down/up
come out	hang out/up	think on/over
cross out	have on	throw out/up
cut (it) out	help out	try on/out (for)
cut up	keep on/out/up	tune in/out/up
drop in	leave out	turn down/off/on/out/up
drop off	look after/into/out/over/up	wake up
drop out (of)	make up	watch out (for)

Tip 8: Check Your Infinitive and Gerund Verb Uses

An **infinitive** is a verb with the word *to* in front of it. It indicates action *after* the time of the main verb, indicates an *effort*, or indicates a *purpose or intention*:

Infinitive (action after): I decided *to paint* the garage.

Infinitive (indicates effort): I tried *to paint* the whole garage in one day.

Infinitive (indicates purpose): I went downtown *to buy* more paint.

A **gerund** uses an *-ing* verb form. Generally speaking, gerunds tend to present facts rather than intentions. A gerund may also indicate an experiment:

Gerund (fact): I finished *painting* the garage before dark.

Gerund (experiment): Try *painting* an entire garage in a single day.

Check to make sure you've used the infinitive and gerund forms of verbs correctly.

Tip 9: Be Careful About Commonly Confused Words

Be careful not to use a word that sounds like another one (a homonym) but isn't the right word for what you want to say. Use the correct spelling. See p. 567 for a list of some of the most commonly confused words in English.

> **Incorrect:** All of *they're* friends *accept* Kiyoshi came to the party.
>
> **Correct:** All of *their* friends *except* Kiyoshi came to the party.

Tip 10: Use a Good Second-Language Dictionary and Use It Well

Travel or minimal translation dictionaries tend to oversimplify a word's meaning or give few definitions. Choose a good, complete English as a Second Language dictionary. A complete dictionary will give you more specific meanings and connotations so you can pick the best English word for the context of the sentence you are writing. Also see if it contains a list of idioms so you can check your verb phrases to make sure they are correct.

ACTIVITY 26-6   Fixing ESL Errors

Directions: *On a separate sheet of paper, rewrite the following paragraph to correct common ESL errors. Refer to the 10 tips in this section for help.*
Answers will vary. Sample answer provided in the IM.

In Saturday I called out my friend Mei-Xing to see if she wanted to hang up with me. We decided going to Museum of Natural History together. I called museum to find on what hours it was open. Is a huge model of a blue whale at the museum. I learned many interesting fact about a blue whale. Blue whales are the largest animals in Earth. The heart of the blue whale is as big as the car. Are the loudest animals too. They make rumbling noises under the waters to communicate with other whales. The noise is louder than jet engine! The whales often swim alone but sometimes travel in pares. Although the whales are huge, but they're diet is composed of tiny, shrimp-like creatures called krill. Blue whales are found on all oceans of the world. But a blue whale is the endangered species. All hunting of blue whales was band on 1966.

LEARNING OBJECTIVES REVIEW

LO 1 What are tone and style, and why are they important? (See pp. 601–604)	**Tone** reflects your manner or attitude toward a subject, and **style** reflects the choices you make about language, diction, and sentence structure. It is **important to** *critically evaluate your* choices to ensure they are the best ones to communicate your message to your audience.
LO 2 What does the term *diction* mean, and why is good diction important? (See pp. 604–610)	**Diction** means word choice, and good diction allows you to communicate effectively. Pick the best word for the idea you are expressing based on the content of the sentence and your intended audience. Be sure to consider both the *denotation* and *connotation* of the words you choose. In academic writing avoid using *slang*, *dialect*, and *clichés*.
LO 3 What is sexist language, and what are some ways to avoid using it? (See pp. 610–613)	**Sexist language** unnecessarily uses gender-specific terms when referring to people's work, behavior, and skills. Only use gender-specific terms when referring directly to men or women. Otherwise, use **inclusive language**, **plural pronouns**, or **parallel terms**, and do not assume an occupation is exclusive to men or women (e.g., all doctors are male, or all caregivers are female).
LO 4 What are the most common usage errors for non-native speaker writing in English, and how can you address them? (See pp. 613–619)	The **most common usage errors** relate to count versus noncount nouns, use of definite and indefinite articles, prepositions, mixing subordination and subordination, use of subject pronouns, correct use of *it* and *there* with deferred subjects, familiarity with phrases and idioms, infinitive and gerund verb uses, and commonly used words. Use Part VI of this text, the Ten Useful ESL Tips, and a good ESL dictionary to help you avoid making these errors.

PEARSON
mywritinglab

For support in meeting this chapter's objectives, log in to www.mywritinglab.com and select **Easily Confused Words.**

LEARNING OBJECTIVES

In this chapter you will learn to

 LO 1 Build up your vocabulary

LO 2 Pronounce words correctly

LO 3 Use context clues to determine the meaning of unfamiliar words

THINKING CRITICALLY

Look at the comic strip above. Then answer the following questions.

1. In your opinion, what is the point of this cartoon strip?

_____

_____

_____

_____

2. How do your word choices and level of vocabulary affect others' impression of you?

_____

_____

_____

_____

621

LO 1   VOCABULARY BUILDING

Did you know that the average educated person knows about 20,000 words and uses about 2,000 different words a week? William Shakespeare, arguably the greatest English-speaking writer, had a vocabulary of between 18,000 and 25,000 words, back when people were happy to have an average of 5,000 words. Why is having a better vocabulary important? Studies have shown that having a better vocabulary increases your success in school and in your career. It also improves your understanding of other people's ideas and arguments in both verbal and written form. Having a command of language is a form of power. Most highly successful business and political leaders have impressive vocabularies and a clear command of the English language.

The best way to increase your vocabulary is to make a conscious decision to learn new words and use them. Don't be afraid to take some risks and make some mistakes as you try out new words, but try not to use an awkward or overly formal or complex word where a simpler one would be better. As Mark Twain once said, "Never use a five dollar word when a ten cent one will do." However, using too many simple words won't necessarily generate more complex arguments and reasoning. Find the right balance for your purpose and audience.

Five Tips for Building Your Vocabulary

Tip 1: Keep a vocabulary log or vocabulary journal. Every time you read or hear a new word, write it in your log, note where it came from (a textbook, lecture, the radio, and so on), write down what you think it means, look it up in a dictionary (right then or as soon as you get a chance), and write down the relevant definition(s). Using a new word helps you remember its meaning, so write a sentence using the new word. Be sure to review your log regularly to brush up on your new words list.

> **Sample Entry**
>
> **pseudonym:** I heard this word in my Victorian literature class when my teacher explained that George Eliot was the pseudonym of Mary Anne Evans.
>
> **My definition:** a fake name

Dictionary definition: pseu•do•nym (**sood**-n-nim) n. bearing a false name; a fictitious name; *esp* : PEN NAME

Used in a sentence: Mary Anne Evans used the pseudonym George Eliot because she was a woman writing in a man's world.

Tip 2: Make a conscious effort to use new words. If you use a word more than a few times, it becomes "yours" and a natural part of your own vocabulary.

Tip 3: Make friends with your dictionary and your thesaurus. Consult a dictionary and a thesaurus regularly to learn new words and to find synonyms for words you tend to use all the time so you can add variety to your vocabulary.

Tip 4: Learn Latin roots, prefixes, and suffixes. A large percentage of words in English are derived from Latin word parts. Becoming familiar with the meanings of these common **prefixes** (word beginnings), **roots** (common word bases), and **suffixes** (word endings) makes it easier to understand new words. For instance, the prefix *de*, meaning *away* or *from*, is used all the time in words such as *derail* (go off the tracks) and *depart* (go away from). The root *tact* means *touch*, as in *tactile* (relating to the sense of touch), and the suffix *ism* means *belief*, as in *pacifism* (belief in settling disputes peacefully).

> **Cross Reference**
> See Chapter 25 for tips on how to use a dictionary or thesaurus and sample entries for each.

Tip 5: Use the Internet. The Internet puts a world of vocabulary tools and vocabulary-building resources at your fingertips. You can look up roots, prefixes, and suffixes as well as definitions of words and **homonyms** (words that sound alike but don't mean the same thing), **synonyms** (different words that mean the same thing), and **antonyms** (words that mean the opposite of each other) in various online dictionaries and thesauruses. Just use your favorite search engine and punch in a word to see what happens!

ACTIVITY 27-1 Keeping a Log

Directions: *Buy a notebook to use as your vocabulary log, and try to keep it with you throughout the day. Keep track of new words that you hear or read this week. Look up their meanings in a dictionary, and then use them when you speak and write.*

ACTIVITY 27-2   Vocabulary Practice

Directions: *Write down two words that appear somewhere in this chapter that you did not know before reading this section. Look up their meanings and then write a sentence using each one.* Answers will vary.

1. _____

2. _____

ACTIVITY 27-3   Vocabulary-Building Techniques

Directions: *In your vocabulary log, complete the following tasks for each word listed below.*

1. *Use an Internet search engine (Google, Ask, or Yahoo!) to look up the meaning of the word.*
2. *Briefly summarize the definition(s) of the word that you find online.*
3. *Write your own definition(s) of the word.*
4. *Create a sentence of your own using the word.*
5. *Try to use the word in conversation or writing this week.*

1. acquiesce

   _____

   _____

2. decorum

   _____

   _____

3. enigma

   _____

   _____

4. palpable

   _____

   _____

5. sanguine

   _____

   _____

LO 2   PRONUNCIATION

Syllables are the number of sounds in a word. For instance, the word *dog* has only one syllable, but the word *Labrador* has three syllables: *Lab-ra-dor*. Syllables help you pronounce words correctly. When you look up a word in the dictionary, you will see it broken down into syllables through the use of hyphens, dots, or slashes. For example, the word *irritable* could be shown in several ways: *ir-it-a-ble*, *ir.it.a.ble*, or *ir/it/a/ble*.

Pronouncing words correctly isn't just about breaking a word into syllables. Dictionaries also provide phonetic (spelling by how a word sounds) pronunciation guides to help you pronounce words correctly. The following pronunciation guide will help you identify the most common consonant and vowel sounds in English.

PRONUNCIATION GUIDE					
Consonant sounds		**Short vowel sounds**		**Long vowel sounds**	
b	bed	a	ham	a	say
d	dog	e	ten	e	she
f	fur	i	if	i	hi
g	goat	o	lot	o	go
h	her	oo	look	oo	school
j	jump	u	up	u (yoo)	use
k	kick				
l	leaf				
m	man				
n	no				
p	power				
r	row				
s	saw				
t	tea				
v	vase				
w	way				
y	yes				
z	zero				
ch	channel				
sh	shop				
th	that				
th	thick				

ACTIVITY 27-4 Practicing Pronunciation

Directions:

1. *Pronounce* each of the following words aloud.
2. *Break the word into syllables* using dashes or dots, and write it in the space provided.
3. *Look up the word in a dictionary.* Make sure you have pronounced it correctly and divided it into syllables correctly. Then read the definition(s) of the word.
4. *Write a brief definition* in your own words.

1. **anachronism** *a-nach-ro-nism*

   My definition: *someone or something that is out of order or belongs to an earlier time*

2. **cacophonous** *ca-coph-o-nous*

   My definition: *having a loud, unpleasant sound*

3. **expostulate** *ex-pos-tu-late*

   My definition: *try to correct someone or persuade a person to change his or her mind*

4. **peripatetic** *per-i-pa-tet-ic*

   My definition: *walking or traveling from place to place*

5. **salubrious** *sa-lu-bri-ous*

   My definition: *making a person healthy; making a person feel good*

LO3 CRITICAL THINKING AND CONTEXT CLUES

Sometimes when you are reading it's not possible to stop and look up a word you don't know. At those times, it is best to figure out a word's meaning as best you can by using **context clues**—clues that come before and after words, in the same sentence or surrounding ones. Figuring out a word using context clues is a skill that you get better at with practice. Moreover, you'll remember the new word longer if you have to figure it out for yourself, which helps you to build your personal vocabulary as you read.

Critical Thinking and Visualization

Think of a jigsaw puzzle that is missing a piece. Based on the pieces surrounding the missing piece, you can figure out pretty accurately what that missing piece should look like.

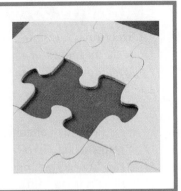

Using Context Clues

To figure out the meaning of a word, ask yourself the following questions:

1. **Does the word have a prefix, root, or suffix I know** that will give me a partial clue to its meaning?

2. **What part of speech is the word** functioning as in the sentence? Is it a noun? A verb? An adverb? An adjective?

3. **Is the word followed by a secondary explanation or an example?**

4. **Is there a word used near the unfamiliar word that may mean the same (a synonym) or the opposite (an antonym)** that I can use as a clue?

5. **What details or descriptive words are used in the sentence that I know?** Do they give me clues to this word's meaning?

6. **What idea is being addressed in the sentence in which the word appears?**

7. **What is the subject of the whole reading?** How does the sentence that this word is part of develop the subject?

8. **What purpose is being developed in this piece of writing?** Does the word in question relate to the overall theme? Does it make sense in that context?

Cross Reference

See Chapter 25 for more on word parts.

If you are *not* able to work out the meaning of the word using these questions, read the next few sentences in the passage and then come back to the word and try again. Sometimes clues appear later in a paragraph or even in the next one. Even if you *are* able to work out a word's meaning, it is always useful to go back later and check a dictionary to make sure you were correct.

ACTIVITY 27-5   Using Context Clues

Directions: *Use the context clue questions on page 627 to help you figure out the meanings of the words in bold print in the following passage. In the spaces provided after the passage, write the meaning of each word, and explain how you used context clues to figure it out. Then double-check your answers using a dictionary.*

Recently I attended a party where the host suggested that we play a game called "Two Truths and a Lie." In this game, each player must tell two true stories and one made-up story about his or her life. The other players try to [1]**differentiate** between the true and false stories, casting a group vote on which story is a "lie."

Most of the guests were enthusiastic about playing the game, but my heart sank. A naturally [2]**credulous** person, I've been teased by friends for being naïve and gullible. I also can't tell a lie to save my soul! I blush furiously if I try to tell even a little white lie, so it's easier for me to just tell the truth or say nothing at all.

I said I wasn't a good story-teller and suggested a couple of other games, but I couldn't [3]**dissuade** the group from playing the game. Offering to go first, my friend, who is a natural [4]**raconteur,** immediately [5]**regaled** the group with three clever and amusing tales. Judging the [6]**veracity** of her stories was not easy, as all three seemed unlikely, and the story that the group identified as false turned out to be true.

The game seemed [7]**interminable;** as the other guests wove [8]**scintillating** tales about their lives, I had plenty of time to worry that my own stories would seem boring and obvious. When it was finally my turn, I [9]**reiterated** that I'm not a good story-teller, but the group encouraged me, so I started talking. The group judged my first story to be false, but I triumphantly announced that the third story was my "lie," prompting laughter and applause. Looking back on that night, I realize that everyone seemed a little shy and serious, but after the game, the atmosphere was one of friendly [10]**levity.**

1. **differentiate:** *recognize the difference*

    Context clues used: *verb has same root as "different"; phrase shows*

    comparison/contrast "between the true and false stories"

2. **credulous:** *too easily convinced, believing too readily*

    Context clues used: *"naïve and gullible" (nearby synonyms)*

3. dissuade: *advise against*

Context clues used: *prefix "dis" meaning "not"; similarity to "persuade";*

context of sentence (trying to get other guests not to play game)

4. raconteur: *someone who is good at telling stories or anecdotes*

Context clues used: *context of paragraph and sentence (story-telling,*

friend who tells "clever and amusing tales")

5. regaled: *entertained*

Context clues used: *context of sentence ("clever and amusing tales"*

entertain listeners)

6. veracity: *truthfulness*

Context clues used: *context of passage, paragraph, and sentence*

(purpose of game is to judge truthfulness of the stories)

7. interminable: *seemingly endless*

Context clues used: *prefix "in" meaning "not"; root "term" (meaning*

"end") familiar from "terminal" or "terminate"; phrases in sentence

("last to play . . . plenty of time")

8. scintillating: *lively or witty*

Context clues used: *meaning of word contrasts with meaning of other*

words in sentence ("boring and obvious")

9. reiterated: *said again*

Context clues used: *speaker repeats "I'm not a good story-teller"*

(paragraphs 3 and 4); prefix "re" meaning "again"

10. levity: *frivolity, lightheartedness, lack of seriousness*

Context clues used: *syntax of sentence sets up contrast ("Before . . .*

serious . . . after . . . levity"); word "laughter" earlier in paragraph

---

▶ NOTE   The reading selections in Chapter 18 include more practice for figuring out the meanings of words using context clues.

LEARNING OBJECTIVES REVIEW

LO1 What are five tips for building your vocabulary? (See pp. 622–624)	The **five tips for building your vocabulary** are **(1)** keep a vocabulary log or journal; **(2)** make a conscious effort to use new words; **(3)** use a dictionary and thesaurus; **(4)** learn Latin roots, prefixes, and suffixes; and **(5)** use the Internet.
LO2 What can you use to help you pronounce words correctly? (See pp. 625–626)	**Syllables** are the units of sounds in a word, and once you know how many syllables are in a word and where the syllable breaks are, it is easier to figure out how to pronounce the word. You can also use the phonetic pronunciation guides in dictionaries.
LO3 What are context clues, and what eight questions can you ask to figure out a word's meaning from its context? (See pp. 626–629)	**Context clues**—clues that appear before and after words, in the same sentence or surrounding ones—can help you figure out the meaning of unfamiliar words. **Eight context-related questions** can help you determine the meaning of a word: (1) Does the word have a prefix, root, or suffix that gives a clue to its meaning? (2) What part of speech is it? (3) Is it followed by an explanation or example? (4) Is there a word nearby that means the same or the opposite? (5) What descriptive words are used in the sentence that provide clues to the word's meaning? (6) What idea is discussed in the sentence in which the word appears? (7) What is the subject of the reading, and how does the sentence the word is in develop the subject? (8) What is the purpose of this piece of writing?

PEARSON

For support in meeting this chapter's objectives, log in to www.mywritinglab.com and select **Vocabulary Development.**

Credits

Index